# The South Since 1865

# The South Since 1865

## Second Edition

## John Samuel Ezell

Macmillan Publishing Co., Inc.
NEW YORK

Collier Macmillan Publishers
LONDON

Macmillan Publishing Co., Inc.
866 Third Avenue, New York, New York 10022

Collier-Macmillan Canada, Ltd.

Library of Congress Cataloging in Publication Data

Ezell, John Samuel.
    The South since 1865.

    Bibliography: pp. 480–492
    Includes index.
    1.  Southern States—History—1865.    2.  Southern
States—Civilization.    I.   Title.
F215.E94    1975          917.5'03'4          74–15132
ISBN 0–02–334750–3

Printing:  1 2 3 4 5 6 7 8        Year:  5 6 7 8 9 0

# *Preface*

THE ORIGINAL PREFACE to this book stressed two things. First were the drastic and dramatic changes which had taken place in the South since the Civil War, a phenomenon which had gone largely unchronicled as a distinct movement in American history. The second point of emphasis was the even more remarkable fact that these modifications and new departures brought the South in line with the prevailing national culture to a greater degree than ever before in its history. At that time no one could have foreseen the fact that the next fifteen years would produce changes so startling that C. Vann Woodward would characterize the decade of the sixties as the "Second Reconstruction."

So profound were the social, economic, and political alterations which occurred that the South of 1960 bears only a nascent resemblance to the region's current profile. What was then a matter of speculation and conjecture is now reality. For example, in regard to the earlier noted tendency toward national conformity, it is ironic that in some aspects the South has more nearly achieved the American ideal than have its regional counterparts. Similarly, more historical research has been undertaken in post-Civil War history, causing a modification in some previously accepted views. Thus, the primary reasons for this revision are to recount and assess the dramatic, and often traumatic, developments of the last decade and a half that make up this revolutionary era, and on the basis of new knowledge to amend the earlier story by aligning it more closely with what historians now believe to be the facts.

Virtually every American is conscious of the Civil War, a struggle which in the last analysis resulted from the inability of national institutions to reconcile the conflicts between North and South. The final Southern decision to strike for independence rather than to submit to Northern demands was bolstered by a belief that the North was insisting upon the surrender of habits, customs, and institutions held dear by Southerners. The new Northern liberalism demanded majority rule through representative government, while the South, on the other hand, felt it must have protection for its unique local interests. To Southerners, this could only be done in a federated union of equals, and therefore they insisted on a confederation to protect minority rights. The South fought for an old liberalism; it wanted equality in the Union and to be left alone with its rights guaranteed. The North felt that some of these rights had to be denied for the good of the whole. Thus the old partnership was rent because of these incompatible viewpoints.

At the end of the Civil War there were, in essence, two nations occupying a formerly united area—one the conqueror, the other the vanquished. What would be the attitudes of the victor and, equally important, of the militarily defeated? Most certainly, one price of reunion would be surrender of some of the treasured Southern customs and institutions. But the South had believed in these enough to go to war, and whether physical defeat alone was enough to convince Southerners that their original loyalties had been misplaced was far from certain. The dilemma thrust upon the nation by the Civil War was, then, that of integrating the South once more into the nation, yet making certain that it would not be in a position to block the goals or objectives of the North. Underlying this were the twin problems of the South's attitude toward its new citizens—the freed Negro slaves who composed one third of the population—and its feeling for the nation it had tried to destroy. What the minimum changes were which the North would accept, as well as what concessions the South would make voluntarily, were the core of Southern history after 1865 and are the theme of this book. It is, therefore, necessarily concerned with the changing society of the South as it yielded to inner and outer pressures to create a "New South"—a region of the United States which eventually became remarkably similar to the rest of the nation, while retaining enough of its historical heritage to remain distinctive. Utilizing an approach which is essentially social and cultural, because of the belief that this is the only one which justifies regional history, this book is the story of the South's return to the "mainstream" of American life.

Any work covering a period of a century must of necessity be the product of many minds. My function has been, therefore, primarily one of correlating and interpreting the research of others and of fleshing out the picture wherever necessary. As to the problem of regional delineation, I have followed the common Southern practice of using the terms "North" and "Northern" to refer to the non-South, except in cases specifically designated otherwise. Moreover, on a subject which excites such wide divergences of opinion, some readers will undoubtedly feel that proper emphasis has not been given to revisionist studies, but the guiding principle on this has been to point out what Southerners believed to be true and therefore what motivated their actions. Often, as Professor William A. Dunning once wrote, "Truth in history is not necessarily what happened, but what men believed happened."

The limitations of space alone prohibit reference to the many sources and individuals that contributed to this study. Citations have been confined principally to manuscript sources, specific monographs, magazine articles, and essays in historical journals—in short, less generally familiar types of materials. The bibliography, likewise, is selective, with emphasis on recent studies and on older ones of particular relevance. Although the breadth of my indebtedness defies verbal, and even conscious, acknowledgment, special mention should be given some. To Professor Arthur M. Schlesinger, Sr., of Harvard University must go the credit for showing me the importance of the cultural approach to history, while Professor Paul H. Buck of the same institution gave me my formal training in Southern history and shaped many of my concepts of that region's culture. I wish also to thank Professors Gilbert C. Fite, Victor Elconin, and Harry Clark for reading sections dealing with their areas of specialization. Professor Jimmie L. Franklin read the entire manuscript and exceeded the claim of friendship by generously sharing his time and knowledge in the preparation of this revision. I am indebted to Mrs. Don P. Bowser of Oklahoma City and her family for permission to quote from papers in their possession. Mrs. Josephine Gil proved endlessly patient and efficient in typing the manuscript, while part of the cost of preparation was borne by the University of Oklahoma Faculty Research Fund. To my wife, Jean McLean, however, must be given my deepest gratitude, for without her encouragement and active assistance in every phase of this undertaking, the task would have been harder and the finished product less worthy.

J. S. E.

# Table of Contents

# The South Since 1865

# 1

# THE SOUTHERN HERITAGE

WHAT IS THE SOUTH? Answering this question has long been a popular pastime with sociologists, psychologists, and professional and self-anointed political, historical, and literary experts of every caliber. Their theories present a mass of contradictory interpretations and unreconcilable differences; while all agree that there is and has been a region with characteristics unlike those of the rest of the United States, they have been unable to reach unanimity about these differences. Their confusion is reflected in a picture which oscillates between snow-white cotton fields and black-smoked blast furnaces; *Tobacco Road* and *Gone with the Wind;* hookworm-ridden tenant farmers and courtly plantation masters; Ku Klux Klan outrages and magnolia-spangled campuses; wild-eyed demagogues and frock-coated, long-haired statesmen; and Franklin Roosevelt's terse remark, "the nation's number one economic problem," and the pride-inspired Southerner's retort, "the nation's number one economic hope."

Geographically, the descriptions vary as widely. The South is variously described as consisting of the states below the Mason-Dixon line, the fifteen governments in which slavery was legal in 1860, or the eleven members of the Confederacy. The "authorities" are of little help in resolving the situation. For example, the United States Bureau of the Census defines the "South" as Alabama, Arkansas, Florida, Georgia, Kentucky, Louisiana, Mississippi, North Carolina, Oklahoma, South Carolina, Tennessee, Texas, Virginia, Delaware, Maryland, the District of Columbia, and West Virginia. The total of seventeen, with the substitution of Missouri for Delaware, is also used in the "Blue Book of Southern Progress" published annually by the *Manufacturers' Record* of Baltimore. On the other hand, Calvin B. Hoover and B. U. Ratchford, in *Economic Resources and Policies of the South* (New York, 1951), included only the first thirteen, while Howard Odum, in *Southern Regions of the United States* (Chapel Hill, 1936), reduced the total to only eleven by further excluding Texas and Oklahoma.

The reason for this dilemma is obvious after a glimpse at a physical map of the United States. Geographical similarity is one of the most common modes of regional delineation, but so widely varied is the topography and soil of the southeastern United States that it is an impossibility to discover any geographical unity. Far from being a unit, the "South" is clearly divided into at least seven physiographic regions, the lines of demarcation running in a northeasterly-southwesterly direction. Such divisions have meant that some parts of the South have more in common with geographically similar Northern areas than with those to their east and west. Furthermore, the region from Delaware south and west to Texas and Oklahoma, embracing roughly one-third of the nation's land and population, is itself composed of as many as twenty-five to thirty subdivisions. Moving westward from the Atlantic coast, the geographer points out the coastal plain, the home of the old plantations, which stretches to the fall line; the Piedmont Plateau of red rolling hills; the pine-covered, infertile Blue Ridge Mountains with their gem-like valleys; the Great Valley, which includes within its limits the fertile Shenandoah and Tennessee valleys; the mineral-rich Alleghenies; the infertile western piedmont, the Cumberland Plateau, barren except in the blue-grass region of Kentucky and the Nashville basin; the Mississippi alluvial lowlands, formed by that river and its tributaries and containing some of the richest lands in the nation; and finally westward into the semidesert stretches of the southern end of the Great Plains. If enough unity exists amid such diversity to justify the term "the South," it has obviously been achieved in spite of, rather than because of, geography.

In the absence of geographical unity, climate has been advanced as an obvious explanation of regional variations. As early as the fifth century B.C., a Greek medical treatise diagnosed a divergence in culture among people of the same physical type as caused by a difference of climate, as well as geological habitat and soil. Ulrich B. Phillips

STATES SOMETIMES CONSIDERED
AS SOUTHERN

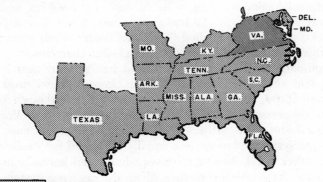

SLAVE STATES 1860

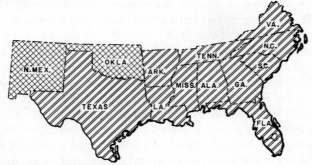

 TERRITORIES OF THE
CONFEDERACY

STATES OF THE
CONFEDERACY

THE SOUTH

began his book, *Life and Labor in the Old South* (Boston, 1929), by writing, "Let us begin by discussing the weather, for that has been the chief agency in making the South distinctive." At a glance it would seem that this statement has validity, for the region has long been noted for mild winters, a long growing season, warm summers, and more sunshine and less wind than other American regions. Except for western Texas and Oklahoma, there is a well-distributed annual rainfall averaging forty inches or more. Certainly the climate has made its mark: it has favored the creation of plantations of cotton, tobacco, rice, and sugar, promoted outdoor life, modified architecture, served as a justification for the employment of labor imported from a hotter land, discouraged immigrants from northern Europe, and perhaps slowed the tempo of speech and action. Yet, if Florida were excluded, the South has the continental climate common to the rest of the nation, and differences must be marked in graduated amounts. Then, too, medical science proved that some so-called "Southern traits" result from such enervating diseases as malaria and hookworm rather than climate.

If not climate, then can its agricultural background explain the South? It is true that the region has always been the most rural part of the United States, with fewer and smaller cities, although twentieth-century concessions to industry, especially since World War II, have weakened the rural attitudes of its people. Furthermore, the South's "unique system," slavery, was usually identified with tilling the soil. On the other hand, however, slavery had been actually only a small part of the total farming picture. Even the one-crop system was not distinctive: the South was no more agricultural than some Western states, nor could it boast a greater devotion to a single staple. Thus, a warm climate and single-crop agriculture were characteristics of the South, rather than explanations of it.

How, then, can the acknowledged similarity among "Southerners" or the recognized differences between them and the people of other parts of the United States be explained? One Southerner, George Fitzhugh, wrote in his *Sociology for the South* (1854), "It is well for us of the South not to be deceived by the tinsel glare and glitter of free society." They, he declared, could boast a more noble heritage. "Our citizens, like those of Rome and Athens, are a privileged class. We should train and educate them to deserve the privileges and to perform the duties which society confers upon them. Instead, by a low demagoguism depressing their self-respect by discourses on the equality of man, we had better excite their pride by reminding them that they do not fulfil the menial offices which white men do in other countries." Furthermore, the differences were more fundamental: "The Cavaliers, Jacobites, and Huguenots who settled the South, naturally hate, contemn, and despise the Puritans who settled the North. The former are master races, the latter, a slave race, the descendants of the Saxon serfs."[1] So readily was this Cavalier tradition embraced by Southerners that it retained popular favor well into the twentieth century, despite the fact that the thesis of selective migration had long been exploded. For the most part, the settlers in both the New England and Southern colonies were basically from the same middle and lower classes of English society.

If, then, the division cannot be made on physical bases, it must lie in intangibles — the special province of the historian and man of letters. Senator John Sharp Williams of Mississippi stated in 1903 that the final history of the South would show that it has been consciously or unconsciously consistent: "that unvarying purpose being this; the preservation of our racial integrity — the supremacy in our midst of the white man's peculiar code of ethics and of the civilization growing out of it."[2] Phillips eventually reached basically the same conclusion. Tangentially, Avery O. Craven explained the South through the continuation of the country-gentleman tradition, an ideal which sought to produce gentlemen within the framework of a Greek democracy or the transplantation of an English aristocracy to America. Poet John Crowe Ransom believed it was the result of men who chose to put their energy in a way of life rather than in acquiring material wealth.

Still others have seen the South as the creation of outside forces. Howard W. Odum wrote, "The rest of the nation never understood the South, and the rest of the nation never ceased to enforce its moral principles; and the South never ceased to resist and resent." This was understandable, for it was, "all told, a paradoxical South, now single-minded, now of multiple trends, now one South, now many Souths, now rapidly developing, now receding, an eager and a puzzled South trying to take stock of itself and its role in the changing nation."[3] Louis D. Rubin, Jr., on the other hand, defined the South in terms of absence of change: "Decades of things as they are, remaining as they are, changing in no appreciable respect, had built in the Southern mind a strong inbred conservatism," and "years and years of enforced stasis had built into the Southern mentality a skepticism of change, a strong inclination to let things be."[4] W. J. Cash saw it as "not quite a nation within a nation, but the next thing to it."

Of the elusiveness of "Southernism" all will agree, and most will

[1] George Fitzhugh, *Sociology for the South* (Richmond, 1854), chap. V.
[2] Quoted by Charles S. Sydnor, "The Southern Experiment in Writing Social History," *Journal of Southern History*, XI (November, 1945), p. 462.
[3] Howard W. Odum, *The Way of the South toward the Regional Balance of America* (New York: Macmillan, 1947), p. 44, and *Southern Regions of the United States* (Chapel Hill: Univ. of North Carolina, 1936), p. 213.
[4] "An Image of the South" in Louis D. Rubin, Jr., and James J. Kilpatrick, eds., *The Lasting South: Fourteen Southerners Look at Their Home* (Chicago: Regnery, 1957), p. 10.

accept the conclusions of the editors of *The Lasting South:* "There *is* a
South, that it is possible to talk of the South, and in doing so to mean
not merely a geographical grouping but a way of life and a state of
mind. . . . The South has gone on being the South, despite controversy
and because of it, and it will continue to go on being the South. 'You
can't understand it. You have to be born there,' a character in a Faulkner novel tells a northern friend."[5] The difficulty of definition in itself
will insure the accuracy of V. O. Key's prediction, "Of books about the
South there is no end. Nor will there be so long as the South remains
the region with the most distinctive character and tradition."[6]

One must therefore be content with the conclusion that history
and not geography made the South, that it is a "state of mind" rather
than a geographical or genealogical development. (Such a conclusion
readily solves the dilemma of those states which did not join the Confederacy, yet whose inhabitants would bitterly resent the connotation
of "Yankee," and those which did secede but have shown characteristics more similar to those of other regions.) Obviously, the Southern
pattern had diverged sufficiently by 1860 to cause its supporters no
longer to feel comfortable and secure within the old union. Observers,
both Northern and Southern, could readily point out basic differences
between the sections in their approaches to class and caste, politics,
economics, and social institutions. In many cases it would take more
than war to convince them that the original choice had been in error.
If history, then, is the key to understanding the post-Civil War South,
what significant legacies did the region inherit from its past?

The Southern caste and economic patterns had their beginnings in
the early colonial period, when the region committed itself to the large-
scale production of tobacco, rice, and indigo for market abroad. The
excessive labor demands of this system led to the adoption of slavery,
and those who succeeded in acquiring the requisite land and labor
quickly developed into the aristocracy of the South. However, market
failures in the years of the Revolution left producers of these staples
in a desperate financial condition, jeopardizing not only the plantation
system but also the existence of slavery and the continuation of aristocratic control. By 1790 many in the South were ready to follow their
Northern neighbors and abolish slavery if only some solution could be
found which would eliminate the presence or threat of the freed Negro.
The fateful die was cast, however, when, in response to European technological improvements which demanded more raw material for cloth,
the planters investigated the possibility of growing cotton. The inven-

[5] *Ibid.,* p. x.
[6] V. O. Key, Jr., *Southern Politics in State and Nation* (New York: Knopf, 1949),
p. ix.

tion of the cotton gin perpetuated the slave economy by making economically feasible the production of short-staple cotton, which would grow almost anywhere with 200 frost-free days. The planters had a new profitable crop adaptable to the plantation system, and thus was also solved the problem of surplus black labor.

Cotton became so important that, in 1855, David Christy could write a book, *Cotton is King,* and Senator James H. Hammond of South Carolina could say to the world, and to the North in particular, "Without the firing of a gun, without drawing a sword, should they [the North] make war upon us, we could bring the whole world to our feet. What would happen if no cotton was furnished for three years? . . . England would topple headlong and carry the whole civilized world with her. No, you dare not make war on cotton. No power on earth dares make war on it. Cotton is King."[7] In truth, cotton had become the most dynamic force of the nineteenth century, and the South controlled this power. So vital was the product in the Southern pattern of thought that it would be only a slight exaggeration to say that it was socially preferable to "go broke" planting cotton than to make money in any other fashion.

Equally as important as the effects of cotton upon the economy were its effects upon the people. The agricultural way of life, with its correlated slave-master social stratifications, dominated all phases of Southern life, and cotton's rise to prominence coincided with the growth of unmistakable evidence that the South was creating a separate, almost opposite, personality from that of its sister states. Legalized bondage was only one of the more obvious distinctions. At a time when the citizens of the North were taking pride in their democratic institutions and holding up the United States as the world's democratic hope, in the South there were people who not only embraced the concept of slavery but who challenged the validity of what they scornfully termed the "glittering and sounding generalities of natural right which make up the Declaration of Independence." It was an early but definite betrayal of the ideals of the Enlightenment, a precursor of a perverted outgrowth of Darwinism. Darwinism was for most thinking men of the nineteenth century a strengthening of their inheritance from the Enlightenment, but for some it provided the ideological basis for racial, and thus national, superiority.

Specifically, the South was bent on maintaining a great void between the white and black races. When the North voiced its opposition to such discrimination, it, too, was declared to be different and therefore inferior. While class distinctions were breaking down in the North, they were increasing in the South. The past, paradoxically, was the

[7] *Congressional Globe,* 35th Congress, 1 Sess., p. 961.

ideal of the Southerners, and to perpetuate a nation of glamorized aristocracy akin to that portrayed by their favorite novelist, Sir Walter Scott, became their goal. A well-ordered society, with well-defined classes resting upon an economic base of self-sufficient plantations, called for each group to know its place and look to the upper class for leadership. Even here lines were drawn, based upon acreage and the number of bond servants. Of one and a quarter million white families in the South, 347,000 owned slaves; yet the highest honors were reserved for the 8,000 who possessed fifty or more Negroes. Not far behind, however, were the lesser planters, the most ambitious group in the South, ever anxious to climb into the ranks of the elite.

These two orders worked for the formation of a real aristocracy. They pictured their caste as motivated by high ideals — honor, chivalry, respect for women, and other imagined traits of a de-scented, imaginary feudalism. They were openly proud of the fact that Southerners had come to accept the planter's occupation as being synonymous with the characterization of "gentlemen." By 1861, although gaps in this aristocratic structure still remained, these were being eliminated.

The planters, though a decided minority, naturally were the leaders in all phases of life: social, economic, and political. The last was exercised by means of their unity in a common cause, their social and economic standing, and their positions as justices of the peace. As members of the county court, after the introduction of that system from England, the planters had controlled county politics by appointing the local officials, supervising admissions to the bar, and making up the unofficial committees who determined nominees for state and national office. Little could happen in any Southern state without their consent. Attacks against their overlordship were met by a united defense. A system of legislative representation by counties was effectively used to thwart their political foes in the back country. Property qualifications were demanded for the right to vote and hold office, and by refusing to reapportion representation, the plantation areas managed to keep control.

The wave of Jeffersonianism, with its democratic connotations, washed futilely against this dike of intrenched privilege. Those portions of Jefferson's philosophy which served the purpose of the ruling caste were adopted, often with distorted meanings, and the rest was repudiated. The decentralized State, with its emphasis upon states' rights, was used as a minority defense. Jefferson's belief that those "who labour in the earth are the chosen people of God, if ever he had a chosen people, whose breasts he had made his peculiar deposit for substantial and genuine virtue," was turned by the plantation elite to their own interests and justification.

The rise of Jacksonianism, however, with its leveling tendencies, created a more dangerous foe. The new Western states were yielding to the clamor for universal, white, manhood suffrage, and the demands of the disregarded masses in the older communities could no longer be ignored. This movement began almost simultaneously with the abolitionists' attacks, making the political overlords even more reluctant to alter the existing order for fear of disturbing the social and economic status quo. Nevertheless, by 1850 all of the South Atlantic states except South Carolina had called conventions for constitutional revision. The liberal goal was equality of representation and extension of the suffrage. The conservatives met these demands by yielding slightly on suffrage and compromising on representation. Although equal county representation was generally abandoned, the same result was achieved by basing representation upon the "federal numbers" (five slaves counted as three whites), total population (including white and Negro), or a combination of population and taxation. Thus, Jacksonianism was virtually repudiated, and most of the larger planters joined the Whig party to emphasize this fact. Southern leadership grew skillful at safeguarding itself against hostile majorities at home, experience which also served it well on the national level.

The largest element in the South was the indeterminate middle class. Mainly ignored by historians, novelists, and essayists, it comprised the great bulk of white society — the non-slaveholding farmers, the business and professional men, and the artisans. By far the largest group was the yeomen farmers. Residing on the fringes of the plantation areas or in the valleys, they grew mostly subsistence crops, with a little cotton or tobacco for extra cash. Southern writers, such as Augustus Baldwin Longstreet in his *Georgia Scenes,* stressed their humor and resourcefulness, while Northerners, such as Frederick Law Olmsted, pictured them as rude and unprogressive. In actuality, they were hard fighters, drinkers, and workers. They had not learned that the white man was supposed to be unable to stand the heat of the sun or that manual labor bore a stigma. Suffering often from isolation, these people were self-reliant and lived in rough contempt of the domestic conveniences cherished by their Northern counterparts. Reading little more than the almanac, their social diversions were chiefly hunting and attending court sessions and political rallies.

On the whole, the Southern yeomen were overwhelming champions of the Southern economic and social order, and it is idle to speak of them as the puppets of the planter-leaders. They were of the same racial stock, and many of the planters of the lower South had only recently risen from their ranks. Their dominant desire was to climb the social ladder themselves or to keep open the way for their children.

They did not always lose in the competition for land, and frequent bankruptcies among the planters allowed them to buy slaves and more land. Blood ties with the upper class were common; intermarriage was frequent, and co-mingling in social and political gatherings was the order of the day. The yeomen were not exploited and could feel as free and independent as the planters.

Yet both recognized a common interdependence. The planter needed the foodstuffs produced by the farmer, as well as his vote. The farmer, on the other hand, depended on his prosperous neighbor for a market, for use of the plantation's cotton gin, press, and wharf, and for political leadership in the English gentry-rule tradition. A common contempt for the slave made all white men brothers and elevated them to membership in the superior class. When criticism of the master-slave relationship arose from outside, the yeoman joined in hatred of the "Nigger-loving scoundrels" — the abolitionists — and when war came, he rallied to the slaveowners' side.

These small farmers of the South, however, like their counterparts throughout history, found themselves teetering between two extremes because of the competition of slaves and the fact that the plantations generally swallowed up the best land. A few of the most successful climbed the ladder to plantership, but those who lost the struggle with the plantations and their fellow farmers fell into the strata of the dis-possessed "white trash," a category known in the similar society of ancient Rome as "free trash." In this lower level of the Southern social pyramid were about one million whites, labeled "crackers," "hillbillies," "clay eaters," "sand hillers," "squatters," "rag tag and bobtail," and "po' white trash." A great favorite with authors, the subject of the poor whites' laziness, poverty, misshapened bodies, and bizarre morals has filled pages from William Byrd II's *History of the Dividing Line* in the 1730's down through William Faulkner. By the mid-twentieth century their characterization had become one of the chief financial resources of a large group of writers.[8] Although it was difficult for a nonresident to make the distinction between poor yeomen and "poor whites," a distinction was made and deemed vital. Men could be poor and white but still be a part of the respected yeoman class. "Poor whites," on the other hand, lay at the bottom of the social as well as the economic structure. It was a difference of kind rather than degree.

Whenever the upper classes deigned to notice these unfortunates at all, they explained the "hillbillies'" existence in accordance with the Cavalier tradition. The "crackers" and their kind were simply the descendants of the indentured servants, debtors, and prisoners shipped

[8] Shields McIlwaine, *The Southern Poor-White from Lubberland to Tobacco Road* (Norman: Univ. of Oklahoma, 1939).

by England to the colonies. However, their large numbers and wide geographical distribution, plus recent knowledge of immigrant origins, argue against acceptance of this theory. Living on the poorest lands in the South, often as squatters, they were merely the weakest element in a frontier society. Their homes — the mountains, red hills, sand barrens, and swamps — were eddies in the stream of progress. Isolation kept them ignorant, and submarginal lands kept them poor. Filth, poverty, and unhealthful surroundings enabled hookworm, pellagra, and malaria to sap any remaining strength of the poor whites, leaving them generally listless unless inspired by corn whiskey.

But these men were genuine Anglo-Saxon Southerners, sharing the aristocratic attitude that manual labor was fit only for Negroes or, at best, women. They were proud of their barren acres and practiced a courtliness of manner which belied their lowly position. Largely ignored by the rest of society, these folk were not exploited, except on such occasions as their misdeeds brought them attention. Since they were not oppressed or mistreated by the governing classes, they shared a lordly contempt for the Negroes, a contempt made bitter in that even the slaves looked down upon them. This skin-color distinction made the poor whites' votes and support readily available to any politician who condemned the Negro or said that the abolitionist wanted to make all men equal. Thus, the poor whites, like the yeomen, found themselves supporting the slave-based aristocracy of the South but having virtually no chance of improving their own position. The only way the planters could be pulled down was to free their slaves, and this the poor whites and the yeomen were unwilling to undertake because of the economic and social misfortunes they believed would result for themselves.

Juxtaposed on this inflexible social order of the white Southerners was the cause of these apprehensions — the Negro slaves — nearly one-third of the total Southern population by 1860. Negroes had been in the New World since around 1500 as explorers, servants, and slaves. Slavery had been introduced to meet a situation in which capital found itself with a market for its goods, abundant cheap land for their production, but a shortage of labor. The slave trade, dominated by the English but including the Dutch, French, and later the New Englanders, was an important economic institution and exerted as much pressure on the South to import slaves as did the necessity for extra labor. Corporations like the Royal African Company of England established posts along the west African coast, where their agents maintained friendly relations with the native chiefs and arranged exchanges of goods and slaves. A company ship would stop at these posts to unload European goods and take on the captured and bartered natives, a healthy young man costing an average of £20 sterling around 1750, the price varying with the age of the slave and the location of the post. When the ship was filled, the long and torturous voyage was begun, with death the ultimate destination of a large percentage of the chained cargo, but the rigors of this notorious "middle passage" from Africa unintentionally assured that slaves would have the physical stamina to withstand the shock of confronting a new climate and society. Although the principal markets were the West Indies and Spanish America, the overflow found an outlet in the English colonies of North America, especially among the labor-starved rice, tobacco, and indigo planters of the South.

Thus, to the shores of North America came these alien and dark people. Gathered from many posts, which in turn had secured the slaves from widely scattered areas, they represented many different tribes with literally hundreds of different dialects and customs. Primarily an agricultural people, they had lived in small villages which often banded together to form kingdoms, ranging in size from family states to federations or even "empires." Governing power was usually held by one family, the eldest male serving as chief of the clan. The family was also the basis of the social organization, and the nobility was comprised of those with the most land and a respected name. Next came the great mass of workers, having no proof of their family tree but claiming a good name. They engaged in fishing, mining, hunting, and other industries. Last were the slaves — chiefly war captives — who, while not mistreated, held no recognized social position.

Religion was an important part of the Negroes' lives; it took strong symbolic forms, with belief in spirits of unlimited powers. Magic was another aspect of their worship and was perhaps a retarding influence on cultural and civic progress. Music was all-important in the religious ceremonies, as it was in the rest of their activities; rhythm flowed through all their actions and expressions. Each tribe, creating its own art forms, was more or less self-contained, for language difference and distances prevented close communication. But in spite of the many diversities among the natives brought to America, there were always certain common characteristics to be found: great respect and loyalty for the family unit and its chief; deep religious capacities which were integrally related to the family alliance; close association with nature; and love of song, dance, and story.

These two different cultures, Southern and African, different yet strangely alike in basic ways, affected each other variously, the amount being a favorite argument among sociologists, historians, and anthropologists. Although possessors of a much higher culture than generally recognized, the Negroes, strangers even among themselves, were inevitably forced to adopt the culture of their white captors to the extent that much of their own cultural inheritance was lost or submerged. While not being absorbed into the white culture, the slaves did ingest much of it — language, customs, and religion — all modified by the dominant and common characteristics of their African background. Correspondingly, the blacks added much to the culture of their owners.

Resting upon a forced migration, the slave trade, before its abolition in 1808, produced one of the greatest mixtures of racial stocks that history has ever witnessed. Literally a new race was created. Beginning in 1619 with the "twenty Negers" brought to Virginia in a "dutch man of warre," by 1790 their totals increased to 697,624 and seventy years later to almost four million. Of this number, moreover, over one-tenth were mulattoes, indicative of yet another blood stream which contributed to the creation of this new race.

By far the greatest number of slaves, 89 per cent in 1790, lived in the South Atlantic states, so the plantation society of that region was the culture to which most of the blacks were exposed. Here class distinctions developed even among the slaves: the house slave, who could often read and write and who was a black counterpart of his master in manners and sometimes dress; the bondsman, who worked as a tradesman or artisan in the towns; and the lowly field hand, who planted and harvested the crops on the plantations. The pattern of this older area was carried to the lower South by both master and slave.

Unique among the blacks were the free ones. Although there was common agreement among the whites by the mid-1830's that the slaves should not be freed, a quarter of a million free blacks were living in the South by 1860. Concentrated most heavily in Louisiana and the upper South, they or their ancestors had been manumitted for special services, humane or economic reasons, or had through unusual industry been enabled to buy their own freedom. Before the whites became alarmed over the abolitionists' activities and the possibility of slave insurrections, these people enjoyed an almost total absence of legal discrimination but were circumscribed by custom. A number, however, were able to acquire considerable property, including slaves, and high business and professional standing.

After 1830, however, their lot was increasingly difficult. There was no place in the Southern master plan for the free blacks. Their very presence, as a potential abolitionist fifth column, was dangerous to planter domination. They were not hired for agricultural work lest they corrupt the slave, and they could not be disciplined by master or overseer. Deprived of economic opportunity in the country, they had little choice but to go to the towns and cities of the South, where all too

often they led lives of petty crime and vice. They were literally walled
off from the whites by law and custom and even from their own race
by the watchful guardians of the Southern system. Exempt from the
control of the slavery system, the freedmen were disciplined by increasingly stringent legal provisions, until at last there could be said to
be little difference between their legal status and that of the slave except the myth of freedom. Consequently, one must wonder at the
report in the New Orleans *Daily Picayune* of April 21, 1861, announcing a gathering of the "most respectable portion of the colored population of the city" to volunteer their aid in case of enemy attack. The
same newspaper reported on November 24, a parade before the governor in which 1,400 free black soldiers participated.[9]

The reaction of the slaves to the willingness of their kinsmen to
fight to keep them in bondage has not been recorded. In fact, the
slaves' attitude toward their own position is a matter of controversy.
Nevertheless, this group of bondsmen, the hewers of wood and drawers
of water, was the foundation of the whites' plan for their economic,
political, and social Utopia. Southerners, in the absence of English laws
governing relations between slaves and masters, adopted Spanish practices or modified old British statutes on indenture and apprenticeship.
These adaptations were in the direction of greater respect for the property rights of the master and increased protection of society against an
alien and savage people. As in the case of the free Negroes, legal restrictions increased with the passage of time, yet the slaves in general
enjoyed a better status than the letter of the law implied. They did
have rights their masters had to respect, but the fact remained that
they were the property of their owners and not in control of their
own fates.

In line with Aristotle's suggestion that some men were intended
"by nature" to be slaves, Southerners justified the Negroes' position
by asserting that the black men, being biologically inferior, were
divinely created to be servants. Merely grown-up children, their Southern servitude rescued them from a more cruel slavery in Africa and
from idolatry and cannibalism. They were Christianized, protected,
civilized, and governed better than were free laborers in the North.
In short, their bondage was not the moral evil it had been proclaimed,
but a positive good, so beneficial, in fact, that further importation
should be legalized to allow more widespread enjoyment of the virtues
of the system. Actually, there appears little reason to believe that the
institution would have been overthrown by a servile revolt. So acqui-
escent were all groups in the South to the status quo that only outside

[9] Donald E. Everett, "Ben Butler and the Louisiana Native Guards, 1861-1862,"
*Journal of Southern History*, XXIV (May, 1958), pp. 202-203.

force, perhaps only a bloody civil war, could produce any drastic social change.

If Southern leaders looked with satisfaction upon their social order, their economic structure was equally comforting. Given an abundance of rich land, an expanding world market, and a large labor force of unskilled Africans, that they had decided to break with the English and Northern agricultural patterns of self-sufficient farming was not surprising. Instead, staple production for an outside market on a plantation scale with forced labor was inaugurated. Land was cheap and labor expensive; thus a policy of mining the soil as rapidly as possible and then moving on to the virgin acres was followed. In the last analysis, it was the threatened check to this Southern geographical expansion which brought the Civil War in 1861.

Cotton was so important that it is easy to overlook other crops in the Southern pattern. The Census of 1850 listed 74,031 cotton plantations (producing more than five bales each), 15,745 tobacco (producing more than 3,000 pounds), and 8,327 hemp, 2,681 sugar, and 551 rice plantations (producing over 20,000 pounds). Although the large plantation was the usual cultivation unit for rice and sugar, cotton and tobacco could be profitably raised by small farmers. Nevertheless, they engaged primarily in growing food crops because of the lack of transportation, capital, and the like. The typical farmer raised rye, barley, oats, or wheat, plus a small number of livestock, but his principal crop was corn, so well suited to climate and soil and so easy to cultivate that the South produced 50 per cent of the nation's output. Corn appeared on the farmer's table in the form of bread, "grits," hominy, roasting ears, whiskey, and meat, chiefly pork.

The overemphasis on staple crops by the principal producers, the planters, left the South with an agricultural imbalance which required the importation of foodstuffs. This situation was growing on the eve of the Civil War, because the high prices for cotton led many to believe that the labor of the slave was more profitably utilized in producing staples. This did not prevent Southerners from grumbling, however, over the loss of money to the North and West for products which might have been produced locally.

Then, too, all Southern agriculturists, except perhaps the sugar planters, felt themselves exploited by the Federal protective tariff. This bite was felt most keenly when their staples were exchanged in European markets for manufactured goods. Thus, not only was the South forced to pay tribute from the crops' return for the benefit of Northern manufacturers, but also the whole system of commerce was geared to the South's economic disadvantage. Its trade was dominated by the cotton, rice, sugar, and grain "factors" — usually agents of

Northern or English firms. To these offices in the principal Southern cities, the planters consigned their crops to be sold or forwarded directly to New York or England. The factors acted not only as sales representatives but also as purchasing agents, and for these services the planters paid a good price of from 2.5 to 10 per cent. Terms for credit ran even higher, and to these had to be added other types of fixed charges, such as insurance and storage.

On leaving the South, the products were shipped either directly to Europe, with the return voyage by way of the North, or to New York and from there to Europe and back by the same route. As the South owned only river vessels, additional opportunities were created for Northern and European levies. It was on the basis of such evidence that John C. Calhoun charged in the *South Carolina Exposition and Protest* that the North deprived the South of cheap manufactured goods and thus increased the cost of cotton production. The tariffs were making "serfs" of the South, who, though representing only one-third of the United States population, produced two-thirds of its exports. Senator George McDuffie of South Carolina placed this Northern toll at forty out of every one hundred bales of cotton raised.

This feeling that the South's devotion to agriculture facilitated its being robbed in purchase of manufactured goods gave impetus to the demand that the region seek economic independence by manufacturing its own products. The South had long engaged in a variety of household industries and as late as 1810 led the nation in the production of homespun cloth. With the coming of the cotton textile industry to American shores during the War of 1812, the South kept pace with the North in adopting the new English machinery and factory methods. However, the expanding market for cotton made planting offer greater returns than manufacturing. So, paradoxically, even in the 1850's, when the region was loudly bemoaning its economic dependence and industrial-minded Southerners like William Gregg were pointing to the dire fate which would overtake the region if war came, only a slight effort was made to remedy the situation. Despite the protests of colonial status and arguments that thus the labor of the poor whites could be utilized and that manufacturing was profitable, in 1860 the single town of Lowell, Massachusetts, had more spindles in operation than did the whole South.

Although agreeing upon the need for manufactures, Southern life was too rigid to absorb the new ideas. It was unable to solve the problems of capital and labor. The planters' resources were non-fluid, and the factors' interests lay in staples; white labor was scarce or uninterested and that of slaves too expensive for turning the wheels of factories. The plantation would probably have had to be destroyed before manufacturing could have prospered. To the eve of war, Southerners still loved to quote Jefferson's strictures against manufacturing and boast that the black slavery of the South was more humane than the white industrial slavery of the North. It was quite problematical in a Southerner's mind that a manufacturer could be a "gentleman." Consequently, the region left manufacturing to the North and took pride in its agricultural unity.

But the decision to cast its lot with agriculture, regardless of immediate and future cost, was not the only different road taken by the South. Confronted by increasingly bitter attacks from the abolitionists, Southerners became convinced that these tormentors were representative of Northern opinion. This belief, in turn, alerted them to the danger of the old practice of sending their children North for an education or else bringing Northern teachers and texts to the students. The region had long since made its choice against the democratic public educational systems and remained true to the English tradition that education should be selective, private, and concerned with the training of leaders. Thus, as a result of Northern influence, the South's future leaders were in danger of being subverted. J. D. B. De Bow, a Louisiana educator and editor of *De Bow's Review*, felt it preferable that "our sons remained in honest ignorance and at the plough-handle" than filled "with doctrines subversive of their country's peace and honor" or in violation of the fundamental principles on which Southern society had been based throughout its history.[10] The answer had to be a "Southern" education for Southerners.[11]

Senator James M. Mason of Virginia saw even the Federal government as a party in this conspiracy. In a speech in Congress, February 1, 1859, in opposing a grant of public lands for agricultural and mechanical colleges, he held that it would lead to the fastening upon the South of "that peculiar system of free schools in New England States which . . . would tend, I will not say to demoralize, but to destroy that peculiar character which I am happy to believe belongs to the great mass of Southern people."[12]

But schools, professors, and texts were not the only problem. Popular literature was also suspect. A Southern Rights Association, formed by the citizens of Prince George County, Virginia, pledged its members to buy from the North nothing which was obtainable at home, to employ no Northern teachers, to withdraw their children from

[10] "Home Education at the South," *De Bow's Review*, X (1851), p. 362.
[11] John S. Ezell, "A Southern Education for Southrons," *Journal of Southern History*, XVII (August, 1951), p. 303ff.
[12] Virginia Mason, comp., *The Public Life and Diplomatic Correspondence of James M. Mason, with some Personal History* (Roanoke, Va., 1903), p. 140.

Northern schools, and to boycott Northern newspapers and books. De Bow asked defiantly, "Who of the North reads a Southern book?" and there appeared new magazines, such as the *Southron,* dedicated to "promoting the literature of the South."[13] The campaign for intellectual independence was vigorous. Orators harangued conventions, editors scolded their readers for being "more familiar with such abominable works as Mrs. Stowe's 'Uncle Tom's Cabin,' and with the abolition sermons of Theodore Parker than with the constitutionalism which has rendered us a nation," and politicians talked to anyone who would listen.

Obviously, religion, too, felt the pull of these divergent forces. The church had played a lesser role in the Southern colonies than in the Northern, and its voice in secular affairs, perhaps even in matters of conscience, was weaker. The King of England's position as head of the dominant Anglican Church made it relatively easy for the South to embrace the revolutionary doctrine of the separation of church and state. From independence down through the 1820's, the region was most tolerant of religious deviations. "The Great Revival" of 1800 deeply imbued the average person with a spirit of evangelical Protestantism to the advantage of such sects, while at the same time there were also many evidences of an increasingly rational attitude toward religion among the upper classes. Leaders such as Thomas Jefferson and Thomas Cooper boldly stated that man should use his reasoning powers fearlessly to probe the mysteries of religion. Minor church groups sprang up, of which the Unitarians were probably the most significant. This group spread into the cities in the decades of the 1820's and 1830's, and Jared Sparks, future president of Harvard, was pastor of such a church at Baltimore in 1819. Catholics, skeptics, and even atheists were viewed with tolerance.

This spirit, however, began to fade in the 1830's. Liberal thought was met by a conservative reaction which was greatly reinforced by the vested interests of Southerners, who felt threatened by all types of liberal forces. The defense of slavery against the rising force of abolitionism and hostile world opinion required the support of a unified, conservative community. The Age of Reason waned; the South became more isolated from the intellectual currents of Europe and the North. Conservative religion, relying heavily upon a literal interpretation of the Scriptures, became one of the most impregnable bulwarks of the status quo. By 1850 both commoner and aristocrat were united in a prevailing orthodoxy of almost medieval intensity. Since abolitionists

[13] Jay B. Hubbell, "Literary Nationalism in the Old South," in Duke University Americana Club, *American Studies in Honor of William Kenneth Boyd* (Durham, N. C.: Duke University, 1940).

proclaimed slavery a sin, defending slavery and the synonymous "Southern civilization" became an obsession with Southerners. Scriptures were searched with diligence, and few proslavery writers failed to quote chapter and verse in vindication of the institution. Many rested their arguments entirely on a Biblical defense.

By this literal interpretation and strict adherence to the letter of the Scriptures, the South became convinced that, to condemn slavery, Northern churchmen had to distort and abandon the Bible. Probably it was with a spirit of equanimity and a feeling of good riddance, therefore, that Southerners pushed the denominational crises which split along the Mason-Dixon line the Presbyterian Church in 1838, the Methodist in 1844, and the Baptist in 1845. Dr. Cooper was forced from the presidency of South Carolina College for his opposition to a law which would ban the carrying of mail on Sundays. Jefferson's policy of a secular University of Virginia was abandoned, and his hope that "there is not a young man now living in the United States who will not die an Unitarian," was not fulfilled, evidenced by the moribund condition of that sect in 1860. In fact, the prevalent orthodoxy of the South was illustrated by the almost total absence of liberal sects in the Census of 1860, which showed only one Swedenborgian, twenty-four Universalist, three Unitarian, and no Spiritualist churches in the slave states.

Feeling under attack upon almost every front, Southerners reacted by throwing into their defense all the talents — literary, scientific, and political — that they possessed. Politically, the South sought to defend itself by emphasizing states' rights, by fighting desperately to maintain its last stronghold in the United States Senate, and by using bluff to force the majority to yield. The most important thing which resulted from the series of political and sectional crises was not the concessions which the Southerners gained, but that they learned to unite. Secession as a final means to redress grievances seemed less and less fearsome. And they were convinced they had grievances. Why, indeed, was the government under the Constitution any more destined for immortality than that under the Articles of Confederation?

By 1860 there was need for compromise in most of the dominant fields of Northern and Southern life. A Southerner writing in 1856 stated his belief that the North and South were two nations, as distinct as the English and French. Based upon institutions, customs, and habits of thought, this difference was so pronounced that he viewed the sessions of Congress not as opportunities to discuss common interests but as conventions "to contest antagonistic opinions and to proclaim mutual grievances and utter hostile threats." The question was whether political organizations could change rapidly enough to take care of the new strains and conflicts, or whether the regional culture and aspirations of the South would have to give way to the national pattern. It was the same old problem of 1776 — acceptance of colonial status.

With the Compromise of 1850, the South surrendered Senate equality, after having lost it much earlier in the House. For the next ten years, hopes for safety within the Union were pinned upon control of the Democratic party and its domination of the national government. But several events destroyed Southern faith in the Democrats' willingness to fight for Southern interests. The failure of a Democratic administration to secure the admission of Kansas as a slave state was one. Democratic support for the Freeport Doctrine of Stephen A. Douglas, which pointed out a loophole whereby the Dred Scott decision, allowing slavery to penetrate any territory, could be circumvented, was compounded by the refusal of the Democratic convention of 1860 to include a plank favoring Federal protection for slavery in the territories. The candidacy of Douglas, a Northern Democrat, on an evasive platform seemed as dangerous to Southern objectives as that of the "black Republican," Lincoln. And so the party split along sectional lines, with the Southern branch of the party nominating John C. Breckinridge of Kentucky on a platform stressing Southern rights.

The Republicans were united and put forth a platform which reaffirmed the Declaration of Independence's guarantee of the equality of men. They denounced the Buchanan administration's efforts to make Kansas a slave state, repudiated the Dred Scott decision, and stated that "the normal condition of all the territory of the United States is that of freedom" and that Congress, territorial legislatures, or individuals lacked authority to give slavery legal existence in any territory. Other planks supported protective tariffs, a homestead policy, and river and harbor appropriations. The Republicans had, in brief, a platform which would not only appeal to abolitionists but also to the small farmers of the West and the industrialists of the North. On the other hand, however, the things they favored were the very things which the South had opposed almost since the formation of the Constitution.

Despite the mild words of Lincoln, the South believed his election would be the first step toward the abolition of slavery, if not worse. A Republican triumph would mean more John Browns. C. C. Clay charged that their real aim was to "free the negroes and force amalgamation between them and the children of the poor man of the South." Robberies, rapes, and murder of the whites by the emancipated blacks were the fears which the press and orators drummed into Southern ears. Why take such a risk? Cotton was still king; the powers of Europe would have to come to the South's aid. An independent South could be prosperous as well as free.

Actually, the South did not believe the nation would choose a party whose election to power, the South had clearly stated since 1854, would give just grounds for secession. The issues were so charged with emotion that only at the last moment did some Southerners realize that the course the Breckinridge Democrats were following was practically assuring the thing they most dreaded. But it was too late: by a majority of 180 electoral votes to 123, although he had received only 39.9 per cent of the popular vote and had not been on the ballot in ten Southern states, Abraham Lincoln was elected president.

The South was stunned. Did the election really mean the South was no longer safe in the Union? South Carolina had no doubts; the legislature without a dissenting vote called a state convention to consider the question of secession, and the latter unanimously passed such an ordinance on December 20, 1860. Any chance for calmer action by the slave states as a body was lost through the precipitous action of the radicals. Before Lincoln could even be inaugurated, six other states followed South Carolina out of the Union and in February, 1861, created the Confederate States of America and chose Jefferson Davis their leader.

Southern nationalism was triumphant. The contagion of secession swept along even those who had at first been opposed. The final act was heralded with spontaneous street parades, band concerts, torchlight processions, and firework displays. Southerners had thrown off their humiliating dependence upon the North and were now going to build the most splendid nation the world had ever seen. Those with less optimistic views either buried them in the secrecy of their diaries or faced the scorn of their neighbors.

The majority of Southerners felt that secession would not result in war, a view shared by their government. The most important problem of the Confederacy, therefore, was to come to terms with its northern neighbor. The most immediate was to induce the United States to surrender the few forts it still held in the lower South, for, until that was done, sovereignty was incomplete. Fort Sumter, at Charleston, South Carolina, was the crux of the matter. It was not evacuated; moreover, Lincoln notified South Carolina authorities that he was sending the garrison additional men and supplies. President Davis and his cabinet reluctantly ordered an attack upon the fort rather than see it reinforced; Sumter surrendered April 13, 1861. Lincoln issued a call for 75,000 troops to suppress the insurrection, thereby placing the slave states which had not yet seceded from the Union in a cruel quandary. They opposed both secession and coercion but now had to choose. In the words of Governor John W. Ellis of North Carolina, rather than be a "party to this wicked violation of the laws of the country and to this war upon the liberties of a free people," four more states, Virginia, North Carolina, Tennessee, and Arkansas, cast their lots with the Confederacy.

An era had ended, however much the Southerner might deny it. Most of them went to war reluctantly, but once in battle they went with spirit. It was a War for Independence, for *their* nation. Slavery might be viewed as the cause, but it was more than a war to retain slavery. Southerners had come to believe that their beloved Southern way of life was something they could not keep if they remained in the Union. And to them all — the planter, the yeoman, the poor white — it was a way of life worth dying for.

This Southern sectional unity had not been omnipresent but was the result of generations of struggle. Geographically, there was no such thing as a solid South, and differences of many kinds had been active to prevent coordinated action until such a time as stronger forces had overcome the natural centrifugal tendencies of the region. Among the more important bonds which served to weld the South into a people ready for common action was the pervading influence of the slavery-based plantation system. Cotton, tobacco, rice, sugar, and hemp planters — all used their political, economic, and social powers to protect their world from the onslaught of the democratic hordes. Whatever threatened cotton threatened planter and farmer alike. Southerners of every class were also made one by a sense of economic wrong. They were convinced that there existed an economic imperialism centered in the North which was determined to make them vassals.

Also, in the South all whites were brothers in the fear that a social revolution could well result from the activities of the abolitionists. They felt themselves to be sitting on a powder keg of race problems while Northern fanatics ran around lighting matches. Then, too, were not they all being insulted by the indiscriminate charges of moral and social degradation being hurled with such abandon by their Northern brethren? The whole Southern people were being condemned for the acts of a single planter or an isolated group or for things which they did not feel to be wrong at all.

In reaction, the South cast its lot with the conservatives. Liberal tendencies in religion, education, literature, government, and the like were viewed as threats. The prevailing Protestant sects, though differing in their plans of salvation, were united in their determination to root out the last vestige of the deistic cults of Thomas Jefferson and Thomas Cooper. Private education was held to be superior to public education, to require strong religious influence, and to be necessary only for potential leaders. Literature was viewed not as a fine art but as a weapon to be used for the defense of home institutions against outside attacks.

The fact that South and North had chosen different and diverging cultural roads not only meant increased difficulty in reaching mutual understanding, but also that Southerners prided themselves on a unique way of life and strove to make it ever more peculiarly Southern. And most important in a political union, they had the growing feeling that the South was a political minority and soon would be unable to protect its heritage against a rival, aggressive, and imperialistic North. They had come to agree with the logic of John C. Calhoun's March 4 speech on the Compromise of 1850: "As . . . the North has the absolute control over the Government, it is manifest that on all questions between it and the South, where there is a diversity of interests, the interest of the latter will be sacrificed to the former, however oppressive the effects may be; as the South possesses no means by which it can resist, through the action of the Government."[14]

Every nation is composed of varied regions, each with what it considers to be its legitimate, if different, interests. If a nation is to endure, it must reconcile yet respect these fundamental regional interests. When this is not done, sectional friction results, and, unless compromises can be worked out, sectional nationalism begins to grow. Just as John Adams said of the American Revolution that it was caused by a change in men's hearts, so could be characterized the revolt which occurred in 1861. The true revolution in the South came when its inhabitants began to feel that their interests were jeopardized by remaining in the Union and to think of themselves as Southerners rather than Americans. Crane Brinton wrote of nationalism as consistent with the rise of a class lacking "cosmopolitan experience and personal knowledge of other lands" and which found the "abstract devotion of the intellectual to all humanity beyond its range." For these, a nation "stood ready to provide the enduring if vicarious satisfactions of 'pooled self-esteem.' "[15]

For four years the South fought to achieve this goal. Finally bereft of its hope of foreign intervention, strangled by the Northern blockade, and overwhelmed by Union superiority in manpower and material, the Confederacy collapsed. Did this mean the end of the unique characteristics which made it so easy for a person to say "the South" in 1840 or 1850 and be sure that his listeners knew with exactness to what he was referring? Would that region be so wholly absorbed into the culture of the victorious North as to lose its identity?

[14] *Congressional Globe*, 31st Congress, 1 Sess., pp. 451ff.
[15] Crane Brinton, *Ideas and Men* (New York: Prentice-Hall, 1950), p. 419.

It was obvious that most of the extreme points of difference, such as political independence, slavery, and the plantation system, were doomed. On the other hand, it was possible that some traits, although largely intangible ones, were too strong to remain submerged and that the war itself had played a role in creating a new "Southerner."

# 2

# THE DEFEATED SOUTH

AS THE thousands of ragged Southern veterans straggled home, still carrying the memories and scars from the war's bitterly futile years, only the most optimistic could look forward to the future without misgivings. Though beaten, they were proud of the past, for the South had given generously of its blood and treasure, equal to over a half-billion gold dollars, nearly a sixth of the non-slave wealth of 1860. And by the final reckoning, the vanquished bore three times as much of the per capita cost of the war as the prosperous victors. The eleven defeated states with a population of around five million whites and three and one-half million Negroes had furnished about one million young men for military service. Over a fourth of those who marched away did not come back; no one even bothered to compile accurate records of those who were wounded or to count the cost in lives shattered by material loss and the demoralization of defeat.

Four years of warfare also deeply etched its physical marks on the land, for the battles had been fought almost entirely on Confederate soil. A resident of Montgomery, Alabama, wrote in May, 1866, "It is scarcely possible to exaggerate the effects of the late desolating war. Where five years ago every thing wore the cheerful aspect of affluence and refinement, where happiness and prosperity abounded, where were apparent domestic and social amenities such as can scarcely be found in any other portion of men's earthly heritage, there is now desolation, poverty, sorrow and suffering; fields are lying waste and unfenced that were then teeming with rich abundance; heaps of ashes and naked chimneys now mark the sites of thousands of splendid dwellings; hopeless misery and helpless despair now brood in sullen silence where but recently princely hospitality and every social and domestic virtue were found in their most attractive forms. In fact, in almost every part of the South the march of hostile armies, the deadly carnage of fiercely contested battles, and all the horrors and devastations of ruthless war may be traced in ruins, blood, and new-made graves. Admit, if you please, that the South was wrong; but has she not suffered a sufficient atonement?"[1]

One thing both Northerner and Southerner could agree upon — the widespread destruction. General William Tecumseh Sherman's report on his "march to the sea" noted, "We have consumed the corn and fodder in the region of country thirty miles on either side of a line from Atlanta to Savannah as also the sweet potatoes, cattle, hogs, sheep and poultry, and have carried away more than 10,000 horses and mules as well as countless number of slaves. I estimate the damage done to the State of Georgia and its military resources at $100,000,000; at least $20,000,000 of which has inured to our advantage and the remainder is simple waste and destruction." His course through the Carolinas was even more destructive, if possible. War had made good General Philip Sheridan's alleged promise in regard to the rich farming land of the Shenandoah Valley: "A crow could not fly over it without carrying his rations with him." The determination of Northern generals to deprive the South of all conceivable resources added greatly to the usual devastation of battle and also created an even greater source of hatred in the Southerners' belief that the North had violated the rules of humane warfare by failure to exclude noncombatants.

Virtually no area escaped unmarked. The battlefields of Virginia reverted to near wilderness; Robert Somers, an Englishman, wrote that the Tennessee Valley consisted "for the most part of plantations in a state of semi-decay and plantations of which the ruin is total and complete." The governor of Arkansas reported that the destruction of his state was beyond description and that two-thirds of the counties were destitute. Governor Robert Miller Patton of Alabama reported, "Of young and middle-aged men killed in war, Alabama lost fully 40,000. About 20,000 were disabled for life, many of whom have since died from this cause. At least 20,000 widows and orphans are left in the

[1] A. Greene, "The Political Crisis," De Bow's Review, I (May, 1866), p. 468.

State. Three-fourths of these are to-day dependent upon Government rations for subsistence."[2]

Nor had the cities and towns escaped. The capital city of Richmond not only suffered a long seige, but its business section was burned and other parts plundered following the withdrawal. The general impression was one of "beds of cinders, cellars half filled with bricks and rubbish, broken and blackened walls, impassable streets deluged with *debris*." It was estimated that less than $10,000 in federal currency was in the city when the victorious Grant entered. In South Carolina, Charleston showed the marks of two fires and repeated bombardments, and in the state capital, Columbia, eighty blocks were consumed by flames. The thriving little pre-war city of Atlanta claimed 35,000 destitute people, half of its buildings in ashes, and its streets littered with the carnage of battle — brick and mortar, scraps of roofing, cannon balls, and wrecked equipment. "Hell had laid her egg and right here it hatched," said one Georgian. Mobile had an obstructed harbor, and nine business blocks were destroyed by an explosion, while Vicksburg, Galveston ("a city of dogs and desolation"), and numerous other towns were similarly scarred. Even New Orleans, which had suffered little physical damage, was like a dead community.

One of the greatest calamities which confronted Southerners was the havoc wrought on the transportation system. Roads were impassable or nonexistent, and bridges were destroyed or washed away. The important river traffic was at a standstill: levees were broken, channels were blocked, the few steamboats which had not been captured or destroyed were in a state of disrepair, wharves had decayed or were missing, and trained personnel were dead or dispersed. Horses, mules, oxen, carriages, wagons, and carts had nearly all fallen prey at one time or another to the contending armies. The railroads were paralyzed, with most of the companies bankrupt. These lines had been the special target of the enemy. On one stretch of 114 miles in Alabama, "every bridge and trestle was destroyed, cross-ties rotten, buildings burned, water-tanks gone, ditches filled up, and tracks grown up in weeds and bushes." Sherman's men had destroyed all railroad equipment within reach — 136 of 281 miles of the Central of Georgia, alone — and added the novelty of twisting heated rails around trees. In Alabama nearly all of its 800 miles of railway was useless. One Mississippi line reported fit for use, though damaged, a total of one locomotive, two second-class passenger cars, one first-class passenger car, one baggage car, one provision car, two stock cars, and two flat cars. Communication centers like Columbia and Atlanta were in ruins; shops and

[2] Robert M. Patton, "The New Era of Southern Manufactures," *ibid.*, III (January, 1867), p. 65.

foundries were wrecked or in disrepair. Even those areas bypassed by battle had been pirated for equipment needed on the battlefront, and the wear and tear of wartime usage without adequate repairs or replacements reduced all to a state of disintegration. Not for a generation were the railroads properly restored, and then largely by Northern capital.

At the outbreak of the war, the South had been self-sufficient only in cotton. The small, promising beginnings in manufacturing which had taken place before 1860 were largely undone. Iron works were worn out or in shambles as the result of military action. Important salt works had been demolished and the cotton mills of Jackson and Atlanta left in ashes. So nearly complete was the erasure of the light mark made by industry on the region's economy that its revival in the 1880's was hailed as the inauguration of a "new" South.

Except for a small number of speculators and war profiteers, everyone was impoverished. An investment in slaves estimated to be two to four billion dollars had been wiped out. Salt water covered most of the rice plantations; broken levees had resulted in the flooding of thousands of acres of the best cotton land. Furthermore, most plantations had been mortgaged even before the war. In 1870 there were nearly half a million fewer horses than in 1860; over 200,000 fewer mules; a million fewer cattle; 1,350,000 fewer sheep and six million fewer pigs. The year before the war, of the first ten states ranked nationally according to per capita wealth, six had been Southern: Louisiana (2), South Carolina (3), Mississippi (5), Georgia (7), Texas (9), and Kentucky (10). Twenty years later, not one of these ranked in the top thirty! Only by 1879 were the cotton states able to reach their yields of 1860. The sugar cane and rice industries all but disappeared. The assessed valuation of property declined 30 to 60 per cent during the decade of the sixties; farm land that had sold for more than $50 an acre brought from three to five dollars, and poorer land could not be given away because of the tax liability.

Banks were engulfed by floods of Confederate paper, and the savings of the people and endowments of colleges which had been put in Confederate bonds were worthless. Insurance companies became bankrupt and defunct. There was little hope that the mines, factories, or mills could be opened in the near future. The losses in personal property equaled the entire official expenditures of the war. Aside from the loss of slaves, the region's total wealth shrank to less than one-third of what it had been before the firing upon Fort Sumter.

Moreover, in many communities violence had not ceased with the surrender of the armies. Portions of Alabama were ravaged by guerrillas and deserters from both armies for over a year; parts of

Texas and Arkansas were virtually no-man's-lands. Nothing of value was safe. Cotton was stolen from the fields, livestock was rustled, river boats seized, and houses robbed. South Carolina was terrorized by gangs of Negro robbers; the petty thievery of the freedmen, which had been viewed with tolerance before the war, became a life-and-death matter to the impoverished whites.

Worse yet, confiscation took a heavy toll of the remaining scanty resources. The Northern consensus was that the property of the Confederate government was the booty of the United States and should be located and seized. Treasury agents, operating on a 25 per cent commission, swarmed over the South looking for cotton which could be claimed under the Confederate tax-in-kind. They quickly developed the tendency to take whatever cotton they found and to turn over to the government only that portion they saw fit. Secretary of the Treasury Hugh McCullock had the personal integrity to admit, "I am sure I sent *some* honest agents South; but it sometimes seems very doubtful whether any of them remained honest very long." He also reported in 1866 that another deviation was causing additional grief to the Southerners: "Residents and others in the districts where these peculations were going on took advantage of the unsettled condition of the country, and representing themselves as agents of this department, went about robbing under such pretended authority. . . . Lawless men, singly and in organized bands, engaged in general plunder; every species of intrigue and peculation and theft were resorted to." All in all, some 3,000,000 bales of cotton were probably seized, as well as livestock, tobacco, rice, sugar, or anything of value, by men who represented themselves as government agents.

The South also had to pay a Federal shipping duty and a special cotton tax of two and one-half to three cents per pound, about one-fifth of the market price. Before the cotton tax was repealed in February, 1868, after having also ruined many Northerners who had become Southern planters, it brought in some $68,000,000, probably more than ample to pay the cost of "reconstruction." Although part of the ill-gotten gains were later disgorged, some 40,000 claimants being repaid for illegal cotton seizures alone, it would not be a great exaggeration to say that all the average white Southerner had left was his land.

The professional men were in an even more desperate condition. Courts, police systems, and governments had collapsed, and even after their slow revival, lawyers could find no practice unless they could prove that they had had no connection with the Confederacy. Doctors lacked even the simplest forms of medicines and could expect little pay for their services. Schools were closed, pupils and teachers scattered. Young men who had stopped their education to serve in the army had to work in the fields to keep their families alive. School funds had been used up during the war; endowments were worthless or confiscated. Churches stood in ruins, with their funds dissipated. Engineers saw plenty of work to do but no money or tools with which to do it. The poet, Henry Timrod, died in utter poverty, and his fellow artist, Sidney Lanier, wrote that "pretty much the whole of life has been merely not dying."

Despite the aid of the Freedman's Bureau, Congressionally created primarily to help the former slaves, and other Northern relief agencies, as late as December, 1865, it was estimated that in Alabama, Mississippi, and Georgia there were over half a million white people without the necessities of life. A press correspondent reported of Georgia that in "many whole counties the merest necessaries of life are all any family have or can afford, while among the poorer classes there is a great lack of even these." Numerous are the stories of once-wealthy families selling the family heirlooms to buy bread, of white women pulling plows, of proud matrons taking in washing, and of aristocrats now willing to accept charity from their former slaves. Confederate generals took to the fields, sold insurance, or worked as day laborers. A colonel peddled his wife's pies to Northern soldiers. The proud George Fitzhugh, one-time lecturer at Harvard and Yale, lived in a hut among his former slaves.

The plight of the Negroes was pathetic. They endured the greatest physical suffering in the social revolution which resulted from the Civil War and, in addition, had to face totally new and often antagonistic situations in a white man's world. While slaves, they had been cared for by their masters; now there were no masters, and the free Negroes were left to their own resources. Upon learning of their freedom, thousands took to the woods or the roads leading to the nearest town. The fact that they had been forbidden to travel while in slavery seemed to make mobility all the more desirable. Some had fled before the invading armies, and others had sought refuge with them. In the "contraband camps" near the army posts, where the government that had freed them was expected also to feed them, and in the Negro colonies which sprang up in the cities, the sanitary conditions were deplorable. Epidemics swept through them unchecked; smallpox and tuberculosis were rampant. Without proper food, clothing, shelter, or medical care, the death toll from starvation, disease, and violence reached the tens of thousands. Children were especially susceptible and almost disappeared in some districts. Estimates of Negro mortality in such areas ran as high as one-third. One of the Negro leaders, Frederick Douglass, said bitterly that the former bond servant was "free from the individual master but a slave of society. He had neither money, property, nor friends. He was free from the old plantation, but he had nothing but the dusty road under his feet. He was free from the old quarter that gave him his shelter, but a slave to the rains of summer and the frosts of winter. He was turned loose, naked, hungry and destitute to the open sky." In this topsy-turvy period, the innumerable Negro men and women who remained true to their families, stayed at home, showed a willingness to work, and were able to maintain a good relationship with their white neighbors were usually ignored, as attention focused on unruly members of the race.

One of the time-honored Southern justifications for slavery was that blacks were irresponsible, like children, and therefore must be disciplined and forced to work. Consequently, many whites expected dire results following emancipation. In this frame of mind, small or isolated incidents were seized upon as signs of black rejection of white standards. Often these events were made to appear general and threatening to the former masters. Black reluctance to sign labor contracts could be cited as proof that they equated freedom from servitude with freedom from the necessity to work. Expressions by ex-slaves of their newly acquired sense of equality were viewed as impudence and intent to overthrow the social structure. Even the deep and honest desire of blacks for separate religious organizations was seen as an attempt to undermine contemporary standards of morality. All in all, for the white citizenry abolition was in many respects as traumatic an experience as it was for their former black servants.

Northerners intently watched the chaotic and unhappy South with a sense of apprehension. Were the Southerners really accepting defeat and ready to admit the errors of their ways? Even though victorious, could it be that the Northern dead would be cheated out of their triumph? No peace treaty existed to guarantee the future good behavior of the defeated, and the victors themselves had not been able to agree on either why they had fought or what should be the final results of their success. At most, they had tacitly assumed three general propositions: secession was impossible and the Union was permanent; slavery should no longer exist; and pre-war Southern leadership had to be replaced.

Southern defeat on the field of battle apparently marked the triumph of these points, but Northern jubilation was quickly tempered by the growing awareness of corollary problems. The Union had been saved, but was it still a democracy? The Negro had been freed, but would Southerners accept this situation? The aristocrats had been overthrown, but could they be kept down and the region be trusted to resume its former place in the Union? These and many other doubts flooded Northern public and private thought as attention focused upon the South for clues to the answers.

What many did not realize was that the answers they found would be colored by their own prejudices. In short, they would see what they wanted to see. The hate and suspicion of four years of strife did not evaporate overnight for either side. Lincoln could say to his Cabinet on April 14, 1865, "We must extinguish our resentment if we expect harmony and Union," and even a future Radical such as Senator Henry Wilson of Massachusetts could write, "I do not consider it either generous, manly, or Christian, to nourish or cherish or express feelings of wrath or hatred toward them." But it was much more difficult for the majority to be as magnanimous.

Right had triumphed over wrong, but whether the wrong appreciated this was debatable. The death of Lincoln by an assassin's bullet six days after Appomattox was at first viewed as the fruit of a Rebel plot. The scores of travelers, newspapermen, and official observers who later went South were not sure. Brigadier General Wager Swayne stated in 1865 that he was "agreeably disappointed in the reasonable temper of the planters." But E. L. Godkin, respected editor of the *Nation*, was not so sure: the South was much too docile to be trusted; undoubtedly it had ulterior motives for its friendly attitude. Northern newspapers commented on the abundance of pictures of Lee, and even a few of Davis, but none of Lincoln were to be seen south of the Potomac. Much also was made of the fact that some Southern clergymen refused to pray for the President of the United States. Lyman Abbott, a Northern minister, explained this recalcitrance by saying, "The clergy who have been for four years preaching slavery and secession, cannot now preach liberty and union. If they attempt it, the people attribute their conversion to fear or self-interest."

Another canker was the snubbing of "Yankees" on the streets by Southerners and the refusal to meet them socially, especially by "women who consider it essential to salvation to snub or insult Union officers and soldiers at every possible opportunity." Throughout the region, thousands of men still wore their Confederate grey uniforms, but few stopped to wonder if this was because of patriotism or lack of other garments. General B. H. Grierson believed an organization operating under the guise of "Historical Societies" was working throughout the South for a renewal of the Rebellion. Every case of friction between the races was hailed as proof that the Negro was not safe in the hands of the local whites. Confederate leaders were viewed with the utmost distrust. When, a few months after his surrender, Lee became president of Washington College in Virginia, *Harper's Weekly* declared him better fitted for the gallows. The *Nation* was more charitable but declared him "not fit" to work with young people. The old abolitionist, Wendell Phillips, said that if Lee were qualified to be president, then Captain Henry Wirz, the "butcher" of Andersonville prison, should be pardoned and made "professor of what the Scotch call 'the humanities.' "

For a true picture, President Andrew Johnson early dispatched as official observers Benjamin C. Truman, a New England journalist; General Ulysses S. Grant; and Carl Schurz, German-American hero of the war. Their reports reflected the mental confusion of the period, for they, also, failed to agree upon what they saw. Truman wrote off the stories of Southern persecution of Northerners as merely a part of the general pattern of falsehoods being woven about the region. He concluded that the South was growing daily in its loyalty to the Union. Schurz, on the other hand, saw just the opposite. He could find no evidence of loyalty to the Republic, but much that revealed a hatred of the North. The Southerner did not consider his past actions treasonous and showed a real lack of "communion with the progressive ideas of the times." The region was controlled by "incorrigibles," making the fate of the Negro indeed dark unless the protecting arm of the United States Army stayed nearby. The "incorrigibles" still "indulge in the swagger which was so customary before and during the war, and still hope for a time when the southern confederacy will achieve its independence." They "persecute Union men and negroes whenever they can do so with impunity, insist clamorously upon their 'rights,' and are extremely impatient of the presence of the federal soldiers," and furthermore, according to Schurz, they formed a numerous and highly vocal group who commanded "the admiration of the women." He dismissed the majority as weak of intellect but as people "whose prejudices and impulses are strong."

General Grant, however, wrote President Johnson that he was "satisfied that the mass of thinking men of the south accept the present situation of affairs in good faith." His observations led him to conclude that they desired self-government "within the Union" as soon as possible and that they would be willing "in good faith" to do anything required by the government which was "not humiliating to them as citizens." It was his one regret that there was not more "commingling" between citizens of the sections, especially by those in authority.

One reason for the confusion of Northern observers and of the public in general as to the state of Southern opinion was that the South, itself, did not know what to expect and therefore was not clear as to what its attitude should be. Northerners had cheered John Brown and during the war had sung that they would "hang Jeff Davis to a sour apple tree." A Northern official had reported that the "only way for this government to make these people its friends is just to keep them down. They have more respect for a man who goes there and shows decision than they do for one who is wavering. . . . I would pin them down at the point of the bayonet so close that they would not

have room to wiggle." He added that if an earthquake should swallow
the South, "the devil would be dethroned and some of them [would]
take his place."

Southerners, ever ready to believe the worst of their erstwhile enemies, took such statements as typical of Northern views. Truman reported that "many of the most intelligent" in the region looked for
"general confiscation, proscription, and the reign of the scaffold." The
defeat of the Southern armies, which they believed to be the only
thing between them and the execution of Union wrath, "threw the
minds of the people into a state of the most abject terror." They lived
in "hourly apprehension" of all that their imaginations had been able
to conceive of "northern vandalism and hideous butchery." The arrest
of Jefferson Davis in May, 1865, and later of Vice President Alexander H. Stephens; of J. A. Campbell, B. H. Hill, S. T. Mallory, J. H.
Reagan, and G. A. Trenholm of the Confederate cabinet; and of such
governors as J. E. Brown of Georgia, Z. B. Vance of North Carolina,
John Letcher of Virginia, and Charles Clark of Mississippi was viewed
as merely preliminary to the blood-letting.

It is not altogether surprising, then, that many Confederates, of
high and low rank, concluded that their only safety lay in rapid flight.
So much the better if this could be done so as to combine an assurance of freedom with prospect of economic recovery. The nearest and
one of the most attractive refuges was Mexico.[3] Its virtues included
the presence of French troops supporting the government of the Arch-
duke Maximilian, the government's friendliness toward the Confederate cause, and knowledge that Southern military experience might be
in great demand if the United States tried to expel the French intruders
from Mexico. There is evidence that the country's attractions had been
noticed even before the end of the war. As early as February, 1865,
General E. Kirby Smith, commander of the Confederate Trans-
Mississippi Department, expressed his hope that "in case of unexam-
pled catastrophe to our arms and the final overthrow of the government"
Maximilian would find his services acceptable. Three months later
he offered not less than 10,000 men "who would rally around any flag
that promises to lead them to battle against their former foe."

Maximilian proved to be interested and encouraging. In September
he declared, "Mexico is open to immigration from all nations," and
offered newcomers liberal inducements. Matthew F. Maury, an agent
of the Confederate Navy Department, was appointed Imperial Commissioner of Colonization. In short order, thousands of Southerners
moved to Mexico, led by such notables as generals Joseph O. Shelby,

[3] For a recent account of colonization in Mexico, see A. F. Rolle, *The Lost Cause:
The Confederate Exodus to Mexico* (Norman: Univ. of Oklahoma Press, 1965).

John B. Clark, Danville Leadbetter, Cadmus M. Wilcox, Thomas C. Hindman, William Preston, William P. Hardeman, E. Kirby Smith, John B. Magruder, Jubal A. Early, and Sterling Price and governors Henry W. Allen, Thomas O. Moore, Thomas C. Reynolds, and Edward Clark. Not only were they welcomed, but soon the Confederate colony of Carlota was thriving.[4]

Almost equally attractive was Brazil.[5] The fact that it alone in the Western hemisphere accepted slavery made it seem ideal. Also, like Mexico, it sought immigrants. Ballard Dunn, an Episcopal clergyman from Louisiana, after exploring the country, wrote a book, *Brazil, The Home for Southerners* (New Orleans, 1866), which made the country very appealing to the discontented. All in all, some 4,000, a cross-section including professional men, laborers, planters, mechanics, small farmers, adventurers, and fugitives from justice, sought a new life in its jungles.

Many fled to other points of the compass — Venezuela, Honduras, Cuba, Canada, Australia, and New Zealand, to mention a few. Judah P. Benjamin made his way to England, where he became Queen's Counsel and an outstanding lawyer. John C. Breckinridge also sought refuge in Europe. Generals W. W. Loring and Charles W. Field became respectively Commander and Inspector General of the Egyptian Army. Robert Toombs stayed abroad until 1867. John Slidell, who played a dramatic role in the *Trent* affair and was Minister to France, never came back to America. A. Dudley Mann, roving Confederate diplomat, who had vowed never to return until the Confederacy was a recognized nation, died in Paris in 1889. Still others simply moved westward in hopes of getting cheap, fertile land and of escaping reconstruction and Negro competition. New York City and other Northern areas which had been friendly or lukewarm during the war soon could boast of Southern colonies. And a few staunch rebels, like the old fire-eater Edmund Ruffin, simply blew out their brains.

As the first hysteria of defeat began to wane, Southerners started reconsidering the advantages of migration. Respected leaders like Lee counseled against it. All, he declared, should stay at home and share the fate of their states. "The South requires the aid of her sons now more than at any period of her history." Conditions did not develop which many a Confederate had anticipated: the bloody purge had not taken place — only Wirz being executed — and only Davis had been imprisoned for a lengthy time. It was true that things were far from

[4] Carl Coke Rister, "Carlota, A Confederate Colony in Mexico," *Journal of Southern History*, XI (February, 1945), p. 33ff.
[5] Blanche H. C. Weaver, "Confederate Immigrants and Evangelical Churches in Brazil," *Journal of Southern History*, XVIII (November, 1952), p. 446ff., and "Confederate Emigration to Brazil," *ibid.*, XXVII (February, 1961), pp. 33-53.

ideal: "We cannot prevent these people from going; we can hardly urge them to remain in a country where Justice, if not dead, sleepeth, where Liberty is bound in chains, where might is right, and Law a mockery. To say that these people are driven away, would not be exceeding the truth," said *De Bow's Review*. But although the present situation seemed most ominous, "hope is not yet dead. You say you are fleeing from the greatest despotism the world ever saw! Granted. But this despotism cannot exist always. Americans will never tamely submit to be held in perpetual bondage by a lawless and unscrupulous faction."[6]

Perhaps more important, no Edens developed to take the place of their homeland. In Mexico, the coming of the rainy season saw many stricken with dysentery and fever and with no proper medical care. Nostalgia took its toll. Governor Henry W. Allen of Louisiana wrote: "When I am sick in this lonely chamber, and I pass hours and hours with no one but my Mexican servant to listen to the impatient ravings of a fevered brain, oh, then, I think of those dear ones I have left in Louisiana, of home, all whom I loved so much." Mexico was in chaos politically: Napoleon was forced to abandon it, and as French troops were withdrawn, the Southerners who had been so closely linked with the imperial regime did not find relations cordial with its successor. By the end of 1867, most of them had gone back home or resumed their wanderings.

Brazil proved little better, and the major portion of Confederate exiles stayed there less than five years. Their experiences were probably summarized by the McCollams, sugar planters from Louisiana. In May, 1866, Andrew and John McCollam joined others in a trip to Brazil. After a while, Andrew wrote in his diary that "with a people who do not speak my language or with whom I cannot talk and in a country where everything is going to decay I must now confess to myself I have not the courage to settle." Eventually he concluded that he had never seen "more idlers and idleness," and even the "once happy but now down-trodden U.S.A." was to be preferred. In 1867 he went to Cuba but was restrained from settling by "the doubt that hangs over the future of this fine island." Giving up the search, he returned to adjust himself to free labor on his own Louisiana plantation.[7]

General Jubal A. Early was one of the most determined migrants, but his adventures were equally as frustrating. Writing a friend on May 10, 1866, he related, "I went to Mexico hoping there might be war with the U.S., but I found the Empire an infernal humbug and no

[6] Charles A. Pilsbury, "Southern Emigration — Brazil and British Honduras," *De Bow's Review*, IV (December, 1867), pp. 537, 544.
[7] J. Carlyle Sitterson, "The McCollams: A Planter Family of the Old and New South," *Journal of Southern History*, VI (August, 1940), pp. 360-361.

chance in that quarter." This disappointment, however, did not change his mind. "I shall never return to the states unless I can come back under the Confederate flag — of which I do not yet dispair [sic]. My hatred of the infernal yankees is increasing daily, if possible. . . . My motto is still 'war to the death,' and I yet hope to have another chance at them." After Mexico, he wandered to Cuba and then to Canada. But, despite his passionate remarks, within three years he was back to open a law office in Lynchburg, Virginia.[8]

But what of those rebellious souls who never left? For some, the war experiences had brought wounds which never healed, and others had jagged, improperly mended scars. These frustrated Confederates were the source of some Northern writers' belief that many white Southerners had not accepted defeat except in a physical sense and that they hoped yet to accomplish by other means those ends which their armies had failed to achieve. These formed the core of Southerners who were neither silent nor discreet and who tortured themselves with bitter memories and carried the seeds of hate and unforgivingness into the next generations.

One of the most outspoken was Albert T. Bledsoe, Confederate Assistant Secretary of War, diplomat, and author in 1866 of a work entitled *Is Davis a Traitor? or Was Secession a Constitutional Right Previous to the War of 1861?* In 1867 he established the *Southern Review*, dedicated to "the despised, disfranchised, and downtrodden people of the South." Published until his death in 1878, the magazine has been described by Paul H. Buck as a "channel of vituperative hatred directed against the North."

Bledsoe was forced to write his journal almost single-handedly, however. The people whose cause he pleaded so passionately were either too poor or too indifferent to help, and support for his family came from his school-teaching daughters. Yet for all those who would hear, he thundered, "Shall we bury in the grave the grandest cause that has ever perished on earth, and so leave the just cause merely because it is fallen to go without our humble advocacy? We would rather die."

Other editors, not so consistently, joined the background chorus. Robert P. Waring of the Charlotte, North Carolina, *Times* was arrested for writing among other things that the Southerner was "the equal if not the superior of the mercenary race which now dominates over him." The publisher of the Macon, Georgia, *Journal and Messenger* was imprisoned and his paper suppressed for stating that in order to take the amnesty oath he had to fortify himself with an extra amount

[8] William D. Hoyt, Jr., "New Light on General Jubal A. Early after Appomattox," *Journal of Southern History*, IX (February, 1943), pp. 113-117.

of "Dutch Courage." A New York *Times* correspondent concluded that "the editors of the South are almost as disloyal and contemptible and almost as malign and mean as the ministers of the Gospel."

It was in the churches however, where festered the greatest intolerance, bitterness, and unforgivingness during the years after Appomattox. In 1861 the Southern Baptist Convention had issued a fiery statement in support of the South, ending with the assertion that they would also pray for their enemies, "trusting that their pitiless purposes may be frustrated." A year later, the Confederate Presbyterians had officially announced that the struggle was "not alone for civil rights, and property and home, but for religion, for Church, for the gospel." Religious leaders preached the righteousness of the Southern cause with such fervor that conversion to a Northern God's will often was more than they could face. Adding fuel to the flames of resentment was the haughty and overbearing attitude of Northern denominational representatives in areas which had fallen under Union control during the war. Afterwards, numerous sermons were preached concerning the godless men who controlled the South's destiny, and common efforts were made to bar participation of Northern army personnel in church services. Bishop Richard H. Wilmer of Alabama went so far as to instruct the Episcopal clergy to omit that portion of the prayer which applied to the Confederate president but did not tell them to substitute that of the United States, since no one desired "length of life" or prosperity to such a government!

The North was justifiably bewildered by performances such as these; yet, it had expected to see unrepentant rebels, and their behavior, being more spectacular and interesting, caught the greater share of attention, just as the squeaking wheel gets the grease. But for those who would listen, both in the North and South, there were spoken quiet words which urged realistic acceptance of the South's shattered world in order to help in its painful rebirth.

General Wade Hampton's counsel to his soldiers upon surrender made no headlines. "My advice . . . is . . . to devote our whole energies to the restoration of law and order, the re-establishment of agriculture and commerce, the promotion of education and the rebuilding of our cities and dwellings which have been laid in ashes." He even wrote to President Johnson that the "South unequivocally 'accepts the situation' in which she is placed" and "intends to abide by the laws of the land honestly; to fulfill all her obligations faithfully and to keep her word sacredly." The revered Lee spoke in the same tenor in August, 1865: "The questions which for years were in dispute having been decided against us, it is the part of wisdom to acquiesce in the result, and of candor to recognize the fact. . . . All should unite in honest effort to obliterate the effects of war, and to restore the blessings of peace."

Alexander H. Stephens, while still in prison after the war, wrote that, if it were permitted, "all my influence and power would be directed to a restoration of quiet, order, and government in Georgia upon the basis of accepting and abiding by the issues of war." Benjamin H. Hill undoubtedly outran public opinion when he stated in 1866, "There was a South of slavery and secession; that South is dead. There is a South of Union and freedom; that South, thank God! is living, breathing, growing every hour." More characteristic, however, were the words of a contributor to *De Bow's Review:* "The stern logic of the late war, if it has not corrected entirely the prevailing fallacy by which these States were led into rebellion, has at least convinced everyone of the absolute necessity of submission to a government so prompt and able to vindicate its authority."[9]

All of these signs, violent and conciliatory, were probably read most correctly by John T. Trowbridge of Massachusetts who wrote, "They submit to the power which has mastered them, but they do not love it, nor is it reasonable to expect that they should." There need not be the least apprehension of another armed rebellion. "Those who are still anxious to see the old issue fought out are not themselves fighting men." Sidney Andrews, correspondent of the Boston *Advertiser* and Chicago *Tribune,* reached the same conclusion. "They are full of ignorance and prejudices, but they want peace and quiet, and seem not badly disposed toward the general government." He admitted that some individuals "rant and rave and feed on fire as in the old days, but another war is a thing beyond the possibilities of time." The North could treat the South as it pleased. "The war spirit is gone, and no fury can re-enliven it." In fact, the ex-soldiers were the "best citizens" in the region.

Quite probably, the feelings of the ex-soldiers were those expressed in an anecdote concerning General Joseph E. Johnston, late of the Confederate army. According to legend, he was approached by a young man who belligerently announced that the "South was conquered but not subdued." The general inquired as to the speaker's war service and was told that circumstances had prevented his being in the army. Johnston replied, "Well, sir, I was. You may not be subdued, but I am." Even George Fitzhugh, the antebellum firebrand, professed himself entirely reconciled to defeat and accepted a minor post as a judge under the "Yankee" Freedmen's Bureau.

The willingness to admit that they had been defeated did not, however, mean that the South had become convinced that its cause had been wrong or that right had necessarily triumphed; nor had the Southerner's belief in the subordinate status of blacks suddenly changed. To admit the power of the enemy was easier than admitting

[9] Greene, *loc. cit.,* p. 469.

that the motives had been bad in 1861; force, Southerners felt, not reason or right, had made the decision. Recognition of this superiority, however, meant that the region had to feel its own inferiority, a situation which automatically denied enthusiasm for the altered circumstances and guaranteed the retention of the South's fundamental beliefs. Although a verdict was accepted which could no longer be contested, and some could say with Robert Toombs that they "had nothing to regret but the dead and the failure," most turned their eyes to the future hoping somehow to find compensation for their children in the new South that they would build from the ruins of the old.

Superbly this sentiment was expressed in a testimony which Charles Henry Reed of Mississippi left for his descendants. "I did the best I could, aimed low and shot to kill. I am proud and always will be so that I had the honor to be a soldier of the Confederacy. When I look at the Stars and Stripes I can't keep back the thought that it represents to me, two homes burned and made desolate, all the life savings of Mother and Father, Grandmother and Grandfather swept away and burned and I can't love it, and don't see how any other old confederate can. . . . However I recommend my Children and Grandchildren to love it for what it represents, a reunited country and the greatest one that has ever been on the earth."[10]

No matter how desperately some Southerners would cling to the past, it was irretrievably gone. Hope, and with it revival, had to lie in the future, whose chief architect would be the North. Any plans which might be made would be deeply influenced by certain conditioning factors. In the first place, the rebuilding would have to take place in a South prostrate, impoverished, and with shattered morale. Not only had the war stamped out secession and the governments that upheld it, but also the economy and social system of the region were wrecked. Any program must therefore be not only political but also one that would encompass immediate humanitarian relief and long-term economic recovery.

Given the frayed nerves, the hatred, and the suspicion which existed on both sides, the chance that a solution would be based entirely on logic was remote. Each had hated the other for a generation; each was ready to believe the worst possible things of its former enemy. The Negro would be very deeply involved in any plan for the future. The slave, once the mudsill upon which the social and economic structure of the old South had rested, was now a free man and the chief labor supply of the region. Still located upon the most fertile lands of the South, he represented a crude mass of labor, without tools or capital assets, that somehow had to be made productive if recovery

[10] In the possession of Mr. John Grady, Blanchard, Oklahoma.

were to be achieved. He would be of little help in working out his own destiny, as he was befuddled, not knowing what his status was to be or what he wanted it to be. He was destined to become the central figure in the South's economic and emotional problems.

And, finally, reconstruction had to be more than mere rebuilding. There could be no thought of replacing the old forms, for their destruction had been one of the primary objectives of the war. Therefore, "Reconstruction" was a misnomer, an impossibility. There could be nothing less than a revolution — economically and socially with the abolition of slavery, and politically with the South surrendering its dominance of the national government for the first time in the nation's history.

3

# THE SOUTHERN DILEMMA

WARS ARE USUALLY FOUGHT to solve problems whose answers cannot be worked out in the normal course of peaceful negotiations. From the first, Lincoln stated that the North's primary objective in the Civil War was the preservation of the Union. In accepting the Senatorial nomination in 1856, he declared, " 'A house divided against itself cannot stand.' I believe this government cannot endure permanently half slave and half free. I do not expect the house to fall — but I do expect it will cease to be divided." In his first inaugural address, he gave his belief "that in contemplation of universal law, and of the constitution, the Union of these States is perpetual," and no state "can lawfully get out of the Union,— that *resolves* and *ordinances* to that effect are legally void, and that acts of violence, within any State or States, against the authority of the United States, are insurrectionary or revolutionary, according to circumstances." After 1862 the abolition of slavery became a second objective, and the determination that a "government of the people, by the people, for the people" should not perish was a primary concern to the mass of Northern people. The Civil War brought victory to those proclaiming these ideals; so, presumably, these goals would be reflected in the peace. However, it is a truism that wars create more problems than they solve.

The Union had been preserved. But what sort of a union could it be when one-third of the country was held in place by force? Slavery was gone — emancipation had brought an end to bondage — but the Negro problem promptly developed. Democracy was left to struggle in a marriage of unequals in the hostile atmosphere of a post-war period.

While these were some of the problems spawned by the war, the solutions of which lay in the future, there were more pressing and immediate concerns. One was the economic situation in the South. James S. Pike, Republican observer from Maine, wrote "Everything went into Confederate securities; everything to eat and everything to wear was consumed, and when the war suddenly ended there was nothing left but absolute poverty and nakedness." This was an over-statement of the situation, but before any plans for the future could be drawn, there obviously first must be direct physical relief.

The twentieth-century American concept that the victor must im-mediately go to the economic aid of his fallen foe was not practiced in the middle of the nineteenth century. There were very few who thought the United States owed the South anything. During this period of "rugged individualism" and extreme laissez-faire, the economic prob-lems of the South were viewed as the concern of individuals rather than of the government. Consequently, the federal government gave only incidental assistance toward their solution. The one exception that Northerners were generally willing to make concerned the freedmen. After all, the slaves had been freed by federal power, so did this not make them after a fashion the wards of the nation? As to the starving white rebels, their suffering was merely the just reward of past evil actions.

Certainly the hand of the Lord had struck the Southerners a mighty blow. Federal officials in Alabama reported white women and children and broken-down men walking thirty to forty miles to beg a little food. Meat of any kind had been "a stranger to their mouths for months." Some had no shelter in midwinter except pine boughs. A Northern reporter stated that in one Georgia county no man had more than two bushels of corn left. The Negroes' situation was impossible. For one thing, they could expect no help from their old masters; Northern reports showed that many of the planters were kindly dis-posed toward their former slaves but could do nothing because of their own destitution, thus leaving the Negro aged, infirm, sick, and helpless particularly in a serious plight.

Conditions in the South brought out two facets of Northern charac-ter. Many saw opportunities for economic profit in the South's prostra-tion. The low price of land and the high price of cotton made farming seem particularly attractive. Practically every Northern state furnished "emigrants" who were sure they could show the natives how money could be made with "Yankee initiative." Southerners were not only willing to sell land but often eager for partners to furnish capital, in the belief that the Negroes would work for Northern men. John Hay, formerly Lincoln's secretary, invested in Florida orange groves; ex-Colonel Henry Lee Higginson became part owner of a 5,000-acre Georgia plantation. Young Union soldiers often settled on land they had coveted while in service, and still others joined companies to exploit the undeveloped mineral resources of the region.

Most of these would-be planters refused advice even when given in friendly fashion by the Southerners. The result was that probably three out of four failed miserably. Higginson, after trying to cope with floods, insect pests, and black labor, sold out and reported that he and his partners had lost well over $60,000. The Negroes did not prove as responsive to their direction as had been anticipated. Truman commented especially on the failure of this group as employers by explaining that they were practical, energetic, economical, and thrifty, while their laborers were just the opposite. This caused the new owners to lose patience, while Southerners had long been accustomed to the Negroes' ways. The Northerners knew the extent of a day's work and expected it to be performed. Truman concluded that it was "the almost universal testimony of the negroes themselves . . . that they prefer to labor for a southern employer."

The number of Northerners who went South for business reasons was augumented by those who were motivated by missionary zeal. During the war, churches both North and South had preached patriotism as a religious duty, and Northern religious forces marched with the army against the common foe. As early as 1863, Secretary of War Edwin M. Stanton had begun the practice of seizing Southern church property overrun by the army and turning it over to corresponding Northern sects. Northern churches interpreted the Union victory as meaning that their brand of religion had also won and that their program of religious reconstruction would be the absorption of Southerners on the Northern churches' own terms. Since the former had "knowingly sinned," they had to prove their repentance. This uncompromising stand made the Southern religious leaders equally stubborn, and only the Episcopalians were able to effect a rapid reunion.

The Presbyterians, Baptists, and Methodists viewed the South as a missionary field. All of them sent their emissaries into every Southern state, determined to recast its society "in a higher mold." The most uncompromising were the Methodists, who continued to hold Southern Methodist Church property until 1878. They also established their congregations among the Negroes and Union sympathizers. While they did succeed in separating the Negroes from their masters, they failed in their objective of changing the South's religious pattern, instead leaving legacies of religious bitterness which a century later had not been completely overcome. The feelings of the white Southern Methodists were summarized at a meeting in 1865 where it was stated that "a large proportion, if not a majority of northern Methodists have become incurably radical."

Showing almost an equally fanatical zeal were the educational envoys from the North. Convinced that the error of the South was rooted in its failure to accept the Northern view of public education for all, they believed salvation lay in speedy repentance. If the whites could not see the error of their ways, then the Negroes at least had to be saved. An army composed mainly of women marched into the South to spearhead the conquest of ignorance.

This combined force of ministers and teachers was supported by considerable Northern financial backing. From 1860 to 1893, the American Missionary Association spent $11,610,000 for church extension and education in the South. The Freedmans Aid and Southern Society of the Methodist Episcopal Church disbursed more than $6,000,000, chiefly on Negro education. The Baptist Home Mission Society contributed some $2,500,000; the Presbyterian Board of Missions for Freedmen spent some $1,280,000 and established fifteen schools. The Episcopal Church divided over $250,000 almost equally between churches and schools, and the Friends supported over 100 schools at a cost of more than $1,000,000.[1] In the most critical years, 1862-1867, an estimated $5,500,000 was given in money and kind by missionary and nonsectarian societies to freedmen's aid. Most of this went for education, and there were 1,430 Northern teachers in the South in 1866-1867 alone.

Through the Freedmen's Bureau and the American Freedman's Union Commission, a federation of most of the nonsectarian societies, over 2,000 schools were established. Before 1878, over twenty-five normal or collegiate institutions were established by Northern agencies, with the Congregationalists and Baptists taking the lead. One of the most influential was Hampton Institute of Virginia, founded in 1868 by the American Missionary Association. Other notable schools included Fisk University in Nashville, begun in 1866, and Howard University in Washington, established in 1867. Northern gifts continued to be, even a century later, the staff of life for many Negro institutions in the South.

[1] U. S. Bureau of Education, "Education in the Various States," *Report of the Commissioner of Education for 1894-1895* (Washington, 1896), pp. 1380-1381.

The bulk of Northern charity went to the Negroes, although some whites had reason momentarily to appreciate the efforts of their former enemies. The federal government also played a minimum role in the economic relief: the Freedman's Bureau, created to help the ex-slaves, did dispense the necessities of life to hundreds of thousands of the needy, white as well as black. The army of occupation contributed indirectly: Union soldiers had money to spend and occasionally shared from their plenty with the less fortunate; the government also often bought locally for their maintenance and for its own convenience reconditioned many of the Southern railroads. But regardless of these scattered facts, Southern whites in the main were left to work out their own economic destinies. They were at first hopeful that there would be a great influx of Northern capital but soon were bitterly disappointed. The North found more attractive investment fields in its own region or in the booming West than in the politically and socially distraught South.

Thrown back upon their own meager resources, Southerners took stock of what they had. Despite threats of confiscation, the greatest portion of land remained in their hands. Equally important, the abilities and spirit of most of the people had not been destroyed. Women cheerfully worked to remake homes or even went into the fields for the first time. The men had been hardened by war, and the region still had competent leadership. Fortunately, the world still needed cotton, though restoration of production would be no easy matter. Seed was lacking, tools and machinery were gone or worn out, work animals were scarce, and labor other than their own was an unknown quantity. Hope and the will to work their land were the principal resources left to the mass of defeated Southerners.

Chiefly, the agricultural South faced two problems: capital and labor. Capital was needed to finance production and to keep the farmer alive until the crop could be harvested. Hopes of Northern money were quickly gone, and most of the small cotton crop of 1864 was seized by federal agents. But by calling into use hoarded gold and by borrowing in Europe and the North, often at ruinous terms, whatever money the promise of cotton would bring forth, a start was made.

The labor problem, above all, proved the most vexing. The whites had the land but not the labor to put it into widespread production; the Negroes were the principal labor source of the region but had no land. Somehow or other, if the South were to recover economically, the land and the labor had to be brought together. Many whites were convinced that the Negroes would never be induced to work without slavery and should therefore be deported to Africa or the West Indies. Even Southerners who were willing to allow them to stay in the South felt that, to prosper, the region would have to attract immigrants or white labor from the North.

But the immigrants did not come and the blacks did not leave. The ex-slaves, therefore, had to be used, but they, too, were uncertain of the future. Many, unsure of their relationship in the new order, proceeded to celebrate by taking off, usually for the nearest town; however, more than 20,000 freedmen found their way to Washington alone during 1865. Others believed that the government would give each of them forty acres and a mule. Sharpers defrauded the gullible by selling red, white, and blue striped stakes with which to mark off their lands when the master's plantation was divided. Also, among those who stayed at home, there often was an uneasy suspicion that the whites would somehow rob them of their freedom.

A writer in *De Bow's Review*, assuming a reluctance on their part, stated that, if the South were to recover, the blacks had to be made to work. The federal government should intervene to insist that "plantation freedmen [make] annual contracts with planters, and to see that such contracts are rigorously enforced." By this means, the laborers could be "*compelled* to work. We have no faith whatever in their being *induced* to do so by any of the motives, which ordinarily govern white laborers." [2]

When the Washington government gave no indication of taking such advice, the newly formed post-war governments of the South decided to take matters into their own hands. Before the war, slavery had been the means by which the black's potential was realized and their legal status determined. After 1865, their legal situation had to be redefined and some other method of regulatory direction installed. The local answers to these problems were the "black codes" passed by Southern legislatures in 1865 and 1866. The authors frankly felt that it was necessary to keep the ex-slaves in a position of social and economic inferiority. By these codes, the region felt that it would be protected against a mob of unrestrained blacks and would be furthering its own material interests and that of the freedmen by inducing them to work. Most states undoubtedly believed that the new leniency more than offset the restrictions by permitting rights that the slaves had never experienced. These laws, Southerners contended, were intended to bridge the gap between slavery and freedom.

Mississippi's was the first and most elaborate. The codes of the other states varied widely in scope and character. Virginia's and North

2 "What the Cotton Industry Requires," *De Bow's Review*, I (February, 1866), p. 198.

Carolina's were mild; Georgia and Alabama had few laws regarding Negroes; Arkansas and Tennessee at first passed none whatsoever. In general, those states with the most Negroes had the most restrictions. Based upon the vagrancy laws of North and South, slavery-time customs, old free-Negro statutes, and British West Indian legislation, the codes generally made the freedmen second-class citizens; they had more civil rights than the slaves but less than the whites.

Negroes were defined as those possessing one-eighth or more of Negro blood. These "persons of color" were forbidden to marry with whites, but slave marriages were validated and their offspring legitimatized. The codes also conferred upon them the essential rights of citizens to make contracts, to sue and be sued, to own and inherit property, and to testify in court, although generally they were not allowed to do so against white men. Some states provided for schools but required separation of the races. In no instance were the Negroes given the right to vote or made eligible to serve on juries.

While most codes included special provisions to protect the Negroes from undue exploitation and swindling, at the same time various restrictions placed them on a lower social plane. Mississippi provided that "any person who shall so intermarry [miscegenation], shall be deemed guilty of felony and on conviction thereof shall be confined in the State penitentiary for life." Another section stated that a "freedman, free negro, or mulatto" could not rent or lease any lands or tenements "except in incorporated cities or town." Other states restricted their property to the country. Louisiana provided that no Negroes could leave a parish (county) without the written consent of their employers, leave their houses after ten o'clock at night, hold special meetings after sunset without permission of the "captain of patrol," preach without a special license, carry firearms or other weapons, or sell merchandise without their employer's permission. Mississippi made it unlawful for them to ride in first-class railroad accommodations. South Carolina forbade them, except under special license, to engage in anything except farming and domestic work.

The most controversial clauses, however, were those which dealt with efforts to force the Negroes to work. Louisiana required all persons engaged as laborers in agriculture to make an annual contract for labor during the first ten days of January, and, while having freedom to choose their place of employment, once having signed, they could not leave until the contract expired. The law further stated that they had to work ten hours a day in summer and nine in winter. "Bad work shall not be allowed." They had to obey all proper orders and take good care of livestock and equipment; furthermore, "impudence, swearing, or indecent language in the presence of the employer, his family, or agent, or quarreling and fighting with one another, shall be deemed disobedience." For any "disobedience" there would be a fine of one dollar. Theft, destruction, or injury to the master's property carried a penalty of double its value.

In most states Negroes were subject to very broad apprenticeship and vagrancy laws. Louisiana required the apprenticing of all females under eighteen years of age and males under twenty who were orphans or whose parents could not or would not provide for them. Mississippi stipulated that preference should be given to former masters in choosing those to whom these wards would be apprenticed. Punishment could be such "as a father or guardian is allowed to inflict on his or her child or ward at common law." Masters, however, were required to meet standards in supplying food, clothing, and su able training.

The definition of vagrancy was expanded to include not only the usual vagabonds, beggars, idlers, etc., but also those "who neglect their calling or employment, misspend what they earn, or do not provide for the support of themselves or their families." Mississippi also provided that, after January, 1866, any freedmen over eighteen who were without lawful employment or business, who were found unlawfully assembling themselves together, or who failed to pay any tax would fall into this category. Alabama included anyone who was "stubborn," "loitered away his time," or refused to comply with any contract without just cause. The penalty for vagrancy could be imprisonment, hard labor, or, more commonly, heavy fines, which, if unpaid, could be collected by selling the services of the offender for a period long enough to satisfy the claim.

While Southerners believed these laws to be "liberal" and generous and aimed at protecting the black against his own ignorance and helplessness, they were certainly impolitic and aroused a storm of protest in the North. To the abolitionists they were violations of the new freedman's rights. The radicals saw evidence that Southerners were not accepting the results of the war but were attempting to have the fact, if not the name, of slavery. The Chicago *Tribune* said that "the men of the North will convert the State of Mississippi into a frog pond before they will allow any such laws to disgrace one foot of soil in which the bones of our soldiers sleep and over which the flag of freedom waves." The fact that Illinois had statutes which severely limited the rights of blacks dating from before the war was conveniently overlooked.

The South's political error in relation to the black codes was in regarding the race problem as purely local and one which could be solved without Northern intervention; the North, however, did not believe in the South's good intentions. For example, North Carolina's laws, which were average, were not chosen as the basis for judgment; instead, Mississippi's extreme statutes were viewed as typical. Although these legal efforts were defended as moderately generous and necessary, they were impolitic in that they would be judged by a region that felt any abridgement of rights was intolerable. The suspicious North concluded that, if the freedmen were to be saved from re-enslavement, the national government had to protect them from their former masters.

This interest in the free Negroes' future had had its origin during the war. Lincoln in his early plans for emancipation had given serious consideration to colonizing the freedmen in other parts of the world. One of his recommendations, which became law in 1862, provided $100,000 for voluntary emigration of the Negroes to Haiti and Liberia. Emigration seemed almost as important to Lincoln as emancipation, as seen in his statement to a group of Negroes in August, 1862: "Your race suffer greatly, many of them, by living among us, while ours suffer from your presence. In a word we suffer on each side. If this is admitted, it affords a reason why we should be separated." The State Department even made inquiries in various parts of the world concerning this possibility of colonization. As late as the end of the war, the President still held to his hope that some of the freedmen could be induced to leave this country.

But until that time might come, something had to be done for them. The first moves were taken by individual army commanders. In December, 1862, Rufus Saxton, commanding the Department of the South, established a general plan to be followed for Negro relief. Every family was allotted two acres of abandoned land for each working hand, with tools to be furnished by the government. Superintendents were appointed to take a census of Negro population and oversee their general welfare. While some overseers showed little interest in their charges, others were conscientious. But even the best of these were handicapped by a lack of available land and interdepartmental squabbles between the War Department and the Treasury concerning jurisdiction over confiscated property. Negro suffering became so intense and a federal relief policy was so slow in developing that private persons, both black and white, had to come to their rescue.[3]

On March 16, 1863, the War Department created the American Freedmen's Inquiry Commission, staffed by Dr. Samuel Gridley Howe and Colonel James McKaye and chaired by Robert Dale Owen. After traveling through the occupied parts of the South, their reports in June, 1863, and May, 1864, held that land and its redistribution among the freedmen and poor whites was the key to the problem. The Ne-

[3] An excellent discussion of early Northern efforts to cope with the freedman problems is found in John Hope Franklin, *From Slavery to Freedom: A History of American Negroes* (New York: Knopf, 1967), chap. XVI.

groes had to have land if they were ever to attain economic independence. The primary source was the large plantations, which could be obtained by forcible seizure, compensated or uncompensated. The Commission also recommended that some scheme should be worked out whereby freedmen could eventually purchase land, if public opinion would not sustain confiscation.[4]

The great need, however, was for a comprehensive and unified program for the freedmen. It was not until the day before Lincoln's second inauguration, March 3, 1865, that such a step was taken, when the Bureau of Refugees, Freedmen, and Abandoned Lands, better known as the Freedmen's Bureau, was created under the War Department to unify the various federal organizations that had been set up during the war to deal with the Negro problem. Originally intended to last for one year after the end of fighting, the Bureau was given general supervision of the Negroes and "loyal [white] refugees." With headquarters at Washington, and hundreds of agents distributed throughout the South, General Oliver O. Howard, the "Christian soldier," was its chief.

The Bureau's first problem was that of direct relief, and between 1865 and 1869 it distributed more than 21,000,000 rations, with about 15,500,000 going to freedmen. In its first year of operation, medical services were furnished 143,000 Negro and 5,600 white inhabitants of the South. By 1867 there were 46 hospitals staffed by the Bureau, and by the end of its career in 1872, it had spent over $2,000,000 in treating 450,000 cases of illness.

The Bureau's major responsibility, the Negroes, involved two groups — those who had stayed on the plantations and those who were homeless, wandering around the countryside or jammed in intolerable conditions in Southern or border cities. The latter were first herded into camps and given "destitute rations"; steps were then taken for their resettlement. Free transportation was furnished more than 30,000 to leave congested areas in hopes of their becoming self-supporting.

In line with previous philosophy, the Bureau law left the impression that freedmen were to be given land. Actually, the Bureau was empowered to divide "such tracts of land within the insurrectionary states as shall have been abandoned, or to which the United States shall have acquired title by confiscation or sale, or otherwise," into forty-acre plots to be rented to its wards for three years, at the end of which period the land could be purchased for about sixteen times the annual rental. The most persistent and vociferous demand of the Negro was for land, some even attempting to seize it by force. On January

[4] John G. Sproat, "Blueprint for Radical Reconstruction," *Journal of Southern History*, XXIII (February, 1957), pp. 40-44.

12, 1865, a group of freedmen, queried by General William T. Sherman and Secretary of War Stanton as to what their race needed most, answered, "The way we can best take care of ourselves is to have land, and turn it and till it by our own labor." But here the Bureau was destined to fail despite its good intentions, for the amount of land that was seized for non-payment of federal taxes, because of its owners' participation in the rebellion, or because it supposedly had been abandoned, came only to 800,000 acres (including urban property). Most of the abandoned property was restored by the amnesty proclamations of Lincoln and Johnson. Expropriation by the Confiscation Act of 1862 was only for the lifetime of the offender, and proposals of additional seizures of private property could not overcome the economic canons of the period. Thaddeus Stevens, Representative from Pennsylvania, introduced such an act as late as 1867, but there was no chance for its passage. Confiscation had never been a tenet of the Republican party; it was viewed even in the North as revolutionary, with implied threats to the sanctity of property. Horace Greeley declared that he knew of no Northerner who favored such a move except Stevens and Benjamin Butler. Nor were the pleas of the landless that the Government lend them the money with which to buy land ever seriously considered by Congress.[5]

Lacking the ability to establish the Negroes as independent farmers, the Bureau thus was forced to seek other ways of dealing with the problem of resettlement. Concurrently, the question had to be resolved as to what was to be done with those freedmen who had remained on the plantations. By what right could they stay on, and how could they make a living? With owners of land wanting labor and a multitude of landless laborers without employment, under normal situations the laws of supply and demand could have been left to work out a system of contracts between the two parties. But as General Wager Swayne, head of the Alabama Bureau, pointed out, "Contracts imply bargaining and litigation, and at neither of these is the freedman a match for his employer." The Bureau therefore not only undertook to regulate the contracts between the two races, affording the Negroes freedom in choosing employers and obtaining fair wages ($9 to $15 a month for men, $5 to $10 for women, plus food, fuel, and cabin), but also to supply special courts, usually consisting of an agent and two citizens, to enforce Negro rights.

Several thousands of these contracts were drawn up under Bureau guidance. Agents consulted with planters and freedmen, urging the one group to be fair in its dealings and trying to impress the other with

[5] LaWanda Cox, "The Promise of Land for the Freedman," *Mississippi Valley Historical Review,* XLV (December, 1958), p. 413ff.

the necessity of working to provide for their families. But these were not normal times or situations. In Virginia and South Carolina the great majority of freedmen were able to secure fairly regular work during 1865-1866, and in Louisiana free labor succeeded when given a fair trial and enough money to pay cash wages. In most of the lower South, however, the problem was more difficult. Here were more Negroes, as well as more general poverty. Planters had little money for wages, and Negroes had even less for rent. Some whites objected to contracts as marks of equality. They did not know what constituted just wages and how to manage free labor; some tried to use the whip. Often, however, the Negroes broke the agreement. Many still dreamed of the forty acres and a mule which the government would furnish. They resented gang work or supervision, and, in the eyes of their employers, they made preposterous demands. Few understood the binding nature of a contract and would work only half a day at a time, rarely seeing the point of laboring after a few dollars had been earned.

The restoration of agriculture, upon which both whites and blacks depended for economic recovery, was not as smooth as anticipated, even the elements of nature seemingly against the South. The crops of 1865, because of uncertainty of labor, lack of proper tools and seed, and a terrible drought, were brutally disappointing, less than half of the last year before the war. The same story was repeated during the next two years, and in 1867 prices fell to half the anticipated level, completely ruining many planters. Although the Negroes were not totally responsible, many white Southerners placed the blame on them. A traveler in Texas in 1865 reported that drought had ruined half the corn and potato crops and that he saw "acres of the finest cotton that ever grew dropping out of the bolls, and wasting for the want of hands to save it. The planters made contracts with their former slaves to remain with them and save the crops, but they proved unfaithful and deserted at the first opportunity."

William F. Samford of Alabama wrote, "The short crop of 1866 causes much dissatisfaction. They [the Negroes] will not engage to work for anything but wages, and few are able to pay wages. They are penniless but resolute in their demands. They expect to see the land divided out equally between them and their old masters, in time to make the next crop." It is not difficult to understand the feelings of the North Carolinian who begged, "Send us forty cargoes of Hindoos, Hottentots, Malays, Chinamen, Indians, anything; we can not be worsted." But without other sources of labor or income, the whites and the Negroes had to learn to live and work together, whether they liked it or not.

Although a few ex-slaves were able to take advantage of the low price of land and become landowners, the eventual replacement for the old plantation turned out to be closer to the Negro's "forty acres and a mule." Planters soon found that the most mutually satisfactory system was to split up their land into small plots with a tenant in charge of each, the returns being divided according to the amount furnished by each party. The formulas for division were many, but the most common was that of one third to the tenant for his labor, a third to the landlord for use of the land, and the remainder to whoever furnished the other necessities besides labor and land. At the outset, since the planters furnished rations, tools, and animals, they commonly received two-thirds of the crops grown. Later, when the Negroes could furnish more, the crops were more equally divided. While the share system remained on a trial basis for about a decade, it gained steady favor among both races, and the Bureau approved it as a transitional stage to final Negro ownership.

But the sharecrop system did not solve all of the agricultural problems. Landlords continued to complain that the Negroes would not fulfill their obligations, that they resented supervision, and that crops were neglected and property abused. On the other hand, the Negroes protested about over-supervision and claimed that they were cheated in their contracts. Despite this, however, the system did have the advantage of making the white landlord's property partially productive and did make possible the utilization of a numerous landless labor force which thereby became at least self-supporting.

Despite the Bureau's hopes, however, the system did not become the transitional stage to Negro ownership. Without the capital to buy land, a mule, and agricultural tools, and with limited credit, the majority of tenants were forced to lease land on the white man's terms. Not only this, but those who were able to become independent were handicapped by unfamiliarity with farm management and marketing. Fifty years after emancipation, there were only 218,000 Negro landowners, and their relative numbers were declining.

The Bureau's failures, first, to secure land for the freedmen, and second, to make tenancy a rapid road to ownership, meant in the last analysis the frustration of the greatest hope of the Negroes and their well-wishers. Perhaps the expectation of forty acres was excessive, but much smaller plots would have been satisfactory and not prohibitive in cost, especially in light of the fact that the same government found it possible to give a single railroad forty million acres of public land. With Southern land selling so cheaply, the entire cost would conceivably have been financed by the receipts from the cotton tax, $68,000,000. But the solution of the South's economic problem by the introduction of sharecropping meant more than failure of the Bureau's economic goal for the Negroes. In the long run, it also doomed the whole Northern plan of reconstruction by leaving the freedmen at the economic mercy of the Southern whites. From economic control to social and political domination was to be a very easy step.

Education, in the Bureau's mind, was closely aligned with land ownership as a means of economic rehabilitation. As already noted, many Northerners were convinced that the redemption of the South lay in the Negro being given the education he had heretofore been denied. Since the Bureau originally was expected to be self-support-ing, it was given no appropriation during its first year, but fortunately there was no shortage of people willing to aid in carrying the gospel of education, and the function of the Bureau became more and more that of coordinating and assisting their efforts.

Booker T. Washington, a Negro who lived through this period, later wrote, "Few people who were not right in the midst of the scenes can form any exact idea of the intense desire which the people of my race showed for education. It was a whole race trying to go to school. Few were too young and none too old to make the attempt to learn. . . . Day schools, night school, and Sunday school were always crowded, and often many had to be turned away for want of room." Such response could not be ignored: a year after the war, there were 366 societies and auxiliaries in the field.

The Freedmen's Bureau undertook to place these activities under some form of systematic supervision. In some states, schools were supported entirely by funds from this agency, but generally it confined itself to furnishing buildings, equipment, and protection from the sometimes hostile whites. On July 1, 1866, it reported 975 schools in fifteen states and the District of Columbia, 1,405 teachers, and 90,778 students.[6] By 1870 there were 4,329 schools and 247,333 pupils. In five years the Bureau spent on Negro schools some $5,262,511, almost a third of its total budget.

The Bureau, by way of summary, sought to install a practicable system of compensated labor, to relieve the suffering, to protect loyal refugees, to afford facilities to aid societies and state authorities in maintaining schools until local governments could take over the bur-den, and to adjudicate disputes, both among Negroes and between Negroes and whites. All this, in addition to political activities that will be discussed later, was done on appropriations that totaled less than $18,000,000 during its seven-year life span.[7]

While the Southern economic and humanitarian problems may

[6] U. S. Bureau of Education, *loc. cit.*, pp. 1377-1379.
[7] For a compact description of typical Bureau activities in a single state, see Eliza-beth Bethel, "The Freedman's Bureau in Alabama," *Journal of Southern History,* XIV (February, 1948), p. 49ff.

have been more immediately pressing, of equal importance was the political dilemma which confronted the nation in 1865. While the South was left to solve its own economic woes, politically no such latitude was allowed, and Northern public opinion was determined that it should have the final say. Most Northerners were also insistent that the triumph of unionism and freedom in the war should be followed by positive measures to insure these goals. Yet beyond these basic objectives, opinion was divided on how these should be implemented.

Reconstruction was widely discussed in the North during the whole war period, and, as would be expected under a constitutional form of government, that document was scanned for answers. Debate centered chiefly on whether the seceded states were in or out of the Union with the crushing of the rebellion. If secession were illegal, then logic declared that the so-called Confederate states were still full-fledged members of the Union. If, on the other hand, secession were valid, they were conquered territory without any rights which had to be legally respected. But the Constitution was no guide on such a thorny problem, for its framers had never foreseen such a situation. Consequently, every theorist was his own supreme court on the issue. The program would have to be worked out pragmatically, within or without the Constitution, and all the plans attempted were extra-constitutional.

The difficulties of the situation were clearly recognized by Lincoln in his last public address:

> By these recent successes, the reinauguration of the national authority — reconstruction — which has had a large share of thought from the first, is pressed much more closely upon our attention. It is fraught with great difficulty. Unlike a case of war between independent nations, *there is no authorized organ for us to treat with* — no one man has authority to give up the rebellion for any other man. We simply must begin with and mould from disorganized and discordant elements. Nor is it a small additional embarrassment that we, the loyal people, differ among ourselves as to the mode, manner, and measure of reconstruction.

As to the question of whether the Southern states were in or out of the Union, that was "immaterial, [and] could have no effect other than the mischievous one of dividing our friends." It was "a merely pernicious abstraction," since all could agree that they were "out of their proper practical relation with the Union." They must be brought back into that relationship, and then, "safely at home, it would be utterly immaterial whether they had been abroad."

But the public could not take so simple a view of the process. Opinion on reconstruction ranged from extreme forgiveness to extreme vengeance. Both were tried, but in each case even the opposition was uncertain of what it wanted to do, and in the end no plan was carried out completely. The most liberal view was that of the "unimpaired rights" theory, based upon the Webster-Lincoln-Johnson argument that the states and Union were indestructible. As Andrew Johnson said of the Southern state, its "life-breath has only been suspended. . . . It was a State when it went into a rebellion, and when it comes out . . . it is still a State." The "States attempting to secede placed themselves in a condition where their vitality was impaired, but not extinguished; their functions suspended, but not destroyed." Any argument as to whether a state could secede had been settled by the war, which proved that it could not. Therefore the states were in the Union, and all that was necessary was for them to elect officers who would swear to support the Union and the Constitution.

This point of view appealed particularly to Southerners and to Northern Democrats. The latter was a minority group in the North after the war, and thus the Southern vote was of prime importance to them. It was to their interest to forget the past and work out as quickly as possible a truce which would readmit their Southern allies. Thus they assumed the role of men of peace and reunion, fighting those who cried for vengeance. But this program forgot the hatred bred by the war, that Southerners could not vote, and that Northern Democrats were bearing the war-time legacy of mistrusted loyalty.

On the other extreme were theories of a more radical nature. To the Republicans it was important that the past not be forgotten nor that a reunion favorable to their rivals be consummated. Senator John Sherman of Ohio said, "We should not only brand the leading rebels with infamy, but the rebellion should wear the badge of the penitentiary, so that for this generation at least, no man who has taken part in it would dare to justify or palliate it." More formal programs were popularized by Thaddeus Stevens and Charles Sumner. As early as 1862, Senator Sumner of Massachusetts proposed the "state suicide" theory, holding that when a state attempted by force to contest the supremacy of the Constitution, it abdicated all of its rights. The "treason" involved worked "an instant *forfeiture* of all those functions and powers essential to the continued existence of the State as a body politic, so from that time forward the territory falls under the exclusive jurisdiction of Congress as other territory, and the state . . . ceases to exist."

In the House of Representatives, Stevens declared the Southern states were "conquered provinces" and "only dead carcasses lying within the Union." The war had broken the original compacts and all ties which bound the two sections together; the "future condition of the conquered power depends on the will of the conqueror. They must come in as new states or remain as conquered provinces." The federal government should force them to eat the "fruit of foul rebellion" by inflicting "condign punishment on the rebel belligerents, and so weaken their hands that they can never again endanger the Union." The property of the "chief rebels" should be seized and used to pay the national debt resulting from the "unjust and wicked war which they instigated." However, he added, how "many captive enemies it would be proper to execute, as an example to nations, I leave others to judge. I am not fond of sanguinary punishments, but surely some victims must propitiate the *manes* of our starved, murdered, slaughtered martyrs." Nevertheless, the "whole fabric of Southern society *must* be changed and never can it be done if this opportunity is lost." All estates worth $10,000 or land holdings over 200 acres should be confiscated and their holders driven into exile or forced to the social and economic level of the common people. These lands then should be resettled by loyal men — preferably Northerners and Negroes.

Secondary to the question of what reconstruction should be was that of who had the authority to institute and supervise the process. During the war the power of the President had been greatly increased. Congress felt that this had been at its expense and that the constitutional balance of power had been upset. That body, therefore, was overly sensitive to any move that to them seemed to be claiming additional jurisdiction. Both Stevens and Sumner, for example, were convinced that Congress alone could determine the pattern of reconstruction.

But Congress, under the control of the Republican party, was divided into three groups on the question of policy. One was the extreme radicals led by Stevens; another was the stern moderates, like William Pitt Fessenden and Lyman Trumbull, who primarily wanted confirmation that the South accepted the verdict of the war and guarantees of future good behavior. Finally, there were those who inclined toward the "unimpaired rights" theory. Yet all three factions were united in a common congressional resentment against what they considered virtual presidential dictatorship, as far as war-time action in the South was concerned. As long as hostilities continued, such criticism was apt to be viewed as unpatriotic, but with the approach of peace, repressed congressional tongues became clamorous.

President Abraham Lincoln had other thoughts. In the first place, he differed from those members who wanted to punish the South. He also felt that reconstruction was an executive function to be accomplished by encouraging the establishment of loyal state governments as military occupation of the region progressed. Unlike Stevens, he considered it to be purely political and as having no concern with economic or social matters. The states merely were out of their proper place in the Union, and the only problem was to get them back. According to the diary of Secretary of the Navy Gideon Welles, Lincoln told his cabinet:

> If we were wise and discreet we should re-animate the states and get their governments in successful operation, with order prevailing and the Union reestablished, before Congress came together in December. . . . There were men in Congress who, if their motives were good were nevertheless impracticable, and who possessed feelings of hate and vindictiveness in which he did not sympathize and could not participate. He hoped there would be no persecution, no bloody work, after the war was over. None need expect he would take any part in hanging or killing those men, even the worst of them.

In these fundamental differences of opinion lay the seeds of a great and long dispute. It was to lead to the impeachment of a president and finally to insure that no one program of reconstruction would be carried to its logical conclusion.

# 4

# RADICALISM VS. CONSERVATISM

PRESIDENT ABRAHAM LINCOLN was little interested in the rhetorical question of whether the Confederate states were still in the Union or had, by secession, lost their legal lives. He had once said that he did not care for the metaphysics of a question but would work out the best practical solution and then argue about it afterwards. To him they were simply "out of their proper practical relation with the Union," and the solution was equally simple —"get them into proper practical relation" once more. Unlike the politicians of his party, he had early devised his own plan — an opportunistic one, as was most of his statesmanship. The President had insisted on waging the war on the basis that it was a rebellion of citizens rather than a revolt of states. Therefore, he felt he could deal with the Confederates on the assumption that they had misled their governments. The function of his office, he believed, was to do whatever was necessary to reorganize these states. His objective, consequently, was merely to promote establishment of loyal state governments as rapidly as possible.

This sensible policy he had pursued throughout the struggle. As early as 1862 he appointed provisional governors with the responsibility of reviving loyal sentiment in each of the seceded states under Northern military control. Moving to the next step, in an amnesty proclamation on December 8, 1863, he formulated what was to become the first plan of reconstruction. In line with his desire to rebuild the Union even as the war progressed and to restore the states to a normal relationship with the federal government as painlessly as possible, he expected to work through the loyal minorities. The stimulus would be the presidential power to pardon. To get the right people in control, his proclamation promised a full pardon, with restoration of all property rights except to slaves (the Emancipation Proclamation having taken effect as of January 1, 1863), to all who would take an oath of allegiance to the United States. The only exceptions were to be those above the rank of colonel in the Confederate army and lieutenant in the navy, those who had resigned seats in Congress or commissions in the United States armed forces to aid the Confederacy, or any who had mistreated prisoners of war. In any state, whenever as few as one-tenth of the number of voters in 1860 took the oath, a government was to be established which would be recognized as the "true government" of the state.

This was a war measure as well as a reconstruction one. It was an effort to break down Confederate war support and build a loyal nucleus around which pro-Union elements could rally. Ten per cent of the voters was too small a group for stable government, but the figure had been set low in an attempt to help end the war by enticing Southerners to be disloyal to the Confederacy. From this point of view it was good, but the plan fell far short of its objective and probably did not shorten the war.

This magnanimous gesture, known as the ten-per-cent plan, was quickly put into effect. Four states, Louisiana, Arkansas, Tennessee, and Virginia, were partly under Union army control, and in these the first new governments were established and recognized by Lincoln. Of the four, Virginia had undoubtedly the most tempestuous and controversial experience. Virginia's secession, on April 17, 1861, had led to a wave of unrest in the western part of the state, culminating in a general loyalist convention which met at Wheeling on June 11. There, delegates elected by local mass meetings in twenty-six counties "reorganized" the government of Virginia, making loyalty to the Union a requirement for officeholding, and created a rival authority to that in Richmond. Claiming eventually to represent fifty counties, it chose Francis H. Pierpoint "Governor of Virginia" and placed his capital at Wheeling.

On May 13, 1862, the "restored" state legislature of about ten senators and thirty-five representatives, acting for all of Virginia, gave its "consent" for the formation of the new state of West Virginia, thus providing at least nominal compliance with the constitutional provision that a state must give its consent to creation of new states from within its boundaries. Although Lincoln disapproved, he did not veto a bill for the admission of West Virginia, and it became a state on June 20, 1863.

Following this action, the Pierpoint government of "Virginia" was little more than a straw one, with its capital moved to Alexandria. Here, a legislature of sixteen delegates and seven senators, controlling but the few miles of Northern-held territory on the south bank of the Potomac and around Fortress Monroe and Norfolk, claimed authority over all of Virginia. Although the ten-per-cent requirement was not enforced and Pierpoint occasionally embarrassed the military officials, Lincoln recognized and supported this government in the hope that it might prove a nucleus for the future reorganization of Virginia. Representation, however, was for the most part denied by Congress, despite the fact that the new state constitution abolished slavery and recognized the Union. When eventually reconstruction was finally completed, it was done by a process which ignored the government of Francis Pierpoint.

Tennessee, also, had a sectional cleavage, the eastern counties being loyal to the Union. It was not necessary for them to break away, however, because of the rapid success of federal troops. As soon as Nashville fell in 1862, Lincoln appointed a native son, Andrew Johnson, as military governor. After a little more than a year of such control, he instructed Johnson to establish a civil government, saying, "You and the co-operating friends there can better judge of the ways and means than can judged by any here." His only suggestion was that it be the "work of such men only as can be trusted for the Union."

A convention was called in September, 1864, for the choosing of presidential electors, electors which Congress refused to recognize even though Johnson was running for vice president on the ticket with Lincoln. This was followed in January by another convention claiming constituent powers, which recommended amending the state constitution by abolishing slavery, renouncing the ordinance of secession, and approving Johnson's actions as governor. At an election of February 22, 1865, the amendments were approved, and W. G. "Parson" Brownlow was chosen governor. One faction claimed this to be full compliance with Lincoln's ten-per-cent plan, although others charged the whole procedure was highly irregular. Nevertheless, this was the only one of the Lincoln governments destined to survive, being recognized by Congress in 1866.

After the capture of New Orleans in the spring of 1862, Lincoln appointed Benjamin F. Butler as military governor of Louisiana and instructed him to hold elections for Congress. The Representatives so chosen were seated, but their colleagues to the Senate were not recognized. In 1863, state elections were held, in which Michael Hahn was elected governor; Lincoln took the additional precaution of appointing him military governor. Following Lincoln's proclamation in December, steps were taken to call a constitutional convention. On March 13, 1864, prior to the meeting of this group, Lincoln wrote Hahn, "I barely suggest, for your private consideration, whether some of the colored people may not be let in [given the franchise to vote], as, for instance, the very intelligent, and especially those who have fought gallantly in our ranks. . . . But this is only a suggestion, not to the public, but to you alone." The new constitution, approved by a vote of 6,836 to 1,566, abolished slavery but did not give any Negroes the right to the ballot. The affirmative vote being more than 10 per cent of the 1860 voters, Lincoln recognized the new government.

After the fall of Vicksburg (July 4, 1863), two-thirds of Arkansas was in Union hands, and a military government was set up. To satisfy the President's wishes, a restoration movement was begun. In January, 1864, a convention at Little Rock repudiated the Confederate debt, repealed the ordinance of secession, and abolished slavery. The new constitution was carried by 12,177 to 226, compared to the 54,000 voters in 1860. Both the convention and election were irregular, and though a civil government was inaugurated in October, it never proved acceptable to Congress.

As a result of Lincoln's determination to use his full powers to make the "road to reunion" short and painless, four states had been reconstructed, but these proved more valuable as precedents than as viable experiments. A great and magnanimous soul like Lincoln was able to be charitable, but most people did not welcome back the prodigals without recriminations. While Lincoln was intent solely on restoring the Union, others, including members of his own party, were anxious that restoration should serve their own desires. Lincoln was willing to accept a promissory oath; others considered this inadequate to protect the fruits of war and insure future Southern good behavior. Some tests, they felt, such as past loyalty, had to be devised before the rebels could be forgiven. It was natural for Northerners to hold the South responsible for the war and to doubt that the region could be trusted to maintain the Union against which it had rebelled; few understood as did the President the difficulties the South would face. In line with his belief that the states had not been out of the Union, Lincoln also wanted to leave the South to settle the Negro problem as it wished; others demanded votes for the freedmen as a guarantee of future good conduct.

Lincoln's policy cannot be criticized as a war measure aimed at ending the rebellion, but it had serious faults as a basis for peacetime reconstruction. A whole nation is seldom magnanimous. In view of the hatreds and suspicions of the period, Lincoln did not make sufficient concessions to Northern feelings, thus subjecting himself to attack as being too lenient. The plan was also put into effect too hastily and without proper considerations of a sensitive Congress, leading legislators to believe Lincoln was intent on grasping more power. Also, the stability of any government by such a very small minority was extremely questionable.

But the strongest support for the dissenters came from Congress, which questioned the President's right even to *begin* reconstruction. Since his policy might well lead to the rise of the Democratic party to power, the Republican majority were bitter that the management of so important a matter had been usurped. They had a trump in that Congress alone had the right to admit Southerners to seats in Congress and the responsibility under the Constitution of guaranteeing a republican form of government in the states. Thus, they claimed the right to make the plans and viewed presidential responsibility as limited to enforcement. There was considerable justice in this stand, and the wise executive tried to conciliate Congress. Lincoln, in his Amnesty Proclamation, carefully stated "that whether members sent to Congress from any state shall be admitted to seats constitutionally rests exclusively with the respective houses, and not to any extent with the Executive."

Already restive over loss of power, Congress, when informed of the Amnesty Proclamation, maintained that a law rather than a proclamation would have been the proper vehicle. Henry Winter Davis of Maryland became chairman of a special House committee to consider the treatment of the Southern states, and Ohio's old abolitionist, Benjamin Wade, took up the matter in the Senate. The result was the denial of admission of "reconstructed" representatives to Congress and the passage on July 8, 1864, of the Wade-Davis bill. The latter asserted the right of Congress to control restoration and proscribed many of the very ex-Confederates upon whom Lincoln had hoped to base his governments. This measure placed control not in the hands of a minority ready to be loyal in the future but required a majority who had records of past loyalty. Provisional governors would be appointed "with the advice and consent of the Senate" with instructions to enroll the white male citizens. If a majority of those enrolled would take an oath to support the Constitution of the United States, they could choose a constitutional convention. But every person known "to have held any office, civil or military, State or Confederate, under the rebel usurpation, or to have voluntarily borne arms against the United States, shall be excluded though he offer to take the oath."

The new governments so created had to declare their submission to the Constitution and laws of the United States. In addition, any person in civil or military office, except those of purely ministerial function or below the grade of colonel, were to be denied the right to vote or to serve as governor or as a member of the legislature. Slavery was to be forever prohibited, and no debt, state or Confederate, "created by or under the sanction of the usurping power" should be recognized or paid. Only after obtaining the consent of Congress was the President to "recognize the government so established, and none other as the constitutional government of the state."

This measure, which appeared vindictive and which would undoubtedly slow down the rate of restoration, marked so fundamental a difference between Lincoln and the Congress that a deadlock was inevitable. Lincoln seldom used the veto, but in this case he applied a pocket veto. Although this required no veto message, he issued an explanation of his action, since an election was pending. He was unwilling to be "inflexibly committed to any single plan of restoration"; he did not wish to see the governments he had established "set aside and held for nought"; he favored a constitutional amendment abolishing slavery throughout the nation, rather than individual state action. But Lincoln did not make the break with Congress final, for he gave the states involved the alternative of choosing the congressional plan if they wished.

But Congress was not so temperate. His statement was answered by Wade and Davis in a manifesto which appeared on August 5, 1864, in the New York *Tribune*. They stated that they had read Lincoln's proclamation "without surprise, but not without indignation." His actions defied the "exercise of an authority exclusively vested in Congress by the Constitution," and a "more studied outrage on the legislative authority of the people has never been perpetrated." He must understand that the nation was supporting "a cause and not . . . a man; that the authority of Congress is paramount and must be respected"; that he must "confine himself to his executive duties – to obey and execute, not make the laws – to suppress by arms armed rebellion, and leave political reorganization to Congress."

Even earlier, some efforts had been made to replace Lincoln as the presidential nominee in 1864, and though these schemes came to naught and he was re-elected, the Radicals were unwilling to concede defeat. In the congressional session of 1864-1865, although the Thirteenth Amendment was passed and submitted to the states on February 1, 1865, these extremists continued to harass the President. Senator Charles Sumner of Massachusetts threatened to block all appropriations unless a bill to recognize Louisiana's government was dropped.

Lincoln signed under protest the joint resolution which excluded from the electoral count of 1865 the votes from his reconstructed states. His pleas for support during the closing months of his life showed that he was clearly apprehensive of his future relations with the legislative branch. In his last public address, he stressed the fact that reconstruction was so complicated "that no exclusive and inflexible plan can safely be prescribed." What terms he might have made with Congress will never be known, for on April 15, 1865, he was assassinated.

The death of Lincoln was quickly used by the Radicals for their own benefit. It was easy for outraged Northern public opinion to believe that the murder was a Southern plot. There was even some talk that God had struck down Lincoln because of his mercy toward the South: "We [the North] thought we might be more merciful than God." They saw in his successor, Johnson, a man more after their own taste; he was known to be a life-long enemy of the aristocrats who had ruled the South. On June 9, 1864, he had stated publicly, "I say that the traitor has ceased to be a citizen, and in joining the rebellion has become a public enemy. . . . Treason must be made odious, and traitors must be punished and impoverished. Their great plantations must be seized, and divided into small farms, and sold to honest, industrious men." It is not surprising that Ben Wade could say with confidence: "Johnson, we have faith in you. By the gods, there will be no trouble now in running this government."

Johnson had had a long and varied career before assuming the presidency. He might have been a great folk hero under different circumstances, but as it was, he quickly made enemies of a strong, well-intrenched minority, who carried out one of the most successful programs of slander ever seen. They said that he was a drunkard, and while certain actions at his inaugural as vice president seemed to prove it, no further evidence was brought forward. They said he was insane, that he had a typical poor-white contempt of the Negro, and that he was trying to rob the North of the fruits of victory.

However, calm reappraisal has shown he was often statesmanlike, a person of integrity, honesty, and ability, and a man of the people with tremendous courage. His background was as humble as Lincoln's. More of a crusading democrat, he was nationally known before the war for his zeal in championing the causes of the laborers and the small farmers. He had sponsored, for example, the Homestead bill, so bitterly opposed by his Southern colleagues. Beginning as a tailor in a Tennessee mountain village and unable to write until taught by his wife, he had risen from the offices of alderman and mayor of Greenville, Tennessee, through the state legislature, to the House of Representatives, governor, and finally the United States Senate. He possessed a powerful though not well-disciplined mind, fine talents as an orator, and a knack for writing that was often the despair of his opponents. As a strict constructionist, he did not believe there was a constitutional right of secession and so stayed in the Senate when Tennessee seceded. During the remainder of his term, he was a member of the Committee on the Conduct of the War and was as zealous as any in urging harsh treatment for rebels. As a War Democrat from a seceded state, he had been placed on the same ticket with Lincoln to emphasize the unionism of the Republican party in 1864.

But there were defects in his character. Lincoln made people feel instinctively that he was one of them. Johnson, on the other hand, gave the impression of being mistrustful and secretive, and he had no confidants. While he was well-mannered in private life, in public he was often brusque to the point of rudeness. He had learned his political tactics in the stump campaigns of Tennessee, where no holds were barred and personal, defamatory attacks were the order of the day. He fought with verbal clubs and, when challenged, was overly pugnacious and too ready to call names. The President of the United States is at a disadvantage; his enemies can call him whatever they choose, but the people expect him to maintain his dignity. But his heritage betrayed him, and Johnson would strike back. Although he knew more about Southern conditions than Lincoln and was industrious and painstaking, he was handicapped by indecision, by saying too much, and by being obstinate. He could not compromise on small details even to win his principles and was fettered by a belief in states' rights which had been outmoded by the war. The combination was to spell disaster for himself and his cause.

On first becoming president, he was, for a short period, a Radical. But after the excitement of the war's end and of Lincoln's death had subsided, Johnson rapidly calmed down and became conservative, giving his former cohorts more reason for hating him. Though Johnson still distrusted the Southern aristocrats, he soon learned that these once powerful foes were now as poor and as powerless as their humblest neighbors. As a Southerner, he also knew first-hand the lack of preparation of the freedmen for the responsibilities of citizenship. Fundamentally he was a states' rights Southern Democrat, as he had always been, willing to go to any length to preserve the Union but wishing to keep the powers of the national government to a minimum. The Southern states were still states and therefore had the responsibility for solving their own problems, including that of the Negroes' future role.

No President was ever in a more awkward position. Johnson had no personal following in either the North or South, having broken with the Democrats without yet being accepted by the Republicans.

Nevertheless, he proceeded alone. The logic of the situation in April, 1865, indicated that sound governmental principles made reconstruction a matter on which President and Congress should cooperate, perhaps involving a special session of Congress. Johnson, however, decided to steal a march on his legislative branch: while Congress was adjourned, he moved to carry on Lincoln's plan of reconstruction.

Though his method was fundamentally Lincolnian, he also borrowed some features from the Wade-Davis bill. By a proclamation on May 9, he declared all "rebel" authority in Virginia at an end and pledged his support to the Pierpoint government. On May 29 came his Amnesty Proclamation and a statement of reconstruction procedures. By the former, he made clear his intention of rebuilding the South with the yeoman class in control. His proclamation offered pardons to the same groups of Southerners as had Lincoln, with the added disqualification of those holding property worth $20,000 or more. On the same day, he appointed William W. Holden provisional governor of North Carolina and in his instructions outlined his scheme of restoration. Within the next two months, similar proclamations for the other six states not recognized by Lincoln were issued. By these pronouncements he appointed as provisional governors Southerners who had opposed secession, though most of them had passively supported the Confederacy. These were instructed to call conventions chosen by the "loyal" citizens of the state, delegates and those electing them being required to take an oath to support the Constitution of the United States. The conventions were to make the constitutional changes necessary to invalidate their old ordinances of secession, to abolish slavery either by adoption of the Thirteenth Amendment or by state action or both, and to repudiate all debts incurred in aiding the Confederacy. It or subsequent sessions of the legislature should also prescribe the qualifications of electors and the eligibility of persons to hold office — "a power the people of the several States composing the Federal Union have rightfully exercised from the origin of the Government to the present time."

With so few requirements, the process of reconstruction moved speedily, and by the autumn of 1865 regular civil governments were functioning in all the former Confederate states except Texas. Mississippi was the first to act, holding its convention in August. Under Provisional Governor W. L. Sharkey, an old-time Whig, the unionists dominated the convention. It was warned that unless it followed the President, the state might be treated as a conquered province. The convention annulled the ordinance of secession and declared that slavery should be abolished, "slavery having been destroyed in Mississippi." This statement, coupled with its failure to ratify the Thirteenth

Amendment as Johnson had suggested, was viewed by some Northerners as a refusal to admit the evil of slavery. Johnson's suggestion that the vote be given to all Negroes who could read the constitution, write their names, and owned real estate or possessed $250, as a means to "completely disarm the adversary [the congressional Radicals] and set an example the other States will follow," was completely ignored by the convention.

Alabama moved next, with a convention which was marked by a division between the unionists from the northern part of the state and those representing the old plantation area. They ended slavery, "whereas slavery has been abolished," only after long debate and did not provide for Negro suffrage. Secession was declared null and void, and the debt repudiated. Representation was based on white population only, a move that gave political control to the northern section of Alabama but was interpreted as an anti-Negro move in the North.

That section also closely watched South Carolina, considered to be the parent of rebellion. Those who expected the worst were not disappointed. Governor Benjamin F. Perry declared to the convention that the Republican party had forgotten that "this is a white man's government, and intended for white men only." A resolution was introduced calling upon the people "to endure patiently the evils of and to await calmly deliverance from unconstitutional rule." The convention repealed, without declaring it null and void, the ordinance of secession. The Negro was emancipated by a vote of 59 to 43, but was not given the vote. The group refused to fly the United States flag over its sessions and failed to repudiate the war debt.

North Carolina's convention was probably the most strongly unionist in the South, but it ignored a memorial from a Negro convention and refused to repudiate the war debt until Johnson sent a telegram ordering that it be done. The decision to fly the national flag came only after a long debate, but the strongest stand of all rebel states was taken on secession — "the said supposed ordinance now and at all time hath been null and void." Georgia refused to fly the flag, repealed rather than declared null and void its act of secession, repudiated its debt reluctantly, and hedged on the abolition of slavery. Elsewhere, the other conventions met without inflammatory incidents.

The unionist elements, chiefly old Whigs or Douglas Democrats,[1] were in control in all these states; yet they played into the hands of the Northern Radicals. None of the conventions had accepted the President's advice to allow some Negroes to vote, nor had they shown any disposition to place political restrictions upon their former leaders.

[1] Thomas B. Alexander, "Persistent Whiggery in the Confederate South," *Journal of Southern History*, XXVII (August, 1961), p. 305ff.

Perhaps more important, none showed signs of the humility expected by the North. In the elections which followed, they cumulatively chose for Congress the vice president of the Confederacy, four Confederate generals, five Confederate colonels, six Confederate cabinet officers, and fifty-eight members of the Confederate Congress. None of these could take the oath of office. In Mississippi, reactionaries succeeded in denying Negro testimony in court, and the governor-elect was not from the eligible list, though Johnson hastened to pardon him. The Georgia legislature made itself conspicuous by asking Alexander H. Stephens to address that body and then, after his bitter speech, elected him to the Senate. These governments were on trial in Northern eyes, and they acted haughtily and talked ungraciously. They resented Northern watchfulness and took for granted that Johnson's will was that of the North and that his recognition meant their final restoration.

But Congress was yet to speak. During the congressional recess, moderates and Radicals alike had watched with increasing annoyance Johnson's actions and those of the Southern states. A few days before Congress met, Thaddeus Stevens of Pennsylvania and some of his fellow Radicals began organizing their plans to undo Johnson's handiwork and to take over control of the Republican party. When the session opened on December 4, 1865, congressional temper was evidenced by the refusal to allow the clerk of the House even to read the names of the members-elect from the South at the first roll call. This raised the question as to the status of these states, and the Radicals declared that action on this issue would have to be postponed until Congress was properly informed concerning the matter. A joint committee of both Houses was created to investigate and report on the status of the former Confederate states. The chairman of the committee was the mild-mannered William P. Fessenden of Maine, but the man who dominated its activities was the acid-tongued Stevens. With a Radical majority, this committee dictated the tactics of the struggle against the President and formulated the final theory of reconstruction.

Although a minority of Congress in December, 1865, by November, 1866, the Radicals had gained control and had defeated Johnson. Why did the North, or at least Congress, swing to the Radicals? The main reason was legislative *esprit de corps*. The office of the President had acquired power during the war at Congress' expense, and the legislature wanted to redress the balance of power between these two branches of the government. Even the moderates were animated by this desire. Then, too, the disposition of the Southern states to claim rights rather than to submit to conditions caused many Northerners to question whether the Southerners accepted the verdict of the war.

The majority of the Southern people were tired, broken in morale, and uninterested in politics, but the North played up the recalcitrance of some of the conventions and took their actions as being representative. Northern reporters exaggerated small incidents and made the resistance of the South appear plausible.

The Black Codes rankled many a Northern liberal. To the South the race problem was a domestic one, but the North did not agree. Once more the North's judgment was not based on the average but on the extreme. It did not believe in the good intentions of the South toward the Negroes and saw the codes as an effort to re-enslave the Negroes in fact if not in name. Constructive efforts to save them from subordination and exploitation were mandatory, and the federal government was urged to protect the freedmen against their former masters.

As evidence that the blacks needed such protection, the North cited outrages committed against them. With civil governments in chaos and wartime violence a living legacy, conditions were ripe for acts of lawlessness. There can be no question that outrages did occur and that the ex-slaves as the weakest element in Southern society were the most vulnerable. Similarly, some politicians saw political advantage in the situation, and reports of the Joint Committee on Reconstruction made racial atrocities appear a common occurence. Some newspapers, also, regularly ran columns entitled "Southern Outrages." Although there was probably a tendency to over-generalize, there were enough documented events to lend credence to even the most exaggerated reports. In May, 1866, a quarrel between a Negro and a white man in Memphis led to a riot in which city police and poor whites raided the Negro quarter, burning and killing indiscriminately. In July a more serious disturbance in New Orleans resulted from a factional dispute over the calling of a constitutional convention. Although the facts are not clear as to which group precipitated the clash, the police became involved and in the melee some thirty-seven Negroes were among those killed. Such incidents naturally fed the inherent suspicions and hatreds which are a normal legacy of any civil war.

Johnson was further handicapped by the fact that the Radical Republicans believed him a turncoat, and he could normally count for support from only the Southerners and Democrats, both of whom were discredited. The South had no votes in Congress, and endorsement by Democrats, whose loyalty had been suspect during the war, embarrassed the moderate Republicans who sought to defend the President against Radical attacks.

But perhaps most important in swinging the Republicans into the Radical position was that they had to enter that camp to insure the continued political supremacy of the party. All factions within the party were united in their desire to become the majority party of the country, as the Democrats had been in the closing decades before the war. The Republicans had had a precarious hold on the government during the late hostilities, depending upon some support from the Democrats for even this. The adoption in December of 1865 of the Thirteenth Amendment, which abolished the old three-fifths ratio of counting population for determining representation in Congress and the Electoral College, had made the Republican situation even worse by giving the South nine additional electoral votes and Representatives.

If the Southern states returned a solid Democratic delegation to Congress, as seemed likely, the reunited Democratic party would have a majority in both Houses, thus enabling it to repeal a good part of the tariff, banking, railroad, and other pro-Northern legislation which the Republicans had enacted. It could become the old government of pre-war times, administered by "rebels" and "copperheads" for the benefit of the South. Thaddeus Stevens freely admitted his partisan purposes on the floor of Congress: his program would insure the ascendancy of the Republicans. "Do you avow the party purpose? exclaims some horror-stricken demagogue. I do. For I believe . . . that on the continued ascendancy of that party depends the safety of this great nation." Furthermore, he added, "I know there is an impatience to bring in these chivalric gentlemen [the Southerners] lest they should not be here in time to vote for the next President. . . . Sir, while I am in favor of allowing them to come in as soon as they are fairly entitled, I do not profess to be very impatient to embrace them. I am not very anxious to see their votes cast along with others to control the next election of President and Vice President." In fact, he felt the Southern states "ought never to be recognized as capable of acting in the Union, or of being counted as valid states, until the Constitution shall have been so amended . . . as to secure perpetual ascendancy to the party of the Union [the Republican party]."

The amendment that Stevens had in mind was for Negro suffrage: "I am for negro suffrage in every rebel State. If it be just, it should not be denied; if it be necessary, it should be adopted; if it be a punishment to traitors, they deserve it." Senator Henry Wilson of Massachusetts estimated that the Republican could count on 672,000 Negro votes in the South, which would partly offset the potential 923,000 white voters and would give the Republican party control of South Carolina, Mississippi, and probably Louisiana, Alabama, and North Carolina. As only six Northern states allowed Negro votes, Charles Sumner counseled, "Their votes are needed at the North as well as the South. There are Northern States where their votes can make the good cause safe beyond question."

Further rationalization by the Republicans led them to claim that if the war victory were to be insured, the party that had produced it had to stay in power; the solid Democratic South had to be split. A strong Southern Republican party could be formed by giving votes to the freedmen, who presumably would vote Republican from gratitude, and by disfranchising the recalcitrant whites. But this had to be done before the states were readmitted to the Union. Johnson's plan, therefore, had to be repudiated.

The Congress which faced this issue was elected in 1864 on a Union ticket. With the war over and Lincoln dead, it had no unified program and was badly in need of a party whip, someone to rally behind. Who would provide the leadership? Given a choice between the leadership of Stevens and Sumner or that of Johnson, which would the Republicans choose? Johnson had never been a Republican and was not responsible to the party, nor it to him. According to Carl Schurz, Stevens, on the other hand, was "the acknowledged leader of the Republicans in the House." One of the most unpleasant characters in American history, this dour old man of seventy-four dominated by sheer force of his driving intensity. He was a cynical democrat who had fought for free schools and against the privileged classes in Pennsylvania. Lame and in ill-health, his driving passion after the war was to devote the few remaining years of his life to the "punishment of traitors." He was determined, with what amounted to almost a pathological intensity, that the South had no rights and that the Republican party must remain in control of the government. Few dared to risk his wrath and face his lashing tongue.

Charles Sumner, Senator from Massachusetts, was polished, well educated, and a favored member of the Boston intelligentsia. He had more personal reason than Stevens to hate the South, for his body still bore the marks of Representative Preston Brook's caning on the floor of the Senate in 1856. With a distinguished record as a champion of good causes, he cherished no vindictive feelings against the ex-Confederates but was convinced that the only way the Negroes could prove their equality was by being given the vote. He had opposed Lincoln on this, and, when Johnson failed to urge such a program, Sumner allied himself with Stevens. He set up five requirements for reconstruction: (1) "the complete re-establishment of loyalty"; (2) the complete "suppression of all oligarchical pretensions" and enfranchisement of all citizens, so that all would be equal before the law; (3) rejection of the "rebel" debt and insurance of the sanctity of the national debt; (4) organization of an educational system for the benefit of all without distinction of color or race; and (5) choice of citizens "of constant and undoubted loyalty" for office.

Faced with a choice between Johnson and the congressional

leaders, the undecided majority in Congress, with no program of its own, naturally leaned toward the well-organized Radicals and followed any policy to keep the Republicans in power. The theory of reconstruction upon which Congress ultimately acted was not actually a clear-cut choice of Johnson, Stevens, or Sumner, but a hybrid proposed by Congressman Samuel Shellabarger of Ohio. As spelled out by the Joint Committee on Reconstruction on June 20, 1866, the "forfeited rights" plan held that "the States lately in rebellion were . . . without civil government, and without constitutions or other forms, by virtue of which political relations could legally exist between them and the federal government." By "treasonable withdrawal from Congress and by flagrant rebellion and war," they had "forfeited all civil and political rights and privileges under the Constitution" and could have them restored only by Congress. Thus was avoided the question of whether such states had been out of the Union. In other words the states were intact, but their governments, for most purposes, were not functional. This made it possible to deny them representation yet accept their ratification of the Thirteenth Amendment.

This policy was so diametrically opposite to that of the President that a clash was inevitable. The first conflict came over the continuation of the Freedmen's Bureau, which originally was scheduled to die one year after the end of hostilities. Angered by the passage of the Black Codes, many saw this agency as the only protection for the Negroes against Southern exploitation. The friends of the Bureau argued that it was a vital organization, that it had saved many Negroes and whites from starvation, that it had looked after the economic and educational rights of the freedmen, and that it had provided courts to insure them justice. Its opponents argued that it was based upon the false assumption that the Negroes needed protection against the whites, that some of the lower officials used their positions to control the Negroes politically and through the Union Leagues were teaching them to be good Republicans, and that the Bureau was enforcing a Negro code of its own and competing for control of the freedmen with the civil governments of the South.

In February, 1866, Congress passed a bill extending the Bureau's life and increasing its powers. It provided not only for care of the freedmen but also gave the officers of the agency many functions belonging to state officials and created an elaborate system of agents, commissioners, clerks, and the like. The army was assigned authority over all cases concerning the immunities and rights of the Negroes. Johnson vetoed the measure on the grounds that it was unnecessary, since it assumed that wartime conditions still existed, whereas the "country has returned, or is returning, to a state of peace and industry, and the rebellion is in fact at an end." He added that the bill was a dangerous extension of military jurisdiction, entailing the denial of trial by jury and allowing court-martial procedures not authorized by law, which would lead to inevitable conflicts between military and civil authorities. It overstepped constitutional limits by making the federal rather than state governments responsible for the care of indigents. And finally, it was the work of a Congress which had denied representation to the eleven states most affected, despite the fact that they "in my own judgment . . . have already been fully restored, and are to be deemed as entitled to enjoy their constitutional rights as members of the Union."

Johnson had a strong case, although his political maneuvering and intemperate remarks were to greatly damage it. On Washington's birthday he was serenaded by a group of his admirers and asked to speak. Johnson responded with a few pleasantries but, encouraged by the cheers of an appreciative audience, soon switched to more intemperate remarks. Always a fiery speaker and given to personal attacks, he asserted that men such as Stevens, Sumner, and Wendell Phillips were as much opposed to the Union as "the Davises, the Toombses, and the Slidells." Such expressions were unfortunate, for the next day the Radical newspapers charged that the President was drunk, both when he made the speech and when he had vetoed the Freedmen's Bureau Bill. His veto had already convinced many that he was willing to abandon the Negroes, and these actions tended to solidify the Republicans behind the Radical leaders.

A second conflict came over the Civil Rights Bill. By bringing such prerogatives under federal jurisdiction, this was to give the Negroes the civil rights not granted them by the states. As passed on March 13, the measure, written by the moderate Lyman Trumbull, provided that the freedmen were citizens of the United States and should have full rights in every state "to make and enforce contracts, to sue, be parties, and give evidence, to inherit, purchase, lease, sell, hold and convey real and personal property, and to full and equal benefit of all laws and proceedings for the security of person and property, as is enjoyed by white citizens." Johnson's friends urged him to accept the bill, but he could not and be consistent. Refusing to suborn his constitutional scruples to arguments of expediency, he vetoed it on the grounds that it was passed without representation from eleven states and that civil rights belonged to the states to confer. This action drove even more moderates into the ranks of the Radicals, and the measure was passed over Johnson's veto on April 9, 1866. Conscious of their advantage, the Radicals then reintroduced a bill to extend the Freedmen's Bureau for two years and on July 16 passed it over the President's veto.

Meanwhile, some of the supporters of the Civil Rights Act had doubts concerning its constitutionality as well as the fear that a later Democratic Congress might repeal it. The Joint Committee on Reconstruction, therefore, recommended that the rights be permanently guaranteed by an amendment to the Constitution. The Chairman announced that "the spirit which animated the rebellion" still existed in the South, and therefore "adequate security for future peace and safety should be required." The resultant Fourteenth Amendment restated the Civil Rights Act and added new conditions. It defined citizenship so as to include the Negroes and stated that "no State shall make or enforce any law which shall abridge the privileges or immunities of citizens of the United States; nor shall any State deprive any person of life, liberty, or property, without due process of law; nor deny to any person within its jurisdiction the equal protection of the laws." Thaddeus Stevens had forced the House to include the right to vote, but to the regret of the more extreme Radicals, the final measure did not confer the right of suffrage, although it did penalize any state not allowing the Negroes to vote. Furthermore, it made ineligible for officeholding all the ex-Confederate leaders regardless of whatever presidential pardons they might hold. (Johnson had pardoned about 13,500 out of 15,000 applicants.) Henceforth only Congress, by a two-thirds vote of each House, could remove disabilities. A final section provided that the United States debts should never be questioned and that the war debt of the Southern states and the Confederacy should never be paid.

If the President had accepted these three disputed measures, everything might have worked out. Under the circumstances they did not go too far; the North was still seeking reassurances as to the South's intentions. Johnson, however, refused to compromise his own convictions and continued to view his own program as sufficient. Even the approval by Johnson just of this Fourteenth Amendment might have avoided the unfortunately extreme reconstruction which followed, but his refusal further alienated the moderates.

The South recognized this new amendment as a blow to states' rights, but the war and the Thirteenth Amendment had prepared them for such drastic changes. The region might have accepted it if nothing better seemed likely to be offered, but now it followed Johnson; every Southern state except Tennessee, under the Radical Governor Brownlow, rejected the amendment in hopes of future concessions. In 1866 Southerners well knew that their preference was unimportant, but they viewed the Fourteenth Amendment as a breach of contract, a further condition applied after they had complied with the earlier ones. Acceptance, they feared, might lead to still additional requirements, would do the South no good, and might hurt its cause in the North.[2]

Besides, the amendment was politically inspired. In the words of an author in *De Bow's Review,* "Of all things a political organization is most unwilling to commit suicide. The Republican chiefs feel that they cannot, in reason, expect the aid of the restored States. They count upon this strength being so much clear gain to the hated opposition." The Republicans therefore must have votes for the Negroes. "Hence, negro suffrage at the South is not merely a fanatical cry, but a political policy. Coupled with this idea of the elevation of the negro at the South as elector, is the depression of those who have hitherto done the thinking of the South." Also, "they imagine they see the phantom of repudiation entering Congress, with members from the South."[3]

Francis Preston Blair, Jr., of Missouri, future Democratic nominee for Vice President, saw even more insidious motives.

> Their object is to buckle on the negro permanently to ride down the South, to exclude white emigrants from its rich and productive fields, by degrading white labor by the presence of the blacks; and as a consequence, reducing white emigrants to the level of negroes, and thus keeping the Southern states poor and weak, incapable of establishing manufactories or prosecuting commercial enterprise on a large scale — incapable of competition with Northern capitalists in any career . . . in a word, incapable of anything save a hopeless effort to stay the decadence of a mongrel race of mixed blacks and whites and mulattoes.[4]

At the time the Fourteenth Amendment was offered for ratification, the congressional elections of 1866 were approaching. When the State of Tennessee showed its subservience by accepting the amendment, Congress in a political move declared it restored to the Union. The fate of the other ten states, which refused approval, then depended upon the outcome of the election. If the Radicals were able to retain control of Congress, Johnson's plan would be ended; if his supporters were able to increase their numbers enough to prevent the overriding of his vetoes, then the President's will could still be paramount. The people would decide.

---

[2] Joseph B. James, "Southern Reaction to the Proposal of the Fourteenth Amendment," *Journal of Southern History,* XXII (November, 1956), pp. 477-497.
[3] "The State of the Country," *De Bow's Review,* I (February, 1866), pp. 134-135.
[4] Francis Preston Blair, Jr., "Shall the Usurpation of Government by the Fragment of a Congress be Perpetuated by Negro Suffrage?," *Negro Pamphlets,* III. University of Virginia Library.

# 5

# THE RADICAL TRIUMPH

EVERYTHING TURNED on the election of a new Congress in the fall of 1866, making it one of the most crucial elections in American history. Johnson accepted the Radical challenge and prepared to rally his supporters. A meeting of the Loyal Unionists of the South which endorsed the Radicals was countered by a National Union Convention of moderates from both North and South which met in Philadelphia to endorse Johnson, but it did not form a new party or set up election machinery; nor was the President able to form a well-defined party. In most congressional districts, therefore, the voter had to choose between a Radical Republican or a Democrat with a poor war record. Faced with this prospect, most of the moderate Republicans entered the Radical camp.

Johnson took the stump personally in a "swing around the circle" but probably did his cause more harm than good. Instead of capitalizing upon the memory of Lincoln and appealing to the finer instincts of the people, he allowed himself to be goaded into the intemperate utterances for which he was famous, and his effort degenerated into an undignified contest in vituperation. The well-organized Radicals systematically set off anti-Johnson demonstrations which sometimes actually prevented his speaking. The Radical press played up his errors in judgment and burlesqued his speeches so successfully as to deceive many of his former supporters. Degrading stories were invented to the effect that he kept in the White House a "harem" of dissolute women. He was repeatedly charged with drunkenness, and even the respectable John Sherman complained that Johnson had "sunk the Presidency to the level of the grog-house." Cartoonists and columnists did their best to make the President appear ridiculous.

The Radicals were remarkably able politicians. They swelled their support by winning over leading moderates, resorting to tricks of party strategy, wooing the more important newspapers, and making the most of the advertising possibilities of the pulpit and of church conventions. Hints were dropped privately among the Northeastern industrialists that their growing prosperity would depend upon a continuation of Radical control, but this was soft-pedaled in public utterances. Also left unsaid was the Radicals' intention of forcing Negro suffrage on the South. They made patriotism their one issue and spread endless propaganda throughout the North concerning Southern "outrages" against hapless Negroes. In the words of Charles Sumner: "Witness Memphis, witness New Orleans [scenes of race riots]. Who can doubt that the President is the author of these tragedies? . . . Next to Jefferson Davis stands Andrew Johnson as [the nation's] worst enemy."

Confronted by an organized political machine, a large portion of the press, and most of the churches of the North, Johnson was almost fore-ordained to defeat. The result of the election was an overwhelming victory for the Radicals, and the next Congress contained 42 Republicans and 11 Democrats in the Senate, and 143 Republicans and 49 Democrats in the House. The Radicals thus had a two-thirds majority with which to override any presidential veto. The questions of who would define and control reconstruction had finally been answered. Congress would call the tune, and the program would be Radical.

The *Nation* summarized the election victory succinctly:

> The first point which has unquestionably been passed upon is, that the people do not trust the South, or its ally, the Democratic party of the North, to rule in our government. The second is, that the South shall not be restored unconditionally to its privileges in the Union. The third is, that Congress, and not the Executive, is to name the conditions of restoration. The fourth, that the conditions already proposed are abundantly liberal to the South.[1]

The victory had gone to the political radicals, who wanted to remain in office; the economic radicals, who hoped to continue the profits

[1] *Nation*, III (November, 1866), p. 390.

made in high tariffs, favorable tax concessions, and a laissez-faire attitude toward business; and the real radicals, who dreamed of a revolution for the masses.

With this mandate from the people, the Radicals were now ready
to act. "I was a conservative in the last session of this Congress,"
Stevens told his fellow congressmen in December, "but I mean to be a
radical henceforth." Determined to have its own way, Congress moved
to so curtail his authority as to leave the President powerless to
interfere. By act of January 22, 1867, the date of the opening of the
Fortieth Congress was moved up, to March 4 from the first Monday in
the following December, to circumvent Johnson's having a period free
from legislative oversight. On March 2, to protect Radical officeholders
from Presidential wrath, Congress passed over Johnson's veto the
Tenure of Office Act, which made it a high misdemeanor to remove
civil officials, including members of the Cabinet, without the consent
of the Senate. (It was on the basis of this law that Johnson was later
impeached, although removal failed by a single vote.) The same day,
executive control of the army was severely curtailed by the Command
of the Army Act, which required that all military orders from the
President or Secretary of War be issued through the General of the
Army, whose headquarters were to be in Washington and who could
not be removed or sent from Washington without senatorial consent.

With Johnson virtually powerless to interfere, Congress was ready
to undertake the major work at hand. On that same fateful day, in one
of the most important acts ever passed by any Congress, and over
Johnson's veto, of course, was enacted the First Reconstruction Act.
Declaring that "whereas no legal State governments or adequate protection for life or property now exists in the rebel States," except
Tennessee, the law overthrew the Johnson civil governments and
divided the ten states into five military districts, each headed by an
army officer of the rank of brigadier-general or higher. Amplified by
additional laws on March 26 and July 19, 1867, and March 11, 1868,
the congressional plan became clear. After restoring peace and order,
the generals were to enroll all males over twenty-one, except those
disfranchised for participation in the rebellion, who would take a long
and complicated oath. These were to elect a constitutional convention,
which would draw up a constitution which provided for Negro
suffrage. When this document was approved by the voters and by
Congress, the legislature then elected had to ratify the Fourteenth
Amendment. When that amendment had become part of the Federal
Constitution, the state might, if the Radicals wished, "be entitled to
representation in Congress." Each newly elected member to Congress

from these states had to take the "ironclad oath" that he had never given voluntary aid of any sort to the Confederacy.

Supplementary acts later strengthened this program. In 1870 was passed an enforcement act so sweeping that it included almost everything a person could do by extending federal jurisdiction over all citizens' civil and political rights. This attempt to prevent the Southern people as individuals from interfering with Negro rights was a serious encroachment upon states' rights and was to be declared unconstitutional in 1875. But, during 1870-1871, there were over 200 cases where union troops were used to support this law. Two acts in 1871 strengthened the penalties and gave the President the power to suspend the writ of *habeas corpus* in counties where organizations such as the Ku Klux Klan were abridging Negro rights. To conspire to deprive a citizen of his rights was made a high crime, and President Grant applied martial law in nine counties of South Carolina. In 1883 this measure was also declared unconstitutional. Finally came the Civil Rights Act of 1875, providing that all persons were entitled to "full and equal enjoyment" of the facilities of "inns, public conveyances on land or water, theaters, and other places of public amusement," but in 1883 the Supreme Court declared this act also unconstitutional, since it applied to actions by individuals rather than states.

Enforcement of the Radical program devolved upon three agencies. The first was the United States Army, which acted directly through military interference at the polls and in the courts under the Enforcement Acts. Second was the Freedmen's Bureau, eventually extended until 1872, which was a valuable aid both officially and unofficially. And finally there was the artificially made and retained Southern Republican party, consisting of Northern "carpetbaggers," Southern "scalawags," and Negroes, that dominated the state governments.

The key, of course was Negro suffrage. As Stevens noted, "the [Republican] white men are in a minority in each of these States. With them the blacks would act in a body, form a majority, control the States and protect themselves. It would insure the ascendancy of the Union party." To the disheartened Southern whites, even more sinister motives seemed apparent. A writer for *De Bow's Review*, December, 1867, saw a "deeper significance" in their actions: "The whole legislation of Congress for the last two years, which has been under the guidance and direction of the New England radicals, shows the deliberate purpose, skillfully planned, but artfully concealed of Africanizing the extreme Southern or Gulf States." The object as he saw it was to create conditions such that the whites would desert the area, leaving it to the Negroes. It would also be unattractive to

Northern whites, who would remain at home to be exploited by the manufacturers. The Negroes thus would become the economic and political slaves of the North.[2]

Both the avowed and the covert purposes were objectionable to the South, and so it attempted to block the first stage, the establishment of military rule. The governor of Mississippi brought suit to enjoin President Johnson from enforcing the Reconstruction Acts of 1867 on the ground that they were unconstitutional, and the governor of Georgia sought to stop Secretary of War Stanton. However, the Attorney-General appeared before the Supreme Court and argued that the executive and his representatives could not be sued; the court, to avoid becoming entangled in a political quarrel, upheld this position.

The army occupation was wrong primarily in two respects: it did not start until two years after the war was over, and it upset existing civil governments. But in retrospect the South liked army rule better than that of subsequent civil governments. The powers of the commanders were almost without limit, not being restricted "by the opinion of any civil officer of the United States." They could use, ignore, or destroy the state governments which they found in their districts. Most of them were good men doing a distasteful job, and some allowed civil government to continue except for replacing civil courts by military commissions and ignoring the black codes. Other military rulers were more reckless with their power, suppressing Confederate veteran organizations, parades, and other symbols of the lost cause. Before military rule was over, the generals had removed thousands of local officials and replaced them with "loyal" men and army officers. The governors of Georgia, Louisiana, Texas, Mississippi, and Virginia were put out of office for coolness toward the reconstruction process. Laws were made through military orders, and taxes were levied and collected by army command. All of this was done by about 20,000 troops, distributed in ten states at 134 army posts.

The main responsibility of these commanders was, of course, to organize new state governments according to the congressional plan. Registrars had to take the "ironclad oath," which eliminated most Southerners, leaving these positions to soldiers, Bureau agents, and Negroes. These registrars were given liberal expense accounts, were paid for each name secured, and had the final decision as to who could register. These officials naturally tried to enroll as many Negroes and as few Southern whites as possible; it has been estimated that about 150,000 whites were disfranchised. When registrations were completed, the totals were 703,000 Negroes and 627,000 whites (not all of whom were Southern). In Alabama, Florida, Louisiana, Mississippi, and

[2] "Designs of Radicalism," *De Bow's Review*, IV (December, 1867), pp. 532-537.

South Carolina, Negro registrants outnumbered white, though only in the last three were the Negroes a majority of the population. Thus, the new electorate was composed of blacks, Southern scalawags, and Northern carpetbaggers. As a group they probably reflected American society of that period: some were able men, others were ignorant; some were honest, and others sought their own interests. And no faction, including disfranchised whites, had a monopoly on virtue.

These groups dominated the constitutional conventions which were called. At the time the Southern whites, who had organized themselves into "Conservative" parties, were uncertain whether to vote, and the number of Negro delegates chosen ranged from nine in Texas to seventy-six in South Carolina. These delegations were, first of all, required to frame constitutions that would facilitate the readmission of their states to the Union. Despite "Rebel" fears, notably absent from their deliberations were black efforts aimed at vindictiveness or breaking the social taboo of Southern whites. While many went beyond the needs of an agricultural people and provided for services which could not be supported by the limited resources available, the finished documents were surprisingly good and almost inevitably more democratic than their predecessors. Generally they established universal male suffrage and granted Negroes equal social and civil rights. Some provided for popular education, abolished property qualifications for holding office, reapportioned representation in the legislature, enlarged the rights of women, and reformed local government and court systems. One difference, an essential clause in each, however, proscribed former Confederates and was usually the point of conflict.

Except for Texas, where the process had been slowed by rivalry between two convention factions, the framing of these constitutions was quickly completed, and by March, 1868, they were ready for submission to the people. The Conservatives, who had been largely disorganized up to this time, now regrouped to defeat the constitutions. In Georgia, where Joseph E. Brown, a local Conservative, had led the convention, the result was less distasteful, and so was accepted by the Conservatives. In Alabama they defeated the constitution by refraining from voting, thus denying approval by a majority of registered voters. Congress hastened to provide that ratification would require only a majority of those voting. In Mississippi the constitution was voted down, and the Virginia document was so vindictive that the military governor refused to submit it for a vote.

In July, 1868, the Fourteenth Amendment was declared in force, and Congress hastened to admit, in time to vote for Grant in the upcoming election, the seven which had approved their constitutions. Texas, Virginia, and Mississippi finally completed the process in

1870 after Grant's suggestion and Congress' approval that they be allowed to vote on the disfranchisement-of-rebels provisions separately. These three, plus Georgia, which fell from grace and had to repeat the process, were also required to adopt the new Fifteenth Amendment as a prerequisite for admission.

The period from 1868 to 1877 was one in which the Radicals were in control, for varying durations, of most of the reconstructed states. In the first elections, four governors, ten of fourteen Senators and twenty of thirty-five Representatives were carpetbaggers, and the rest were scalawags or Negroes. Throughout the period, nineteen carpetbaggers went to the Senate. Some of these Northerners were honest, like Daniel H. Chamberlain, a native of Massachusetts and a Harvard and Yale student, but were forced to yield to party pressures. Others were corrupt, like Henry Clay Warmoth of Illinois, who came to Louisiana a poor man and left office a rich one and William Pitt Kellogg of Vermont, a name which became synonymous with scandal.

In Virginia, North Carolina, Georgia, Tennessee, and Texas, the scalawags came to be the dominant faction. While the term "scalawag" was used to denote those Southerners who cooperated for various reasons with the Radicals and carpetbaggers, it gradually became a term of opprobrium. They were not always, however, men who had sold out their section for office or financial reward. In Mississippi[3] and Louisiana,[4] for example, they were respectable citizens, often old-line Whigs and bitter opponents of the Democrats. As wealthy businessmen, they naturally turned to the national party dominated by business. They were inclined to accept the inevitability of Negro participation and so entered the party in hopes of controlling it, securing better terms for their states, and restoring peace and harmony.

In no state was a Negro elected governor, although they became lieutenant governors in South Carolina, Mississippi, and Louisiana. They held other state offices in some states at one time or another, but the majority of Negro office holders were federal appointees or local officials. Twenty Negroes were sent to the House of Representatives from Southern states, but only two were elected to the Senate —

---

[3] David H. Donald, "The Scalawags in Mississippi Reconstruction," Journal of Southern History, X (November, 1944), pp. 447–460, Allen W. Trelease, "Who Were the Scalawags?," Journal of Southern History, XXIX (November, 1963), pp. 445–468; Warren A. Ellem, "Who Were the Mississippi Scalawags?," Journal of Southern History, XXXVIII (May, 1972), pp. 217–240.
[4] T. Harry Williams, "The Louisiana Unification Movement of 1873," Journal of Southern History, XI (August, 1945), pp. 349–369. For the role of Whigs in other Republican governments, see also Thomas B. Alexander, "Persistent Whiggery in the Confederate South," Journal of Southern History, XXVII (August, 1961), p. 319ff.

Hiram R. Revels and Blanche K. Bruce — both from Mississippi. While black office holders were usually much more able men than generally recognized, in no state did their numbers approach black percentage of the electorate.[5]

The Union or Loyal Leagues organized the freedmen politically. These had begun in the North as patriotic organizations, but with peace they became rich white men's clubs. Introduced into the South with added rituals and ceremonials, they admitted the Negroes and trained them to vote Republican. The prettiest Negro girls were hired to recruit membership, and the recalcitrant men were ostracized, deserted by wives and sweethearts, kicked out of churches and lodges, or beaten. Similar smaller orders were the Red Strings of North Carolina, the Alcorn Club of Mississippi, and the Lincoln Brotherhood of Florida. One of the reasons for the formation of the Ku Klux Klan was to oppose these movements.

The administrations of some of the reconstructed states were clearly characterized by extravagance and/or corruption. Yet even with honest intentions, inflation and the new responsibilities alone assumed by these governments in public education, social welfare, and the like would have caused state and local debts to mushroom. The public debt of the ten reconstructed states increased about $132,000,000 during the period 1868-1872. In 1874, ten Southern states owed $292,000,000, while the debt of the other twenty-seven totaled no more than this amount. In fact, the indebtedness of the South by the end of the period was more than the states of the Confederacy could have been sold for according to their assessed evaluation in 1865.

Taxes, of course, rose steadily. Considering their financial bankruptcy, Southerners became the most heavily taxed people in United States history. In Louisiana, for example, the state tax rate rose from 3.75 mills in 1867 to 21.5 in 1874. Montgomery, Alabama, reported 200 applications for bankruptcy in a single day in 1868. By 1870 the eleven Southern states were paying four times as much taxes as in 1860, yet property values had dropped by half. Part of this increased taxation was legitimate; much was also the result of corruption, waste, and financial naivete while trying to promote internal improvements. Almost any enterprise had a good chance of having public money or credit voted toward its support, regardless of how unsound it might be. Cost of government skyrocketed, with one session of the Radical Louisiana legislature costing ten times more than any before 1860. The governor explained this money "was squandered in paying extra mileage and per diem of the members for services never rendered; for an enormous

[5] John Hope Franklin, *Reconstruction After the Civil War* (Chicago: Univ. of Chicago, 1961), pp. 133–138.

corps of useless clerks and pages, for publishing the journals of each house in fifteen obscure parish newspapers, some of which never existed, while some never did the work; in paying extra committees authorized to sit during the vacation . . . ; and in an elegant stationery bill which included ham, champagne, etc."

NIGGER, SCALLAWAG, CARPET-BAGGER.

*A Contemporary Caricature*

After a trip to the South, editor Horace Greeley of the New York *Tribune* was asked if the reports of carpetbag corruption were true. He was reported to have answered, "Yes, gentlemen, I regret to say to you that he [the carpetbagger] is a mournful fact, and the attitude in which I have most generally found him is with both arms around the negro's neck and both hands in his pocket."[6] There is reason to suspect that the high tax rate, especially on land, was partly deliberate in order to keep land cheap and to have it confiscated by the state, giving the

[6] As quoted by Charles E. Hooker, "On Relations between White and Colored People of the South," *Negro Pamphlets*, V, 3. University of Virginia Library.

freedmen an easier road to land ownership. Certainly that was the effect. In Mississippi, about a fifth of the state was advertised for sale for back taxes; sixteen pages of a newspaper were needed to list the delinquent lands in Arkansas. But even taxes could not carry the load, and bonds were issued in such numbers that some governments made no effort to keep count of their total. So much of the funds was used to pay interest charges that little was left for proper use by the governments.

One of the favorite subjects for bonds was railroads. Aid was given in several states before the roads even were built, and some lines profited without ever laying a mile of track. Where the assistance took the form of loans, more was advanced per mile than the completed systems were worth, leaving the state the loser when the lines were forfeited. Every state suffered these dishonesties except Mississippi, which had a constitutional prohibition against issuing bonds. Part of these losses, however, were made up by selling charters, even including one for a college, to people who desired to enter business.

The widespread Southern corruption was matched by the political depravity current in the North at the same time; witness the scandals of the Grant administration and the Tweed Ring of New York, which reduced graft to a science, a process the carpetbaggers might well have envied. In the North the foreigners were herded to vote in much the same fashion as the Negroes were being used in the South. About the only difference in the two sections was that these practices were going on in an economically prostrate South but in a prosperous North.

This, needless to say, was cold comfort to the Southerners. They felt that they were badly treated by reconstruction and were bitterly resentful. This feeling did not die out with the return of home rule to the section and became one of the factors which account for the continuance of a "self-conscious" South long after the last federal troops had been withdrawn. Almost every Southern family perpetuated legends of "what might have been" but for some atrocity committed during reconstruction. Oddly enough, the feeling of bitterness engendered by the legends of reconstruction was not based entirely, nor can be measured exactly, by the degree of harshness in each state. Citizens of states where reconstruction was easy felt just as bitter as those living where the sordid drama was played out to the last act.

Virginia, for example, avoided a period of Radical rule. The state was under military rule until it approved its constitution without the disqualifying clauses and was admitted in 1870. Two parties sprang up — one radical and the other conservative — both claiming to be Republican and splitting the Negro vote between them. The "Conservative" party, consisting of Confederate Democrats, "True" Republicans, "Old Line" Whigs, and Negroes won the first election by 20,000 votes. Since either party could serve Northern Republican political purposes, the Grant administration refused to interfere. In 1872 the state voted for Grant but then was Democratic until 1928.

Georgia, also, had a mild time. The first election in 1867 saw the Republicans elect their candidate for governor, Rufus Bullock, by a narrow margin, with one house of the legislature avowedly Conservative. Twenty-eight Negroes were elected to the legislature. The state was readmitted to the Union on July 25, 1868, and in September certain Negro members were expelled from the legislature on the grounds that, although the new constitution gave them the right to vote, they did not have the right to hold office. Former Confederates were seated in direct opposition to the reconstruction laws and the Fourteenth Amendment. The Radicals in Congress expelled Georgia and put it back under military rule. The commander then threw out twenty-four Conservatives, giving the Radicals control, and in January, 1870, the Negroes were readmitted. Six months later, the state was restored to the Union.

All in all, Georgia had only about two years of Radical rule, but this was time enough for the state debt to mount from less than $1,000,000 to $18,000,000 and for scandals to develop over moving the state capital to Atlanta and state endorsement of bonds for thirty railroads. Perhaps Georgia's most colorful figure in this period was the manager of a state-owned railroad who explained that the "exercise of the most rigid economy" enabled him to save $30,000 each year out of his salary of about $3,000!

In the 1870 elections, the Conservatives won both houses; in October, 1871, Governor Bullock resigned rather than face impeachment charges over the issuing of several millions of dollars of bonds during his administration. In the special election of 1871, no Republican candidate was offered, and the Conservatives thus took complete control of the government.

Tennessee and Texas had about three years of Radical rule each. In Tennessee, Parson Brownlow's Radical government, with the aid of the state militia, held control until 1869, managing somehow to increase the debt of that poverty-stricken state by over $21,000,000 from 1866 to 1869. When Brownlow gave up the governorship to become Senator in 1869, the Republicans split, and a Conservative was elected. Texas, in the first election held under the reconstruction acts (1869), elected the extreme candidate E. J. Davis, along with a Radical majority in the legislature. Davis was honest but arbitrary in his actions. The legislature was dishonest and despite increased taxation left a debt of

$4,500,000. Davis vainly sought federal help but was defeated by a Conservative in the election of 1873, and the state passed out of carpet-bagger hands.

In North Carolina, Johnson's appointee, W. W. Holden, now a vindictive scalawag, became the first Radical governor of that state. His legislature was dominated by Republicans, by three to one in the senate and two to one in the house. Although personally honest, he was surrounded by crooks. Over $27,000,000 in railroad bonds were endorsed by his administration, and taxes rose to $1,000,000 annually on an assessed property evaluation of only $120,000,000. Despite this expenditure, very few miles of railway were actually constructed. In the close election of 1870, two Conservative counties were declared in insurrection, and the state militia was put in control. Nevertheless, the Conservatives won control of the legislature, impeached and removed Holden for his use of the militia, and thus redeemed North Carolina from Radical rule. Yet even in this short period the state's indebtedness was increased some $20,000,000.

In Alabama, since the Conservatives had stayed away from the election in hopes of defeating the constitution, almost every office was filled with Republicans. The governor, William H. Smith, was a Confederate deserter and a weak man, though probably not a corrupt one; in 1870 the Radicals elected Robert B. Lindsay, a Scotchman by birth. In the first legislature, there were Radical majorities of thirty-two to one in the senate and ninety-seven to three in the house, and it has been estimated that the members of this body as a whole paid less than one hundred dollars in taxes.

Under these two administrations, Alabama was a fertile source for railroad promoters, for the governor was empowered to endorse bonds at the rate of $16,000 a mile. So carelessly was this done that it is impossible to know just how many were issued, but estimates of the figure lie between seventeen and thirty million dollars. School funds were embezzled in several counties, and conditions in the Radical-dominated university caused its boycott by white students. Negroes were particularly active in the state because of a very strong Freedmen's Bureau. Current expenses of the state government increased 200 per cent and the tax rate 400 per cent. Taxes in Montgomery County quadrupled, and real estate fell to less than one-third of former value; the indebtedness of state and local governments reached 65 per cent of the value of all Alabama farm property by 1874. But in 1872 a scalawag, hostile to the corrupt elements in his party, was elected governor, and the Democrats won the legislature, bringing the worst excesses to a halt; two years later, the Conservatives took control of the state.

Although Arkansas chose as its first governor one of the more enlightened carpetbaggers, its road through reconstruction was a rough one. General Powell Clayton had been a federal cavalry officer, who, after a short period of conservatism, became a Radical with the stated purpose of turning control of the state over to loyal Negroes. To enforce his rule from 1868 to 1872, he had to rely upon a large state militia. In addition, operating under the guise of militia activity, white desperadoes from Missouri and native freedmen ravaged the state. At one time, fourteen counties were under martial law. Graft and corruption were rampant, with an outside reporter stating that he could hear of only one honest tax collector in the whole state. Specific cases included a Negro who was given $9,000 for repairing a bridge which had originally cost only $500 and a group of twenty men who got state loans of more than $5,000,000 for railroad projects. Not surprisingly, current state expenses rose 1,500 per cent. The state, which had a debt of only $3,500,000 in 1868, seven years later owed $15,000,000 plus an additional $5,000,000 in county and local obligations, a per capita indebtedness of $175. For these burdens, the state could show little more than a few miles of railroad.

In 1872 the state Republican party split into two factions. Both vied for the white and Negro votes, and this led to the Brooks-Baxter War. Joseph Brooks headed the reform group and was supported by moderate Republicans and the Conservatives (Democrats). Elisha Baxter, the Radical, won the election and was recognized by Grant. But by refusing to issue more railroad bonds, he soon alienated his supporters, who switched and supported Baxter, and both sides claimed the government. At one point, active civil war broke out in the state, claiming some 200 lives. A compromise ended in a constitutional convention, which took steps to insure white supremacy, election of a Conservative governor, and the permanent restoration of home rule in 1874.

Mississippi's reconstruction history was different, primarily because of the failure there of an attempt under the leadership of James Lusk Alcorn to establish a Republican party resting upon the common white man. Alcorn, an old-line Whig, enemy of secession, and one of the wealthiest planters in the state, hoped to unite the old Whigs and control the Negroes through the recognition of their legal equality.[7] The state had rejected its first constitution and had been admitted only in 1870, with Alcorn as its first governor. In the legislature there were thirty-five Negroes, and men of that race were chosen as Senator and secretary of state. Elected Senator in 1871, Alcorn resigned as governor. His plan to build a white Republican party had been opposed by the

[7] Donald, *loc. cit.*, pp. 447–460.

son-in-law of Benjamin F. Butler, General Adelbert Ames, a Maine carpetbagger who, after having been provisional governor, had been elected to the Senate. "Addle-pate" or "Onion-head" Ames, as he was called by his enemies, had a sincere belief in his duty to protect Negro rights, which he felt were being neglected by Alcorn.

The showdown came in 1873, when the two men both decided to run for governor, causing a split in the Republican ranks. Ames won by a large majority. Alcorn then took his former Whigs into the Democratic ranks and joined the fight for white supremacy. Under Ames, the offices of lieutenant governor, secretary of state, superintendent of education, and commissioner of immigration and agriculture, the presiding officers of both houses, and sixty-five members of the legislature were Negroes. However, Vernon L. Wharton, in *The Negro Mississippi, 1865-1890* (Chapel Hill, 1947), concluded that, although Negroes formed majorities in thirty counties, few held local offices.

The Mississippi constitution forbade state aid to railroads, closing that avenue of graft, but a serious scandal developed out of aid to river navigation. The annual cost of state printing soared from $8,000 to a high of $128,000. Current state expenses of government multiplied 1,400 per cent, while the state indebtedness more than doubled. Over 6,000,000 of 30,000,000 acres of land had to be forfeited for taxes.

In Mississippi, the Negroes outnumbered the whites. When the latter used force and threats of violence to keep the freedmen from voting, Ames appealed to Grant for troops and organized two regiments of Negro militia. This angered the whites even more and led to a serious race riot at Vicksburg on December 7, 1874. By the time of the election of 1875, the state was on the verge of civil war, with armed Negroes facing armed whites. General Philip Sheridan was sent to restore peace, and Ames and the Democrats signed a treaty which provided on one hand that the militia would be disbanded and on the other that a free election would be allowed. Nevertheless, the whites waged a campaign of intimidation, known as the "Mississippi plan," and the Democrats won by a majority of 31,000 votes. Ames resigned, and after five years of Radical rule, Mississippi was restored to Conservative hands.

Louisiana's story is one of the most sordid of all, with a Radical period stretching from 1868 to 1877. Under the reconstruction acts, 84,436 Negroes and 45,218 whites were registered as voters. In the election of 1868, Henry C. Warmoth of Illinois, a carpetbagger with a poor war record who had been indicted in Texas for embezzlement and appropriating government cotton, was elected governor. Although he accumulated a personal fortune of over $500,000 on a salary of $8,000 a year, he did not claim any personal virtue other than that he was no more dishonest than other politicians. With Warmoth were elected a Negro lieutenant governor and two other carpetbaggers as Senators. Warmoth was a real spoilsman, and graft was the order of the day in all branches of government. A tax collector in New Orleans received over $60,000 a year in fees and commissions, and the vote of a state senator sold for a flat $600. The state printing bill over a three-year period reached a total of $1,150,000, though it had never before exceeded $60,000 a year; a building previously valued at $84,000 was bought by the state for $250,000; a state-owned railroad on which the government had spent $2,000,000 was sold for $50,000 after higher bids had been rejected. The state university went four years without an appropriation.

Warmoth organized a machine which rested upon Negro votes and could boast the support of James F. Casey, brother-in-law of President Grant. It manipulated elections through its control of municipal police and constabulary and through its returning board, which canvassed the vote. This board juggled figures and estimated "what the vote ought to have been." Its actions in the election of 1872 were characterized by a congressional committee as a "comedy of blunders and frauds." There were also levee frauds and the usual railroad graft. The state debt grew malignantly: in January, 1869, it was $6,777,300; a year later, $28,000,000. By November, 1870, it had reached $40,000,000. Government expenses rose by 500 per cent and the tax rate by 800.

With such abundance of graft, a falling-out among thieves was not surprising. The "Customs House Gang," headed by Casey and federal marshal Stephen B. Packard, led the ultra-Radicals in a bid for control in 1872. Warmoth supported the Democratic candidate John McEnery against the Radical William P. Kellogg. After the election, he declared McEnery to be the winner and turned the government over to him. The Kellogg faction created its own returning board and, without benefit of any ballots or returns, declared Kellogg and the Republicans the victors. A federal judge agreed. Both groups set up governments, but Kellogg was inaugurated with the aid of federal troops. Many Democrats and Liberal Republicans refused to pay taxes, and McEnery issued proclamations and held his own legislature of Democrats. Actual civil war resulted in a number of localities, and the state was in anarchy. A compromise was finally reached whereby the Democrats were given control of the lower house, and Kellogg was free to amass a personal fortune in relative peace.

In the election of 1876, frauds were again the order of the day, and the following January both Francies R. T. Nicholls, the Democrat, and Stephen B. Packard, the Republican, claimed victory and established governments. The state also dispatched two sets of presidential election returns to Washington, contributing to the confusion of the disputed national election of 1876. The White League of Louisiana, leading the struggle for the return to home rule, dominated the state to the point that Packard's control barely extended beyond the capital city. As part of the settlement of the national election, Hayes agreed to withdraw federal troops from the South, and when this was done in April, 1877, the Packard government collapsed.

South Carolina vied with Louisiana for the dubious distinction of having the worst reconstruction. Negroes outnumbered whites in the state by three to two, with almost every freedman a member of the Union League, and had majorities in the legislature from 1868 to 1874. Of the group elected in 1868, not more than twenty-two could read and write, and the members paid a total of only $635 in taxes. These legislators were described in James S. Pike's classic picture of "carpetbag rule" as the "most ignorant democracy that mankind ever saw."[8] Added to this was the fact that the first two governors, Robert K. Scott of Ohio and the scalawag Franklin J. Moses, Jr., were extremely corrupt, helping to make South Carolina the most graft-ridden of Southern states.

Elections, judicial decisions, votes, and franchises were openly bought and sold. Both Scott and Moses had a lucrative business in sale of pardons, and the latter confessed to accepting bribes and to spending ten times his salary on extravagant living. A Negro member of the supreme court dispensed justice to the highest bidder; a congressman sold an appointment to West Point; one Negro legislator admitted accepting $5,000 for his vote — in order to keep the money in the state! Almost no source of graft was too small to be overlooked, and on one occasion Moses, then speaker of the house, was reimbursed $1,000 by that body for money which he had lost on a horse race. The state house was refurnished at exorbitant costs, with furniture bought for $200,000 which was worth less than $18,000; a restaurant for legislators cost $125,000 for one session; every and anything was charged as legislative supplies: hams, whiskies, rugs, corsets, bustles, bedsteads, imported cigars, diamond rings, corkscrews, wash tubs, ad infinitum. The lawmakers apparently agreed with a Massachusetts carpetbagger who declared, "The State has no right to be a State unless it can pay and take care of her statesmen."

[8] James S. Pike, *The Prostrate State: South Carolina under Negro Government* (New York, 1874). Although Pike has since been proven a biased source, his work had much influence on public opinion.

There were heavy railroad expenditures, and printing costs, which had totaled less than $1,000,000 from 1800 to 1860, rose to $500,000 for a single session. The state property tax was raised to the point that it was confiscatory, and tremendous amounts of land had to be forfeited to the government. Legislative expenditures multiplied six-fold, and the state debt increased from $7 to $29 million. Bonds totaling $1,590,000 were issued to redeem $500,000 in state banknotes, and more millions in bonds, some signed by a burlesque queen, were sold at twenty-five cents on the dollar. Approximately $750,000 was spent in buying land which was so poor and wornout that it was virtually worthless for resale to Negroes. To keep the whites under control, his political opponents claimed Governor Scott had enrolled 90,000 Negroes in the militia and furnished 20,000 with arms. Fourteen regiments, costing $374,000 in one election alone, terrorized the freedmen and kept the whites from voting.

After three terms, two for Scott and one for Moses, a respectable Republican carpetbagger from Maine, Daniel H. Chamberlain, was elected governor in 1874 and began to clean up some of the worst mess. Two years later, the South Carolina whites united behind Wade Hampton in hopes of carrying the election for the Democrats against Chamberlain's bid for a second term. They adopted a policy of simultaneously coercing and wooing the Negro voters: Negro Democratic clubs were organized, Negro officeholders were nominated, and support was promised for the Thirteenth, Fourteenth, and Fifteenth amendments. Democratic rifle clubs (Hampton's "Red Shirts") were organized and, using the "Mississippi plan" or the "Edgefield" or "shotgun" system, broke up Republican rallies and intimidated Negroes and white Radicals into voting Democratic. More ballots were cast than there were voters, both sides being guilty of irregular practices; each party claimed victory and installed rival legislatures. A visit to President Hayes by the two rival governors in March, 1877, was followed by withdrawal of federal troops on April 10, and the next day, after denouncing Hayes, Chamberlain gave up the governor's office.

Florida's nine years of Radicalism differed from that of Louisiana and South Carolina only in that a smaller population was involved. The state's registration lists showed 11,148 whites and 15,434 Negro voters. The Radicals were firmly in control and left little to chance. Ballot boxes were stuffed before the polls were opened, and gangs of freedmen went from precinct to precinct voting under assumed names. On occasion, Democratic members of the legislature were falsely arrested to provide Radical majorities. Negro legislators regularly received sealed envelopes with cash enclosed and at one time established a "smelling committee" to discover "money schemes," only to be betrayed by the chairman of the group, who failed to divide the spoils. The state also had its railroad graft, and the cost of printing in 1869 was more than that of the entire government in 1860, as current government expenses increased by 200 per cent.

In 1874, Marcellus L. Stearns, who had been accused of stealing relief supplies as an agent for the Freedmen's Bureau, was elected governor, as the Radicals took their last fling. In the 1876 election, Florida whites put into effect a milder "Mississippi plan" and secured the victory for the Democrats. Although Stearns' supporters threatened to refuse to give up control, the native whites, bolstered by Georgians who came in to help, succeeded in inaugurating their candidate in 1877.

Southern reaction to carpetbag government was bitter and often violent. With legitimate victory at the ballot box usually viewed as impossible, the region struck back through extra-legal means. The most common method was formation of secret societies, of which the Ku Klux Klan was the most famous. As early as 1866, a group of young men organized it as a secret social lodge at Pulaski, Tennessee. The idea spread rapidly throughout the South, and the groups were united in 1867 as the "Invisible Empire of the South," primarily to counteract the Union League, check the carpetbaggers, and give resistance to Negro militia units. In efforts to break up Radical political organizations by intimidation and terrorization, night rides of white-robed and-hooded men played upon the fears of the superstitious Negroes, always with the threat of horrible punishment if warnings were ignored. Some Negroes, carpetbaggers, and scalawags were shot, hanged, drowned, or burned, in addition to those who were flogged. Weird notices in newspapers and on posters added to the mystery. One read:

> Thodika Stevika! Radical plan
> Must yield to the coming of the Ku Klux Klan!
> Niggers and leaguers, get out of the way,
> We're born of the night and we vanish by day.[9]

At first many of the best Southerners supported the Klan, but it quickly outgrew their control, and in 1869 its leader, General Nathan Bedford Forrest, ordered all Klansmen to unmask. The majority of respectable men withdrew, perhaps only out of respect for Forrest, but it continued as a vehicle of vengeance and private gain.

Similar organizations on a smaller scale also existed. Among these were the Pale Faces of Tennessee, the Constitutional Guard and White Brotherhood of North Carolina, the Knights of the White Camelia in

[9] As quoted by E. Merton Coulter, *The South during Reconstruction, 1865-1877* (Baton Rouge: Louisiana State Univ., 1947), p. 167.

Louisiana and Arkansas, the Council of Safety in South Carolina, the
Men of Justice in Alabama, the Society of the White Rose in Mississippi, and the Sons of Washington in Texas.

To meet these threats to Radical rule, Congress appointed a joint
committee (whose report covered thirteen volumes) to investigate
such activities and stepped up its use of military force through three
enforcement acts, the most important being those of 1870 and 1871.
Some 7,373 indictments were found under these acts, and martial law
was declared in nine South Carolina counties. With such measures,
these organizations were effectively dispersed, virtually ending in
1871.

Gradually, Northern opinion changed. The public became tired of
their reformers, were alarmed by excesses in the South, and greater
sympathy developed for the Southern whites in their struggle for home
rule. As E. L. Godkin, editor of the *Nation,* pointed out, the establishment of an ignorant, just-freed group as the controlling factor in the
states was an open invitation to crooked leaders. Gradually, pressure
also mounted for a general amnesty. Shifting Northern opinion, along
with the increasing strength of the Democratic minority, the rise of the
Liberal Republicans, and the counter efforts of the Southern Republicans, brought under attack the provisions of the Fourteenth Amendment which denied the right to hold office to approximately 100,000
white Southerners. A bill was passed by the House in 1871 and by both
houses in May, 1872, which reduced the number of disqualified to
under 500. During the next eight years, practically anyone who petitioned was pardoned and was free of federal restrictions in exercising
his political rights.

The Radicals had made the mistake of viewing all Southern whites
as bad and excluding them from the Southern Republican party. This
drawing of the color line was distasteful even to Northerners, and
racial prejudice aided the Democrats. Many Northerners in the South
deserted the Republican party when membership in it hurt their business and social acceptability, and even the Negro support became unreliable when distribution of the spoils was not equal. Carpetbagger
and scalawag factions appeared, and the Southern Democrats made the
most of their economic and social positions.

In the presidential election of 1872, a large segment of the Republican party (the Liberal Republicans) opposed the Radical policy and
threw its support to an independent candidate pledged to civil service
reform and the ending of the Southern problem. Although Grant was
re-elected, the Liberals, allied with the Democrats, were sufficiently
strong to tie the Radical hands, and the Panic of 1873 further distracted Northern attention. When the Democratic-controlled House

elected in 1874 took office, any further anti-Southern legislation was impossible.

The presidential campaign of 1876 saw both major candidates promising to end Radical reconstruction. When President Hayes, true to his promise, withdrew federal troops from the South in 1877, the last carpetbag governments fell. Political reconstruction was over, except for the post-mortems and the smarting scars. On June 11, 1877, former governor Chamberlain of South Carolina wrote the old abolitionist, William Lloyd Garrison, "Your prophecy is fulfilled, and I am not only overthrown, but as a consequence I am now a citizen of New York." Looking backward over the events which had produced this situation, he concluded that it resulted, first, from the fact that "my defeat was inevitable under the circumstances of time and place which surrounded me. I mean here exactly that the uneducated negro was too weak, no matter what his numbers, to cope with the whites." In addition, he saw that the Radicals "had lost too, the sympathy of the North," and that the "Presidential contest [of 1876] also endangered us and doubtless defeated us. The hope of electing Tilden incited our opponents, and the greed of office led the defeated Republicans under Hayes to sell us out."

The scars of reconstruction included many real and fancied wounds. The most painful was the specter of Southern whites under the political control of their former slaves. Not even the exorbitant taxes or the plundering of state revenue equalled this humiliation in Southern eyes. The attempt to give the blacks equality by giving them the ballot was a failure and was recognized as such by Northern and Southern whites alike. Although the Radical *National Republican* explained the defeat by blaming the carpetbag governments for ineffectiveness, an outside party which had excluded the former governing class and relied upon the "native menial classes" was too "abnormal" to endure. The Negroes had been forced to come to terms with their old masters, "the persuasive power in hunger and cold" being stronger than moral convictions and what was often "empty privilege."

The blacks, of course, should not be scapegoats. They had not sought any power, only freedom. The role of the freedmen in reconstruction is one of the most perplexing questions in American history, with prejudice entering on both sides. During the war, Northern humanitarians had claimed there was no difference between the races but skin color. Afterwards, Southern extremists were anxious to keep him "in his place," a position not far removed from slavery. Moderates in both sections, who believed the Negroes should have training before getting full rights, were shouted down. As Booker T. Washington pointed out, the race was given more rights than it knew how to use and then was penalized ever after for its inexperience. When the Negroes were suddenly given these privileges, even before educated white females were entrusted with them, they had not had time to develop a code of ideals, leaders, or even race consciousness.

It was obvious after 1865 that the freedman would be exploited and led, but by whom? Southerners thought they would do it and attempted to create a status midway between slavery and freedom for him. Northerners, on the other hand, promised him education, churches, suffrage, and equality, and so he turned to the Northerners. The venal carpetbagger, as a representative of the saviors, was obviously impossible to eliminate without depriving the Negro of his political power. From this alliance, racial antagonism developed which caused trouble for years to come. One reason for Southern memorialization of reconstruction nightmares was the desire to keep the Negro subordinate, so the freedman and the tradition of an evil reconstruction were inseparably linked together. The corruption, however, was not necessarily the result of the Negro in government but the coexistence of factors which also dragged the moral level of the national and state governments in the North to a low plane. Significantly, graft in the South did not end with the removal of the Negro and carpetbagger from power.

How much did the South actually suffer? James Bryce, an impartial English observer, was one of the first to say that reconstruction had been quite lenient in comparison to aftermaths of European civil wars. Though Southerners continued to think it unusually harsh, Jefferson Davis was not executed and was about the only one persecuted, while unreconstructed rebels such as A. T. Bledsoe and Robert Toombs were allowed to rant on unharmed.

What about economic ruin? In the first place, the corruption of reconstruction state governments has been exaggerated in the public mind. Democrats as well as Republicans were willing to be bought by business. The appropriations of these Southern governments seemed high, primarily in comparison with the pinch-penny planter governments of the antebellum period, but their extravagances were not incompatible with the era of expansion which swept the nation; all governments used public funds lavishly in the name of progress. Every Northerner who came South was not motivated by evil desires. Many were honest citizens, looking for better economic opportunities, who would have been welcomed anywhere else.

Some Southern states were well administered by the Radicals. How much of the opposition was due to misrule and how much was caused by objection to Radical personnel is impossible to say. Not many Southerners would have liked these governments regardless of their merits. But they did have merits. Unlike the constitutional conventions of 1865 which were intended primarily only to make required changes in the old frameworks of government, those of 1867-1868 embarked upon basic constitutional reform. The liberal concepts of equalitarianism of the past half century, which had been largely ignored in the South, were for the first time given a sympathetic hearing. Almost without exception, the new constitutions provided for more democratic government than their predecessors.

Their innovations are worthy of notice. To them must go credit for introduction of the concept of universal male suffrage, abolition of property qualifications for office, popular election of county and additional state officials, liberalized homestead exemptions, and reform of penal systems with a lowering of the number of crimes punishable by death. The Radicals wrote mandatory provisions for free public education and provided for uniform taxation to support these systems. They rebuilt the ruined facilities of the region; they instituted many new social services by the government. Above all, they included the Negro in the American dream. If this had not come when the South was powerless to resist and the North was reform-minded, the principle of Negro equality might never have been included in the national charter. This is as much a part of the legacy of reconstruction as the better-known corruption and imposition of alien rule. But all this took money and meant increased taxes, another source of grievance to property owners who were unaccustomed to paying for services for poor whites and Negroes.

While it is true that in 1865 the South was economically prostrate, it recovered very rapidly even under Radical rule. Much of postwar poverty cannot be blamed upon reconstruction but upon the results of war and emancipation, which revolutionized the economic systems of the region. While the corruption and extravagance were heavy burdens and much land was forfeited because of mountainous taxation, still, economic recovery did come under carpetbag rule.[10]

A final myth born in this era which has haunted the South was the belief that the Ku Klux Klan was responsible for overthrowing Radical reconstruction. As has been shown, it was broken up during 1870-1871 and affected redemption very little. The ultimate triumph of home rule was more the achievement of responsible Southerners working through

[10] Many historians have sought to re-evaluate reconstruction. Among these are Howard K. Beale, "On Rewriting Reconstruction History," *American Historical Review*, XLV (1939-1940), pp. 807-827; Francis Butler Simkins, "New Viewpoints of Southern Reconstruction," *Journal of Southern History*, V (February, 1939), pp. 49-61; T. Harry Williams, "An Analysis of Some Reconstruction Attitudes," *Journal of Southern History*, XII (November, 1946), pp. 469-486; and Jack B. Scroggs, "Carpetbagger Constitutional Reform in the South Atlantic States, 1867-1868," *Journal of Southern History*, XXVII (November, 1961), pp. 475-493.

able leadership. The Southern whites never lost economic control of the freedmen and had invented new ways of controlling them politically. Most important, the Northern public got tired of Radical excesses. But the legend of the Klan set the dangerous precedent that extra-legal methods are justified and honorable against bad laws. As Hamlet said, "There is nothing either good or bad, but thinking makes it so."

The war and reconstruction contributed to later Southern unity by giving the region a common and unique history: the memory of defeat and a "lost cause." In the words of Sir Winston Churchill, "The victors forget, the vanquished remember." The total defeat of what they considered to be a superior way of life and the loss of control of their own destiny gave Southerners a feeling of uncertainty which amounted to a regional inferiority complex. A common defense reaction caused them to stifle self-criticism, indulge in self-praise, view outsiders with suspicion, and feel themselves an embattled minority within a hostile nation. The excesses of reconstruction and the role of the freedmen merely reinforced the low opinion which Southerners had traditionally held of the Negroes' ability and united them in a greater determination to maintain white supremacy.

# 6

# THE CONSERVATIVE TRIUMPH

THE FALL OF THE CARPETBAG GOVERNMENTS made a political decision mandatory. Radical reconstruction had marked a tremendous effort by the victorious North to eradicate the Southern political structure, blamed for having caused the "Rebellion." A prime objective had been to break aristocratic political control of the South by force from outside and by social and political revolutions from within. The former leaders had been disfranchised, and Negro suffrage and the Republican party had been grafted to the tree of politics. Now when the external pressure was about to be removed, the question was: Would the new hybrid be accepted as Southern?

Contrary to the hopes of Northern Republicans and of Southerners such as Andrew Johnson and James L. Alcorn, who viewed reconstruction as an opportunity for the common man to come into his political own, the people of the South, in their zeal for "home rule" and in revolt against the alien concepts which had been forced upon them, turned to the Conservatives. As state after state was "redeemed" from carpetbag rule, not only were the Republicans repudiated and new constitutions often drawn up, but conservative ideals and leaders came into control. Yet, while locally repudiating Republicanism, nationally the new leadership found the business-oriented Republican program more to their taste than the archaic state-rights policy of the Democrats. As Professor C. Vann Woodward has so graphically shown in *Reunion and Reaction* (Garden City, 1956), these Southern Conservatives cooperated to secure the election of President Hayes in 1877 in return for promises of patronage, economic assistance to Southern enterprises, and a voice in his government. The new officials, who would rule until challenged by the agrarian revolts of the 1890's, endorsed few liberal ideas and preached neither reform nor economic heresy. To many, these "Redeemers" appeared merely a reincarnation of the oligarchy which had ruled before the war. They were familiarly known as "Bourbons," from the epithet applied by their political enemies, who sought to imply that Southerners, like the French monarchs, had "learned nothing and forgotten nothing," that the plantation clique was back in control.

This was not true. During their hegemony, neither the planter as such nor agricultural protagonists were to dominate, for the political, economic, and social center of gravity was shifting from the country to the town. Very few of the new leaders were primarily interested in agriculture. Some were planters, it is true, but even they had other interests. In Georgia not one of the antebellum leaders remained a dominant figure. Of the new, only General Alfred H. Colquitt was a planter-aristocrat, but he had also wide business interests and was a railroad promoter as well. In 1880-1881, only 38 per cent of the Georgia legislature had any agricultural interest, and even fewer depended solely on the soil for income. In Alabama the Louisville and Nashville Railroad dominated politics and furnished the leaders. The Louisiana Lottery Company was a force in that state, furnishing the money which helped win the disputed state election of 1876. Mississippi passed into the hands of a triumvirate of corporation lawyers, while South Carolina leaders, though of planter origin, were spokesmen for the business interests. The redemption governor of Florida owned the largest store in the state and had extensive lumber interests. As a group, these men were of middle-class origin, having but nominal connections with the old planter regime and with primarily an industrial, capitalistic outlook.

In the different states, Bourbon government reflected the regional characteristics. Alabama Bourbons were among the more liberal, the new constitution of 1875 containing advanced provisions about matters such as public education and popular election of some officials. Nevertheless, the new regime was mainly conservative and economical, taking steps to reduce the debt and control the Negro more effectively. It, too, sought greater industrialization, though with fears of monopolistic corporations.[1] Although Kentucky had not seceded, it was quickly dominated by the Conservatives and business interests. Their spokesman was Colonel Henry Watterson, editor of the Louisville *Courier-Journal,* who advocated conciliation with the North and attraction of Eastern capital. The government responded with subsidies, tax exemptions, and privileged franchises. Redemption in Tennessee was achieved by General John C. Brown, railroad promoter, who at his death was president of the Tennessee Coal, Iron and Railroad Company. His successors were men of the same mold.

The Georgia Bourbons were more industrially minded, chiefly because of the influence of the city of Atlanta and of Henry W. Grady. Grady, son of a Georgia major killed during the war, had borrowed $20,000 from Cyrus W. Field of Atlantic cable fame to buy an interest in the Atlanta *Constitution,* and he became the leader of a group who wanted to build up industry in the South with Atlanta as its center. In addition to Grady, there were three politicians in the Atlanta Ring, which ran the state politically for decades. First was John B. Gordon, a handsome man with long flowing hair who had become a general while still in his twenties. He had played a leading role in the Ku Klux Klan and for many years was commander of the United Confederate Veterans. He was adept at appealing for the soldier vote, praising the lost cause, as well as being a great favorite with the ladies. He enriched himself through railroad speculation and numerous ventures in insurance, publishing, mining, manufacturing, and real estate. General Alfred H. Colquitt, a planter-aristocrat by origin, whose tenants produced large amounts of cotton, attracted the landlord group, although he had extensive holdings in railroads, textiles, fertilizer manufacturing, and coal mining.

Finally, there was Joseph E. Brown, the most interesting of them all. Of humble origin and a self-made success, he was a past master at changing sides and coming out ahead. As a war governor, he resisted Jefferson Davis in the name of the common man; he was a Republican during reconstruction but left the party to help in the fight for home rule. Wealth came to him as president of the Western and Atlantic Railroad, the Southern Railway and Steamship Company, the Walker Coal and Iron Company, and the Dade Coal Company, but even as a businessman he never lost his touch with the farmers. These three men restored home rule and afterwards ruled Georgia with an iron hand. One was governor and one or two were Senators throughout the period.

Mississippi also had its triumvirate: Lucius Q. C. Lamar, Edward

[1] Allen J. Going, *Bourbon Democracy in Alabama, 1874–1890* (University, Alabama: Univ. of Alabama, 1951).

C. Walthall, and James Z. George, all United States Senators and all corporation lawyers. Lamar was born a plantation aristocrat and had played an active role in the negotiations which led to the withdrawal of troops from the South in 1877. Walthall was a wealthy railroad lawyer, and George, who had come up from the working class to become well-to-do, took pride in his title, "The Commoner," and kept his appeal to the farmer class. The governorship was restricted to an equally small group, two allies dominating it for twenty years. Operating under the title of Democrat Conservatives, Mississippi Bourbons sought industry, were friendly toward railroads, preached reconciliation, and agreed upon control of the Negro vote. A policy of rigorous economy was followed, and it was not until 1886 that annual disbursements reached $1,000,000.[2]

Virginia was restored to the Union in 1870 by the Conservative party, a mixture of pre-war Democrats, "True [conservative] Republicans," old-line Whigs, and Negroes. Business interests were largely predominant, especially concerns in Richmond. By 1876 the Republican party virtually ceased to exist except as a patronage group, but even the opposition to the Bourbons was led by a railroad organizer and executive, General William Mahone. All of the governors were Confederate veterans, and the chief issues during these years were the state debt, the state's interest in its railroads, and public education. These Bourbons surrendered their railroad interests to Northern capitalists, allowing them, however, to keep all the benefits of state ownership. The Funding Act of 1871 was equally advantageous to the moneyed interests.

In South Carolina the leaders were General Matthew C. Butler, lawyer, planter, and one of the chief organizers of the "Edgefield" or "Shotgun policy" which had helped redeem the state, and General Wade Hampton. Hampton had once been the richest planter in the South, prospering from the labor of 3,000 slaves; he declared himself bankrupt in 1868, with personal debts of over $1,000,000. He had taken no active part in the Klan but had defended its motives and sought to get Northern lawyers to defend those members who ran afoul of the law. In 1876 he ran for governor on a platform of "Reconciliation, Retrenchment and Reform." Campaigning as a friend of the Negro, he won in a contested election featured by activities of the Red Shirts or Rifle Clubs, which killed or intimidated Negro and Republican voters and indulged in wholesale stuffing of the ballot boxes. The Negro vote, however, continued to be an important support for Hampton, with fifteen freedmen serving in the General Assembly in 1882 and with representation there as late as 1896. Negroes also held a number of

[2] Willie D. Halsell, "The Bourbon Period in Mississippi Politics, 1875-1890," *Journal of Southern History*, XI (November, 1945), pp. 518-537.

county and municipal offices. Hampton, to the consternation of his white supporters, even dined with them and urged that the University of South Carolina be merged with a Negro college. But his attitude was that of a master-servant relationship.

As governor for two terms, Hampton also allied himself with the business interests, joining his friends General John B. Gordon and Benjamin H. Hill in organizing the Southern Life Insurance Company of Atlanta. To carry out his pledge of strict economy, he leased state prisoners to private contractors. After he moved to the Senate for two terms, he continued to control the state through hand-picked governors.

There was a strong leaven of old Whigs and Whiggish tendencies among the redeemers. Tennessee was first restored under a former Whig, General Brown, and his successor, James D. Porter, had also been a member of that party. Other governors with similar backgrounds were George F. "Millionaire" Drew of Florida and Robert Lowry of Mississippi. Even the name Democrat fell into general disuse in the first decades of home rule. The term "Conservative," widely used to designate those opposed to "Radical" rule, was adopted as the official name of the party. Wherever the denomination "Democratic" was used, it was almost always combined with "Conservative"— a practice in Alabama for forty years after the war. By 1880 this Whiggish or business-minded group had gained control of the Democratic parties in nearly all the Southern states, and as long as the national Democratic party was in the hands of conservative Easterners, these Southerners had little temptation to consider national affiliation with the Republicans.

These men, whether of Whig or Democratic antecedents, shared a common reputation with their electorate of having won the right to leadership by services during the war and its resultant upheaval. They were the heroes of the Confederacy and reconstruction. War-time leaders, further endeared by defeat, were rewarded for their valor and failure with indefinite leases of political power. So prominent was their role that the period was sometimes referred to as the Reign of the Brigadiers. But there was also recognition for the less glamorous. A man who claimed little distinction other than having on one occasion held the bridle of Lee's horse, Traveler, was assured of political tenure. To have a Confederate record and a Conservative label during reconstruction became indispensable to political success, other qualifications being negligible in comparison. Typical were the Congressional delegations from Alabama and Georgia in 1878, when their sixteen seats were occupied by fifteen Confederate veterans. These "natural" leaders successfully and perpetually identified themselves with the romantic cult of the Old South and the war years.

In the antebellum South, political control had rested on a narrow basis of gentry rule, and it quickly returned to a restricted base once the experiment of reconstruction had been concluded. The balance of political power still rested in the counties of the black belt, a fact that these new leaders recognized as they sought to align themselves with these landlords, the growing manufacturing groups of the cities, and their rising merchant class, rather than with the farmers. In fact, now that all Negroes were counted in determining representation, these counties were over-represented, since the freedmen did not vote or cast their ballots as directed. As a political device to promote white solidarity, the Bourbons kept alive memories of reconstruction excesses and the constant threat of somnolent Negro power. Control of the Negro vote rather than disfranchisement was the aim of the redeemers, control which would make it available to the Bourbons or deny it to the Republicans.[3]

Furthermore, the Radical abuses during reconstruction killed off the chance to build up a truly democratic common man's party in the South and aided the restoration of conservatism. So detested and such a formidable foe was "black Republicanism" that middle- and lower-class whites had little choice but to join the gentry in the fight against Radical government. Home rule had been the one all-encompassing issue from 1865 to 1877, and when it was finally accomplished, the region found itself without a single major political issue, a situation conducive to political indifference among the rank and file. The practical effect of this was that protestors against the victorious Conservatives had no place to go even if they were able to generate some interest. Thus, politics in the South became one-party, without fundamental issues.[4] The Republican party virtually disappeared, becoming chiefly a clique of federal officeholders, increasingly white in complexion.

Under this new dispensation, certain characteristics became evident. An almost complete break with the past was represented by the professionalization of political careers. Wide distribution or rotation of offices became an exception to the rule. The state party became a closed corporation, with positions passed around within a small group who remained in office for long periods at a time. Dissenters were summarily kicked out, and the loyal were rewarded after long faithful apprenticeships in lower positions. Generally, these officeholders were intellectually shallow but in compensation were good speakers, confirmed exponents of white supremacy, and models of the ideal of

[3] Donald N. Brown, "Southern Attitudes toward Negro Voting in the Bourbon Period, 1877-1890" (unpublished Ph.D. dissertation, Dept. of History, University of Oklahoma).

[4] Dewey W. Grantham, Jr., "The One-Party South," *Current History*, XXXII (May, 1957), pp. 261-262.

chivalry. They did not abandon all the political practices developed during reconstruction, occasionally using devious means to protect their own control. The dangers of party division were preached with such fervor that bolting the party became the unpardonable sin. As one Southerner declared, "There is but one party for true Southern men, . . . and that is the Democratic party."

The Bourbons made a fetish of proclaiming governmental economy and political honesty. Most of them found their states in varying degrees of bankruptcy, often the result of the graft and corruption of preceding administrations. In Louisiana, government expenditures were reduced from $7,587,148 in 1871 to $1,617,164 in 1882. Texas, too, followed a program of retrenchment, but it was not until 1879 that the state treasury could meet its obligations without delay. Total Alabama expenditures had reached $2,237,200 in 1873; two years later, after the overthrow of the Radicals, they were $874,164 and were kept under $1,000,000 until 1883. At the end of the century they averaged only about $2,000,000 a year, the increase going chiefly to schools and Confederate pensions.

The Georgia constitutional convention of 1877, under the leadership of the old "warhorse" Robert Toombs, so restricted taxation and expenditures that Toombs declared that they "had locked the doors of the treasury and thrown away the key." The legislature could instigate taxation only for support of the state government and elementary education, payment of the public debt, the suppression of insurrection and invasion, and the defense of the state in time of war. Other purposes had to be authorized later by constitutional amendment.

The Bourbon's oft-repeated claim of scrupulous honesty was not justified, however, although state appropriations were usually too small to permit larceny on a grand scale — perhaps some theft might even have resulted from the penny-pinching salaries paid. Scarcely a state escaped without some evidence of official corruption during this period. For example, state treasurers in Virginia, Tennessee, Alabama, Kentucky, Mississippi, and Louisiana failed to uphold the creed of honesty; in Georgia the comptroller was convicted on eight counts, and the commissioner of agriculture was forced to resign. Generally, nevertheless, the Bourbons' reputation was maintained by the reverence accorded their war records, the closely-knit nature of the governing ring, and the absence of effective opposition from the Republican party.

The mania for economy resulted not only from a reaction to past extravagances but also from the Panic of 1873 and the general poverty of the region. Under reconstruction, the South, when viewed according to its wealth, bore a load of oppressive taxation which has probably never been equalled in the United States. Low taxation, therefore, became an essential of good government. Salaries were often cut in half, and $5,000 was considered a munificent reward for governors and beyond the ability of most states to pay. Large numbers of offices were abolished and departments slashed to the bone as most of the expanded functions of previous administrations were eliminated. Government activities were kept to a minimum; a penny-pinching group, the Bourbons gave little to education, condemning public schools as "Yankee" institutions, and maintained a hostile attitude toward most social legislation. Consequently, the needs of prisons, the insane, the blind, public health, and the like, were virtually ignored.

The Bourbon period was marked also by wholesale repudiation of state debts. The precedent had already been set in North Carolina, South Carolina, and Louisiana under the carpetbaggers, but repudiation or "readjustment" became epidemic under the Conservatives, with only Mississippi, Texas, and Kentucky forbearing to use this method of lightening the load on the government. The total amount by which state liabilities were reduced cannot be determined with accuracy but probably reached a total of not less than $150,000,000. Reduction became an issue in almost every state, with the country people favoring readjustment as a way to lower taxes.

When the Redeemers came into power, they found the fiscal records in such a chaotic state that it was impossible to determine the exact indebtedness. Accounts had been so carelessly kept or maliciously destroyed that estimates varied as widely as 100 per cent. In South Carolina, for example, the state debt was estimated from $15,700,000 to $29,100,000, with liabilities of counties, cities, and other subdivisions past discovery. Some of the states' indebtedness had been secured by valuable property such as railroads, but most just vanished. Many reasons accounted for the tremendous totals. A part of the debts was for obligations contracted before 1860 and for civil services during the war. More was for war debts, repudiated by the Fourteenth Amendment, but the greatest proportion was that incurred during reconstruction. There is little doubt but that the first two of these four categories were legally binding, but the status of the reconstruction debt was more difficult. Unquestionably, much of it represented corruption and as such was viewed with repugnance. States were bankrupt, or nearly so, and therefore used the nature of the carpetbagger debts as an excuse to repudiate them and sometimes all of the other types as well.

Virginia, which had escaped Radical rule almost entirely, nevertheless had the largest debt and also the greatest difficulty in reducing it. Most of this was pre-war, originally contracted in aid of transportation, but with the accumulation of war and reconstruction interest it had increased by 1870 to some $45,000,000. Against this were assets of approximately $10,000,000 in railroad stocks and bonds. Private debts had also been increasing by leaps and bounds, while agricultural prices declined. In 1871 the legislature passed the Funding Act, which assigned one-third of the indebtedness to West Virginia, the rest (approximately $31,000,000) to be paid with interest of approximately six per cent. This interest alone was more than half the total revenue of the state, making the annual deficit approximately $1,000,000. This brought an effort to repeal the act, but the Virginia supreme court declared it irrepealable in 1872. There was little alternative then but drastic economy. Schools, asylums, and veterans were put on short rations, officeholders and salaries slashed, property taxes raised to the point of diminishing returns, and new taxes of all types introduced. Nevertheless, in 1877, when Virginia was rocked by the full effects of the national panic, the deficit was still over $500,000.

Increasingly, people began saying that the War and reconstruction interest debt was not binding because, by the law of nations, debts follow the soil and thus interest stops when war begins. Since the state was actually bankrupt, the debt should be "readjusted." As a result of these issues, three factions appeared. Beside the Bourbons, who stood for "sound finance," there was also a strong Negro voting group, especially in the Fourth and Fifth Congressional districts, under the control of General William Mahone. (The Negroes played an important role in Virginia politics until 1901 and furnished members of the legislature as late as 1891.) The third faction was the whites of the western counties. These were the same people, with the same stubborn opinions, who had given the tidewater aristocrats so much trouble before the war. Even with the separation of West Virginia, they were still important.

Discontent with the Bourbons centered geographically in the western part of the state and politically among those opposed to raising taxes to pay state debts; there were also irreconcilables who wanted to discard democratizing social ideas, such as public education, projected in the Underwood constitution under which Virginia had been restored to the Union. Former Confederate Major General William Mahone played upon this growing discontent, running for the Conservative gubernatorial nomination in 1877 on a platform calling for readjustment of the debt, by force if necessary. Although he lost, "readjusters" in the legislature passed such a bill in 1878, only to have it vetoed by the governor.

When the readjusters were kicked out of the Conservative party, they became the Adjuster party and continued their fight to make sure that "the state's creditors should be compelled to share in the general loss occasioned by the war and reconstruction." Both sides appealed for the Negro vote, and Mahone was supported by the national Republicans who hoped to overthrow the Bourbons and bring Mahone into the Republican party. The whites of the west and the Negroes of the east gave the Adjusters approximately two-thirds of that party's votes and the Conservatives a new argument for Negro disfranchisement. Bourbon support by the cities and town was not enough, and in 1879 Mahone's forces gained control of the legislature. Two years later, his candidate became governor. The Riddleberger Bill of 1882 set the amount of the public debt at $21,000,000, a cut of some ten million, interest rates were reduced by half, and all special privileges were abolished.[5]

Though temporarily successful, Mahone could not hold his coalition together, and by 1882 his party was a part of the Virginia Republican party. In 1883 the Conservatives accepted the readjuster's plan for debt reduction, invited the bolters back, and changed the name of their party to Democratic. Soon they were firmly in the saddle, and although accepting some of the readjuster social reforms, they continued their pro-business program.[6] The Riddleberger settlement was declared unconstitutional by the United States Supreme Court. Finally in 1890, the Virginia legislature successfully reduced its share of the debt to $19,000,000, with interest payable at rates of two and three per cent. After fifty years of controversy with West Virginia, the two governments compromised their difference, with the latter agreeing to responsibility for $14,500,000 of the original indebtedness.

Elsewhere, the same result was obtained with less resistance. Arkansas, with a reconstruction indebtedness of nearly $18,000,000, cut the amount by approximately one-half. Close to $4,000,000 in Florida bonds were repudiated as being "issued in violation of the constitution, and in fraud upon the taxpayers of the state." In Alabama, debt repudiation began under the carpetbaggers, and so the total cannot be ascertained with accuracy, although a commission in 1874 fixed it at over $30,000,000. By the time the Bourbons were through, this had been scaled down by about two-thirds. One of Georgia's first acts of home rule was to investigate the bonded debt. Approximately $9,000,000, mostly railroad bonds, was nullified on the grounds that the authorizing act had not been complied with, and the constitutional convention of 1877 forbade its ever being paid. Thus Georgia cut the debt in half.

North Carolina in 1879 repudiated the reconstruction debt and

[5] C. C. Pearson, "The Readjuster Movement in Virginia," *American Historical Review*, XXI (1915-1916), pp. 734-749.
[6] Allen W. Moger, "The Origin of the Democratic Machine in Virginia," *Journal of Southern History*, VIII (May, 1942), pp. 183-187.

funded the rest at less than 40 per cent, achieving a reduction of about $22,000,000. No one has ever accurately estimated South Carolina's debts, for the reconstruction legislatures disavowed them freely. Eventually the state assumed responsibility for some $7,000,000. In Tennessee, the debt was a political issue for fourteen years, reaching a total of some $42,000,000; in 1882 the decision was made to pay only about $16,500,000. Louisiana had a public debt of $22,589,628 in 1870, plus a contingent liability for endorsed railroad bonds. This last brought the total close to $50,000,000 by the end of reconstruction, despite a constitutional limit of $25,000,000 adopted in 1870. Later, all bonds issued after 1870 were declared void, and in 1874 the state's obligations were refunded at sixty cents on the dollar. After the state defaulted on payment of seven per cent interest, this rate was lowered. All told, the Louisiana debt was cut by some $38,000,000.

The net result of these actions, as might be expected, was to ruin the credit of the states. But to the Bourbons this was a minor problem. Northern and foreign bondholders fought bitterly but were never successful in their efforts to collect. Needless to say, outside capital was hesitant to enter the region for a time, but the fact that interest was promptly paid on the accepted portions of the debts, the favorable tax situations under the Bourbons, and the lure of cheap labor eventually overcame the unpleasant memories.

Regardless of how much the Bourbons sang the praises of the Old South, farming was considered less important than merchandising, money-lending, railroad promotion, factory building, and the development of natural resources. Convinced that the future of the South lay in diversification, the Bourbons allied themselves with the forces of capital — the landlords, merchants, and industrialists. They were willing, if necessary, to sacrifice agrarian traditions and states' rights to partake in the industrialism which had brought prosperity to other regions. There was little interest or consideration of the small farmer and tenant, except the vague belief that he would somehow benefit in the general prosperity which would result. The Redeemers had no definite agricultural policy, so in general allowed the farmers to work out their own salvation. On the other hand, numerous lien laws and statutes dealing with debts were passed to strengthen the hand of the landlord and merchant in his relations with tenants.

Another area challenged the Bourbons. In 1861 there were 47,-700,000 acres of federal land in Alabama, Arkansas, Florida, Louisiana, and Mississippi, but it was reserved for homesteaders. With the attractions of timber and iron and coal deposits, Southerners demanded free access, charging that the North feared Southern economic rivalry and was trying to hinder its progress. To the Bourbons, natural resources

existed for exploitation, and they fretted at all restrictions. The aggressive Bourbons forced through a repeal, and a horde of lumbermen
and speculators surged in for the spoils. Between 1877 and 1888,
5,692,259 acres of these federal lands were sold. Before the region
realized that the anticipated prosperity had not come, Northerners
had bought the most desirable areas and taken away the cream of the
best stands of timber.[7]

Businessmen of every sort learned that they could expect favors
in the form of tax exemptions and other special privileges, and many
of the politicians themselves were front-men for industrial concerns.
Railroads, in particular, found the South a happy hunting ground. As
noted, Tennessee elected a line of governors whose chief interest
seemed to be the railroads in which they had investments; in Kentucky
and Alabama, it was the Louisville and Nashville Railroad. Virginia
politicians sacrificed the state's valuable railroad property chiefly to
the benefit of Northern lines. Under such favorable conditions, a great
railroad revival took place in the 1880's; New Orleans and San Francisco were joined by the Southern Pacific in 1883. In the same year,
other lines joined St. Louis with Southern cities, and by the 1890's
Northern financiers such as J. P. Morgan brought order into the chaotic
situation along the South Atlantic seaboard by creating the Southern
Railroad network.

The Bourbons were also careful to hold in check any democratic
tendencies which might threaten their control. They had risen to power
by driving out the Republican-Negro factions which had dominated
the Southern states, and efforts were exerted to make sure that they
could not regain control. Negroes were still legally entitled to the
privileges of voting and holding office under the war amendments to
the Constitution, and although the election of large numbers of freedmen was no longer tolerated, they occasionally were permitted to hold
office, some even going to Congress during this era. While publicly
calling attention to the horrors of Black-Republican rule, privately the
political rulers of the South encouraged the legacy of pre-war paternalism toward the Negroes and were willing to accept them in public
life so long as they were clearly subordinated to Bourbon wishes.

Where the Negro vote continued a threat, rather than an asset, it
was neutralized by fraud and intimidation if necessary. This was done
by legal procedures of various sorts. In South Carolina, for instance,
the election code of 1882 provided for the "Eight Ballot Box Law,"
which established the use of separate boxes for the different classes
of elected officials. A vote to be valid had to be placed in the correct

[7] Paul Wallace Gates, "Federal Land Policy in the South, 1866-1888," *Journal of
Southern History*, VI (August, 1940), pp. 303-330.

box, thus establishing a crude type of literacy test. As many counties in the black belt were controlled by Negroes or in danger of falling into their hands, state authority over county governments was strengthened to assure these counties of white government. In North Carolina the legislature named the justices of the peace, who in turn chose the county commissioners. The governor of Louisiana was empowered to appoint all officials not specifically subject to election, including all registrars, most local officials, and even school boards and the like. In Florida the appointive power was even more sweeping. Gerrymandering was used when necessary, as well as the various forms of fraud and chicanery developed during reconstruction.

Since such tactics might well be viewed with alarm in the North, the Bourbons took every opportunity to stress that their campaign against the Negroes and the Republicans was not racially inspired or anti-Northern; rather, it was depicted as an effort to restore good government and harmonious relations between the sections. John B. Gordon of Georgia said to a Northern audience, "The causes that divided us are gone, and gone forever. The interests which now unite us will unite us forever." Although Henry W. Grady supported white supremacy before Southern audiences, he was Bourbonism's most effective voice in the North. In his famous speech on December 21, 1886, before the New England Society of New York, Grady left many of his listeners in tears and some shouting enthusiastically. He declared that former foes had learned to love each other and that the South was no longer mourning lost battles; the Southerners were the best friends of the Negro, and therefore race problems should be left to them. "We have found out that in the summing up the free Negro counts for more than he did as a slave. We have planted the schoolhouse on the hill top, and made it free to white and black. We have sowed towns and cities in place of theories and put business above politics." In the final speech of his life, before the Boston Merchant's Association in December, 1889, he reiterated the theme that Northerners should never allow Negro rights to separate them from their Southern friends. "Never before in this Republic has the white man divided on the rights of an alien race. . . . The red man was cut down as a weed because he hindered the way of the American citizen."

Recalcitrant Southerners had also to be converted. In an address to the graduates of the University of Mississippi, George Washington Cable, the Louisiana author, said on June 28, 1882:

> When the whole intellectual energy of the Southern states flew to the defense of that one institution which made us the South, we broke with human progress. We broke with the world's thought. We have not entirely in all things joined hands with it again.

When we have done so we shall know it by this — there will be no South. We shall be Virginians, Texans, Louisianians, Mississippians, and we shall at the same time and above all be Americans. But we shall no more be Southerners than we shall be Northerners.

In general, the North accepted the situation in the South. Absorption of European immigrants was difficult enough to make Southern racial problems seem less unique. The Republican party committed itself to sectional reconciliation, and the Negro was the sacrificial lamb offered up in interest of harmony. President Rutherford B. Hayes added a Tennessee former Confederate, David M. Key, to his cabinet, and Garfield showed no intention of reviving the issues of reconstruction. In his first annual message to Congress in December, 1881, President Chester A. Arthur made no special mention of the South, and journalists were quick to note that this was the first time such an omission had occurred in forty years, hailing it as a happy omen that the troublesome issues of the past had been laid to rest. The United States Supreme Court openly admitted in 1883 that federal courts could not guarantee the Negroes their rights under the Fourteenth and Fifteenth Amendments, on the grounds that Southern violations were subject to state regulation. In 1885, under the first Democratic administration since the Civil War, Southerners were given additional evidence of acceptance. Under Grover Cleveland they held two cabinet posts, as well as Speaker of the House and Chairman of the Committee on Ways and Means. Patronage once more began to flow south in something more than a gratuitous trickle.

Thus the Bourbons, who had found their states in disorder, brought order to their constituents, though often at the expense of democracy and in violation of established prejudices. Limited, liberal concessions were made in the form of additional funds for education, token regulation of railroads, and the like. While various Southern citizens claimed that the anti-Negro reaction had not been carried far enough, that landlords got too many favors, that state services were insufficient, and that they suffered rule by oligarchy, still the average person did not bother to vote or voted Bourbon to play safe.

The Bourbons thus not only pointed with pride to their political acceptance by the North but also claimed to have put the region back on the road to economic recovery, thus creating a "New South." As industrialization made spectacular advances and the South prospered, to shrug off the charge that they had allied themselves with the Republican-industrial North in order to exploit the manpower and resources of their homeland was easy. Ignored were these facts: this prosperity was unevenly divided, and the price was the loss of important Southern resources to outside capitalists and the sacrifice of functions which progressive states should assume.

# 7

# SOUTHERN AGRICULTURE, 1865-1930

WITH POLITICAL RECONSTRUCTION OVER, the South was free to give full attention to its economic recuperation. Normally, an agricultural civilization recovers from a war more easily than an industrial one, for though other kinds of wealth and property may be destroyed, the land remains. But in the South, land was worth only half as much in 1865 as before the war and often had to be mortgaged to finance a new beginning. Most of the small crop of 1864 was seized by federal agents, and the following year brought more poor harvests. Even these small returns, however, were subject to the federal tax on cotton, and the Negro labor supply was in a perpetual state of unrest.

Before 1860 the region had raised chiefly cotton and tobacco for outside markets. Cotton had become important in the early 1800's with the universal demand for a cheap textile — a demand which grew with the increasing population. Prices rose and fell, but the world always needed cotton. The tobacco trade, which had lagged in importance from 1800 to 1840, began to revive, accelerated after the war with the rise to prominence of bright-leaf tobacco. The staple-crop system before the war had been a result of certain economic factors which were not changed by the conflict, thus fore-ordaining that the practice would continue.

Gradually, the Southern scene took on a familiar look as high post-war prices encouraged the resumption of cotton- and tobacco-growing. The road back, however, was not easy. William F. Samford of Alabama wrote in 1870, "We are today . . . poorer than we were on the day of the surrender of the Southern armies. . . . All this great staple producing region is essentially upon the sheriff's block." In fact, only thirteen years after the war did the South produce as much cotton as it had in 1860. This slowness was caused not only by the lack of capital but also because of the necessity for a revolution in the method of production. Obviously, the old system based upon slave labor could not be reinstated.

Another of the more thorough changes was the redistribution of land. The attempt to resume agriculture on a large-scale basis proved impossible in the face of heavy taxes, lack of operating capital, and an uncertain labor supply. Plantations which had cost from $100,000 to $150,000 before the war were sold for $6,000 to $10,000 after Appomattox, if buyers could be found. Many planters were forced to sacrifice their land for low prices, not only to Northern men but also to yeomen, poor whites, and the few Negroes who had the money. For the Northerners, here was another frontier to exploit; for the poor whites, the chance of a lifetime, their first opportunity to escape from the piney woods and swamps to a more normal life; for the former slave, a dream come true.

An indication of what was happening appeared in Mississippi's reporting in 1860 only 563 farms of less than ten acres and twenty times as many in 1870. South Carolina had 33,171 farms in 1860, while Louisiana had 17,328. Twenty years later their respective figures were 93,328 and 48,292, and there were 1,500,000 farms of all sizes in the South, more than double the number in 1860. By the end of the century, another 1,000,000 swelled this total. Some of this increase came from the opening up of new lands, but the majority resulted from the subdivision of the great plantations.

These figures, however, do not represent a similar growth in land ownership, for they refer to units of operation. After failure of the wage system, many who had not sold their land and others who had bought sizable numbers of acres divided their plantations into "one-horse" and "two-horse" farms for cultivation by tenants. In the 1910 census, officials studying 325 black-belt counties found that more than a third of the land holdings were in "tenant plantations" averaging 724 acres in size. But even here, there had often been a change in ownership. It was estimated as early as 1881 that not one-third of the cotton plantations in the Mississippi Valley were held by their pre-war owners.

As has been seen, the share-crop or tenancy system grew out of the post-war adjustment, which was characterized by the lack of credit and the breakdown of the labor supply. This new technique made it possible for planters to obtain labor without paying wages and for landless farmers to get soil without buying it or paying cash rent. Instead, the owners and the tenants agreed to share the proceeds of the crop. As a temporary expedient which they thought would benefit all, most of the freedmen and many of the poorer whites entered into the arrangement. Time, however, proved that the system was self-perpetuating and that escape was, at best, extremely difficult, although the advantages for anyone became very doubtful. Each year the number of tenant farmers increased, and profits and soil fertility declined. As early as 1880, for example, one-third of all farmers in the lower South were tenants, and forty years later the proportion was two-thirds.

The desired goal of any agricultural area is to develop a population of land-owning, prosperous yeoman farmers. This might have been possible if the Negro had been given land or if a system of wages had been worked out, but neither occurred under tenancy. In 1860, 64 per cent of Southern farms were operated by owners, the figure dropping 11 per cent by 1880. By 1930 the ownership total was only 44 per cent, and four-fifths of these farms were under mortgages. The following chart approximates the various divisions of the farmer population.

SOUTHERN FARMERS IN 1930

|  | White | Negro |
|---|---|---|
| Total number | 2,945,000 | 1,393,000 |
| 1. Land owners | 42% | 13% |
| 2. Cash tenants | 5% | 7% |
| 3. Share tenants | 19% | 15% |
| 4. Croppers | 13% | 28% |
| 5. Wage laborers | 21% | 37% |

The wage laborers were often a sub-tenant class of drifters or squatters who moved with the demand for cotton pickers and other forms of agricultural labor. The croppers provided only their labor, while the share tenants had some capital and/or equipment, such as a mule. The elite of the tenant group was the cash tenant, who faced no restrictions as to what he could grow and who worked entirely free of supervision; he also rented for a fixed sum. All other arrangements entitled the landlord to a certain share of the cash crops — a fourth, a third, a half, or, on occasion, as much as three-fourths. Those tenants who received one-half or less were the sharecroppers. The cash tenant usually furnished all the work, stock, feed, fertilizer, and tools, while the other groups generally supplied these things to lesser degrees, which determined their tenure status.

In 1930, four-fifths of the Negro farmers were in the lowest three levels, while approximately one-half of the Southern whites lived in similar circumstances. These farmers had very little opportunity for advancement. They were untrained in the better techniques of farming and, since they moved frequently, were interested only in the existing crop. The tenant farm had no orchard, few gardens, and few animals except for work. Furthermore, the sharecroppers were "kept" men, in a sense, dependent upon the local merchants or their landlords for food and clothing. Without their consent, diversification of output was impossible, for they insisted that labor and borrowed capital be devoted to the old staples. Moving on the average of once every two years, these migrant farmers had no interest in keeping up their houses and barns or engaging in soil conservation. Children were not properly schooled or personal property accumulated. The standard of living of both white and black was pitiably low, and the environment played havoc with home life, citizenship, and the instinct normally associated with inherited ownership of the land. In short, tenancy led many Southerners into a situation much akin to that of the lowest European peasantry.

Another unhappy result of the Civil War, and an important stimulant to the growth of tenancy, was the inadequate credit system of the South. The region, which had not had a sufficient number of banks in antebellum days, found itself practically without financial institutions at the end of hostilities. Even in 1870 only thirty-six national banks existed in the six states of Virginia, North Carolina, South Carolina, Georgia, Alabama, and Louisiana, and these had a combined capital of only $7,000,000. There were only a few state banks, and what money they had was scattered and not readily available for credit. Progress in the concentration of these resources was so slow that by 1895 there were only 417 national banks in the ten cotton states, more than half of which were in Texas, and more than 100 counties in Georgia had no banking facilities whatsoever. Small wonder that agriculture was unable to compete successfully for the little money available.

To meet this enduring crisis was created a unique credit institution: the country store. Here the merchant performed the functions of the banker for large and small farm owners. The landlord of croppers had to furnish teams, tools, food, clothing, and shelter while his tenants produced the crops. The landowner seldom had sufficient cash and had to turn to the local merchant for credit. Land was worth so little that it alone was not often accepted as a basis for credit, and so the plant-er's share of the crop was pledged for security.

There were two periods during which most of these stores were established — immediately after the Civil War and later in the 1880's. These businesses, sometimes known as "furnishing merchants," took over the functions of the pre-war "factors," serving as a source of commodities and capital. They were also the local contacts for the big wholesale mercantile houses, fertilizer manufacturers, meat packers, and the grain, feed, and cotton speculators. The country storekeepers did not expect to sell for cash, for few of their customers had any. They sold on credit and, to protect themselves against loss, took crop liens and, if possible, chattel and land mortgages also. If the farmers were tenants, the liens were taken only on the tenants' shares, though often the landlords were required to underwrite the loans.

Between January and planting time, the farmer made his arrange-ments with a storekeeper to furnish the necessary supplies for making a crop and supporting his family. The amount, known as a "limit," depended upon his credit standing and the crop to be planted. No money changed hands, but credit to his "limit" was extended, secured by a crop lien. After the lien note had been signed, the customer was then permitted to purchase goods at the rate of so many dollars a month, chargeable against his account. Goods were sold in these stores for two prices — one for cash and one for credit. How much mark-up was made for credit was an individual matter governed by the mer-chant. C. H. Poe, writing in 1915, said, "They charge from 25 per cent to grand larceny." Bad debts, tenants who had skipped without paying, taxes, interest, and the like, were all figured in the price of goods. True prices were concealed from the customer by use of code marks which indicated, but only to the store's owner, the cost and the cash and the credit prices. As Thomas S. Stribling shows in his book, *The Store,* once a crop lien had been signed, there were no "sales" for the debtor, he had to take what was offered, usually of the lowest grade, and he could not shop other stores for bargains.

By use of this mark-up the storekeeper protected himself against bad debts and insured himself a good profit if all customers paid, an uncommon situation. Some items yielded as much as 50 to 200 per cent, while others carried mark-ups only of 10 to 20 per cent. Added to these increased prices were 8 to 15 per cent interest charges. Studies of merchant accounts show that, contrary to supposition, there was no conscious effort to cheat the debtor; errors favored the purchaser about as often as the store. At the end of the year, the debits were added and interest charge entered. If the amount of credit were extended, interest rates increased. If the landlord "stood for" his tenant or allowed him to buy on the landlord's account, the tenant usually paid the landlord a separate interest charge for his risk.[1]

No ordinary business can stand such a carrying charge of from 25 to 75 per cent, and so it was not surprising that tenants who had hoped to become landowners instead found themselves hopelessly mired in debt. Farm owners also found the crop-lien system a greased path to tenancy, and many yeomen fell this way. Solvency for renters and owners alike depended upon crop prices, putting them at the mercy of forces beyond their control. The quantity and quality of the product depended not only on the efforts of the workers but also on the condition of the soil and the hazards of weather. According to crop-lien laws in most states, a tenant could not dispose of the fruits of his labor until he had paid all the back rent and bills at the local store. He was seldom consulted about how to sell his crop or to whom, and he had to take the landlord's word as to the price received and the merchant's statement on what had been advanced and how much interest had accrued. If the bill exceeded the tenant's power to pay, he was bound to trade with the same merchant the next year at an even higher rate of interest. The plight of the farmers ensnared in the system was always hard, for few could plan their expenditures to break even at the end of the year. Many, therefore, chose their only means of escape and fled the community. Not surprisingly they became fatalists, and many felt like Jeff Wilson, an ignorant tenant in Dorothy Scarborough's sensitive novel of a few years ago, *In the Land of Cotton:* "If I was to start to hell with a load of ice, there'd be a freeze before I got there."

On the merchant's side, he had to charge high rates. He had become a banker, since the risks were so great that no bank would take them. He in turn obtained advances from a wholesaler or jobber, and the chain of credit ran back to the Northern manufacturer and his banker. Some storekeepers made money and accumulated considerable cash savings, while others acquired large land holdings, but it is doubtful that many became rich. A series of crop failures or low prices, plus the characteristic shiftlessness, illnesses, and flights among his customers, might well mean that the merchant would receive next to nothing for his heavy outlays of credit and be forced into bankruptcy by his own borrowing. "A chain of debt bound tenant, planter, merchant, and banker together, and in their efforts to extricate themselves the banker exploited the merchant, the merchant exploited the tenant, and the tenant exploited the land."

[1] Good accounts of the operation of these stores are found in Thomas D. Clark, "The Furnishing and Supply System in Southern Agriculture since 1865," *Journal of Southern History*, XII (February, 1946), pp. 24-44, and Jacqueline P. Bull, "The General Merchant in the Economic History of the New South," *ibid.*, XVIII (February, 1952), pp. 37-59.

Concurrent with the credit system as a means of holding the farmer in tenancy was his dependence upon a single crop. This was especially true of cotton and, to a lesser degree, tobacco. With all of his economic eggs in one basket, the chance of calamity was enhanced, for there were no subsidiary crops upon which to fall. This devotion to a single staple defied logic, but, nevertheless, it continued because of factors beyond the control of the victim. A chief reason for lack of an alternative cash crop was inadequate transportation facilities, which restricted farmers to non-perishable products which could stand rough handling and the crudest kind of processing for marketing and storing. Second, there were no markets for other crops; taste for the new and a large-scale demand had first to be created.

The argument for the South's producing its own food supplies ignored the fact that to have done so would have reduced its cash income. Cotton and tobacco furnished the easiest means of securing money and were bolstered by a legal structure to protect production and sale. There were established markets with strong precedents and experience behind them. Cotton could be hauled with relatively small loss, its storage was simple, and at the end of the war it offered the quickest means of raising needed capital. The storekeepers were often compelled to rely for part of their own credit needs upon advances from cotton-buyers, who could be paid off in cotton rather than cash. Not only did tradition favor the continuation of the pre-war staple agriculture, but the margin of profit of most small Southern farms was too narrow to allow departure from accustomed usage. The one crop, of necessity, was therefore a reasonably safe crop; farmers knew how to grow it and could always market it at some price.

But the longer the Southern farmers depended upon the one-crop system, the more closely they found themselves bound to it. As prices dropped, crop liens increased, and often crop liens could be obtained only by continuing to grow the staples on which the merchants were willing to make advances. The South, therefore, became the locale of an agriculture of small farmers with little mechanical aid, devoted to raising a cash staple with hand tools and a mule, with direction supplied by his landlords and his suppliers of credit.[2]

With the passage of time, variety in the types of landlordship developed. There were the great company-owned plantations, especially in the lower Mississippi Valley. One of the more famous was that of the English-owned Delta & Pine Land Company, with 37,000 acres in Mississippi. These plantations were not worked by gangs, as in slavery days, but divided into forty- to fifty-acre tracts for individual cultivation. The labor was furnished by tenants, usually Negroes, who were

[2] Thomas D. Clark, "Southern Common Folk after the Civil War," *South Atlantic Quarterly*, XLIV (1945), pp. 130–145.

paid with part of the crop rather than in cash wages. They were managed by a resident superintendent who saw that the cotton was planted and tended at the proper times. The companies ran their holdings efficiently, saving by common purchases of supplies, by common insurance and warehousing, and by taking early advantage of new machinery and techniques.

Another type of landlordship — the merchant farms — resulted from the lien laws where, as a result of the credit system, storekeepers found themselves the possessors of farm acreages. When a tenant found that his share of the crop would not pay his account at the store, often the balance due was assumed by the landlord. The landlord, probably already in debt and unable to pay his annual store account, in time lost part or all of his land to the merchant, thus moving the land along the common road of ownership. Some merchants avidly sought land, while others took it because they could not help themselves. Once in possession, it was naturally put to use, and so the merchants, some of whom eventually owned huge acreages, became landlords in their own right and competitors with their customers. More and more as time went on, the landlord and the storekeeper tended to become the same person.[3]

Some owners were resident on their land, working part of it and renting out the rest. They were in a position to oversee their tenants with some degree of regularity and often got into the business of selling them supplies as well. Others were absentee landlords, living in town and making only occasional trips of inspection. This type was predominant, for example, in the lower counties of South Carolina, where the tenants were chiefly Negroes working with little supervision. With such semi-independent tenants, the landowners just hoped for the best. To the easy-going cropper, absentee landlordism was regarded as a blessing rather than a hardship, much to be preferred to the constant supervision of a landlord neighbor.

As a result of the devotion to one-crop farming, the South found itself restricted to a system of unprogressive agriculture. The plight of the region showed up in comparison with the agricultural practices in other parts of the United States. The United States Department of Agriculture divides American farms into eight categories: (1) large-scale mechanized one-crop farming, such as wheat-raising in the Dakotas; (2) truck farming in the Gulf and Atlantic coastal plains; (3) sheep and cattle ranches; (4) all-around animal farms, raising corn for hogs and hay for cattle and selling meat, milk, butter, and cheese to the cities — an exception in the South; (5) the self-sufficient farmer

[3] For a discussion of the merchant-landlord and his effect, see Charles H. Otken, *The Ills of the South* (New York, 1894), chap. III.

of the pioneer type, a frontier survival on the lowest level, found chiefly in the Appalachian region of the South; (6) the all-around diversified farm with a fair balance between meat, food, and cash crops — an ideal farm found commonly in Ohio and Illinois but rarely below the Mason-Dixon line; (7) small-scale unmechanized farms devoted to cash staples, raising very little food, found predominantly in the South; and (8) unmechanized but coordinated large-scale farming by directed gangs of hands, as characterized by the sugar belt in Louisiana.

Of these types, the cotton farms (7) were the most prevalent in the South. Cotton had been king before the war and continued a despotic rule afterwards. The limit of its realm was drawn only by temperature and rainfall, and the history of the South is, in effect, the story of cotton. The introduction of commercial fertilizer made it possible for the crop to be grown in some of the poorer untapped regions, but the chief expansion came with the opening of new fields in Texas and Oklahoma. The old pre-Civil War process of wearing out land and then moving on to new fields continued for a while, but this soon became geographically impossible, and the area gradually stabilized. By 1930, cotton ruled supreme in a broad crescent of land, 125 to 500 miles wide and extending 1,600 miles from eastern North Carolina southwestwardly into Texas and Oklahoma. Along the way it reached northward into Tennessee, Arkansas, and one or two counties in Missouri. This area was ideally suited for growing cotton and supplied the bulk of the world's needs. But cotton was not a benevolent despot, and by 1930 approximately 80 per cent of the cotton growers were tenants. Nevertheless, because of the need for money, lack of knowledge of how to grow other crops, and an absence of competition, the area continued to limit production to cotton.

In the fifty years from 1860 to 1910, cotton output rose from 3,841,000 bales (of approximately 500 pounds each) to 11,609,000, and twenty years later climbed to 13,932,000. On three per cent of the world's land area was grown 60 per cent of the world's cotton supply. More than half the total acreage harvested in the South in 1929 was in farms dependent upon cotton for at least 40 per cent of their gross income. So important was the crop that the life of the whole area was characterized by activities and attitudes resulting from its cultivation. Social life and institutions, such as schools, churches, and the like, were all geared to the cycle of planting, cultivating, harvesting, and sale. The need for hand labor perpetuated field labor by women and children, thus encouraging a high birth rate; its demands upon the time of the farmer caused him to limit his diet to the easily raised pork, corn, and molasses. Since cotton needs the most attention coincidentally with the rush period in other crops, if one had to be slighted, the non-cash crop was usually ignored.

That cotton was vital to the American economy and furnished directly or indirectly a livelihood for millions cannot be denied. But, on the other hand, whether cotton benefited the South as much as it cost in social values is questionable. Of the wealth it created, only a small part remained in the region and that in the hands of a small and selective group. Significantly, the states most completely devoted to cotton were the least prosperous and cultured by almost any standard. In the words of Hodding Carter, "Cotton devoured land and men, requiring and creating poverty as its handmaiden."

Cotton production was a complex system, with three main aspects: financing, growing, and marketing. As has been shown, the credit system was very expensive and was furnished by merchants, banks, cotton brokers, and fertilizer dealers. With all its faults, however, it did save the poorer farmers by permitting them to engage in agriculture. Production was almost entirely unmechanized, requiring the labor of a whole family. Planting was done in the spring, cultivating in the summer, and picking in the fall. Mechanization for the first two operations was achieved in the twentieth century, but there was little incentive to use machines, since hand labor was required for the picking. Even with primitive equipment, one man could plant and cultivate more cotton than he could pick, for 30 to 100 man-hours were required to hand-pick an acre of cotton in Mississippi, a time expenditure which could grow and harvest three acres of corn in Iowa.

This problem was a challenge to inventors as early as 1850, and since that time almost a thousand patents have been issued on new or improved mechanical pickers of varied sorts, stripper and spindle-type pickers receiving the greatest attention.[4] But only after World War I was much effort made to use these devices, and then they proved unsatisfactory, being crude sled-like affairs which stripped off ripe and unripe bolls alike, as well as any remaining leaves. After 1924, experiments with more selective pickers were carried on by the International Harvester Company and by individual inventors like John and Mack Rust.[5] Though these machines were offered for commercial sale, they never have become popular over all the South.

One big reason for this is that cotton is a temperamental plant, the bolls not all ripening at once. Machines cannot tell the difference between fully ripened and partly ripened cotton. Three pickings by hand usually are necessary to clear a field. Since most mechanically

[4] Gilbert C. Fite, "Recent Progress in the Mechanization of Cotton Production in the United States," Agricultural History, XXIV (January, 1950), pp. 19-28.
[5] John Rust, "The Origin and Development of the Cotton Picker," West Tennessee Historical Society, Papers, VII (1953), pp. 38-56.

picked cotton contains trash and unripe cotton, many gins in the South cannot handle it. The more successful pickers are large and bulky machines which cannot be adapted to the rolling, gullied land of the older sections of the region. Mechanization has advanced farthest in the Arkansas-Mississippi-Yazoo Delta, the coastal plains of Texas, and northwest Texas and southwest Oklahoma, where the fields are relatively large, fairly level, and free from stumps, gullies, and other impediments.

Then, too, most cotton farms are too small and the price of the machinery (over $10,000) too high to justify such equipment. Much of the nation's cotton is produced on irregularly-shaped, rolling farms of less than thirty acres. Over half of the cotton farms in 1940 produced less than four bales each. Tradition and custom are also potent factors in retarding mechanization; a cheap and adequate supply of labor reduces any pressure to substitute machinery. Indeed, an economic and sociological problem of tremendous magnitude would result from the creation of surplus labor if cotton yielded to large-scale mechanization.

The hiatus of the Civil War also brought changes in marketing techniques. The "factor" system, which had been the chief means of selling cotton before 1860, largely disappeared. Afterwards, the cotton usually was purchased by the local cotton merchants, who staked the growers while the crop was being raised. The merchants, in turn, sold it to the "cotton buyers," or "brokers," located in the interior markets or ports of the South; these buyers sold to the domestic mills or their brokers, or to importing merchants who then sold to the European mills.

The price paid for cotton depended upon world demand, with variations according to grades assigned on the basis of such characteristics as cleanliness and length of fiber. Demand, and consequently price, for each grade was reflected by quotations on the cotton exchanges, the most famous being the Liverpool Cotton Association (1870) and the New York Cotton Exchange (1871). The farmer received the current exchange price for his grade of cotton minus a deduction for insurance, profit, freight, and other charges.

Some of the transactions on these exchanges concerned the sale, purchase, and delivery of cotton for cash. But more important were the sale and purchase of contracts for future delivery. Trading in cotton futures began in the troubled days after the War, when great demand, small crops, and wildly fluctuating prices led purchasers to seek stability through future contracts. A mill owner, needing supplies of cotton throughout the year, contracted for future deliveries. Cotton brokers and speculators contracted to make delivery at stipulated prices, gambling that in the meantime they could acquire the cotton for less than the price for which they had agreed to furnish it. If the price of cotton went up, they stood to lose, but if it went down, they could make a good profit.

As acreage and production increased, cotton prices declined. As early as 1878, the price dropped to ten cents per pound, and in the next twenty years the trend generally was downward, plunging finally in 1898 to below five cents, the cost of production. Down to the early 1900's, there was not a year in which the average return per acre from cotton was more than $15. The only times that the crop could be said to have brought in more than a bare living were the periods of the Spanish-American War and the first World War.

The second-ranking agricultural staple in the South was tobacco. Its culture is quite different from cotton, but it had the same tenant setup and financing and was also grown on small unmechanized farms with the handwork of the entire family being necessary. Its production was highly speculative, varying yearly from a good profit to a severe loss for its growers.

Tobacco is a curious plant which grows in all types of soil and has been grown in virtually every state of the United States, but nearly 90 per cent of the country's acreage is found in five Southern states. This area is divided into three zones according to the nature of the tobacco, for changes in soil, as well as curing methods, cause the plant to develop variations in fragrance, color, structure, size of leaf, delicacy of fiber, and the like. Pale sandy soils grow a yellow leaf, red clay the heavy dark export tobacco, and limestone the white burley.

Northern Tennessee and western Kentucky produce the dark fire-cured tobacco popular in Europe; the Kentucky blue grass region is the source of white burley, an air-cured tobacco used chiefly for chewing; and the bright-leaf belt of coastal Florida, Georgia, and the Carolinas grow the light flue-cured tobacco used in cigarettes. The South grows, on the average, five-sixths of the tobacco produced in this country, with nearly half of it being exported, England, Germany, Italy, France, the Netherlands, and Spain in that order, being the principal markets.

As in the case of cotton, the Civil War brought changes to the industry. Since much of the war was fought in the heart of tobacco-land, every single state reported a smaller crop in 1870 than in 1860, output falling from 403,975,915 pounds to 227,139,646. The great fields of 100 to 500 acres occasionally seen in the pre-war years disappeared. Hard-pressed owners and tenants whose soil was unsuited for cotton cultivated small plots of one to four acres in an effort to get much-needed cash. Soon, about half of all tobacco was produced by tenants.

The increase in tobacco consumption in the United States was enormous after the Civil War — from 1.6 pounds (1861-1865) to 5.5 pounds (1901-1905) per person — and the European market grew rapidly, if less spectacularly. Much of this was the result of the growing popularity of the cigarette, made of bright-leaf tobacco. This variety had been discovered in 1852, when two brothers in the sand-hill area of North Carolina planted tobacco despite a neighbor's protest that it would not grow. The seed they used had produced dark heavy tobacco in Virginia, but in North Carolina the leaf was at first a golden yellow and finally lemon-colored, with a sweet aroma. It immediately brought a high price, but the war interrupted the experiment. Afterwards, everyone planted tobacco, quickly redeeming piedmont North Carolina with its wornout land. By the 1880's, bright-leaf had spread northward into Virginia and southward into Georgia. Following in this path came railroad construction, new trading centers and revival of old ones, and the economic rise which helped make North Carolina the most progressive state in the South. Demand for bright-leaf continued to mount, as per capita consumption of cigarettes grew from 32 to 2,607 per year between 1900 and 1951, a jump from two to 75 per cent of the total national tobacco consumption.

Tobacco farming is much more complicated than cotton; it also wears out the land and the men, women, and children engaged in it. Only three to six acres are planted, but the crop is expected to furnish nearly all the cash income. Because of the large degree of care and selectivity necessary, machinery is used for very few of the stages of production. Work begins in January or February with preparation and planting of the seed bed, usually on new soil. A field is prepared in April and then comes transplantation by hand. All of these steps fully occupy the farmer and his family from the time the young plant is moved in May until the final picking in September. Cultivation, usually requiring a field to be worked over six times, calls for more hand labor. The plants must be thinned and replanted, with almost constant hoeing and plowing to keep the weeds out and the plants upright. Inferior leaves and "suckers" have to be picked off to improve the quality of those remaining. Because most insecticides discolor the leaves or affect the taste, insects are sometimes also removed by hand. The selected leaves are picked as they reach maximum size, so the harvest begins in late July and continues into the middle of September. As the leaves are picked, they are taken to the curing barn to be heat-dried, a process which must be done with care, for changes in temperature can damage the leaf. After drying and preserving comes the process of sorting the leaves, tying them in bundles, and placing them on huge trays to be carried to the market. Unlike cotton, tobacco is taken to local warehouses where it is sold by auction.

Profits depend upon two variables, the weather and the market —

neither controllable by the farmer. Because of the great variation in quality, grading is the all-important factor. Cotton is graded by United States government standards, but tobacco is rated by the buyer according to his own mysterious standards. The same kind of tobacco does not serve for all types of tobacco products, and most are often-changed blends of several sorts. Cigarettes use 50 to 55 per cent flue-cured and 30 to 35 burley, pipe tobacco uses 25 to 30 per cent flue-cured and 40 to 50 burley, and so on. The buyer alone knows what he wants and what he will pay for it, thus having the farmer almost completely at his mercy. Tobacco which one year may have brought a good price may be unmarketable the next. This change in demand means change in methods of curing, types of plants, and areas suitable for cultivation. Until 1941 the average price per pound was usually below twenty cents, exceptions, such as a high of 43.8 cents in 1919, being rare.

Yields varied, with an average of 500 to 750 pounds per acre from 1866 to 1933, though later intensive cultivation produced over 1,000 pounds per acre. The cost of labor and fertilizer approximated $200 per acre. The landlord usually received one-fourth to one-third of the crop, but if the tenant had more than four acres in the crop, he was usually assisted by "croppers" who got half of what they produced, with the tenant getting a quarter and the landlord the remainder.

Rice culture underwent drastic changes after the Civil War. The pre-1860 production of the Carolina and Georgia coastlands had been based upon slave labor and tidal flows. Actual devastation came to many plantations, while disuse ruined others. Broken dikes admitted salt water, and weeds and bushes took over fields which once sold for as much as $300 an acre. Rice cultivation demanded more capital than did cotton, and the work was so distasteful that tenants who would work in the swamps were hard to find. Consequently, production dropped from 6,732,627 bushels in 1860 to 2,648,742 in 1870, and by 1900 it had declined in these three states to barely 1,000,000.

This area had to contend with many woes. New insect pests and diseases were joined by ruinous competition. In the 1880's, farmers from the northwestern wheat fields began to settle along the coast of Louisiana and Texas and, under the direction of Seaman A. Knapp, head of a large colonization experiment and later a representative of the United States Department of Agriculture, utilized wheat-farming techniques for rice production. Here a strip of coastal prairie was quickly transformed into the best rice-producing land in the world. Cultivation was based not on tidal flow but upon artesian wells, which gave a level, steady flow when needed and lacked the dangers of the former system. The area was far enough from the coast to be relatively free from storms but close enough to get the coastal rainfall and the warm and humid climate. More important, the fields were level, with a subsoil of clay which would hold water but when drained would dry quickly and support heavy machinery. This region, along with an area in Arkansas developed after 1909, transformed rice farming into an operation of highly mechanized, large-scale production, employing few tenants and using equipment adapted from that used in wheat farming.

Not only did this new area force the older rice fields out of contention, but it quickly dominated American production. The only big rice producer outside the South was California, which ranked second to Louisiana in 1919; by 1929 California had dropped to fourth place, behind Louisiana, Texas, and Arkansas, with a production of a little less than 5,000,000 bushels out of a total crop of 33,468,983. This Southern tri-state area not only produced more rice than the United States could consume, but the use of machinery and superior organization allowed one man to cultivate about one hundred times more land and produce sixty to seventy times as much rice as an Oriental farmer. A Texas rice farmer could have undersold Japanese rice in Japan had it not been for the tariff.

Another agricultural product influenced by tariffs, but this time the American tariff, is sugar. Sugar cane is a tropical plant which is grown in the semi-tropical area of southeastern Louisiana. Even there, its cultivation requires far more labor and must be replanted more often than in tropical sugar-producing regions. Cuba, for example, can produce sugar two or three times more cheaply than Louisiana. Without a protective tariff, the state could not compete.

Like the other crops, sugar, too, had a long antebellum history. Unlike them, however, only the wealthy could afford the business, as sugar-producing establishments ranged in value from $50,000 to $500,000 or more. The war temporarily destroyed the industry because of the grower's need for large gangs of laborers, and only in the 1890's did it

### SUGAR CANE PRODUCTION IN LOUISIANA

| | |
|---|---|
| 1861 | 235,856 tons |
| 1865 | 9,289 |
| 1870 | 75,369 |
| 1890 | 215,834 |
| 1900 | 270,338 |
| 1911 | 352,874 |
| 1930 | 208,000 |

reach pre-war production totals again. Expansion after 1870 was not from opening virgin areas but more basically because of improved cultivation methods and new seeds sponsored by the Sugar Planters' Association after its formation in 1877. The high crop in 1911 was grown on 310,000 acres, while by 1930 the output had stabilized at 208,000 tons from 171,000 acres.

Tenancy was unable to get a foothold in this empire, which demanded large investments in land and mills. Only large-scale production was profitable, and the risks were great. Profits not only depended upon the weather, frosts and storms being a particular menace, but, as mentioned, also upon the tariff policy of the United States. The large amount of manual labor needed, particularly at cutting time, was furnished by hired gangs, employed for that season alone from migratory workers or from the fishing and trapping population of the bayous. After the 1890's the industry faced its first home competition with the rise of the beet sugar farmers in the West. But even at its best, the Louisiana sugar producers could furnish only a fractional part of the demand of the American market.

The developing urban life in the last decades of the nineteenth century was the primary incentive for the agricultural diversification which took place in the post-bellum South. The Grange and other farm organizations had been preaching the need for change, capital had been slowly accumulated, and transportation facilities had been extended. Farmers also became aware of the growing city markets as a new opportunity for profit and, as Americans in general began to place more emphasis on fruits and vegetables in their diets, began turning their land into truck farms, orchards, and gardens. Not only did the South have the advantages of earlier growing seasons, but the older forms of Southern agriculture were depressed. The boll weevil was playing havoc with cotton. Migrating from Mexico, it crossed into Texas in 1892 and moved northward and eastward at a rate of forty to fifty miles a year. In its wake, the pest-infested fields were planted with vegetables, fruits, and other new crops and brought substantial profits.

Soon, steamers sailing out of Norfolk, Virginia, carried early vegetables to winter-bound Baltimore, Philadelphia, New York, and Boston. By 1889 the area within a ten-mile radius of Norfolk was producing three to four million dollars annually in truck produce. Railroads were quick to see the trend, and the six refrigerated cars extant in 1887 increased to 60,000 in 1901. Other regions of the South saw new opportunities, also. The first shipment of truck produce left New Bern, North Carolina, in 1887; the next year Charleston, South Carolina, sent its initial consignment, and a carload of oranges left Florida for the North. The Gulf Coast, like the Atlantic seaboard, soon entered the picture, and the whole coastal area from Delaware southward to the Rio Grande began exploiting its earlier growing seasons. With centers at

Norfolk, Wilmington, Charleston, Savannah, all of Florida, Mobile, east Texas, and the Rio Grande Valley, truck gardening by 1900 was producing an annual income of nearly $80,000,000 for the South. In 1930, Florida alone realized $33,998,000 from this source.

Generally, vegetable growing was done on small plots owned by the farmer. When additional labor was needed, it was hired. The production of these crops called for the most intensive type of culture, being chiefly "hand-and-knee" work. On a larger scale but closely related was the cultivation of fruit and peanuts. Georgia had 100,000 acres in watermelons by 1900, the piedmont sections of the Carolinas and Georgia were being planted with peach orchards, and apples became a major Virginia product. Peanuts became a primary source of income in northeastern North Carolina and Virginia; Twelve Southern states were producing 740,710,000 pounds annually by 1930. The little town of Enterprise, Alabama, where peanuts alone brought in as much money as cotton had formerly, indirectly praised the "goober" with a monument whose inscription read: "In Profound Appreciation of the Boll Weevil and What It Has Done as the Herald of Prosperity."

In spite of these variations, Southern agriculture in 1930 was still primarily what it had been before the Civil War — one-crop production of tobacco or cotton. A bad system of labor — slavery — had been exchanged for another unfortunate one — tenancy. Production of wheat and corn in the South increased after the war but not enough to maintain their pre-war percentages. Cotton and tobacco reigned supreme because they were in demand, and at least in the United States the South had a monopoly on their production. By tying their agricultural future to a single crop, Southern farm prosperity rose and fell with the fluctuations in the prices of cotton or tobacco. The farmers could not or would not change.

These two crops, however, had made it possible for the South to regain its feet economically. When the high post-Civil War prices inevitably skidded downward, the farmers of the region willingly joined the disgruntled agrarians of the West in the farm revolts of the 1880's and '90's. But the Spanish-American War spearheaded new prosperity, and between 1900 and 1910 the value of all farm property increased 110 per cent, while farm bankruptcies declined. However, the good times were not equally shared. During these years the landholders profited, but they were a minority. Tenants found that the soaring land prices made it harder and harder to become owners, and their number increased in this and following decades, as it had in every previous one. Eight Southern states in 1910 had a majority of their farms operated by sharecroppers, and the cotton belt contained half the tenant farmers of the nation.

The first World War brought unprecedented prosperity, especially to the cotton farmers, leading them into greater expansion and indebtedness. With the 1920's, however, this era collapsed. High cotton prices had encouraged foreign competition to enter the market. In 1920-21 the total yield of cotton outside the United States was 6,964,000 bales; by 1929-30 it was 11,535,000 and destined to climb. Concurrent with this rise was a drop in American cotton exports from 10,926,614 bales in 1927 to only 3,326,840 in 1939. Moreover, landowners saw their fields devastated by the boll weevil, forcing thousands of tenants and sharecroppers to migrate. Farm income fell almost twice as much as expenses; gross value of produce declined by two-thirds in many states. The average annual return per acre for all Southern cotton farms during 1920-27 was approximately $30, whereas the average in 1919 had been $60. Finally, much of the land on the older farms showed the inevitable effect of years of abuse. From one-fifth of the national income, the South paid three-fifths of the nation's fertilizer bill.

Mechanization, thought to be the salvation for the South, was not generally adopted. In 1920, for example, each South Dakota farm had farm implements and machinery worth an average of $1,500; the average equipment value per farm in the cotton belt was $215. Ten years later, it was still much the same. The East South Central states specifically could count only a single tractor for every 43.5 agricultural establishments.

### AVERAGE VALUE OF FARM EQUIPMENT, 1930

| Region | Tractors 1 for each | Trucks 1 for each |
|--------|---------------------|-------------------|
| South | 26.92 farms | 15.28 farms |
| New England | 8.85 | 3.29 |
| East North Central | 3.88 | 4.88 |
| West North Central | 3.49 | 6.15 |

Despite the lack of farm prosperity, the average Southerner in 1930 was a farmer. The total population of the region was approximately 31 per cent of the nation's and about 50 per cent of the farm population. On roughly one-third of the country's area were produced crops valued at nearly $3,200,000,000, or 37 per cent of the crop value of the United States. But in gross value of farm products per adult male worker, the South averaged scarcely half that for the rest of the nation.

Almost 80 per cent of all the farms in 1930 in eleven Southeastern states were smaller than 100 acres (more than half of the total number of farms of this size), and fewer than one per cent were larger than 500 acres. Most of the small plots were operated by tenants, 719,402 whites and 614,298 Negroes being in this category. At a time when one-third of the farms in the Middle and Northwestern states were run by tenants, 65 per cent of the farms in South Carolina, 68.2 in Georgia, 72.2 in Mississippi, 66.6 in Louisiana, 61.5 in Oklahoma, and 60.9 in Texas were tenant operated.

PERCENTAGES OF NATIONAL FARM OUTPUT FROM THE SOUTH IN 1930

| | | | |
|---|---|---|---|
| 1. | Cotton | 96 per cent | |
| 2. | Grapefruit | 96 | |
| 3. | Sweet Potatoes | 94 | |
| 4. | Tobacco | 87 | |
| 5. | Rice | 84 | |
| 6. | Strawberries | 37 | |
| 7. | Apples | 33 | |
| 8. | Corn | 29 | |
| 9. | Dairy Cattle | 25 | |
| 10. | Swine | 20 | |
| 11. | Sheep | 18 | |
| 12. | Beef Cattle | 9 | (excluding Texas and Oklahoma) |

The South had many natural advantages which were not used profitably. It had two-thirds of all the land receiving forty inches of annual rainfall or better and nearly half the land on which crops could be grown for six months without danger of frost. Yet, in comparison with the Middle West it had only a third as much first-quality land and a little more than half as much second-quality land. Sixty-one per cent of the nation's badly eroded land was in the South, and at least 22,000,000 acres were ruined beyond repair, with an estimated $300,000,000 worth of fertile topsoil continuing to be lost annually through erosion.

The credit-single-staple-tenancy-erosion cycle operated to produce poverty for most and economic insecurity for all. Howard Odum described the deficiencies of the South as including

> the lowest per capita farm income, the lowest income per worker, the lowest return per unit of horse power, the lowest ratio of income from livestock production, the lowest percentage of total sales coming from cooperative sales, the lowest per capita purebred livestock, the lowest production of milk and dairy products, a low ratio of pasture land, a low carrying capacity for pasture lands, and extraordinarily large drain from erosion and waste lands, a phenomenally high expenditure for commercial fertilizers, a low ranking in the various mechanical techniques of

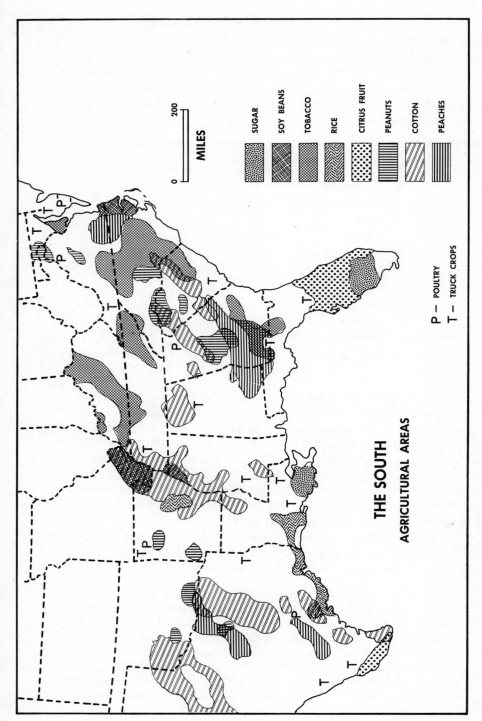

THE SOUTH

AGRICULTURAL AREAS

MILES

0 ____ 200

SUGAR

SOY BEANS

TOBACCO

RICE

CITRUS FRUIT

PEANUTS

COTTON

PEACHES

P – POULTRY

T – TRUCK CROPS

From Introductory Economic Geography by Klimm, Starkey, Russell and English, © 1937, 1940, © 1956 by Harcourt Brace & World, Inc. and reproduced with their permission.

farming and living, such as tractors, water, lights, telephones, and many others, in addition to deficiencies in health, literacy, education, and general cultural activities.[6]

Too much emphasis on plant production and the disregard of animal culture automatically created an economic disbalance. Southern farmers needed better business methods, along with the opportunity and incentive to take advantage of technological improvements. With few exceptions hoes, one-mule plows, and hand labor continued to be the hallmark of Southern agriculture. The Great Depression which hit the nation in 1929 was nothing new to the farmers of Dixie, for most of them had known little other than hard times.

[6] Howard W. Odum, *Southern Regions of the United States* (Chapel Hill: Univ. of North Carolina, 1936), p. 343.

# 8

## SOUTHERN INDUSTRIALIZATION BEFORE 1930

THE CROWNING GLORY of the Bourbon era was its sensational success in attracting manufacturing to the South. But the Redeemers could not claim full credit; for one thing, history had aided them. Their "New South" in terms of industrialization was not new in the true sense; they merely resurrected it. The region did not suddenly become industrial; it only became suddenly industrially articulate. As Professor Robert S. Cotterill has stated, "The beginning was not in manufacturing, but in publicity."

A few Southerners, such as James D. B. DeBow and George Fitzhugh, had long preached the blessings of industrialization and a diversified economy to relieve the hated colonial status of the South. Agricultural supremacy had yielded sufficiently by 1860 for Southern industry to employ 131,979 wage earners, occupy 15 per cent of the manufacturing establishments of the country, and produce approximately eight per cent, worth some $193,462,521, of the national total of such goods. But that this was not enough was quickly evident. Before the war was over, Southern armies were paralyzed for lack of equipment which the Northern armies possessed in abundance. Domestic shortages occa-

sioned by the blockade clinched the point. The almost inevitable reaction, once the war was over, was that the South had to imitate its
conquerors. Some, like Robert Toombs and Albert T. Bledsoe, refused
to admit that the pre-war agrarian tradition must give way, but these
links between the old and new were soon to be shoved aside and
quickly left behind.

Many factors tended to push the South toward this new way of
life. One was a labor surplus. Governor Robert M. Patton of Alabama,
writing in 1867 about the widows and orphans left by the war in his
state, noted that from this "unemployed and impoverished class of
women, boys, and girls there might be employed 20,000 or 25,000 efficient factory operatives. . . . The truth is, that the employment of this
large class of sufferers is a matter of pure necessity. Without it a large
portion of them will necessarily continue a charge upon the Public
Treasury."[1] Even the Southern Grangers felt the need to support manufacturing when it became obvious that agriculture could not use all the
available Negro and white labor without forcing the whites down, not
merely to economic equality with the Negro but to a standard lower
than either had previously known. Helping, also, to convince Southerners that manufacturing was not only a complementary but a superior
form of economic activity were the declining values of farm products.
Cotton dropped from $.23 a pound in 1868 to $.15 in 1870 to $.07 in
1878. Wheat fell from $2.18 a bushel to $.77 in the same period. In the
South of 1880, with less than eight per cent of the country's manufacturing wage earners, there was a correspondingly lower wealth distribution: $5,725,000 of the $47,642,000 in estimated true valuation of
property in the United States; $375 per capita wealth against $1,086
elsewhere.

Consequently, by the 1880's the industrial road to wealth had become almost a religious crusade. The "New South" was a Mecca for
those who believed in the development of manufacturing and diversified farming rather than in the old one-staple economy. This was purely
a Southern development, not one brought in from the North. Viewing
the drive for factories as a means to provide employment and thus
escape competition with the Negroes, energetic citizens of all classes
joined the campaign to raise capital. Many enterprises had hundreds of
small shareholders. In the Carolinas, camp meetings spread the religion
of industry along with the religion of Christ, as for example the revivalist in Salisbury, North Carolina, who told his listeners that "next to the
grace of God, what Salisbury needs is a cotton mill!" Though profits
were promised, the factories were viewed not so much as businesses

[1] Robert M. Patton, "The New Era of Southern Manufactures," *De Bow's Review,*
III (January, 1867), p. 65.

but as social enterprises. In the words of Gerald W. Johnson, "People were urged to take stock . . . for the town's sake, for the poor people's sake, for the South's sake, literally for God's sake." Another observer wrote, "Every little town wanted a mill; if it couldn't get a big one, it would take a small one." As the fire of enthusiasm spread, mills were built without any investigation of the adequateness of the location; only rarely were they managed by men with business experience, but instead by doctors, lawyers, teachers, planters, and even clergymen.

Even the Northern press began to point out the business opportunities in the South, and books appeared entitled *How to Get Rich in the South* and *The Road to Wealth Leads through the South.* But there was no stampede. While there was little Northern hostility to building up the South economically, there was skepticism over the chances of success, and not until around the Panic of 1893 did Northern capital go south for investment. Money was safer in the booming Northern industry, or the Western cattle ranches, farms, and mines seemed more attractive. Only when Northerners could profit through cooperation with the South did they cooperate. Thus those Southerners who hoped that help would come to them were temporarily disappointed. In the long run, this was probably a fortunate thing for Southern morale, for from the war until the 1890's the region was forced to rely mainly on its own resources and do it alone.

Myriad were the Southerners who goaded the people and politicians of the South to act. Among the earliest was Francis W. Dawson, an Englishman who had joined the Confederate Navy and remained as the influential editor of the Charleston, South Carolina, *News and Courier.* He argued that the war had taught three things: that slavery had been the cause of all pre-war ills, that the Southerner could not live by cotton alone, and that the great significance of the war was that it had emancipated the white man from slavery and cotton. Now there was no longer any reason for poor schools, unstable wealth, prejudice against industry, or the practices of too little manufacturing, wasteful farming, and the absorption of all energy and capital by cotton and slavery. Henceforth the new Southerner should be less interested in tradition and honor and more in material things. The region would focus its brains and brawn toward improving the land, bettering schools, extending railroads, and encouraging manufacturing. Not only would mill towns provide many jobs which were preferable to agriculture, but also the booming industrial cities would furnish markets for the farmers' food crops.

A better-known prophet was Henry W. Grady. Descended from antebellum tradesman stock and having married into a pioneer cotton-manufacturing family, Grady, editor of the Atlanta *Constitution,* did

not, in the words of one of his contemporaries, "tamely promote enterprise and encourage industry; he vehemently fomented enterprise and
provoked industry until they stalked through the land like armed conquerors." Grady loved to tell Southern audiences of a funeral he had
once attended of a "poor one-gallus fellow." Though he was buried in
the heart of a pine forest, his pine coffin was imported from Cincinnati;
although interred within touch of an iron mine, the nails in his coffin
and the shovel came from Pittsburgh. Even though he had grown cotton all his life, the deceased was buried in a New York coat, Boston
shoes, Chicago trousers, and a Cincinnati shirt. After he ennumerated
the other ingredients used at the event, Grady's clincher was that the
"South didn't furnish a thing on earth for that funeral but the corpse
and the hole in the ground!" On the other hand, he bragged to the
North that, "We have let economy take root and spread among us . . .
until we are ready to lay odds on the Georgia Yankee . . . against any
downeaster that ever swapped nutmegs for flannel sausages in the
Valley of Vermont."

Other men of vision and enthusiasm included Walter Hines Page,
Daniel A. Tompkins, and Richard H. Edmonds. Tompkins, a manufacturer himself, and Edmonds, editor of the *Manufacturers' Record,*
added their own embellishment to the industrial gospel — that the
"New South" was not a departure but actually in harmony with the
best traditions of the region. Edmonds pointed to the amount of manufacturing and mechanical skill in the Old South. Tompkins pictured the
pre-cotton period as a golden age when Southern manufactures had
been more prosperous than those of any other section and its people
more mechanically inclined. All this, by their account, had been ruined
by the rejuvenation of slavery. But the war had ended that problem,
and the South was free once more to travel the road to happiness and
prosperity. Industry was just a good old Southern custom, and its supporters were patriots working in loyalty to the past.

The most spectacular success of these crusaders lay in their efforts
to "bring the cotton mills to the cotton fields," an industry with roots
which went far back into Southern history. The new mills were located
on the Piedmont crescent, running from Lynchburg, Virginia, southward to Georgia and westward to northern Alabama. There the growing season and soil favored cotton, and many mills were located in the
fields. Land was cheap, with plenty of room for expansion and space
for gardens and the like. The area was bound on the west by the in-
accessible Blue Ridge Mountains and on the east by the Coastal and
Gulf plains. It had an abundance of water power and easy access to
transportation. Cotton could come up the rivers from the black belt,
and the Southern Railroad ran along the Piedmont from Birmingham

to Washington, where it joined with the Pennsylvania Railroad to reach Northern markets, while interconnecting lines gave access to the rest of the country. The Piedmont, also, was close to the coal fields of West Virginia to the north and of Alabama and Tennessee to the south, meaning cheap steam power when it was necessary.

As already noted, the agriculture of the area was not progressive, with a great deal of tenancy and little cash income. Mill jobs which paid cash were therefore very attractive and could tap an almost inexhaustible supply of cheap labor — the mountaineers to the west and white tenants to the east. The warm climate and abundant local timber meant that houses and factories could be inexpensively constructed and maintained and that work could continue the year round.

The textile industry also benefited from a favorable political climate and the fact that falling agricultural prices meant less competition for capital. New markets for cotton cloth were developing; the Orient wanted cheap cloth, and this the South could produce. Also at this time, new inventions in the manufacturing process had reduced to a minimum the amount of skill necessary to produce inexpensive and medium quality cloth. Almost the only skilled men needed were foremen and repairmen, and these could be brought in from the North if necessary. Better still, the price of cotton manufacturing machinery was declining. As Northern machinery companies expanded, they had surpluses on hand and were eager to sell even on liberal, long-term credit arrangements.

Leadership in the rising textile industry was supplied by a group similar to men active in other manufacturing fields. A study of 300 Southern industrialists showed that about 80 per cent of them came from non-slaveholding parents, and only 13 per cent were Northern by birth, about half of whom had moved south before the war. Typical cotton-mill success stories were those of Henry P. Hammett, George A. Gray, and Daniel A. Tompkins. Hammett (1822-1899) was of yeoman ancestry, born in North Carolina. As a youth he went to Augusta, Georgia, to work in a cotton broker's office. This experience led to a position as business manager, buying cotton and selling cloth, for the Batesville mill in South Carolina, one of the leading pre-war mills in the South. He married Bates' daughter, inherited the establishment, which he sold in 1863, and began speculating in railroads. But textiles remained his first love. In 1873 he organized the Piedmont Manufacturing Company, capitalized at $200,000, but was struck by the Panic of that year. With a loan from a Northern machinery manufacturer he was able to pull through, and by 1890 he had three mills. He originally made sheeting, but as he prospered he found it easier to get Northern money and began to make better grades of cloth, build more mills, and add more spindles. His labor consisted of poor whites under Northern supervisors, and his buildings and villages became models for other mills, while his plants served as training schools for future owners and managers.

Younger than Hammett was George Gray (1851-1912). His father had been a farmer who gave up agriculture in 1853 to become an ordinary worker in a cotton mill. The father died in 1859, leaving a large family, and eight-year-old George went to work, earning ten cents a day for a twelve- to fourteen-hour stint sweeping out the factory. His only schooling was for one year, when a badly mangled arm prevented his working in the mill. But he was a natural mechanic and soon attracted attention by improvements which he made in the machinery. Gray worked his way up to superintendent of the mill and became recognized as an authority on textile machinery, one who would install equipment and oversee the beginning operations of factories for others. In 1888 he set up for himself the Gastonia Cotton Manufacturing Company at Gastonia, North Carolina, and soon made it an important center. By 1907 he had about a half dozen plants of his own but continued to help others establish factories in North Carolina, South Carolina, and Georgia. He was always the first to make use of new and improved machinery and was an early user of hydroelectric power.

Different in origin was Daniel Augustus Tompkins (1851-1914), born on a cotton plantation at Edgefield, South Carolina. His family survived the war without being impoverished, and so, after attending the University of South Carolina, he went to Rensselaer Polytechnic Institute in New York to study engineering. After graduating in 1873, he went to work for the Bethlehem Iron Company. Nine years later he moved to Charlotte, North Carolina, going to work as an engineer, machinist, industrial contractor, and "industrial missionary." His specialties were advising on construction of all types of plants and using his Northern connections to raise money. He was an excellent promoter, adept at selling the idea of a mill, and his various skills, to a community. He was also one of the first to stress the possibility of exploiting the by-products of cotton manufacturing, especially cottonseed oil. He became chief owner and president of three large mills, director of eight, and a stockholder in many more. He also owned three newspapers and wrote numerous pamphlets and articles on the necessity of industrialization.

Although expansion had become a symbol in virtually every field, it was most notable in textiles. These mills often differed little in organization from the plantation. Often they lay outside the town limits and jurisdiction. The owners built private villages on their own land, controlled the stores, provided the schools and churches, hired the

teachers, ministers, and police, and in general furnished the same paternalistic oversight which had characterized the plantation. Negroes
got almost no chance to work in the textile factories. This was justified
by the abundance of white labor and the belief that the two races could
not be worked together; to have white women working on the same
premises as Negroes was viewed as especially objectionable. Unspoken,
but probably more important, was the desire to reassure investors, including Northerners, that racial peace would not be broken nor profits
interrupted by interracial factory friction. Segregation would also assure white operatives a greatly desired economic and social superiority,
while leaving both groups to be exploited with impunity.

The number of textile mills mounted steadily, from 161 in 1880 to
239 in 1890 and 400 in 1900. Many of these were equipped with more
modern machinery than their competitors in the North. In the same
two decades, the total number of operatives rose from 16,741 to 97,559,
and capital investment from $17,375,897 to $124,596,874. In the 1880's,
profits of 20 per cent were average, and a return even as high as 75
per cent was not unknown. These facts were reflected in the region's
standing in national statistics bearing upon the number of spindles, a
measure of productive capacity. The decade of the 1890's marked the
beginning of Northern mill migrations to the South, and if only active
spindles were counted, the figures would be even more in the South's
favor: 53 per cent in 1920; 72 in 1930.

SOUTHERN PERCENTAGE OF SPINDLES IN THE UNITED STATES

| Year | Percentage |
|------|------------|
| 1840 | 7.0 |
| 1860 | 6.0 |
| 1870 | 4.5 |
| 1880 | 5.0 |
| 1890 | 11.0 |
| 1900 | 23.0 |
| 1910 | 39.0* |
| 1920 | 43.0 |
| 1930 | 60.0 |

* This total represented more spindles than the entire country had in 1880.

The decrease in Northern mills was simply because they had been
unable to equal the abundance and cheapness of the Southern labor
supply. The workers were easily trained and were not inefficient, despite the common legend of Southern laziness. Most of them were from
farm families who were accustomed to low standards of living, poor

diet, long hours, low income, and all members of the family having to work. They were old American stock, who were forced to the mills by the declining condition of agriculture. Some were tenants who moved to escape Negro competition; others were Appalachian mountaineers. These people found the mill villages attractive, and they worked willingly. They felt themselves to be much better off than farm laborers: they could work in the shade, had better living conditions, company, and amusements, and were paid in cash. Accustomed as they were to economic repression, it is not surprising that most complaints about their condition originated from outside the region.

Though wages were low, they included the right to live in a mill house free or for a dollar or so a week, often with the privilege of garden space, room for livestock, and free utilities. Cash wages ranged from twenty cents a day for bobbin boys, through forty to sixty cents for spinners, up to seventy cents to a dollar for weavers. North Carolina's average annual mill wages in 1929 were from a low of $698 at Salisbury to a high of $1,028 in Charlotte. Although it was no abundant life, it was better than that to which most of the workers had been accustomed and an improvement over slum life in the cities.

The advantage of Southern mill owners becomes quite apparent through statistics. In 1900 Massachusetts' cost of labor per yard of cloth was 200 per cent higher than in South Carolina, 190 in North Carolina, and 170 in Georgia. Hours were also longer in the South. In 1890 Massachusetts had an average 60-hour week, compared to 66 in Alabama and 68 in North Carolina. Even by 1928, Massachusetts had an average week of 49 hours compared, for example, to 56 in North Carolina and 55 in South Carolina. Not even the advent of protective labor legislation did much to end the difference, because the Southern states were the last to be affected, and their laws were weaker and enforcement poorer. To be successful, unions had to have a class consciousness and a solidarity which could come only from a stable labor force. Southern labor was too fluid and content, and unions had to wait until the New Deal era before making progress south of the Potomac.

Before the first World War, Southern mill owners generally left weaving of the finer fabrics to the North, although some variations occurred among the states, with North Carolina making better goods than Georgia and Alabama because of more skilled labor. There was a great demand for cheaper goods, plus the advantage of less competition from other fabrics which rivaled fine cotton. The asset of being located in the cotton fields did not prove too vital, because most of the marketing centers were still in the North, and New England enjoyed an advantage in freight rates.

After the war the trend in Southern textiles was toward merger of existing mills and construction of larger factories to meet the growing competition from the Far East. Production of finer fabrics increased for the same reason. Northern migration into the Southern textile field, which had begun in the 1890's, became a steady stream. Usually a Southern branch was first opened and the Northern plants abandoned altogether as they wore out. Deeper and ever deeper into the South they came, looking for cheap labor. By 1930, even though the South was still an agricultural region, it not only had taken over textile supremacy from New England, but Kannapolis, North Carolina, could boast the largest towel mills in the world, Durham the largest hosiery mills, and Greensboro the largest denim and the largest men's knit underwear factories. The value of cotton manufactures, almost $1,000,000,000, was double that of New England, and the cotton-growing states had about 60 per cent of the cotton mill workers.

Coincident with the development of the textile industry was the utilization of cottonseed. This by-product was viewed variously as trash in 1860, fertilizer in 1870, cattle feed in 1880, and table food in 1890. When it was realized that the seeds were rich in oil, chemists made from them cheap substitutes for such expensive items as olive oil, lard, and butter. They soon were furnishing the basic ingredient in soap, cosmetics, and other oil-based products. The crushed seeds, after the oil was removed, were still rich in nitrogen and could be turned into fertilizer or pressed into oil-cake and fed to cattle. By 1880 forty-five mills were producing some 7,000,000 gallons of cottonseed oil for export alone. Northern capitalists and consumers once more became interested, and in 1884 the American Cotton Oil Trust, controlling 88 per cent of American production, was formed. By 1900, Texas and Georgia ranked first and second in an industry of 353 factories, which by 1914 was producing over $200,000,000 in products.

Cottonseed alone could not furnish all of the fertilizer needed by the farms of the South. The commercial chemical fertilizer industry in the United States had its Southern origin in Baltimore in 1853, based upon imported materials. The discovery of phosphate rock in South Carolina, Florida, and Tennessee changed this, and the three states took the lead in phosphate production. The construction by the federal government during World War I of two nitrate plants at Muscle Shoals in Alabama gave the region a great potential in that important ingredient of fertilizer, although it was not capitalized upon until after 1932. Nevertheless, by 1930 the South was producing and consuming well over half of the nation's fertilizer.

Paralleling in many ways the exploitation of cotton was the rise of the tobacco industry. It, too, had a pre-war background, was based upon a major staple, used local labor, and was begun on a small scale with local capital. This industry, however, enjoyed certain advantages denied the textile mills. It had competition from no well-established producers, there being only scattered small cigar, snuff, and chewing tobacco factories. The tremendous development in tobacco was the result of the post-war demand for a new product, cigarettes; the cigarette rolling machine, was invented in 1880 by a Southerner, James A. Bonsack, and was available to the South from the beginning. The greatest advantage of all was that tobacco products had a steadily increasing demand. The United States was the largest market, the world market being small by comparison. In the forty years after the Civil War, the national per capita consumption increased 267 per cent, from 1.5 pounds in 1860 to 3.2 pounds in 1870, 4.5 in 1890, and 5.5 in 1900. It continued to rise after that. There was more money spent in 1900 on tobacco than on men's clothing, boots, shoes, and the like, and in 1947, citizens of Oklahoma spent more for cigarettes than on any item in the school budget except salaries. It was one industry which was not seriously hurt by depressions.

In 1859 the Virginia-North Carolina area had manufactured 61 per cent of the country's smoking and chewing tobacco. During the Civil War, Northern soldiers grew accustomed to Southern brands and, after Appomattox, wrote back for more to the towns where they had been stationed. Enterprising Southerners, such as Washington Duke, took advantage of the opportunity to expand their markets. Duke, a North Carolina anti-slavery farmer who served in Lee's army, returned from the war to find his farm in ruins except for a barn of bright-leaf tobacco. He and his son, James Buchanan Duke, therefore began peddling their own brand of smoking tobacco known as "Duke's Mixture."

The revolution in the methods of tobacco processing and the shift in public taste to cigarettes gave young Southerners like Duke, William T. Blackwell, James R. Day, Julian S. Carr, and Richard J. Reynolds an unprecedented opportunity. Reynolds opened his first factory in 1875 with a capital of $7,500. Like many sons of the New South, Duke passed up a liberal arts education and went north to business college; he returned to Durham determined to emulate his model, John D. Rockefeller, and began manufacture of cigarettes in 1881.

Not only did Duke decide to go into cigarettes, but he also determined to dominate the whole industry. As Southern men tended to view them as effeminate, three years later he decided to try for the Northern market. He undertook a nation-wide sales campaign and hired Russian Jews to teach his Negro workers the best techniques. (Like the coal and iron industry, but unlike textile mills, blacks were widely used in tobacco factories. Most of the work there called for little skill, they would work for less, and whites objected to the heat and odors in the factories.) It soon became obvious that mechanization was the key to competition and production. Cigar making was the slowest to yield to this process. Because of the necessity for leaf selection, machinery was used only in cheap cigars, where this feature could be ignored; the best cigars were handmade and tended to be produced in small plants scattered from Florida to New York and catering to their local markets. In other types of tobacco manufacturing, machinery superseded skilled labor almost from the time of its introduction and drastically reduced the need for crude labor. By 1905 only five per cent of the cost of production was due to labor.

The period of the 1880's saw a tobacco war in which domination and survival were decided. As some plants became larger, pressure built up on the smaller. More extensive advertising of the better-established brands took away much of the small producers' trade, forcing production cut-backs. Their best helpers left to secure more regular employment; the farmers often found it more profitable to sell their choicest tobacco to the larger firms; and the railroads often gave the bigger producers special rates.

James Duke, by 1890 a devout Bourbon, now combined the five largest plants into the American Tobacco Company, capitalized at $25,000,000 and chartered in New Jersey. This was a period of cut-throat competition. Duke secured exclusive rights to the use of the Bonsack cigarette-making machines, the best then available, putting him in position to control that aspect of the industry. Two things prevented Duke from achieving a complete monopoly: he could not control the distribution of other cigarette-making machinery or buy all the tobacco sold. His dominance, however, did allow him to set the selling price for the field, a weapon he used with great success against independents. Those that he could not force out, he bought out and formed into allied companies (Liggett & Myers, 1899). As a result, the number of tobacco factories in North Carolina, for example, declined from 253 in 1894 to 33 in 1914.

In 1901 the Duke interests were put under a large holding company, the Consolidated Tobacco Company, and efforts were begun to monopolize fields other than cigarettes. A company was organized to buy up cigar manufacturers. Cuba was invaded in 1902 to end competition there, and by 1908, control of half the cigar production of that country was achieved. Simultaneously, the trust organized the United Cigar Stores as a chain-store system to sell its products. The trust had 150 factories by 1904 and controlled 90 per cent of the American tobacco industry and 40 to 60 per cent of the foreign. In that year all of these companies and the holding company were combined into the American Tobacco Company, capitalized at $300,000,000, a figure which was later almost doubled. This giant managed by 1906 nearly 100 per cent of the stogie trade, 96 per cent of the snuff, 82 per cent of the cigarette, 82 per cent of the plug, 81 per cent of the fine cut, and 71 per cent of the smoking tobacco, as well as purchasing 80 per cent of the total Southern tobacco sold for domestic consumption, a fact on which farmers blamed the low prices received. There might have been some question as to whether the South was spiritually back in the Union, but at least one of the most complete trusts in the great trust era existed there.

The supremacy of the American Tobacco Company came not from the usual methods of freight rebates or monopoly control of the basic raw material but from the economies of large-scale production and ruthless tactics in competition. The very size of its working capital enabled it to force competitors to sell out at ruinously low prices. Very commonly, it would undersell a small rival in his own local area while keeping prices up elsewhere. In 1901 the trust actually priced cigarettes for less than the revenue tax on them. Jobbers were given rebates if they would push trust products. Cheap imitations of competitive brands were sold at reduced prices; coupons which amounted to a 10 per cent rebate were placed on packages of trust goods. The United Cigar Stores naturally gave all possible advantage to its parent's products. On occasion, the American Tobacco Company was able to corner the market on constituents of cigarettes such as glycerin, sugar, and licorice, additives which made up 75 per cent by weight of the finished product. The public taste, after becoming accustomed to these flavors, demanded them, and thus prohibitive prices could be charged for them by the trust.

While never 100 per cent dominant, the trust did attain a very high degree of control and kept competition from rising above a very low point. The Progressive era brought the American Tobacco Company under attack along with its Northern counterparts, and in 1911 a unanimous decision of the Supreme Court ordered it dissolved. When finally broken up, the company did not, however, become a host of small ones but an oligarchy — a few great concerns which used essentially the same tobacco and the same curing and manufacturing processes. Markets were primarily created by fictitious or assumed advantages built up with advertising. After the split, the big four were the American Tobacco Company, R. J. Reynolds, Liggett & Meyers, and P. Lorillard. Two other companies specialized in buying for the foreign trade: the Imperial Tobacco Company and the Export Tobacco Company. This concentration of buying power is without parallel in the history of the United States. This also meant concentration of productive facilities, 80 per cent of all tobacco products being manufactured in only eight cities, mostly Southern; in 1929 Winston-Salem had the largest tobacco factories in the world, and North Carolina produced nearly half the nation's total.

Scarcely less impressive than the developments in textiles and tobacco were those in the iron and coal industry. The existence of rich coal and iron deposits in the Southern mountains was known long before the Civil War, but comparatively little effort at exploitation was made. When development came, the iron industry, like textiles, was concentrated in a well-defined area — the Birmingham-Chattanooga district of northern Alabama and eastern Tennessee. In the 1870's, a group of enterprising pioneers from both North and South, operating usually with Northern or foreign capital, began work in the area. The first pig iron was made in Birmingham in 1876, and three years later the Pratt mines of coking coal were opened, events destined to create the future "Pittsburgh of the South." Birmingham had been founded in 1871 at the junction of two railway lines and in 1880 was a town of only 3,000 inhabitants. At approximately the same time, an English syndicate opened its first furnace in Tennessee, but the Alabama town developed more spectacularly, spurred on by the Louisville & Nashville Railroad, whose stock was also mostly owned by foreigners.

Nature had been especially kind to the area, depositing in close proximity the three major ingredients needed for iron-making: coal, iron ore, and limestone. As early as 1883, Northern producers discovered that foundry iron could be made more cheaply in the South than in Pennsylvania and Ohio, and Southern pig iron was shipped regularly to Northern mills. By the end of that decade, the South was producing far more pig iron than the whole nation had produced before the Civil War. Northern manufacturers began negotiating in earnest for furnace properties. In August, 1890, of thirty-six furnaces under construction in the United States, twenty-five were in the South.

The only problem facing the region was that its product was not chemically adaptable to the contemporary processes for making steel. But new techniques soon removed this difficulty, and in 1888 Birmingham put its first ton of steel through the furnaces. Between 1880 and 1890, the city's population jumped to 26,000, and production of iron and steel increased ten times, more than twice the combined output of her nearest Southern rivals, Tennessee and Virginia.

By the turn of the century, the South was producing 1,965,000 tons of pig iron, compared to 212,000 twenty years earlier, and employing about one-fifth of the total workers in the nation's blast furnaces. Birmingham ranked fifth in production of iron and steel. Northern infiltration was accented by the United States Steel Corporation's purchase in 1907 of the Tennessee Coal, Iron and Railroad Company, the chief operator in the Birmingham area, at a time when 70 per cent of all iron smelted in the South was produced there. Birmingham had a population of nearly 260,000 by 1930, and the South had raised its output of iron to 4,480,000 tons.

Coal mining also came into prominence. Before the Civil War, it had been limited chiefly to Maryland, western Virginia, and Kentucky, although beds had been found in other states. The initiative of Southerners and the demands of Northern industry guaranteed that this vast resource was soon to be exploited. Alabama quickly became an important source for the iron foundries and by 1875 was producing 67,200 tons. The first modern methods of exploitation of the bituminous coal beds were introduced in the 1880's, while new railroads simultaneously opened up these areas to the markets of the world. Between 1880 and 1890, Southern coal output spurted from 6,000,000 to 26,000,000 tons and ten years later reached 50,000,000. (At the same time Alabama ranked second nationally in production of coke.) Over 202,000,000 tons were mined annually by 1930. In the twentieth century, West Virginia and Alabama remained the primary centers, followed by Tennessee, Virginia, and Kentucky, with smaller deposits in Arkansas, Oklahoma, and Texas.

Less spectacular, but still important to the total picture, was the role played by other Southern minerals. Operations on seams of copper near Ducktown, Tennessee, which had supplied the Confederacy, were expanded in the 1880's, and Pennsylvania entrepreneurs opened mines on the Virginia-North Carolina border. Arkansas became the only state to produce diamonds, while Georgia, North Carolina, and Texas were minor producers of gold and silver. The Gulf Coast area developed into a major source of sulphur after discovery of a new extraction process in 1903. Granite and marble from Georgia and Tennessee were soon competing with the best offered by New England's quarries. Production of long-used lead mines was stepped up, and new metals, such as manganese, came into importance. Mineral clays became the basis of a growing pottery industry, and local sources of cement, stone, and gravel made possible the good roads program undertaken in the 1920's by most Southern states. All in all, by 1930 the South was responsible for a fourth of the mineral output of the United States.

Another obvious opportunity for wealth was the tremendous forest resources of the South, over 60 per cent of the nation's total. Lumbering took on added status with the disappearance of Northern timber sources, and soon Southern yellow pine was competing strongly with the white pine and hemlock of the Northwest. Lumber production rocketed, doubling between 1880 and 1890, and led to the most ruthless destruction of forests known in history. Southerners, Northerners, and foreigners took advantage of relaxed land laws and the newly released federal lands to acquire large holdings. One English firm bought 2,000,000 acres in Florida; another purchased 4,500,000 acres in Texas. By 1895 the South furnished over seven billion board feet of pine, five hundred million of cyprus, and over three billion of hardwood, leading the nation in total production. The greatest advance, however, came after 1900, when lumbering was the largest industry in the region, employing one of every three wage earners and producing half the nation's total. By World War I, however, abuse and bad logging practices had taken their toll, and production began to slump, although in 1930 the South could still claim 47 per cent of the total.

Far too often, Southerners contented themselves with the mere sale of lumber. However, manufacture of cyprus shingles was carried on in Alabama, Louisiana, North Carolina, and Arkansas. Southern hardwoods proved easily adaptable for furniture making, and this industry began in High Point, North Carolina, in 1888; by the turn of the century, that town was threatening Grand Rapids, Michigan, as the furniture capital of the nation. By 1928 North Carolina surpassed all other states in production of lumber used to manufacture furniture, and the South produced one-third of such equipment. The ancient naval stores industry, long a virtual Southern monopoly (17,565,000 gallons of turpentine in 1880), remained so through development of new techniques and migration into more southerly regions. By 1930, it contributed around $40,000,000 a year to the region's wealth.

Power resources were not overlooked either. A natural advantage of the region was its abundance of water power. Hydroelectric power and its auxiliary, steam-electric power, were first successfully introduced into the North in 1882. About five years later, it made its way into the South, and the first electrically-driven cotton mill opened in Columbia, South Carolina, in 1894. Afterwards, electricity not only swept the textile industry but spread through other types of manufacturing as well. James Buchanan Duke very quickly realized the potentials, and his Duke Power Company was supplying electricity to one-third of the spindles of the South by the 1920's. North Carolina, Alabama, and South Carolina ranked third, fourth, and sixth in the nation in water power development in 1930. By that time the South had a generating capacity of 5,460,000,000 kilowatts, or 17 per cent of the total electric power of the United States. With the exception of Duke's holdings, most of the Southern power companies were under control of large non-Southern holding companies.

The search for oil spread into the South shortly after the Drake discovery in Pennsylvania in 1859. It was a slow beginning, with West Virginia producing 120,000 barrels in 1876 and Texas only forty-eight in 1889. In this interval small finds had also been made in Kentucky and Tennessee. All of that was changed magnificently, however, on January 10, 1901, with the discovery at Spindletop, near Beaumont, Texas, of one of the greatest gushers of all times. Oil fever quickly raced over adjoining states,[2] and strikes followed in quick succession in Oklahoma and Louisiana. By 1908 the South was producing 75,908,329 barrels, with Texas contributing eleven million, Oklahoma forty-five, and Louisiana almost seven. Production had reached such proportions by 1927 that the market was glutted, and the governors of Texas and Oklahoma called out their militias in an effort to close down production until a fair price could be reached. By 1930 the Southwest was the greatest oil-producing area in the United States, and its 150 oil refineries processed about 40 per cent of the nation's crude petroleum.[3]

Of equal and vital importance in the progress made in industrialization was the railroad development which took place. The war had left in virtual ruin the 10,000 miles of track in the South. During reconstruction, while the railroads had been the plaything of the carpetbaggers, some two or three thousand additional miles of track were laid. Northern and foreign capital hesitated about entering other forms of Southern industry, but the railroads were a potent lure. State governments not only gave favorable tax considerations, but some aided with land grants, Texas alone giving 32,400,000 acres to some twelve lines. In the 1870's, Southern mileage east of the Mississippi River increased 24.9 per cent, while at the same time a ruthless railroad war to integrate and consolidate the lines was inaugurated in both the North and South. Railroad "pools" to avoid rate cutting, such as the agreement of twenty-five companies in 1875 to fix uniform rates and apportion profits, became common.

The real railroad boom got underway in 1879, when twice as much mileage was laid as had been in any preceding year. Within the next two years, over $150,000,000 was invested by outside capital; some 180 new companies opened their lines in the Southeast in the 1880's. The Interstate Commerce Act of 1887 outlawed the pools which had given stability to Southern railroads, and the efforts of the agrarian-dominated state legislatures to regulate rates added to the confusion. This led to a period of rate cutting and further consolidation, all the more bitter because mileage far exceeded traffic potential. The Panic of 1893 hit Southern lines hard and furnished further opportunities for strengthening Northern control by such as J. P. Morgan, the Belmonts, and the

[2] For an example of "oil fever" in another Southern state, see John S. Ezell, "Mississippi's Search for Oil," *Journal of Southern History*, XVIII (August, 1952), pp. 320-342.
[3] Carl Coke Rister, *Oil! Titan of the Southwest* (Norman: Univ. of Oklahoma, 1949).

"Pennsylvania Group." In 1900 only two major lines were free of Northern financial domination. By 1930 the South had 82,000 miles of track, or one-third of the nation's total, as well-supplied in that regard as any other region. The only real ground for complaint was a differential in freight rates. Southern roads from the beginning charged higher rates per mile than Northern on the basis of sparse population and seasonal and one-way traffic. This had the approval of the Interstate Commerce Commission, despite the resultant handicap to Southern manufacturers.

Despite such obstacles, however, the progress of Southern industrialization was little short of a miracle. Between 1880 and 1900, the number of wage earners and the value of manufactured products increased about threefold, from some 209,000 to almost 600,000 and from $315,000,000 to $953,000,000, respectively. The South's proportion of the nation's wage earners advanced from eight to thirteen per cent and the value of manufactures from six to eight per cent.[4] During this period Benjamin H. Hill of Georgia wrote exuberantly: "Our taxes were scarcely ever so low. Our credit was never so high. Capital and people and machinery are flowing in, and everybody is brushing away the tears of war, and laughing with a new hope in a new era!" Another contemporary showed the full extent to which the philosophy of the New South had triumphed when he noted that "the nonsense that it is beneath the dignity of any man or woman to work for a living is pretty much eliminated from the Southern mind."

Except for the period between 1909 and 1919, the South developed steadily in the early twentieth century. By 1929 the value of its manufactured products was 11.7 per cent of the national total; more than

SOUTHERN INDUSTRIAL WAGE EARNERS — 1929

|  | Percentage of South's | Percentage of National Total |
|---|---|---|
| South | 100 | 15.1 |
| North Carolina | 16 | |
| Georgia | 12 | |
| Texas | 10 | |
| Oklahoma | Less than 4.0 | |
| Arkansas | "    "    " | |
| Mississippi | "    "    " | |

one-sixth of the nation's manufacturing establishments were in that region, as were a seventh of the production workers, who were paid ap-

[4] U. S. Department of Labor, Bureau of Labor Statistics, Bulletin 898, *Labor in the South* (Washington, 1947), p. 6.

proximately one-tenth of the nation's manufacturing wages. The textile industry, including spinning and weaving, was first in importance, followed by lumber and food manufacturing — these three accounting for about half the area's total industrial employment. On the eve of the great depression, the South had 35,570 industrial establishments employing a total of 1,338,131 people for wages of $1,182,000,000.[5]

Except for wages, however, a great part of the wealth created by the industrial boom left the South. Although in 1892 Georgia claimed eleven millionaires, Kentucky had twenty-four, and New Orleans alone boasted thirty-five, the dream of a wealthy class to rival the industrial barons of the North largely went unfulfilled. In 1926, for example, the proportion of Southerners with incomes large enough to require filing a federal income tax return was only one-third as great as in the nation as a whole. Four years later the South had but one-fifteenth of the nation's millionaires and paid only 22 per cent of the federal tax receipts.

The continued and accelerated flow of Northern capital brought an increasing degree of control. While the number of Southern businessmen increased, all too often they were the agents of the North. J. P. Morgan was the biggest name in Southern railroads, the iron and steel industry was dominated by United States Steel, and the oil industry paid homage to the Mellons and Rockefellers. Even the one Southern financial giant, James Duke, transferred his headquarters to New York. Still, too, the South continued to send the products of its mines, farms, and forests North or abroad in the form of raw or crudely processed materials. The colonialism of which pre-war Southerners had complained had not been ended but had merely shifted emphasis. Nor had the hold of agriculture upon the region's economy been broken by 1930. Despite all efforts of the Bourbons and their successors, the "New South" had not achieved a revolution. The region, instead, remained essentially rural and agricultural in economy and in patterns of thought, with only a veneer of industrialism.

[5] Calvin B. Hoover and B. U. Ratchford, *Economic Resources and Policies of the South* (New York: Macmillan, 1951), p. 116.

# 9

## THE REVOLT OF THE FARMERS

SOUTHERN FARMERS originally hailed the drive toward industrialization as portending a valuable supplement to agriculture, since the movement seemed highly unlikely to offer any harm to them and was a way to use the mass of workers not yet assimilated by established economic pursuits. Some farmers, too, were probably influenced by claims of such as Francis W. Dawson that new markets would be created for the rural producers and that, by the breaking of the Northern manufacturing monopoly, the farmers also might expect lower prices for the things they had to buy. The Bourbon leaders reassured them of all these benefits, and certainly most farmers were willing to give manufacturing a chance.

While awaiting the "promised land," the people of the soil found their own recovery much more difficult than had been anticipated. Their dire plight attracted the sympathetic attention of others, too. In January, 1866, Oliver Hudson Kelley, a clerk in the Department of Agriculture, was sent south by President Andrew Johnson to see what could be done to revive agriculture. Kelley was also motivated by a personal desire to do what he could toward sectional reconciliation. Deeply impressed with the poverty, isolation, fears, and backwardness of Southern farmers, he decided to help them by establishing a "Secret Society of Agriculturalists," an organization somewhat along the lines of the Odd Fellows, and opening it to the farmers of all sections. On December 4, 1867, Kelley, with William Saunders and a few other government employees, organized the National Grange of the Patrons of Husbandry, based on the principle: "We cherish the belief that sectionalism is and of a right should be dead and buried with the past. Our work is for the present and the future. In our agricultural brotherhood and its purposes we shall recognize no North, no South, no East, no West."

The Grange, as it was most commonly called, and its program of healing the wounds of war were soon subordinated to the broader and more appealing objective of providing economic, social, and cultural uplift. According to its "Declaration of Purposes," the Grange sought to improve the comfort and attractions of farm life, make better farmers, dispense with the "surplus of middlemen," encourage transportation, oppose monopolies, fight for agricultural education, promote non-partisan but clean politics, end sectionalism, and advance the position of women — in short, to "educate" the farmers.[1]

Although initiated for the benefit of the South, the Grange was viewed with suspicion. The organizers were accused of ulterior motives, especially since their headquarters were in Washington. One dark rumor circulated was that its purpose was to stir up racial strife, while the admission of women to membership made it seem extremely radical to others. Finally, in 1871, the Grange was successfully introduced into South Carolina, Mississippi, and Kentucky, and a year later spread widely throughout the South. By the end of 1872, South Carolina ranked next to Iowa in having the largest number of local units. The Grange boasted 210,000 members in the former Confederacy by 1873 and two years later numbered 6,400 local units.

Through the Grange, Southerners discovered that they had interests in common with other farmers. Its frequent meetings and social gatherings, in which women were allowed to take full part, played important parts toward the relief of the loneliness of the farmer and his wife. Picnics and cake auctions satisfied more than their physical needs, and in secret conclaves, with carefully guarded rituals, they could speak their minds without fear. Farmers were taught to work together, to study their peculiar economic problems, to read agricultural literature, and to be aware of their material, social, and cultural welfare. At each regular monthly meeting, committees reported on agricultural progress, the condition of the crops, quarrels between members, relief for the

[1] John Trimble, "The Grange," in E. A. Allen, *Labor and Capital* (Cincinnati, 1891), pp. 429-448.

needy, and the conduct of business enterprises such as money lending, cooperatives, and insurance. Often recommendations were made concerning sympathetic merchants and doctors who should be patronized. Overall, the never-ending theme was the need for crop diversification and soil preservation.

Locally, the interests of the Grange varied according to the more pressing needs. In Alabama, members pledged to withhold employment and shelter to anyone known to be a thief and in the state convention in 1874 petitioned for better protection against theft of agricultural products and for a state geological survey.[2] Often the Grange was active in working for home rule, which led to accusations of being an adjunct of the Ku Klux Klan. Seeking to escape the high prices of merchants and middlemen, members began to appoint purchasing agents and set up cooperative stores. One Alabama grange built a warehouse for storing cotton, forcing down the prices for such services, and Mississippi, at least, had a representative in Liverpool to look after consignments of cotton. Kelley consistently opposed most such ventures. "This purchasing business," he said, "commenced with buying Jackasses; the prospects are that many will be *sold*," a prophecy often justified.

Essentially, the Southern Grange was a movement of small, white farmers rather than planters and was geographically oriented toward the "up country" rather than the "low country." Chapters were allowed discretion as to the admission of Negroes, and a few were given membership in local units. Most of them, however, went into a Negro equivalent, the Council of Laborers, which had in each local council two white Grangers as advisers. The Grange also supported the idea of Southern industrialization and refused to get as excited over the railroad problem as their colleagues in the West; in most of the South in the 1870's the need was for greater transportation facilities, and railroads were sought. In some instances, however, Bourbon legislatures were persuaded to pass moderate rate regulations. In general, Southern farmers were unwilling to undertake independent political action, white unity being necessary to reclaim or keep their states in the hands of the Conservatives. Since the Granger period in the South coincided with the battle against Radical reconstruction, the region confronted the immediate and pressing problems of labor, capital, and credit more than did Grangers elsewhere.[3]

After the mid-seventies, the Southern Grange declined sharply. Its opposition to the crop lien system and efforts at cooperative buying and

[2] Hiram Hawkins, "Achievements of the Grange in the South," *ibid.*, pp. 477-493.
[3] Theodore Saloutos, "The Grange in the South, 1870-1877," *Journal of Southern History*, XIX (November, 1953), pp. 473-487, and *Farmer Movements in the South, 1865-1933* (Berkeley: Univ. of California, 1960).

selling made enemies of the powerful landlord and merchant classes. There is evidence that some landlords and credit sources boycotted Grange members, although to determine how extensive such actions were is impossible. Southern farmers were also more apathetic, by comparison with those of Kansas and Iowa, and lacked aggressive leadership; simply too many downtrodden farmers were concerned only with day-to-day existence. At least, however, the movement fostered the beginning of class consciousness among farmers and directed attention to such economic evils as the crop lien system. Most important, moreover, the idea was planted that laws could be a valuable weapon against poverty and injustice.

As long as unity against the carpetbaggers was imperative, white men cooperated under the leadership of the Conservatives regardless of economic conflicts. But the basic, historic lines of social cleavage still existed: the black belt, or low country, still hated and feared the hill country and was repaid in kind. Once redemption was achieved and the need for unity relaxed, emotions which had been restrained by political expediency broke out into the open. Antagonism began developing throughout the South by the 1880's, and Bourbon leadership was challenged by the "up country." Independent candidates ran for local offices and seats in the legislature. Local third parties organized, calling themselves Readjusters, Independents, Greenbackers, Laborites, the People's Anti-Bourbon party, and the like. Sometimes they carried whole districts and, as in Virginia in 1879, entire states.

This was essentially a country *versus* town cleavage; the rural elements were repelled by the social or economic doctrines of the Conservatives. Farmers resented the economic competition of the Negro; as residents of chiefly white counties, they objected to the manner, especially the rewarding him with minor offices, in which the black belt, both Republicans and Bourbons, used the vote of the Negro to curb the power of the white uplanders. "White supremacy" seemed to be working for the political benefit of only a small portion of the whites. The plutocrats, a small clique of Conservatives, were in control; as farm leader Benjamin R. Tillman of South Carolina said, 76 per cent of the whites were farmers and should rule the state, but they did not. The Bourbons practiced machine politics and were not above using the same tactics against these independents that they had used against the Republicans.

The farmers were faced with mounting debts and falling prices. From 1880 to 1890, the number of recorded mortgages in Mississippi more than doubled, and the percentage of farms operated by owners dropped sharply. Agriculture languished in the midst of prosperity, a condition not attributed to overproduction but creating the conviction that someone had a hand in the farmer's pocket. This villain was generally conceded to be the Eastern capitalist — Wall Street — or his Southern ally, the Bourbon. The political alliance of the Bourbons with Northern conservatives did little for the material welfare of the farmers.

Cotton prices dropped by almost half in the period of the eighties and early nineties. In 1870-73, prices averaged $.15 a pound; 1874-77, $.11; 1878-1881, $.095; 1882-84, $.091; 1885-87, $.083; 1888-90, $.078; and by 1894-96 was down to $.058, although a Senate committee in 1894 placed the cost of cotton production at about $.07 a pound. These represented market prices, and it is a known fact that the grower always gets less than that. Ferdie Deering once described a dirt farmer as a "man who starts out with nothing, loses on everything he grows and comes out even at the end of the year. Nobody knows how he does it. He doesn't know himself." While this might be normally true, the dirt farmer of the eighties and nineties knew full well he was not coming out even!

These grievances were expressed in the following song sung by Southern farmers:

> My husband came from town last night
> As sad as man could be,
> His wagon empty, cotton gone,
> And not a dime had he.
>
> Huzzah — Huzzah
> 'Tis queer I do declare:
> We make the clothes for all the world,
> But few we have to wear.

They blamed the "conniving" middlemen. As chronic debtors, the Southern farmers suffered from the national policy of currency contraction, and a high tariff was clearly a disadvantage to a section which sold raw stuffs abroad but was unable to buy cheap foreign manufactured goods in return. Inadequate banking facilities and high interest rates added to their woes. The new lien laws, which favored the Bourbon proprietors, dissatisfied them, and the Northern-owned railroads with their high and discriminatory rates, political activity, and pools were incarnate enemies. The jute-bagging trust, the cottonseed-oil trust, the tobacco trust, the fertilizer trust — all affected the farmers and gradually led them to view industry as an evil rather than a boon.

And finally, there was the antiquated tax structure in the South, which placed an unequal burden upon the agriculturists. Traditionally, land had always borne the greatest load. To get railroads and industry in the South, the Bourbons had granted them great economic favors, and what taxes were assessed against them were often evaded. The

Bourbon fetish for low taxes and governmental economy was often used as an excuse to deprive the farmers of additional services such as increased educational advantages, state boards of agriculture, experimental stations, and agricultural colleges such as were being furnished in Western states. Since the political alliance of the South with the industrial East was not to the farmer's liking, the Southern rebel began to call for union with the agrarian West, where people like himself already were clamoring for action.

But how could the uneducated and unprosperous Southern farmers be effectively organized? Unrealized by most, the seed had already been sown by the Grange. With its decline, other agricultural societies had sprung up throughout the South under such titles as the Farmers' Alliance of Texas, the Arkansas Agricultural Wheel, the Brothers of Freedom, and the Farmers' Union of Louisiana. The oldest of these was formed in 1875 by small farmers in Lampasas County, Texas, for protection against cattlemen and other enemies. After a struggling existence, it reorganized in 1879 on a state-wide basis as the Farmers' State Alliance, a "secret benevolent association," claiming 50,000 members by 1885. The next year Doctor Charles W. Macune, former resident of Wisconsin, California, and Kansas, became president, determined "to organize the cotton belt of America so that the whole world of cotton raisers might be united for self protection."

In furtherance of this goal, the Alliance in 1887 united with 10,000 members of the Farmers' Union and took the name Farmers' Alliance and Cooperative Union. The next year it absorbed the half million members of the six-year-old Agricultural Wheel, organized by W. W. Tedford, and again changed its title to the Farmers' Alliance and Industrial Union. Under Macune's aggressive leadership, the Southern Alliance, as it was popularly known to distinguish it from a similar organization in the Northwest, flourished. Sometimes Macune's organizers found local farm orders in operation and induced them to join forces with the Alliance; other times they had little to work with but the existence of smoldering discontent. Success was contagious, and local chapters based upon the Texas model appeared in nearly every Southern state. The Alliance became a closely knit national organization with headquarters in Washington, D.C., claiming as many as 3,000,000 members in 1890. In addition, there were a reported 1,250,000 in the Colored Farmers' National Alliance and Cooperative Union, which had been organized in Houston in 1886.

This farmers' organization, although some other "country" occupations were included in its membership, had objectives which were almost solely agricultural and similar to those of the old Grange. It sought to better farm conditions mentally, morally, and financially; to suppress

personal, sectional, and national prejudices; to uphold the doctrine of
equal rights and equal chances; to educate farmers so that rural life
would become less lonely and more social; to prevent exploitation by
the middlemen and secure the highest price for produce and the lowest
for purchases; and to encourage non-partisan political discussion.[4] The
announced strategy was "agitation, education, organization." Frequent
meetings were held to "break up the isolated habits of the farmers,
improve their social conditions, increase their social pleasures, and
strengthen their confidence and friendship for each other." The farmers
would receive facilities and encouragement to study the laws of business and trade and to learn the best methods of buying and selling.
Without partisan strife, members could learn to "discuss and investigate" laws and governmental policies which affected them and to "approve the good and condemn the bad through the ballot."[5] Numerous
social meetings would relieve the drudgery of daily living.

The chief appeal, however, was the chance for economic improvement. At first the Texas Alliance sought this through the "contract
store," an agreement whereby a merchant in each county sold at a dis-
count to Alliance members in return for their buying exclusively from
him. This arrangement failed to be wholly satisfactory, and Alliance
men decided to go into business for themselves, with local chapters
taking care of their own needs. Alliance stores, warehouses, gins, and
newspapers sprang up throughout the South. The most ambitious undertakings, however, were the Exchanges, a scheme of Macune's in
which state groups undertook to market the farmers' cotton directly
to the mills. In 1887 in Texas, for example, he sought capital of $500,000
to buy buildings and equipment and to finance the farmers until their
crops had been sold.

Business interests naturally opposed all these activities. In some
communities, Alliance stores were wrecked and the storekeepers beaten
and occasionally killed; its newspapers were boycotted or had their
plants wrecked. But the Alliance businesses failed mainly from internal
weaknesses rather than opposition. Management was amateurish and
too optimistic; it tried to save the members too much; and too great a
volume of business was undertaken for the capital. The problem of
finance was never solved. Macune failed to raise the half million dollars
he needed for the Texas Exchange and had to borrow at very heavy
rates of interest. The Texas Exchange lasted only two years, while those
in Florida and Georgia lingered on for five and six. Most such ventures
had failed by the time of the Panic of 1893.

[4] Leonidas L. Polk, "The National Farmers' Alliance and Industrial Union," in
Allen, *op. cit.*, pp. 494-508.
[5] Homer Clevenger, "The Teaching Techniques of the Farmers' Alliance: An Experiment in Adult Education," *Journal of Southern History*, XI (November, 1945),
pp. 504-518.

It was soon obvious to the Alliance that the task of underwriting the welfare of the farmer was too great for its own resources. Consequently, its thoughts turned more and more toward political measures as means of securing relief. Despite the fact that during the Alliance's early years it was proclaimed non-political, much of its program could be obtained in no other way. Therefore, in 1888, Alliance men in several states supported candidates for the legislatures who agreed to help the farmers. But these legislators were generally ineffective. In Texas and Arkansas, third parties were formed but with so little success that the decision was made to gain control of the state Democratic parties and make them over in the Alliance pattern, thus respecting the legend of the one-party system as a means of maintaining racial unity.

The plan was furthered by the election of Leonidas L. Polk, a leader who had long advocated political action, as Alliance president. Most typical of the Alliance politicians, Polk was born of sturdy yeoman stock in North Carolina.[6] Prominent in politics during the Confederacy and reconstruction periods, Colonel Polk remained a farmer at heart. He advocated creation of a state department of agriculture in 1870 and seven years later became its first commissioner, a position which he held until 1880. He eventually became editor of the *Progressive Farmer*, published in Raleigh, and was quickly recognized as the leader of the informed farm press.

At first his editorials were concerned with technical agricultural improvements, but they grew increasingly political. He advocated class consciousness among the farmers and the formation of farm lobbies to force the legislature to grant desired reforms. With rural support he was able to secure the founding of a state agricultural college and get the federal Morrill Act funds diverted to it from the state university. When the Alliance movement reached North Carolina, he became the leader of the state organization. He became national vice president in 1887 and then president in 1889. Under his leadership, the Alliance probably reached its height, for he was a rough and forceful speaker with a national reputation as a champion of the farmer. In 1890, North Carolina Alliance men gained control of the machinery of the state Democratic party, forced the convention to endorse the "efforts of the farmers to throw off the yoke of Bourbonism," and elected agriculturally-inclined legislators and congressmen.

Without official announcement, the Alliance early in 1890 had moved to capture control throughout the South of state Democratic nominating conventions from the Bourbons and to force all candidates to give written pledges to support its demands. In the general elections of that year, many candidates ran as Democrats with Alliance plat-

[6] Stuart Noblin, *Leonidas LaFayette Polk: Agrarian Crusader* (Chapel Hill: Univ. of North Carolina, 1949).

forms; some were frankly Bourbons; others made politicians' promises and regarded them lightly; some led genuine democratic revolt movements. After the elections, the Alliance claimed majorities in eight state legislatures; six governors and more than fifty congressmen had won under its banner. In Tennessee the governor, J. P. Buchanan, almost half of the state senators, and 40 per cent of the house were Alliance men; in Mississippi, it successfully backed two congressmen. Florida Alliance men elected a majority of the legislature and one Senator, although their candidate for governor was defeated. In North Carolina they claimed eight congressmen, all of the state Democratic officers, and half of the Republican. In Alabama, Reuben F. Kolb, commissioner of agriculture, was defeated in his race for governor by black belt votes, although the legislature and a Senate seat were secured. Georgia farmers elected William J. Northen governor, three-fourths of the legislature, and six congressmen, and in other states, candidates were successful on farm programs although they were not officially connected with the Alliance movement.

The Alliance political programs varied yearly and from state to state. Local issues included extension of public education, prison reform, good roads, and the like. In general, however, they demanded strict regulation or government ownership of railroads; inflation of the currency to not less than fifty dollars per capita; abolition of national banks; prohibition of alien land ownership; cessation of trading in futures in agricultural produce; a fairer system of taxation; and more equitable legislative representation with fairer elections. An original proposal, submitted in 1889, called for the adoption of the so-called Sub-Treasury plan, whereby the government would establish warehouses for farmers to store non-perishable farm produce. In exchange, the farmer was to receive a loan of legal tender money up to 80 per cent of the market value of his produce, which might be repaid at one per cent interest when the depositor wished to sell his crop. This proposal had the triple advantage of allowing the farmer to borrow on his produce at a low rate of interest, to wait for a favorable market before selling, and to profit by an expanded and flexible currency.

One of the colorful figures of the period who rode such a platform to victory was James S. Hogg, a product of the Texas farmers' revolt.[7] His family migrated from Alabama just before the Texas Revolution, in which the elder Hogg was a leader; later, he served as a general in the Confederate army until his death at Corinth (1862), when Jim was eleven years old. The mother died the next year, leaving a large family of children to shift for themselves. Jim grew up as a farm hand and

[7] Robert C. Cotner, *James Stephen Hogg: A Biography* (Austin: Univ. of Texas, 1959).

typesetter and later editor of a small country newspaper. He took up the study of law in 1871 and in 1877 became attorney-general of Texas on an anti-monopoly platform. During his two terms in this position, he attacked insurance companies, forced recession of much of the lands granted by the state to railroads, and fought for state ownership of these lines and finally for a regulatory railroad commission.

In 1890 he secured the Democratic nomination for governor on a platform promise to establish such a commission. Supported by country editors, the Alliance, and the farmers in general, who were attracted by his very name, this massive man, weighing nearly 300 pounds, quickly proved that he knew the heart of the common man and spoke the language of the farmer. Once elected, Governor Hogg urged passage of radical legislation against the railroads and other corporations, abolition of the convict-lease system, a revision of the criminal code, free schools for at least six months in the year, and an endowment for the University of Texas. When he sought renomination in 1892, the state convention was the most riotous in Texas history, with nearly every seat contested. Two chairmen were elected, and each attempted to address the convention simultaneously to the accompaniment of some fifty fist fights on the floor. The split continued, and Hogg and his rival were both named as Democratic nominees. After a turbulent campaign, in which Edward M. House managed Hogg's affairs, Jim was re-elected governor by a large majority.

Another agrarian governor coming into power in 1890 was Benjamin R. Tillman.[8] A hard-hitting, back-country South Carolinian, he was typical of the new type of leader rising in the South. Born of farmer ancestry in 1845, he was the youngest of seven sons. His father found it necessary to supplement his farm income by operating a run-down inn in his home on the stage line. At seventeen, Ben tried to get into the Confederate army but fell ill, losing the sight of one eye. (Despite this original patriotism, he eventually referred to the Civil War as a rich man's war and a poor man's fight.) Two brothers were killed in the war, one died of disease, and two others were killed in feuds, leaving only Ben and George, a lawyer who served two years in prison for killing a bystander in a gambling duel. Ben tried reading law, but in 1868 he married and settled down on a 400-acre farm. At first he was able to make money on his up-country farm, enlarging his holdings. In 1881, according to his account, he "ran thirty plows, bought guano, rations, etc., as usual, and the devil tempted me to buy a steam engine and other machinery, amounting to two thousand dollars, all on credit."

[8] Francis Butler Simkins, *The Tillman Movement in South Carolina* (Durham: Duke Univ., 1926), and *Pitchfork Ben Tillman: South Carolinian* (Baton Rouge: Louisiana State Univ., 1944).

His prosperity soon vanished through drought, crop failures, and high interest charges, however, and he had to sell much of his land, causing his family to suffer actual want.

Up until this time, Ben's political activities had been routine. He was a member of Hampton's Red Shirts in the fight for redemption and in 1882 an inconspicuous delegate to the state Democratic convention. Unimpressive in appearance, with a rasping voice, and seemingly without any of the attributes of leadership, he had, however, become convinced that his farming was a failure and that the other farmers in the state were in a similar condition. The cause, he decided, was betrayal by the lawyers and politicians of the common man.

Tillman's rise to prominence began on August 6, 1885, in the small, sleepy farming town of Bennettsville. A speech which should have been routine and Democratic became instead a bitter attack upon the merchant-lawyer-politician clique headed by Wade Hampton, the enemy of the farmers. Ben's answer to the problem of financial insecurity which troubled most of his audience received immediate approval, and instinctively he called upon them to capture the Democratic party of the state. In 1886 he organized the Farmers' Association of South Carolina, which demanded greater economy in government, more efficiency from officials, and cheaper and more practical education. Failing to win the election that year, the organization renewed its efforts in 1888. A new issue had been given them by a Northerner, Thomas G. Clemson, who had willed his estate to South Carolina for establishment of a state agricultural college. The Bourbons opposed acceptance of the gift, claiming that it was not enough to pay for the project and therefore additional money would be taken from taxes. On this one issue, the "wool-hat boys" came within less than twenty-five votes of controlling the Democratic convention and did force the party to accept the gift.

Thoroughly convinced that he was the only man who could lead the farmers to victory, Ben Tillman announced his candidacy for governor in 1889. His radical platform was spelled out in one of his frequent letters to the Charleston *News and Courier*. The famous Shell Manifesto, written by Tillman but published under the name of G. W. Shell, president of the Farmers' Association, fully expounded his views. The document claimed that the farm movement represented a majority of the people and had failed so far only because of the superior political tactics of the opposition and the lack of organization on the part of the farmers. It stated also that South Carolina had never had a democratic government in its history; the fear of a division among the whites permitting a return of Negro rule had kept the people quiet, and they had "submitted to many grievances imposed by the ruling faction because they dreaded to risk such division." Therefore the Association had decided to make its fight within party lines, "assured that truth and justice must finally prevail." The agricultural college had to be established; the fertilizer trust in the state be broken; and protection be given against the "greed of the gigantic corporations owned by the North, which regard South Carolina as a lemon to be squeezed and care nothing for the welfare of our towns, our State or our people." Furthermore, the railroad commission had been "tamed" by the railroads; "rotation in office is a cardinal Democratic principle, and the neglect to practice it is the cause of many of the ills we suffer"; the penitentiary was mismanaged; and the legislature should be reapportioned according to population. The Manifesto closed on a ringing note: "Fellow Democrats, do not all these things cry out for a change? . . . Can we afford it [the state] longer in the hands of those who, wedded to ante-bellum ideas, but possessing little of ante-bellum patriotism and honor, are running it in the interest of a few families and for the benefit of a selfish ring of politicians?"

His campaign against the Bourbons rocked the state and gained national attention. After a hard fight, aided by the Farmers' Alliance, he won the Democratic nomination, normally tantamount to election. The Bourbons, however, ran an independent candidate against him, made special efforts to solicit the Negro votes, and heaped ridicule upon Tillman and his followers. The *News and Courier* referred to him as "the leader of the Adullamites, a people who carry pistols in their hip pockets, who expectorate upon the floor, who have no toothbrushes and comb their hair with their fingers." Perhaps there was some truth in the accusation, but Tillman and his followers swept into control of South Carolina.

The legislature, however, was not as quick to do his bidding as he desired, and in 1892 he appealed successfully to the "red-neck boys" for a legislature which would follow him implicitly. His four years as governor marked one of the most turbulent periods in the state's political history. The Bourbons fought him bitterly, but Tillman was master, kicking Wade Hampton out of the Senate and, in 1894, forcing through a proposal to call a constitutional convention to protect the gains made by his group. This was approved in the same election in which he defeated M. C. Butler for the United States Senate; one of his devoted followers took his place as governor. During his term, Tillman had organized a centralized tax administration; secured an increased royalty from the companies developing the phosphate deposits; established a state dispensary system for sale of liquor; appropriated more money for education; diverted funds from an overstaffed State University to Clemson and Winthrop College, a teacher training school for women; and revamped the railroad commission for better control of that farm

enemy. He had kept his promises to his faithful followers, although
many of his economic reforms were later to be largely nullified.

The capstone of his program, however, was the constitution of
1895. It was designed to reapportion the state's voting districts to break
black belt control and to secure the disfranchisement of the Negro.
The latter was inspired by the fear that the Negro votes would return
party control to the Conservatives and the general dislike of the wool-
hat boys for their black competitors. Senator Tillman returned from
Washington to lead the convention in person. Addressing the delegates
upon the necessity for disfranchisement, Tillman repainted the horrors
of reconstruction and placed the blame on the Negroes. It was they
who "put the little pieces of paper in the box that gave the commission
to these white scoundrels who were their leaders and the men who
debauched them." The Negroes, "like the viper that is asleep," could
"be warmed into life again and sting us whenever some more white
rascals, native or foreign, come here and mobilize the ignorant blacks."
The only solution "as patriots and as statesmen" was to "take from them
every ballot that we can under the laws of our national government"
by property qualifications and a literacy provision. Tillman's constitution became South Carolina's and was hailed as the beginning of a
new era.

Tillman was viewed by the nation as a wild man from the South
rising in unison with other wild men in the West. His reforms and the
over-all conditions in South Carolina were not known to all of the country. Tillman won his Senatorship and his nickname, "Pitchfork Ben,"
by promising to stick his pitchfork into conservative President Grover
Cleveland's ribs. As a Senator, his continued criticism embarrassed
Cleveland on many occasions, since, after all, Tillman was a Democrat.
With the revolt of the inflation-minded Democrats, Tillman aspired to
the Democratic presidential nomination in 1896, but with a harsh
speech at the national convention ruined what little chance he might
have had.

Thus forced to be satisfied with his Senate seat, Tillman kept public attention by radical moves. He opposed the Spanish-American War
as a product of the armor-plate trust, openly justified lynching, and
tried to repeal the Fifteenth Amendment. At first he was an important
supporter of the progressive program of Theodore Roosevelt, but the
two split when the President withdrew a dinner invitation at the White
House after Tillman had engaged in a fist fight on the Senate floor with
the other South Carolina Senator. Senator and President, both self-
proclaimed "friends of the people," fought each other verbally, trying
to prove the other a hypocrite. Tillman won easy re-election to the
Senate in 1900, 1906, and 1912, keeping control of the state until his

death, but became more conservative as he became more prosperous and as the discontent of the farmers lessened. Gradually a political balance was reached in South Carolina between the farmers and the conservatives. In the final analysis, Tillman's significance lay in the fact that, by perfecting a technique of exploiting ugly passions to win elections, he had achieved a victory over the Bourbons and seized control of the Democratic party in the most conservative of Southern states.

Economically, the 1890's proved worse than even the eighties. The Depression of 1893 hit the South earlier and harder. Business failures were considerably higher than in the rest of the country, and industrial unemployment became a serious problem for the first time, accompanied by riots, strikes, and use of state troops. But the agricultural people suffered most. Alliance successes had not brought the hoped-for results. While more money was obtained for education and some control of railroads and other forms of business was attempted, little was done to improve rural credit conditions and the general economic problems of the farmer. Crop prices continued to fall, and mortgages and tenancy increased as the lien system tightened. In 1892 the boll weevil made its appearance; the Mississippi River flooded each year from 1891 to 1893; also in 1893 heavy storms struck the Georgia coast; the Gulf area was ravaged by a yellow fever epidemic; and the disastrous freeze of 1894-95 was followed by drought in 1896. During all of this, the Democratic administration did nothing for the South, despite the prominent place occupied by Southerners.

Members of the Alliance in the West had long since despaired of effective relief from either of the two major parties and were advocating creation of a third party which would be responsive to the farmers' needs. To most Southerners such a course seemed dangerous. If the white voters of the South were divided, the Negro vote might dominate, and the horrors of reconstruction might be repeated. Southern Alliance men, therefore, preferred to work within the framework of the Democratic party, where they could already point to some considerable success. There was, of course, one great objection to such a technique. The Southern wing, however strong it might be, could not hope to dominate the national party. Though Alliance control could achieve a certain amount of useful state legislation, reforms such as efficient railroad regulation, currency inflation, and the Sub-Treasury plan could be carried out only with congressional action.

This demand for national action was seen in the formation of the Farmers' National League to secure just representation and treatment for agricultural interests in state legislatures and Congress. This movement, originated in Massachusetts in 1889, moved southward into Maryland, Virginia, West Virginia, Arkansas, Kentucky, Georgia, and

Missouri. To many farm men, however, such an approach seemed too slow. In May, 1891, a call was issued to the leading farmers' organizations, Union and Confederate soldiers, and the Knights of Labor to attend a conference at Cincinnati. Fourteen hundred delegates appeared, composed mainly of Westerners and a few Southerners, and the People's, or Populist, party was formally launched as a national third-party organization.

An ominous omen could have been seen in the lack of enthusiasm on the part of Southerners and labor unions. The following February in St. Louis, a convention representing delegates from all the farm orders tried to achieve closer union but was unsuccessful. Only a common platform ensued. President Polk of the Southern Alliance, presiding officer of the convention, was loathe to break off with the Democratic party but reluctantly agreed to support the Populists. Efforts to interest labor in a united front found only the old and weakened Knights of Labor signifying any interest in cooperation.

The call to support a third party split the Southern Alliance. Many farmers could see no need for such action in the light of the successes in 1890; breaking away from the Democratic party could also have adverse social and political effects, not to mention the threat to white supremacy. But in all Southern states, the Populists organized and nominated a ticket before the election of 1892. The political strategy of the Southern Populists called for alliances between the South and West, of farmers and factory workers, and in the South among white and Negro farmers and laborers, elements which the Bourbons had sought to keep apart. In the South Populists elected blacks to office and gave them a voice in party organizations, and their platforms denounced lynching, the convict-lease system, which rested most heavily upon the blacks, and called for protection of black political rights.

The Populist movement was a direct challenge to the Conservatives. Agrarian rebels in the South joined their fellows in the West in castigating Eastern Democratic leadership, Wall Street financiers, and corporations, and in proposing a comprehensive program of governmental activity which seemed almost rank socialism. Ancient cleavages which the Bourbons had not been able to heal completely were exposed. Political status quo was threatened, along with the imminent collapse of the one-party system. The Bourbons invoked the race issue on the one hand while seeking Negro support on the other, shouted the dangers of bolting the party, and used their control of the governmental machinery to beat off attacks.

North Carolina's Leonidas Polk might well have been the presidential nominee of the Populist party except for his sudden death in June, 1892, a factor which further weakened the movement in the

South. With Polk gone, the nominating convention at Omaha, Nebraska, selected Virginia's James G. Field, a former Confederate general, for the vice presidency, and James B. Weaver of Iowa, former Union general, early leader of the Prohibitionists, and the Greenback presidential candidate in 1880, for first place on the ticket. General Weaver was personally distasteful to many potential Southern voters because of his war record and the activities of other Union officers in his behalf. A circular depicting Weaver raiding Southern henhouses appeared in the South. When he went into that region during the campaign, he was bitterly attacked by Bourbon newspapers and bombarded with eggs when he attempted to speak. After one such occasion, an observer remarked that Weaver was made "a regular walking omelet by the Southern chivalry of Georgia."

Farm leadership in the South was also split, with Tillman and Hogg refusing to cooperate with the Populists in their states. But, in general, with its liberal fringe going over to the Populists, the Southern Democratic party became more conservative than ever. Many wavering Southerners were shocked by the intemperate language of Populist orators like Thomas E. Watson of Georgia and the fact that the Populists were willing to cooperate with Negroes and Republicans.

On the other hand, the Bourbons hired Negro orators, shamelessly purchased Negro votes, supported Negro candidates, provided entertainment for Negro voters, and even imported Negroes from adjoining states to vote on election day. They instituted boycotts and social ostracism against those who supported the Populists and appealed for campaign funds from Notherern business and political interests. Populist orators were mobbed, fifteen Negroes were killed in Georgia, and, where necessary, returns were altered to insure Conservative victory. In Florida the state president of the Farmers' Alliance was badly defeated as a candidate for governor on the Populist ticket. Reuben Kolb of Alabama was either defeated or counted out in his second bid. In Georgia, Negroes were brought from South Carolina and taken from one polling place to another. Defeat of the Populist rural counties was all-important, and in the case of the town of Augusta, a Democratic majority greatly in excess of the voting population was returned. Throughout the South, so successful were Conservative tactics that 1892 saw the Bourbons gain back what they had lost in 1890, except in South Carolina, where Tillman had stayed in the Democratic party.[9] In no Southern state did Weaver receive more than 37 per cent of the vote, and the Populists for all their efforts failed to dent the "solid South."

Convinced that they had been robbed of numerous offices by the

[9] For events in Mississippi during this period, see Albert D. Kirwan, *Revolt of the Rednecks: Mississippi Politics, 1876-1925* (Lexington: Univ. of Kentucky, 1951).

Bourbons, the Populists got renewed hope from the Panic of 1893 and the refusal of President Cleveland to take steps to relieve the situation. Cleveland became increasingly unpopular in the South, along with the Bourbons, and in the 1894 Congressional election, the Agrarians, working more closely than ever with the Republicans, made an all-out effort. The violence, intimidation, and frauds of 1892 were repeated, more violent in some cases than those of reconstruction. Despite these frantic maneuvers, the Populists made great gains and reached their zenith in the South. In North Carolina, where, by fusion with the Republicans, they successfully wooed the Negro vote and were permitted by law to participate jointly in the control of the election machinery, they carried the state by a 20,000-vote majority. The governorship and control of both legislative houses were captured and a Populist and a Republican sent to the Senate.

In both Alabama and Georgia, the Populists also made strong gains. In the former, polling over 47 per cent of the total vote, they elected a Congressman and had their gubernatorial candidate, Kolb, defeated only by vote manipulation in the black belt. In Georgia, they got over 44 per cent of the vote, and it is probable that the Bourbons saved the day only by wholesale fraud, justified on the grounds that those "damned Populists would have ruined the country!"

Typical of Southern Populism was the career of Thomas E. Watson (1856-1922) of Georgia, who became leader of the Southern group after the death of Polk.[10] Watson was the son of a well-to-do slaveholder, but the family was impoverished by the war, an experience which left him deeply embittered. After an unhappy experience as a farmer, he spent two years as an underpaid country schoolteacher before turning to law as a path upwards. He suffered from an inferiority complex which made him aggressive and supersensitive. Although he later made a sizeable fortune at law, the profession remained petty haggling to him, failing to provide a return to pre-war status. It did allow him, however, to buy back the old family plantation, and he publicly thrashed the landlord, who he believed had mistreated his family.

Watson first appeared on the political scene in 1880 as a red-headed youth of 23, when he called for a revolt in the Georgia Democratic convention against the renomination of Colquitt. Tom was convinced that the state's zeal for the "New South" was responsible for the lack of attention to the serious plight of the plain farmers. To him the enemy of the common man was personified in the "Atlanta Ring," the landlords, merchants, and railroads, and their spokesman Henry Grady. He was a bitter enemy of Grady, accusing him of betraying the South. Grady was trying to integrate the South with the industrial North,

[10] C. Vann Woodward, *Tom Watson, Agrarian Rebel* (New York: Rinehart, 1938).

while Watson's ideal was a return to the agrarian civilization of the pre-war period and union with Western farmers. While Henry Grady was telling an audience how "plenty rides on the springing harvests," Watson was replying that "plenty rides on Grady's springing imagination" and that a "billy-goat would have to labor twelve hours a day for living" on the average farm in Georgia. The agrarian rebels, however, were quickly overwhelmed by the bought Negro vote which supported their opponents, and Watson went into political eclipse for ten years.

As agricultural discontent actively flared in the 1880's, Watson's star rose once more. In the election of 1890, he was elected to the House of Representatives as a Democrat on an Alliance platform, but he refused to support the Democratic candidate for Speaker because of the candidate's opposition to farm principles. When the Bourbon leaders of Georgia pressured Watson to behave, he boldly broke with his party, becoming the first Southern Congressman to admit he was a third-party man. He then began to assault the Democrats with all the emotional bitterness at his command and became in Washington the personification of the Southern dirt-farmer revolt. As official leader of the little group of Populists in Congress, he introduced several farm-sponsored measures.

Watson attempted to build up a third party in Georgia by politically combining the Colored Farmers' Alliance with its white counterpart, declaring that they were kept separate by the Bourbons so that each might be robbed more easily. The Populist party had to concern itself with the interests of both in order to get them to vote the same ticket. He opposed lynching and terrorism and demanded equal justice for the Negroes. Efforts in Georgia and South Carolina to disfranchise them were denounced, a stand which caused him to be hailed as the savior of the Negro. With many whites, however, this stand was so unpopular that often Watson and some of his Negro supporters were forced to speak from behind the shelter of armed guards.[11]

In campaigning for re-election to the House, Watson viciously assailed the bankers, merchants, railroad owners, corporations, and the prosperous. Since most of these lived in urban areas, he made the cities his whipping boys. By gerrymandering his district, the Democrats were able to defeat him in 1892, probably by sheer fraud. He redoubled his efforts but in 1894 was once more fraudulently beaten in a bloody campaign which brought him recognition as a national hero and symbol of the Populists.

Although the Conservatives defeated Watson in 1894 and managed to hold most of the South, they realized they were in a bad spot. It was

[11] C. Vann Woodward, "Tom Watson and the Negro in Agrarian Politics," *Journal of Southern History*, IV (February, 1938), pp. 14-33.

doubtful that they could continue to manufacture majorities, and Cleveland was becoming increasingly unpopular in the region because of the depression and his uncompromising stand for hard money. Some concessions, they felt, had to be made to radical demands. A meeting in Memphis, June 12, 1895, dominated by conservative Southerners, debated whether to form a free-silver third party as favored by Tillman. Instead, they decided to control the next Democratic national convention and win back the Populists. Allied with Western Democrats, who faced the same problems, they succeeded in nominating William Jennings Bryan on a liberal platform.

These actions presented the Populists in 1896 with a serious dilemma; they finally decided also to nominate Bryan as their candidate for the presidency, with Watson as the vice-presidential nominee. Watson had fought this fusion and lost, and his choice was probably a sop. The Populists expected or hoped that the Democrats would withdraw their vice-presidential candidate and support Watson, but they did not, desiring no connection with the radicalism of Watson and his type. Tom considered himself ill-used but stumped the West for Bryan. He got no help from the Democrats and few votes. Locally, only in North Carolina, where they allied with the Republicans, were the Populists successful, getting a firmer grip on the legislature and county and state offices and electing a number of Negroes to office in the process. Whatever the national union of the Populists with the Democrats might have meant in the West, it was fatal in the South.

Confronted on the one hand with the alliance of farm rebels and big business (Populist-Republican) and on the other with a combination of white supremacy (Southern Democrats) and Negroes against white farmers, that the average Southern voter became confused and apathetic is not surprising. Tom Watson pronounced the epitaph of the Populists when he said, "Our party, as a party, does not exist any more. . . . The sentiment is still there, but confidence is gone." The defeat of Bryan, along with improving economic conditions and the region's patriotic response to the Spanish-American War, helped dissipate any remaining strength of the movement.

Although gone, the Populist party left its mark. The class consciousness of the farmers had been aroused to the extent that they became one of the most self-conscious groups in American history. The agrarian revolt also forced the Democratic party for a time to be almost as progressive as the Populist, resulting in gains for popular education and social and economic reform.[12] The status of the common man was improved, but on the debit side were the demagogical tactics often used,

[12] Arthur S. Link, "The Progressive Movement in the South, 1870-1914," *North Carolina Historical Review*, XXIII (1946), pp. 175-180.

the unsoundness of much of the legislation, and the treatment of the Negro. The end result was that the rebels returned to the Democratic party with their hats in their hands, convinced through their lack of success in wooing the Negro vote away from the Conservatives that the Negro must be denied the franchise. North Carolina had had riots and race wars when the Populists put some Negroes into political office, and now both rebels and Conservatives were convinced that when their votes were divided, the Negro might rule — a danger to be avoided at any cost. Even Watson, once a supporter of the political rights of blacks, became a rabid negrophobe, as well as anti-Semitic and anti-Catholic. Thus Watson and Populism, as symbols of a democratic revolt, ended by siring the antithesis.

# THE SOUTHERN BLACKS, 1877-1930

DURING THE CLOSING DAYS of reconstruction, the whites tacitly agreed that Negro rights would have to be sacrificed in the interest of sectional reconciliation. The era had opened on the issue of whether the North or South would control the freedman. To a great extent the contest had ended as a draw. On the surface, it appeared that after the overthrow of the black codes, political control, at least, had gone to the North. In actuality, however, Southerns still maintained economic domination and, even during Radical rule, exercised considerable political influence in a number of states. Despite the North's self-appointed role of "protector" of the Negro, the withdrawal of federal troops and the fall of the carpetbag governments marked the desire of people in general to disengage from the unsavory Southern situation and to leave it up to the Negro to protect himself.

Bourbon politicians were quick to reassure the North that there was nothing to fear so far as Southern treatment of the Negro was concerned. Since many Northerners had viewed the franchise as the Negro's chief weapon for self-protection, conservative Southerners were quick to reply that no wholesale disfranchisement was impending just because home rule had been attained. The Arkansas Democratic state convention in 1878 included a plank in its platform stating that "it is the sense of the convention that the colored population . . . are identified in interest with the great Democratic part of the State" and "fully realizing the importance of a more harmonious feeling between them, embrace this opportunity of inviting them — the colored people of the State — to an active cooperation with us in furthering our common interests."

In a symposium in the March, 1879, *North American Review*, Alexander H. Stephens, L. Q. C. Lamar, and Wade Hampton, three of Dixie's most illustrious sons, tried to allay Northern fears on this score. Lamar went so far as to make the extreme statement that he knew of no Southerner of importance or influence who considered the taking of the vote from the freedman as politically expedient. Hampton added the factor of self-interest, expressing his opinion that "as the negro becomes more intelligent he naturally allies himself with the more conservative of the whites, for his observation and experience both show him that his interests are identified with those of the white race." Two months earlier in the same magazine, Henry Watterson, influential Kentucky editor and politician, had implied the same thing when he wrote, "No true friend of his [the Negro] but would take him out of politics as a factor or leading issue."

But the issue was not that simple. The North had to be mollified to the extent that it would not interfere, and the Negro had to be convinced that his interests were coincident with those of the Southern whites. But in case he did not see the light, the Bourbons, as has been seen, stressed the need for white solidarity. Restriction of Negro political activity was justified on the grounds, expressed by Chief Justice H. H. Chalmers of Mississippi, that the freedman "will be bought and sold, and led to the polls." The white conservative approach, therefore, became fourfold: to appease the North, to solidify the white vote for the Democrats, to encourage the Negro to vote Democratic, and to nullify the voting strength of those who would support the Republican ticket.[1]

Under this program Negroes voted to a much greater degree than has been recognized. In Louisiana, for example, the constitution of 1879 stated that "no qualification of any kind for suffrage or office, nor any restraint upon the same, on account of race, color, or previous condition of servitude shall be made by law." Consequently, in that state black enrollment continued to be greater than white during the Bourbon period. In 1878 their respective totals were 78,123 to 77,341. Eleven years later the ratio had increased to 128,150 to 125,407. Out-

[1] Donald N. Brown, "Southern Attitudes toward Negro Voting in the Bourbon Period, 1877-1890" (unpublished Ph.D. dissertation, Dept. of History, University of Oklahoma).

numbered, the white politicians had to come to terms with the black voters and their leaders. The usual Bourbon tactic was to give them offices, either as Republicans or Democrats, in return for their support in the state races. From 1876 to 1900, Negroes served continuously in the Louisiana legislature, eleven in the house and four in the senate in 1880, for example. Four years later the totals were twelve and four, and in 1888, nine and four, respectively. There, as elsewhere, dissatisfaction with the major parties made third party and reform movements attractive; in several counties blacks almost completely dominated the Greenback organizations. James S. Hogg received important support in his fight against the Bourbons, and black participation in the People's Party was widespread.

In Arkansas, Democrats nominated Negroes for minor offices, while Republicans chose them as delegates to state and national conventions. Before 1898, Texas' Black-Belt counties normally had some black commissioners, justices of the peace, and constables, and this area elected nearly three score of that race to serve in the legislature or in constitutional conventions. There was not a session of the legislature which did not include at least one Negro. Tennessee had nine Negroes who won seats in the house of representatives in the eighties and nineties. Mississippi, with approximately 109,995 white and 130,483 Negro voters, made common use of "fusion," whereby Negroes would be given some offices in return for their support of the Democratic ticket.[2]

In Virginia the Negro vote held the balance of power and played an important role in the fight between Mahone's Readjuster-Republican party and the Bourbon Democrats. The only Negro sent to Congress from that state was elected in 1888 as a result of the successful wooing of the Negro vote from Mahone. The Democrats controlled the election machinery and, when necessary, used intimidation and stuffed ballot boxes, all the time declaring the necessity of saving white civilization from Negro-Republican domination.[3]

In South Carolina, where the Negro population was in the majority, fusion tactics were also used. Governor Hampton appointed Negroes to minor offices, and vigorous efforts were made to capture their votes from the Republicans. Before the mid-1890's, both Republican and Democratic Negroes held seats in the state legislature and occasionally in the House of Representatives. Negroes also belonged to the

[2] Lawrence D. Rice, *The Negro in Texas, 1874-1900* (Baton Rouge: Louisiana State Univ., 1971); Vernon L. Wharton, *The Negro in Mississippi, 1865-1890* (Chapel Hill: Univ. of North Carolina, 1947).
[3] Allen W. Moger, "The Origin of the Democratic Machine in Virginia," *Journal of Southern History*, VIII (May, 1942), pp. 199-205.

Democratic precinct clubs during the same period. As late as 1889, Governor John P. Richardson said, "We believe that the whites must dominate, but at the same time we do not refuse local offices to the blacks."[4]

Throughout the South white factions vied with each other for Negro support with dances, barbecues, and plenty of whiskey. Some landlords mobilized their tenants to vote as they did to pick cotton. A few candidates sought Negro votes by supporting issues favorable to them. In 1882, for example, Tom Watson demanded free schools and abolition of the convict-lease system. But if cajolery and promises were not enough, there was always the implied threat of force. The Copiah, Mississippi, *Signal*, on October 18, 1883, editorialized, "If they [the Negroes] will not vote with the Democrats, it would be better for them and the county that they refuse to participate in the election. The weather might be warm that day and they might possibly get sunstruck." However, the Atlanta *Journal*, on July 29, 1890, claimed, "We have said repeatedly that the only interference in this state with the Negroes in their right to vote was by Republican Negroes intimidating those of their color who are disposed to vote the Democratic ticket."

Whether there was or was not intimidation of the Negroes, their voting habits were clear. The situation was summarized by the Fort Smith, Arkansas, *Weekly Elevator*, on November 26, 1886: "Talk with the people who have lived in the rural districts of the Gulf States, or go and reside there yourself, and you will learn that the negroes generally vote the democratic ticket." This success of the Bourbons in controlling or eliminating the Negro votes explains why the agrarian reformers launched an attack against the Negroes as one of the ways of destroying the power of the dominant conservatives.

Since reconstruction, a certain amount of Negro disfranchisement had been going on, at first by extra-legal means featuring intimidation and violence. This, in turn, was supplemented by statutory devices. Control of elections was highly centralized, being placed in the hands of the state instead of local officers, thus making it possible to alter returns from the counties. Areas with a heavy concentration of Negroes were divided by gerrymandering to render the Negro vote ineffective; Virginia shifted its voting districts five times in seventeen years for just this purpose. Very elaborate and confusing registration and voting procedures were set up, which allowed many opportunities for mistakes and subsequent throwing out of the ballots. Limits were placed on the time a voter could spend in the voting booth; registration and elections were held in areas far from Negro settlements and shifted suddenly

[4] George B. Tindall, *South Carolina Negroes, 1877-1900* (Columbia: Univ. of South Carolina, 1952).

without notification to Negro voters; and names of candidates were printed on the ballot by office rather than party. Most election laws required that the number of ballots had to match the voting population of the district and be reduced by lot when a surplus occurred. This encouraged stuffing of the ballot boxes with illegal votes, a practice made easier by the use of tissue-paper ballots. Bigamy, petty larceny, and other crimes more commonly filed against blacks were added to the long list of grounds for voter disqualification.

Then came the discovery of the value of the poll tax. This tax was not, as often supposed, a Southern invention. Poll taxes had been used all over the United States since the colonial period, but usually for school revenue and not primarily as a voting qualification. From 1865 to 1900, Pennsylvania, Delaware, and Massachusetts, as well as the South, required payment of some tax for voting. The reconstruction constitutions applied the device for school revenue, but only in Tennessee was payment a condition for voting. There seems to be little evidence that it was initially a means to disfranchise; its payment was merely a symbol of a good citizenship. Georgia's new constitution of 1877 required payment of all taxes to vote, and Virginia collected a poll tax for voting from 1876 to 1882.[5] But as adopted in the late eighties and the decades which followed, state laws demanded a poll tax payment from all registrants, paid well in advance, the receipt to be presented at voting time. The tax was not large, although some states made it cumulative. But the theory was that most Negroes did not care enough about voting to pay for the privilege, especially months before they even knew who the candidates would be. Then, too, even if the tax were paid, the receipt might be lost. In some cases Negroes were encouraged to give their receipts to one person, perhaps the local minister, and then they would be mysteriously stolen from him. On other occasions, a circus would tour the black belts and take poll tax receipts for admissions.

These earlier disfranchisement techniques were dangerous devices. They quite obviously violated the spirit and stated intent of the Fourteenth and Fifteenth Amendments, presenting the possibility of a federal election law as a result of the anger of Northern Republicans and humanitarians. Also, Southern congressmen could be unseated. That these were not idle fears was seen in the House of Representatives' passage of the Lodge "Force Bill" of 1890, providing for federal supervision of congressional elections. The efforts to nullify the Negro vote also often violated state constitutions, while another fault was that inner conservative cliques could, and increasingly did, use these meth-

[5] Frank B. Williams, Jr., "The Poll Tax as a Suffrage Requirement in the South, 1870-1901," *Journal of Southern History*, XVIII (November, 1952), pp. 469-496.

ods against white progressives. A frustrating effect upon the Democrats themselves was apparent, as white illiterates were often unable to fulfill the voting requirements. And a factor of underlying significance was that, since the Negroes had the legal right to vote, their ballots were courted in times of political stress. Therefore the white conservatives decided that to avoid fraud, the chance of Negro votes holding the balance of political power, and the loss of political participation by ignorant, but Democratic, whites, constitutional disfranchisement of the Negroes was imperative.

Those states where the Negroes outnumbered the whites were the first to act. As early as 1880, a move for a constitutional convention got underway in Mississippi because of the need for reform and the general objection to living under a carpetbag document. The Negroes in the state voted Republican, and the techniques used to void their votes were extra-legal. The introduction of the Force Bill in 1890 made a change even more imperative. A constitutional convention was called for that year, with suffrage reform the principal issue. The convention was made up largely of Confederate veterans; a single Negro delegate represented the more than 65 per cent Negro majority in the state.

In the convention it was frankly admitted that, in order to suppress a large portion of the Negro vote, there had not been a fair election count in the state since 1875. Both the black-belt and the "white county" delegates wanted the Negroes disfranchised but were divided as to the method. The white counties wanted to make sure that no white was excluded, but the black belt was willing to sacrifice some whites in order to remove the Negroes. The white counties also were anxious to control the legislature, and they consequently opposed any literacy test. At the same time, the black belt objected to legislative reapportionment, which would endanger their control. After much debate the legislature was reapportioned, and the suffrage problem solved thus: a voter had to be twenty-one years old, sane, and a resident of the state for two years and of his district for one year; he must have no convictions of certain crimes, including theft and bigamy; he had to pay a two-dollar poll tax eight months before elections; and he must be able to read a passage from the state constitution or understand it when read to him *or* give "a reasonable interpretation thereof." Lack of provision for bipartisan and bi-racial representation on the registration boards gave many opportunities for discrimination. Poor whites could be given an easy section of the constitution and be required to explain it; Negroes could be given a difficult one and find it impossible to explain to the satisfaction of the white board.

The Negro convention member, a former slave of Jefferson Davis' brother, supported the new constitution in his hope of restoring

# THE SOUTH SINCE 1865

180  THE SOUTH SINCE 1865

onfidenceonfidence

180 THE SOUTH SINCE 1865

# THE SOUTH SINCE 1865

confidence and honesty, saying he "believed that the white people, if let alone, would do the right thing." This despite the fact that it obviously would convert a potential Negro majority into a white one of 40,000. The constitution was not submitted to popular vote, and its success was made clear in the next election, when the Negro votes declined 70 per cent.[6]

In South Carolina the Tillman constitution of 1895 reflected the desires of the agrarian reformers, who wanted to lessen the Negro vote, and of the Bourbon wing which opposed the lenient policy toward the Negroes pursued by Hampton. It was not so much a fear of a Republican victory, for the Republican vote had been cut from 91,870 to 13,740 between 1876 and 1888; rather, it was a desire to eliminate the Negro franchise. The vote on the referendum for a constitutional convention had been 31,402 for and 29,523 against, generally featuring low-country opposition and up-country support. The convention contained 112 Tillmanites, 42 Conservatives, and 6 Negro Republicans; the Committee on Suffrage had 8 Tillmanites and 3 Conservatives, with Tillman as chairman. The suffrage provisions provided for residence of two years in the state, one year in the county, and four months in the precinct, and for payment of the poll tax at least six months before the elections. The chief control measure was the literacy requirement. Each registrant had to prove to the satisfaction of the board that he could read and write any section of the constitution. There were, however, two vital alternatives: ownership and payment of taxes on property assessed for at least $300 and ability to "understand" the constitution when it was read aloud. Specially aimed against the Negroes was a list of crimes punishable by disfranchisement, including those the whites believed to be most frequently committed by Negroes. The document was approved by a vote of 116 to 7 and put into effect without submission to the people.[7]

The specter of white men appealing for Negro votes and the decisive role which such ballots had often played in the Populist Revolt buried internal sectionalism after 1896, and white conservatives and liberals joined in the movement to curtail the Negro vote. All classes joined in the campaign which swept the remaining Southern states down the path blazed by Mississippi and South Carolina. This crusade saw so firm a union among the whites that even the state Republican organizations disavowed their Negro supporters and took on a "Lily White" complexion. The only issue became the maintenance of white

[6] William Alexander Mabry, "Disfranchisement of the Negro in Mississippi," *Journal of Southern History*, IV (August, 1938), pp. 318-333.
[7] George B. Tindall, "The Campaign for Disfranchisement of Negroes in South Carolina," *Journal of Southern History*, XV (May, 1949), pp. 212-234.

supremacy, and everything else was subordinated to implementing and perpetuating this idea.

Tom Watson, who had been known earlier as the "savior" of the Negroes, showed this rapid conversion. After his successive defeats, he more and more characterized the Negroes as a constant barrier to his program of reform. He was not afraid of Negro domination but was convinced that the conservatives would not disenfranchise the race because Negro votes were needed to beat off political insurgents. Watson, therefore, offered to support any Democrat who would make a disfranchisement pledge, for with the Negro threat removed, "every white man would act according to his own conscience and judgment in deciding how he should vote." As he became older, Watson decided the only solution was repeal of the Fifteenth Amendment and even sank to justifying lynching.[8]

Carter Glass of Virginia was more forthright than most Southern leaders. When asked the motives which activated the disfranchisement drive in his state, he answered on the floor of the constitutional convention: "Discriminate! Why that is precisely what we propose; that, exactly, is what this convention was elected for — to discriminate to the very extremity of permissible action under the limitations of the Federal Constitution, with a view to the elimination of every negro voter who can be gotten rid of legally, without materially impairing the numerical strength of the white electorate."[9]

Even old friends deserted the Negro. In an open letter to James Bryce of England, D. H. Chamberlain, Massachusetts-born carpetbagger governor of South Carolina, wrote in 1904 that he hoped he was much wiser than thirty or forty years earlier. "Regarding the negro problem in this spirit, I find myself forced . . . to say that perhaps our first practical aim should be to undo, so far as possible, what we have heretofore done for the negro since his emancipation — namely the inspiring in him the hope or dream of sharing with the white race a social or political equality; for whoever will lay aside wishes and fancies and look only at realities, will see that these things are impossibilities within any measurable range of time, if ever."[10] During the same year, Andrew Carnegie announced his opposition to unlimited suffrage in the South on the grounds that the Negroes were "steeped in ignorance of political responsibilities to a degree impossible for northern people to imagine." This was not a fault of theirs, but "an educational test for

[8] C. Vann Woodward, "Tom Watson and the Negro in Agrarian Politics," *Journal of Southern History*, IV (February, 1938), pp. 14-33.
[9] As quoted by Paul H. Buck, *The Road to Reunion, 1865-1900* (Boston: Little, Brown, 1937), p. 287.
[10] D. H. Chamberlain, *Present Phases of Our So-Called Negro Problem* (n. p., 1904), p. 6, in *Negro Pamphlets*, I. University of Virginia Library.

suffrage should be adopted and strictly applied, applicable to white and black alike, for ignorance in the whites is deplorable."[11]

One faction of the national Republican party favored elimination of the Negro vote, hopeful of making the party respectable in the South and permitting the white men to divide politically. The North was now absorbed in imperialism and problems resulting from the Spanish-American War, and even the federal government was guilty of practicing racial discrimination in its newly-acquired dominions. The United States Supreme Court in 1898 gave its stamp of approval by accepting as constitutional the Mississippi suffrage provisions (Williams *v.* Mississippi, 170 U. S. 213). Disgust with corrupt elections and black-belt domination, the desire by some conservatives to eliminate some whites, the wish of whites to divide on basic issues, the hope that the Negro could be forced to give up false hopes and accept his place — all sparked the South to action, a drive to which resistance was negligible.

One unexpected result was a corresponding drop in white voter participation. To what extent this was a result of planning is debatable, despite assertions such as Dunbar Rowland's that in Mississippi the "avowed and confessed object of the convention was to eliminate the ignorant voter whether white or black."[12] Whether or not there was conservative malice aforethought, the white masses were given positive assurance that they would not lose their vote. Probably the conservative Democrats had no strong objection to disfranchisement of the ignorant whites, who often had been politically active against them, but they could not afford to say so.[13] Certainly the long-range result was that many of the lower classes lost the right or desire to vote; the poll tax, for example, proved to be a joker, after elimination of the black by effectively checking the white man, especially during periods of economic depression.

One concession to ease this situation was made in 1898, when Louisiana changed her constitution, adding residence requirements, literacy tests, and poll taxes. To protect those whites threatened with loss of suffrage, the state produced the so-called "grandfather clause," which exempted whites from property and educational tests by automatically placing on registration all male applicants whose fathers or grandfathers had been eligible to vote in 1867. The rest of the South quickly followed this example. North Carolina took the step by constitutional amendment in 1900; Alabama in 1901; Virginia in 1901-02; and Georgia

[11] "The Work and Influence of Hampton," Armstrong Association, *Proceedings* (February, 1904), p. 6, in *Negro Pamphlets,* I. University of Virginia Library.
[12] Dunbar Rowland, *A Mississippi View of Race Relations in the South* (Jackson, 1903), p. 12, in *Negro Pamphlets,* V. University of Virginia Library.
[13] For a discussion of intent to disfranchise whites, see V. O. Key, Jr., *Southern Politics in State and Nation* (New York: Knopf, 1949), pp. 542-550.

in 1908. Oklahoma, although having only a small Negro population, attempted in 1910 through its "grandfather clause" to eliminate Negroes permanently while permitting white illiterates to vote, only to have it struck down by the Supreme Court in 1915 (Guinn *v.* U. S., 238 U. S. 347).

The two most common barriers to Negro voting were literacy and property qualifications, with the former prevailing in eight states. Four others allowed an alternative to literacy tests, in the form of possession of property worth from $300 to $500, but the tendency in some states to undervalue property for tax assessment made this loophole almost invisible. The "understanding" and "grandfather" clauses took out some of the sting for poorer whites, but all Southern states had poll taxes with few exemptions.

By 1910 the Negro disfranchisement movement was virtually complete. The effects were already obvious. Not only had most of the Negroes stopped voting, but the great loss in white participation left the conservatives once more in firm control. It became even harder to lodge crusading protests, for effective disagreement was restricted to within the Democratic party. The South had erased itself from the national political equation: the national Democratic party counted Southern votes as assured; the Republicans had no hope there. Consequently, the Republicans in the South became a party of federal officeholders and, to exist at all, had to become "Lily White." Political apathy settled over the region, and only the specter of Catholicism in 1928 caused the voter participation rate of 1896 to be equalled, despite the doubling of the electorate through woman suffrage. In Louisiana between 1897 and 1904, the total of registered voters declined from 294,432 to 93,058, with a drop of almost 73,000 in white registration and 129,002 among the Negroes (from 130,344 to 1,342). Voting declined in Texas by half; Mississippi registration dropped 42,100 among the whites, and the number of Negro voters cascaded from 147,205 to 8,615. The average vote in congressional elections fell about 56 per cent in Virginia, 60 in Alabama, 69 in Mississippi, 80 in Louisiana, 34 in North Carolina, 69 in Florida, 75 in Arkansas, 50 in Tennessee, and 80 in Georgia. In one of the hardest-fought presidential elections in United States history, that of 1912, only 15 to 24 per cent of potential voters in the lower South went to the polls, while the figures for the upper South, including North Carolina, ranged from 26 to 48 per cent. The average for the entire region was only 33 per cent, compared to the national average of 60. In the lack-luster election of 1920, the Southern vote varied from eight to 44 per cent, averaging 21 per cent of the potential voters.

Disfranchisement in the South was reinforced around 1910 by a fundamental process which proved more effective than either threats or constitutional restrictions. This was the twisting of the democratic process of primary elections into the "closed" or "white" primary, on the theory that a private association, the Democratic party, might discriminate as it chose. The primary election was the real election in the one-party South, and if Negroes could be barred from it, little matter if some voted in the general election. As early as 1890, the Tillmanites had inaugurated a rule that no Negro could vote in the Democratic primaries unless he had voted Democratic continuously since 1876. As the direct primary came to rest on statute rather than party rule, local and state party committees were empowered to prescribe qualifications for voters in the primaries. Variously by state party rule and by county party rule, participation came to be formally limited to whites. By 1930 all Southern states except Florida, North Carolina, and Tennessee barred Negroes by state party rule.

Rules or no rules, however, some Negroes continued to vote throughout the period. In the border states or states of the upper South, where there were strong Negro leaders or where the Negroes were higher in the economic scale, small groups continued to exercise the ballot. This was usually in the cities, where there was less a sense of economic competition and where the more intelligent Negroes and whites lived. In rural areas Negro voting was unpopular, even if they paid poll taxes and passed a literacy test. Generally, however, when the Negroes did vote, they usually voted Democratic in local elections and, as a gesture, cast a Republican ballot in the national elections. In the main, not surprisingly, the Negroes looked upon politics as a white man's game and cynically concluded that the effort to vote was not worth the trouble. Many, too, followed the advice of Booker T. Washington: that they should be concerned primarily with economic factors; when they became economically indispensable, their political rights would follow.

Along with the drive to isolate the Negroes politically came an effort to segregate them socially[14] and economically as well. Segregation had been impractical under slavery, with the races often living in the same houses, sharing a common family life, and attending the same churches. As long as the Negroes had been enslaved, the circumstances which later gave rise to the segregation codes could not exist. Reconstruction saw the initiation of only a few elements of race separation, chiefly in churches and schools. In the case of churches, the whites generally desired to keep the Negro membership, but it flocked into new organizations which sprang up spontaneously or were sponsored by Northern missionaries. By the end of reconstruction, the Protestant church organizations and worship services were almost entirely

[14] C. Vann Woodward, *The Strange Career of Jim Crow* (New York: Oxford, 1955).

separate. In public schools, regardless of the Fourteenth Amendment and reconstruction constitutions, separation was the universal policy.

Even with the return of home rule, practically no effort was made to expand segregation into other fields. The Bourbons, although believing the Negroes to be inferior, saw no essential connection between white supremacy and the need to humiliate the Negroes publicly. Some Northerners even criticized the degree of commingling between white Southerners and Negroes. Negroes were admitted to theaters, at least in most cities, and were served at bars, soda fountains, ice cream parlors, and general merchandise stores. Parks and public buildings were usually open without discrimination, and the practice of using a common cemetery continued for many years. They rode street cars and were unrestricted on the railroads except by the custom which barred them from "ladies" cars except in the capacity of servants. Some Negroes served on juries, and they continued to work with whites on political committees and sit in political conventions. There were no strenuous efforts at geographical residential segregation. Only in hotels was discrimination likely to be encountered, and this lacked the force of law. On the contrary, the federal Civil Rights Act of 1875 was reinforced by similar Southern state legislation which was passed without protest. When the Supreme Court declared the federal law unconstitutional in 1883, few Southern blacks dared or cared to protest, and there was no wholesale rush by Dixie legislatures to take advantage of the situation or repeal their own similar laws — none of which seems to have been vigorously enforced.

During slavery there were no laws requiring segregation, and afterwards blacks continued to be admitted to stores and such facilities because of habit. This did not, however, imply equality for in personal relationships involving individual choice, blacks and whites seldom intermingled. Whenever crowds collected, the two races tended to group themselves separately, only with the rise of white-dominated democracy, coupled with Negro invasions of up-country towns and the increased economic competition on the farms and in the labor markets, did demands begin for segregation. Coincident with the militancy of the Alliance movements came efforts to kick the Negro down the social and economic ladder. Between 1887 and 1907, all Southern states separated the races on railroads and other public transportation, a move which was sanctioned by the United States Supreme Court in 1896 in Plessy v. Ferguson (163 U. S. 537), upholding the policy of "equal but separate accommodations." Only three states, however, required separate waiting rooms, and Georgia alone applied segregation to street cars. South Carolina's civil rights law was not repealed until

.1889, and not until 1898, after a ten-year fight, was segregation on trains approved by a single vote in the senate.

The segregation of train passengers was the only instance, apart from in the schools, of legal separation in the majority of states before 1900. With the all-out drive for political disfranchisement came an increased tempo in laws providing greater social barriers. Separation in penal and charitable institutions, parks, beaches, playgrounds, factories, barber shops, restaurants, and hotels — in short, nearly everywhere except in stores and in the streets — became common. Wherever the association of the two peoples might suggest social equality, there the color line was most firmly drawn. By 1910 many Southern cities introduced residential segregation laws, only to have them voided by the Supreme Court in 1917 (Buchanan *v*. Warley, 245 U. S. 16). Thereafter the same goal was achieved by more ingenious techniques.

Extreme racism was possible only because of the relaxed vigilance of the Negroes' supporters in both the South and North. The Southern upper classes, which had formerly protected the Negroes, now felt compelled for political reasons to join the lower class against their traditional enemy; the North was busily preaching the doctrine of Anglo-Saxon superiority to justify imperialism. In a speech on February 12, 1904, President Charles W. Eliot of Harvard stated that both Northern and Southern opinions were agreed upon the necessity for keeping the race pure. "Put the prosperous Northern whites in Southern States, in immediate contact with millions of Negroes, and they would promptly establish separate schools for the colored population, whatever the necessary cost." It was his belief that, after personal contacts with Negroes, the desire for segregation by the Northern white was stronger than that of the Southerners, who were accustomed to Negroes. The main difference he could see between the sections was that no Northerner connected political equality with social equality, as did the Southerners. He concluded that the "Northern whites are beginning to sympathize strongly with their Southern brethren in respect to the peculiar burden which the action of the National Government in liberating the Negroes has imposed on them."[15]

The South's segregated "Jim Crow" society proved expensive, despite the fact that facilities for Negroes were not equal, and troublesome to defend. Nevertheless, the region was determined to maintain it. In the first place, the Negro was considered inferior, a stand based on alleged Biblical support, on the bad connotation given to the word "black," and upon a misinterpretation of Darwin's theory: the Negro was a race lower on the scale of evolution and not merely one of God's children only partially developed. To abolish segregation, therefore,

[15] Armstrong Association, *loc. cit.*, pp. 9-15.

would be to flaunt "natural law," not to mention God's will. Nor could the freedman escape the stigma of slavery and the object lesson of his roles in reconstruction and during the Agrarian Revolt. There was also a widespread feeling that the newer class of Negroes had lost the virtues (i.e., humility) of their forebears while acquiring many new vices. Some white Southerners justified Jim Crowism on the grounds that segregation was needed to protect the innocent Negro from bad white men. The whites knew what was best for the Negro, and so he was not harmed by segregation.

Although seldom mentioned, two basic factors underlay the defense of segregation. One was the desire to end economic competition; the other was the concern with "race purity," with its chief objective that of preventing amalgamation.[16] The fear of miscegenation, and particularly intermarriage, was so great that social equality had to be rejected and segregation and discrimination of the Negro extended to nearly every sphere of activity. The fact that the Negro already was poor and socially inferior made such a move seem even more plausible.

Determination to keep the Negro in his place made the whites passionately resent any gesture by the black man which seemed to suggest equality. The accustomed use of force against the Negroes consequently increased and was justified as racial and patriotic. The white woman, perpetuator of the "superior" race, was placed beyond approach by the inferior black man, even to the extent of condoning lynch law. The color line was also apparent in law enforcement, with Negroes not only excluded from jury panels but also often receiving heavier penalties than whites for comparable crimes. Consequently, there arose a class of Southern politicians which made political capital out of the fears of racial equality.

This treatment associated with segregation aroused the race consciousness of the Negro, providing him with an incentive which spurred his ambitions. It created a whole separate system of society and economy on the dark side of the color line, with Negroes fabricating an imitation of the white capitalistic society. Ironically, the black professional and businessman was able to make gains as his white counterpart forfeited such trade to him. Although separation imposed racial peace, at the same time, it also caused the whites to lose contact with the educated and upper-class Negroes and, more importantly, was conducive to "forgetting" to provide the minority group with equal rights and opportunities.

The inferior position of the Negroes was concretely illustrated by their economic status. For ten or fifteen years after the Civil War, the destruction of the old plantation system had led to some improvement

[16] Gunnar Myrdal, *An American Dilemma* (New York: Harper, 1944), pp. 58-59.

in their status, but their economic level soon was permanently depressed by the perpetual debts which were an inherent part of the sharecropping system. In competition for the better types of employment, they met constant defeat by white labor. From the 1880's to World War I, there was a period of debate over the value of the Negroes as workers. Many whites held that they were incapable of doing skilled work or of operating machines, that Negroes got sleepy when running machinery and on the whole lacked mechanical aptitude. As a race, they met wholesale accusations of general unreliability, lack of aptitude for sustained mental activity, "childishness," immaturity, a lack of initiative, disinclination to learn new skills, willingness to work only when necessary, and generally lower intelligence. On the lone positive side, they were credited as being superior to whites in agricultural labor, as having a special affinity for such work.

Nevertheless, the industrial revolution, which held out such great promise to Southern whites, attracted Negroes from the farm as well. Because of the predominantly white female population in the textile industry, the Negro workers usually found that business closed to them except for heavy, outside work or as strike breakers. During the nineties, in search of still cheaper labor, some South Carolina mills experimented with the employment of Negroes. This often resulted in pitched battles between the two races, with the Negro workers being chased off the job. When one mill which hired only Negro labor failed, the failure was blamed on lack of efficiency in the labor force, and further experimentation along this line was discontinued. Negro men had more success in getting the heavy, dirty, and distasteful jobs in cotton-seed oil mills, sawmills, furniture factories, foundries, boiler works, and machine shops, and Negro women became predominant in tobacco factories. A mere 196 Southern industrial employers used only 7,395 Negroes in 1891; by 1910 the number of Negro factory workers had increased to more than 350,000.

In the skilled labor field, the Negro was faced with the problem of obtaining membership in labor unions, while the control of apprenticeships by white unions often kept him from learning certain trades. Prejudice, along with the refusal of many whites to work with him, acted as invisible bars to membership. Some unions set up percentages of Negroes which could be employed. Although on the national level both the Knights of Labor and the American Federation of Labor were willing to accept Negroes as members, in order to secure Southern white membership they often ignored discrimination in the region.

Excluded from recognized unions, but drastically in need of such protection, the Negro worker attempted to fill the gap by creating independent unions of his own in occupations in which he had won a sub-

stantial place. An effort was made in 1919 to federate the various
Negro labor unions in the National Brotherhood Workers of America,
the strongest element of which was the employees in the shipyards
and on the docks at Newport News, Norfolk, and Portsmouth, Virginia.
Although this group made an effort to attract field workers as well as
craftsmen, opposition of the AF of L, general hostility of the whites,
and Negro apathy caused its collapse in 1921. The slight progress made
in independent unions was restricted almost entirely to railway workers, leaving the great bulk of Negro workers untouched.[17]

The Negroes were also unable to hold their own in trades which
they had dominated before the Civil War. Negro percentages of total
national employment fell by 1890 to 16.1 in carpentry, 28.2 in masonry,
10.9 in painting, 33.2 in plastering, and 2.5 in machinist work. Some
sought to enter business for themselves, but here again they met the
caste system which limited them only to the service of Negroes. They
also faced the almost insurmountable problem of securing finances. An
1899 survey of Negro businessmen in South Carolina with stocks of
goods for sale or with $500 or more invested capital counted only 123
merchants, almost half of whom were located in Charleston. The most
striking exception came in 1898 with the organization of the North
Carolina Mutual Life Insurance Company which soon became the
world's largest black business. Most of the Negroes who went to the
city had to content themselves with jobs in personal service, mainly
domestic, accounting for 31.4 per cent of all Negroes so employed in
1890. Often the urban blacks found themselves in worse condition than
they had been on the farm and with no way to survive without drifting
into petty crime.

On the farm the way upward was equally difficult. Three-fourths
of the Negro farmers were still croppers or tenants in 1900. Although
the Negro farmers constituted one-third of the Southern population, by
1925 they owned only one-seventh of the farms. That the land they
owned was less desirable was shown in 1930, when the average value
per acre of their land was $19.93, while that of the land they worked
as tenants was $31.18. The annual gross income of Negro farm owners
during the years 1920-1930 was less than $600, of cash and share ten-
ants about $550, and of croppers less than $500. During the period before 1930, the absolute right of the Negro to work was not challenged,
except by some labor unions. His place in the Southern economy at the
bottom of the ladder was assured; his chances of climbing were few.

In the years after 1877, many Negroes sought relief from their

[17] The best discussion of the Negro and organized labor is Sterling D. Spero and
Abram L. Harris, *The Black Worker: The Negro and the Labor Movement* (New
York: Columbia Univ., 1931).

problems through migration. Uprooted and disillusioned, some were attracted by the idea of leaving the United States entirely. Organized movements to go to Liberia sprang up in many Southern counties, and in South Carolina in 1877 the Liberian Exodus Joint Stock Steamship Company was organized to provide the transportation. After moving approximately 300 persons, the company collapsed because of poor management. Unfavorable reports from those who had migrated quickly choked off interest in Africa.

Interest rekindled only during the decade of the First World War, when, once again disillusioned, the American Negro was vulnerable to the blandishments of a remarkable West Indian Negro, Marcus Garvey. He declared that while the whites might fight for democracy abroad, they continued to oppress the Negroes at home, and the race must forego all hope of aid and understanding from them. As president of the newly-formed Universal Negro Improvement Association in the United States, he proposed a sort of African Zionism, proclaiming that the "hour has come when the whole continent of Africa shall be reclaimed and redeemed as the home of the black peoples." He exalted everything black. It was imperative for the Negroes to organize and build a country of their own, compelling the world to respect them. Needing an army, he created one. The Black Star Line would transport them. He formed throughout the United States, while awaiting the day of the exodus, cooperative grocery stores, laundries, hotels, restaurants, and printing plants, with the *Negro World* his official newspaper. As provisional president of Africa, he had a flag and a host of sub-officers, including a nobility.

When opposed by local Negro leaders, he appealed to the rank and file. The awe in which he was held by the lower classes is seen in the comment by one of his disciples: "So at this time, God has sent a Daniel after us to take us back home to our motherland in Africa whose name is Marcus Garvey who is the greatest leader in the world today, and we Negroes ought to feel proud of him everywhere even in the four corners of the world for he has stood the test and is standing it yet." According to his follower, Garvey was even mentioned in the Bible: "The church that is at Babylon elected together with you, saluteth you; and so doeth Marcus my son."[18] The bubble burst, however. After involving millions of Negroes, Garvey was prosecuted for using the mails to defraud in connection with stock sales in his steamship line and was deported as an undesirable alien.

By far the greatest number of "exodusters" confined their hopes to finding better opportunities outside the South but within the United

[18] Zebedee Green, *Why I am Dissatisfied* (n. p., 1924), p. 34, in *Negro Pamphlets*, V. University of Virginia Library.

States. In the 1870's and '80's, the West was the first lure, with Kansas as the main attraction. Led by men such as Henry Adams and Benjamin "Pap" Singleton, thousands of Negroes moved westward from the states of the lower South. The majority came from Louisiana and Mississippi because of their proximity to easy river-boat transportation. Between March and July, 1879, over 5,000 Negroes descended upon the unprepared citizenry of Kansas alone, and between 1860 and 1880, the Negro population of that state increased from 627 to 43,107.[19] All told, some 200,000 sought new homes in the West before the movement waned. Many of these aided in the creation of black towns not only in Kansas but also in what is now the State of Oklahoma. Some, such as Edwin McCabe, entertained the idea of an all-black state in the West. This was an early "black power" dream which never materialized.

As early as 1897, it was obvious that the Negroes were moving North as well and in considerable numbers. From 1870 to 1910, Southern-born Negroes in the North increased at an average of about 67,000 in each ten-year period. The great migration, however, began during and after World War I, with nearly 2,000,000 moving into the industrial centers of the North and Middle West by 1930. White acceptance of jobs formerly monopolized by the Negroes in the South, the westward shift of the cotton belt, the ravages of the boll weevil, and droughts in 1916 and 1917 — all helped give the Negroes a "push." A new growth in race consciousness developed when the War stirred up the Negroes and moved some into new areas, often where their race was better treated. Industrial expansion in Northern cities, the draft, and the cessation of foreign immigration made them welcome in the North.

The desire for economic improvement was the Negroes' chief motive for heading north. A Negro minister wrote in the Montgomery *Advertiser*: "The Negro farm hand gets for his compensation hardly more than the mule he plows; that is, his board and shelter. Some mules fare better than Negroes." The desire for social betterment followed closely in appeal. A high premium was placed upon education, and the greater freedom, excitement, and anonymity of city life appealed to many rural Negroes. This pattern of migration, once started, formed its own undertow and ballooned the Negro problem into a national one.[20] Approximately 90.6 per cent of all Negroes had lived in the South in 1870; this figure had dropped by only one per cent by

[19] Glen Schwendemann, "Negro Exodus to Kansas: First Phase, March-July, 1879" (unpublished Master's thesis, Dept. of History, University of Oklahoma, 1957).
[20] R. H. Leavell and others, *Negro Migration in 1916-1917* (Washington: Government Printing Office, 1919).

*The South Woos the Negro Migrants*

1900. But by 1930, however, the approximate percentages were 78 for the South, 20 for the North, and one for the West; Mississippi had the only Negro majority.

The migration of the Negro workers placed the white Southerners in a dilemma. Frankly recognizing this was a South Carolinian who said, "Politically speaking there are far too many negroes in South Carolina, but from an industrial standpoint there is room for many more." Some, like Senator Matthew C. Butler of the same state, denied this and claimed in 1879 that "the departure of 100,000 darkies from the South would prove beneficial," while later he raised that figure to 200,000 from South Carolina alone! But as usual, economic interest supplanted political and social ones, and white farmers throughout the South protested the loss of their labor. Some even used shotguns to hold their tenants, and state legislatures hastened to the landlords' aid.

Generally, two methods were tried to solve the problem: encouragement of white immigration to replace the Negro, and attempts to halt the exodus. Newspapers published scare stories of the horrible fate awaiting migrants to the North. Labor-contract legislation prescribed heavy fines for breaking written or verbal contracts and often left the laborer under a condition similar to peonage. In some Southern areas, Negroes were forced to sign a contract for a year in order to get a job and were treated like fugitives if they left earlier. Other laws attempted to discourage the activities of emigrant agents. In 1916 Florida enacted a penalty of $1,000 for any person convicted of enticing a Negro to leave the state, while Georgia set the fine at $500. A labor agent for a big Chicago firm escaped arrest only by being able to outrun the local police in a race to an outgoing train. In Macon, Georgia, the police used force to disperse 1,000 Negroes who had gathered to leave for Chicago, threatening to use rifles if they persisted. At small-town stations Negroes had to explain where they were going and would be sold tickets only for short distances. As one lamented, "It is now almost as difficult for a colored man to leave some parts of the south as it was in the day of the 'underground railroad' of sixty years ago."

But the majority of Negroes, whether from inertia or lack of opportunity, had to work out their problems in the South. From this sprang one of the most progressive ideas to come out of the reconstruction period — industrial training for the colored race. Generally credited with this concept was General Samuel Chapman Armstrong, a former Union soldier who had come south as an agent of the Freedman's Bureau. In 1868 he managed to open Hampton Normal and Industrial Institute with the basic aims of teaching respect for labor, building up character, and providing graduates with an economically useful trade.

The best example of a Hampton product was Booker T. Washington, who rose from a humble position to that of the most distinguished American Negro of all times. Born in slavery in 1857 or 1858 — he was never sure which — he worked in a coal mine after emancipation until he heard of Hampton Institute. Penniless, he was allowed to work his way through the school and there pledged himself to give his fellows in the lower South the same chance given him. In 1881, following the

Hampton idea, he formed Tuskegee Institute in Alabama with a borrowed log shanty, one teacher, and thirty students. He became an educator for his race in the broadest terms. Opposing migration, he counselled the Negroes to "cast down your bucket where you are." It was "through the dairy farm, the truck garden, the trades, and commercial life that the negro is to find his way to the enjoyment of all his rights." Friction would "disappear in proportion as the black man, by reason of his intelligence and skill can create something that the white man wants or respects." If the Negro owned the mortgage on the white man's house, said Washington, the latter would not drive him from the polls. Although he might be denied the vote once a year, there was "a little green ballot" that could be passed through the teller's window, and "no one will throw it out or refuse to count it." There would be no necessity to pass laws to force men to come into contact with a "negro who is educated and has $200,000 to lend."

Washington, likewise, had much to say to whites. His people's mistakes he did not deny: "We began at the top. We made those mistakes, not because we were black people, but because we were ignorant and unexperienced people." To an Atlanta audience, whose whites probably missed the import of his statement that the laws of changeless justice binds oppressor with oppressed, he gave his solution for racial tensions: "Agitation of questions of social equality is the extremest folly." In matters "purely social we can be as separate as the fingers, yet one as the hand in all things essential to mutual progress." The Negro should be more interested in education and economic opportunity than in the franchise. The race that made itself indispensable would find its problems solved, and so the Negro should remain aloof from politics.

In line with his belief, Washington aimed at building up a class of Negro businessmen who would become the leaders of his people. He organized in 1900 the National Negro Business League, so that "through the promotion of commercial achievement" the race could be led to a position of influence in American life and thus pave the way to economic independence. The League was to function as a national center for local business leagues, Negro chambers of commerce, and the like. By 1907 there were 320 of these local leagues in the United States.

It was easy to criticize Washington's approach. He accepted the white man's version of the Negro's "place," but he did not relinquish the right to eventual full equality in all respects. He did not insist upon "rights" but asked for tolerance and some material assistance. His views were a reflection of the white philosophy on race and business, but it is doubtful if he could have successfully upheld any other program, considering the time and place. He was a great politician, serving as an advisor on black affairs and on political appointments to Presidents Theodore Roosevelt and William Howard Taft, until his death in 1915.

Dissent did arise, however, and from some of his own people. Negro intellectuals, particularly in the North, fretted over Washington's virtual monopoly in leadership and political patronage and in 1901, through the Boston *Guardian,* began a vocal opposition. Leadership of the protest movement fell to W. E. Burghardt Du Bois, Massachusettts-born and educated at Fisk, Harvard, and the University of Berlin. He became a professor of economics and history at Atlanta University in 1896, at a time when racial violence was the order of the day. In 1903 he published *Souls of Black Folk,* bitterly attacking Washington's strategy, his submission to caste discriminations, and his materialistic concept of education. Industrial education would not produce the leaders needed by the race; salvation could come only through aggressive political action to insure the Negroes of every single right which belonged to any American.

In the summer of 1905, twenty-five Negro intellectuals met at Niagara Falls to form a national protest organization to battle all forms of segregation and discrimination. Although similar meetings were later held, several years passed before an effective program developed. Following a severe race riot in Springfield, Illinois, in 1908, a group of whites organized to prevent future such occurrences, and in 1910 they merged with the leaders of the Niagara movement to form the National Association for the Advancement of Colored People (NAACP). All the officers were white except Du Bois, who gave up teaching to become Director of Publicity and Research and its guiding spirit. Interracial at the top, the NAACP was practically all-Negro in the branch organizations. It served as a watchdog over Negro rights and intervened whenever anything adverse to Negro interests developed. Using publicity as a tool, it lobbied on national and state levels with great stress on legal redress of grievances. A pamphlet issued in 1919 set its objectives thus:

> 1) To abolish legal injustices against Negroes; 2) To stamp out race discriminations; 3) To prevent lynchings, burnings and torturings of black people; 4) To assure every citizen of color the common rights of American citizenship; 5) To compel equal accommodations in railroad travel, irrespective of color; 6) To secure colored children an equal opportunity to public school education through a fair apportionment of public education funds; 7) To emancipate in fact, as well as in name, a race of nearly 12,000,000 American-born citizens.

In addition to their own organizations, numerous other national, state, and local groups were concerned with the Negro problem. The

Communists, for example, made strong appeals to the Negroes to join in a war against their common natural enemy, the capitalists, and promised at one time the creation of a black republic in the cotton belt. More in line with the American tradition, however, was the work of such groups as the University Commission on Southern Race Problems, the Commission on Interracial Cooperation, the Urban League, and interracial groups sponsored by organizations such as churches and the Young Men's Christian Association. Many individual Southerners, newspapers, and chambers of commerce devoted themselves to actively fostering better race relations. Negroes also received a large share of the funds, especially for education, supplied by men such as George Foster Peabody, John D. Rockefeller, Julius Rosenwald, and Edward S. Harkness.

Given at best a minimum of opportunity, blacks could show some progress. Despite ignorance, poverty, and caste discriminations, by 1900 one in every five Negroes owned his home; their farms were valued at nearly $500,000,000. That they had taken advantage of the educational opportunities was evident in the rise of their literacy rate from nearly zero to 56 per cent. This increased knowledge was also reflected in a slow but steady improvement in morals and family relations. One-room cabins were being replaced by two- or even three-room houses. In 1915, although they existed to serve their own people, Negroes in the South could boast of owning 30,000 businesses, including 1,000 millinery and 7,000 grocery stores, 100 drugstores, 200 sawmills, 50 banks, and 120 insurance companies. Some 34,000 Negroes were employed as teachers.

With the outbreak of the First World War, Negroes were eager to do their part. Some 400,000 were drafted, and 200,000 went to France. Not a single Negro was convicted of disloyalty during the war. The period also saw some improvement in economic situations, with both farm and industry bidding for their services. Negro college enrollments increased over sixfold between 1917 and 1927. More Southern high schools were built for the race between 1918 and 1928 than had ever been erected before. By 1930 a higher percentage of Negroes than whites was gainfully employed: in industry the number had risen to 1,024,656; there were 136,925 in the professions; and some 70,000 were in businesses of their own. Standing alone, these figures are impressive; yet comparatively they are less so as the blacks still lagged behind the whites to about the same degree as the South trailed the North.

This progress was not without continued difficulty, however. First of all, the illusions and high hopes of the race that its loyal service at home and abroad during World War I would be repaid by better understanding from the Southerners was met instead by increased fear and suspicion. The revitalization of the Ku Klux Klan and a wave of lynchings and race riots made Garvey's plan for migration to Africa seem more plausible. In the second place, all too often the great prosperity which swept the nation did not filter down equally to the Negroes. The agrarian population, which included the majority of Negro citizens, was left without means to enjoy the opulence of the twenties. When the crash came in October, 1929, Negroes already knew their own depression.

# 11

## LABOR IN THE SOUTH

IN THE FIRST BURST of enthusiasm for industrial development, promoters of the "New South" had little concern that they were creating an essentially new social class of Southerners. Industrialization was hailed as a means of economic salvation and a way to put the idle to work. The problems of whether the poor whites were willing to work, a stumbling block in antebellum manufacturing, and whether they had the requisite skills or aptitudes for such labor, were ignored. Apparently no serious consideration was given to the possibility of using the traditional labor supply of the region (the Negro) except in agriculture. If people and talents were not available, they could be acquired by the same method used in the North, i.e., immigration. It was believed that skilled foreigners and Northerners would be happy to come in and make up any labor deficit, since slavery, the traditional barrier to immigration into the South, no longer existed.

From 1865 to 1907, state governments, spurred on by planters, land speculators, railroad officials, and industrialists, sought unsuccessfully to attract immigrants. Planters led the movement because of their dissatisfaction with both the quality and quantity of labor by the free Negro. During the 1870's, farm organizations in South Carolina, Tennessee, and Louisiana adopted formal resolutions favoring imported labor, and units of the Patrons of Husbandry published foreign-language pamphlets to lure immigrants. Land companies, of course, hoped to sell their large, undeveloped tracts, while railroads also had land to sell and, in addition, coveted the foreigners as laborers. Cotton mills, mining, and other industries also were looking for skilled and docile labor.

South Carolina set up a state immigration agency in 1866, but the office had succeeded in bringing in only 400 people by the time it was abolished, perhaps because of Negro influence with the carpetbag government. James S. Pike reported in *The Prostrate State* that in an 1871 debate over tax exemptions for railroads and other types of manufacturing, a Negro leader claimed that Southern industries hoped to crowd out the freedman by foreign immigrants and declared that though they "might bring on their immigrants, they would find the blacks ready for them." However, South Carolina renewed its immigration campaign in 1882. Meanwhile Georgia had set up an agency in 1869, with one of its most outspoken advocates, Henry Grady, desiring 100,000 immigrants for his state, three-fourths of whom he would place in factories. Louisiana had an immigrant bureau from 1866 into the 1880's; Virginia operated one from 1866 to 1888, sending recruiting agents to Great Britain and Germany. Similar steps were taken by Tennessee, Arkansas, Alabama, Florida, Texas, Mississippi, and North Carolina before 1875.

Commercial conventions were also active. In 1883 the Southern Immigration Association of America was organized at Louisville and a year later held its first annual meeting, with representatives from each Southern state, in an effort to promote interstate cooperation. By 1888 it was defunct, but other similar organizations replaced it. The Southern Railway Land and Industrial Agents' Association was formed in 1902 to promote immigration, while eleven railroads also maintained such departments, some with agents in Europe.

Georgia claimed such labor was vital for cotton picking, railroad building, cotton mills, and the iron industry. Governor Robert B. Glenn of North Carolina, supported by his South Carolina counterpart, seriously suggested repeal of the Chinese Exclusion Act. In the fall of 1881, South Carolina phosphate manufacturers experimented with hiring Italian laborers, who worked on the railroads in the summer and were attracted by mild Southern winters. Foremen commenting upon their virtues usually stressed the beneficial effect upon the Negro workers. "They have a capital effect on the negroes, and show them, in a practical way, that the miners are not alone dependent upon them for their labor." After the large building program in 1899, textiles claimed a pressing need for foreign labor. The South warmly welcomed 1,500 Italians to New Orleans in 1904, and by 1910 there were at least thirty-five such communities in the South. A few Poles came in, and several Slovak colonies were established, but nowhere occurred the mass influx which had been anticipated.

The movement was greatly handicapped by foreign governments' investigations of the conditions faced by their citizens (South Carolina phosphate miners complained of the Italians' tendency to run to their consuls). More telling was a 1907 federal decision that state efforts to bring in immigrants violated the law against contract labor importation. But generally, immigrants avoided the South because of the tendency there to treat all foreign labor on the same basis as Negroes. By 1900 the South had 620,000 foreign-born inhabitants, who provided only seven per cent of the iron and steel workers, an industry very desirous of their labor. Ten years later, the region's immigrant population dropped to less than a half million, or two per cent of its total population, as compared to approximately 20 per cent for the rest of the nation.[1] After some forty years of effort, the percentage of foreign-born Southerners was smaller than before the Civil War.

While disappointing, the failure of foreigners to come into the South in significant numbers was not a serious handicap. By the end of reconstruction, economic control of the Negro was firmly re-established, and his labor, such as it was, was generally available. More important, a new and plentiful source of white labor opened up from several sources: the destitution from war, the unprogressive nature of agriculture and the steady rise of tenancy, increased openings for employment, and a changing attitude toward manual labor. Before the War many whites had viewed manual labor as "nigger work" and beneath a white man, but necessity had convinced even the proudest aristocrats of their error. Charles Nordhoff reported in his *The Cotton States in the Spring and Summer of 1875* that

> employments are becoming more varied, and there is more work for me-chanics of different kinds. It is among the factory workers and the small farmers of Georgia that one finds the chief prosperity of the State. Here . . . there are patient, hopeful labor, thrift, and enterprise, which affect, as it seems to me, the whole population. I heard here and there of instances of poor young mechanics working steadily and earnestly, in a New England way, at their trades, making labor respectable, accumu-lating property, and making honorably places in their communities.

Talking to such men showed him that there was "a new born hope of better things in the poor white people of the State."

Spurred on by the gospel of the "New South," eagerly sought by

[1] Rowland T. Berthoff, "Southern Attitudes toward Immigration, 1865-1914," *Journal of Southern History*, XVII (August, 1951), pp. 328-360.

employers, and anxious to better their conditions, by 1880 there were some 209,000 white and black wage earners in the region, a figure which had almost tripled by 1900. Labor conditions in the South differed markedly from the North, which was building its industrial society at the same time. For one thing, Southern children in great numbers worked for low wages. Whites from the poorer lands of the piedmont and from the mountains furnished the bulk of the skilled labor, while the Negroes worked in the mines, blast furnaces, and lumber mills. Only the rarest instance found the two races side by side at the same task. Where both were used, a division of labor separated them, with the inferior positions regularly assigned to the Negro workers. In the textile industry, a great attraction was the opportunity for a whole family to earn money, women and children working almost universally. Although hours were long, sometimes as many as seventy-five per week, so were the hours on the farm. And though wages were low, usually from 30 to 40 per cent less than those paid in the rest of the nation, the whole family's total income was much larger than could be reaped from a rundown Southern farm.

The lower wages in the South mainly resulted from the dominance of low-income agriculture and the relatively large supply of labor competing for jobs in comparatively few industries. Other factors besides the large number of potenial laborers included the decentralization of industry and the lack of legal controls. In fact, there were few if any restrictions on hours, working conditions, and age and sex of operatives, except those imposed by the worker's degree of anxiety for a job. Cotton mills in the nineties paid adult males forty to fifty cents a day, and children normally received ten to twelve cents. Male spinners averaged around $2.50 a week, females slightly more. Cigar makers received approximately twenty-five cents an hour, and stemmers ten cents. Skilled tanners of leather could hope for about eleven cents per hour; printers about twenty-six cents; bricklayers about forty; and carpenters about twenty-five cents an hour.

Management enjoyed a favorable position in public eyes and used this to its advantage. The construction of factories came to symbolize recovery and a new life. Builders were hailed as models of patriotism who brought employment and community development to a disinherited people. The Nashville *Republican Banner*, as early as May 26, 1867, pontificated that "capital . . . must lead, impel, direct and control; it must build; it must invest. . . . On the other hand, labor . . . must take care of the lesser and irresponsible jobs." In this basically agricultural society, the worker was viewed, if considered at all, as a person apart, one who should be thankful for what he got from the benevolent owner.

Favored by such philosophy, most Southern mills and factories soon developed along definitely paternalistic lines. Someone had to provide houses for the workers, and so the management did it. The "company" also came to own the streets, stores, schools, churches, and utilities. It provided only such schools and churches as it deemed desirable and hired both the teachers and the preachers. Inevitably, it also controlled the local administration and police. The "village" was literally outside the adjoining town, and the inhabitants, most of whom worked for the company, could remain only with the consent of the owners. To the country people who flocked in, these conditions contained no hidden dangers. The houses of the village were better than those on the farm, and the company stores were convenient and charged about the same as others. The churches, schools, and even the mines and factories gave opportunities for community living never before experienced by most of the employees.

Most Southern workers, with no standard except unprogressive agriculture against which to evaluate their new positions, thought themselves well off. But if they had complaints, there were no normal avenues of protest. The organized labor movement, usual protector of the working man, was still in its infancy. Before the Civil War, skilled craftsmen in the North, who were gradually losing their independent position, had organized unions, some of which claimed to be national in scope. The Panic of 1857, however, devitalized the entire labor movement, and by 1861 only a few struggling unions maintained a precarious existence. Even with the rise of big business in the 1870's, American trade unions enrolled less than five per cent of the laboring classes and had not advanced beyond ten per cent by the outbreak of the first World War.

The unions in the North at least had the advantage of a past history; labor organizations in the South virtually had to introduce a new and alien concept. In the 1870's the region did have a craft labor movement, smaller but similar to those in Northern cities. In general, however, its leadership was inept and disagreed on objectives. Some favored political action, and workingmen's parties were formed in Nashville, Memphis, and Chattanooga in 1877.[2] Most of these were short-lived, although the National Greenback Labor party of Tennessee in its 1882 platform condemned "the barbarism which imposes upon the wealth producers a state of perpetual drudgery as the price of bare animal existence." Another point of controversy was the Negro. Although there were so few Negro craftsmen that they often could be ignored, in a few trades they were a factor. In some cases they were included in the unions, while in others they set up their own groups.

[2] Constantine G. Belissary, "The Rise of Industry and the Industrial Spirit in Tennessee, 1865-1885," *Journal of Southern History*, XIX (May, 1953), pp. 209-211.

The Longshoreman's Protective Union, originally chartered in 1869 in Charleston, South Carolina, had a long record of successful operation with a mixed membership. The Bricklayers Union Number 1 of South Carolina, organized in 1881 and affiliated with the International Bricklayers Union, also had both white and Negro members. The Negro carpenters, however, had their own organization, to eliminate the "large number of 'saw and hatchet' jacklegs who were constantly coming into competition with them."

The National Labor Union, organized at Baltimore in 1866 by an array of diverse organizations, some of which could hardly have been regarded as labor unions, had little evident effect upon the labor movement in the South. Support of many reforms which had little to do with labor and backing of the abortive Labor Reform Party of 1872 served to discredit the organization, and it collapsed in the Panic of 1873. On the other hand, the Knights of Labor, formed in 1869 on the principle of "one big union" to which all workers, skilled or unskilled and regardless of race, color, and occupation could belong, showed a very definite interest in the Southern workers. As early as 1878, it sent fifteen organizers into the region, and "assemblies" were started in Alabama and Kentucky as early as 1879. Growth, however, was painfully slow until 1884. In that year it went into North Carolina,[3] organizing white and Negro, male and female, though Negroes were often in separate assemblies. By 1886 the Knights had a membership of about 30,000 in ten Southern states and two years later claimed 487 "locals" in that area, with 101 in North Carolina, sixty-five in Louisiana, sixty-four in Alabama, fifty-six in Kentucky, and fifty-four in Virginia. Farmers and wage earners made up the bulk of memberships.

During these years the Knights of Labor led strikes in the cotton mills of Augusta and Roswell, Georgia; Cottondale, Alabama; Greenville, South Carolina; and Maryville, Tennessee. Coal strikes were sponsored at Whiteside, Tennessee, and at Pratt Mines, Alabama, while similar support was given to sugar and lumber workers in Louisiana and Alabama and to railroad men in Texas.[4] The Knights of Labor also started many cooperative stores in the South and actively participated in politics in some cities. The Workingman's Reform party, backed by the Knights, gained control of nearly all departments of the Richmond, Virginia, government in 1886. The next year the party claimed a Congressman and eleven of fifteen city council members in Lynchburg, Virginia, a majority of city and county offices in Macon,

[3] H. M. Douty, "Early Labor Organizations in North Carolina, 1880-1900," *South Atlantic Quarterly*, XXXIV (1935), 260-268, and "Development of Trade-Unionism in the South," *Monthly Labor Review*, LXIII (October, 1946), pp. 555-582.
[4] United States Department of Labor, Bureau of Labor Statistics, Bulletin 898, *Labor in the South* (Washington, 1947), pp. 149-176.

Georgia, and strong political influence in such Alabama towns as Anniston and Mobile.

These gains were not enough to insure the union's existence, however. Management was hostile; many of the strikes were lost; increasing racial tension made the Knights vulnerable because of its attitude toward Negroes; skilled labor was restive in union with the unskilled; many of the farmers drifted away into Populism; and the organization was tarred with the brush of anarchism. By 1888 national membership dropped to less than 260,000, and the order disappeared entirely in the early nineties.

The death of the Knights of Labor did not mean an end to labor's efforts at unity. The American Federation of Labor had organized nationally in 1881 on a craft union basis and, led by the able Samuel Gompers, quickly filled the void left by the Knights. Generally ignoring the Negroes and the unskilled, it made a successful entry into New Orleans in 1898, adding thirty new chapters and raising the city's total of craft unions to ninety-five. In a strike involving forty-two locals and over 20,000 workers, a reduction in the working day and all of their demands except that for a closed shop were gained for New Orlean's workers. Despite this success, progress was slow in the South. The union movement was virtually dead among textile workers, and even the trades showed little activity. Eugene V. Debs reported that he could find only one craft union in all of Georgia in January, 1898, and it had little influence.

That year, however, was the turning point. Although two AF of L organizers sent to work among the textile operatives in Alabama and Georgia in 1894 had been withdrawn for lack of funds, the convention in 1898 instructed the Executive Council to send organizers back into the South. That same year, Prince W. Greene, a young Southerner, organized a local union in the Columbus, Georgia, mills and took the workers out on strike after a wage cut. Applying for affiliation with the national organization, Greene was referred to the newly-organized National United Textile Workers' Union. This had been formed in part for the specific purpose of entering the South, where the cheap wages had stagnated the New England cotton-mill industry. Southerners quickly dominated the textile union, Greene becoming its president. Gompers then appointed him to head a general campaign for the South.

For three or four years following 1898, Southern labor activity was substantially successful. Only the tobacco and lumber industry showed little signs of penetration. Gompers reported in 1899 that the "workers of the South are manifesting their appreciation of our efforts by forming unions, and uniting with our fellow workers in all parts of the country." During this period the textile union claimed a high of 235 locals, and organizers reported encouraging results with plumbers, typographers, marble cutters, gas fitters, and the like. The United Mine Workers entered the Alabama coal fields not long after that union's formation in 1890 and by 1902 it had enrolled 65 per cent of Alabama miners.

The first tests of actual strength came at the turn of the twentieth century, much to the unions' regret. In 1899 eleven textile mills in Augusta, Georgia, crushed a strike in eight of their plants by a co-operative lockout. Violence swept the Carolinas the next year, involving thirty mills in North Carolina alone. In Danville, Virginia, even the personal assistance of Gompers himself could not win a 1901 strike. Textile unionism took its last big chance in Augusta, Georgia, in 1902 and lost. Northern unions contributed about $10,000 to help the Georgians, but management, backed by the Southern Manufacturers' Association, stood firm, locking out some 8,000 employees from all the mills in the vicinity. After fifteen weeks, the union conceded defeat, and, having lost virtually all of its strikes, the United Textile Workers temporarily withdrew from the South. Defeat of the United Mine Workers in a major strike in 1908 also broke that union's hold in the region. Organized labor declined to such an extent that before the end of the decade only ten Southern cities had central labor organizations, and there was not a single state federation.

Union activity from 1902 to World War I was confined largely to the skilled trades and farmers.[5] The Farm Labor Union of Texas, in the preamble to its constitution, stressed the common interest of farmers and laborers, who "have been slaves for years of the manufacturers, the gamblers, and the speculators of every type." In 1909 the Renters Union appeared in Oklahoma. It was strongly socialistic and sought better tenant-landlord contracts and establishment of "Agricultural Arbitration Courts." A year later the Brotherhood of Timber Workers was formed as an independent order in Texas, Louisiana, and Arkansas, and soon claimed about 35,000 members, about half being Negroes. It joined the radical Industrial Workers of the World (IWW) but died after losing a bitter strike in 1915. The Mexican Protective Association, organized in Texas in 1911 to unionize Mexican cottonfield workers, illustrated the diversity of types attracted by the appeal of unity, but the United Textile Workers were defeated in their comeback effort in a big strike in Atlanta in 1913. In the following year, some 9,000 farmers, 95 per cent of them tenants, combined in the Farmers Protective Association to fight farm conditions and usurious bank charges. In

[5] United States Department of Labor, Bureau of Labor Statistics, Bulletin 836, *Labor Unionism in American Agriculture* (Washington, 1945), pp. 256-342.

Oklahoma and Arkansas, a militant secret organization known as the Working Class Union sought abolition of rents, interest, and profit-taking, and favored government ownership of utilities and free schools and textbooks.

During World War I, union activity was extensive in tobacco, textiles, iron, and steel. The United Mine Workers re-entered Alabama in 1917, and bitter textile strikes occurred in Anderson, South Carolina, in 1916 and at Columbus, Georgia, in 1918. In Georgia the mill owners, supported by troops, newspapers, and the general public, won a complete victory. In eastern Oklahoma, some 2,000 tenants, small farmers, and laborers staged what came to be known as the "Green Corn Rebellion"; 450 participants were arrested, and eighty-five were convicted. These men were probably influenced by the Industrial Workers of the World, a strong Socialist party, and by their opposition to the draft act of 1917.

Organized labor intensified its drive after 1918. In eight months of 1919, sixty-seven new locals sprang up in textiles, chiefly in North and South Carolina. At the same time, the tobacco organization won its first union agreement in the South, and the region's mine workers participated in the national coal strike of 1919. Once more, this stepped-up labor activity produced violent counter-reactions. Anti-union vigilantes murdered the leader of the lumber workers in Louisiana. A year later, in a state-wide Alabama coal strike over union recognition, when almost half of the 27,000 miners walked out, the national guard had to be called. After five months without work, the workers began to weaken, and the governor of Alabama, who was sole arbiter, ruled against the union on every count, thus temporarily killing the labor movement in his state. Some 9,000 textile operatives went on strike over lay-offs in North and South Carolina in 1921 but lost, and that union suffered a sharp drop in membership. By 1922 unionism as a positive force ceased to have any importance in major Southern industries and again became overwhelmingly characterized by locals of skilled craftsmen alone.

This decline had its antecedents. Unions had found members relatively easy to get but hard to hold. The worker was willing enough to join the union as a novelty and to go on strike as an opportunity to air his grievances and take a forbidden holiday. But when it came to holding fast to a cause and methodically preparing for a strike by regularly paying union dues, the Southern worker reneged. There were class divisions among the workers themselves and between industries, which made cooperation psychologically difficult. The workers were rural in background, with the farmer's sense of independence. This was strengthened by the fact that in the early days of industry a man could advance by merit alone, and he wanted no organization which could limit him by seniority rules. There was also the eternal race problem. To white unionists, the Negro was not merely an outsider trying to get into the union; he was also a social and racial inferior trying to force the white man to associate with him as an equal. In short, the workers felt no common tie or any sense of unity.

The employer, on the other hand, was also an individualist, also class conscious. In his desire to deal with his employees as individuals, he was braced by public opinion. "Yellow Dog" contracts, by which the worker certified that he was not a member of any union and agreed not to join one while employed by the company, were common and occasioned few protests. The Southern public, even more conservative than in other regions, was sold on the idea that the South's economic salvation lay through industrialization. Strikes and union interference were therefore viewed as being, if not "un-American," at least anti-Southern. Politicians, even the agrarians as well as the Bourbons, were usually hostile to anything which would upset the status quo. They were indifferent to labor as a movement and were quick to use the forces of government against it.

As discouraging as the situation was, there were, however, signs of improvement, especially in the attitudes of the laborers themselves. The twentieth century saw a sharp increase in literacy in the South, making the average worker better educated and more susceptible to union propaganda. Boom years after World War I brought some added benefits in the form of improved housing and wages, and the spread of installment buying helped increase standards of living. For the first time, large numbers of people got a taste of the better things, while new and broader experiences made the laborer more conscious of the important role he played in the overall economic scheme. Consequently, he became anxious not to lose any of his material and psychological gains and even to increase them.

The years 1920 and 1921, however, saw a general slackening in nearly every field of business. Although industry made a speedy recovery and began a rise to new and greater heights, agriculture and labor were unable to regain their former degree of prosperity, and the contrast between their status and that of industry became more painfully apparent. During 1927 and 1928, a new concerted effort was made by the national unions to crack the anti-labor "solid South." In textiles the situation became explosive, as owners, faced with growing competition and falling prices, introduced the "stretch-out" system, which multiplied the number of machines attended by each worker. Discontent swept the Southern textile region, and in October, 1928, delegates from six Southern states met at Chattanooga to plan resistance.

The National Textile Workers' Union, a Communist-controlled group, entered the picture early the next year and quickly recruited membership among the discontented. To meet this threat, the AF of L put fifty organizers into the field; by September of 1930, it claimed organization of 112 new locals in the South — eighty-one in industries other than textiles. The greatest success came among the hosiery workers, where as early as 1926 the Philadelphia union of full-fashioned hosiery workers had followed the industry southward. Alfred Hoffmann, its organizer, skillfully wooed the support of craft unions in Virginia and the Carolinas and prepared the state federations for greater activity.

These new labor efforts, combined with the growing dissatisfaction over local conditions, reacted with unexpected suddenness early in 1929 in Elizabethtown, Tennessee. Over 5,500 rayon workers, supported by their unions, struck for higher wages and improved working conditions. But the companies' call for troops was quickly answered, and the District Court forbade picketing. Workers were evacuated from company housing and refused credit by local stores. Mobs attacked the strikers, and the union organizers were driven from town. When government arbitration was finally accepted, few gains were posted by labor.

Even before this strike had been settled, the Communists made their bid at Gastonia, North Carolina. Demanding an eight-hour day, five-day week, and a minimum wage of twenty dollars, the textile strikers were roughly handled by the state militia, and their economic grievances were ignored as political beliefs became the principal issue. A mob of masked men destroyed the headquarters of the strikers, and a woman striker was killed when a truck in which she was riding was fired upon. The chief of police was killed as he tried to break up a workers' meeting. For this, seven labor leaders were sentenced to from five to twenty years for "conspiracy to murder." This strike's principal achievement was, as W. J. Cash explained it, "to fix solidly in the minds of the great mass of Southerners the equation: labor unions + strikers = Communists + atheism + social equality with the Negro."

Other strikes broke out in the Carolinas and Tennessee. Some were led by unions and others were unorganized; at one time the total number of strikers was over 10,000. All were largely doomed to failure because of the reservoir of surplus labor and the determined opposition by management, stockholders, and the majority of Southerners. The pattern of suppression was identical. Strikers were evicted from their houses and dropped from church rolls; court injunctions forbade picketing; the militia was called out; mob violence occurred in the form of kidnapping, flogging, and attacks upon groups of strikers; and finally, trials freed the strike-breakers and penalized strikers. In these series of events, eight people were killed, seven of them workers, the majority at Marion, North Carolina, when strikers fleeing from tear gas were fired upon by deputy sheriffs.

In general, labor's immediate demands for wage increases, adjustment of the stretch-out, and union recognition were defeated. But the efforts had not been in vain. Management became more cautious, even making concessions to avoid strikes. Workers throughout the South learned that they had to have local leadership and gain the support of public opinion, but that all workers did have a common cause. For these bitter years, organized labor could point to increased craft-union activity, the beginning of tobacco unionism in the Carolinas, and the temporary addition of thirty to forty thousand textile workers. On the negative side, the lower levels of industrial and city labor had scarcely been touched, the Negroes continued to be ignored by most locals, and nothing had been done for agricultural workers.

Lost strikes, shortages of funds, and the deepening depression struck Southern labor movements hard. The depression years of 1931 and 1932 were marked by two unorganized labor uprisings. In High Point, North Carolina, workers of all types commanded the streets for several days; Kentucky coal miners struck because of "Yellow Dog" contracts, intolerable working conditions, the ruthless profiteering in company stores, and wages which averaged from eighty cents to a dollar a day, when work was available. The laborers were again defeated, but assistance was soon to come from an unexpected source.

In March, 1932, President Herbert Hoover signed the Norris-La Guardia Act, outlawing "Yellow Dog" contracts and explicitly limiting the use of injunctions by providing that "no persons participating in, or affected by, such disputes shall be enjoined from striking, or from striving for the success of the strike by customary union effort, short of fraud or violence." That fall, national elections brought in the Democrats, who were pledged to a "New Deal" which included labor. Organized labor could use one. Total membership in the AF of L had fallen from 4,000,000 to 2,500,000 between 1920 and 1932. Under the new President, Franklin D. Roosevelt, labor enjoyed a favored position. The federal laws designed to better wages and working conditions were especially significant for the South, where the worst situations existed. The National Industrial Recovery Act of 1933, through its section 7(a), established minimum wages, shortened hours, banned child labor, and guaranteed labor the right to bargain collectively through representatives chosen by the workers.

Under the banner, "The President wants you to join the Union," labor organizers re-entered the South. Although the NRA provisions left much to be desired (they permitted wage differentials between races, sexes, and regions), Southern workers flocked into the unions in unprecedented numbers. The United Mine Workers made substantial gains in Tennessee and by 1935 reported more than 23,000 Alabama members, about half Negro. The Tobacco Workers Union organized most of the workers in the American Tobacco Company and in Liggett & Myers; the iron and steel, petroleum, lumber, and furniture industries were penetrated. But the most spectacular development came in textiles. On September 1, 1934, about 100,000 operatives joined a general strike. Their employers had resumed the practice of "stretch-out" to offset the higher wages required, and the textile code authority sanctioned a cut in mill production. The strike was poorly prepared and timed. Union violence in the form of "flying squadrons" to force non-strikers off the job aroused governments and the general public against the workers, and the strike ended with few gains.

When the NRA was declared unconstitutional in May, 1935, the Southern labor movement was in a much stronger position than it had ever been. Before union enemies could take advantage of the loss of this protective shield, the National Labor Relations Act, which continued and strengthened the old collective bargaining provisions, was passed two months later. This was bolstered by the Fair Labor Standards Act of 1938, placing in effect a minimum wage of twenty-five cents an hour and a maximum forty-four-hour week, with future plans to raise wages, lower hours, and iron out the regional differential. The South again was the chief beneficiary from these actions, and by 1941 wages had increased an estimated $100,000,000 annually, an augmentation of purchasing power which also greatly benefited business in the region.

One of the most important developments of this period was the emergence of the Committee for Industrial Organization. This body set out to organize all workers, disregarding such factors as race, skill, and type of work. For the first time, two large segments of Southern labor, the Negroes and the unskilled, found a labor organization which was interested in them. The AF of L, while officially against racial discrimination, had never done anything to check such action by its members. As late as 1942, one union excluded Negroes by ritual, sixteen did so by constitutional provision, five refused them membership by tacit consent, and seven supported Jim Crow auxiliaries. The CIO determined to correct this by convincing Southerners that their economic bargaining power would remain weak unless every worker was part of a union.

Agricultural labor organizations were also active during the thirties. Among these were the Veterans of Industry; the Workers

Alliance; the Workingmen's Union of the World; Catholic Workers Union; Agricultural Workers Union (Communist); Agricultural Workers Labor Union (AF of L); United Cannery, Agricultural, Packing & Allied Workers of America (CIO); Share-croppers Union (Communist); Farm Laborers and Cotton Field Workers Union (AF of L); and the Southern Tenant Farmers' Union. The most notable were the Southern Tenant Farmers' Union and those dominated by the Communists. In 1935 the Share-croppers Union attempted a general strike during cotton-picking time by some 12,000 members in Alabama, Louisiana, Mississippi, Georgia, and North Carolina. The threat to the plantation interests, plus the race and political issue, led to a miniature civil war in Alabama that was lost by the union.

The most dramatic landlord-tenant strife during the thirties, however, occurred in Arkansas, where the strongly socialistic Southern Tenant Farmers' Union was organized in July, 1934, by a small group of white and Negro tenants. The union attempted to force an increase in cotton-picking wages, to get a fairer distribution of Agricultural Adjustment Act payments, and to prevent tenant displacement by the AAA program. Its implication of racial equality and its radicalism alarmed the average cotton farmer, and planters and authorities attempted to check its development by violence and intimidation. Despite floggings and night-riders, it boasted 328 locals and 30,827 members throughout seven Southern states before affiliation with the CIO in 1937.

Agricultural unions were not the only ones to face public disapproval. The police commissioner of Memphis warned in 1937, that no CIO organizers would be allowed to enter town. The resurging Ku Klux Klan also capitalized upon anti-union sentiment, centering its hostility against the CIO because of its racial-equality stand. The thirties and forties saw the Klan particularly active in Florida, South Carolina, and Georgia in this respect. It was suspected of having a hand in the disappearance in 1934 of Frank Norman, a Lakeland, Florida, citrus-worker organizer. Another agent in Tampa was murdered and his body mutilated. Union representatives were flogged in Georgia and South Carolina, and fiery crosses were burned on the lawns of many Southern mill villages. Although some employers were beginning to realize their potential stake in the greater purchasing power of labor, others continued to terrorize their workers by dismissal and blacklisting.

The outbreak of World War II in Europe and America's subsequent entrance in 1941 brought new markets to business and some increase in wages. Determined to hold and expand the gains previously made, unions increased their activity. A *Fortune* magazine poll in 1943 showed that only about 30 per cent of Southern industrial workers and 12 per cent of Southern Negroes were organized, as compared to almost 54 and 44 per cent respectively for the nation. Textiles (outside of cotton), tobacco, steel and iron, coal mining, ship building, petroleum refining, and pulp and paper making had the largest memberships. Virtually untouched were lumber and food processing, while furniture and the chemical industries were very weak and the agricultural labor movements essentially dead.

With the end of World War II, the CIO and AF of L launched "Operation Dixie," with the former announcing in 1946 a goal of more than a million workers the first year. The prosperity of the post-war years worked against the unions, for six years later, after the expenditure of over $11,000,000, the results were obviously not as great as hoped. The CIO counted about 500,000 dues-paying Southern members, and the AF of L, around 2,000,000. With the United Mine Workers' 125,000, plus the independents, total union membership in the region was perhaps 2,750,000 out of a non-agricultural working force of approximately 9,300,000. A mere 700,000 Negroes were unionized.[6]

Although "Operation Dixie" continued, its progress was slow. In addition to hereditary conservatism and prosperous times, it bucked a new weapon wielded by its enemies: the "right to work" laws, state legislation which banned the union or closed shop. Florida acted first in 1944, but most such laws followed the passage of the Taft-Hartley Act in 1947. By 1958 eighteen states, ten of them Southern, had such provisions. An eleventh, Louisiana, passed one in 1954 but repealed it in 1956.[7] Despite federal threats to annul these laws during the sixties, "right to work" remained a stumbling block for unions. State governments defended them as necessary to attract industry and soft-pedaled the facts that they were anti-union and designed to protect traditional concepts of wage levels. By the mid-seventies nineteen states still had such laws, with Louisiana the only exception in the deep South.

Nevertheless, labor unions made slow, if not spectacular, progress. It was spotty and varied from state to state and from industry to industry. For example, in 1966, the Carolinas had less than 10 per cent of their non-agricultural labor in unions. In the deep South only Arkansas had over 20 per cent, the rest falling between 10 and 20 per cent. Five years later, when the national average was slightly better than one-third of the non-agricultural workers unionized, North Carolina still had 7.5 per cent; South Carolina, 14.4; Georgia, 17; with Louisiana's high of 37 per cent. These deviations are largely explained

6 "Setbacks for Unions," U. S. News & World Report, XXXII (February 22, 1952), pp. 60–61; George S. Mitchell, "How Far Has Southern Labor Advanced?" Nation, CLXXV (September 27, 1952), p. 262.
7 "Why the Big Fight Over 'Right to Work,'" U. S. News & World Report, XLV (October 24, 1958), p. 85.

by the success of unions in specific industries, such as aluminum, pulp and paper, petro-chemicals, and shipbuilding, and a continued frustration in textiles and manual labor-oriented concerns. It is interesting that from 1960 on, the black worker more readily joined a union than did his white counterpart, and much of the statistical gain came through such enrollments. The South paid a price, however, as reflected in the fact that in 1970 American manufacturing industries paid a national average hourly wage of $3.36; but nine Southern states averaged below $3.00. Yet labor in general had benefitted as state and federal laws specifically attempted to give the worker greater protection and outlawed most of the obvious abuses.

Chief among these was that of child labor. In the glare of publicity, it was made to appear a Southern problem, when actually it was very old and existed on a national scale. As Northern textiles felt the bite of Southern competition, increasingly they denounced the South's use of child labor, although their own hands were far from clean. Most of the writers of these exposés were Northerners, and all were crusaders. Consequently, the literature tended to concentrate on the Southern situation and to play up extreme cases. It was true, of course, that Southern children were often victimized by the connivance of employers and incompetent or greedy parents who were careless or too blind to see the difference between working on the farm or in the factories. Generally ignored, however, was the fact that in the beginning cycle of every industry there had been use of child labor which was later discontinued. The protest against the system was a relatively new development the world over. There had been, for example, wide acceptance of the custom of having children join their parents in fieldwork and even in craft work carried on under the parental roof. Nor did working always deprive a child of an education. In many areas no schools were available. Moreover, the conditions under which industry was begun in the South should be recalled. As Broadus Mitchell wrote of this period in his *The Rise of Cotton Mills in the South:* "The great morality then was to go to work. The use of children was not an avarice then, but philanthropy; not exploitation, but generosity and cooperation and social-mindedness."

Cotton mills and vegetable canneries soon became second to agriculture in employing child labor, and at one time or another, children could be found in virtually all occupations, including coal mining. Beginning in 1870, when Southern mills employed 2,300 children under sixteen years of age, the total of industrially-employed children rose in proportion to the expansion of the textile industry. Consequently, this industry came under the greatest degree of attack. Most of the children worked in the spinning rooms, where the girls proved deft in mending broken threads of yarn, while the boys worked as "doffers," removing full bobbins and replacing them with empty ones. Wages were usually below thirty cents a day, and legal protection was nonexistent. An Alabama law of 1887 limiting a child's working day to eight hours was repealed in 1895 upon the demand of a Massachusetts company which was constructing a large mill in the state.

In 1880, 25 per cent of Southern cotton mill workers were under sixteen years of age, as compared to 14 per cent in the North. The Census of 1890 showed 23,0000 children employed by industry in thirteen Southern states. The South accounted for 256,000 of the 400,586 male children between the ages of ten and fourteen, and 130,546 of the 202,427 girls of the same age, gainfully employed at any type of labor in the United States. The 1900 Census showed 1,077,950 Southern children under sixteen worked for a living, with North Carolina using the most, 26,883.

DIVISION OF CHILD LABORS IN THE SOUTH, 1900

| | |
|---|---|
| Farm and agriculture | 843,494 |
| Textile mills | 27,902 |
| Messenger, errand, and office | 7,700 |
| Mining | 4,235 |
| Tobacco industry | 3,780 |
| Dressmaking, millinery, and tailoring shops | 2,899 |

By 1900 the older industrial states of the North had laws, though poorly enforced, regulating the labor of children, and a clamor began for the South to have similar legislation. Northerners allowed themselves to become very vocal on Southern problems. Reactions to these attacks were equally intemperate: "The agitation is simply a 'Yankee trick' and started in New England, the home of 'Uncle Tom's Cabin.'" It was an effort to destroy Southern industry; such laws would be an opening wedge to Socialism and would mark the beginning of the end of all individual liberty. Worse yet, they would be unchristian, for they violated the Biblical right of parents to govern their children. Child labor, Southerners admitted, was not good, but they claimed that it was better than letting the children run wild or having needy families and ruined industry. If working children were not physically abused and preferred working to an education, it was the sole concern of themselves and their parents. The South still thought of its problems in terms of the agricultural society idealized by Thomas Jefferson; for the state to regulate either industrial or agricultural labor was improper.

The initiative for reform in the South was provided chiefly by humanitarians and organized labor. State labor bureaus furnished the ammunition. Beginning with Massachusetts in 1869, state after state had created these agencies, which were empowered to collect information, as defined in North Carolina, regarding labor's "relation to capital, the hours of labor, the earnings of laboring men and women, their educational, moral and financial condition and the best means of promoting their mental, material, social and moral prosperity." Between 1879 and 1900, Missouri, Maryland, North Carolina, West Virginia, Kentucky, Tennessee, Virginia, and Louisiana established such bureaus.

As early as 1900, the AF of L had campaigns under way for child-labor legislation in the South.[8] It was joined by clergymen, women's clubs, and groups with a special interest in promoting public education. Sparked by ministers such as Edgar Gardner Murphy of Alabama and Alexander J. McKelway of North Carolina, reformers took advantage of the Progressive movement sweeping the country during the early years of the twentieth century. Preoccupied at first with conditions in textiles, they eventually broadened their campaign to include canneries (where little girls "snipped" sixteen hours a day or capped forty cans a minute), mines, cigar factories, night messenger boys, and the like. Despite a strong lobby of manufacturers, the reformers aroused so much indignation that they were able to write their first law in North Carolina in 1903. Arguing that child labor was a national problem rather than a purely regional one, the Reverend Murphy secured the formation of the National Child Labor Committee on April 15, 1904, which united efforts of both Northern and Southern reformers and attracted the support of politicians such as Ben Tillman and Hoke Smith. Spurred by President Theodore Roosevelt, Congress in 1907 undertook an investigation of child labor which resulted in a nineteen-volume *Report on Conditions of Women and Child Wage-Earners in the United States*. While the North did not escape censure, wide publicity was given to the fact that 23.8 per cent of Mississippi's mill employees were under sixteen and that, of fifty-nine North Carolina mills investigated, forty-four hired children under twelve. Three employees were as young as seven years of age, and one worker, aged six, was discovered in South Carolina. Twenty-seven North Carolina factories had children under sixteen working on night shifts. Also in that state, over half the laboring children under fourteen could not read or write, while the percentages in South Carolina and Virginia were 50.3 and 70.4 respectively.

Remedial progress was slow in the South, lagging always behind the North. By 1909 the percentages of children under sixteen in total mill population had dropped to 18.9 in North Carolina and 18.7 in

[8] Samuel Gompers, "Organized Labor's Attitude toward Child Labor," *Annals of the American Academy of Political and Social Science*, XXVII (March, 1906), pp. 79-83.

South Carolina, as compared to Massachusetts' figure of 5.7. All Southern states had adopted age and hour limits by 1912, with some sort of regulation concerning night work. These were generally far from satisfactory because of the twelve-year age limit and the sixty-hour week, both with many provisions for exemptions and few for enforcement. Parents could connive and lie about children's ages, a practice aided by the absence of registration of births in many towns. People would not testify against the operators for fear of losing their own jobs. All of this, plus poor enforcement of laws in the North, began to culminate in a demand for federal regulation. A child-labor bill which had languished in the United States Senate for almost four years passed quickly in 1916 under President Wilson's prodding. This closed interstate commerce to products produced by children under fourteen. Southern representatives voted 41-43 against the measure, with the Carolinas, Georgia, Alabama, Florida, and Mississippi voting almost as a unit.

When this law was declared unconstitutional by a Supreme Court vote of 5-4, Congress levied a 10 per cent tax on the net profits of employers of children, but this action also met the same fate in the Court. On June 2, 1924, Congress passed and submitted to the states a constitutional amendment which provided that "the Congress shall have power to limit, regulate, and prohibit the labor of persons under eighteen years of age." The growing strength of labor, introduction of new machinery unadaptable to child labor, and the massive unemployment of adults during the Depression helped make the nation more receptive to curtailing the work of children. A provision of the NRA prohibited labor by children under sixteen, and later the Fair Labor Standards Act regulated the practice. By the end of the 1930's, all Southern states had strengthened their laws, though qualifying exceptions weakened many of them. Most set the minimum age at fourteen, although Virginia permitted children of twelve to fourteen years to work in canneries during the summer. They also exempted agricultural labor but required school attendance, although Mississippi and South Carolina required only eighty days of school a year and Texas exempted those twelve years of age who had finished the fifth grade. All prohibited night work for minors under sixteen. In the slow pace of democracy, the constitutional amendment proposed in 1924 still lacked the necessary number of state ratifications well past the middle of the century.

Parallel to the problem of working children was that of female labor. Just as the child was a mainstay of nascent Southern industry, women were likewise in great demand as workers, particularly in textiles. In Alabama, for example, the number of female employees increased 75 per cent between 1885 and 1895. Here, too, there was no protection as to wages, hours, or conditions of work. Reform in this field was slower, for the low wages for men in the South frequently made it imperative that wives and daughters help in the burden of family support. The National Emergency Council's *Report on Economic Conditions of the South* in 1938 pointed out that the region had a larger proportion of its women working under fewer safeguards than elsewhere in the nation. Two of the four states which had no laws to fix maximum hours for female workers were Southern, and only one had established an eight-hour day for women in any industry. Only four Southern states had a week as short as forty-eight hours, and only two a minimum wage for women. There were no organizations fighting for them comparable to the National Child Labor Committee. Most improvement in this field came through the efforts of unions, general improvement in economic conditions during and after World War II, and a gradual enlightenment of public opinion.

Other benefits for labor were also more slowly adopted in the South than elsewhere.[9] While Maryland was the first state to provide a workmen's compensation law (1902), its courts declared the law unconstitutional. In 1930 four Southern states still failed to provide such protection. In the field of employer liability, the South lagged behind the rest of the nation, as did its laws governing safety devices on hazardous machinery and insurance protection against accidents. Most commonly, also, Southern rates of compensation were lower and more difficult to collect. As late as 1947, Mississippi, Tennessee, Texas, and Virginia had no machinery at all for conciliation and mediation of labor disputes. By the seventies, however, federal laws, court decisions, and threats to withhold funds had forced a high degree of uniformity in employment practices, industrial safety, maximum hours and minimum wages, and compensation for accidents and unemployment.

[9] U. S. Dept. of Labor, *Labor in the South*, pp. 118-137; Charles F. Sharkey and Marian L. Mel, "State Labor Legislation in the South," *Monthly Labor Review*, LXIII (October, 1946), pp. 535-554.

# 12

## SOUTHERN SOCIETY BEFORE 1930

OFTEN OVERLOOKED in standard historical surveys is the social revolution, in many respects more important and all-pervasive than the political, which resulted from the Civil War. For example, it is common knowledge that after the War not only was the black man free, but texts abound with details concerning the political struggle, first, to enfranchise and, later, to disfranchise him. Less often considered is the question of what happened to him socially in a mixed society and what culture he developed after obtaining more control over his destiny. Equally important, however, were the impacts of the War and of the free Negro upon white society and modes of living.

Two primary social revolutions took place in the South between 1865 and 1930. The first of these was a realignment of white society occasioned largely by the War and the development of a Negro social structure. This was primarily a Southern phenomenon, since the Civil War did not force a radical readjustment upon the North, although social changes did result. The second revolution was a Southern phase of an American evolutionary process which simply did not reach the region below the Potomac until after the Civil War. This was the crumbling of a predominantly rural society and the accompanying rise of city life, with the consequent development of a strong urban culture.

Traditionally, not only had the South been overwhelmingly agricultural, hence rural in orientation, but its social structure also had been largely rigid and aristocratically dominated. Before 1865 the slave-holding planters controlled the region socially, economically, and politically, and were willingly followed by the yeomen, both farmers and townsmen, who hoped that they or their children could move into the planters' golden circle by acquiring slaves and lands. Beneath these were the "poor whites," usually ignored by the ruling clique, as they did not fit into the aristocratic society, but nevertheless tied to the upper class by shared membership in the white race and by their mutual antipathy toward the Negro. When war came, they joined the rest of their color in fighting for a way of life which they viewed as their own. At the bottom of the social ladder was the Negro. The slave was the mudsill upon which the aristocratic structure rested, but the free Negro was an outcast, viewed with suspicion by a white-dominated society in which he had no recognized position.

The emancipation of the slaves had the immediate effect of forcibly removing the foundation upon which the Southern class system rested and, at the same time, of multiplying by millions the free Negroes who had never been successfully integrated into antebellum life. Furthermore, the top of the South's social pyramid, the planters, were also dislocated. This was, politically, a result of the Northern theory that the mass of Southern whites had been betrayed into war by their leaders. In Northern eyes, and of some Southerners, such as Andrew Johnson, the planter class became the "war criminals" of that day. A primary objective of reconstruction was to see that never again would they be in a position to exercise their wills upon Southerners, white or black. The stereotype of the planter lolling on the broad veranda of his mansion, sipping his mint julep and being fanned by an industrious "darkey" as he expounded on local politics to obsequious neighboring white farmers, or gazing through the magnolia trees toward the distant fields where his white overseer drove his slaves to ever greater exertions — these scenes had to be forever blotted out.

The planter aristocrat suffered far more than the loss of his slave property and the general destruction and decay of his plantation occasioned by the war itself. In the first place, they were barred by Johnson from general amnesty, and as former civil and military leaders of the Confederacy, they were excluded from political participation by Presidential proclamation and the Fourteenth Amendment. The planters were fair game to be plucked by the reconstruction governments, and discriminatory taxation turned their property from assets into distinct liabilities. Thousands were forced to sell their land for whatever price was available, and those who held on had to adjust themselves to the post-bellum system of labor and land tenure, even to working in the fields with their families. There were no longer any rich planters, but simply the land poor, whose struggles to hold their property together incited more pity than envy from their neighbors. A few tried to keep up past appearances with long-tailed coats, tired old carriages, and faded silk or satin dresses, but no one was fooled.

The low prices for land and the breaking-up of estates by sale or tax forfeiture marked the downfall of the ruling class. Having set the standards for polite and political society before 1861, the old planter aristocracy was broken, scattered, and churned into a heterogeneous society to such a degree that for a generation their names almost disappeared from public affairs. Vanishing with them went not only their leadership but also their way of life. The ladies came down from their pedestals and, for the first time, learned to work. The cult of ancestor worship suffered a serious blow. Confronted with the cruel realities of a post-war world, Civil-War generations quickly found that the "virtues of an ancestry wear out like the effect of vaccination." "Personal honor" became less a matter of one's good name and more the protection of what one still possessed. A South Carolinian writing in 1877 stated that nine men out of ten carried pistols, but that there had been "only eight or ten duels in South Carolina since the war, hardly as many as used to occur every year. Men will rarely fight duels when death may mean starvation to their families." The proverbial mint julep ceased to be a sign of graceful living and instead became a means of escape, as the same author related that "many Southerners were driven to drink by their misfortunes, and drunkenness . . . is deplorably prevalent to this day."[1]

Work virtually became a religion, with the objective of securing enough wealth to be freed from further necessity for labor. Push and hustle were the order of the day. As one contemporary admitted with a hint of nostalgia: "Our people are becoming 'Yankeeized': our sons and daughters are brought up to depend upon self, to work and to place a value upon the wages of work of every kind. The dignity of labor is admitted and asserted by all. The children of our oldest and best families do manual labor in field or shop, and do not lose caste."[2]

The worst aspect of pre-war provincialism, aristocratic arrogance, disappeared to a great extent when it became obvious that birth and gentility were of small importance for the solution of the problems of

1 "A South Carolinian," "South Carolina Morals," *Atlantic Monthly*, XXXIX (June, 1877), pp. 467-475.
2 As quoted by Roger W. Shugg, *Origins of Class Struggle in Louisiana* (Baton Rouge: Louisiana State Univ., 1939), p. 279.

the post-war age. Only a few of the gentry, like Wade Hampton, were able to make their voices heard during the early efforts to adjust to the new way of life. Some Southerners lamented the "great *mania* of Southern planters for transforming their sons into lawyers, doctors and merchants," while others were equally sure that what the region needed was "smaller farms, more villages, less pride, more industry, fewer stores and clerks, and more laborers."

Whatever was believed to be right, the planters did lose Southern leadership; new men rose to take their place, men whose rise duplicated the Northern success pattern of crude energy and calculating shrewdness. Even the few leaders of gentry origin were largely "self-made" men. The ambitious, hard-working middle class — farmers, lawyers, merchants, manufacturers — furnished most of the sons destined for prominence. Success in all fields, as well as politics, was determined largely by the extent to which the menace of poverty was defeated. The young men saw the post-war disorder not as defeat but as an opportunity. They crowded into business and felt pride in attaining distinction as merchants, doctors, journalists, teachers, or engineers. The old semi-feudal set of rural ideals crumbled, as commerce brought the desired wealth and prestige formerly possessed by the landowners, and city life gained in importance as compared with the country. The planters, submerged by the social and economic revolution and the gradual rise of new groups with a "go-getting" ideal, were no longer able to set the standards of conduct.

This new pattern of thought dominated politics, as a result of the rise of the "New South" with its emphasis upon manufacturing and diversification of agriculture. The new idolization of the businessman was evident in the words of the Nashville *Journal of Commerce*, of January 3, 1874: "A man of wealth who uses that wealth to improve his country, to reward labor, and to benefit his fellow man, is worth all praise, and deserves our warmest thanks." Three years later, the Knoxville *Daily Chronicle* was even more specific in stating that the "man who builds a rolling mill or a blast furnace, or a cotton factory is of more real benefit to us than all the nasty politicians that could be mustered in all the states."[3] This new business leadership could not be called an aristocracy, since it was neither closely knit nor inherited. Moreover, its composition was constantly in a state of flux.

Although the old leaders and aristocrats were pushed to the back of the political and economical stage, they continued to hold an honorary position in Southern society. A South Carolinian noted in 1877 that they were sought for speeches and to serve as trustees and direc-

[3] Constantine G. Belissary, "The Rise of Industry and the Industrial Spirit in Tennessee, 1865-1885," *Journal of Southern History*, XIX (May, 1953), pp. 193-215.

tors of the new businesses, although they could furnish little except their names with their historical connotations. "Insurance companies invariably select ex-Confederate generals for their state agents, and their lower agents, as well as those of the sewing-machine companies, are members of the aristocracy." They kept as much of their old customs and traditions as poverty would permit, and whenever the aristocrats were forced to mingle with the old middle and lower classes, they were treated with "a respect which is positively amazing." If they had to work, they generally entered one of the professions, becoming lawyers, doctors, ministers, and teachers. "Consequently over three fourths of the members of the learned professions in the South are aristocrats. Especially is the bar stocked with them. . . ." Moreover, hundreds of their impoverished wives and daughters became teachers in boarding schools and grammar schools for girls.[4]

Thus, the upper class of the New South came to be composed of two groups, separated by a fine but well understood line of demarcation. There were the "old aristocracy," who owed their position solely to the fact that their families had always been the "best" people. They tried to keep the old patterns of behavior which had been established during past periods of wealth. Lacking money, they became preoccupied with lineage, although after the War money as the final arbiter of rank was even more important than property had been before 1860. Nevertheless, the older group, full of possessiveness for ancient distinctions, snubbed the newcomers to the upper class at every safe opportunity.

These newcomers, the *nouveaux riches,* were recognized by the public as "aristocracy but not old." Convinced that the achievement of wealth had automatically transformed them into gentry, they were determined to be recognized as such. Consequently, their behavior was patterned upon that of the "old aristocracy." Upon failure to acquire, either by marriage or by purchase, a ready-made past in the form of an antebellum home, they retaliated by making a more splendid show than their tormentors could match. This group of native Southerners was later augmented by the Northern management people who followed their capital into Southern industries.

The post-Civil War social upheaval not only made possible new entries to the white upper class, but it also provided increased opportunity in the lower groups as well.[5] In the Old South there had been no clearly defined middle class as had been created in the North by the

[4] "A South Carolinian," "South Carolina Society," *Atlantic Monthly,* XXXIX (June, 1877), pp. 670-684.
[5] Good descriptions of the Southern class structure can be found in John Dollard, *Caste and Class in a Southern Town* (New Haven: Peter Smith, 1937), and Allison Davis and others, *Deep South* (Chicago: Univ. of Chicago, 1941).

earlier industrial and urban revolution. But in the New South, many small farmers obtained additional land as a result of the breakdown of the plantation system, and the commercial and professional men received new recognition. A middle class, so constituted, reached a level determined by material possessions, with membership based on small capital holdings or skillfulness which augured a potentially larger income. This group placed emphasis on individual wealth; "appearances" were particularly important, and the occupations which carried the most prestige were followed. These men were among the most energetic and acquisitive of all Southerners, holding higher standards of personal behavior than those either above or below them in any status. The dominant class in social significance, they were inclined to be faithful church-goers, staunch advocates of education, active club members, and ever zealous in their efforts to climb still higher in all of these endeavors.

The existence of large numbers of Southerners lumped together under the denomination of "poor whites," or more contemptuous titles, had been virtually ignored before 1865. Scattered through the swamps, pine barrens, and the mountain ridges of the Appalachians, these people were of special interest to Northerners and travelers after the War. Freedmen's Bureau officials commented upon their misshapen forms, ignorance, low moral standards, slovenly habits, and general laziness, when, as avowed unionists, they came begging for help and calling for confiscation and division of the Rebels' lands. Charles Nordhoff, a Northern reporter, wrote in 1875 that the

> Southern white population differs from ours in one or two important respects. . . . The numerous class of poor white farmers are a kind of people unknown among us. Settled upon a thin and unfertile soil; long and constantly neglected before the war; living still in a backwoods country, and in true backwoods style, without schools, with few churches, and given to rude sports and a rude agriculture, they are a peculiar people. . . . They are ignorant, easily prejudiced, and they have, since the war, lived in dread of having social equality with the negro imposed upon them.

Another visitor, writing two years later, declared that they lived as poorly as Negroes and that most of them were "inveterate beggars."

In some respects the post-war social revolution most affected this group by giving them opportunities for escape which had not previously existed. The breakdown of the plantation system and the rise of tenancy allowed the more ambitious to swap their backwoods cabins for sharecroppers' huts. Though only a little improvement, there was always the hope that this foothold could lead to life as a cash renter and perhaps even as a landowner. With the rise of manufacturing, especially the cotton mills, the lower classes also found a ready market for their labor, and if the male were inclined to continue the slothful habits of the past, he could live off the wages of his wife and children. The mill workers, miners, and foundrymen, though fewer in number than the tenant farmers, were like them in constituting a new economic and social class in Southern life. Together, these two segments of the poor-white population formed a group without parallel in Southern history — a class without capital, talent, or ancestry to give it preferential claims. Denied equality with other whites except perhaps at political rallies, the resulting economic and social frustrations were often vented upon the Negro. If denied membership in the Klan, the poor whites undertook on their own to take all "sassy niggers down a peg." Proposals for Negro equality caused fear that the equalizing would start at their own doors.

While seldom moved by ambition to change his mode of life, the poor white was more often motivated by necessity. The ever-encroaching development of the New South forced him from his havens. Artificial fertilizers made the soil where he squatted potential cotton and tobacco land; rich men fenced the acres around him as game preserves; truck farms, orchards, and winter resorts encroached still farther; the lumber and turpentine business destroyed his pine barrens; coal mines bored into the mountain sides, bringing industrious thousands to live in company towns; and railroads and highways cut across formerly isolated areas. Only in the most remote swamps and desolate mountains could he find refuge. In these isolated pockets, social change came very slowly. As late as 1883, an English observer commented that the women still did the outdoor work, while the men sat smoking. Early marriages were still the rule, and fifteen children were not uncommon. These people remained provincial, usually dying without having been more than a few miles from their homes.

The majority of the lower class, however, adjusted to various new lives on tenant farms, in mill towns, and in mining communities. The listless hunter-fisher-farmer poor white of antebellum days was eventually eliminated by the twentieth-century campaign against hookworm and malaria. Thus this group, which was for the most part the purest Anglo-Saxon stock in America, predominantly holding the fundamental beliefs of the Baptists and Methodists, became incorporated into the life of the South, albeit on the lowest level.

After the Civil War, therefore, caste replaced slavery as a means of maintaining the essence of the old status order in the South. Caste delineated a superior and inferior group, based upon biological, not cultural, features, and regulated the behavior of each. For the white Southerner skin color became the line of demarcation. The key element in any democratic society — equality — was sacrificed to the expediency of reducing racial animosity, and the black was assigned the lowest classification. Eventually some achieved wealth and positions that would have entitled a white, at least, to middle-class status. But even the best Negroes still ranked below the lowest whites in social relationships; the guiding factor in segregation was that in the inescapable meetings of the races the superior-inferior differential had to be maintained.

According to the 1860 census, 94.9 per cent of all the Negroes in the United States lived in the Southern slave states. Thus, their postwar social status was primarily a regional problem, and a whole new orbit had to be created for them. After the War, but before caste distinctions were firm, the Negroes had greater social freedom than they were later to enjoy. Whites would ride on the same seats with Negroes, as long as the latter were traveling as servants, nurses, and the like. In South Carolina in 1877, the sight of freedmen in first-class railroad compartments and on street cars was "so common as hardly to provoke remarks." They were freely admitted to theaters and other exhibitions, but "a wide berth is given them by the white audience if the hall be not crowded." One characteristic of the old Southern order that lingered far into the new was the intermixture of residences in the older cities and towns.

Special conditions, however, created special needs. For example, most of the Negroes had no last name, and generally they adopted names at random or took the family names of their former owners. Often, people were startled to read in newspapers that some supposedly eminent person had been arrested for public drunkenness or petty larceny. Emancipation also left a serious problem as to the marital status of the freed Negroes. Many states enacted special statutes to determine and recognize their unions. The Missouri law of 1865 requiring legal marriage of former slave couples was interpreted by some Negroes as a chance to leave their slave-day companions and take new wives or husbands. Maryland, on the other hand, took no legal notice of blacks born out of wedlock until 1888. In Mississippi the proposal to put the freedmen on the same basis as the whites in the marriage relationship led a native son to exclaim, "Why, Sir, that so-called constitution elevates every nigger wench to the equality of mah own daughters."

Although the reconstruction governments and the federal government sought to improve the social position of the freedmen in such legislation as the Civil Rights Act of 1875, their efforts were largely nullified following the restoration of home rule. The Negro was left to the economic mercy of the whites by his failure to secure land, and the dominant race found little difficulty in enforcing caste restrictions of its own making. The grasp of tenancy and the allocation of the desirable

jobs to the whites led to Booker T. Washington's conclusion that
the only way the Negro could rise politically and socially was by first
rising economically. Progress in both respects was slow. The census of
1890 showed that 41.1 per cent of all Negroes were gainfully employed,
a higher percentage than among the whites, but that over seven-eighths
of the Negroes were still farmers or servants. The houses they occupied were 19 per cent owned and the rest rented.[6]

### DISTRIBUTION OF NEGRO EMPLOYMENT, 1890

| Type of Employment | Percentage |
|---|---|
| Professions | 1.1 |
| Trade and Transportation | 4.7 |
| Manufacturing | 5.6 |
| Personal Services | 31.4 |
| Agriculture | 57.2 |

Nevertheless, by 1892 a government representative reported a
steady improvement in the manners and morals of all classes of Negroes, although matings without benefit of clergy and divorces of equal
informality still occurred. Housing had improved over the slave quarters and early tenant houses: dirt floors were disappearing and some
glass was coming into evidence. There was still gross overcrowding,
with little privacy or beauty, and an absence of sanitation. Because of
the inability of the males to get work or to support large families on
small incomes, the mothers were often the more important breadwinners. Family life consequently suffered because of this necessary
employment of women, but the race as a group was imbued with the
hope of something better, if not for themselves, at least for their
children.

Hardly true in general was a statement in 1925 by a former president of Wilberforce University about the Virginia Negroes: "Virtually
all are members of a church and of one or another of the many fraternal societies. . . . Most of the Negroes have automobiles and many own
victrolas." A few years later, on the other hand, William T. Couch
wrote that the chain gang was one of the few public institutions where
Negroes and whites could associate freely. Nevertheless, despite caste,
unequal treatment before the law, voting restrictions, local acts of mob
violence, inferior school accommodations, injustices in sharing farm
profits, discrimination on common carriers, denial of courtesy to educated Negroes, and lack of opportunity for full employment, slow
improvement continued.

[6] United States Bureau of Education, "Education in Various States," *Report of
Commissioner of Education for 1894-1895* (Washington, 1896), pp. 1384-1405.

Another minority group, the foreign immigrants, had given the average Southerner little reason for concern before 1860, since few migrated into the region in the face of competition with slavery. As earlier indicated, in the years after the War the South attempted to attract immigration but with little success. Then, with the waning of the economic pressures which made immigrant labor seem so necessary, the immigrants themselves became less desirable. The white population of the South remained unusually homogeneous. Only 450,000 inhabitants in 1880 had been born outside the region; by 1890 there were still fewer than 600,000, and foreign-born residents numbered no more than one in fifty. These foreigners, while free to progress without the handicap of the color line if they worked as quiet and industrious individuals, found the natives suspicious of all alien groups, particularly if their religious views differed from the predominant protestantism. One notable exception was the Jews. Probably in no other region of the United States have they been so integrated with the general population or subjected to less discrimination. Most came into the South after a period of assimilation in the North. They were welcomed because of their business connections, which fitted in well with the philosophy of the New South, and they quickly occupied an important position in the retail dry-goods business.

Occasionally, some foreigners met with violence, however. In the 1880's a colony of Sicilians settled in New Orleans, working mainly as longshoremen. Membership in secret-oath societies, differences in language, religion, and customs, and a tendency toward lawlessness quickly antagonized local opinion against them. When the chief of police was assassinated and three Sicilian suspects were acquitted, a mob lynched eleven Sicilians, creating an international incident. Twice in 1896 the Catholic church at the Italian settlement at Tontitown, Arkansas, was burned, and Mississippi at one time had a law barring Italian children from the public schools.

Regional hostility, as distinct from local, was slow to develop, partly explained by the fact that immigrants were so few and usually isolated. The American Protective Association, organized in 1887 by Henry F. Bowers in Iowa as basically an anti-Catholic movement, claimed 2,000,000 members by 1894. Yet it numbered few Southerners and had little influence except in the border states of Kentucky and Tennessee. The Populist stand in favor of immigration restriction was largely ignored by Southerners.

However, after 1900, as the South began to demand white solidarity in the fight to isolate the Negroes politically and socially, views on immigrants also underwent a change. The immigrants, especially if they were Catholic, became an object of suspicion. The Richmond meeting of the Farmer's National Congress in 1905 proposed restriction of immigration, a stand supported by state branches of the Farmers' Educational and Cooperative Union after 1907. Tom Watson, who earlier had supported immigration, helped found the Guardians of Liberty, a Protestant-nativist group, in 1912. Ben Tillman underwent a similar conversion, supporting literacy tests to prevent making a "hell-broth" of American population, a stand supported by all but seven Southern members of Congress. During this period Southerners backed such nativist organizations as the Junior Order of American Mechanics and the Patriotic Order of Sons of America. The weak organized labor movement joined in, the Georgia Federation of Labor objecting in 1907 to "flooding the South and Georgia with a population composed of the scum of Europe," who might "foment race troubles and tend to destroy the cherished ideals of every loyal Southerner. . . ." By World War I the region was probably more solidly nativist than any other in the United States.[7]

Another group which found its status immensely changed after 1865 was the white female. The antebellum code of chivalry had enthroned women, theoretically exempting them from having to confront the harsher aspects of life. While practice fell far short of theory, Southern white women nevertheless were undoubtedly the most sheltered of all American women. Perhaps because of this, the women as a group had the most difficult time emotionally adjusting to the results of military defeat. As late as 1873, Jefferson Davis declared he had never seen a reconstructed Southern woman. Numerous female societies were formed for the avowed purpose of refusing to bend the knee to the conqueror or even to speak to a federal soldier. The ladies were the ones who worked hardest to get Davis released from prison, who first began erecting monuments to Confederate dead and providing them with proper burial, and who, at Columbus, Georgia, in 1866, originated the idea of a Southern Memorial Day.

Not only were the women forced to adjust to the emotions of defeat but also to the changed social and economic circumstances which ensued. Before the War they could not work for money or have a career outside the home. Even the mere opportunity for self-support was denied them. But the War left thousands of widows, and wives with crippled husbands, who were forced then to become breadwinners or paupers. Repudiation of bonds, bank failures, and various other disastrous circumstances left them no choice but to become economically productive. The years of reconstruction continued the burdens of war and even imposed new troubles. There was no alternative but to bestow respectability, even at the risk of defeminizing her, on a woman en-

[7] Rowland T. Berthoff, "Southern Attitudes toward Immigration, 1865-1914," *Journal of Southern History,* XVII (August, 1951), pp. 328-360.

gaged in any work to make a living. Many not only had to pick up the management of farms or estates, as well as run a home with scant resources, but some also went to toil in the fields, doing the roughest sort of work. Editors gave lavish praise to the gentle-born lady who could "chop wood, drive a two-horse wagon, go to market, and do all the housework." Others opened boarding houses, sought money as authors, and taught, the last a pursuit combining good style with patriotism.

The desirability of teaching as a career for women brought passionate demands for better education for girls. One educational authority described the Southern women of the nineties as being the greatest single educational force in the region. During this period they displaced men in the teaching field, and women's colleges were opened, while coeducation also began to take root. To retain domination of the teaching field, the women needed better education themselves, and the Peabody Fund established Peabody Normal School in Nashville in 1875. Females made up 51.2 per cent of all Southern teachers by 1880, a figure which grew to 58.9 ten years later. Mississippi established the first state normal school in 1884. Special colleges for women were founded, such as Agnes Scott in Georgia, and state universities began opening their doors in the eighties. Soon over half of the "higher institutions for women" were in the South. Much of this progress was built on the philosophy that "when you educate a man, you educate one person; when you educate a woman, you educate an entire family."[8]

A better education and more freedom to take care of themselves made marriage less essential for women. No longer did they lose caste by working and not marrying. Instead, social scorn descended if an able-bodied woman allowed herself to be a burden on her relatives. A college president stated in 1891 that one-fourth of the girls at his institution expected to support themselves upon graduation. The same year, a writer for *Century Magazine,* while lamenting that much less deference was now paid to women by the rising generation of young men, concluded that the "crowning glory of the present age is that every woman is free to develop her own personality."[9]

This was an exaggeration. While the Southern girl was freer than ever before to make a living, her total emancipation was far from complete. In 1890 one authority estimated that of the 346 economic opportunities for women in the United States, Southerners had access only to some 20 to 40. These were chiefly work which could be done in the home, although women outnumbered men in teaching and in textile-mill work. Socially and politically, the Southern female was much less

[8] Marjorie S. Mendenhall, "Southern Women of a 'Lost Generation,'" *South Atlantic Quarterly,* XXXIII (1934), pp. 334-353.
[9] Wilber Fisk Tillett, "Southern Womanhood as Affected by the War," *Century,* XLIII (November, 1891), pp. 9-16.

advanced than those in the North. The idea of her voting or speaking in public was still extremely distasteful to the males. Editors referred to her as the "strongest power in the South, that sweet-voiced, gentle, womanly creature we call the Southern girl," and always raised a tear by referring to sacrifices of the women during the War. But voting would divest her of the "crowning attractions, and chief graces of her sex." Even farm journals alluded to the agrarian agitator, Mrs. Mary Lease, in such unflattering terms as that "old hell-raising Kansas heifer." Women were scolded for being slaves to fashion, for having too much interest in clothes, for wearing too many, and later for wearing too few. When in the eighties the Southern woman, following Northern trends, became club-minded, joining societies for humanitarian purposes, entertainment, or self-improvement, many men became alarmed. An editorial of 1886 warned against women's clubs as the probable cause of the prevalence of divorce in the North. That the warning was not heeded was evidenced by the Memphis *Commercial Appeal's* list of forty-eight women's clubs in that city in 1895.

Clubs were not the only worry of the masculine sex. A writer in the *Southern Review* for October, 1871, put it thus:

> We have been accustomed to view the woman's rights movement as too insignificant and too absurd to deserve serious attention. But . . . this move is assuming proportions and manifesting a spirit which inspire some of our most thoughtful minds with no little alarm. . . . For, in fact, the sun shines not more clearly in the heavens than this law does in the word of God. . . . "The man," says St. Paul, "is the head of the woman." The family, as organized by Christ, is constituted on the principle of autocracy, and not on the principle of equality in power and dominion between man and wife.

Legally, laws made by masculine legislatures reflected the Southern woman's inferiority. In many states she could neither sell her real estate without her husband's consent nor deprive him of a life interest in her estate. In some areas the husband controlled his wife's earnings, he was the legal guardian of their children, and only on his authorization could she appear in court. Whereas South Carolina banned divorce entirely, North Carolina, Kentucky, and Texas as late as 1898 allowed it only for adultery when the wife was the offender. Some states refused to grant females admission to the bar or licenses to practice medicine. Nevertheless, although some conservative practices continued in nearly every Southern commonwealth, the trend toward civil equality was so strong that, by the beginning of the twentieth century, it was merely a matter of time until the few remaining discriminations were removed from the statute books. The fight for the right to vote, one of women's most spectacular crusades against discrimination, is discussed in a later chapter.

Woman's emancipation did not come without cost. The female of the New South became a "woman" rather than a "lady," although much of the aroma of the old sentimentalism still lingered. Her freedom alarmed some; a nationally-circulated etiquette book of 1906 lamented that, in "many parts" of the South, "society" granted a girl the "privilege of visiting places of public refreshment or amusement alone with a young man, or of accepting his escort to or from an evening party."

Servants were hard to obtain and often undependable, even if they could be afforded. This shortage made changes in the way of living. A contemporary remarked that whereas the kitchen had formerly been separated from the house and the cooking done over fireplaces, now the white women would not carry dishes across the yard, and stoves came into general use. "Not only stoves but sewing-machines and other household utensils are much more common than before the War. The whites, having to do their own work are clamorous for conveniences in which they would not indulge their slaves." The necessity for doing their own housework was the reason given by the writer that "hospitality has been below par." However, the Southern woman tended more to stay married for life than did her Northern contemporary, although the rate of divorce rose steadily. In a region where cities were fewer and economic opportunities limited, wives were more willing to accept their lot in life.

Birth rates in essentially rural areas are traditionally high, and the South was no exception. Children were welcomed not only as potential helpers but also as additional wage earners. While life for a Southern child was not one of unrelieved drudgery, the necessity of working was an accepted part of being. The mill owner's son might well take a turn in the mill, and rural schools dismissed for cotton-picking time. Even when the number of Southern cities multiplied, the birth rate remained high. In 1920 North Carolina had 827 white children under five years of age per 1,000 mothers, Alabama 786, South Carolina 777, and Arkansas 798, while California had only 341, Connecticut 371, Massachusetts 359, and New York 362. Ten years later, Texas, with the lowest rate in the South, had 514 per 1,000, while Kansas had 498, Ohio 446, and New York 351. In a region where child labor lingered as a substitute for mechanization, and large families were viewed as an economic blessing, there were few advocates of birth control. As late as June, 1931, the Southern Presbyterian General Assembly withdrew from the Federal Council of Churches after that national organization endorsed birth control.

The antebellum glorification of the farmer and agriculture clashed with the philosophy of the New South. Conditions on post-war farms made the life much less attractive. The average farmhouse in the seventies was an ugly frame structure, and the furniture was sparse, cheap, and worn. In winter the home was likely to be so poorly heated that the family would cook, eat, and live in a single room for comfort. The farmer and his sons dressed in denim trousers and cheap cotton shirts, while his wife and daughters wore faded calico. Pork was the year-long staple, supplemented by cornbread and "greens." Work was hard, involving the whole family, and in the main financially unrewarding, as many lost the struggle and descended into tenancy.

The agrarian revolt was one by-product of this drabness of farm life. Another was migration. Bankrupt farmers began moving westward, especially into Arkansas and the interior of Texas, in hope of more favorable conditions. Alarmed newspapers and politicians tried to check this movement by praising the opportunities of the South and describing Texas and the West in unfavorable terms, playing up every story of misfortune in that "godless country." Only when it became clear that the agricultural West offered little improvement did the direction of migration change.

The city next became the lure. While Southern agriculture staggered under its burdens, a new urban South was rising to prosperity. After the Civil War the young people, in particular, felt the urban attraction, and often only the old were left at home on the farms and plantations. Charles Nordhoff commented in 1875 that everywhere except in Louisiana, Mississippi, and perhaps Arkansas, he had noted an increase in towns with new buildings under construction. Even Southerners were beginning to comment upon this phenomenon. Nordhoff believed that the money formerly invested in slaves was now being turned into houses, town improvements, and "above all," factories of various kinds. John C. Reed wrote the next year that a "new system is slowly developing, and can be plainly discerned among the rubbish of the old. The change from former days most noticeable now is the multiplication, increased energy, and continually growing trade of the smaller towns." Northern travelers pictured not only deserted farm shanties but also hundreds of old mansions going to decay, "the glass broken in the windows, the doors off hinges, the siding long unused to paint, the columns of the verandas rotting away and bramble thickets encroaching to the very doors." Owners had sold their land for whatever they could get and moved to the cities or towns to educate their children and escape the intolerable conditions surrounding them.

In 1860 New Orleans, with 168,675 people, was the only metropolis in the South. In fact, there were only sixty-two settlements of over 2,500 inhabitants in thirteen Southern states, and there was not a single town of 10,000 population in North Carolina, Florida, Mississippi, Arkansas, and Texas. Whereas the nation's urban population had grown from 5.1 to 8.8 per cent between 1790 and 1830, that of the Southeast had grown only from 1.8 to 3.4. Thirty years later, the national percentage was approximately 20; that of the South was about six. After the Civil War, however, hundreds of dozing market villages in the South came alive, built factories, and began dreaming of future greatness. The rapidly expanding railway systems sent currents of trade flowing in new directions and in greater volumes. Strategically located inland towns like Atlanta, Memphis, and Dallas became distributing centers. Birmingham, settled in 1871, had 3,086 people by 1880, while Dallas exploded from 1,500 in 1872 to 10,300 in 1880. Slightly less than 10 per cent of the Southern people lived in towns or cities by this time, compared to a national average of 33 per cent.

CITY GROWTH IN THE SOUTH, 1860-1900

|  | 1860 | 1880 | 1900 |
|---|---|---|---|
| New Orleans | 168,675 | 216,090 | 287,104 |
| San Antonio | 8,000 | 20,500 | 53,321 |
| Charleston | 40,500 | 50,000 | 55,807 |
| Richmond | 38,000 | 63,600 | 85,050 |
| Atlanta | 9,500 | 37,400 | 90,000 |
| Memphis | 22,623 | 33,592 | 102,300 |
| Nashville | 16,988 | 43,350 | 80,800 |
| Birmingham |  | 3,086 | 38,400 |
| Dallas |  | 10,300 | 42,000 |

As the full force of the New South's increasing industrialization and declining agriculture was felt, the flow to the towns and cities accelerated; new business enterprises, railway shops, machine shops, wholesale houses, department stores, banks, hotels, insurance firms, and a multitude of small stores of every variety were begun. Before the turn of the century, Atlanta grew to 90,000, Memphis 102,300, Nashville 80,800, Birmingham 38,400, and Dallas 42,600. By 1930, city populations were double or better, with individual cities showing extraordinary gains: Birmingham reached 259,600, Atlanta 270,300, and Dallas 260,400. By that year, 32.1 per cent of the population of the South was in urban areas, as compared to a national average of 56.

Despite the fact that the region was still more rural than the rest of the nation, its rate of urbanization was greater. For example, in the first twenty years of the new century, the percentage of urban gain was 114, as against 71.6 for the rest of the nation. Cities of 10,000 or more showed a gain of 132.4 per cent, as against 80.3 elsewhere. Between

1920 and 1930, Southern farms lost some 2,973,900 people, while the towns and cities gained 1,547,500, with migrants between ten and thirty years of age composing 67 per cent of the former total.

The growth of urban population brought the final development in the social and cultural revolution of the South which began at the end of the Civil War. Before 1860 the social life of the country dominated the social life of the town; by 1900 the reverse was true. "If King Cotton still reigned, his throne was in the mill and his council was the chamber of commerce." The polite society of the planters gave way to the urban high society of the newly rich, a more pretentious and ostentatious life, more responsive to world fashions and more like that of the North and West. The Southern social world became filled with names like Duke and Reynolds (tobacco), Candler (Coca-Cola), Cheek (Maxwell House Coffee), Cannon (textiles), and Patten (patent medicine), and Hogg (petroleum). Few of the newly rich were college-trained; most were of yeoman stock who had grown up during the cultural famine which followed the War and reconstruction. Correspondingly, they went through the same "gilded age" which had earlier characterized their Northern counterparts.

Although often lacking the polish and interest in culture which was synonymous with the old aristocracy, the new leaders at least gave lip service to the old tradition.[10] The aristocratic ideal was rejuvenated in the cult of ancestor worship: efforts to trace connection with the planter group, buying of country estates, perpetuation of antebellum architecture, and the continuation of the planter's church, the Episcopal, as representing high society. Ironically, the rich, upon achieving prominence and money in the city, returned to the rural life and to the traditional plantation pattern, a mold which they or their fathers had helped destroy.

The city's attractiveness was not limited to the whites alone. Often the first thing a freed Negro did was to go to the nearest town. Although the Freedmen's Bureau endeavored to return them to the country, here, too, the Negro followed the white pattern. In 1860 only 6.7 per cent of Southern Negroes lived in urban areas, comprising 19.3 per cent of such populations. Thirty years later Negroes owned 110,000 city homes, and by 1900 some 14.7 per cent of the Negroes lived in urban areas. About twenty-two per cent of the Southern Negroes were city dwellers in 1910, making up approximately one-fourth of the urban population of the region. Between 1910 and 1920 in the South Atlantic states alone, nearly 235,000 moved from country to city, a flood which continued unabated until checked by the Depression of 1929. By this

[10] Francis B. Simkins, "The South's Democratic Pose," *Georgia Review*, IV (1950), pp. 255-262.

time one-third of the race had become city residents. While the number of Negro city inhabitants increased, it did not increase in proportion to the total population growth of the city, as the urban areas drew from many sources.

Unlike the majority of whites who arrived in the city, the Negro often found this condition of living worse than it had been in the country. While a few made better homes, others collected in the slums or back alleys in Southern cities. Some were housed on the grounds of affluent whites, but their quarters were usually confined to a different part of the town. Not only were the houses shamefully inadequate, but the occupants also were cruelly exploited by their landlords; rentals often yielded 15 to 20 per cent of the cash value of the property. The shacks were one-room affairs in the most unhealthy sections of town, with conditions worsened by yards and alleys full of garbage, stagnant water, and pig and poultry pens. Often a single outhouse or toilet served as many as a dozen families. The crowding was responsible for much of the often-cited high death rates and promiscuousness, with Negro sections often being the worst.

These conditions, plus the fact that economic opportunities were very limited, inspired the Negro to leave the South altogether. He was not alone. In February, 1867, *De Bow's Review* estimated that 20,000 Southerners had moved to New York since the War. White migration was most pronounced after 1880 and Negro after 1910, and almost without exception the number increased each decade, reaching a peak in the twenties, when the Southeast lost more than 1,500,000 people. From 1915 to 1928, about 1,200,000 Negroes moved North, and about one-fourth of all Negroes in the United States lived in the North and West by 1930. In all, the South lost some 3,800,000 of its total population in the first thirty years of the twentieth century. One-third was white, mostly from the Southern border states, while the Negroes chiefly left the lower South.

The typical Southern city was small, serving a limited agricultural area, though some became identified with varied types of production. Durham and Winston-Salem, North Carolina, became associated with cigarettes; Newport News, Virginia, with shipbuilding; Birmingham and Chattanooga with coal and iron; Tampa with cigars; Houston with petroleum; and Natchez, Charleston, Williamsburg, and Miami with tourists. The textile industry generally did not locate within city limits but established its own villages on the outskirts, usually with several hundred people living in cheap housing along a single street ankle-deep in dust. Few Southern cities had many paved streets before 1880, and a goodly number could boast none. As they grew in population, they often remained little more than overgrown country towns. The most progressive introduced horse-drawn trolleys in the late sixties; fire-fighting became a civic function; gas lighting was common in the larger communities; and police forces were expanded, although the typical policeman was a "poor white" with legal sanction to use a weapon but with low social prestige and little training.

The most serious problem resulting from the rise of the city was that of health. Urban sanitation was virtually unknown in any American city at the time of the Civil War; the basically rural South lagged even further behind in cleanliness. Memphis, in 1870 a city of 40,000, had practically no sewage arrangements or health administration, while Charleston and Mobile were as nauseating. Nashville, also, was notoriously unclean: streets were poorly drained, sewers were open, and foul garbage heaps poisoned the air. The state penitentiary and several slaughter houses poured their wastes into streams flowing through the town, and banks formed which had deposits of "every imaginable abomination which lies rotting, seething and weltering in the unobstructed summer sun." Four cemeteries, a community garbage dump, a tannery, and numerous outdoor toilets drained into the river a short distance above the intake pipes of the water reservoir.[11] New Orleans was one of the most unhealthy cities in the world. A writer in the Tenth Census (1880) said that the "soil is saturated almost to its surface . . . very largely with the oozings of foul privy vaults, and the infiltrations of accumulations on the surface of the streets and in the rear of houses."

Such examples could be multiplied almost endlessly. It was not surprising, therefore, that Southern cities became the prey of frightful epidemics. A yellow fever outbreak in 1873, along with smallpox and cholera, took the lives of 2,000 out of 5,000 victims in Memphis. In 1878-1879 this plague swept through the Gulf states and reached as far north as Missouri, killing 16,000 out of 74,000 afflicted. From Mobile to Galveston, cities were placed under quarantine, and railroad operations ceased in much of the area. Memphis, hardest hit of all, found its very existence in jeopardy after 5,150 deaths.[12]

Doctors were helpless before such onslaughts. They knew little of the reasons for disease or the treatment of victims. They generally believed that epidemics were caused by the filth of the city and decaying wooden pavement, if not by divine wrath. Once an epidemic struck, the only safety was believed to lie in fleeing to higher ground and waiting for the return of cold weather. For those who could not leave, perfume, onions, assafoetida, and sponges over the face were used to

[11] F. Gavin Davenport, "Scientific Interests in Kentucky and Tennessee," *Journal of Southern History*, XIV (November, 1948), pp. 500-521.
[12] Gerald M. Capers, Jr., "Yellow Fever in Memphis in the 1870's," *Mississippi Valley Historical Review*, XXIV (1937-1938), pp. 483-502.

ward off the disease. These experiences caused Americans to grasp the new germ theory just coming into prominence and greatly spurred efforts toward public health. In 1874 Nashville reorganized its city board of health, which had been disbanded in 1868, and three years later Tennessee set up a state organization. Elsewhere, similar moves were taken, and most cities were beginning to put in effective sewers by 1880. Although the president of the State Board of Health of Louisiana reported in 1881 that New Orleans gutters and streets were choked with garbage, filth, and mud, Mark Twain found the next year that the gutters were being flushed out with running water two or three times a day. By 1890 its unsanitary practice of relying upon open gutters for sewage disposal had been completely abandoned, and by World War I most Southern towns of size had undertaken or were seriously considering construction of modern establishments for water supply and sewage disposal.

Progress was also evident in other phases of city life. Ice-making plants first appeared in the South in 1870 and spread northward. New Orleans in 1871 boasted a factory which could make seventy-two tons daily, reducing the price from as much as $60 per ton for imported ice to $15 for the local product. By 1882 even a community the size of Natchez had such a plant capable of producing thirty tons a day, and the price of ice fell to six or seven dollars a ton. The South had about 350 miles of street railways, chiefly horse-powered, by 1880. The incandescent light, developed that year, was quickly utilized in the more advanced Southern metropolises. Mark Twain described New Orleans in 1882 as the best-lighted city in the nation, electrically speaking, with more and better lights than even New York. By the mid-eighties, the telephone had ceased to be a city novelty and in the next decade penetrated the rural areas. Cobblestone streets and boardwalks were replaced with modern pavement in many areas by 1890, and the latest developments in waterworks and fire and police methods had been introduced.

One of the earliest uses of the electric trolley was in 1885 in Montgomery, Alabama. The first financially successful effort came when Frank J. Sprague, "Father of the Electric Railway," was given a contract for $110,000 to construct a twelve-mile street railway in Richmond, Virginia. By February, 1888, it was in commercial operation, with cars getting current from an overhead wire fed from a central powerhouse. The success of this line led to adoption of the technique by Boston and other Northern cities. By 1890 the South had 1,239 miles of street railway, two-thirds operated by animal power; the figure was 2,203 miles by 1902, and mules were a thing of the past, only thirty-one miles being so operated.

The South showed itself alert to other types of transportation and communication. With the outbreak of the Civil War, the major cities were already linked by two principal telegraph systems in the South: the American Telegraph Company and the New Orleans and Ohio, sometimes known as the Southwestern Company. After consolidation, these were in turn taken over by Western Union in 1866, at a time when they were operating 20,000 miles of wire. After the turn of the century, three companies, Western Union, Postal, and the Cumberland Telegraph and Telephone, insured that the region was relatively as well-served as any other. Only three commercial telephone systems preceded the development of such networks in the South, the first below the Potomac coming in 1885 in South Carolina and West Virginia. From there, the spread was rapid. By 1888 there were twenty-three commercial systems in the country — thirteen Southern. Following the expiration of the Bell patents, systems and subscribers mushroomed, until by 1900 there were over 800 companies and 368,000 telephones, or one for every sixty people, in the South.

Public highways did not become a serious concern until 1885, when agitation for good roads reached noticeable proportions. Conventions were held in nearly every state during the next decade to agitate the matter, and the National Road Parliament was held at Atlanta in 1895. The establishment of the Office of Public Roads in the Department of Agriculture in 1893 provided an agency which did yeoman labor in acquainting the national public as to the need for and proper methods of good road construction. By 1920 the campaign had reached almost religious fervor. The Southern press was outspoken in support, and all the Southern states had created highway commissions. The first progress came with wide-scale use of convict labor in road construction, but it soon became obvious that the Southern states with their restricted finances could not solve the problem on a pay-as-you-go basis. The decade of the twenties eventually marked the great highway expansion program, usually financed by bond issues, which placed a number of the states of Dixie in the forefront of the good roads program.

The opening up of the region by good transportation and communication did much to break down local provincialism. With the passage of time, Southern cities became more and more like their Northern counterparts in every way, even to the appearance of skyscrapers, which had little justification other than local pride. The absence of equal wealth usually meant that improvements were later and on a less lavish scale, but, aside from a more rural atmosphere, by 1930 there was little to distinguish Southern cities from Northern and Western ones of similar size.

Day-by-day life in the South reflected the conflict between the old and new forces at work in the region. Rural conservatism was seen in religious attitudes, and local prohibition found a ready acceptance in most of the area, sweeping to victory in the 1880's. Even in the cities, most stores, except for occasional tobacco and confectionary vendors, were closed on Sunday, a dispensation allowed because tobacco was used by nearly every man and boy, and some women, in the South. As late as the 1930's, the Georgia legislature reaffirmed an ancient law against fishing on Sundays, and South Carolina had a law making church attendance compulsory as late as 1885. This conservatism, though yielding slowly in the cities, was still so strong in the South that in the 1920's the president of the University of Florida was quoted with approval for having said that the "low-cut gowns, the rolled hose and the short skirts are born of the Devil and his angels, and are carrying the present and future generations to chaos and destruction." The Virginia legislature seriously considered a bill outlawing female dresses which exposed "more than three inches of . . . throat."

Old traditions of violence yielded slowly. Nearly each issue of every newspaper published before 1920 furnished documentary proof that the South was a land of violence, where knife, pistol, brass knucks, razors, clubs, and even fence rails took their daily toll. As a region, it had the lowest rate from suicide an the highest from homicide. The lynchers and the Klan were warped inheritors of the Southern pattern of direct, personal action. Homicides among both whites and blacks exceeded the highest records of larger cities of the North.

Yet, conditions of life showed steady improvement. The threadbare garments which had marked the post-war period began disappearing by 1877, and Northern fashions were imitated by the wealthy and aspired to by the common folks, both white and Negro. Homes reflected the improved financial condition of the region. By 1880 a Southerner could write that already the average houses of the South were much better than they had been before the War, with better furniture and greater provisions for comfort. Mark Twain left a classic description of the upper class homes of the period, "the residence of the principal citizen, all the way from the suburbs of New Orleans to the edge of St. Louis." It was a big, square, two-story, white "frame" house which featured a large parlor with an "ingrain" carpet and a mahogany center-table supporting copies of "Friendship's Offering," *Ivanhoe*, and a current number of *Godey's Lady's Book*. A polished, air-tight stove supplied the heat, and the mantelpiece featured baskets of fruit done in plaster or wax. A piano was piled with music such as the "Battle of Prague" and the "Bird Waltz." Homemade works of art covered the walls, such as pious mottoes done in grass or yarn, along with portraits of relatives, lithographs and steel and copperplate engravings of Napoleon Crossing the Alps, Moses Smiting the Rock, and the Return of the Prodigal Son. In the corners were whatnots featuring shell collections, Indian arrowheads, painted toy dogs, homemade wire baskets, old lockets with circlets of ancestral hair, wax figurines, and more daguerreotypes of relatives. Uncomfortable horsehair chairs and sofas completed the parlor furniture.

Bedrooms were bare or had rag carpets; bedsteads used cords, usually sagging in the middle, for springs and had feather mattresses. Cane-bottom chairs, a split-bottomed rocker, an inherited bureau with a small mirror in a veneered frame, and a brass candlestick and tallow candle completed the furnishing. There was no bathroom in the house, and "no visitor likely to come along who has ever seen one."[13]

By the turn of the century, the incandescent light was finding its way into middle-class homes, at least in the city, and the way was opening for other domestic uses of electricity. Southern use of electricity increased 212 per cent from 1913 to 1923, while elsewhere the increase was only 148 per cent. Telephones were beginning to appear elsewhere than in business offices. The bathroom was brought into the house, and better plumbing and kitchen fixtures simplified housekeeping. Rugs replaced carpets, and smaller rooms displaced the wondrous arrays of bric-a-brac. The new emphasis was on austerity, and the "living room" was put to use for daily living. The cannery, the bakery, and the steam laundry took over many of the former functions of the housewife, and the trend toward smaller families and lighter duties allowed her more free time.

These gains for the middle class, it should be pointed out, were not available for the majority of Negroes and poor whites. Many who flocked to the city, for example, failed to find adequate and low-cost housing. In 1890, of the eighteen cities in the United States with under 20 per cent home ownership, eleven were in the South. As late as the 1920's, most of the newly-built city housing was small and flimsy, in scrubby suburbs and undesirable locations, and with cost and rent completely out of proportion to the earnings of the inhabitants. A large part of the labor in the larger and more rapidly developing cities was living in slum or semi-slum conditions. The South's efforts to align itself in the national pattern of urban society had, indeed, succeeded in emulating many aspects, good and bad. Much had been done, but much remained to be accomplished.

[13] Mark Twain, *Life on the Mississippi* (New York: Harper, 1904), pp. 295-299.

# 13

## THE RISE OF EDUCATION FOR
## THE MASSES

THE EDUCATIONAL SYSTEM of the Old South had been a good one of its kind, but it was vastly different from the national or American philosophy of education. Southern education from the 1830's to 1860, was based upon an excellent system of private tutors and academies, with the student bearing the financial responsibility. Based upon an aristocratic society, it was selective and geared to producing leaders. Excluded from its benefits were not only the Negroes, a fact which was considered unimportant and even desirable, but also the lower and many middle-class whites. The democratic movement for public schools which swept the North made only a faint impression on the South, in general taking the form of paper provisions which were largely unimplemented. Where actual efforts were made to broaden the scope of education, they usually were in the form of charity, thus stigmatizing the public school as a pauper's institution and fixing in the Southern mind the conviction that private education was superior to public.

After the Civil War, Southern school systems had virtually no assets, historical or economic, upon which to rebuild. Collapse of the Confederate and state financial setups had closed nearly all schools before the end of 1864. Pupils and teachers were scattered, while school funds were nonexistent. Young men who had interrupted their education to fight came back to labor in the fields. The poverty of the post-war South made even light taxation seem oppressive and education a luxury rather than a necessity. Southern education was additionally handicapped by accumulated prejudice, for the overthrow of the Southern aristocratic system had not necessarily convinced the late Confederates that they were wrong. The inherent problems which arose from the region's basically rural nature and the new question of the Negroes and poorer whites haunted educators. In the latter case, both had larger families and little taxable property; the freedmen, alone, made up around 36.5 per cent of the population. And finally, if the Negroes were to be educated, would it be in the same schools with the whites?

Reform made a poor start because of the fact that public education was looked upon as a "Yankee" attack upon Southern institutions. As has been shown, the end of gunfire signaled an invasion by a new army of Northern educators, determined to win the war on this front. The North was convinced that the South had no public education and, what was more important, was opposed to it. They believed that pre-war false education had provided the basis upon which secession and rebellion had grown and that the exploiting of the ignorance of the poor whites had made the Confederacy possible. The greatest point of argument, however, was the belief that difference in educational opportunity alone explained the backwardness of the Negroes, a differential the Southern leaders were believed determined to continue. The president of Harvard told the National Teachers' Association in 1865 that the "present hour opens particularly inviting fields of labor for those engaged in teaching . . . and in the new work of spreading knowledge and intellectual culture over the regions that sat in darkness." And the *Nation* argued that education would make Southerners Republicans!

These Northern hopes did not picture the attitude of all whites, however, but did correctly suggest the Negroes' susceptibility, if not eagerness. At first, Northern educators tried to attract the poorer whites, but quickly alienated them by their patronizing attitude and Northern bias. Next came concentration on the freedmen. Spearheading the educational movement were some 366 Northern aid societies and their auxiliaries, whose aim was musically expressed by the words:

> We go to plant the common schools,
>     On distant mountain swells,
> And give the Sabbaths of the South
>     The ring of Northern bells.

The Negroes showed an almost unnatural zeal for education; over 150,000 were in some sort of school by 1886, and their numbers continued to grow. Three years later, 9,503 teachers were working with the freedmen alone. Although a few of the instructors were Southerners, the majority of white teachers came from the North. At the same time, the number of Negro teachers increased, and gradually they took over supervision of some of the schools for their race. Financing, however, remained a strictly Northern function carried on by the Freedmen's Bureau and private organizations. The American Missionary Association, for example, annually spent an average of $100,000 and maintained eight colleges, twelve normal and high schools, and twenty-four common schools.

Although their students might be eager, the lot of these teachers was far from pleasant.[1] Southern whites were generally very hostile to these Northern educators. In some areas this took the form of overt action, such as burning of schools and terrorizing of teachers. Social ostracism was the rule of the day. Some of this was because the teachers were outsiders who were trying to remodel society along radical lines; some resulted from their own tactlessness. Teachers who lacked a deep dedication quickly despaired under the social pressure and the backwardness of their pupils, but others gave long and fruitful years of humanitarian service and successfully nurtured the Negroes' enthusiasm for knowledge.

Coincident with the educational drive developed the quarrel as to whether Negro education should be "classical." The New England pedagogue had little concern but to educate the freedmen as he himself had been schooled. To the Southerners this seemed a worthless effort, smacking too much of racial equality. On the other hand, the Southerners felt that if the Negroes had to be educated at all, it should be done in a way which would make them more desirable servants and laborers. Proponents of vocational education pointed out that it continued the skilled-artisan tradition which had existed among the Negroes before the War; it would be less expensive and would allow the student to earn part of his maintenance at school. Students could erect buildings, grow their own food, and the like. Opponents, however, feared that it would not provide the type of leadership the race needed and would keep Negroes out of the higher and more general culture of America. The arguments finally crystallized in the opposing positions of two Negro leaders, Booker T. Washington for practical education and W. E. B. Du Bois for equal and similar instruction to that given whites. Generally, although there were notable exceptions, the vocationalists carried the day. Historians, to this very day, continue to debate the merits of the two approaches. Since numerous Southern whites, however, accepted the vocational approach, the idea

[1] Henry L. Swint, *The Northern Teacher in the South,* 1862-1870 (Nashville: Vanderbilt Univ., 1941).

of education for blacks was saved from entire destruction when Southerners regained political power.

Some leaders were outspoken on their behalf. John B. Gordon of Georgia ran for public office in 1866 on a platform which included free schools for the Negroes. The same year, J. L. M. Curry of Alabama issued a public appeal for local whites to aid in the freedmen's education. The Mississippi State Teachers' Association went on record in 1867 as favoring public schools for Negroes, and leading politicians such as Wade Hampton of South Carolina and Benjamin H. Hill of Georgia fought for better treatment and schooling for the former slaves. Blacks, too, in the long tradition of self-help, pushed for educational opportunities.

This interest in the freedmen resulted from the partial acceptance by some Southerners of the necessity for public education for all. As the Johnson governments took steps in this direction, Arkansas passed a good law in 1866 providing for tax-supported schools. Alabama provided for a state superintendent, local county authorities, and schools for children from ages six to twenty, although attendance was not made compulsory. On January 9, 1867, Montgomery appropriated $5,000 to open two schools for "education for the poorer classes of this city." Georgia, too, set up a system of public schools, to be supported by county taxes. Other states, like Texas and Mississippi, discussed the question. Before any concrete steps could be taken, however, these governments were overthrown by the onset of Radical reconstruction.

When the carpetbag governments took over, scarcely a physical trace of a state-supported school system could be found in most of the South. There was not even a normal (teacher-training) school in the entire region, and the old academies had disappeared. During the Congressional period, every Southern state provided admirable systems of schools in their laws, but mainly they were concerned only with the early grades, while high schools existed only in cities and a few towns. This was a period of turmoil, corruption, and misuse of funds. The Alabama Superintendent of Education was defeated for re-election in 1870 by charges of graft. No state was able to put into full operation the systems provided for by law. Funds were withheld or squandered. Taxes were beyond the ability of the people to pay, school boards were often composed of politicians and inexperienced Negroes, and the issue was clouded by demands for mixed schools.

Only in South Carolina, Florida, Mississippi, and Louisiana were bi-racial schools authorized. In its 1868 constitution, South Carolina provided for a system of public schools open to both races, with one school in each district to be maintained for at least six months in each year. The General Assembly was admonished to require at least a total of twenty-four months' attendance by each child between the ages of six and sixteen years. The school law of 1870 financed the system by poll taxes, legislative appropriations, and voluntary local taxation. By 1876, South Carolina had 2,776 schools; 123,085 pupils, of whom 70,802 were Negro; and 3,068 teachers, about one-third of whom were Negroes.

Elsewhere, the North Carolina convention could not reach a decision on mixing the races, and so the constitution was silent on the matter, but the legislature set up separate schools. Segregated classes were provided in Alabama, but localities could have mixed schools by unanimous consent. Since the Mississippi constitution made no definite statement, it was interpreted as authorizing mixed classes, but enforcement was lax. Virginia required that its system of public free schools be administered impartially between the races. Only 59,000 Virginia children were in school in 1870 – the 10,000 Negroes being in institutions established by Northern societies and the Freedmen's Bureau. Seven years later, the state had an enrollment of 205,000 in public schools – 140,000 white and 65,000 Negro. Louisiana's constitution required the General Assembly to establish at least one free school in each parish, to which all children between the ages of six and twenty-one should be admitted without distinction of race, color, or previous condition. It also stated emphatically that there should "be no separate schools or institutions of learning established exclusively for any race by the State of Louisiana." The whites retaliated by boycotting the schools.

All of the states had good laws on paper, but they failed to achieve their goals. At best, the schools were inadequate in numbers, funds, and caliber of instruction. The greatest failure, however, was that Radical educators in the reconstruction years did not establish a popular confidence in the importance of the public school system. The carpetbaggers cannot be blamed entirely, however; equally at fault was the poverty of the region, and also the presence of large groups of underprivileged people, Negroes and poor whites alike, who not only were unacquainted with education but also were actually hostile to the idea. The South had not yet developed a democratic philosophy of education and did not feel its need. It would have been amazing, moreover, if such a maturing had come while the South was still suffering from the legacies of war – loss of morale, inertia, and destruction of life and property.

Nevertheless, to the credit of the carpetbaggers, some accomplishments were made. Illiteracy was reduced, with the most impressive gains among the Negroes. More than 85 per cent of the Negroes ten years of age and older could not read or write in 1870; in one decade this proportion was reduced by 10 per cent. The Radicals wrote into their new state constitutions the first mandatory provisions for systems of free public education. And for the first time, provisions were made for uniform systems of school taxation and for education of Negro children. Normal schools were also instituted; as early as 1871, eight — four for each race — were proposed in Alabama, and the first one was given a charter in 1872.

This was the spark of democracy handed to the Southern "Redeemers" upon the restoration of home rule. While some Bourbons, like Wade Hampton of South Carolina, could speak with enthusiasm of the need for educational development, even those with the best intentions were confronted by the practical problem of schooling "two populations out of the poverty of one." In March, 1877, the Louisiana General Assembly pledged itself to "secure the education of the white and the colored citizens with equal advantages," yet school receipts of that state a scant five years later allowed only forty-five cents for each school-age child, and the *Louisiana Journal of Education* declared the public school system was as "dead as Hector."[2] Faced by similar problems, Governor F. W. M. Holliday of Virginia declared to the legislature, "Public free schools are not a necessity. The world, for hundreds of years, grew in wealth, culture, and refinement, without them."

Despite the fact that the poverty and debts of war and reconstruction led to sharp cuts in all taxes, including educational levies, the biggest obstacle to schools was the Southern people themselves. In addition to viewing public education as a "Yankee" notion, many resented what they considered an invasion of parental authority. Others objected to its leveling tendencies, especially if it included both races, even in separate schools. A South Carolina editor wrote that no "sophistry or false reasoning can ever convince us that the industrious and self-denying citizen should be taxed to educate the children of indolent and immoral parents," and another added that the arguments for public schools could apply equally to free public meat markets! The South Carolina superintendent of education reported in 1886 that the "largest and most dangerous" group of dissenters were those who opposed education of the Negro upon the ground that to "educate a Negro is to spoil a laborer and train up a candidate for the Penitentiary."

Numerous are the accounts which make it clear that the average Southerner did not feel the need for general education. Sir George Campbell reported after a tour of the South in 1879 that the "blacks are very anxious to learn — more so than the whites." Christopher G.

[2] United States Bureau of Education, "Education in the Various States," *Report of Commissioner of Education for 1894-1895* (Washington, 1896), p. 1304.

Memminger of South Carolina, antebellum educational reformer and Confederate Secretary of the Treasury, wrote Colonel Edward McCrady, Jr., in 1881, favoring a literacy test for voting on the grounds that some "additional stimulus upon the white man is necessary to forward education. It is unfortunate that the whites, in many cases, do not make use of their privilege to attend the schools, while every negro uses his to its fullest extent."[3] The English observer commented again a few years later on the Negro's greater interest in education, while in 1888 a bill was introduced in the Alabama legislature to abolish that state's normal schools.

Even the most altruistic must have been daunted by the magnitude of the task confronting them, however. In 1879 the enrollment in ten Southern states was 1,590,000 out of a school-age population of over 3,000,000. The proportion of Southern whites over ten years old who could not write was almost one-fourth, and for Negroes it was over three-fourths. At the same time, the region had 1,242 minors of school age for every 1,000 adults, with a net wealth per child of $851; the Northern child-adult ratio was only 909 per 1,000 and the net wealth ratio, $2,225. The Southern states among them had less taxable wealth than did New York State alone, and only five spent as much as $2 per child, while only three Northern states spent less than $5.

It is not surprising, therefore, that as early as 1878, representatives of nine Southern states at a Southern Educational Convention in Atlanta called for national action to distribute the receipts of federal land sales on the basis of illiteracy. Ironically, the Blair bill, which proposed this, passed the Senate on three different occasions only to die in the House. This was the result of combined opposition of state-rights Southerners and those Northerners who were unwilling to have the lion's share of the money go to the South.

Fortunately, Northern philanthropy tried to fill the gap. Undoubtedly the brightest spot in the darkness of Southern education of the period was the Peabody Educational Fund. George Peabody had amassed a fortune as a merchant and financier in England and America and, like other wealthy men of his generation, was interested in good causes. He gave money in England for lower-class housing to improve slum conditions as a means of pacifying the class struggle. The prime American problem to him was reconciliation of the sections, and he decided that public education would win the South back into the Union. By gifts in 1867 and 1869, he established a trust fund of over

[3] This letter is attached to a McCrady speech, "The Necessity of Raising the Standard of Citizenship and the Right of the General Assembly of South Carolina to Impose Qualifications upon Electors," found in the Dawson pamphlets. University of North Carolina.

## SOUTHERN EDUCATIONAL STATISTICS, 1879*

| | Whites | | | Negro | | | Total Expenditure both races |
|---|---|---|---|---|---|---|---|
| | SCHOOL POPULATION | ENROLLMENT | % | SCHOOL POPULATION | ENROLLMENT | % | |
| Ala. | 217,590 | 107,483 | 49 | 170,413 | 72,007 | 42 | $375,465 |
| Ark. | 181,799 | 53,229 | 29 | 54,332 | 17,743 | 33 | 238,056 |
| Fla. | 46,410 | 18,871 | 41 | 42,099 | 20,444 | 49 | 114,896 |
| Ga. | 236,319 | 150,134 | 64 | 197,125 | 86,399 | 45 | 471,029 |
| La. | 139,661 | 44,052 | 32 | 131,184 | 34,476 | 26 | 480,320 |
| Miss. | 175,251 | 112,994 | 64 | 251,438 | 123,710 | 49 | 830,704 |
| N.C. | 291,770 | 136,481 | 47 | 167,554 | 89,125 | 53 | 352,882 |
| S.C. | 83,813 | 61,219 | 73 | 144,315 | 72,853 | 50 | 324,629 |
| Tex. | 171,426 | 138,912 | 81 | 62,015 | 47,874 | 77 | 753,346 |
| Va. | 314,827 | 152,136 | 48 | 240,980 | 68,600 | 28 | 946,109 |

* Report of Commissioner of Education, 1880, p. lvii.

## SOUTHERNERS AGED 10 YEARS AND UPWARD UNABLE TO WRITE, 1879*

| | Whites | Negro |
|---|---|---|
| Alabama | 24.7% | 80.6% |
| Arkansas | 25.0 | 75.0 |
| Florida | 19.9 | 70.7 |
| Georgia | 22.9 | 81.6 |
| Louisiana | 18.4 | 79.1 |
| Mississippi | 16.5 | 75.2 |
| North Carolina | 31.5 | 77.4 |
| South Carolina | 21.9 | 78.5 |
| Tennessee | 27.3 | 71.7 |
| Texas | 15.3 | 75.4 |
| Virginia | 18.2 | 73.7 |

* Compendium of the Tenth Census (1880), pt. 2, pp. 1646, 1650.

$3,000,000, part in Mississippi bonds which were later repudiated. He stated that he gave "to the suffering South for the good of the whole country . . . for the promotion and encouragement of intellectual, moral, or industrial education among the young people of the more destitute portions of the Southern and Southwestern States." The trustees, headed by R. C. Winthrop, a conservative Bostonian with considerable political experience, were empowered to use the interest and up to 40 per cent of the principal. Barnas Sears, one-time president of Brown University, was chosen as general agent. After Sears' death in 1880, he was succeeded by Jabez L. M. Curry, who retained the post for over twenty years, except for a short time when he served as Minister to Spain.

The Fund was most fortunate in its choice of agents. Sears was not the conventional, uncompromising Yankee most familiar to the South. Curry, a Southerner, was already well-known as a result of military and political service and had been a Baptist minister and professor. He was a great orator, with unusual personal magnetism, and was dedicated to the cause of education. He quickly became the most persuasive Southern champion of schools for both races. The Fund needed his and all the talent it could find. As Curry later said, "At the origin of the Peabody Fund not a single Southern state within the field of its operations had a system of free public schools and only in a few cities were any such schools to be found. No state organization existed through which this fund could reach the people."

The trustees wanted free schools for all, a task obviously beyond their financial resources. They therefore wisely decided not to squander their slim resources where there was no spark of interest in public education, but to help only those states willing to help themselves. None of the money would be used to originate schools, nor would help be given to private or sectarian schools. Not only did the Fund discriminate between states, but also between areas within states and between towns and cities, with the most progressive getting help first. The trustees' attitude on mixed schools was illustrated by Sears' reply to the Radical superintendent of education in Louisiana in 1870: "[We] raise no question about mixed schools. We simply take the fact that white children do not generally attend them, without passing on the propriety or impropriety of their course." If, however, this could be removed, "we could act in concert with you." By the same token, the trustees later prevented white governments from ignoring Negro education by threats to withhold funds. Throughout the Bourbon period, the meager school revenue was divided with less discrimination between the races. South Carolina, for example, spent more on its Negro than its white schools in 1880.

The Peabody agents made speeches, propagandized, cooperated with state officials, helped localities plan school systems, and then gave cash assistance. In key areas they tried to create model schools which could influence the surrounding district. They were not engaged in charity, for self-help had first to be present, but instead followed a program of concentrating help on a few schools rather than dispersing it over many. A corollary to their efforts for better schools was an interest in establishing normal (teacher-training) schools for preparation of both white and Negro teachers. George Peabody College for teachers at Nashville, Tennessee, became the best known product of this program. If a college course were impossible for teachers, then counties or smaller communities were encouraged to have summer institutes. Another special concern was to attract women into the field previously dominated by males.

Almost without exception, Southern communities were eager to have Peabody help and supervision, indicating the region's willingness to accept alien institutions presented in an acceptable fashion. The Peabody work not only kept alive Southern public opinion favorable to education during these dark years but also helped develop sentiment sympathetic to tax-supported systems. It set up many city and state plans, preached a general responsibility for educating the Negro at a time when some were advocating limiting state expenditures for Negroes to the amount furnished by their taxes, and encouraged education of teachers. The basic goal of George Peabody was also fulfilled, for his foundation's efforts removed much bitterness and sectionalism, served greatly to reconcile Southern individuals and Northern institutions, and probably as much as anything else insured the basis for the development of a Southern school system akin to that of the national one.

The work of the Peabody Educational Fund was supplemented by the Slater Fund. In 1882, John Fox Slater, a textile manufacturer of Norwich, Connecticut, gave $1,000,000 for "uplifting the lately emancipated population of the Southern states and their posterity by conferring on them the blessings of Christian education." Rutherford B. Hayes was chosen as first president of the trust, and the Reverend A. G. Haygood of Georgia was the general agent until the position was combined with the Peabody agent, Curry. The trust was used almost entirely in helping students and preparing teachers in the industrial and vocational training of Negroes.

The greatest local spur to education in the South grew out of the development of the Agrarian Revolt. One of the original arguments of its supporters was the extent to which the city-based Bourbons had ignored rural education, especially vocational training for the whites. The Shell Manifesto of South Carolina in 1890, for example, castigated the neglect of "the free schools which are the only chance for an education to thousands of poor children, whose fathers bore the brunt in the struggle for our redemption in 1876." The neglect was obvious from the fact that South Carolina in 1890 had the second highest illiteracy rate in the nation, surpassed only by Louisiana. But these two were not unique. Some 18.2 per cent of the whites over ten years of age in Alabama and 69 per cent of the Negroes were illiterate. In 1893, Curry was able to say to the members of the Georgia General Assembly, "None of you, perhaps, were educated in the public schools."

The concurrent drive for disfranchisement of the Negroes also played its part in broadening educational opportunities. After setting up educational qualifications for voting, the whites wished to make their own position secure by providing adequate school systems for their race. The role of education as an adjunct to white supremacy was emphasized by the chairman of the education committee at the South Carolina constitutional convention, who said, "It is foolish to say any other race can get control of this State if we are educated." This view prevailed in the convention, illustrated by an increase in the property tax for schools from two to three mills, the tax being permissive above that rate.

While white education improved somewhat as a result of Agrarian efforts, that of the Negro child declined. In South Carolina, for example, where Negroes had previously received a fair division of funds and in some years even had the advantage, more than twice as much, and nearly three times as much per pupil, was spent in 1895 on white schools. The segregation of pupils was also on the rise. In 1895, of the thirty-two colleges, seventy-three normal schools, and fifty-seven secondary or high schools for Negroes in the United States, only six were outside the former slave states.[4] Discrimination and separate schools became more and more marked, and the practice received legal approval when, in 1896, the United States Supreme Court placed its blessing upon segregation and established the separate-but-equal doctrine which was to endure for more than half a century. In Plessy v. Ferguson, it held that segregation laws were valid exercises of the police powers of the states and did not imply racial inferiority.[5]

Despite the Peabody and Slater funds, the increased desire of whites for knowledge, and the efforts which had been expended, all of Southern education, and not just the Negroes' portion of it, was by modern standards still in a pitiful condition by the turn of the century. Poor economic conditions, the sparse and isolated population, depressed morale, the conservatism of Bourbon politics, and a bi-racial system — all fostered poor schools. Less than half of the region's approximately 8,000,000 eligible children attended school regularly. Only three states had more than half the whites in regular attendance, with Negro enrollments ranging from 23 per cent in Texas to 46 per cent in Tennessee. Only one Southern state, Kentucky, had a compulsory attendance law, although in the rest of the Union all but two states had them. By 1900 the South still had 1,198,744 white and 2,637,774 Negro illiterates over ten years of age, for approximate percentages of 12 and 50 per cent, compared to an over-all national illiteracy rate of 4.6.

[4] U. S. Bureau of Education, *loc. cit.*, pp. 1332-1336.
[5] 163 US 537, 16 Sup. Ct. 1138, 41 L.Ed. 256 (1896).

Total Southern school revenue was around $24,000,000. Compared to Massachusetts' $39.10 and the national average of $21.14, Alabama's funds averaged only $3.10 per child, North Carolina's $4.56, and South Carolina's $4.62. To make matters worse, there was the added differential between urban and rural systems and between white and Negro. In the former slave states, white children averaged $4.92 and Negro children $2.21. The child-adult ratio was still highly unfavorable. Compared to 1,250 adults per 1,000 children in New York, 1,350 adults in Massachusetts, and 1,340 in Connecticut, there were only 660 adults to 1,000 children in North Carolina and Mississippi, and 610 in South Carolina. The amount of taxable wealth per school child in Massachusetts was $6,407, against $1,301 in North Carolina.

Southern school terms averaged less than 100 days a year, while the national average was 145. Only one Southern pupil in ten who enrolled reached the fifth grade, one in seventy achieved the eighth, and there was a great gap between the elementary schools and colleges, since only a few cities and towns had high schools. The meagerest instruction was given, for less than one-fifth of the elementary school teachers themselves had a high school education and less than half had any adequate professional training. While salaries nationally averaged $310 a year, a teacher in the South could expect around $159, slightly less than the cost of feeding a prisoner in a county jail for the same period. Often, schools were not graded, and students studied from any books available. Schoolhouses averaged a mere $276 in value and were poorly lighted and furnished. Despite the fact that St. Louis, Missouri, had established the first public kindergarten in 1873, only Maryland, Alabama, Mississippi, Louisiana, and Kentucky had followed by 1900 — these, of course, were in the larger urban areas. Tenure was brief and pay poor for school administrators. Generally, with politicians, struggling young lawyers, and broken-down preachers as state and county superintendents, there was little supervision, and each school was often a law unto itself.

But effects of changes in the later decades of the nineteenth century were to be felt in the twentieth. The effort to eliminate the Negroes as voters pointed up the ignorance among the whites and put a stigma upon illiteracy. Segregation gave a temporary answer to the social problem and shelved the race issue in education. The North also became more sympathetic as it recognized the unique Southern problems and began to cooperate rather than dictate. Especially was this true of churches that gave money. Development of industry and the introduction of truck farming, along with the growth of towns and cities, especially in the Piedmont Crescent, meant more taxable property and greater state incomes. From 1890 to 1900, the taxable wealth of the region increased nearly 50 per cent. This, in turn, led to the growth of an ambitious middle class, with the corresponding pride and desire for improvement via education. Tillman and the Agrarian reformers found that demands for more and better schools were a vote-getting issue, as farm and Populist newspapers stressed its importance.

For the first time, also, the South produced a new and potent group of educational leaders. Among these were Walter Hines Page of North Carolina, Atticus G. Haygood of Georgia, and Edgar Gardner Murphy of Alabama, as well as such progressive governors as Charles B. Aycock of North Carolina, who soon made his state the leading one educationally in the South, Andrew Jackson Montague of Virginia, Braxton B. Comer of Alabama, Napoleon B. Broward of Florida, and Hoke Smith of Georgia. Some of these men have never received just attention, but their contributions were among the greatest in Southern history, and much that the South became can be traced to them. Individually, they were not too important, but as a group they were vital.

By 1900 the theory of public education had at least taken root in the South, although its fruits were not prize specimens. The states had paper provisions for a public school system, but needed was a well-organized and directed agency to vitalize them and to lead the Southern people to realize a broad definition of the educational function. Once more, Northerners supplied much of the initiative, but for the first time Southerners were equal partners. As early as 1898, a group of interested Southerners and Northern philanthropists met at Capon Springs, West Virginia, to discuss Southern educational problems. Much of the motivation and financing was furnished by Robert Curtis Ogden, a New York capitalist and churchman. This became an annual affair but attracted little attention until its fourth meeting, held at Winston-Salem, North Carolina, in April, 1901. Delegates from all over the South were joined by influential Northerners such as Ogden, John D. Rockefeller, Jr., and William H. Baldwin, Jr.

One of the most prominent Southerners was Walter Hines Page, a North Carolinian who had first attracted attention as editor of the Raleigh *State Chronicle* with his demands for public education. Moving to the North, he expanded his reputation as a crusading journalist and as a spokesman for things Southern. He became a gadfly, a prodder, who said that what the South needed was some first-class funerals and even suggested the occupants for the coffins. In 1897, as an editor of the *Atlantic Monthly*, he had returned to North Carolina and spelled out his ideas in an address, "The Forgotten Man," by whom he meant the poverty-stricken Southerner denied an education by unprogressive leadership. Three ghosts, he said, haunted the South — the Confederate dead, religious orthodoxy, and Negro domination — and the region had to "lift dead men's hands from our life." Page's knack of dramatizing Southern needs appealed to the North and to interested Northern philanthropists, especially John D. Rockefeller, Jr.

The 1901 conference decided that the time had come for action rather than talk. They formed the Southern Education Board, with Ogden as president, Edgar Gardner Murphy as executive secretary, and George Foster Peabody[6] as treasurer. The board, in addition to the officers, included Charles D. McIver, Wallace Buttrick, Edwin A. Alderman, H. B. Frissell, Charles W. Dabney, H. H. Hanna, Page, Baldwin, Albert Shaw, and Walter B. Hill. J. L. M. Curry was chosen as supervising director. The treasurer guaranteed funds of about $40,000 a year for the first two years, and the board decided that its money would be used "exclusively for the purpose of stimulating public sentiment in favor of more liberal provision for universal education in the public schools." It was organized strictly for propaganda and publicity, with its chief purpose being to get appropriation money, since most states had authorized school systems but failed to finance them. A short time later, largely as a result of Page's influence, Rockefeller created the General Education Board, on the theory that the Southern problem was really a part of a national one. Between 1902 and 1909, he endowed it with $53,000,000. The two boards virtually merged and began a concentrated effort in the South.

In state after state, intensive drives were undertaken to secure more adequate financing. North Carolina became the target in 1902; Tennessee in 1903; Georgia in 1904; South Carolina, Alabama, Virginia, and Mississippi in 1905; Louisiana in 1906; Kentucky and Arkansas in 1908; and Florida in 1909. It was insisted that the gains must not be restricted to the white race alone. Almost everywhere, the agency met with success, and an unparalleled enthusiasm for public schools swept most of the South. Other philanthropists were attracted. In 1905, Miss Anna T. Jeans of Philadelphia gave $200,000 to the General Education Board to help improve Negro rural schools. Two years later, she gave an additional $1,000,000, which was also set aside and used to pay salaries for teachers doing industrial and extension work in such schools. The Phelps-Stokes Fund (1910) provided money for specialized studies of educational problems to help in planning future programs, and Julius Rosenwald offered in 1911 to pay one-third of the cost of construction of Negro school buildings in the South. Within twenty years, the Rosenwald Fund had aided in the construction of more than 5,000 buildings in fifteen Southern states.

All of these efforts paid dividends, as the South experienced the

[6] Care should be taken not to confuse George Peabody (1795-1869) and George Foster Peabody (1852-1938).

greatest educational awakening in its history. Constitutional and statutory provisions for education were strengthened. School revenues were increased an average of 100 per cent between 1900 and 1910, with some states doing much better. In the same decade, the average school term was lengthened from 96 to 121.7 days, and 61.3 per cent of the white and 47.7 per cent of the Negro school-age population was in attendance. Illiteracy declined from 27 to 18 per cent. Teacher training improved markedly, with approximately forty normal schools, eleven for Negroes, in thirteen Southern states. Six states added free public kindergartens, and high schools became accepted and integral parts of the school system. More and more states legislated compulsory attendance, since the drive was often tied in with the movement against child labor. If children were forced to stop working, then they should be educated. By 1910, for the first time, the principle of universal education along the same lines as in the rest of the nation existed in the South.

Progress continued in the second and third decades of the twentieth century. Total educational expenditures rose by 1913 to $71,400,000, and Virginia devoted half, and Alabama more than half, of its net state revenues to schools. Public high schools continued to increase in number, spreading to Negro systems after 1918, although the greater bulk of colored students did not progress beyond the elementary grades. Of state-accredited four-year high schools in 1925-1926, more than 5,000 were for whites and about 200 for Negroes. Three years later, the percentage of children from five to seventeen years of age in school rose to 81 per cent, only slightly below the national average, while the school term averaged only seventeen days less.

By 1930 the South had taken great strides toward realizing the ambitions of the educational agitators of 1900. Annual appropriations for public schools had multiplied during the thirty years from $24,000,000 to $415,000,000. Most Southern states were spending a greater percentage of their total income for education than the rest of the nation; state governments correspondingly took over much of the responsibility from local administration. Consolidation of schools and better transportation improved the lot of Southern rural pupils; more than one-third of the nation's school buses were for their use. A larger portion of the total population was at school in Southern states than in Northern counterparts, and concern was already developing for those adults who were past the usual age for schooling. Many towns and cities could, and did, boast of schools the equal of similar communities outside the South. Negro Southerners also had reason for pride: that race went from more than four-fifths illiteracy to less than one-fifth, from the legal deprivation of the right to learn to an approximate

2,000,000 pupils with 40,000 teachers. Some states by 1930 were spending more on Negro education alone than had been appropriated for all races in 1900.

Although much had been accomplished in mass education, obvious shortcomings remained. Southern schools, though improving, did not catch up with the Northern, which were making continuous progress also. The average child below the Potomac not only went to school fewer days in the year but dropped out two years earlier than the child in the North and West. In the percentage of children in high school, many Southern states were at the bottom of the list; estimates stated that nearly 500,000 white children alone still did not have access to a high school of any kind. School administration had improved, but there remained obvious weaknesses, especially in the fact that most superintendents were selected on a strictly political basis and usually by popular vote. Average annual salaries for supervisors, principals, and teachers were only about 58 per cent of the national average.

Rural schools lagged behind those in the cities, and most of the region's population was rural. Density of school population in the North was from three to ten times greater than in the South. Only a few Southern states had more than ten white children of school age to the square mile, and probably none had an average of ten Negro children. This handicap was also compounded by the high farm tenancy rate, a rate nearly double that of other parts of the country. Thus, added to the adjustment of school terms to farm needs, such as closing down during cotton-picking time, was the constant shifting of school populations by tenant families who moved about once a year.

Neither had the South faced the problem of inequality between Negro and white schools. Segregation had put the Negro out of sight, and in the absence of strong Negro-support groups and the opportunity to make his needs known through the ballot, discrimination was easy. Some whites still felt that the Negro should be given only what he paid for, and since he usually had a large family and small resources, that meant very little. Although the total amount spent on Negro education had increased since 1900, the over-all percentage had declined. For every seven dollars spent on white schools, Negro education received only about two. School property, especially in rural areas, was markedly inferior, and teachers' salaries were often lower by as much as 50 per cent.

These socio-economic problems which plagued Southern education in 1930, such as bi-racial systems, unfavorable child-adult ratio, and lower regional standard of wealth, would continue. Separate schools would always be more expensive to maintain than integrated systems. Moreover, there were more children for fewer adults to support and less with which to do it. With one-third of the nation's children in school, the South had only one-sixth of the total educational revenues. The estimated average true value of all property per child of school age in the Southern states was approximately one-third less than that of Northern states and one-fourth less than that in the West. Legislatures in the South were already sacrificing many desirable programs to secure the funds for education, yet the average expenditure per child was still far below the national average. The problem of the future was how far could such sacrifices be extended and how long could these states continue to spend the major part of their total revenue on schools? Could the educational gap between the North and South ever be closed?

# 14

## HIGHER EDUCATION

IN THE FIELD of higher education, the antebellum South had a long and distinguished tradition. Not only could the region claim the first attempt to establish a college in the colonies (Henrico, 1619) but also the second permanent institution (William and Mary, 1693) and the first state university. For this last honor, there were two claimants: Georgia, which issued the first charter (1785), and North Carolina, which offered the first instruction (1795). The University of Virginia, brainchild of Thomas Jefferson, was responsible for many of the innovations in American college training in the nineteenth century. The Southern states concentrated their educational efforts upon development of the culture of the upper classes, and the pre-War South had a larger proportion of college-trained men than any other region of the country. On the eve of the Civil War, the South's 260 colleges represented one-half the total in the United States, and its annual expenditure of $708,000 for support was double that of the wealthier New England states. While some of the so-called colleges were obviously not worthy of the name, the quality of Southern higher education matched that of the North, and the better institutions could vie on equal terms for distinguished professors.

The outbreak of the Civil War disrupted college life. Although school officials desperately tried to keep their students at their books, faculty members and young men, fearing that the war would end before they claimed their chance of glory, enlisted in the army. Probably those few who remained achieved little because of the excited conditions. The University of Mississippi closed its doors at the outbreak of hostilities, while its sister institutions in Georgia and South Carolina did likewise in 1863. Many college buildings were used for hospitals and barracks, while others fell under the torch of Northern armies; the library of Cumberland University in Tennessee was so destroyed. Military damage was so great to William and Mary that Congress later gave it $64,000, while the University of Alabama received an additional grant of public land for its restoration.

The general economic collapse after the War was the felling blow for other schools. The small resources of the few endowed institutions usually had been invested in Southern railroad bonds or those of the Confederate government. Few were so fortunate as Guilford College, a North Carolina Quaker school, which had deposited its funds in Philadelphia. The denominational colleges, always dependent upon the gifts of the faithful, shared the general poverty of their church members. State institutions were even in worse plight, for they most often had been the target for invading armies, and state governments in their distress could not repair the damage or even furnish operating funds in some cases. Alabama and Mississippi in 1866 and 1867 desperately turned to lotteries as a source of revenue for this purpose.[1]

Nevertheless, most attempted to reopen their doors. The University of Alabama could count only one student in 1865, so quickly closed, but Louisiana State University struggled on with four enrollees. General Robert E. Lee showed his faith in education by agreeing to become president of war-stricken Washington College, an institution with four professors and forty students. The University of South Carolina opened the next year, as did the University of Virginia, which boasted an enrollment of 500.

The onslaught of Radical reconstruction bestowed new wounds. Besides interjecting the issue of bi-racial schools, the graft and corruption naturally affected the financial picture. In 1870 the total college income from all sources in New York State was $2,260,000, while in Georgia it was only $222,000. As a result of Radical control, the University of North Carolina was forced to close its doors from 1870 to 1875. The carpetbag government of Alabama did reopen that university in 1868, but the school staggered along with Northern teachers and an enrollment of from ten to thirty until 1871. While the University of

[1] John S. Ezell, *Fortune's Merry Wheel: The Lottery in America* (Cambridge: Harvard Univ., 1960), pp. 233-234.

Mississippi had several carpetbaggers and scalawags on its board, at least it got money. In South Carolina the entrance of the first Negro student resulted in faculty and student resignations, until the university became primarily one for Negroes, with a Northern faculty. It continued to function as such until the restoration of home rule, when it was quickly closed and its students and faculty dismissed. This action left that state in the unique position of supporting a college for the Negroes (South Carolina Agricultural and Mechanics Institute) but none for whites.

Louisiana State University was kept alive by a devoted faculty who served without pay from 1873 to 1877, although during one term it was reduced to four professors and six students. President David French Boyd wrote in his diary, July 23, 1874, "This day finds our poor school in very bad condition — terribly in debt, ourselves so poor that we are in actual want — no money and no credit — and the impression pretty general throughout Louisiana that the University cannot long stand." The institution had been abandoned because "we are not presumed to be in accord with the ignorance and villainy of the powers that be, and very little supported by the people of Louisiana because of the general law . . . which makes it obligatory on all schools, supported in whole or in part by the state, to receive *negroes* as students." On August 16, he wrote, "What is to become of us if we stay here much longer, or if I should die, God only knows. I have not a dollar, owe a great deal, and what money is due me from the University I may never get."[2]

Private and denominational schools, being relatively free from Radical control, carried most of the burden of higher education for whites during these reconstruction years. Their financial support was, however, at best very precarious. The period, however, made distinctive contributions in the field of higher education. The passage by Congress of the Morrill Act of 1862 gave land subsidies to states which would appoint at least one college to give instruction in "agriculture and the mechanic arts" without excluding "other scientific and classical studies." This measure did much to strengthen or initiate Southern as well as Northern colleges. Arkansas had not had a state university until it got one from the Radicals in 1872 as a by-product of this act. The same year, in South Carolina, Morrill funds were used to establish the South Carolina Agricultural College and Mechanics Institute for Negroes, and the site was selected for Alabama Polytechnic Institute.

The period also marked the beginning of higher education for Negroes in the South. In addition to the induction of freedmen into

[2] As quoted by Walter L. Fleming, *Documentary History of Reconstruction* (Cleveland, 1907), II, pp. 199-201.

previously white colleges and universities, numerous schools for them were created, usually with outside assistance. The American Missionary Association alone maintained eight colleges. Every Southern state established normal schools for them, and some so-called universities were created. The school which became Howard University was incorporated in 1867 in Washington, D.C. Within a few years after the War, most of the notable Negro schools had been established: such as Morehouse, Hampton Institute, St. Augustine's College, Atlanta University, Fisk University, Storer College, Shaw University, and Straight University. Kentucky saw the formation of Berea College, in which no racial distinctions were made. In general, intelligent Southerners kept silent, as long as the educating was not done by Northern teachers in mixed classes. Even the white governments divided Morrill Act funds with Negro schools, and Georgia gave Atlanta University as large an appropriation as the state university.

A part of the philanthropic giving which largely sustained education for the freedmen also helped the whites as well. Aside from some church assistance, most important were Vanderbilt University in Nashville, made possible by a $500,000 gift in 1873 from Cornelius Vanderbilt, previously mentioned Peabody Normal College in the same city in 1875, and Johns Hopkins University in Baltimore in 1876 — the last soon setting the pace for graduate work in the United States.

College education also came under the influence of the "New South" philosophy. As early as 1866, General Daniel Harvey Hill, later a college president but then editor of the *Land We Love*, wrote that, while the old system of education had produced orators and statesmen, it had done "nothing to enrich us, nothing to promote material greatness." The South, in his opinion, had to "abandon the aesthetic and the ornamental for the practical and the useful." This point of view was accentuated with the rise to power of the Bourbons, when the demand increased for scientists, engineers, and the like. Many of the old-school educators fought a bitter rear-guard action, but others, like Robert E. Lee, symbol of the Old South, quickly surrendered. At Washington College, Lee promoted departments of chemistry, practical mechanics, applied mathematics, modern languages, history and literature, and journalism. More and more schools abandoned the old rigid classical curriculum and adopted the elective system introduced by the University of Virginia even before the War.

While this expansion and flexibility were on the whole desirable, they were not without their drawbacks. Bourbon governments favored these broader courses of study, but their program of economic retrenchment did not supply the necessary funds, leaving the institutions to stagger on with inadequate library and laboratory equipment and with miserably paid instructors. Actually, most of the expansion in state and private colleges came at the expense of the long-suffering faculties. The number of subjects and hours taught by some of these men seems fantastic by modern standards. Remarkably, however, some individual professors managed to do work of a caliber which won them national recognition. Such was the case of Basil Gildersleeve in classics and philology at the University of Virginia and at Johns Hopkins. George Frederick Holmes offered some of the earliest sociology courses in the nation at Virginia. A. W. Chapman, author of *Flora of the Southern United States,* contributed highly important work in botany.

The average teacher, however, could not claim any distinction in letters or scholarship, and his formal training was often most meager. A few, fortunate enough to have been trained in German seminars, were able to sow a few of the seeds of modern scholarship in the more progressive universities. More than likely, however, the professor was completely unaware of the newer trends in education which were coming overseas from Germany and only vaguely cognizant of the revolutionary concepts being introduced by Johns Hopkins. He was, on the other hand, devoted to his school and students. Most were men of character and personality who made strong impressions upon their students. At a salary of less than $1,000 a year in even the better colleges, the Southern professor was still a force of social and intellectual inspiration in his community.

But devotion and local influence were not enough. By the middle of the Bourbon period, Southern higher education began showing definite flaws. Strong religious orthodoxy and lingering sectional prejudice often interfered with freedom of intellectual inquiry and exchange of ideas. A Southern educator, writing in 1884, graphically described the problems.[3] "We have too many so-called colleges and universities, and too few preparatory schools. There has been no great advance, if any, in college work in the South since the war, and in preparation for college there has been a positive decline in most of the States." He stated that, in six years of teaching, he had found "few men whom I consider fully prepared, both in quantity and equality of work, for a good Freshman class." The problem of maintaining proper college entrance requirements was magnified because of the almost complete disappearance of the antebellum academies, which formerly had prepared students for college. The academies had bowed to poverty and to competition from the growing public schools, which were still too immature to be a satisfactory substitute. Public schools were "generally in the hands of young women and others, who are incompetent to

[3] Charles Forster Smith, "Southern Colleges and Schools," *Atlantic Monthly,* LIV (October, 1884), pp. 542-557.

prepare young men for college." Tennessee had only four public high schools, none taught Greek, and only one offered sufficient Latin to qualify for most freshman classes.

Students were also bothered by the spirit of the times and were too eager to get into active employment. Young men would not take the time to get ready for college and could not do the work to stay in when they got there. Nearly half dropped out before completion of their course, the majority during the first year. Since endowments had been swept away and appropriations were inadequate, colleges were forced to live on tuition fees. This led to "an unseemly competition for numbers . . . until the colleges and universities have entered into competition with the very preparatory schools." In 1880 Tennessee had twenty-one male colleges and universities and ten degree-granting female colleges — nineteen of them with preparatory departments, while many of the others offered little more than preparatory work at best.

Paradoxically, it was the pre-war collegiate heritage that constituted one of the major problems. The region had been and was still oversold on the value of higher education. Every little town and every denomination had to have its college, and sectionalism within the states produced even more state schools and an over-duplication of facilities, with much competition for students and the scant funds available. Moreover, since the older state universities were solely for males, when the demand for female education became irresistible, additional schools were established, and they, too, got state aid. The growth of teacher training saw the creation of still more separate institutions, as did the development of agricultural and mechanical studies. Thus, in addition to the state university, each state could usually boast, and did, of at least one woman's college, several for teachers, and an agricultural college. Also, there were colleges supported by every major religious denomination, and several by the larger ones, not to mention privately endowed institutions. In 1884 the states of Georgia, Kentucky, North Carolina, South Carolina, Tennessee, and Virginia had sixty-seven male colleges, while the six New England states had only seventeen.

Despite the existence of five "universities" in Louisiana, the president of Tulane remarked, "There is not a single youth pursuing within the borders of the State what can be justly called a university course. They have no opportunity to do so." In 1881, all of the 123 Southern colleges and universities had an income of $1,089,187 and a total of 668,667 volumes in their libraries. (Harvard alone, at the same time, had $357,431 and 214,000 volumes.) Of these Southern institutions, sixty-nine each had property in buildings, grounds, and equipment valued at not more than $50,000, while fourteen were worth less than

$10,000. In New England, on the other hand, not a single college valued its holdings under $100,000.

In line with progressive traditions, thirty-five institutions had adopted the elective system by the eighties. Unfortunately, this was done generally not on the grounds of improving offerings, but because the system was more adaptable to the irregular preparation of the students! Another complaint by students, and probably the faculty as well, was the common practice of long examinations. An examination in trigonometry at one school took the students from six to nine hours to finish; for a student to be examined for six hours a day for five days in succession was not uncommon. When Vanderbilt first opened, there was no time limit for tests; one professor was held in the classroom two days in succession from 9 A.M. till midnight. After this experience, the faculty put a limit of five hours on all tests.

Meager provisions were made for new subjects. History was lacking in many schools, and sociology, economics, modern languages, and education were touched but lightly. Libraries were not only small but also poor in content from bad administration and over-dependence upon gifts. As late as 1906, the United States Commissioner of Education reported only four Southern institutions with libraries of 50,000 volumes. Sectarian education was an increasing problem. In that same year, the Methodist Episcopal Church South was supporting twenty colleges, and the Southern Baptist forty. Ten years later, the largest branch of the Presbyterians reported eighteen. Not only did the denominational schools vie for students but often denounced the state institutions as ungodly and tried to cut down or cut off their appropriations on the grounds that state colleges were unnecessary. Especially bitter were the internal battles when institutions attempted to throw off denominational control. Higher education was also handicapped by isolation and lack of effective contacts outside the region and by public opposition to many of the new scientific and social ideas which were sweeping the intellectual world.

Improvement in these problems came slowly, aside from the expansion of agricultural training pushed by agrarian reformers. The Englishman James Bryce, writing in the 1890's, said of the numerous Southern colleges that none "except the University of Virginia attains first rank; and the great majority are undermanned and hampered by the imperfect preparation of the students whom they receive." A Southerner writing in the *Sewanee Review* (May, 1893) stated that it was "notorious" that few schools prepared students adequately for any "reputable or self-respecting" college, thus increasing immensely the "amount of purely mechanical teaching needed during the freshman year."

To accomplish its miracles, the University of Alabama received a state appropriation of only $10,000 for the school year of 1900, and those of Kentucky, Mississippi, and Tennessee apparently received none at all. Endowments were still small or lacking entirely. Of Alabama's nine colleges, seven had no endowment; in Texas, this was the situation of eleven of sixteen. The region as a whole had only two of the thirty colleges in the United States with endowments of over $1,000,000 — Vanderbilt and Tulane. Seventy-three colleges in the South, excluding technological, professional, and women's, had a total of less money in 1901 than Harvard alone. The region had only 14 per cent of the national value of college buildings and grounds and library holdings and only 10 per cent of the productive funds. Southern institutions had only about $1,000,000 invested in scientific apparatus, as against the national total of $17,000,000.

By 1900 there were 216 institutions of higher learning of varying degrees of excellence in the South, only fifty-six free of some sort of denominational control. Ninety-five of these "colleges" were for women alone, although the quality of instruction probably did not warrant the name in most cases. All of the new state universities were coeducational, and of the older ones, only Virginia, Georgia, and Louisiana refused to admit women. Some private institutions, such as Tulane, had coordinate women's colleges. Altogether, the 216 could make an aggregate claim of only 28,000 students, 1,500,000 library books, and an annual income of $2,500,000.

Higher education in the South, along with primary and secondary, began to emerge from the doldrums of the post-war period after 1900. Many new schools were founded and old ones revitalized. Most spectacular was a gift of $40,000,000 by James Buchanan Duke in 1924 to Trinity College (Duke), with provision for a similar sum in his will. Quite naturally, colleges and universities shared in the improving financial situation in the South and also in the efforts of the General Education Board and other organized philanthropic organizations to raise endowments, improve equipment, and expand school functions. The General Education Board alone gave $3,000,000 by 1914, with the requirement that it be matched four-for-one by private donations, and legislative appropriations increased by such leaps and bounds that in 1930 the Southeastern states were spending .30 per cent of their total income on higher education, a greater ratio than the rest of the nation. The South as a whole funneled approximately 20 per cent of its total expenditures to state-supported educational institutions.

This one-fifth ratio came from a region which claimed only 12 per cent of the national wealth, however. Despite this tremendous increase in expenditures, enrollment, faculty, buildings, and facilities, Southern colleges still ranked low in comparison with the best in the country. On the eve of the Great Depression, the South had 171 colleges and universities, thirty-six teachers' colleges, and thirty-nine technical and professional schools. There were ninety-six Negro institutions, and of the ten largest colleges for women, five were in the South. Total enrollment, exclusive of junior colleges, was over 155,000. Junior colleges, a new innovation, numbered 143, with Texas alone furnishing 36.

Yet, despite this multiplicity of institutions, including roughly one-fifth of the publicly-supported and a fourth of the privately-financed colleges and universities, the region could not point to a first-ranked agricultural or engineering college or to a school of national prominence in the fields of politics, business administration, and the like. Salaries were still about one-third lower and teaching loads about one-third heavier. There were even fewer Ph.D.'s on the faculties and considerably fewer books in the libraries. In June, 1935, Edwin R. Embree, president of the Rosenwald Fund, stated that "not one of the Southern universities came within hailing distance of the first dozen centers of higher learning in the United States"; only one of 206 "distinguished" departments was found in the South.

Nevertheless, some progress was evident. The South was more willing to accept professors from outside its culture. As to per capita attendance, it ranked nationally in the third quarter, showing up especially well in urban areas. Fourth in wealth, it was third in educational expenditures. More professional students were graduated in proportion to its population than in any other section of the United States, and a large share of the nation's good professors were Southerners. Moreover, in 1937-1938, when women made up 40.5 per cent of national college enrollments, in the South they comprised 45.9 per cent.

Much also was done to overcome the problem of deficient students. Vanderbilt had long set an example by refusing to admit those without adequate preparation. In 1895 the Southern Association of Colleges and Secondary Schools was organized to raise standards of scholarship and coordinate entrance requirements. Twenty-eight institutions could claim membership in this group by 1913, although admittedly some could qualify only by liberal interpretations of the requirements. Church school standards were raised in 1898 by the Southern Methodist Church's creation of an Educational Commission to set minimum requirements of admission and graduation for its institutions, and the Carnegie Foundation for Advancement of Teaching refused assistance to those colleges which did not meet its standards. Although, in 1930, many high schools still turned out poorly prepared students and some colleges maintained only fictitious entrance requirements in their desire for increased enrollments and tuition funds, the general situation was undoubtedly improved.

The South was still distinctive from the national pattern in ways other than lack of money. Southern higher education was characterized by a greater religious atmosphere. An older and stronger Protestant religious heritage demanded more respect for the form and organization of religion. Even the largest state university was held responsible for overseeing the morals and personal conduct of its students. This heritage naturally did not encourage independent religious thought. The South also showed a closer adherence than the rest of the country to the classical tradition of education; college leaders were generally educational and economic conservatives.

The South had at least four levels of education in colleges and universities, despite severely limited financial capacity. Sharp divisions existed between colleges of different functions. Normal, business, and agricultural schools were separate, with the last type said to be the answer to accusations that the state university existed solely for the children of the rich and snobbish. Kentucky, for example, had four teachers' colleges plus the state university, and Alabama had four teachers' colleges and several normal schools offering less than four years of work, in addition to departments of education at the university and Alabama Polytechnic Institute. Another division came with separate schools for men and women. Despite the rise of coeducation, a greater degree of separation according to sex was evident, not only in state-supported but also in denominational colleges. Still another was this church-state dichotomy, with schools of both types competing for public favor, money, and students. And finally there was division by race, with no other colleges attempting the Berea experiment.

Negro colleges were one of the reasons for the lower educational standing of the South. If Negro colleges were excluded from Southern statistics, progress was extraordinarily good. But Southern Negroes, like the whites, suffered almost from the start of higher education for that race from an overly-abundant number of colleges, certainly more than could be supported with the meager funds available and the weak educational background of students. In short, Negro colleges were infected with the same, but intensified, evils of the white schools. Handicrafts which had been replaced by machine production continued in the curriculum. Moreover, the few resources which came to the Negroes were sometimes squandered to add unnecessary frills in imitation of their white counterparts.

Originally, until about 1875, the principal source of income for Negro colleges had come from Northern reform groups, churches, and the reconstruction governments. By the 1880's, these had pretty well ceased, and although some individual philanthropists continued to help, the Negro schools had to depend more heavily upon themselves. One notable example of self-help was the highly successful tours of the

Jubilee Singers of Fisk University, who traveled in Europe and throughout the United States providing entertainment and raising money for
their institution. Even at best, the years before 1900 were ones of poverty and want as far as Negro colleges and universities were concerned.
In view of the general condition occupied by the race, its neglect, and
the increasing segregation from white society, the statement by Paul B.
Barringer, chairman of the faculty of the University of Virginia, came
close to being correct: "In short the only things gotten from the present
system of Negro schools that stick to the pupil throughout life are an
intense hatred of the white race and false ideals of life."[4]

Things were bad, but not quite that bad. Thirty-four institutions
for Negroes gave college training in the South by 1900, and the doors
of Northern schools were being opened to them. More than 2,000 graduates had degrees, and some 700 were enrolled. Already Virginia, Arkansas, and Georgia had set up state colleges for the race, as the South
began to experience a great educational awakening. The General Education Board eventually assisted with money for fellowships, libraries,
and other educational facilities for Southern Negroes, and aid from the
Rosenwald Fund, Carnegie Foundation, and many small funds increasingly made select Negro colleges more stable.

Traditionally, Negro colleges were of three types: church, pri-
vately-endowed, and publicly-supported. The first two had been especially hard hit by decreases in contributions from wealthy individuals,
and the most notable growth after 1900 occurred in those with public
funds. Since most private schools could not secure such support, they
were forced to curtail their programs, consolidate, or close, while the
great and continually increasing desire of Negro students for a college
education compounded the dilemma. In 1916 the Negro colleges in the
United States, most of which were in the South, had a total enrollment
of 2,637. But a survey made by the United States Office of Education
showed that only thirty-three were teaching any subjects on a college
level. Most damning of all was its finding that only three — Howard,
Fisk, and Meharry Medical College — had "a student body, teaching
force, equipment and income sufficient to warrant the characterization
of 'college.'"

This report, plus the relative prosperity of the South and the increasing tendency of Southern whites to aid rather than oppose Negro
higher education, led to slow but steady progress in the years following
World War I. Enrollment of Negroes in the South doubled by 1922 and
more than doubled again five years later. By 1930, Negroes could point
to more than ninety Southern colleges, around 12,000 students, and en-

[4] Paul B. Barringer, *The American Negro: His Past and Future* (Raleigh, 1900),
p. 18, in *Negro Pamphlets,* I. University of Virginia Library.

dowments of nearly $25,000,000. With the exception of a few institutions chiefly supported from outside the South, however, no Negro college approximated the best white Southern schools. The Negroes had also been ignored by the junior college development. In 1933-1934, there were only five Negro public junior colleges, with 706 students, in sixteen Southern states.

The Depression of 1929 was a cruel blow. More Negro institutions closed or consolidated, but enrollments continued to mount, reaching nearly 34,000 in 1938, a mere 3.7 per cent of the Negroes in that age group. Despite inequitable distribution of funds — South Carolina in 1938 spent $82,500 on Negro higher education and $1,445,900 on white, while Alabama appropriated $76,000 and $1,900,000 respectively — some aspects did improve. Higher standards became the goal of Negro professional organizations such as the Association of Colleges and Secondary Schools for Negroes and the American Teachers Association. Regardless of their best efforts, however, in 1939 the Southern Association of Colleges and Secondary Schools gave a class "A" rating to only eighteen senior and four junior colleges for Negroes.

White institutions, too, were hard hit by the Depression. Their rapid expansion usually had not been backed by cash reserves, for while Southern states during the twenties had greatly increased their bonded indebtedness, it had been for enlarged road programs and the like, and so educational finances had been forced to the background. Nevertheless, progress in collegiate training was continuous. The statistics for 1940 showed that 4.7 per cent of the nation's adults over the age of twenty-five were college graduates, while the South's average was 3.5. Likewise, the percentage of those with some college work was 9.08 in the South and 10.32 in the non-South.

Southern colleges, like those throughout the nation, met the challenge of World War II by offering their facilities to the national government in cooperation with its mobilization program. Acceleration was undertaken and special courses offered to meet the demands of the military. In some cases, only through such services were small, weaker colleges able to continue at a time when many young men were going into the armed forces. With the return of peace, Southern campuses were engulfed in the flood of young men eager to pick up their disrupted careers and by the additional tens of thousands whose attendance was made possible through the benefits of the "G.I. Bill," which gave financial aid to veterans in college. As a result of the massive overcrowding which followed, Southern colleges and universities became attractive to large numbers of enrollees from outside the region, and the previous one-way flow of students and professors was checked.

Government financial assistance also made higher salaries and improved facilities possible, and by the mid-fifties the South claimed about one-third of the nation's colleges and almost a fourth of the students and full-time staff members. Salaries for instructors and assistant professors matched those outside the region, while higher ranks trailed by one to two thousand dollars. Quality-wise, the South had many good schools, with probably the greatest weakness in the fields of professional and graduate education. But it still lacked one equal to the best in the nation — one which would attract faculty and students from throughout the United States and the world. This slow development of graduate work had been of necessity: fewer Southern teachers had higher degrees; they were overburdened with undergraduate courses; their institutions were unable to keep their own most promising students for graduate work; and long years of financial stringency took its toll of libraries and laboratories. In 1934 the American Council of Education found only forty "adequate" departments for granting the Ph.D. in the South, as against 623 in the rest of the country. Four years later, the region had 9,600 graduate students; yet, in 1940, the South had only four of thirty-three centers of learning whose graduate facilities were deemed sufficiently comprehensive to permit membership in the Association of American Universities. In the same year, the region had only six of the forty-four largest library collections in American colleges. As late as 1942, it was impossible to get a Ph.D. at any school in Alabama, Arkansas, Mississippi, or South Carolina, and the degree was given for only a few subjects in other Southern states. In 1950 the South granted just five per cent of the nation's Ph.D.'s, and its 39,822 graduate students were 14,000 fewer than those in the state of New York alone. The bulk of higher degrees continued to be awarded in the field of "education," and the fewest in technology.

Professional education, largely a product of the post-Civil War period in the United States, went through a long period of gradual development, with progress being slower in the South than in the rest of the nation. Southern medical training was short, and entrance requirements were minor, if any. It was not until the 1880's that most medical schools required as much as three years' work for a degree and not until World War I that a high school education was needed for entrance. In legal training, none of the law schools at first had any entrance requirements, and all felt that one session was enough. The University of Virginia limited its course to one year until 1894, although the University of North Carolina required two in 1887. Not until 1920 was a third year generally added, and even in the 1950's, some states required only two years of law school for admission to the bar. Dentistry was even slower, and as late as 1960, several Southern states still did not offer such training. Only in theological seminaries could the

South boast a sufficiency; the Southern states had 135.6 clergymen per 100,000 population in 1930, while the national average was 121.2, but in the other professions the South ranked lowest of all the regions.

This deficiency had a marked effect upon the South's problem of racial segregation. The perplexity of inadequate finances and facilities for graduate and professional training increased as more and more Negroes sought higher degrees. Although such institutions as Howard, Fisk, and Atlanta universities attempted to meet the demand, to do so on the scale needed or in all fields was impossible. There was also a growing feeling that the Negro should be provided, at public expense, with the same training as the whites in these areas. The obvious impossibility of having two systems, because of the expensive equipment, libraries, museums, and expert teachers needed, cracked the wall of separate schools. As early as 1933, a North Carolina Negro tried by court action to force the University of North Carolina to admit him to the school of pharmacy, and in 1935 the University of Maryland had to enroll a Negro in its law school. But the system of segregation was not abandoned quickly or gracefully. States attempted to get around the situation by appropriating money for out-of-state graduate training for their Negro citizens.

This escape route was barred in 1938, when the United States Supreme Court ruled that it was not enough for the states to furnish tuition for outside training.[5] An attempt to establish a regional university for Negroes supported by all Southern states was blocked by Congressional refusal to provide sanctions necessary to set up an interstate school. Efforts to provide separate schools were checked in 1950, when the courts ruled that a special Negro law school set up in Texas was not "equal."[6] Beginning as early as 1947, the border states began to give up the fight and allow Negro students to enter white universities. In 1950 more than 200 Negroes were enrolled in twenty-one graduate and professional schools in eleven of the seventeen states where separate schools had been decreed by law.

Aside from the admission of Negroes to all-white schools, the most significant development in Southern post-graduate education took place in the 1947 annual meeting of Southern governors. Pressed to provide professional training facilities and faced with the facts of the obvious retarding effect upon the states of the lag in graduate and professional training — Florida, for example, had neither dental, medical, nor veterinary schools — the executives approved the general idea of regional cooperation in education and appointed a committee to develop such a

---

[5] Missouri ex rel. Gaines *v.* Canada, Registrar of the University, et al. (305 U.S. 337).
[6] Sweatt *v.* Painter (339 U.S. 629).

plan. A special meeting of the Southern Governor's Conference was held early in 1948. At that time, the governors of Alabama, Arkansas, Florida, Georgia, Kentucky, Louisiana, Maryland, Mississippi, North Carolina, Oklahoma, South Carolina, Tennessee, Texas, and Virginia signed a regional compact which "provided for all their citizens, through cooperative effort, sound, comprehensive and high quality educational opportunities, with special relation to the professional, technical and graduate fields."[7]

A permanent agency, the Board of Control for Southern Regional Education, usually referred to as SREB, was created, with headquarters in Atlanta, Georgia. Its duties were to submit plans and recommendations for establishing and operating regional educational institutions to the legislatures of the member states. The membership of this board consisted of three citizens — including one Negro — from each state. Its program was to be supported chiefly through legislative appropriations and grants from philanthropic organizations. At first, construction of a major university center was debated, but eventually better use of existing schools and a pooling of resources was decided on. The director, Dr. John E. Ivey, Jr., explained that "a state shares the school it has in one field and . . . [uses] a school elsewhere in a field in which it is deficient" — a process described by Florida's Governor Fuller Warren as "the greatest bargain since manna fell on the children of Israel."

Through "contracts for services," states lacking facilities for training in dentistry, medicine, veterinary medicine, and social work contracted with an existing Southern institution to send a specified number of students there each year. The state then paid the school $1,500 a year for each medical and dental student and a lesser amount in the other fields. This was not a fellowship, for the student still paid all but out-of-state fees. During the first year, 1949, some 207 white and 191 Negro students were exchanged. There were 867 students by 1952, and the states involved appropriated $2,429,000. Four years later, over 1,000 students were benefiting, and two additional states, Delaware and West Virginia, had joined the compact.

In addition to overseeing contracts, the SREB assumed responsibility for preventing duplication of facilities and for creation of a sort of educational NATO. By 1956 the Board had worked out programs to coordinate Southern educational efforts in such fields as city planning, forestry, research library cooperation, marine sciences, nursing, pulp and paper, petroleum sciences, statistics, and educational television.[8] Although a great infusion of federal and state money into higher edu-

[7] *Regional Cooperation in Higher Education: A Summary of the Development of the Regional Council for Education* (Tallahassee, 1948).
[8] *The Southern Regional Education Program* (Atlanta, 1956).

cation in the sixties lessened some of the urgency previously faced by the SREB and permitted an increase in duplication of facilities, nevertheless, by 1963 some 11,000 students had been involved and exchanges made in some thirty different fields.

In other ways, Southern higher education followed the national pattern. Despite a flurry of opposition, fraternities dominated the social life and often the campus politics of Southern schools. As late as 1897, the Legislature of South Carolina banished fraternities from its state university, although sister institutions in Alabama, North Carolina, Georgia, and Tennessee had by then repealed or allowed to drop into disuse their anti-fraternity laws. One church college, it was rumored, was not allowed to institute a chapter of Phi Beta Kappa because of opposition by its trustees to Greek-letter organizations. Although the classical tradition lingered longest in the South, the region generally conformed in curriculum changes to meet common patterns; administration, buildings, over-emphasis upon mass education, big-time football, and the like — all fell into a common mold. All had not learned the lesson that institutional standings in football and productive scholarship were not necessarily correlative. On the other hand, high ranking in sports has nationally advertised young colleges, thus perhaps attracting students from other regions.

The influence of great Eastern graduate centers on Southern higher education was marked. In the period of growth after 1900, Columbia and Chicago attracted numerous Southern students. Many of these graduates became the administrators back in the South and patterned their institutions on those where they were trained. Southern universities, moreover, perhaps because of these outside contacts, have been more conscious of their region's problems and have attempted to do more about them than was usually the case; the University of North Carolina has made outstanding contributions in Southern sociology, North Carolina State in textile research, and Louisiana State in sugar culture, for example. Highly critical attitudes toward Southern society were voiced, and, next to the newspapers, the universities were the most vocal group calling for improvement. Their extension divisions have tried to aid in the solution of political, social, and economic problems. Their presses poured out books dealing with the multitudinous concerns of the region, but, unfortunately, the chief reading public for these books has been in the North and not the South.

Presses of the University of North Carolina, Oklahoma, Duke, and Louisiana State long ranked among the top in the nation, both as to quantity and quality of their productions. By 1974, sixteen of the 69 members of the American Association of University Presses were Southern. Among the better-known faculty-sponsored magazines, there were the *Virginia Quarterly Review* (University of Virginia), *William and Mary Quarterly, South Atlantic Quarterly* (Duke), *Sewanee Review* (University of the South), *Books Abroad* (Oklahoma), *Southwest Review* (Southern Methodist), *Social Forces* (North Carolina), and the *Journal of Southern History* (Louisiana State, Vanderbilt, Kentucky, and Rice University). Vanderbilt and Louisiana State developed centers of literary criticism and creative writing, while Baylor University and the University of North Carolina became notable for original work in the field of drama. Southern scholars, despite the continuation of heavier teaching loads, became productive far beyond what could have been predicted at the beginning of the century.

The improving intellectual climate of the region can be seen in migration rates. It was long axiomatic that the South's best brains deserted it for other regions. In the 1932-33 *Who's Who*, of 6,015 native living Southerners of sufficient importance to be listed, 37.1 per cent did not live in the South. A similar study made in 1939 again showed that the loss of "eminent" persons was nearly three times greater than white losses in general.[9] During the next twenty years, however, not only did such migration decline, but there was some evidence that the South may actually be gaining more highly-educated people — people in the professional, semi-professional, proprietor, manager, and official groups — by in-migration than it loses.

Another evidence of progress was improved faculty tenure and academic freedom. Historically, the main causes of friction were not economic radicalism, as in the North. Religious fundamentalism — especially over evolution and the conflict of science and religion — and questioning of the bi-racial setup of the South were the chief causes for faculty dismissals, although in a few cases a wrong interpretation of the Civil War has also led to unemployment. The majority of the cases occurred in private rather than state schools, and probably most were caused by lack of tact, poor adjustment to environment, and personal deficiencies.

Perhaps the most notable case occurred in 1903, when the historian John Spencer Bassett of Trinity College (Duke) said in the *South Atlantic Quarterly* that, except for Robert E. Lee, Booker T. Washington was the greatest man produced by the South in the nineteenth century. Josephus Daniels, editor of the Raleigh *News and Observer*, led the attack. He raised the race issue and referred regularly to the professor as "bASSett," while demanding his dismissal. Despite calls for a boycott, not a single student left, and backed by the president, fac-

---

[9] Wilson Gee, "The Drag of Talent Out of the South," *Social Forces*, XV (March, 1937), pp. 343-346; H. L. Geisert, "The Trend of Interregional Migration of Talent: The Southeast, 1899-1936," *ibid.*, XVIII (October, 1939), pp. 41-47.

ulty, trustees, and the Duke family, Bassett remained. Professor William P. Trent, author of an excellent study of William Gilmore Simms, was saved from the uproar caused by his critical remarks concerning the Old South only by the firm stand of the administration of the University of the South (Sewanee).

Many of these men were able to get jobs in other Southern schools and in some cases were later hired by the dismissing institution. A study of the professors dismissed from 1893 to 1914 showed that the total number of cases termed violations of civil liberties was far greater in the North and West than in the South. The American Civil Liberties Union in 1931 listed seven institutions where violations occurred with greatest frequency, and no Southern school was named. Its list of the eight most flagrant dismissals in the preceding five years did not show a Southern example. There was a fear, that proved unjustified, that the passions engendered by federal efforts at integration would result in an increased pressure for faculty conformity.

Progress in higher education in the South in terms of quantity was phenomenal after the Civil War, and particularly after 1941. By the mid-seventies the South claimed some 456 colleges and universities and over 190 junior colleges. In 1965 alone, thirty-two community junior colleges were established to lead the nation in such new starts. With an average of approximately forty institutions of higher learning per state, the South struggled to cope with the rising flood of enrollments, one of every two high school graduates. Every state had at least one institution which awarded the Ph.D., whereas thirty years earlier, four had none. Between 1960-1965 there was a 40 per cent increase in doctorial programs, and graduate enrollments increased by 54 per cent. Production of doctorial degrees in the South had increased 67 per cent (*versus* 47 per cent nationally), and the region was producing 16.6 per cent of the nation's new doctorates as compared to 9.1 fifteen years earlier.

Southern college enrollments tripled between 1960 and 1970, with the number of graduate students increasing 232.6 per cent (*versus* 159.6 per cent nationally). Federal aid to Southern schools doubled, between 1965 and 1970, and state funding rose by 342 per cent in the decade of the sixties. By 1971 the American Council on Education ranked the University of Texas among the top ten nationally. On the basis of percentage of increase in state appropriations to higher education, 1963-1964 to 1973-1974, nine Southern states ranked above the median (twenty-fifth), and only Arkansas and Louisiana were below it.

Unfortunately, however, problems were never far away. In 1970 federal grants to higher education began to drop while state appropriations started to level off. With sharply rising inflation, endowment returns declined, as did private foundation support. Even at the height of available resources only five Southern schools were in the top twenty of the 100 state-supported institutions with the largest annual appropriations, and South Carolina ranked 88th. In white colleges and universities during the 1970's, professors' salaries still lagged some $2,000 below the national average, and despite exceptional improvements in libraries, the South could still not match the best in the North and West. Furthermore, appropriations per student per year were about $200 below the national average. No Southern school could boast a single Nobel Prize winner. The region still lagged far behind in the percentage of its college graduates seeking advanced degrees. In seventeen professions studied by a Columbia University research team in 1973, Southern schools were ranked in the top five nationally only in seven fields. The next year the director of Duke University's Center for Southern Studies stated that not one of the region's Schools of Business could be termed "first rate" in MBA programs.

In black colleges, the situation was even more regrettable. In 1967 the Commission on Higher Educational Opportunity of the SREB reported concerning the 104 traditionally black institutions, that (despite important contributions and valiant efforts of the past) they were still unable "to provide equally high educational opportunity for their students." They were unable to match their white counterparts in "admission standards, breadth and depth of curriculum, quality of instruction, or preparation of students for employment." These schools were training about one-third of all blacks (about 15 per cent of blacks of college age were attending some college, *versus* 44 per cent for Southern whites), yet only seventy-one colleges were accredited, only twenty-one offered graduate and/or professional degrees, and only one gave the Ph.D. Sixty-five had less than 1,000 students, and faculty salaries were $1,500 lower than in comparable white schools. In 1973 federal pressures for integration focused upon black institutions, and they began to seek white students; but by the mid 1970's their loses still outweighed their minor gains as many of their brightest students and faculty were lured to white schools, often outside the South.

Despite the fact that in the 1970's the region continued to appropriate a larger share of its personal income and a higher percentage of its total taxes than the national averages to higher education, the gap had not been closed. With over 150 unaccredited schools, there was also a quality problem. Money, leadership, and, most important, a desire for excellence were the ingredients most needed by Southern higher education as it faced the last quarter of the twentieth century.

# 15

## THE SOUTHERN LITERARY RENAISSANCE

IN 1852 THE EDITOR of *De Bow's Review* of New Orleans had plaintively asked, "Who of the North reads a Southern book?" Five years later, the Northern *Putnam's Monthly Magazine* for February sarcastically reported a Southern debate over the state of letters in that section: "Resolved, say these lovely wags, that there is no southern literature. Resolved — that there ought to be a southern literature." Such comments naturally lead to the conclusion that before the War the South was a literary desert. That the antebellum South produced no great literature was true, but it was not without a certain literary tradition. Southerners such as William Gilmore Simms had been productive but were the unhappy victims of their time and place. The social mores had not been conducive to a life of letters; nor had the rural nature of the region, the absence of cities and publishing houses, absorption of literary effort by the slavery controversy, and the tendency to look to England and the North for reading matter. These all contributed to literary backwardness.

But the South was conscious of its need, shown by the concern for developing a "Southern" literature. The Confederate Congress, in its final plea for support, listed among the horrors connected with defeat the necessity of having to "drink the cup of humiliation even to the bitter dregs of having the history of our struggle written by New England historians."[1] When defeat became an undeniable fact, Southerners took up their pens in place of weapons, and the writing profession became more respectable than it had been. Two factors motivated them. Paul Hamilton Hayne, the poet, wrote in *Scott's Monthly* for September, 1866, that having been bested "in our efforts to establish a political nationality by *force of arms,* we may yet establish an intellectual dynasty more glorious and permanent by *force of thought.*" Less idealistically, he added, the region had to state its case before the bar of history and refute the expected distortions of Northern writers. As early as 1866, the idea was advanced that historical societies should be created to preserve the records of the heroic acts of the Southern people, and in May, 1869, the Southern Historical Society was formed in New Orleans for that purpose. General Lee seriously considered writing a tribute to his men, and though he gave up the project, he recommended it to others.

Not only did the need for self-justification spur such activity but also the pressure of poverty. The Southern magazine *Land We Love,* whose very title illustrated the first point, stated in February, 1867, that the "pursuit of letters is not now a recreation, but an earnest effort for a livelihood." With seemingly no capital necessary and only pen, paper, and ink needed for equipment, scores of men and women, especially women, sought their fortunes through the printed page. The obstacles in the way of success should have daunted all but the most optimistic and desperate; at the end of the War, the South was without publishing houses or magazines of its own, while in the North few editors, publishers, or readers had a real interest in anything written about the South unless it conformed to their own views and prejudices.

The mere nature of the first post-war writing was such as to close the doors of the North. Much of Southern writing was frankly sectional and designed as a literature of defense. Alexander H. Stephens, vice president of the Confederacy, wrote *A Constitutional View of the Late War Between the States,* and Jefferson Davis issued his *Rise and Fall of the Confederate Government.* Countless military men sought to glorify their victories and explain their defeats. Other former Confederates spent their time in prejudiced and partisan appeals or gave way to a spirit of hopelessness and despair. In spite of the North's indifference, they were determined to produce a literature distinctively Southern for their own people, ignoring the fact that poverty would probably prevent purchase even if desire were present. Albert Taylor Bledsoe, former assistant secretary of war in the Confederacy, after rushing out a book in defense of Jefferson Davis, founded the *Southern Review* at

[1] *American Annual Cyclopedia,* V (1865), p. 198.

Baltimore in 1867 and for the next decade lauded everything about the Old South without seeing anything good in the New. Two years later William Gilmore Simms, leading literary light of the region, with a group of associates established the *XIXth Century* at Charleston as an additional outlet for such views.

With some exceptions, most of the literary production of the late sixties and early seventies can be dismissed as pot-boilers, shoddy journalese, and sleazy verse. James Wood Davidson's *The Living Writers of the South* (New York, 1869) listed 241 authors, of whom 112 were poets. Most of these were amateurs without skill or experience, motivated by aims contrary to the production of good literature. But as long as the shock of defeat gripped the South and the carpetbaggers controlled the governments, it was almost impossible for writers to view their homeland with the detachment necessary for honest appraisal.

The financial lot of the most talented, or professionals, was pathetic. Simms, who had been the South's answer to the Abolitionist charge that a slave-owning people could not produce a literary genius, was so disillusioned with the defeat and by the events of reconstruction that he composed little before his death in 1870. Henry Timrod, "Laureate of the Confederacy," wrote a friend in 1866 that the past year had meant for him "beggary, starvation, death, bitter grief, [and] utter want for hope" and that his family had survived by eating "two silver pitchers, one or two dozen silver forks, several sofas, innumerable chairs, and a huge bedstead." He expressed his willingness to deliver every line he had written to "eternal oblivion, for *one hundred dollars in hand.*" He died in October, 1867, to tuberculosis, leaving some sonnets which were among the best produced in America up to that time. Sidney Lanier, who had contracted the same disease in a federal prison camp, struggled almost futilely against ill health and poverty until his death in 1881 at the age of thirty-nine. Paul Hamilton Hayne, wrecked in health and fortune, retreated to a shack which he built himself in the Georgia woods, swearing to make a living as a poet and as a poet alone. Here he lived, virtually on the edge of starvation, until his death in 1886.

Of these early writers, only Lanier's and Hayne's reputations have stood the test of time. Hayne's importance as a poet was chiefly as a link between the Old South and the New. A personal friend of many Northern authors, he used his influence to try to open the doors of publication for other Southerners. Critics generally agreed that he himself wrote too much and revised too little. Most of his poetry was too removed from life to interest the general readers and too delicate and refined, faults which had characterized most antebellum Southern poetry. He was a good, competent poet, who, despite his shortcomings, was then recognized as one of the prominent literary leaders of the South. But he found it difficult to adapt his writing to the taste of a new age, and with little sympathy for the New South, he remained unreconstructed in some respects until his death.

Sidney Lanier (1842-1881) was undoubtedly the most important writer of this transition period. Born in Macon, Georgia, and educated at Oglethorpe University, he plunged with youthful zeal into support of the Confederate cause. After four months in a prison camp, he was sent home seriously ill, never to regain his health. Despite his war experiences, Lanier harbored no bitter sectional feelings but became convinced that his Confederate dreams were a delusion. Hampered by his health, he roamed the South working as a hotel clerk, teaching school, and practicing law to support his family. In 1873 he determined to devote his remaining time and energy to literature and music. A gifted musician, he obtained employment playing the flute in the Peabody Orchestra of Baltimore. His love and knowledge of music convinced him that there was an identity of poetry and music, a theory he tried to prove in his own poetry. His poem "Corn," a plea for agricultural diversification, published in *Lippincott's Magazine* in 1875, first brought him national recognition. "The Symphony" showed not only his efforts to combine music and poetry but also his fear that the new industrialism might destroy the finer graces of the soul. He rejected alike both the genteel tradition and the ideals of the rising middle class. Although only one volume of his poems was to appear during his lifetime, he was honored otherwise by being chosen to write the cantata for the Philadelphia Exposition of 1876 and by appointment to the faculty of Johns Hopkins in 1879. One of the better poets of the late nineteenth century, his primary fame came from his experiments in techniques of verse and for his series of poems dealing with his native Georgia, such as "The Song of the Chattahoochee" and "The Marshes of Glynn." Although often his poetry was overwrought and over-elaborate, he showed a special talent in the mastery of sound.

Hayne expressed doubts in 1873 that Southern literature could survive. Yet within a decade, a score of young writers were busily and profitably exploiting native materials, and the South became the most popular setting in American fiction. This innovation was possible for several reasons. In the first place, bitter experience had proven that the South was not sufficiently interested or able to support a sectional literature. Second, while Congress was trying to force the South to conform to the national pattern, Northern literary men were holding out the hand of friendship to Southerners of their trade. Even John Greenleaf Whittier, who had been so fiercely against slavery, could write to Hayne in 1870, "At any rate, their [northern and southern] literary men should have no prejudices." Usually more willing than the general public to let bygones be bygones, Northern writers helped Southerners re-establish connections with editors and publishers and were quick to offer friendship and encouragement. The new generation of Southerners, further removed from the prejudices of war, were also more willing to grasp the proffered hand. They realized that the cultural milieu, as well as the political and social aspects of Southern life, had to change. Most important, hard logic dictated that literary output had to win approval by Northern editors to secure publication and by Northern readers to become profitable. Writers on both sides of the Mason-Dixon Line accepted the necessity of reconciliation, and, in the opinion of Professor Jay B. Hubbell, improvement of relations between the sections "owed far more to the work of the men of letters than to that of the politicians."[2]

By the eighties the South was the locale of a literature of surprising vigor, which quickly found patrons among the Northern publishers of books and magazines. The end of reconstruction saw continued Northern interest in things Southern. The success of Bret Harte and his Western mining-camp stories in the early seventies had stimulated development of the "local color" school in American literature, and Southern writers quickly saw that they could adapt themselves to this trend. In fact, their region provided perhaps the richest of all sources for this particular type of literature. Local color abounded in the South's geographical diversity as well as in its social and racial contrasts inherited from the past. There were, for example, the "Creoles" of Louisiana, the "crackers" of Georgia, the mountain folk of the Appalachians, and the rich lode of the Negroes and plantation aristocracy. The new generation of writers accomplished the task of presenting Southern life in a manner acceptable to the general American reading public. They broke with the attempt to establish a literature for Southerners alone, and their desire to preach their regional prejudices was suppressed. A tacit literary compromise was reached whereby Southern writers were admitted to Northern publication with the understanding that they were neither to defend slavery and secession nor to attack the North. On the other hand, the North tolerated such views as the racial inferiority of the Negro. Thus were Dixie authors able to write about life in the South without violating their own beliefs.

As a group, Southern writers were untrained but wrote simply and successfully of Southern customs, scenes, and traditions. More important than their personal success was their setting the stage for later authors by demonstrating the permanent values of Southern themes in

[2] Jay B. Hubbell, *The South in American Literature, 1607-1900* (Durham: Duke Univ., 1954), pp. 702-703.

literature. They firmly fixed the necessity for integrating such themes into American literary patterns and brought to light the amazing receptivity of Northerners to literature about the South. Among the reasons for this almost inexhaustible appeal of the South to its former enemy, aside from a war-born legacy of curiosity, was that such literature afforded Northerners an escape from the worries and harassments of the enveloping industrial age by reading about an almost unreal region untouched by such ills. In addition, Southern writers pushed the lure of the glamor, the glory of defiant pride, and the mystery of the "lost cause." A third appeal developed with the new and unique problems of the eighties and nineties — the Negro problem, tenancy, the poor white — materials which provided for sociological novels and also furnished the first hint of critical interpretation by native Southerners.

Soon the fictional world swarmed with dashing, if somewhat decadent, Southern gentlemen, ladies of the old régime, faithful "darkies," resourceful poor whites, picturesque mountaineers engaged in bloody feuds, mysterious Creoles, and talking animals, all glossed over in mellow tones and shadowy coloring, with close attention to local dialects and customs. It was as though the South were determined to make up in a single generation for its long neglect of literary pursuits. By 1888 a writer in *Forum* could say without much fear of controversy that American literature had become "not only Southern in type, but distinctly Confederate in tone." A foreigner judging by fiction alone would "undoubtedly conclude that the South was the seat of intellectual empire in America."

The way to this era of Southern dominance had been paved by the nostalgic poetry of Lanier, Hayne, and the lesser known transitional figures. Richard Malcolm Johnston (1822-1898) showed the close kinship of the antebellum humorists with the local colorists of the New South. In his early years, he was a contemporary of such established figures as Augustus Baldwin Longstreet and later a friend of the young Joel Chandler Harris. Beginning to write near the close of the War, Johnston's *Georgia Sketches from the Recollections of an Old Man* (1864) and his *Dukesborough Tales* (1871) continued the humorous portraiture of Georgia crackers first begun by Longstreet and pointed up their potentiality for local color. The spirit in which he wrote was shown by his dedication "to the Memories of the Old Times: The Grim and Rude, but Hearty Old Times in Georgia."

John Esten Cooke (1830-1886) brought out the possibilities of the plantation legend of Virginia. Cooke, who had been writing with amazing regularity since long before the War, wrote two of his best-known novels during reconstruction, *Surry of Eagle's Nest* (1866) and *Mohun* (1869), and was reputedly the best-paid Southern man of letters before

1870. In both of these, he idealized and found nobility in antebellum Tidewater Virginia, paving the way for Thomas Nelson Page. Sherwood Bonner (Katherine Sherwood Bonner MacDowell) (1849-1883) celebrated the mountaineers of Tennessee and the hillbillies of her native Mississippi. Although she made some use of Negro dialect, the Negro's adaptability was first dramatized by a fellow Mississippian, Irwin Russell (1853-1879). Although his untimely death prevented his giving a complete portrait of the Negro, his best poem, "Christmas Night in the Quarters" (1878), captured the genuine exuberance, the mingling of humor and religion, the dialect, and the picturesqueness of the race as never before.

These writers, although failing to produce lasting masterpieces, kept open the way for the more talented who followed. Thomas Nelson Page (1853-1922) took up the mantle of Cooke. Born of a Virginia family of distinguished ancestry, he began his career as a lawyer. He first broke into print by writing Negro poetry in the style of Irwin Russell and achieved prominence in 1884, when *Century Magazine* accepted his short story "Marse Chan." Emboldened by this success, he quickly became a prolific producer of short stories, novels, and essays. His best-known work, *In Ole Virginia,* appeared three years later and won national acclaim. In addition to his short stories and novels, he wrote children's stories and books of social criticism, the best-known in the last category being *The Old South* (1892) and *The Negro: The Southerner's Problem* (1904).

Page set his novels and stories in the idyllic days of the Old Dominion and always handled his characters with the utmost sympathy. "That the social life of the Old South had its faults," Page once wrote, "I am far from denying. But its virtues far outweighed them; its graces were never equalled. . . . It was I believe, the purest, sweetest life ever lived." Page had the good fortune to be born at the right time, a time when Northern muckrakers were pointing out the rottenness of American industrial life. He was a past master at stirring up sentiment for the simple rural life. He not only converted the North to the glory of the Old South but also reassured Southerners that they had an origin and history of which to be proud. His stories emphasize the loyalty of the slave to a kindly master and of the planter to his state and code of honor, along with the necessity of sectional reconciliation. His chief characters were the great planters and the faithful house servants, the loyal old slaves whose utopian existence on the plantation was forever destroyed by the War. Despite his overemphasis of the attractive side of such life and his blindness to its faults, he assured himself a secure place among Southern writers by his well-constructed plots and his skillful use of Negro dialect.

Of those who followed these footsteps, the greatest was Joel Chandler Harris (1848-1908). Born in middle Georgia of the marriage between the daughter of a prominent family and an Irish day-laborer (who deserted his wife before the baby's birth), Harris at thirteen became a type-setter on a plantation-published newspaper, the *Countryman*. Here he not only learned his profession but came into intimate contact with the people who later became his literary stock-in-trade. When his employment ended, he found other work with various newspapers as a type-setter and writer of humorous paragraphs. Finally, in 1876, he joined the Atlanta *Constitution* under Henry Grady. As early as January, 1877, that newspaper published a few of his songs in Negro dialect, followed by character sketches of Uncle Remus and occasional animal stories. The Northern publishing company D. Appleton-Century approached him with an offer to combine these into a book. The first, and probably best, collection of Uncle Remus tales appear as *Uncle Remus: His Songs and His Sayings* (1880). The popularity of this collection in the North and South, sales averaging over 4,000 copies a year for the next 25 years, led to some additional nine volumes. While his major fame resulted from these tales, he produced a number of other stories about mountaineers, reconstruction, slavery, aristocrats, and poor whites, as well as several novels.

Despite his fame Harris always insisted that he was a "cornfield journalist" and his success a "lucky accident." He was not a propagandist and preferred to picture Georgia country life as it was and to write of the country people. "What does it matter," he asked, "whether I am Northern or Southern, if I am true to the truth? . . . My idea is that truth is more important than sectionalism, and that literature that can be labeled Northern, Southern, Western, or Eastern, is not worth labeling at all." In his editorials he showed that he was a realistic critic of the South, and taken as a whole, his writing did much to reduce the sectional hostility which still lingered. In his early stories of Uncle Remus, he surpassed all in his ability to combine accurate research on Negro life and language with a good style, appealing to both old and young. A more authentic and artistic reproduction of Negro dialect has never been achieved by a white author.

As Harris placed his locale in the Georgia which he knew best, George Washington Cable (1844-1925) found his in Louisiana. Born in New Orleans of a Southern father of Virginia slaveholding stock and a Northern mother of New England Puritan background, he served in the Confederate cavalry and later held jobs as a clerk, surveyor, and bookkeeper. In 1869, to earn extra money, he began writing successful articles for the New Orleans *Picayune* but did not have the self-discipline to become a full-time reporter. He turned to short stories of the haughty Creole aristocrats, the Creole gamblers on the river, and the beautiful Quadroons of New Orleans. But he was unable to get a publisher for these, even when he offered to pay the cost. By 1873, however, he got some of his stories printed in *Scribner's Monthly*, and his first book, *Old Creole Days*, came in 1879, after a friend guaranteed the publishers against loss. This, quickly recognized as a landmark in portraying life among the French-speaking people of Louisiana, was soon followed by other works on the same general subject of the exotic and dying Creole culture.

Like succeeding local colorists in the South, Cable was completely reconstructed. He had no objection to writers choosing Southern subjects —"only let them be written to and for the whole nation." William Dean Howells described him in 1881 as the "loyalest ex-rebel that lives." In fact, he was so reconciled as to find it uncomfortable. His Creole sketches angered many of the citizens of Louisiana, including Grace King, who became a writer primarily to offset the impressions which he presented. When Cable became enmeshed in the social issues of the day, the local reaction was great enough to bestow the label of "Southern Yankee" upon him. As a propagandist and social critic, he argued for the abolition of the convict-lease system, changes in the election laws, and prison reform, and most vehemently against the injustices to the Negro. Castigation of his *The Silent South* (1885), which set forth many of these ideas, probably was a factor in his move to New England the next year. There he tried to change his material as well as his residence. These later works suffered from too heavy dosages of reform propaganda and often from slovenly and careless craftsmanship, but his narratives always fascinated and his characters lived, even if exaggerated. Whereas others had chosen their material from everyday situations of Southern life, Cable tended to stress the unusual, the bizarre, and the exotic, and his early tales of Creole Louisiana were those which brought him his lasting fame.

Charles Egbert Craddock was in reality a well-educated, partially crippled Tennessee spinster, Mary Noailles Murfree (1850-1922). Born on a 1,200-acre plantation in middle Tennessee, Miss Murfree did not follow Page's glorification of plantation life but depicted the mountaineers of the Cumberland and Great Smoky mountains. After placing short stories in *Lippincott's* and the *Atlantic Monthly*, she published her first collection, *In the Tennessee Mountains*, in 1884, and her first novel, *The Prophet of the Great Smoky Mountains*, the next year. Readers throughout the country were quickly attracted to these simple, down-to-earth people, whose strength of character seemed to stem from their close contact with nature. Miss Murfree took great care with the reproduction of the customs and dialects of her region, and readers even a century later, although distracted by weak plots, lengthy scenic descriptions, and tedious dialect, could feel that they had associated with real mountaineers.

The Kentucky Bluegrass region found its champion in James Lane Allen (1849-1925). Descended from a long line of non-slaveholding farmers, Allen's early work glorified an idealized plantation life. His first short story appeared in *Harper's Magazine* in 1885, but literary success did not come until 1891 with the publication of *Flute and Violin and Other Kentucky Tales*. Writing with careful artistry of human passion and conflict, his best known work was *A Kentucky Cardinal* (1894). Although criticized by his contemporaries for his frankness on social issues and by twentieth-century readers for sentimentality, Allen nevertheless placed his native state firmly in the literary picture.

The success of these writers, to which are sometimes added the names of "O. Henry" and Samuel Clemens, although the latter left the South in 1861,[3] was so great that they undoubtedly influenced *Harper's Weekly*, on December 27, 1884, to state that the "South has become a part of the modern world," and "there is no longer a North or a South in business or in Society." Although the local colorists' contribution to reconciliation and to literature was large, they were not without faults: absorption with the picturesque, a tendency to gloss over true but uglier aspects, oversentimentality, and a fetish of the use of accurate dialect as to be almost unintelligible to later readers. So successful were Southerners with their local-color stories that eventually no one would attempt to write any other kind, and they were soon turning out hack work. An anonymous critic in 1907 accurately delineated the extent to which local color had fallen: "We all know to our sorrow what local color is. The novel of today reeks with it — dialect so carefully spelled as to be unintelligible, passages of precise description of persons and place, meticulous attention to costumes, forms and custom. It is realism run mad."[4]

Ignoring the trend toward naturalism which was sweeping the world's literary front, Southern writers continued to exploit the charming past and were blind to the rapidly changing face of the region about which they wrote. Despite the impact of progressivism, no Southern Muckrakers appeared. Instead, Southern men of letters happily reacted to the vogue of the historical novel which swept the nation in the years following the Spanish-American War. Twelve Southerners wrote thirty-four of the seventy-two most popular novels dealing with the American scene between 1895 and 1912; twenty of the thirty-four

[3] See *ibid.*, p. 822ff., and Richard Croom Beatty and others, *The Literature of the South* (Chicago: Scott, Foresman, 1952), p. 596.
[4] "The Worship of Local Color," *Nation*, LXXXIV (January 24, 1907), p. 75.

dealt with the Civil War or reconstruction; four of the seven historical novels which sold more than 500,000 copies were by Southerners. Led by Mary Johnston, Thomas Dixon, Jr., and John Fox, Jr., they wrote voluminously and successfully, if not technically well. So badly out of touch with reality were these writers that, in 1920, critic H. L. Mencken described the South as an intellectual and literary desert from which came no great literature, art, or music.

Yet at that very moment, the literary South was in the throes of a Renaissance soon to evolve into the great era of Southern literature. Several decades earlier, realism or naturalism had made its way from Europe to the Northern United States, but it took longer to be felt in the former Confederacy. Whereas literature by the previous generations had celebrated the amenities of life and escaped from its vexations, the later writers were destined to magnify the vexations and repudiate the amenities. This new group was determined to hold a mirror to Southern society and show the ugly and evil as well as the novel and picturesque.

The forerunner of this period in Southern writing was Ellen Glasgow (1874-1945), daughter of a prominent Richmond, Virginia, family, who produced some twenty-one volumes. Probably as a reaction against the verbal portraits of Thomas Nelson Page, her first novel, *The Descendant* (1897), begun when she was eighteen, showed her determination to achieve realism. She took as her central figure "one of the despised and rejected of society, an illegitimate offspring of the peasant or 'poor white' class," who was also a Socialist. Despite the shock to Richmond society and relatives' advice — "If you must write, do write of Southern ladies and gentlemen" — she declared that what the South needed was not idealism but "blood and irony," and set herself the task of writing a true picture of Virginia and the South from 1850 to 1912. When she was through, she had produced an ironic chronicle of the social transformation of Virginia and, by implication, of the South. She pictured the mutation not only of a society but of a culture, including not only the impact of the Civil War and reconstruction, but of wealth, the rise of the farmer, the workingman, and the industrialist, and the advent of new ideas and new values. There was no romance, unless it was the romanticism of the small and commonplace things. Her heroes were ordinary people, who envisioned a better life in trying to break from the dead past.

In *The Voice of the People* (1900), the agrarian revolt was described through the story of another poor white who overcame class prejudice and studied law to become governor of Virginia. *The Battleground* (1902), her sole treatment of the Civil War, ignored the actual battles but emphasized their impact on Southern civilians. In *The*

*Deliverance* (1904), she explored the clash of interest between the tenant farmer and his landlord. *The Romance of a Plain Man* (1909) recounted the rise of the city workers, along with the trials of an aristocratic lady married to a poor white. *The Sheltered Life* (1932), a story of the strength of family ties, and *Barren Ground* (1925) were her best novels, the latter being one of the best produced by a Southern writer. An allegory of the rise of the New South, it was the grim story of a woman's fight to make her barren acres produce after generations of abuse.

Although she could be unconventional in portraying sex and Negroes, and her women were not fictional Southern belles but human beings, she never allowed her realism to become "hard boiled." Throughout her novels can be seen the battle between progressive and reactionary forces in the South — between the individual's right and the Southern legacy. Whereas at first she threw her energy wholeheartedly to encouraging the New South, by the 1920's she felt that the threat to her region lay no longer in the past, but the present. Her work then began to show dissatisfaction with the vulgarity and emptiness of the new day and a greater appreciation of the virtues of the old; her satire became compassion. *In This Our Life* (1941), for which she was awarded the Pulitzer prize, she contrasted unfavorably the new generation with the old, concluding that it was no longer happy or enlightened.[5]

Another Virginia writer to achieve popularity in the twenties was James Branch Cabell (1879-1958), who caused even Mencken to change his mind concerning the barrenness of the South. Beginning to write while the historical romance was still in vogue, Cabell published *The Eagle's Shadow* as early as 1904. But it was in 1919 that the attempted legal suppression of *Jurgen* for alleged obscenity brought him to national prominence and made him the special favorite of the young intelligentsia. Much of his appeal stemmed from his wit, general tone of disillusionment, and frank treatment of sex. Some of his works, such as *The Rivet in Grandfather's Neck* (1915), were based in Virginia, but more often the locale was a land of his own creation, the kingdom of Poictesme. His theme was ironic and full of romantic disillusionment. Finding his region "an inadequate place in which to live," he sought to escape from it into a world of imagination and dreams. Throughout, his one ambition seemed to be to prove that modern civilization was a sham or fraud. Especial targets were the stale chivalry and perfunctory religion of Virginia, the bourgeois morality, the sentimental deification

[5] For an evaluation of Miss Glasgow as a literary figure, see John E. Hardy, "Ellen Glasgow," in Louis D. Rubin, Jr., and Robert D. Jacobs, *Southern Renascence: The Literature of the Modern South* (Baltimore: Johns Hopkins, 1953), pp. 236-250.

of women, and the insensitiveness of the New South to beauty. He was a perfect stylist, and his lasting appeal primarily lay in his carefully polished prose.

More directly in the Glasgow tradition was T. S. Stribling (1881-1965), son of a country storekeeper in Tennessee. Although trained for law, he soon began writing for popular magazines. The publication of his first novel, *Birthright* (1922), the story of an educated Negro who came to the South to try to help his race, focused national attention upon him as a writer of high promise. Generally his stories were based in Tennessee, but he did not picture its inhabitants as charmingly as had Miss Murfree, but showed them leading a harsh, cruel type of life. In 1931 he published the first of a trilogy which was planned to be a history of a Florence, Alabama, family from just before the Civil War to the 1920's. *The Forge* dealt with the Civil War and reconstruction, *The Store* (1932) marked the rise of the New South, and *Unfinished Cathedral* (1934) brought the family into the twentieth century. By far the best was the second, for which he received the Pulitzer prize and which dealt with the conflicts between the old and the new and chronicled the rise to power of the storekeeper. Stribling will probably not be considered a great writer, as he had too little to say and said it too often and at too great a length. Even with his weak style, however, he was a good storyteller. Although a Southerner, most of his white characters were villains, and he saw nothing good in the Southern heritage.

Rediscovering the Negro in realistic fashion was Paul Green of North Carolina, who in his plays and stories followed a contemporary rather than traditional approach. Although he experimented with short stories and novels, he is best known for his plays, the most esteemed being *In Abraham's Bosom,* for which he was awarded a Pulitzer prize in 1927. Julia Peterkin wrote classic sketches of Negro life in the coastal area of South Carolina in her *Black April* (1927) and her Pulitzer prize-winning *Scarlet Sister Mary* (1928). She was probably a better interpreter of Negro life than Harris, although she did not create a single outstanding character like Uncle Remus. DuBose Heyward of South Carolina wrote of the Negroes that he had learned to know on the Charleston waterfront, producing *Porgy* (1925), which later appeared in two dramatic forms on Broadway with great success. Another Southerner to have similar success was Roark Bradford, whose *Ol' Man Adam and His Chillun* (1928) became the basis for the highly popular *The Green Pastures.*

Others to win acclaim in the field of drama included Lula Vollmer of North Carolina, who wrote a number of plays with Southern backgrounds which reached Broadway during the 1920's and 1930's. Hatcher

Hughes' comedy of North Carolina mountaineers, *Hell-Bent for Heaven,* won the Pulitzer prize for the 1923-24 season. Lawrence Stallings of Georgia collaborated with Maxwell Anderson on three plays, the most successful being *What Price Glory?* (1924), and wrote the book and lyrics for an opera, *Deep River,* about New Orleans.

In virtually every field during the decade of the 1920's, there was evidence of the flowering of Southern literary talent. Some 300 volumes of various kinds by Southerners had been issued by national publishers since the first World War, and critics were safe by 1927 in prophesying "that the Renaissance is only beginning." This came true in the 1930's, when Southern writers exploded with works of outstanding brilliance. The critic Edward Weeks wrote of these years,

> Curiously enough, it is the Depression which really marks the fountainhead of Southern genius, and it is exciting to see such brilliant writing come to the surface from so many different areas. In *Look Homeward, Angel* we hear Tom Wolfe speaking in the accents of North Carolina. In *God's Little Acre* and *Tobacco Road* Erskine Caldwell is creating characters who fit anywhere from Virginia to Florida. Robert Penn Warren makes his bid from Tennessee. In New Orleans we hear from Roark Bradford and DuBose Heyward, the author of our poignant *Porgy and Bess.* Chapel Hill is a beehive. . . . And in Greenville, Mississippi — in a town no bigger than Concord, Massachusetts, at its flowering — we have a whole bevy of writers. . . . No area in the North or West could match that quality of competition.[6]

The comments of W. J. Cash concerning the thirties were equally enthusiastic. After pointing out the rise of Thomas Wolfe, William Faulkner, and Erskine Caldwell, Cash noted that "thereafter the multiplication of Southern writers would go on at such a pace until in 1939 the South actually produced more books of measurable importance than any other section of the country, until anybody who fired off a gun in the region was practically certain to kill an author."[7] Rising as it did amid the depths of the 1929-41 depression, this literature was probably marked by the economic conditions. Whereas the twenties had brought cynicism and disillusionment as a theme, the literature of the thirties pulsed with an anger and pity which Vernon L. Parrington called "pessimistic realism," Henry S. Canby labeled the "school of cruelty," and others tagged with such titles as the "bad dreams of reality," "weird realism," the "Southern Gothic school," and "primitivists and irrationalists." This was all true, in that the fictional characters indulged their natural instincts as casually as animals and that subhuman louts too often were emphasized.

[6] Edward Weeks, "The Peripatetic Reviewer," *Atlantic,* CIC (June, 1957), p. 81.
[7] W. J. Cash, *The Mind of the South* (New York: Knopf, 1941), p. 376.

Towering over this school were giants such as Thomas Wolfe, William Faulkner, and Erskine Caldwell. Wolfe (1900-1938) was born in Asheville, North Carolina, of a "naturalized" Southern father and a mother descended from a prominent mountaineer clan. After an education at the University of North Carolina and Harvard, Wolfe began to teach and write, emerging in the 1920's as a self-conscious member of the "lost generation." His was the story of a man at odds with an environment which both bewildered and charmed him. A prolific writer, he wanted to represent everything in his works, and the finished product was often of prodigious length, his second novel reaching some 912 pages. Before his untimely death, he was able to publish only four books, which cumulatively might be considered a single novel and his autobiography: *Look Homeward Angel, the Story of a Buried Life* (1929), *Of Time and the River: a Legend of Man's Hunger in His Youth* (1935), *The Web and the Rock* (1939), and *You Can't Go Home Again* (1940). His central theme was, in his own words, the fact that "Man was born to live, to suffer, and to die, and what befalls him is a tragic lot. There is no denying this is the final end. *But we must . . . deny it all along the way.*" Artistically, Wolfe can be criticized on the grounds that he wrote too much and too loosely; intrinsically, his value was his penetrating insights, insights tinged with genius.

William Faulkner (1897-1962) was born in Mississippi of a family of governors and other important figures. He drifted from one job to another before settling down to a serious career as a writer. Two themes dominate his works: violence and the disintegration of the ideals of valor and honor. Creating his own literary world with "Jefferson," Mississippi, as its capital, a world which reached back in time to the origins of Southern culture and forward to prophecies of its extinction, his stories concern primarily four families — the Sartorises, the Compsons, the Sutpens, and the Snopeses. The first three were aristocratic and traditional, destroyed economically and spiritually by the Civil War and its aftermath. On the other hand, the Snopeses benefited, because they were not bound by a code of honor but were free to use ruthless and unscrupulous methods of the new era against the impotent old. He created a "lightless and gutted and empty land." His characters usually followed their native heritage into blind alleys and to tragic ends; yet no one ever totally lost all sense of values.

Faulkner experimented in style, which often makes his narrative difficult to follow. He wrote stories within stories. *The Sound and the Fury* (1929), for example, was not only about the innocence and corruption within a family but was also a parallel of the conflict between the decaying landed aristocracy and the rising commercial classes. *As I Lay Dying* (1930), *Sanctuary* (1931), and other novels likewise dealt with the New South. His Southern world was peopled by idiots, poor-white moonshiners, prostitutes, perverts, and suicides, whose primary occupations were murder, rape, and incest. Viewed by many critics as the most outstanding twentieth-century American fictionist, in 1950 he was awarded the Nobel prize for literature, followed five years later by a Pulitzer prize.

Writing in the same vein at the same time was Erskine Caldwell (1903-    ), born the son of a Presbyterian minister in Georgia. As an itinerant worker, he learned about the seamy side of Georgia life and took as his special theme the Jukeses and Kallikaks living on the exhausted land which had once been the prosperous farms of their ancestors. Caldwell's controversial career began in 1929 with publication of *The Bastard*. Although constantly denounced in the South as sex-dominated and unnecessarily sordid, his stories actually featured the deadening of normal emotions by poverty, and he wrote with simplicity, imagination, and humor. He enjoyed amazing popularity, with the stage version of *Tobacco Road* (1932) running for 3,180 consecutive performances. The author of over twenty-four books, the most important are generally accepted as being *Tobacco Road, God's Little Acre* (1933), *Kneel to the Rising Sun and Other Stories* (1935), *Georgia Boy* (1943), and *Tragic Ground* (1944).

Such themes were directly in line with those enjoying national popularity from such writers as Theodore Dreiser, F. Scott Fitzgerald, Sinclair Lewis, John Steinbeck, and Ernest Hemingway. Yet, dominated as the 1930's were by stark realism, there was also a counter-reaction in the South. As early as 1926, Elizabeth Madox Roberts of Kentucky returned, but with less sentimentality, in *The Time of Man* to the locale of James Lane Allen. Although writing of the poor whites of central Kentucky and their hopes and ambitions, she subordinated their miseries. Marjorie Kinnan Rawlings showed the same sympathetic tendency in her stories of Florida, such as *The Yearling* (1938). Stark Young of Mississippi, unlike Faulkner, began writing of a genteel South of charming tradition, vigorously defending traditional attitudes and customs, the "flower of Southern civilization," against the encroachments of modern industrial society. He asked his readers to accept the best of the new but also to preserve the good in the past. His *River House* (1928) and *So Red the Rose* (1934) were admiring recreations of Mississippi plantation society in which he defended provincialism and tradition as the only positive protection against the anonymity and rootlessness of modern life.

Stark Young had already predisposed the nation with shaded pictures of all that was best and most gracious about the Old South when *Gone With the Wind* dealt realism a terrific blow. This Pulitzer prize-winner by Margaret Mitchell regilded the old traditional legends of the South and took both the North and South by storm. A massive novel, it portrayed the triumph of a Southern woman over adversities and charmingly pictured the graciousness of the plantation, the human drama of the Civil War, and the rise of Atlanta, Georgia, from its ashes. It made a pleasant antidote in 1936 to depression worries. As a result of its success, more Southern writers began to look with more contentment upon the past, to see less need for attacking it, and, even as Ellen Glasgow did, to suggest that perhaps the old way was the best after all.

In the ensuing conflict over how Southern life should be interpreted, whether with cold realistic overtones or sympathetic understanding, both sides claimed the attention of young writers. One of the twentieth century's best known playwrights, Tennessee Williams of New Orleans, pictured seamy characters and situations in his successful plays, such as *The Glass Menagerie*, *A Streetcar Named Desire*, *Rose Tattoo*, and *Cat on a Hot Tin Roof*, and won two Pulitzer prizes. Truman Capote and Robert Penn Warren were likewise concerned with weaknesses in Southern culture. On the other hand, Katherine Anne Porter and Eudora Welty showed more evidence of sympathy and nostalgia, while Lynn Riggs' *Green Grow the Lilacs* swept the theatrical world in the form of a musical, *Oklahoma!*, and went far toward blotting out the impression of that state made by *The Grapes of Wrath*. In any event and whatever the inspiration, the fountainhead of Southern literary production appeared everlasting.

Many of those who made their mark in the novel or in the short story were also good, if lesser-known, poets. From the 112 poets listed in 1869, poetry continued to have appeal as a vehicle of expression. An "avalanche of Poetry," mostly mediocre, swept the South. However, with the departure of Hayne and Lanier from the field, Southern poetry was in a slump, from which it did not begin to recover until after World War I. In 1920 the Poetry Society of South Carolina, with a membership of 400 and a "waiting list," was founded under the leadership of DuBose Heyward and Josephine Pinckney, starting a movement which spread to nearly every other Southern state. Undoubtedly the most important factor in the poetical renaissance, however, was the work of a Nashville group, centered at Vanderbilt University, which published its own magazine, *The Fugitive* (1922-1925). Led by John Crowe Ransom, it featured, in addition to the works of such authors as Allen Tate, Donald Davidson, Merrill Moore, and Robert Penn Warren, some of the best criticism ever written in the South. Since that time, the region has produced its share of poets, although their appeal, like most modern versifiers, has been chiefly to other poets.

The humorous tradition, so much a part of antebellum literature, continued after the Civil War. A transitional figure in the Longstreet-Baldwin tradition was Charles Henry Smith (1828-1903) of Georgia, with his character "Bill Arp" who commented upon the war and post-war period. Others, who also used the newspapers as an outlet, were Irvin S. Cobb of Kentucky and Will Rogers of Oklahoma.

The newly freed black also contributed to the Southern drive for self-expression. Booker T. Washington's *Up From Slavery* became a classic in American biography. By the twentieth century the race was producing literature of high quality as seen in the work of Charles Chesnutt, James Weldon Johnson, Jean Toomer, and in Richard Wright's controversial stories, *Uncle Tom's Children* and *Native Son.* Ralph Ellison's *Invisible Man* is considered by some as one of the most creative works since the turn of the century. Blacks could also boast poets Anne Spencer, Joseph Seamon Cotton, Jr., Melvin Tolson and Margaret Walker, and their own poetry circle in Houston, Texas.

The region was also productive in areas other than traditional literature. In the scientific field the South could claim, but seldom hold, such eminent writers as Lucien Carr in ethnology, Ellen Churchill Semple in human geography, Edward E. Barnard in astronomy, J. Lawrence Smith in chemistry, and Nathaniel Southgate Shaler, Robert Peter, and John R. Proctor in geology. In history Southerners not only became more objective in viewing their past but also produced men recognized nationally for their historical writings and teaching. Among the most outstanding were William E. Dodd, Ulrich B. Phillips, and Douglas Southall Freeman. A figure of special importance was Carter G. Woodson, founder of the Association for the Study of Negro Life and History and the first editor of the *Journal of Negro History.* His numerous books and articles have caused him to be viewed as the "Father of Black History."

In the first half of the twentieth century, the South contributed no less than 5,000 book-length titles to the cultural resources of the United States: some 1,000 volumes of fiction, 500 of biography, 400 of poetry, and 125 of drama. In addition, there were approximately 800 of history, 800 on the race question, and some 400 more on various aspects of the Southern scene. Something of the quality of this quantity shows in the fact that Southern writers won nine Pulitzer prizes for fiction, five for drama, and four each for biography and poetry, as well as one Nobel award and innumerable lesser-known prizes, between 1900 and 1960. Of the eleven best-sellers claiming sales of approximately a million copies each, ten were products of Southern writers and used themes dealing with the South.[8]

[8] Howard Odum, "On Southern Literature and Southern Culture," in Rubin and Jacobs, *op. cit.*, pp. 85-86.

Much of the credit for the high-caliber literature of Southerners since 1900 must go to the development of Southern literary criticism. Not only were writers subjected to the penetrating analysis of outsiders, but increasingly they also set higher standards for themselves. Some of the most effective criticism came from the pages of *The Fugitive*, the *Southern Review*, the *Kenyon Review*, and the *Sewanee Review*, and from the creators of the so-called "New Criticism," such as John Crowe Ransom, Allen Tate, Cleanth Brooks, Robert Penn Warren, Donald Davidson, and Randall Jarrell. Also important was the rivalry among the various schools of Southern authors. Each was ready to point out the shortcomings of the other.

The death of Faulkner in 1962 could be said to mark the end of his literary generation, and the direction of the succeeding one is not clear. Faulkner's contemporaries, the pre-World War II writers, were enmeshed in a period of transition in the South. Their works reflect this as they viewed the old with eyes of the young, yet the new was seen in terms of old values. The sharp contrasts in the South which allowed this viewpoint, however, were missing in the post-war years, and new influences appeared in contemporary writings. For example, whereas the earlier giants were from small towns, the 1970 leaders — William Styron, Eudora Welty, James Agee, Truman Capote, *et al.*, are urban products, and thus write from a different frame of reference. The Pulitzer prizes since 1960 of Harper Lee, Shirley Ann Grau, Katherine Anne Porter, William Styron, and John Crowe Ransom indicate that there is still vitality in the "Southern Renaissance," however, and reason for pride as well. Despite these achievements, the South as a whole probably remains unaware of its literature. Until a Southern author earns a national reputation, he is a prophet without honor in his own land.

# 16

## OTHER ASPECTS OF SOUTHERN CULTURE

ALTHOUGH THE LITERARY FLOWERING of the South was its most spectacular development during the hundred years after the Civil War, the region was not without achievements in other fields. Closely allied was magazine and newspaper publishing; in fact, these two had always been the principal outlets for the literary efforts of the Old South. Even so, the antebellum South had been a graveyard for magazines, with the large birthrate one reason for the high rate of fatalities. At least fifty-seven periodicals had been started in Georgia alone during 1790-1860, but none lasted more than five years. Charleston, South Carolina, initiated over thirty, yet only two survived until 1861. Nevertheless, the region boasted successful periodicals such as the *Southern Review* (1828-1832), the *Southern Quarterly Review* (1842-1857), the *Southern Literary Messenger* (1834-1864), at one time edited by Edgar Allen Poe, and *De Bow's Review,* founded in 1846 and published intermittently until 1880.

Few magazines survived the War, but immediately afterwards the number multiplied almost beyond reason and certainly beyond the capacity of the prostrate section to support them. Perhaps magazine editing, like literature, was viewed as a means of livelihood by those whose talents were not physical, as demanded by the times; the fact that most of these editors were amateurs without experience partially explains their foolhardiness. By 1880 the number of magazines ranged from none in Florida to thirty-three in Virginia. These ran the whole gamut of subject matter — religion, children, women, agriculture, literature, literary criticism, and music. Regardless of subject matter, however, most were devoted to the idea of a Southern literature and to defending the concepts which the Confederacy had lost on the battlefield — in other words, presenting and preserving a good picture of the South.

From this chorus of voices, ranging from good to indifferent, a few became famous beyond their locale. Even at their worst, however, these journals were almost the only medium available to older Southern writers, and they contain some of the early writing of men later to make a national reputation. One of the earliest of the new magazines was *Scott's Monthly* (1865), established by the Reverend W. J. Scott, which preached the need not only for industry but also "beyond all else, literary elevation and enfranchisement." The *Sunny South* was a popular literary weekly also published in Atlanta. The *Land We Love*, subtitled "A New Monthly Magazine Devoted to Literature, Military History, and Agriculture," was one of the more successful and, under the editorship of General Daniel H. Hill, served as a sort of Confederate veteran's journal. Part of its success also was probably because it was one of the few which could pay contributors. The *Manufacturers' Record* of Baltimore took up where *De Bow's Review* left off, and the freedman was represented with the *Southern Workman,* published at Hampton after 1872.

The Richmond *Eclectic* lived a hectic life for almost a decade. Begun in 1866, it was moved to Baltimore two years later and given the title of the *New Eclectic*. After absorbing the *Land We Love,* it became the official publication of the Southern History Association, and in 1871 the title was changed once more, becoming the *Southern Magazine*. Most controversial of these journals was the *Southern Review*, edited by Albert Taylor Bledsoe. As learned and philosophical as any in the country, it was, on the other hand, completely unreconstructed in tone. Even when it became the official organ of the Southern Methodists in 1871, it could not claim financial success. The *South-Atlantic* of Wilmington sought to follow the tradition of the *Southern Literary Messenger,* whereas the *Southern Bivouac* of Louisville devoted itself to war memoirs and the like, becoming the mouthpiece for the Southern History Association after the death of the *Southern Magazine* and until its absorption by *Century* in 1887.

The abnormal growth of magazines in the unnatural climate of the post-war years diminished before cold realities by 1880. When writers found that they could write acceptably for Northern magazines and be well paid for so doing, they began seeking these markets. Southern journals could not compete with the greater and established magazines for the work of the very authors they had helped to develop. The editors had also made the mistake of appealing to the educated and not the masses, and the educated were insufficiently interested to respond with money. *Scott's Monthly* had only 5,000 subscribers in 1867, and the *Land We Love* counted only 12,000. There was also the difficulty of collections. The editor of the *New Eclectic* wrote in 1870 that it had a "very good subscription list, if all would pay; but our trouble is they take the magazine and won't pay for it. . . ." Two years later he lamented, "If we had but 10,000 circulation . . . we could give such prices to contributors as would bring the best work of the best men. . . ."

Not only were the editors naive, but they also lacked printers or business managers who were proficient in marketing their wares. In the final analysis, however, failure of the magazines to take root in Southern soil must be blamed on the people themselves. While all of the magazines could not have succeeded, enough potential subscribers existed to support several good journals. The simple fact was that, apart from local newspapers and farm and religious journals, there was little demand for the unprofessional Southern product.

The end of reconstruction removed even the incentive for a distinctive Southern literature. Editors complained with justice that the people preferred Northern magazines, regardless of how trashy and libelous they might be. In 1887, Margaret J. Preston stated the epitaph of Southern magazines when she wrote, "I was sorry to see that the Southern Bivouac had gone down, as all its predecessors have done and that we are now actually without a printed sheet in the South that can be called literary. . . . The truth is our people do not care for home-wares. They prefer the foreign product." General Hill, in an 1868 survey, found that Northern magazines outsold Southern even in their own cities by as much as 240 to 1. Another editor estimated that *Godey's Lady's Book* or the *New York Ledger* had a larger circulation in most Southern towns than all the Southern magazines put together.[1]

After the 1880's, it was impossible for a distinctly Southern magazine to survive. The nearest exception was *Holland's Magazine* of Dallas, Texas, founded in 1876, which enjoyed a wide circulation throughout the South before finally succumbing to rising printing costs and loss of subscribers in 1953. Joel Chandler Harris issued *Uncle Remus's Magazine* from Atlanta in 1907, hoping to make it typical of

[1] Jay B. Hubbell, *The South in American Literature 1607-1900* (Durham: Duke Univ., 1954), pp. 716-726.

the South but national in scope. After his death the next year, however, it lost its primary appeal and became defunct some four or five years later.

With the obvious fact that the region could not compete in journals of a general nature, emphasis was placed on specialization. Success most often followed these periodicals, usually subsidized and initiated by universities or university communities. Oldest of these was the *Sewanee Review,* established at the University of the South in 1892 by William P. Trent, eminent biographer of William Gilmore Simms. Specializing in literary criticism, it claimed to be the "oldest living quarterly in the United States" and was very fortunate in having some of the most competent literary men in the South as editors, including Allen Tate and Andrew Lytle. Historian John Spencer Bassett established the *South Atlantic Quarterly* at Trinity College (Duke) in 1902 as a journal of opinion and history. In 1915, Stark Young launched a literary journal, the *Texas Review,* from the University of Texas, but in 1924 it was transferred to Southern Methodist University in Dallas and its name changed to the *Southwest Review.*

The literary Renaissance of the 1920's was similar to the period after the Civil War; little literary magazines sprang up all over the South. Although many journals gave some space to poetry, it was not enough, and scores of little poetry magazines were founded, with Dallas, Texas, alone fostering six. The *Double Dealer* of New Orleans was established to encourage and print "real" literature. The *Reviewer* of Richmond set the development of young Southern writers and general improvement of literary style as its task. Under the leadership of Emily Scott and Paul Green, contributions from most of the outstanding literary figures of the South were secured. The *Virginia Quarterly Review,* begun in 1925, became one of the "quality" magazines of the nation. The University of Oklahoma in 1927, founded *Books Abroad,* a unique quarterly publication devoted to comments and reviews of recently published foreign literary works, which quickly won an international reputation. The region also hosted a number of professional journals, such as the *Mississippi Valley Historical Review* and the *Journal of Southern History,* which commanded the respect of specialists throughout the country.[2] Unfortunately, circulation for all of these was quite small, a not surprising condition in light of the fact that the region also trailed the rest of the nation in purchase of national magazines as well. Consequently, the mortality rate for Southern publications continued high.

Newspapers, on the other hand, had more vitality and longer

[2] Jay B. Hubbell, "Southern Magazines," in W. T. Couch, ed., *Culture in the South* (Chapel Hill: Univ. of North Carolina, 1935), pp. 159-182.

lives. The South was always articulate through its press; many papers were often the oldest businesses in their area, such as the Augusta *Chronicle,* begun in 1785, and the Charleston *News and Courier,* one of the first American dailies. Before the Civil War, some of the ablest minds, including William Gilmore Simms, Augustus Baldwin Longstreet, and Henry Timrod, were in this field, and newspapers served as one of the principal literary outlets of the section. While the War had struck them a heavy blow, 182 weeklies survived and with their scathing comments became thorns in the sides of the reconstructionists. Soon after 1865 every county and major town had its own newspaper. By 1868 there were 499 weeklies, and by 1885 some 1,827. Of the 1,500 in 1880, mostly weeklies, forty-one were at least fifty years old. Since practically all which had survived the War were Democratic by inclination, numerous sheets sprang up to defend the Republican faith during reconstruction and feed on governmental printing contracts. These were owned and edited by carpetbaggers and quickly folded with the fall of that regime. Since most of the Republican papers depended primarily upon the Negroes for mass readers, the period also marked the beginning of Negro journalism in the South. With the death of the carpetbag journals, other papers devoted to the interest of the race were established. South Carolina alone by 1895 had ten, seven published weekly and the rest semi-monthly — the oldest being the sixteen-year-old *Pee Dee Educator.* Only two of these were continuous, and by 1899 the total was only six, for as might be expected, the mortality rate was much higher for the Negro press. Most of the Negro papers in the South were weekly or less frequent. In 1900 there were three dailies in the country, in Kansas City, Norfolk, and Washington, but Georgia and Texas each had no less than twenty-three Negro weekly newspapers, while North Carolina had ten, with the other states close behind.

Although an active press had existed before the Civil War, the profession was even more attractive afterwards. Publishing ranked with storekeeping and mill supervision as the most desirable jobs in the New South, requiring scant capital and offering more rapidly attainable prestige than perhaps any other line of work. Editing also had the advantage of being an excellent springboard to other professions. Politicians, lawyers, teachers, and even preachers found it a good sideline. A common-school education, ambition, and a little mechanical sense were about all that were needed to put a man in the business. A single room often served the purpose completely, and the equipment could usually be bought on easy credit terms. Development of "ready print" and "boiler plate" matter furnished by syndicates cut the labor to a minimum. Ready print sheets with two blank pages were available, so that all an editor had to do was to fill the empty sheets with local news, editorials, and advertisements. Boiler plate came in columns ready to go to the press and could be placed anywhere in the paper. Patent medicine advertisements and public printing contracts could be counted on as a source of revenue to implement subscriptions. Something of the low cost of production can be seen in the small subscriber lists which sustained the papers. Subscription rates for weeklies ranged from one to three dollars per year, and circulation varied from 300 to 1,000, with an average of approximately 500 before 1900 and 1,000 afterwards.

Before 1860 the function of the newspaper had been almost purely political, but afterwards it was much broader in scope. The major emphasis was on local events and personal news, community economics, morals, welfare, and politics, and the race issue. Editorials, heavily larded with the editor's personal opinions, were pungent and specific, and often his personal comments were mixed in with news items. Moreover, the editor was expected to back up his judgments to the point of violence.

The Southern journalist, even on the smallest weekly, was a firm advocate of the New South. Following the lead of Henry Grady of the Atlanta *Constitution* and F. W. Dawson of the Charleston *News and Courier,* he spoke long and loud of the better days to come as a result of diversified farming and industrialization. Liberal space was given to excerpts from the *Manufacturers' Record.* He was strong for attracting immigrants and the exploiting of Southern resources; Southerners had to be kept in the South, unless they were Negroes or there was a labor surplus, and Northerners should be welcomed if they were settlers or investors. For over seventy years, the editor preached the need for railroads and better highways. He was for education and soon opposed the convict-lease system and public executions. Often he had courage enough to speak out against lynching and the Ku Klux Klan. To the editor, the Negro was good as long as he behaved, and the South knew more about what he needed than did Northerners. But the freedman, in the editor's opinion, should not be allowed to vote until he was educated and free from outside influence.[3]

In brief, the Southern press was called upon not only to furnish news but also to lead and encourage all popular movements and to act as educator and advisor. Some went even farther than that. Before 1900 no newspapers in the country gave more space to or showed more interest in industrial development, mining, agriculture, and home

[3] Thomas D. Clark, "The Country Newspaper: A Factor in Southern Opinion, 1865-1930," *Journal of Southern History,* XIV (February, 1948), pp. 3-33; and *The Southern Country Editor* (Indianapolis: Bobbs-Merrill, 1948).

literature than those in the South. They were preponderantly journals of opinion, and the editorials were more widely read and thus more influential than elsewhere in the United States because of the rural nature of the region and the absence of other forms of mass communications. They were also distinguished by the fact that nearly all were Democratic in their political views because of the one-party system which prevailed in the South. Some from time to time bolted the Democratic party, e.g., during the Populist revolt and the presidential elections of 1928, 1952, 1956, and 1960. Since 1950, however, the Southern press has seldom spoken with a single voice.

The South continued to depend heavily upon the press for its information. With the growth of cities, the number of dailies increased without seriously diminishing the total of those published. The number of daily journals continued to increase until the 1940's, when their numbers began to level off, while the total number of all journals dropped slowly. In 1949 there were almost 9.5 persons for each morning newspaper, 7.5 for each evening, and 5 for each copy of a Sunday edition. In the nation as a whole, the ratios were 7, 5, and 3.[4]

SOUTHERN NEWSPAPERS, 1921-1972 *

| Date | Dailies | Weeklies | Semi- & Tri-Weeklies | Total, all types |
|------|---------|----------|---------------------|------------------|
| 1921 | 505 | 3,110 | 162 | 4,313 |
| 1931 | 530 | 2,748 | 128 | 4,339 |
| 1941 | 541 | 2,720 | 109 | 3,390 |
| 1952 | 533 | 2,464 | 124 | 3,139 |
| 1960 | 541 | 2,306 | 101 | 2,962 |
| 1972 | 529 | 2,232 | 138 | 2,964 |

* Included in the totals are the District of Columbia, Delaware, Maryland, Virginia, North Carolina, South Carolina, Georgia, Florida, Alabama, Mississippi, Louisiana, Texas, Oklahoma, Arkansas, Tennessee, and Kentucky.

These shifting figures and declining totals indicate that Southern newspapers underwent the formative influences common to the nation as a whole. The urban movement of population lessened the need and demand for country weeklies. Increased costs made the profession more hazardous and competition more bitter, resulting, if not in death, in combinations or absorption into national newspaper chains. In fact, by the 1930's, Southern journalism could be said to differ but little

[4] Harry Estill Moore, "Mass Communications in the South," *Social Forces*, XXIX (May, 1951), pp. 365-376.

from journalism elsewhere; largely departed were the individualistic editors of yesteryear. Standardization moved rapidly through the formation of the Southern Press Association, the growing dependence upon national syndicates, and the influence of the Associated and United Press associations. In news content, feature material, and editorial policies, little distinguished a Southern newspaper as such. The press associations furnished the same general news, and the syndicates supplied the funny papers and special features without distinction as to region. Publishing became a business, and control passed from the editor's office to that of the accountant.

The mid-twentieth-century newspaper, however, continued to be one of the most liberal forces in the South. Many city papers, in particular, advocated better treatment of the Negro and did much to educate the region against the appeal of the demagogue. They were primarily responsible for agitation and improvement of the freight rate-differential problem. On the other hand, these papers were generally conservative on economic questions, usually reflecting the anti-labor bias of the South, and refused to view industrialization critically. They also reflected their constituents' extraordinary sensitivity to outside criticism.

This conservatism of the white press was an additional spur to Negro journalism in the South. The results were first and foremost race papers, devoted primarily to advancement of the Negro people. They were usually published weekly and served as supplements to the white newspapers, which did not always cover Negro news events. The Negro papers operated with editorial policies that Negroes were equal and should be treated as ordinary Americans. While usually considered sensational, actually the Negro press was radical only on the race issue.

A large proportion of the Negro newspapers read in the South were published in the North, however. During the first World War, when the Negro people were migrating to the North in great numbers, some efforts were made by Southerners to keep this literature out of the South. Northern papers were almost uniformly more "radical" on the race issue than their Southern counterparts. In a year of Northern and Southern race riots, Somerville, Tennessee, decreed that no Negro newspaper could be sold there and that everyone should read a paper edited by a Confederate veteran. Two years later, an agent for the Philadelphia *American* was lynched in Athens, Georgia.

The number of Southern Negro newspapers increased steadily after World War I. This was because none of the white papers had the desired editorial policies or news interpretations; generally the Negro was ignored by white reporters except for news of his crimes. A few liberal white papers printed noncontroversial news for the Negro community, and some sold a special edition in which the Negroes got a whole page to themselves, but none of them consistently expressed the Negro protest or gave the race national coverage. Although the number of black-oriented newspapers reached 300 by the early 1970's, most were weeklies and outside the South. With small circulations, they were vulnerable as a result of trends toward consolidation and wider coverage of "black news" by the "white" press.

All in all, with the obvious exception of ignoring the black Southerner for so long, the record of white Southern journalism since 1865 has been a good one. It produced perhaps more than its proportionate share of well-known names. Probably no editor ever had more influence on any state than Francis W. Dawson, English-born editor of the Charleston *News and Courier*. During reconstruction he fought for an end to sectional bitterness and afterwards became a powerful voice demanding industrial and agricultural development. A supporter of reform, he was chiefly responsible for a South Carolina statute outlawing dueling, but ironically his death resulted from a bullet wound suffered during a quarrel. His position as a leader of crusades was taken over in the state by Ambrose E. and N. G. Gonzales of the Columbia *State*, who supported laws against lynching and child labor and favored better schools with compulsory attendance.

Henry W. Grady and Joel Chandler Harris made the Atlanta *Constitution* one of the most liberal newspapers in the South, and Grady's name came to personify the New South. At nineteen, Grady was associate editor of the Rome, Georgia, *Courier* but resigned when forbidden to attack local corruption. After taking part in several unsuccessful journalistic ventures, he acquired a quarter interest in the *Constitution* in 1880, at that time one of the half-dozen largest papers in the lower South. As managing editor, he increased the circulation of the weekly edition to 140,000 — the largest weekly in the United States. His influence extended far beyond the borders of Georgia because of the reprinting of his views by smaller papers and his own popularity as a public speaker.

Succeeding Grady and Dawson as the most outstanding Southern editor was brilliant and eloquent Henry Watterson of the Louisville *Courier-Journal*. Joining the paper in 1868, he, like Grady, became an ambassador of good will, and the *Courier-Journal* was soon recognized as the most widely-read and influential in the South. He defended the Negro, opposed the Klan and prohibitionists, and was an important figure in national politics. With a flair for memorable phrases, his editorials were widely copied, and his paper rivaled the New Orleans *Picayune* for the honor of being the largest Southern daily.

At least two Southern editors made even larger contributions to the national scene. Walter Hines Page took over editorship of the Raleigh *State Chronicle* in 1883 and lost no time in attacking the most cherished prejudices of the South and in leading a hammering fight for public education. After two years he went to New York, where he had a distinguished career as editor of *Forum, Atlantic Monthly,* and *World's Work,* as a crusader for a better South, and later as a diplomat. Adolph Simon Ochs, raised in Knoxville, Tennessee, began his career as a newsboy and finally bought the Chattanooga *Times* in 1878, lifting it to national prominence. In 1896 he purchased the bankrupt New York *Times,* making it a national monument to responsible journalism in defiance of the sensationalism which then dominated the field.

Into the twentieth century, the South continued to furnish crusading papers and editors of national repute. Under Virginius Dabney, the Richmond *Times-Dispatch* became for a while one of the most liberal newspapers in the nation. Jonathan Daniels made the Raleigh *News and Observer* a constant champion of the underdog, while J. E. Dodd produced one of the South's best in the Charlotte *News.* The crusades of Hodding Carter made the Greenville, Mississippi, *Delta Democrat-Times* probably the best-known small-town paper in America. The Richmond *News-Leader,* Norfolk *Virginian-Pilot,* Montgomery *Advertiser,* and Birmingham *Age-Herald* and *News* all became recognized for their relatively liberal leadership. The courageous stand of the *Arkansas Gazette* and its editor, Harry S. Ashmore, in the Little Rock crisis was rewarded by Pulitzer prizes in 1958. Two years later, Lanier Chambers and the Norfolk *Virginian-Pilot* received similar recognition for editorials on school integration.

The eminence of the Southern press was obvious in ways other than leadership. Its quality was shown by the fact that of the thirty-eight Pulitzer prizes for editorial writing awarded by 1960, eleven went to Southern papers, and ten won gold medals for "meritorious public service"; by 1972, the totals were fourteen and fifteen respectively. Another evidence of alertness came in 1939, when the Southern Newspaper Association took the lead in establishing a $6,000,000 print mill at Lufkin, Texas, for the use of Southern pine. Members of the association furnished a third of the money in 1948 for a similar plant at Childersburg, Alabama — the largest cooperative venture in the history of American newspapers.

One reason for the continued heavy responsibility carried by Southern newspapers was the relative weakness of other means of mass communication. In 1946, for example, the South had only 14.09 telephones per 100 persons, as compared to a national average of 24.2. Only 58 per cent of the people owned radios, as compared to 73 per cent nationally. In book purchases, the region ranked at the bottom of the list.[5] Cheap radios, omnipresent television, and the region's improved economic status brought changes in these statistics by the 1970's, although the South still lagged in book purchases.

In the general destruction of the Civil War, libraries suffered physically and professionally, for afterwards they were allowed to languish behind problems viewed as more pressing. The wave of library enthusiasm which swept the Northern states and led to the formation of the American Library Association in 1876 did not reach the South. Only one Southern librarian was a charter member of that organization, and in the same year, the librarian of the Charleston (S. C.) Library Society wrote, "We must say with regret that notwithstanding the occasional instances of favorable progress . . . a view of the condition of public libraries in the Southern States presents after all but a barren prospect. In proportion to the population their number is exceedingly small, they are poorly supported; are conducted on no general or fixed system, and are confined usually to the large cities. . . ."

Interest remained small. Representation at national library conferences was limited to one or two dedicated persons from the South. In 1897, a Georgia library association was organized, and the meeting of the American Library Association in Atlanta in 1899 greatly stimulated the formation of library clubs and state associations. Although they were able to expand library facilities and secure passage of scattered laws which permitted localities the option of taxing themselves for libraries, these groups were still voices whispering in the wilderness.

The twentieth century brought to libraries stimulation through gifts by Andrew Carnegie and other philanthropists. While these were helpful, more urgent were the needs for organization and public awakening to the necessity for such services. Not until 1920 did real concern develop, resulting in the formation of the Southeastern Library Association in that year and of the Southwestern in 1922. In 1926 the South was spending a mere $1,864,670 annually on libraries and 72 per cent of all Southerners and 817 of 1,284 counties were without any library service. Responding to this need, the Rosenwald Fund set aside $500,000 in 1929 for experimentation in country library service.

In 1930, when the Depression caused sharp cuts in the already inadequate budgets, the South was still at the bottom in national library spending, with per capita expenditures ranging from two to eighteen cents, as compared to a national average of thirty-three. By 1935 all Southern states had permissive municipal and county library

[5] *Ibid.*

laws, but the tax provisions were generally unsatisfactory. Five still lacked state library extension agencies, and of those with such agencies, only two, North Carolina and Louisiana, provided annual appropriations of over $10,000. Some 66 per cent of Southern people were still without access to a public library. The region spent $2,558,-262, or eight cents per capita, as compared to a national thirty-seven cents, and had .2 books per capita, a total of 7,830,353 volumes. Of 1,284 counties, only 52 spent as much as $1,000 a year, only 127 spent anything at all, and 782 had no library facilities within their borders. No collection in the South, public or institutional, possessed as many as 500,000 books. The color line was in effect in this field also, with only ninety-five libraries which would serve blacks.[6]

In some respects, the Depression was beneficial to the library systems. PWA funds were used to construct new buildings, while WPA workers rebound books, indexed newspapers, catalogued collections, and did dozens of other jobs which improved service and facilities. TVA, in attempting to provide library services for thousands of workers in an area of few books and periodicals, operated through state and local library boards to furnish "bookmobiles." This activity became the nucleus in Tennessee, Alabama, and North Carolina of permanent regional systems which were tax-supported and open to non-employees as well.

In 1939 the South had 774 public libraries, an increase of 209 over the preceding nine years. Prosperity brought a steady improvement in the status of libraries. In 1945, book service was available to 58 per cent of the Southern people, the unfortunate 42 per cent being mainly blacks or rural-dwelling whites. The latter group did benefit however from the extensive adoption of the bookmobile. As a dollar-stretching device, the bookmobile was more widely used in the South than elsewhere.[7] By 1956 over half such vehicles were located there.

In 1956 the U.S. Congress passed the Library Services Act making federal funds available to individual states for the improvement of library services to rural areas. Matching grants were required, but, according to each state's ability to pay, the federal share might cover between one-third and two-thirds of the cost of the programs. The same funding provisions were applied in titles I, II, and IV of the Library Services and Construction Act of 1964, which extended coverage to urban areas and authorized funds for establishing or extending facilities, construction of libraries, improvement of institutional li-

[6] Tommie Dora Barker, *Libraries of the South* (Chicago: American Library Association, 1936).
[7] United States Department of Health, Education, and Welfare, Bulletin 9, *Public Library Statistics* (Washington, D.C., 1953).

braries, and library services to the handicapped. Title III of the LSCA authorized the federal governments's half of the cost of establishing regional, state, or interstate networks of libraries for coordinating services and resources.

In the South LSCA grants stimulated general increases in library budgets. For example, Mississippi in 1956 was spending 37 cents per capita, and by 1970 was spending $1.97, a five times increase.

Between 1955 and 1970 five southern states show decreases in the number of county and regional libraries, possibly a consequence of consolidation of several libraries for more adequate resources and services, often with title III funds. In this period, Mississippi, with an almost stable population, was able to cut the number of county libraries from 50 to 44 while extending services to include all her people. The number of county and regional libraries increased in six states. Florida, whose population swelled by 150 per cent, increased the number of county libraries from four to twenty-six, but still left over a million and a half of her people unserved.

In the fifteen year period of LSA and LSCA, total expenditures for library construction and services in the South almost quadrupled, volumes per capita showed a 60 per cent increase, and percentage of population served rose to 92 per cent, 1.3 per cent below the figure for all states. However, resources and expenditures remained low in relation to the rest of the nation; no southern state exceeded the national mean in expenditures or volumes per capita.

In arts other than literary, the record of the South is less impressive. The so-called fine arts have ever been recognized as exotic flowers which flourish only under the most ideal of circumstances. At a time when civilized Europe spoke contemptuously of the barbarism of a money-mad United States, and even Americans referred to their era as "The Gilded Age," it would have been little short of miraculous if the South could have pointed to a better record. True, the destruction of the Civil War furnished architects with great opportunities, and the rash of memorial statuary could have lent support to artistic Southern sculpture. Moreover, the heroics of the conflict could well have served as stimuli to great music and drama. But none of this happened. While the wealthy aristocrats of the Old South had been appreciative of the ornaments of culture, their roles had been those of importers and consumers only, and their tastes were geared to Europe. Painting and musical performances were poses which were applauded in females; no one would have seriously proposed them as vocations for males. The economic stringency of the post-war period put an emphasis on the practical and utilitarian and gave life a sense of urgency which boded ill for the creative spirit. Literature, at least, was justified on the grounds that it was salable in the North, if not at home. Most other forms of creative genius were stifled or taken to more appreciative audiences. Consequently, before 1900, aside from accidental expressions on the folk level, the South made virtually no direct and permanent contribution to the aesthetics of the nation.

Architecture was a perfect example of the South's inertia. The region had already produced the regional styles of Williamsburg, New Orleans, Charleston, and Natchez, and in the 1850's added the prevailing national modes — Greek Revival, Gothic Revival, and other romantic manifestations. This trend was rudely checked, however, by the Civil War and the poverty which followed. From this background, two architects emerged. Henry Hobson Richardson, the most prominent American architect of the seventies and eighties, was born at the Priestley sugar plantation in Louisiana before the Civil War. Educated at Harvard and the École des Beaux-Arts in Paris, he created original adaptations of the Romanesque style which stood in splendid contrast to the Gothic or Victorian efforts of the prevailing jerry-builders and engineers. However, they graced not his native region but the North. John Wellborn Root, Georgia-born in 1850 and a pioneer in the development of the skyscraper, won his fame entirely in the North.

The plantation system, which had produced the wealth to build the show places for the planters' homes, often constructed with imported labor and supervision, was gone, along with the opportunity for genteel living. The average post-Civil War home was contrived by a carpenter and not only reflected the poverty of the region but also the combined lack of skill of the builder and taste of the owner. Churches, which before the War had often been the most beautiful structures in the South, were replaced by uniformly uninspired buildings or, worse, by architectural monstrosities of a pseudo-Gothic style. Public buildings, first hampered by the penurious tendencies of the Bourbons, were further handicapped by the prevailing American belief that an architect was quite unnecessary to construct a public building. When a United States treasury politician was allowed to design acres of hideous federal buildings, what hope was there for beauty on a state and local level?

The delayed industrial revolution in the South brought more money, but while the merchants, bankers, and industrialists of the New South had the wealth to indulge good taste, they lacked both the incentive and the imagination. The region became rich in the architecture of the late industrial revolution — that of the self-made man, of the business tycoon who rose from factory hand to president of the local textile factory. The most pretentious efforts were characterized by over-ornamentation and ostentation. Scroll work, mansard roofs, useless gables, narrow windows, small dark rooms, narrow halls – all showed the determination to copy the poor taste of their Northern counterparts on a small scale if not in full. Soon, all the mistakes of other earlier industrial civilizations were being repeated, with congested, slum-breeding cities and closely-placed houses.

By the twentieth century, most of Southern architectural improvement came not so much from local initiative but from the tendency to adopt prevailing styles in other parts of the country. As one author said, the South regaled itself in "borrowed finery." Consequently, the newer sections of most Southern cities were a medley of styles and variations which seldom took advantage of the unique attributes of their locale. The average building cost in 1928 for single-family dwellings was less than $3,000. The region was still swamped with mediocrity and vulgarity in its buildings. One important reason was the lack of conviction for the need of expert advice. In 1930 the South ranked at the bottom in the number of architects, with 7.1 per 100,000 population, as compared with 26.4 in the Northeast, 30.7 in the Far West, and 17.9 nationally.

During the Depression the South, as elsewhere, received government aid for its public buildings. This architecture suffered from a sterile, bureaucratic control which stifled imagination and creative initiative. In fact, during this period, architecture languished almost to the point of completely disappearing as a social art. The architect, largely replaced by the engineer, degenerated into a mere decorator of facades, and architectural schools reflected the trend by their emphasis upon the architectural-engineering approach.

New forces were developing, however. Nationally, Frank Lloyd Wright "stood almost alone in the Western world against the decadent creations of the period from 1900 through the 1930's" with his insistence that "form follows function." In Germany, Ludwig Mies van der Rohe placed the emphasis upon architectural expression through the materials used. Nationally, and in the South, architectural schools slowly changed from mere draftsman training to a dedication to the new architecture. Better copies of the colonial style were reflections of the restoration of colonial Williamsburg. Local individuals played their part; Neel Reid, for example, convinced many citizens of Atlanta to harmonize their dwellings with their environment, helping make the residential areas of that city one of the most beautiful in the South.

The change was less slowly felt in non-residential buildings. Sheer ugliness remained the hallmark of business sections in most Southern cities. The main streets primarily continued to be a succession of rectangular buildings without distinction. In the larger cities, this monotony was broken by an occasional skyscraper built along Northern lines and usually for reasons of local pride. Evidence of increasing wealth showed up in public buildings; yet few governments anywhere were as daring as Louisiana with its state capitol constructed by Huey P. Long. Its classical simplicity, spacious gardens, wealth of decorative design, and soaring tower mark it as unique among American state-houses. With regard to churches, a host of elaborate edifices proclaimed the piety of the South, but, while often beautiful, they were still unoriginal copies of Gothic or classic styles. Construction on Southern university campuses most often repeated existing models rather than adapting to local conditions. Thus, Duke University became a Gothic Oxford amid the forests of North Carolina, with no concern for the heat of the sun.

The over-all change became more evident by the 1950's. This was especially true in public-school construction, and a comparison of the new schools of the South with those of other states clearly showed that the leading architects of the South were earning a high respect. In meeting the needs of the teeming universities, the region led the nation in willingness to accept new ideas. Florida Southern College, at Lakeland, Florida, boasts the largest aggregation of Frank Lloyd Wright buildings in the world, and structures by Arkansas-born Edward D. Stone grace the campuses at Vanderbilt and the Universities of Arkansas and South Carolina. Large expanses of glass, ornamental screens, and refrigerated air conditioning were but a few of the adaptations made to temper the humid climate.

By 1950 the number of architects in the South had increased five-fold, mostly since 1930. But the region had about one-fourth of the nation's urban population and new construction and only one-fifth of its professional architects to advise it. Southern schools of architecture, however, expanded, and studies show that most of their graduates stayed in the South. Increasingly, the region showed a willingness to employ the great Northern architects and pointed with pride to works of Stone and Wright; in 1959, Ludwig Mies van der Rohe designed the Cullinan Hall addition to the Houston Museum of Fine Arts.

The Southern tradition of gracious living continues to be overlooked in the rush to industrialize and urbanize. Prior to the 1960's and 1970's, the major failure of Southern architecture was concentrating on individual building, thereby not seeing the city as a complex of buildings making up an architectural environment.[8]

---

[8] Lewis Mumford, *The South in Architecture* (New York: Harcourt, Brace, 1941); Edward and Elizabeth Waugh, *The South Builds* (Chapel Hill: Univ. of North Carolina, 1960).

With the availability of matching federal funds for "urban renewal," most of the region's major cities began completely rebuilding their "inner city" along aesthetic and architectural lines that rival the best in the nation.

Musically, the South could claim greater distinction. Much of the religion of the region was expressed through song, and Southerners had long composed hymns in abundance. They also bought song books by the millions, and the prevalence of "all day singings" and music parties testified to their love of music, generally making it the most popular of the arts. Southerners literally fought the Civil War with a song on their lips, and the battles had hardly ended before music shops reopened. Music also benefited with the growth of magazines, the Savannah *Southern Musical Journal* appearing in 1871 and the Richmond *Baton* six years later. Private clubs were organized by music lovers, and many towns and cities had their own brass bands. Traveling musicians could almost always find a hospitable welcome in the South.

Creatively, however, Southern composers did little. Sidney Lanier, torn between music and poetry, ended by trying to combine the two, writing for the flute, voice, and piano. His early death left unfinished a Choral Symphony, a Symphony of Life, and a Symphony of the Plantation. A mid-twentieth-century historian of American music declared of Lanier, "The music he left is the work of a gifted musician and a true artist. . . . The fact that circumstances did not permit him to develop his creative genius to the full is one of the major tragedies of America's music."[9]

For years after the Civil War, the region satisfied its soul with inherited music and folk songs. The Negro had long since taken over many of the hymns of his old master and made them his own. In the simple but vigorous religious music, the trials of the New South were momentarily forgotten by white and Negro alike while singing of the heavenly home which was "bright and fair," where there would be "rest for the weary" in the "land that is fairer than day." There were all-day singings, at which community vied against community and individuals against individuals for prizes before "dinner on the ground." "Sacred Harp" singers, using a musical form derived from early British music, held conventions attended by thousands from within and outside the state.

In addition to the sounds of religious music from the South was vigorous folk music of a secular kind. Not only were the old ballads still in vogue but also storied songs of local people whose misfortunes offered dramatic possibilities. "Come all you young people, and listen

9 Gilbert Chase, *America's Music* (New York: McGraw-Hill, 1955), pp. 344-345.

while I tell the fate of Floyd Collins, a lad we all knew well," and the flaming death of Casey Jones in the "Wreck of 97" were known throughout the region. The death of William Jennings Bryan led to a ballad which ran:

> He fought the evolutionists, the infidels and fools
> Who are trying to ruin the minds of children in our schools,
> By teaching we came from monkeys and other things absurd,
> By denying the works of our blessed Lord and God's own Holy Words.

There were whoopee and funny songs. One called "The Boll Weevil" ran for twenty-seven stanzas and taught the moral, "The boll weevil says to the farmer, 'I'll learn you a little sense; I'll learn you to raise your own food stuffs and cut down your expense.'"

The fiddle was the favorite instrument for a majority of Southerners. Not only did it usually supply the music for the numerous rural and small-town dances, but the fiddler was a man of importance throughout the region. Fiddlers' conventions, where master fiddlers vied, were almost as common and popular as all-day singings. Here local favorites from far and near contended for public favor by rendering such classics as "Devil in the Woodpile," "Arkansas Traveler," "Turkey in the Straw," "Pop Goes the Weasel," "Mississippi Sawyer," "Cackling Chickens," "Chicken Reel," "Billy in the Low Ground," "Grey Eagle," and "Alabama Girl."

This folk music made its national contribution in the form of the "hillbilly" music, which swept the country with the advent of radio. Throughout the United States on a Saturday night, millions of people listened to the "Grand Ole Opry" from Nashville or local counterparts, and in the 1970's "country music" swept the nation, as popularized by Johnny Cash, Roy Clark, and Charlie Pride. Negro folk music, too, came into vogue. The North had first become aware of Negro spirituals in the years following the Civil War, when the first efforts were made by Northerners to collect them. They were further popularized by tours of Negro choral groups, such as those of Fisk University and Hampton Institute, and "Swing Low, Sweet Chariot," "Roll Jordan Roll," and similar songs became national favorites. Huddie Leadbetter, more familiarly known as "Leadbelly," in nation-wide tours brought attention to the more secular types of Negro ballads.

The Negro's greatest gift to popular music, however, came from the role he played in creation of ragtime, blues, and jazz — the last being sometimes described as "the first important American contribution to music." Ragtime, like blues, was a tributary of jazz, sweeping the country in the Gay Nineties, even making considerable impression in Europe. Negro syncopation, involving the "ragging" of popular songs, was the origin of ragtime. It probably started in the minstrel shows' cakewalk rhythm as interpreted by Negro bands, banjoists, and pianists. New Orleans was the original center, evolving from the large number of Negro brass bands in that city. These groups, usually consisting of five to seven players, were given a role of honor in Mardi Gras processions, the frequent parades, and celebrations of all kinds — weddings, funerals, and picnics. Negro fraternal groups, labor organizations, and the like all had their own bands. Many of the musicians could not read music, and they liked to play it "hot." New Orleans was also the center of the ragtime piano, especially in the notorious red-light district of "Storyville." From there it spread up the Mississippi and its tributaries to cities like Memphis and St. Louis, which furnished water-front dance houses and other places where it could flourish and be further exported by white as well as Negro performers.

The most important names associated with ragtime were those of Scott Joplin and Ferdinand "Jelly Roll" Morton. Morton, from New Orleans, was noted for his piano playing and for "King Porter Stomp," published in 1906. Joplin, born in Texarkana, Texas, in 1869, began his career as an itinerant musician before ending up in St. Louis as a pianist. He published some thirty-nine piano rags, the best known being the "Maple Leaf Rag" (1899).

Blues on the other hand, developed from the Afro-American folk songs and was widely sung throughout the rural South in the final decades of the nineteenth century. Black musicians carried it with them to the cities in the nineties. Generally recognized as the "father of blues" was William Christopher Handy, born in a log cabin near Florence, Alabama. The son of a Methodist minister, he became a song writer because the "songs of the South were pinin' to be written." His writing career began with a campaign song for Edward H. "Boss" Crump which later became famous as "The Memphis Blues." This was followed by his even better-known "St. Louis Blues." "I took the humor of the coon-song," said Handy, "the syncopation of the ragtime, and the spirit of the negro folk-song, and called it blues." Handy, thus, predated a later revival of blues and such black artists as Bessie Smith and the currently popular "King of the blues," B. B. King, as well as a host of others who through their music have told of a folk culture not usually recorded by historians.

As this combination of mood and sound moved northward, it was called jazz. White musicians began to pick it up, and Northerners, such as Irving Berlin, began to capitalize on its possibilities. By the time of the first World War, it so dominated the period as to give it the name of the "Jazz Era," and respectability came through the works of George Gershwin and Paul Whiteman. Although declining in popularity during the depression years of the 1930's, it began a revival during World War II. By mid-century it was widely hailed by European audiences and produced its own annual festival at Newport, Rhode Island. Although played and composed throughout the country, many of the important jazzmen, white and Negro, were Southerners — Louis Armstrong of Louisiana, Jack Teagarden of Texas, and Fletcher Henderson of Georgia.

In serious music, the South had little to offer as popular as jazz, and its composers are virtually unknown except to other musicians. John Powell, born in Richmond in 1882, became one of the few distinctly regional composers of stature that the United States has produced. His *Symphony in A* was first performed by the Detroit Symphony Orchestra in 1947. Mainly a pianist, however, he stressed the rich Anglo-American folk music of the South in his compositions such as *Negro Rhapsody, Sonata Virginianesque, In Old Virginia,* and *Five Virginia Folk Songs.*

When conductor Leonard Bernstein of the New York Philharmonic presented three "musical pioneers" to a Carnegie Hall audience in October, 1958, two were Southern-born: Wallingford Riegger of Georgia, whose symphonic works earned him a number of awards but little money, and Kentucky-born John J. Becker, a musical experimenter and author of seven symphonies. Others who could have spiritually shared the platform were William Grant Still, born in Mississippi in 1893, composer of two symphonic works and two operas, along with shorter pieces, which depicted the musical background of the American Negro, and Lamar Edwin Stringfield of North Carolina, whose *From the Southern Mountains* won a Pulitzer prize in 1928.

The radio, and later inexpensive record players and tape machines, made music, classical and popular, available to Southerners as never before. Although more time was probably spent listening to news, country-western music, and the like, lovers of classical music who formerly suffered from rural isolation had a source of supply for the first time. The great gains in public education during the twentieth century encouraged music as a part of the curriculum in most of the larger and many of the smaller schools. As early as 1930, there were sixty-eight conservatories and university and college music departments, over half of which were twenty-five years old and a third of which had been in existence for half a century.

Urbanization and growing civic pride were reflected in increased musical opportunities. All of the good-sized cities and many of the smaller ones had annual public concert series which presented national artists at moderate admission prices. New Orleans had had opera as early as 1791 and, after a short hiatus during the Civil War, hosted good French troupes; along with New York, it was the only American city to boast a resident opera company. In its tours, the Metropolitan Opera Company of New York annually received a warm response from audiences of the South. Music clubs flourished in towns, small and large, and college and university communities served as focal centers of musical interest.

In addition to performances of bands, college groups, and assorted musicians on every level, the larger Southern cities undertook more pretentious activities. There were eight symphony orchestras in the region in 1930; by 1958 the states of Alabama, Florida, Georgia, and Mississippi alone claimed twenty-six. Southern cities by 1960 were as active in this field as any in the nation of similar size, although because of insufficient endowments no Southern orchestra was of the first rank. Nevertheless, the orchestras of Dallas, San Antonio, and Houston, the last under the batons of Leopold Stokowski and Sir John Barbirolli, were attracting national attention. The Louisville Symphony, under Robert Whitney, was one of the most active in the country in encouraging new compositions. The interest in symphonic music was not restricted to the metropolitan areas alone, however. The Community Music Bureau of the University of North Carolina, for example, stirred up such interest that the North Carolina Symphony, supported in part by state appropriations, annually barnstormed the entire state.

The Birmingham Civic Opera Association not only presented operas using local talent assisted by well-known artists but also took pride in its success as a workshop for operatic talent. An event of national importance in 1957 was the formation of the Dallas Civic Opera Company with the renowned Maria Meneghine Callas as its star attraction. Even the more exotic field of ballet was not ignored, as local dance studios were reinforced with the organization of the Southeastern Festival Association, the first regional ballet group to be organized in the United States. The University of Oklahoma in 1961 began offering instruction in ballet under its native daughter, famed ballerina Yvonne Chouteau, who, with Oklahoman Maria Tallchief, brought luster to the American ballet.

The South, as well as the rest of the nation, thrilled with pride to the European success of Texas-born pianist Van Cliburn. But in the fifties the great reservoir of black talent still went virtually unrecognized outside the field of popular music. The internationally applauded contralto Marian Anderson was denied use of a Washington, D.C. concert hall, and the Metropolitan Opera's Leontyne Price had to leave Mississippi to gain recognition. The following decade brought a remarkable change. To the gratification of blacks and many whites it became possible to witness talented blacks performing before desegregated audiences in centers formerly reserved "for whites only."

The fields of painting and sculpture suffered even more in the

South than in other regions because of a lack of popular interest. As art forms, they long were viewed as things apart and not natural media of expression. Despite the region's consciousness of history and profusion of monuments, it generally was satisfied to import its sculptors. Before 1930 only four names of relative importance can be linked with the South. Edward Kemeys, who specialized in statues of Indians and animals, was born in Savannah but grew up and achieved his fame in the North. Ephraim Keyser, best known for the Chester A. Arthur Memorial in Albany, New York, was born in Baltimore. Elisabet Ney, born in Germany, had made her name celebrated in Europe before migrating to Texas, where she produced monuments to Sam Houston, Stephen F. Austin, and General Albert Sidney Johnston.[10] Edward Virginius Valentine, born in Richmond in 1838, returned to his native city in 1865 after study abroad, and made a reputation as a sculptor of Confederate heroes such as Beauregard, Mosby, Stuart, Jackson, and Lee. His fame depended primarily upon his studies of Lee, a bust made from life and the well-known recumbent statue in the chapel of Washington and Lee University. While others have been active, the *American Art Annual* listing some thirty-three native Southern sculptors in 1931, none distinctly connected with the South have achieved national prominence. Most creative activity of this sort has been restricted to fine arts faculties. Edward Higgins of South Carolina was probably the best known sculptor during the 1960's.

Richmond, Virginia, prided itself on becoming a city of monuments, and most Southern cities of size have some sculptured works. Most of it, however, could charitably be described only as second-rate. Among sculptors of note whose works can be found in the South should be mentioned Daniel Chester French, Lorado Taft, Herbert Adams, William M. McVey, Augustus Lukeman, and Sir Moses Ezekiel. One of the most massive projects of carving to be found in America was begun by the United Daughters of the Confederacy as a memorial to the Confederacy. In 1923, Gutzon Borglum was hired to carve on the face of Stone Mountain, near Atlanta, Georgia, a great panorama featuring Southern heroes of the Civil War. Financial problems and artistic squabbles halted the work with only the three main figures of the central group—Davis, Lee, and Jackson—partially finished. Efforts to raise additional money and to use other sculptors delayed dedication of the Confederate memorial until 1970. The South, like the rest of the nation, has yet to achieve an understanding and appreciation of sculptural art.

Painting was somewhat more popular. Prior to 1860 the region had been a market for canvases, if for nothing more than ancestral portraits;

[10] Henry B. Dielmann, "Elisabet Ney, Sculptor," *Southwestern Historical Quarterly*, XLV (October, 1961), pp. 157-183.

Thomas Jefferson in 1779 had proposed a bill to amend the charter of William and Mary College to provide for "inclusion of professors who should instruct in the fine arts as well as in ancient languages." By 1970, however, the South had yet to produce a painter of international reputation, despite the 1922 organization of the Southern States Art League to hold annual exhibitions of local artists and to send their best works on tour and the fact that in 1932 the region counted seventy schools of art. The number of Southern novices did increase with the national vogue for "weekend" painting, but the region has remained primarily a consumer rather than an important producer of this form of art. Whenever any recognition has come to Southern painters, it has been chiefly as pictorializers of local scenes.

The South became more conscious of art, however. Practically every city claimed an art club by 1950, and while most of the members were enthusiastic amateurs, they were important educationally, with exhibitions of their own works and efforts to acquire traveling exhibits for their communities. The WPA, as part of its relief program during the Depression, gave encouragement to many struggling artists and commissioned numerous murals in public buildings. Like music, art made its way into the public schools, and many college fine arts departments offered special classes in painting for non-students.

The growing appreciation of painting showed up in the increasing market. A private collection in San Antonio listed a splendid El Greco and one in New Orleans a noted Renoir. An art store was virtually unknown in the South in 1930; yet by 1959, Dallas and Houston between them supported twenty-five art galleries, one of which grossed $80,000 in a single month. Atlanta had two galleries and Nashville one. Several art schools attained regional prominence, while still failing to rival the great art centers of the East. Most of these were connected with university centers or museums, although the James Lee Memorial Academy of Arts, founded in Memphis in 1925, offered free instruction. To many Southerners, however, contact with art came almost exclusively from museums.

Although lagging far behind the rest of the nation in this form of institution, the South at least has credit for establishing one of the first American art museums, at Charleston, South Carolina, in 1773. Since then, creation of additional museums was slow until the twentieth century. Despite the fact that the South in 1948 had no great comprehensive collection to match the best in the United States, an historian of American art museums could list fourteen "important" Southern museums.[11] Only seven states south of the Potomac were

[11] Walter Pach, *The Art Museum in America* (New York: Pantheon, 1948), pp. 269-287.

included, indicative of how far the region neglected its responsibilities in this field. Most heartening, however, was the increasing interest shown by state governments. The Virginia Museum of Fine Arts (established in 1937) began operating in 1953 the nation's first "artmobile" to take its treasures to the people. Another high point was the opening of the North Carolina Museum of Art at Raleigh in 1956. Nine years previously, the state, as the result of the offer of Samuel Kress to donate $1,000,000 in art if it were matched, appropriated $1,000,000, the largest amount ever provided for art by any United States legislature. The resultant collection, covering from the fifteenth through the nineteenth century, by 1961 was probably the outstanding collection in the South and a perfect example of what could be accomplished by an enlightened state.

The field of drama had wider public support, for the dramatic has always appealed to Southerners. As will be shown, the region was the scene of the last stand of the showboat and chautauqua, where every town and city boasted an "opera house" and where visiting troupes, however lacking in ability, could usually count on an attentive and largely uncritical audience. But this consumption was not offset by original contributions to the national theater. Aside from the purchase of tickets, the South served chiefly to produce names which had no other connection with the region except in natal statistics. To mention only the most important before 1900, such a roll includes Augustin Daly (North Carolina, 1838), a theatrical manager and playwright of whom it has been said, "Modern American drama begins with Augustin Daly"; Edwin Booth (Maryland, 1833), brother of John Wilkes Booth; Adah Isaacs Menken (Louisiana, 1835); Minnie Maddern Fiske (Louisiana, 1865), considered the cleverest actress of her generation; and E. H. Sothern (Louisiana, 1859), noted for his character roles.

After 1900 the South was left to produce its own plays. The traveling theater died as a result of increased expenses and the competition of the motion pictures. Curiously, even a Southerner was largely responsible for this turn of events. Most famous of the early directors of motion pictures was the son of a Confederate officer, David Wark Griffith, who was reared in the romantic tradition of the Lost Cause. He developed numerous camera techniques which were sensationally successful in his feature film *The Birth of a Nation* in 1915. This picture, an adaptation of *The Clansman,* written in 1905 by another Southerner, Thomas Dixon Jr., glorified the Ku Klux Klan as the defender of white civilization and pictured the Negroes as passionate brutes. This film did much to perpetuate the romantic stereotypes of the South, revitalize the Klan, and secure a firm foundation for the infant motion picture industry. Since that time, the South contributed its share of actors and actresses to filmland; Francis X. Bushman, Charles D. Coburn, Joan Crawford, Melvyn Douglas, Joseph Cotten, and Miriam Hopkins, to mention only a few.

Left to its own devices for live dramatic entertainment, the South filled the void with amateur performances. Colleges, high schools, and civic clubs organized drama groups for local productions. The little-theater movement which swept the United States in the years following the First World War had its Southern disciples, and soon a list of the "leading" little theaters in the country found the South credited with a fourth of the total. Some, such as the Dallas Little Theater and La Petit Théâtre du Vieux Carré, won national reputations for the excellence of their productions and ingenious stage techniques. College departments of drama also made their contributions, some undertaking a serious and complete study of playmaking, as well as presentation. Probably the best known of the latter are Paul Baker's at Baylor University in Waco, Texas, and the Carolina Playmakers of the University of North Carolina. In 1918, Professor Frederick H. Koch became Professor of Dramatic Literature at the University of North Carolina and began to encourage his students not only in acting but in writing dramas drawn from the rich source material around them. The Playmakers gave productions, often of their own creation, throughout the state. A community drama bureau of the same university was instrumental in setting up permanent historical dramas, the most famous being Paul Green's *The Lost Colony* on Roanoke Island, which not only entertained North Carolinians but annually attracted thousands of tourists.

The twentieth-century South pointed not only to increased dramatic activity but also, as previously discussed, to a number of celebrated playwrights and performers who grew up in the South. In addition to Lula Vollmer, DuBose Heyward, Paul Green, Tennessee Williams, and the like, Joshua Logan of Texas made a national reputation as a playwright, director, and producer, while the names of Mary Martin and Tallulah Bankhead, to mention only two performers, are familiar to theater-goers throughout the nation.

By the mid 1970's the South could feel a certain degree of satisfaction from its cultural achievements after the Civil War. With the exception of the literary and musical arts, this was not because of original contributions. Rather it was in the greater availability of cultural opportunities for all of the people. In many respects it was not until the 1940's that a sizable number of Southerners had the time and money for any arts much beyond the practical. After that, greater affluence helped create a desire for the arts, and also the means to satisfy it. The National Foundation on the Arts and Humanities, through its state programs, was a generous patron of the arts, carrying drama, art exhibits, and other such programs to even the remote Southern villages. While so far the South has remained somewhat a passive consumer, the widening acquaintance with the "finer things in life" will in turn spur creative genius. It is hoped that in the future the necessity for Southern artists to seek their fame and fortune outside their native region will be greatly reduced.

# 17

## THE SOUTH AT PLAY

FROM VIRTUALLY THE END of the seventeenth century, when the religious vigor of the Anglican Church began to wane, down almost to the middle of the nineteenth, the aristocratic South had the reputation of being the most religiously relaxed region in the United States. Its religion, lacking the stern overtone of puritanical morality, made few strict rules concerning relaxation and play. Consequently, the South generally amused itself without twinges of conscience over wasted time or from harsh strictures by religious leaders. Traditionally, the planter led a life characterized by extravagant hospitality and the relentless pursuit of pleasure. Even the poorer classes usually felt no great limitation on their social freedom.

The defensive attitude of the South in the decades of the 1840's and 1850's was reflected in an increasing demand for religious conformity and stricter orthodoxy; the usual moral relaxation, nevertheless, occurred during the Civil War and its aftermath. In this period of many troubles, Southerners hunted eagerly for escape from the grim realities which surrounded them. In fact, some forms of play, such as hunting, fishing, nutting, and berrying, became for a time a means of livelihood for whites and Negroes alike. Large-scale gambling was also justified by the revenue it furnished depleted treasuries and worthy beneficiaries. The legal lottery, a once-popular device, had gradually died out in the two decades before the Civil War but was quickly revived by the poverty-stricken Southern states.[1] On February 3, 1866, Alabama incorporated for twenty-five years the Tuscaloosa Scientific and Art Association with a three-fold purpose: to encourage art, replace the war-destroyed state university library, and establish a scientific museum. Tickets were sold in drawings which featured prizes of books, paintings, statues, scientific instruments, and other useful or ornamental property. This was followed in October, 1868, by the creation of a Mutual Aid Association to raise funds for common schools by lottery. Georgia, meanwhile, had also empowered the Masonic Orphans' Home to hold a series of such drawings to purchase land and erect buildings. At the same time, the carpetbag legislature of Mississippi created the Mississippi Agricultural, Educational and Manufacturing Aid Society, with a twenty-five-year lottery monopoly, in return for $5,000 down and annual payments of $1,000, plus one-half of one per cent of the gross to the state college. In Kentucky a similar grant was made to help a library, and an old franchise was renewed.

But all of these efforts were quickly dwarfed by the monster created in Louisiana. Contrary to precedents set by the state constitutions of 1845 and 1857, the document of 1864 granted legislative power "to license the selling of lottery tickets and the keeping of gambling houses." An act of 1866 gave this revenue to the New Orleans Charity Hospital, up to a maximum of $50,000. Two years later, the Louisiana Lottery Company was given a monopoly for twenty-five years in return for an annual payment of $40,000. The company moved quickly to take advantage of its grant, claiming the honesty of its drawings was assured by the supervision of former generals P. G. T. Beauregard and Jubal A. Early. Once a month for ten months of the year, 100,000 tickets priced from two to twenty dollars were offered. Every six months, "extraordinary drawings" of 100,000 chances, priced from ten to forty dollars, were held. The capital prizes in these semi-annuals steadily increased to $600,000, while total prize values fluctuated between $265,-500 to $2,000,000. In addition to the monthly lotteries were daily drawings with high prizes of approximately $5,000.

Illegal sales throughout the United States brought the company fantastic profits, and in 1890 it offered $1,250,000 a year to the state for a renewal of its franchise. In a popular referendum, it was turned down and subsequently operated outside the country, smuggling in its tickets. While most of the lottery tickets undoubtedly had been bought all over the United States, many a Southerner, both white and Negro, dreamed for a while that his dismal lot in life would be ended by the

[1] Ezell, *Fortune's Merry Wheel.*

ticket for which he had denied himself and family the necessities of life; however; the time for such opportunities being offered for so little under a legal sanction was quickly over.

But the means of spending a "sporting dollar" did not vanish. There was always a small market for chances in the Mexican and Cuban lotteries and the Irish Sweepstakes, law notwithstanding. Endless, although surreptitious, opportunities were afforded by cockfighting, horseracing, and the booths of the county fairs and carnivals. Although, by 1890, the predominantly Protestant ethics of the South would not approve legal gambling, resort towns quickly acquired the reputation of being wide open. Miami, New Orleans, Galveston, and Hot Springs, to name only a few better-known examples, enjoyed such immunity from police interference as virtually to claim legal approval.

Other illicit fruits were available for tasting. Prostitution was slow to become important in the rural South, but by the late nineteenth century, the larger cities reported this occupation to be growing. New Orleans, the most cosmopolitan of Southern cities, had its famed or infamous "Storyville," one of the most gaudy and elaborate "red-light" districts in America. The nearby presence of many army camps during World War I greatly fostered the growth of prostitution in even smaller communities. Although the second World War again spawned the practice in the vicinity of military establishments and defense plants, the return of peace found police goaded by reforming citizens at least to drive the practice underground, if eradicating it proved impossible. The continued presence of the "call girls" indicated, however, that Southern cities, like their Northern counterparts, had not eliminated this "oldest" of professions.

But the average Southerner resided in a rural community or small town, part of a middle-class society. His opportunity to partake of the fleshpots was limited. In fact, his actual experience was often what he had heard of the evils of the big city and the tawdry glimpse afforded by the visit of a cheap carnival or "girly show." His ministers were usually quick to denounce the very appearance of evil, and the penalty for detected participation was often social ostracism and a promise of hell's fire in the future. Consequently, his pleasures were of a less dramatic type, more like the life he led. There was little choice in recreation, a man having to be satisfied with intensity rather than variety. The average man's circle of acquaintances was limited, and so community life became a tightly-knit affair in which he filled a place. His group activities of necessity were religious, fraternal, or social.

For the farm family, the great social events of the year, besides those provided by the Grange and Alliance, were Christmas and the Fourth of July, with picnics, the circus, political rallies, fairs, and often a public execution supplying additional excitement. Between these momentous occasions, to break the monotony of planting, chopping, and picking cotton, there were the free pleasures of every-day life: camping out; hunting rabbits, quail, opossums, coons, and other small animals; fishing; school parties; church suppers or dinners on the ground; and splashing in the old swimming hole. Draughts and marbles were popular during warm weather. A Georgia country newspaper reported that "from early morn to dewey eve the unemployed citizen humps his spine over the fascinating board, or stands at 'taw.'" During the summer months, country and small-town newspapers also abounded with accounts of barbecues and basket meetings at springs, lakes, and water-mill sites, with speeches and dancing. Wagon loads of watermelons were given away; big barbecues took at least two days and nights of preparation. In the winter were spelling bees and singing meets, and any time of the year tent shows roamed the neighborhood. A big favorite, because it was free, was the medicine show, dispensing entertainment and "cure-alls." The Kickapoo Indian Show, for example, drew a crowd of 5,000 for one performance in Fayetteville, North Carolina.

Before 1900, when a general revulsion set in against the practice, hanging day was a holiday in the South. While the main feature cost no admission, there were also such attractions as tightrope walkers, medicine men, and perhaps even a small carnival. Bottles and jugs of whiskey were in plain sight, and swearing, fist fights, and pistol shots were the order of the day. The event was attended not only by the males but also by large numbers of women and children. As the time for the event approached, the audience assembled in a large outdoor area, preferably a natural arena large enough to hold thousands of spectators, dominated by the heavy wooden gallows. The heavily-manacled prisoner was brought forth with great ceremony. Ministers prayed over the crowd, and then the prisoner made his address, often for as long as twenty-five minutes, with frequent interruptions in the form of hoots and catcalls. Occasionally there was group singing before the prisoner's family was marched to the platform for its final farewells. To the participants and contemporaries, these revolting exhibitions were considered merely an old English institution for punishing the enemies of society and as an exemplary warning to others.

For the more refined tastes, there was the circus of animals and clowns. The Civil War had scarcely ended before the circus returned. P. T. Barnum's Great Traveling Museum and smaller outfits of every sort featured such thrills as ventriloquists, conjurers, trained animals, humorous lecturers, or even electric shocks from a battery at ten cents each. In the South the circus season extended from April to December, bringing in an exotic world to break the humdrum existence of rural life. Often families set out for the grounds a day ahead, sleeping in or under their wagons and cooking over a campfire, in order to be present at the unloading and to get favorable positions for the parade and balloon ascensions which marked the opening ceremonies. Excursion trains brought customers by the hundreds. As one country editor wrote, "Circus coming, old fogies are relaxing in their views and some even propose to take their children to see the animals which the Lord made."

While the circus' popularity was universal, its most ardent support came from among children, Negroes, and the poor whites, where white and Negro shared the same tent but usually sat on opposite sides. The circus reached the height of its popularity in the last quarter of the nineteenth century, with nearly forty organizations on tour annually, traveling by train or wagon. Sharpers and pickpockets often followed the circus, and it was also an occasion for drunks and fights, frequently arousing religious and community leaders. Owners, however, were wise to the way of the South, advertising their circuses as highly educational, classical, and Biblical, featuring chariot races, religious tableaux, and the like. Consequently, moralists preached in vain. Most famous of the outfits which toured the South were John Robinson's Circus and Menagerie, W. C. Coup's Monster Shows, and the Grand New Orleans Menagerie and Circus, boasting "150 men and horses," clowns, athletes, the usual menagerie, and Mademoiselle Eugene leading uncaged lions and tigers down the street. One proprietor, Adam Forepaugh, claimed to have 1,500 animals, birds, and beasts. The claims always exceeded the truth, but who could afford to miss the chance of a lifetime? In the twentieth century, the circus tradition was kept alive in the South, as Florida served as the winter quarters for America's largest troupe and one of its educational institutions received national attention for the amateur productions of its students.

A South Carolinian wrote in 1877 that in addition to the circuses, photographers traveled the countryside, finding extensive patronage among the whites. Magic-lantern shows under canvas, minstrel companies, and itinerant jugglers reaped a rich harvest among the poorer whites and Negroes, with the latter predominating in the crowds at the cheap shows and circuses.[2]

The amusement fare was more varied in the larger towns and cities. The pre-war theatrical tradition of the South was renewed with amazing promptness at the end of fighting. Before the turn of the twentieth century, every town of any size and pretension had a theater or "Opera House." The *Official Theatrical Guide* for 1904-1905 listed thirty-nine in North Carolina alone. In 1861 the established Charleston

[2] "A South Carolinian," "South Carolina Society," *Atlantic Monthly*, XXXIX (June, 1877), pp. 681-683.

Theatre, generally recognized at that time as one of the best in America, had offered a season which ran from October through May, and performances continued on a limited scale throughout the War. Three days after Lee's surrender, New York producers presented a play to a large audience, starting a run which lasted until July. An Italian company sang grand opera in 1866 and was followed by a legitimate drama. The 1869 season was highlighted by a German grand opera company, the English Opera Bouffe, and two appearances of the Parisian Ballet Troupe. In the summer of 1869, Charleston constructed the Academy of Music, with a theater to seat 1,200 people, which at its zenith could boast such performers as Laura Keene, James H. Hackett, Edwin Forrest, Junius Brutus Booth, Joseph Jefferson, Ellen Terry, John Drew, and Sarah Bernhardt.[3]

In Atlanta, Davis Hall, seating 4,000, was built even before the debris of battle had been cleared. Wilmington had opened its legitimate theater in 1858 and, like Charleston, managed to keep it going during the War, even in the black days of defeat. By 1869-1870 there were fifty nights of entertainment, featuring such variety as Shakespearean plays, Italian opera, and magicians. Until 1900 it averaged about forty performances a season, although during 1880-1881 it had 108.[4]

New opera houses also sprang up all over the South, and old ones were refurbished after the War. The St. Charles of New Orleans continued to boast that it featured more famous names than any other theater in the South. Dallas constructed its first in 1872; Little Rock and Louisville built handsome new structures the next year. Smaller towns were also captivated by the drama, with theaters being constructed in Salisbury, Greensboro, and Charlotte, North Carolina, in 1873 and 1874.[5] The new Macauley in Louisville cost some $200,000, and simultaneous with its grand opening, Harriet Beecher Stowe was giving readings, "Macbeth" was at a rival theater, the Masons were giving a promenade concert for the plague sufferers of Memphis, the Vaudeville Theatre was featuring the "Carnival of Fun," and the German opera season was scheduled for two days later.[6] All of this in a community of approximately 100,000 people!

Programs varied widely in type and between large and small

[3] W. Stanley Hoole, "Charleston Theatricals during the Tragic Decade, 1860-1869," *Journal of Southern History*, XI (November, 1945), pp. 538-547.
[4] Donald J. Rulfs, "The Professional Theater in Wilmington," *North Carolina Historical Review*, XXVIII (1951), pp. 119-136, 316-331, 463-485.
[5] Donald J. Rulfs, "The Era of the Opera House in Piedmont North Carolina," *North Carolina Historical Review*, XXXV (1958), pp. 328-346.
[6] West T. Hill, Jr., "Opening of Macauley's Theatre, Louisville, Kentucky, October 4, 1873," *Filson Club Historical Quarterly*, XXXII (1958), pp. 151-166.

towns. Whereas old established theaters such as those of Charleston, New Orleans, and Wilmington boasted fantastic arrays of the best talent of Europe and America, often the features in smaller communities were less renowned, and rarely did a star come their way. Salisbury's Meroney's Hall in its first season presented the Swiss Bell Ringers and the Thespian Dramatic Company in *Ten Nights in a Bar Room*, Greensboro's first professional performance was by a lady lecturing on "Fashion — Its Follies and Changes," and Charlotte's theater opened with a magician and marionette show.

Altogether, however, theater patrons often saw programs which would be envied by twentieth-century devotees. Among Southern favorites were such famous names as Ole Bull, Norwegian violinist, and the New York Symphony under Walter Damrosch; Edwin Forrest, E. H. Sothern, Helena Modjeska, Maurice Barrymore, Otis Skinner, De Wolfe Hopper, Anna Held, Maude Adams, and Lillian Russell; the D'Oyly Carte London Opera Company; and John Philip Sousa's Band. Popular favorites, but less renowned, were the Armstrong Brothers Minstrels and Brass Band, the Representative Pantomime Company, the Negro pianist "Blind Tom," the New Orleans Jubilee Singers, Ford's Juvenile Opera Company, General Tom Thumb and a company of midgets, and Buffalo Bill Cody with his Indians.

Stock companies usually ran a week at a time, offering eight performances, with Wednesday and Saturday matinees, and a change of program each day. After the 1870's, however, stock companies lost popularity. They were replaced by the star system, featuring a nationally or internationally famous person on tour supported by an inferior cast for only a single performance. Broadway hits were also sent on the road after 1900, with musicals by Franz Lehar, Oscar Straus, George M. Cohan, Victor Herbert, and Jerome Kern exceedingly popular. By World War I these operettas had largely displaced opera and classical music on Southern stages. They, in turn, were to yield to the attractions of vaudeville. By 1910 vaudeville had reached the smaller theaters in the South. Featuring a wide variety of acts, it offered three performances a day, separated by numbers by a chorus consisting of six to eight female dancers. Often, vaudeville was presented in connection with supplemental motion pictures, but the roles were eventually reversed, the movies becoming finally the major attraction.

The 1920's saw the professional theater in the South moribund. Its decline was the result of increased railroad rates and operating expenses, the monopolistic practices of New York booking syndicates, and, probably paramount, the increased quality and quantity of moving pictures. Most theaters surrendered and became motion picture houses. In time, even the fair, carnival, and circus found themselves unable to compete with the glamor of the silver screen, and lodge night and church suppers seemed tame by comparison. With the advent of sound in 1928, the motion picture completed its sweep of the entertainment field, reigning despotically until challenged by radio and, later, television. Although many Southerners viewed the movies with distrust as a result of publicity about the morals of the stars, the lure was great enough to capture paying audiences. Most Southerners who grew up in small towns during the 1920's and 1930's long recalled with nostalgia the Saturday shows, permitted by most indulgent parents, featuring the contemporary Western hero and probably a Tarzan serial.

Besides the "opera house," two other media of mass entertainment rose and declined by the 1930's. Most spectacular was the showboat, which steamed and paddled the rivers of the Atlantic seaboard and the Mississippi and its tributaries. It began its travels as early as 1831 but reached its greatest peak from 1878 to 1910. Thrilling thousands of patrons were such vessels as Augustus French's *New Sensation,* John McNair's *New Era,* Edwin Price's *Water Queen,* and Norman Thom's *Princess.* As a rule, these and dozens like them presented highly respectable family shows, featuring sentimental musical numbers, minstrel jokes, a comic political speech or sermon, acrobatics, a fiddler's contest, feats of magic, and a short farce. The inhabitants for miles around were notified of the showboat's arrival by the shrill tones of the calliope, and, if the settlement were large enough, the main program was preceded by a parade and a free calliope concert. In many isolated communities, these boats were almost the sole contact with the outside world of fun, and the audiences were enthusiastic rather than critical.

With the coming of automobiles, better roads, and the motion pictures, the showboats faced greater competition. To meet it, they built "floating palaces" such as the *Cotton Blossom,* the *Sunny South,* and the *Goldenrod,* which would often seat as many as 900 persons. To contest the movie's appeal, they began to specialize in dramatic productions, giving such favorites as *The Parson's Bride, From Rags to Riches,* and *Ten Nights in a Bar Room,* as well as the most popular New York hits. Their efforts were largely in vain, however. In 1910 some twenty-two showboats were working along the Mississippi; in 1938, only four; and in 1943, one.[7]

Another unique institution for amusement and instruction was the Chautauqua. Beginning as a "Sunday-School Teacher's Assembly" at Lake Chautauqua, New York, in 1874, it took to the road in tents in 1903, offering a program of culture and entertainment to the nation. It owed much to the old Lyceum movement, which had featured circuits

[7] Phillip Graham, "Showboats in the South," *Georgia Review,* XII (1958), pp. 174-185.

of speakers and entertainers for urban areas. The novel departure was
made to furnish the tent and entertainers for towns which wanted their
own Chautauqua. The community took the financial risk and accepted
what it got. The Chautauqua's stay of one or two weeks featured programs of magicians, music, drama, operas, humorists, Hawaiian dancers, Swiss yodelers and bell ringers, quartets, solos, bands, harpists,
Gilbert and Sullivan productions, impersonators, dramatic readers, and
speakers upon almost every conceivable subject. Julia Claussen, prima
donna of the Chicago Grand Opera Company, sang in 120 towns in
one summer, beginning in Florida and working her way through the
South to Chicago. The inspirational lecture was the backbone of the
series, however. Russell H. Conwell's "Acres of Diamonds" speech was
delivered some 6,000 times in his career. William Jennings Bryan was
almost equally famous for his "Prince of Peace" and was probably the
biggest drawing attraction. Lecturers were of either sex, and top politicians such as Eugene V. Debs, William Howard Taft, Champ Clark,
Alfred E. Smith, and Robert M. La Follette were presented as speakers.

The South was more or less the private domain of two groups in
the Chautauqua system, the Alkahest of Atlanta, Georgia, and Radcliffe
Attractions of Washington, D.C. Alkahest, featuring a seven-day circuit,
covered forty towns in Florida, Georgia, Alabama, Mississippi, Louisiana, Texas, Arkansas, Kentucky, and North Carolina. Radcliffe ran
three circuits in the South, covering over 200 communities. A third
organization, Redpath, while not limited to the South, ran two circuits
in six states, which served around 200 towns. Enjoying the sponsorship
of the churches and local merchants and with a program for every age,
the Chautauqua was often the one bright week in a hot, dusty Southern
summer.[8] The Big Spring, Texas, *Herald,* for March 11, 1921, listed the
following attractions: six lectures, including Dr. Frank Dixon and
Henry Adrian, the Montague Light Opera Singers in *Broadway Jones,*
the Philharmonic Ladies Orchestra, and a violinist. The caliber of talent
suffered under the stress of daily performances, however, and the Chautauqua found itself no longer able to compete with the movies, automobiles, and the radio. The movement reached its peak in 1924 and
by 1932 was gone.

In addition to such organized circuits, local talent also performed.
Confederate officers were in vogue as traveling lecturers, with Admiral
Raphael Semmes describing the cruise of the *Alabama* and General
John C. Pemberton refighting the battle of Gettysburg. Bill Arp gave
his humorous lectures, and phrenologists analyzed cranial bumps and
sold charts. Steamboat races were occasions of excitement for those

[8] Victoria and Robert O. Case, *We Called It Culture: The Story of Chautauqua*
(Garden City: Doubleday, Doran, New York, 1948).

along the river, and in 1882 Mark Twain was entertained in New Orleans at a cock fight and at a mule race featuring fashionable riders and stands full of the city's fairest. "Tournaments" were revitalized, in which colorfully dressed young men in the fashion of Sir Walter Scott's romances exercised at feats of skill, on foot or horseback, to win the esteem of a young lady denoted the "queen of love and beauty." The Civil War had scarcely ended before dancing societies were once again in full operation, the only concession to the times being the popularity of "calico balls." Excursion trains and steamers furnished other occasions for entertainment.

Every capital city and most county seats boasted a fair grounds, where once each year, usually after harvest time, exhibitions of agricultural products, machinery, and the like were held. In addition to such booths, the race track, originally featuring horses and later automobiles, and the "midway" or carnival area demanded attention. Not only could the farmer compare his agricultural skill with his neighbors, but he could become acquainted with the "bearded lady" and "dog-faced boy" and try his hand at guessing under which walnut shall lay the pea and which was the fastest horse in the daily race.

Individual towns and cities had their own days of glory and fun in elaborate festivals of every type. Most famous and colorful was the Mardi Gras celebration of New Orleans, revived immediately following the Civil War and quickly imitated by many smaller communities. Lasting for weeks, these celebrations featured parties, dancing, parades, and general hilarity for all segments of the population. As Mark Twain said, "It is a thing which could hardly exist in the practical North for the soul of it is the romantic, not the funny and the grotesque." Other localities established special days or weeks in honor of some specific product or characteristic, such as apple blossom, tobacco, cotton, peach, tulip, azalea, dogwood, strawberry, citrus, oleander, rose, forest, and peanut festivals, to mention only a few. Featuring parades of floats and an inevitable selection of a reigning beauty as queen, such occasions were welcomed as an opportunity for fun by the many and for ringing cash registers by the merchants. Small and sad, indeed, was the town which could find no worthy object to commemorate by a festival, and the number of Southern "queens" became legendary.

Also attracting national and even international attention were the regional expositions, the pride of the Bourbons. America became exposition-conscious following the 1851 London Crystal Palace and 1876 Philadelphia Centennial expositions. By 1907 the South had held eight major expositions, the result of competitive sectional rivalry, local pride, and the profit motive. They were especially the vehicle for spreading the New South propaganda. Although they were regional in orientation, they received considerable northern aid. The first, suggested by a Northerner as a means of sectional reconciliation and profit, was the Atlanta World's Fair and Great International Exposition in 1881. Desirous of overcoming what was considered an inadequate representation of Southern industry at Philadelphia, the Georgia show featured cotton and other Southern products. This exposition ran for three months and was attended by some 225,000 people. Two years later, Louisville hosted the Southern Exposition that attracted 375,000 and boasted fifteen acres of floor space for exhibits. The National Cotton Planters Association sponsored the World's Industrial and Cotton Centennial Exposition in New Orleans in commemoration of the first shipment of cotton in 1784. Congress loaned the group some $1,000,000, and the federal government spent $300,000 on buildings. This exposition surpassed the Philadelphia Centennial in size, to the great delight of Southerners, while bringing the industrial potentialities of the region to the attention of Northern capitalists.

This success was quickly followed by Atlanta's Piedmont Exposition in 1887, featuring the interdependence between agriculture and industry in the piedmont area of the South. Spurred by the acclaim given the Chicago World's Columbian Exposition of 1893, Atlanta launched in 1895 the Cotton States and International Exposition. This was a daring move in view of the Panic of 1893, and as its president said, "the courage, zeal, the defiance of difficulties . . . were exhibited in scarcely higher degree when they so rapidly rebuilt Atlanta from the ashes of war than they are in the history of this Exposition." Attracting over 1,200,000 sightseers, it featured the industrial awakening of the region and made a special attempt to promote increased trade. Displays were furnished by all South American, as well as many European, countries, and fifteen states constructed special buildings. The exposition also did much to foster racial reconciliation through the prominent role assigned Booker T. Washington, the great Negro leader.

Two years later, Nashville's Tennessee Centennial and International Exposition stressed Tennessee history and especially the importance of the coal and iron industry. The South Carolina Inter-State Exposition and West Indian Fair at Charleston (1902) once again featured the region's interest in international trade, while the biggest and most expensive undertaking, promoted chiefly by women's patriotic organizations, was the 1907 Jamestown Tercentenary Exposition. Stressing the role of the South in the foundation of the nation, a theme repeated fifty years later, it featured displays of naval power and in six months attracted approximately 2,800,000 visitors. Other later expositions included the Texas Centennial sponsored by Dallas and Fort Worth in 1936 to celebrate Texas independence. All of these various expositions were not only sources of Southern pride in actual accomplishments but also stimulated the spirit of progress and education. Equally important, the commingling of thousands of vistors from all regions of the country made the expositions a means of fostering reconciliation and nationalism.

When fairs and expositions were not in progress, other excursions for the travel-minded were available. Conventions of the Masons, Grangers, and similar organizations were held annually at some key city, and the railways spurred attendance by reducing fares by half. Trips to the nearest Confederate cemetery for Memorial Day furnished the chief occasion for glorifying the Old South and the Confederate cause. Although reconstruction officials had looked with suspicion upon veteran's organizations, such groups appeared in parts of the South, and as time went on, frequent reunions were held by survivors of old brigades and regiments. The former soldiers did not join into one body, however, until 1889, with the formation of the United Confederate Veterans. Memorial associations for the women, which had proven quite popular for raising money for local monuments, were the foundation of the United Daughters of the Confederacy established in 1894.

Although Union veterans had organized much earlier, there was still latent suspicion of the Southern counterpart. However, the attitude of the former Confederate soldier was probably expressed by a resolution adopted at their sixth reunion: "With no humble apologies, no unmanly servility, no petty spite, no sullen treachery, he is a cheerful citizen of the United States, accepting the present, trusting the future, and proud of the past." Highlighting veteran activities and important times of sectional reconciliation were the occasions on which the Blue and Gray met on old battlefields to hold joint reunions. Fitzhugh Lee had led Southern troops to take part in the Bunker Hill Centennial at Charlestown, Massachusetts, and soon their presence became common at celebrations of famous events in American history, as the stings of the Civil War began to mellow more and more into a glorious memory. Both hailed the Spanish-American War as an opportunity to prove national unity and Southern patriotism and fighting ability. A joint reunion was held in 1910 at Atlantic City, a practice which became more common as partisan feelings, along with survivors, declined.

As soon as the first shock of the Civil War had declined and finances improved, Southerners renewed their accustomed habits of traveling to summer resorts and Northern cities. Fewer made their way north, to the great advantage of local mountain resorts, watering places, and mineral springs. Virtually every state had its attractions, but the most popular were the "spas," springs featuring waters of supposedly medicinal powers and entertainment for young and old. When at their heyday, several hundred sought patronage in the South. Some had rude log cabins, but others boasted impressive multi-story hotels. Bath houses, dance pavilions, game rooms, and private cottages — all were to be found at one spring or another. Some travelers came in search of health, but the majority were "taking the cure" because it was a fashionable fad. They were also there to escape the harsh climate of coastal areas, to enjoy the amusements provided, and to make possible matrimonial contacts for eligible daughters. With the advent of modern transportation and increased recreational opportunities, the attractions which once seemed so compelling began to fade, and so by the middle of the twentieth century only a handful of these spas were still in operation — White Sulphur Springs in West Virginia, Warm Springs in Georgia, Hot Springs in Arkansas, and Mineral Wells in Texas being about the best-known.

Gulf and Atlantic beaches were slow to rise as rivals for mountain springs as summer resorts, but Florida, because of its warm winter climate, soon became attractive especially to Northerners. By 1874 the population of several Florida cities, notably Jacksonville, doubled every winter. The great playland of southern Florida, however, lay virtually empty until the twentieth century because of the lack of transportation. In 1910, Miami had only 5,400 inhabitants. The extension of the Florida East Coast Railway, the automobile, and Northern promoters brought a flood of people from all regions of the United States and the great land boom of the twenties, checked only temporarily by periodic hurricanes and depressions.

But for those who stayed at home, there was also plenty to do. Southerners had always been social creatures, demonstrated by eagerness to join clubs of all sorts. The church became the social arbiter of the unsophisticated Southern world of the nineteenth century, especially in the small towns. As it often frowned upon dancing, card playing, theatrical performances, and motion pictures, it in turn provided less worldly entertainment in the form of Ladies' Aid, Christian Endeavor, and missionary societies, which vied in production of socials, fairs, and festivals. The South also teemed with fraternal organizations, both old and new, and every community had one or more lodges with memberships which embraced every element in town and even had auxiliaries for the women. The elaborate cermeonies and rituals, colorful costumes, and mysterious titles helped members escape the humdrum aspects of their daily lives. Sons of Temperance, Good Templers, Knights of Pythias, Red Men, Woodmen of the World, Odd Fellows, Masons, and the Grangers were favorites. By the twentieth century, they had been joined by service organizations such as the Rotary, Kiwanis, and Lions clubs. Country clubs catered to the more exclusive, yet managed to grow in membership and number.

Female social clubs of every description also flourished, usually masquerading under educational titles. The first meeting of the original American garden club was held in Athens, Georgia, in January, 1891. So club-minded were Southern women that, in 1909, of the 350,-000 organized club women in the General Federation of Women's Clubs, 45,000 were in the South, not to mention tens of thousands of others that were not so recognized. Education, libraries, civic projects, and literature vied with the Daughters of the American Revolution (1890) and the Colonial Dames of America (1892) for feminine attention and support. Symptomatic of their changing position was the formation of the Southern Association of College Women in 1903. For the children, the Boy Scouts came into the South in 1910, and in 1912, Mrs. Juliette Gordon Lowe of Savannah formed the Girl Scouts of America. Soon, Southern youths could claim membership in all the national movements of this type.

The Negro showed himself a good Southerner and American by the eagerness with which he joined societies. Barred from white organizations, he quickly formed his own. He was particularly attracted by the mysteries and ceremonies of the fraternal orders. After 1900 the women's club movement spread to this race, resulting in the formation of a National Association of Colored Women's Clubs with substantial Southern membership. If anything, the Negro seemed more ready to join a club than his white neighbor, a tendency explained by President Robert R. Moton of Tuskegee as being a substitute for the political activity Negroes were denied. Few of their organizations, however, had the primary purpose to protest against inequalities or to fight for racial improvement. In the 1930's, between 300 and 600 benevolent and mutual aid societies for Negroes existed in New Orleans, and over 200 Negro associations were to be found in 1935 among the 7,500 colored inhabitants of Natchez.[9]

Amusement fads, usually originating in the North, swept the South from time to time. Walking marathons, croquet, mah-jong, bicycling (Columbus, Georgia, held races for the state championship in 1884), bridge in the cities, miniature golf with its green cotton-seed-hull fairways and mazes of pipes and trap doors, and myriads of others claimed Southern attention from time to time. The South was not even totally immune to such vogues as flagpole-sitting, goldfish-swallowing, telephone-booth-packing, and similar collegiate fads.

For a period, the South was the center of prizefighting activity, with the legalization of prize fights by Louisiana in 1890. Even before that time, covert cooperation of police permitted exhibitions. In 1882, John L. Sullivan challenged the national champion, Paddy Ryan, and

[9] Gunnar Myrdal, *An American Dilemma* (New York: Harper, 1944), pp. 952-954, 1430.

knocked him out in Mississippi City, Mississippi. Seven years later, Sullivan defeated Jake Kilrain in seventy-five rounds at Richburg, Mississippi, for $20,000 and a diamond-studded belt offered by the *Police Gazette* in the last bare-knuckle championship fight in America. He was beaten in 1892 in twenty-one rounds at New Orleans by James J. (Gentleman Jim) Corbett for the championship and a purse of $21,000. The last of the major, old-time fights came in 1894 at Jacksonville, Florida, when Corbett bested Charley Mitchell. More sympathetic Northern legislatures allowed the fights to move to the more populous centers, but cities in Florida, Louisiana, and Texas continued to sponsor local bouts and local boys, with an occasional championship contest. The success of Joe Louis, who reached the heavyweight championship of the world from Alabama *via* Detroit, greatly excited Southern enthusiasts, especially members of his own race.

Horse racing, the traditional sport of Southern gentlemen, suffered a severe blow as a result of the Civil War's effect upon livestock, the ensuing poverty, and the growing influence of Protestant middle-class moral standards. Nevertheless, a Kentucky Derby was held each May at Churchill Downs in Louisville after 1875, reaching great fame in the twentieth century. By 1877, "A South Carolinian" reported that every Southerner was ambitious to own blooded horses and that "horse racing and, to a less degree, cock-fighting are popular to excess." Jockey clubs were fashionable and cities such as Memphis, Montgomery, Little Rock, and Nashville held meets attracting spectators and horses from throughout the region. For a time, enthusiasts were checked by growing feeling against gambling, but by the twentieth century many Southerners took pride in the feats of Man o' War and other famous horses of Southern origin, as well as patronizing tracks in Kentucky, New Orleans, Miami, and Hot Springs, to mention only a few of the better-known centers.

Baseball, the "national game," also became the pride of the South. Introduced into the North before the Civil War and with New Orleans teams playing it in 1858, it had such appeal that it was a popular wartime game in both camps. According to legend, games were even played between units of the opposing armies on quiet sectors. With peace, the game literally swept the South; amateur clubs sprang up everywhere, with even the Negroes organizing teams, and every town and school had its representatives until a single community might field a dozen or more teams. The Montgomery *Advertiser* wrote in 1867, "This disease has broken out in this section of the country. It is a good game." A few weeks later, it editorialized that "no better relief from the depression which overhangs our unhappy country could be found and so we hope, that with picnics, ball games and excursions, the dull

dull summer can be whirled away." Five Alabama towns organized the Alabama Association of Base Ball in 1868, and by 1872, sandlot baseball flourished in Texas. All classes of society took the game seriously; in a Georgia contest, three people were shot and two killed. Tom Watson, of later Populist fame, was captain and pitcher of the "Up and At Em Club," which in 1877 defeated the "Skunk Em" group, 57 to 27.

Professionalism entered the picture in 1869, when the Cincinnati Red Stockings became the first club openly to hire players, and in 1876 the National League of Professional Baseball Clubs was organized, with Louisville as one member. Professional status was given recognition elsewhere in the South in 1885 with the formation of teams in Georgia, Alabama, and Tennessee into the Southern League. This, in turn, was replaced by the Southern Association in 1891. After that, numbers of minor leagues were organized, many with their own versions of league playoffs and series, with perhaps the best known being the Dixie Series between the Southern Association and the Texas League (1888). Southerners have long insisted, that their region has been responsible for producing more big league players in proportion to population than any other. From Ty Cobb to Willie Mays to "Hammering Hank" Aaron, a season never passed which did not find a number of stars who claimed the South as their birthplace.

Football was much slower in winning Southern approval. Although the first collegiate games took place in the North in the 1860's, not until the late seventies was it tried below the Potomac, the Alert Football Club at Virginia's Richmond College in 1878 being one of the first. At a time when Ivy League games were drawing as many as 40,000 spectators, football was introduced at the University of Virginia in 1888. Tulane, Washington and Lee, and Georgia Tech began organized programs in the nineties. The game reached Alabama in 1891, and the University and Auburn fielded the first college teams in that state in 1892. In 1894, Texas defeated Texas A&M in the first intercollegiate football game played in the Southwest. Approximately thirty Southern colleges were playing football by 1894, and in that year they organized the Southern Intercollegiate Athletic Association.

By the turn of the century, football was played by most men's colleges. Very little national attention had been attracted, however, except for an occasion like the game in 1890 when Princeton defeated Virginia 115 to 0. The general belief was that the Southern climate was unfavorable to such strenuous activity. Except for momentous upsets, such as Vanderbilt's victory over Carlisle of Pennsylvania in 1906, Virginia's defeat of Yale in 1915, and the even more astonishing success of little Centre College's "Praying Colonels" over Harvard in 1921, Southern colleges had little of which to boast until after World War I. From that time, the center of football power shifted into the South. Throughout the thirties, Southern teams became familiar and were often successful participants in the Rose Bowl in California, the reigning "World Series" of collegiate football.[10]

With the national recognition of Southern football, Southerners embraced the game with such enthusiasm that ethics were sometimes forgotten. "Tramp" athletes, who wandered from school to school without worry about grades and eligibility, gave some institutions the reputation of being "football factories." Under pressure from victory-hungry alumni, often the desire to have a college of which the football players could be proud was forgotten in the pursuit of national ratings and successful seasons. After 1915, football swept the secondary schools, becoming almost a mania. Soon, most of the bad things which forty years earlier had been said about Northern football were true also of the South. As a result, athletic conferences were established at the college, and often lower, level, empowered to police the activities of their members.

Local chambers of commerce quickly found that the Southern climate could make football pay in more tangible forms. Not only were stadiums built, often at relatively small schools, which rivaled any in the country, but the region became the home of the football bowl games, boasting such nationally-known organizations as the Orange, Cotton, Sugar, and Gator bowls, as well as a host of smaller ones. The continued success of collegiate football was evidenced by Southern schools having more than their proportionate share of teams ranked in the top twenty-five on the basis of won-lost records over the past forty years. Although professional football arrived late, by 1974 it could boast seven Southern teams, the Super Bowl Champion, and a strong role in integration. It, like baseball, sought the best players, even in previously ignored black schools, a practice that spread to collegiate ranks.

With the exception of hunting, fishing, and baseball, most recreational sports were like football in that they were slow to win general acceptance in the South. Most Southerners were too busy with the economics of dollar-chasing to consider sports as a proper or needed activity of the adult. Tennis and golf, introduced from the North, reached the lower South in the late 1880's and 1890's respectively. When Montgomery established a golf course in 1898, Savannah, Georgia, was the only Southern city with one. Outside of colleges, golf and tennis were generally viewed as not only on affectation of wealthy Northerners but also as somewhat effeminate. With the development of more wealth

[10] Alexander M. Weyand, *The Saga of American Football* (New York: Macmillan, 1955), pp. 113-122.

and leisure time, the two games proved more attractive, particularly in cities and tourist areas such as Florida. Soon, however, country clubs and park movements made swimming pools, golf courses, and tennis courts an accepted part of the landscape. When Robert T. "Bobby" Jones of Atlanta set the record of winning the American and British Amateur and Open golf championships in 1930, that game was assured of Southern approval. The Depression indirectly gave impetus to such sports when, by 1937, the WPA constructed some 440 municipal swimming pools, 123 golf links, 1,500 athletic fields, and 3,500 tennis courts in the South.

Because the South remained the most rural of all regions and because of its abundance of both fresh and salt water, the traditional sports of hunting, fishing, and boating remained important. A contemporary reported in 1877 that "every man, white or black, rich or poor, aristocrat or plebian" kept a gun and was nearly always a first-class marksman. It was probably not by coincidence that the first national trap-shooting tournament was held in New Orleans in 1886. The spread of good roads and more intelligent game laws made the twentieth-century South the hunting and fishing capital of the nation, attractive to citizens throughout the country. Money and leisure brought boating into an all-time high of popularity. The sporting boat became a status symbol, with the artificial lakes, bayous, and rivers becoming crowded with yachts, sailboats, outboard-motor enthusiasts, and water skiers.

Interest in sports broke down class barriers, even racial ones, as Southerners had the money, time, and inclination to indulge themselves. Thus in play, as in other areas of activity, the years after reconstruction saw the South come more into line with national habits and customs. Recreation was accepted as an integral and necessary part of living and as big business. Yet, even in its acceptance, enough distinctive traits were kept to make its play recognizable as "Southern."

# 18

## RELIGION IN THE SOUTH

A RECOGNIZED HISTORICAL THESIS is that religion can be one of the strongest bonds of nationalism. However, in the United States, the presence of denominations which spread across regional boundaries before the Civil War was not a bond able to withstand the stress of sectional conflict. Under the strain of the slavery controversy, this spiritual link snapped.

Perhaps in the background of this development lay the fact that although the denominations were theoretically united, in essence most denominations contained diversities of opinion that would prove a source of weakness in time of trial. Religion did not play the role in the colonization of the South as it had in the North, and the Anglican Church became the established one in all of the Southern colonies. Dissatisfaction, however, developed, in the "back country" in particular, over the aristocratic tendencies and lack of religious zeal of the Church of England. This fostered the rise of dissenting sects which differed in theology and objected to the favored position of the Anglicans. Therefore, following the Revolution, the separation of church and state in the South was relatively easy to secure. The "Great Revival" of 1800 deeply affected the middle and lower classes of Southern people, strengthening the cause of evangelical Protestantism.

Not only did this revival benefit directly the denominations most involved — Presbyterians, Methodists, and Baptists — but it also strengthened the concept of democracy in religion with its intense emotionalism and its doctrine that salvation was equally open to all. It featured self-trained and lay preachers whose zeal and direct effectiveness more than compensated for the lack of formal schooling in theological doctrines. It made the matter-of-fact presumption that man was morally and spiritually a free agent, responsible for his sins. While obligated to seek salvation, one did so with the assurance that if he were earnest, it would not be denied him, reflecting the needs and outlook of a migratory population that had largely freed itself from the traditions of an educated leadership. Although each denomination theoretically identified itself with the whole of society, actually it tended to serve the needs of a particular stratum. Under this force, the region entered probably its most liberal period. During the 1820's and 1830's, the Unitarian Church expanded in the urban South, while Thomas Jefferson and Dr. Thomas Cooper expressed opinions which would not have been tolerated in other regions, then or even at a much later date. Cooper went so far on one occasion as to refer to the Book of Genesis as a collection of "absurd and frivolous tales." The University of Virginia, handiwork of Jefferson, was deliberately fashioned to break the hold of religion on education.

When, however, the South came under Northern critical attack in the 1830's, it reacted defensively. A great resurgence of religious orthodoxy began to regiment thought to protect Southern vested interests. Dr. Cooper was removed as president of South Carolina College in 1834, and Jefferson's policy of secular instruction was abandoned by the University of Virginia. The 1860 Census showed an almost complete absence of liberal sects. With the Bible and religion used to justify slavery, orthodoxy prevailed. Liberalism brought threats to the *status quo;* therefore, Southern reaction was conservative in religion as well as in politics.

The first cleavage within a church was between Presbyterians over doctrinal issues which were essentially liberal *versus* conservative. By 1850, the Methodists and Baptists had severed connection with their Northern brethren over slavery and established their own organizations. By avoiding the question of human bondage, the Episcopalians held together until the formation of the Confederacy, as did the few Lutherans in the South. Only the Catholics were able to preserve their unity through the ensuing years.

Thus, by 1860 the average Southern church member had long since ceased to feel a common religious tie with his fellow Northern Christians. To him, the North had once been religious and conservative but now was a land of heresies, infidelities, and superstition in the grasp of doctrines subversive of "established tenets respecting religion, law, morality, property and government." The Apostle Paul had described the abolitionists in I Timothy, chapter 6:

> Let as many servants as are under the yoke count their own masters worthy of all honor, that the name of God and his doctrine be not blasphemed. And they that have believing masters, let them not despise them, because they are brethren; but rather do them service because they are faithful and beloved, partakers of the benefit. These things teach and exhort. If any man teach otherwise, and consent not to wholesome words, even the words of our Lord Jesus Christ . . . he is proud, knowing nothing, but doting about questions and strifes of words, whereof come envy, strife, railings, evil surmisings, perverse disputings of men of corrupt minds, and destitute of the truth, supposing that gain is godliness: from such withdraw thyself.

To the Southerner, his Christian duty was clear: "From such withdraw thyself."

The middle and lower classes, or nearly three-fourths of Southern church-goers, in 1860 were Methodists and Baptists. The aristocratic churches were Episcopal and Presbyterian, although the former represented only about five per cent of the church membership. Religion, especially among the masses, was a force of almost medieval intensity, and the churches were active in disciplining members and in enforcing creeds. Given the influence of three decades of orthodoxy, it is easy to understand the ease with which religious leaders led their flocks into support of the War against the anti-Christian Yankees and how even Protestant bishops saw nothing incongruous in laying aside their ecclesiastical robes for the grey uniforms of the Confederacy. In fact, as Professor Sweet wrote, the "Civil War was considered by Church people in both North and South as primarily a moral and religious struggle, and it appealed more strongly to religious zeal than any war in modern times."[1] Thus, religious fanaticism was added to political bigotry to heat the flames of fratricidal war.

The conviction that God was on the side of the South made defeat all the more unintelligible. Some of the faithful, such as Henry W. Ravenel, held that defeat should be accepted as the will of providence or of "the great Umpire of nations." Others viewed it as divine punishment for lack of faith and past sins and wrapped themselves more tightly in the mantle of fundamentalism. God, they comforted themselves, chastens those He loves. Ministers preached that although the proud Yankees seemed dominant, God's will might even yet let the

[1] William Warren Sweet, *The Story of Religion in America,* revised edition (New York: Harper, 1939), p. 470.

South triumph, if it only held true to the faith. In this time of stress, when deliverance was obviously beyond their own power, Southerners clung more closely than ever to religious hope, invariably embracing the more primitive faith of the past as being the safer refuge.

Northern religious emissaries strengthened Southern antagonism by their wartime zeal in deposing Southern brethren and by their postwar attitudes. Basically, the Northern churches felt that since slavery had produced the denominational splits, victory and the death of that institution had proved the righteousness of their cause. There should, therefore, be a religious reconstruction parallel to the political one. Northern insolence and the demand for repentance usually served to check early moves toward reunion. Northern churchmen had not only supported the War but also backed Congress in its Radical reconstruction program, even praying for the conviction of President Johnson. Southerners easily convinced themselves that Northern denominations were "incurably radical" and too politically minded. Particularly resented, also, were the efforts to wean away the Negro membership of white churches. One Northern missionary was even reported to have told his Negro congregation that Jesus Christ was a Republican! Only in the Protestant Episcopal Church did reunion come easily. Slavery had not been the divisive factor, and the national organization had never recognized the withdrawal of their Southern members, keeping their activities during reconstruction more discreet. The prodigals thus were welcomed back without recriminations.

With this exception and that of the Catholic Church, which did not split, Southern denominations faced religious problems similar to those in politics: conflicts between white and Negro and between North and South. Northern sects for a period after the War had the upper hand. During the struggle they had been given special consideration by federal agencies, such as the War Department order surrendering to the Methodist Episcopal Church all buildings of that faith in the South "in which a loyal preacher appointed by a loyal bishop does not officiate." They usually, also, enjoyed the support of the army in their religious and educational activities. Ambitious leaders attempted to extend their ecclesiastical jurisdiction into areas claimed by rival Southern organizations, and while little headway was made among the whites, they were much more successful in wooing the Negroes.

Southern ministers opposed this infringement by increasing their attention to their Negro membership, but in the long run, neither Northern nor Southern whites were able to dominate the Negro religiously. Southern churches tried to keep control by making provision for allied congregations and associations, but this failed to satisfy the

Negro. Separation was of the Negro's choosing, and gradually the local whites decided to aid them — assisting in organization and construction of churches. Catholicism, in particular, suffered as a result of this trend, as there were no Negro priests to serve the new parishes and Southern white Catholics who had previously supported this work were impoverished. Then, too, the Church nationally was more concerned with its immigrant membership of the North than with the Negroes of the South. All in all, however, separation was accomplished with a minimum of racial bitterness, a unique achievement in that period.

This separation of churches was inevitable.[2] No longer were there laws to restrict Negro preachers or forbid separate organizations. Political and economic freedom made religious freedom attractive, also, even if it were not compulsory. Most Negro church members before 1860 had attended white churches, but after the War they began to withdraw and create their own congregations. Freedmen set up in 1865 an organization called the Colored Primitive Baptists in America, and four years later a secession movement from the Presbyterian Church led to the formation of the Colored Cumberland Presbyterian Church. By 1870 five Negro conferences had been organized among the Methodists and the first Negro bishops consecrated.

Not only did the former slaves set up their own churches, but membership also grew by leaps and bounds, spurred on by the knowledge that this was one social institution which they controlled. Their denominational preferences were approximately those of their white neighbors. In general, they were not attracted by the intellectual atmosphere of the Episcopal and Presbyterian faiths but to those sects more marked by emotion and whose form of government made it easier for the members to exercise control. By 1906 the Baptists outnumbered the combined membership of all other Negro denominations as a result of its evangelical work among the poor and the fact that its congregational form made it possible to organize individual churches without reference to any church hierarchy. The most important denominations after the Baptist were the African Methodist Episcopal, African Methodist Episcopal Zion, Colored Methodist Episcopal, Presbyterian, Reformed Episcopal, and Protestant Episcopal. One reason for the increase was exemplified in the zeal of a former slave who organized more than forty churches in thirty years. So numerous were those "called to preach" that Booker T. Washington recalled one Negro congregation of 200 with eighteen ministers. The Census of 1890 showed 860 Negro Baptist churches in South Carolina alone. Ten years earlier,

---

[2] John Hope Franklin, *From Slavery to Freedom: A History of American Negroes* (New York: Knopf, 1948), pp. 305-306.

the denomination had reached the point that the National Baptist Convention had been organized in Montgomery, Alabama.

The church played a vital role in the life of the Negro besides furnishing an outlet for religious expression. In the existing state of social dislocation, it provided a focus for group cohesion and self-help and a sense of belonging. In addition to the opportunity for face-to-face contact, the church became a center for the Negro community, supplying opportunities for recreation and relaxation, and serving as a social arbiter, and its message for many provided escape from the despair of everyday living. The fact that the ministers were usually the race leaders, even in politics, made the fact that separation had come without prior preparation especially significant. Most of the preachers had a minimum of education — as late as 1933, scarcely more than two-fifths had grammar-school training. One nineteenth-century contemporary, speaking of the Negro clergyman, said that he "does his best according to his lights. But the lights are so dim." Considering that the preachers were usually better educated than the flock, "Heaven only knows what diverse, tangled and mistaken ideas and theories these poor darkened minds do extract from the shapeless mass of confused words, sentences and metaphors hurled upon them by their teachers."[3]

The majority of Negro churches were small, unpretentious wooden structures, unpainted or whitewashed, box-like in form, and with gabled roof and a belltower rising above the entrance. The interior was almost painfully sparse, with a few plain wooden benches confronting a home-made pulpit. The cemetery which flanked the building was characterized by boards or small stone markers. In contrast to these drab surroundings, the services were lively and enthusiastic, featuring mass participation in singing, prayers, and sermons. The discourses were highly dramatic, with great emphasis upon "sin" and the "Devil" and strongly against loose sex and drink. The audiences responsded with "Amen," "Preach it," and "Yes, Lord," until sometimes the congregation began "shouting." Since "getting religion" was stressed, the revival played an important role in the church's activities.[4] A white observer wrote in 1898 that the Negroes "sing and shout, and dance the holy dance, and jump over the benches, and have a regular jubilee time." Despite the fact that many whites, especially the more educated, were prone to look with scorn or amusement upon such antics, most of these expressions of piety could be found in rural churches among the poorer whites. Aside from perhaps a greater degree of emotionalism,

[3] As quoted by George Brown Tindall, *South Carolina Negroes, 1877-1900* (Columbia: Univ. of South Carolina, 1952), p. 203.
[4] E. Franklin Frazier, *The Negro in the United States* (New York: Macmillan, 1957), pp. 347-366.

separation had not brought significant religious changes or innovations to the freedman.

The Protestant clergy, both white and Negro, enjoyed an unchallenged position as leaders of the South during the last part of the nineteenth century. Religious zeal was abnormally intensified, and church membership skyrocketed: membership in the Methodist Church alone doubled in the first fifteen years of peace. The decade of the eighties saw this fervor take the form of extraordinary revivals, largely the work of the Baptists and Methodists, who came to claim nearly 90 per cent of all church members in the region. The increased fervor was seen not only in enlarged memberships but also in an astonishing increase in the value of church property, despite the War's destruction and the poverty of the period. Between 1860 and 1890, the value of the property of the Episcopalians and Presbyterians doubled, while that of the Baptists and Methodists quadrupled. The next two decades saw Protestant gains to the degree that every Southern state but four showed a greater increase in communicants than in population. Much of this was due to the Negroes, as their church membership totals grew 40 per cent while the race increased only 31 per cent. This 20-year period saw the white Southern Baptists augmented by 1,003,000, or 78 per cent, and the Methodist Episcopal South by 641,173, or 53 per cent. Total church membership rose from 6,139,023 in 1890 to 9,260,899 in 1906. Given such conditions, it was not surprising that among the professions the South ranked high in only one, the percentage of clergymen per 100,000 of population being 135.6 as compared to a national average of 121.2.

Before the Civil War, scarcely 20 per cent of the Southern people were affiliated with any church; yet after 1865 the Southerner soon found it difficult to believe that any person could be decent in morals and manners who was not a church member. The Puritan overtones of this were evidenced in the increasing "blue laws," rising strength of the prohibition movement, and hostility to secularization of the Sabbath. Just as the churches had been the principal antebellum supporters of the *status quo*, they often became post-war centers of resistance to Northern innovations. At first they opposed the New South but then became its advocates. Although each church might have its individual brand of revealed truth, in general they buttressed a conservative social philosophy with an orthodox theology. This, in turn, enabled them to ignore the social implications of Southern change — problems of the Negro, the sharecropper, and the mill worker.

The insistence on theological and denominational orthodoxy led to numerous small churches and sects, whose numbers increased with every religious controversy. Finding agreement among themselves difficult, that the churches made slow progress toward reunion with the North is not surprising, only the Northern and Southern branches of the Methodist Episcopal Church (1939) emulating the Episcopal. A major reason for this was the domination of the "old-time" religion. Not only was heresy still heresy to most Southerners, but any liberalization was also generally so viewed, especially if it were Northern in origin.

Congregations found additional thrills in denominational competition. With each sect advertising its own special road to Heaven, the revival and camp meeting served an important role in instructing the laity in the fine points of doctrine. This technique, already familiar among the evangelical sects, particularly on the frontier, was strengthened by desire to counteract the post-war moral slump and the rising tide of skepticism. While part of a national religious movement, the Southern phase was more colorful and lasted longer. The rural areas featured the camp meeting, lasting from a week to ten days. The focal point was the tent or "brush arbor" in which the services were held. Families camped around it, living out of wagons and sleeping in tents or lean-tos or under their wagons. The day began for the faithful with a 6 A.M. prayer meeting. After breakfast the song service began and was followed by the morning sermon, attended by people driving in from the surrounding area. The afternoon was free for visiting and doing chores around the camp. The big and popular service came in the evening, when the ceremonies would be conducted by three or four ministers speaking in rotation. The highlight came with the call for repentance and the trip to the mourner's bench by those seeking salvation.

The counterpart of the camp meeting in towns, and even in the country as transportation improved, was the annual revival, or "protracted" meeting. These, too, were usually held about the time that the cotton began to "boll up" and the tobacco was "laid by." Stores closed, and farmers drove into town to hear the visiting evangelist and song leader. Sometimes services would run all day, with dinner on the ground. In both the camp meetings and small-time revivals, it was not unusual for the services and audience to become supercharged with emotion, shouting, speaking in unknown tongues, and "holy rolling."

Some ministers had special talent for these types of services and built up regional and even national reputations. The pre-eminent Northern revivalist Dwight L. Moody was not too popular in the South. His Southern counterpart was Samuel Porter Jones, a pioneer Methodist preacher from Alabama. A pulpit orator of astonishing powers, he became an itinerant preacher throughout the nation. After 1900 he concentrated on the South, where he preached a fiery version of the old-fashioned gospel with a hell for sinners and the joys of Heaven for the righteous. The colorful Billy Sunday was one Northerner who was well-received, although general preference was given to Southerners such as J. Frank Norris of Texas, Mordecai F. Ham of Kentucky, and "Cyclone Mack" McLendon of South Carolina. The Englishman Gypsy Smith, Jr., also had a strong Southern following. Revivalism continued to flourish in the rural South long after it declined elsewhere, and from here came the most renowned Christian evangelist in America and probably the world, Billy Graham of North Carolina, who in 1972 attracted over 75,000 young people to Dallas' "Explo 72."

The religious inclination of the people, plus the conservative orthodoxy, made the South one of the most devout sections of Christendom, with a more homogeneous religious quality than any other region in the United States. Rigid theology, emotionalism, and the emphasis upon individual salvation helped divert attention from the ills of society; further, religion was used to justify social segregation. Drunkenness, however, was a personal sin, and churches organized temperance societies in support of the Anti-Saloon League and the Women's Christian Temperance Union. Local option had its greatest success in the South, and most of its states were totally or in the larger part "dry" before the Eighteenth Amendment.

Only shortly after reconstruction and its accompanying menaces, Southern religion received a challenge which imperiled the very bastion of orthodoxy. The one solid element in many Southerners' lives had been their certainty of the unchanging character of God and His Church. From here had come the strength to face post-war realities. Now, even this "Rock of Ages" was endangered by new findings in research and science. Soon the pious were engaged in one of the recurring conflicts between orthodoxy and heterodoxy, between fundamentalism and modernism, between the old and the new. The dangers came from three areas: science, Biblical criticism and the study of comparative religions, and the "social gospel," which disputed the role of the church in this world. The "new science" seemed to attack the validity of the Bible, especially the story of creation and the miracles. Some churchmen argued that religion and science occupied mutually exclusive areas, others that the Bible if properly interpreted actually supported the findings of science; still others saw no possibility for coexistence. Textual criticism, with its rigorous historical analysis, showed the conglomerate nature of the Bible and seemed to question its infallibility and the belief in verbal inspiration. New knowledge of other religions, especially Oriental, indicated that all good was not a monopoly of Protestantism.

Since the majority of Southerners were originally unmoved by these intellectual waves, the chief battlegrounds were in the colleges. In 1878 geologist Alexander Winchell was dismissed from Methodist Vanderbilt for his belief that man existed before Adam's creation. The Tennessee Methodist Conference denounced him as an emissary of "scientific atheism" and "untamed speculation." C. H. Toy was soon afterwards forced to resign from the Southern Baptist Seminary at Louisville, Kentucky, for his interpretation of the Old Testament. In 1884 Heidelberg-educated Dr. James Woodrow was removed from the Presbyterian Theological Seminary at Columbia, South Carolina, for believing, among other things, that the Bible did not teach science. This removal on the grounds of heresy was supported by the General Assembly of the Southern Presbyterian Church. Sam Jones and other ministers attacked Lyell's geology and Darwin's evolution with vigor. A revision of the New Testament in 1881 and of the Old Testament four years later to "adapt the King James' Version" to new findings in Biblical scholarship and changes in the English language was likewise denounced for the changed readings and, in some instances, changed meanings as an effort to undermine the inspiration of the Bible and its inerrancy. In the words of W. J. Cash, "Darwin, Huxley, Sherman, Satan – all these came to figure in Southern feeling as very nearly a single person."

The increased tendency toward liberalism was balanced by factional splits, establishment of new sects, and the creation of "Bible Institutes" to teach "Fundamentals." Fundamentalists were those who proclaimed certain traditional doctrines as fundamentals of the Christian faith. They held to the inerrancy of the Scriptures, believing the literal truth of the miracles and repudiating any teaching which seemed to disagree. The Modernists (or Liberals) were those who tried to reconcile their beliefs with scientific thought, discarding those that were out of date but retaining that which was essential and intellectually respectable. The Fundamentalists complained that the Liberals sapped religion by interpreting it symbolically in a manner never intended by the church fathers.

These two forces met in titanic battle in the years following World War I. Throughout the United States, this era of the "lost generation" was characterized by its challenges to the *status quo*. In the South it was a period of uprooted emotions, as conservative Southerners reacted in blind anger to all that seemed to threaten their world, the Ku Klux Klan being but one of their weapons. For many, Modernism extended far beyond its religious connotations. Coupled with the new Darwinian science was the "social gospel," which contained implications alien to an individualistic agrarian society. In the past, Protestant ministers had refrained from politics and direct action in social reform. The new concept that the church had a responsibility for prevailing ills not only ran counter to past practice but also violated the tenet that problems and sins were personal, not social.

The field of science was most vulnerable in the South. Only since 1900 had public education won acceptance, with science incorporated even later. Both areas lacked the security of position conferred by institutional maturity. Liberal professors and denominational schools were attacked first. The Southern Baptist Convention of 1922, for example, stated, "One can understand the Bible and evolution and believe one of them, but he cannot understand both and believe both." The Fundamentalists then turned on tax-supported education, as illiterates and the semi-educated put pressure upon their legislators to outlaw the teaching of evolution or face the loss of the powerful rural vote.

William Jennings Bryan lobbied for anti-evolution laws in one Southern state after another. Nearly half of the states of the Union had bills introduced to bar the teaching of evolution (thirty-seven bills in twenty legislatures between 1921 and 1929), but the real marks were made in the South. Through interdenominational organizations such as the Bible Crusaders of America, the Anti-Evolutionist League, the Bryan Bible League, and the World's Christian Fundamentals Association, they sought to hold firm to Scriptural literalism.[5] The years 1921-1922 saw such measures fail by one vote in the Kentucky house and struck out by a joint committee after unanimous passage by the senate in South Carolina. Such legislation was introduced by Georgia (approved by committee but failed to reach the floor), Florida, Alabama, Texas, West Virginia (defeated by popular vote), and Oklahoma in 1923. Florida passed a resolution condemning the teaching of Darwinism but provided no penalty for offenders; the Texas bill passed the lower house by better than two to one but died in the upper house.[6]

In February, 1923, Oklahoma house bill 197, providing an educational appropriation to buy school books, was amended to state that no text should be adopted "that teaches the 'Materialistic Conception of History' (i.e.) The Darwin Theory of Creation vs. the Bible Account of Creation." The prevailing mood was expressed by Representative J. L. Watson, who declared that he had "promised my people at home that if I had a chance to down this hellish Darwin here that I would do it. . . . If you want to be a monkey, go out and be a monkey, but I am for this amendment and will strike this infernal thing while I can." The measure passed the house by 87 to 2 to the applause of the

[5] Kenneth K. Bailey, "The Enactment of Tennessee's Antievolution Law," *Journal of Southern History*, XVI (November, 1950), pp. 472-490.
[6] Virginius Dabney, *Liberalism in the South* (Chapel Hill: Univ. of North Carolina, 1932), pp. 288-298.

Oklahoma Baptist Sunday School convention. The senate concurred, 29 to 7, to make Oklahoma the first state to pass such legislation, but the next year a bill to fine those who taught that man descended from a lower order of animals was defeated, 46 to 30, in the lower house. In 1923 the Baptist State Convention voted also to withhold funds from their institutions which failed to repudiate evolution.[7]

In 1924 and 1925, Congress prohibited the teaching of "disrespect for the Bible" in Washington, D. C., schools, and Arkansas Baptists provided that no one, even janitors, that believed in evolution would be hired by their institutions. State boards of education in North Carolina, Georgia, and Texas barred teaching of evolution in 1925 after efforts to achieve this objective by law had failed. Simultaneously, the issue was raised in Florida, South Carolina, West Virginia, and Tennessee, but only in Tennessee was there success. Despite such comments as that "the missing link . . . might be found near Capital Hill," the measure passed the Tennessee house, 71 to 5, and the senate, 24 to 6, making it unlawful to teach "any theory that denies the story of the divine creation of man as taught in the Bible, and to teach instead that man has descended from a lower order of animals," on penalty of from $100 to $500 and dismissal.

John T. Scopes, a young instructor at the Dayton, Tennessee, high school, together with some friends decided to test the law by a deliberate violation, with one of the conspirators acting as accuser. Upon his arrest, the World's Christian Fundamental Association brought Bryan in to help with the prosecution; Scopes' liberal supporters chose Clarence Darrow, one of the country's most successful defense attorneys and an avowed agnostic, for the defense. The Civil Liberties Union furnished two additional counselors. The ensuing trial attracted international attention: over one hundred newspapermen poured into the small village, Western Union furnished twenty-two telegraph operators who sent out over 2,000,000 words of coverage, and the proceedings were covered by motion picture cameramen and broadcast by station WGN of Chicago.[8]

Almost from the very beginning, the trial took on many of the characteristics of a vaudeville performance. Bryan announced that the event would be "a duel to the death between Christianity and evolution," while Darrow retorted that "Civilization and not a school teacher is on trial." On the day that Bryan was placed on the stand as an authority on the Bible, the crowd was so great that court was held

[7] This account of Oklahoma's anti-evolutionary experience is based primarily upon research done by Elbert Watson, Gadsden, Alabama; see also R. Halliburton, Jr., "The Nation's First Anti-Darwin Law: Passage and Repeal," *Southwestern Social Science Quarterly*, XLI (September, 1960), pp. 123-135.
[8] Frederick Lewis Allen, *Only Yesterday* (New York: Harper, 1931), 201-206.

out-of-doors. Bryan affirmed his belief in the literal details of the Bible but was forced into the admission that he had studied no other religions, knew little science, had formed his opinions as a boy, and was willing to legislate matters of conscience and to jail men because of religious beliefs. The exchanges were so violent that Darrow was fined for contempt of court, and the remarks between the two were stricken from the record. To those who took their religion lightly, the reaction was that God may not have made man out of a monkey but that Darrow did make a monkey out of Bryan.

The trial ended the next day, July 21, with the foregone verdict that Scopes was guilty, and he was fined $100. Bryan and the Fundamentalists had won, but it was a costly victory. They had been made to appear before the world as bigots and ignoramuses. When Bryan died four days later, he was hailed as a Christian martyr and, as noted before, entered the folklore of the Southern mountaineers.

Blind to shifting public opinion, the Fundamentalists stepped up the attack. Itinerant ministers spoke from courthouse steps in hot, sleepy county-seat towns to audiences of visiting farmers, Negro idlers, and little boys. They challenged the believers in evolution to cease praying "My Father which art in Heaven" and intone instead "My heavenly Father up a coconut tree." In 1926 the Southern Baptist Convention passed a resolution declaring that "this convention accepts Genesis as teaching that man was the special creation of God and rejects every theory, evolution or otherwise, which teaches that man originated in or came by way of a lower animal ancestry." The same year, Mississippi adopted such a measure despite one opponent's proposed amendment to make the penalty for teaching evolution "death by burning at the stake, it being the spirit of this bill to restore the Spanish inquisition." In 1927 such bills were unsuccessfully introduced in Alabama, Arkansas, Florida, Louisiana, Missouri, North Carolina, and Oklahoma (the 1923 law had been repealed in 1926). Such measures came up in 1928 in Kentucky and Arkansas, the latter adopting an anti-evolution law by popular referendum by a vote of 108,000 to 63,000. However, although spasmodic efforts to secure such legislation continued, Southerners reconciled themselves to living with science, and religious leaders found more pressing foes, especially Catholicism, as epitomized by the candidacy of Alfred E. Smith for the presidency.

Historically, the South was more anti-Catholic than anti-Semitic. Despite the fact that Catholics made up only a fraction of the religious population of the South, traditionally they were the least Southern of all Southerners — the French in Louisiana, the Mexicans in Texas, and city immigrants. Louisiana was the only Southern state in which the Protestants were in a minority. In 1868, out of a population of over

1,000,000, North Carolina had only 800 Catholics. Two years later Georgia, with over 2,500 Baptist and Methodist churches, had but 14 Roman Catholic edifices, and only Kentucky, Louisiana, and Maryland had as many as 100. Catholics furnished a mere 769,973 members out of a total church membership of 6,682,615 in fifteen Southern states in 1890, and in Louisiana alone did they have a majority (56 per cent). By 1916, when nationally one of every three church members was Catholic, in the South the ratio was one in twelve, and only in Louisiana had they made a gain in percentage. While Southern Catholic membership increased 288,000 during the next decade, affiliation with all churches rose nearly 2,500,000. By 1936, when Catholic communicants numbered 2,000,000, total church membership was 13,500,000. By 1970 the Church claimed 6,290,000 adherents in sixteen states and the District of Columbia, but Roman Catholics still comprised only 35.5 per cent of the total population of Louisiana and ranged between 5.7 and 1.2 in such Protestant strongholds as Virginia, the Carolinas, Georgia, Alabama, Mississippi, and Arkansas.

One of the principal objections to foreign immigrants had been their Catholicism. But immigrants in the South were few and usually isolated, and the comparatively small total of the resident Catholic population kept anti-Catholicism at a low level. For example, only a small number of Southerners joined the American Protective Association, organized in the Midwest in 1886. By 1910, however, some leaders, such as Tom Watson, were crying in alarm at what they considered papal threats to the United States. Watson, who was said to have spent $200,000 fighting the Pope, was one of the founders of the Protestant-nativist Guardians of Liberty in 1912. By the first World War, the entire country was swept by a wave of anti-Catholic feeling. In the South the movement was not only characterized by the violent words of Watson but by such events as the election in 1916 of a professional anti-Catholic, Sidney J. Catts, as governor of Florida (24,000 Catholics out of a church population of 324,000), and Georgia's (18,000 out of 1,000,000) enactment of the Veazey Convent Inspection Act to supervise convents and monasteries.

This antagonism undoubtedly was partially responsible for the rise and spread of the second Ku Klux Klan. Professing to be a Christian Protestant organization, it worked closely with the more fundamentalist denominations, often receiving open or tacit support of individual clergymen, with as many as sixteen Protestant ministers serving as officials.[9] The Klan's anti-Catholic teaching bore fruit even after the

[9] Robert M. Miller, "A Note on the Relationship between the Protestant Churches and the Revised Ku Klux Klan," *Journal of Southern History*, XXII (August, 1956), pp. 355-368.

parent organization weakened and virtually vanished, seen in the frenzy in 1928 over Al Smith's nomination: he was not only a Catholic but also a "wet," enough to stir the most lethargic Fundamentalist into action. The campaign in the South, led by Bishop James Cannon, Jr., of the Methodist Church, turned primarily on these two issues, with the Methodist Preachers' Association in Atlanta adopting the resolution: "You cannot nail us to a Roman cross or submerge us in a sea of rum." The fact that the first significant break in the "Solid South" came with the revolt of seven states from the Democratic ranks was not without significance.

Anti-Semitism was not dominant, despite Watson's being a frenzied anti-Semitic by 1913 and the Klan's opposition to Jews. The South had relatively few Jews, ranging according to a 1956 report from 3.4 per cent of the population in Maryland to 0.1 in North Carolina, Mississippi, and Arkansas — certainly not enough to constitute a Jewish problem in any rational minds. There were, of course, the facts that these people were traditional scapegoats and that they refused to be assimilated in a region which demanded conformity. There was also the element of economic competition. Nevertheless, aside from isolated cases of persecution, anti-Semitism made little headway, even in Watson's home state of Georgia (0.5 per cent), and the region's record in this form of intolerance is good.

Despite the apparent strength of the Fundamentalist organizations, it was soon obvious that their most radical stands had been discredited in the eyes of the educated. By the 1930's, liberal ministers were beginning to raise their voices against using orthodoxy as a cloak for reaction. A majority of the high-ranking theological professors and city ministers were Modernist, reconciled to science; they emphasized a "social gospel" of religious responsibility for world conditions. This development did not, however, imply the decline of orthodoxy. It merely meant that the region saw no need for the old militant organizations outside of the church. All of the churches, rural and urban, faced continued pressures, especially from their younger members, for liberalization of their approach — shorter sermons, less theology, and more tolerance toward dancing, smoking, card playing, and the like. Yet in many ways the tendency remained of preaching the New Testament while living by the narrower tenets of the Old.

Moreover, not until 1970 was the anti-evolution law finally killed—by action of the Mississippi supreme court. (Missouri in 1959 considered banning the teaching of evolution as a "fact.") "Bible colleges," following the Genesis account of creation, were established in the South but made almost no impact upon Southern thought. Camp meetings, brought up-to-date with public address systems and air conditioning, still had their attractions. Yet the public made at least an uneasy peace with two other traditional enemies: liquor and the Catholics. A Gallup Poll in 1940 showed that 51 per cent of the Southerners interviewed would vote for a Catholic for president, while eight per cent answered "don't know." Fifteen years later, the percentages were 53 and 12, respectively. Those opposed expressed their fear of a Catholic spoils system, with the "Catholics getting all the jobs," and of "the Pope running the country for us." But in 1960, Southern votes for John F. Kennedy, a Catholic, helped in his victorious election. Alcoholic beverages also were legalized in one form or another in all of the Southern states by the end of the sixties. Thus was largely ended another social contradiction — that of voting "dry" and drinking "wet" and the political alliance on this issue of ministers and bootleggers.

The religious inclination of the Southern people, such a dominant unifying force in the nineteenth century, persisted powerfully into the twentieth. The forces of industry, science, and urbanization, which were responsible for declining church attendance elsewhere, actually assisted the expansion of Protestantism below the Mason-Dixon Line. Scientific conflicts made the Southerner feel that he could not be neutral in what was viewed as a fight between good and evil, leading him to identify himself with a church. The great wave of industrialization which swept the South was often church-encouraged and brought into Southern cities and factories, not immigrant hordes as in the North, but tens of thousands of native, rural people — a group strongly imbued with the "old-time" gospel. The collecting of these into compact masses made possible religious activity heretofore largely denied because of isolation.

According to the Census of Religious Bodies issued in 1926, Protestants in the prior twenty years experienced a greater rate of growth in the South than in any other region, the Southern Baptists showing a greater expansion than any other of the major churches. Denominational lines held firm, however, and sectional suspicion remained strong. Each sect undertook to supply college training for its constituency, and factionalism was represented by the existence of six kinds of Baptists, seven of Presbyterians, and so on. Actually without exaggeration, only the illiterates and the badly isolated in Southern society — white and Negro — had failed to identify themselves with some church, and the eventual progress of education and roads increased the harvest among those unredeemed.

By the 1930's, the ministry lost much of its position of leadership, and many churches became vestry- or deacon-dominated. But even the concessions made to modernism failed to shake the church as one of the more powerful conservative forces in the region, reflecting the attitudes of its membership. Social distinctions were accepted, and certain classes joined particular churches. There was also class distinction within denominations, especially in cities, leading to rival congregations of the same faith. The lower classes, neglected by the more respected sects, found refuge in pre-millennial cults such as the Holiness Church, founded in Tennessee in 1907. Climbing the social ladder via church membership became a common Southern practice.[10] Edward McNeill Poteat, Jr., in 1935 classified the major Southern denominations thus: the Episcopalians were few and the aristocrats; the Presbyterians, more numerous, were the Bourbons; and the teeming Baptists and Methodists were the proletarians.[11] Yet despite ecclesiastical differences, the basic social philosophy of Southern churches was the same.

These characteristics knew no color line. As has been seen, Negroes flocked into churches in even greater percentages than did their white neighbors. By 1936 there were 23,744 Negro churches in the rural South and 9,486 in its cities. More than two-thirds were Baptists, and most of the rest Methodists. Their progressives, too, suffered from dissatisfaction with their leadership and Biblical interpretations. As social distinctions developed within the race, they were reflected by withdrawals from the Baptists and Methodists and union with the Presbyterians and Episcopalians. The lowest classes set up new denominations and made one indirect contribution to the national religious scene when, in 1932, George Baker of Georgia, a Negro evangelist, entered Harlem as Father Divine, and his "Peace, it's wonderful" became a part of America's vocabulary. Gunnar Myrdal found in 1944 that Negro churches in the South stressed the glories of Heaven rather than the faults of earth, largely ignoring the practical problems of their members. Yet their appeal was strong. Savannah, Georgia, for example, had 47,000 Negroes, ninety churches, 100 active preachers, and another 100 "Jack legs."[12]

By 1930 the Southeast had 61.4 per cent of its adult population enrolled in some denomination, and the Southwest 48.3. With 19.7 per cent of the national adult population, the South had 33.4 per cent of the adult Protestant church membership and 22.3 per cent of total church membership. There were more smaller churches, an average congregation numbering 137, compared to the national average of 235. They also had a better record of financial contributions to their denominations on the basis of personal income than did the membership of any other region.

The *Yearbook of American Churches, 1937* showed the Southern Baptists as the largest single group of non-Catholics in the nation. Of

[10] Francis B. Simkins, "The Rising Tide of Faith" in Rubin and Kilpatrick, *op. cit.,* pp. 92-103.
[11] Edwin McN. Poteat, Jr., "Religion in the South" in Couch, *op. cit.,* pp. 251-266.
[12] Myrdal, *op. cit.,* pp. 873-877.

its factions, the Primitive Baptists, sometimes called "Hardshell," had 103,135 communicants and 2,700 churches. In the following chart, the major denominations are listed:

MEMBERSHIP IN MAJOR SOUTHERN CHURCHES, 1936

| Denomination | Members | Clergymen | Buildings |
|---|---|---|---|
| Southern Baptist | 4,389,417 | 21,917 | 24,537 |
| Methodist Episcopal | 2,751,354 | 7,790 | 16,245 |
| Presbyterian | 477,465 | 2,460 | 3,541 |

Twenty years later, the same source showed that church membership had continued the long-established habit of growing faster than the whole population. The Methodists had reunited in 1939, but the Baptists, with the national record for new church construction, had 30,340 buildings and a membership of 8,467,439, an increase of 2.9 per cent over the previous year (total membership of all religious bodies in the United States increased nine-tenths of one per cent the same year). The Southern Presbyterians had 3,853 churches and 810,917 communicants, and the Roman Catholics 2,177 buildings and 3,563,317 members. Splinter groups were also increasing. For example, the Apostolic Overcoming Holy Church of God (Negro), incorporated in Alabama in 1919, had 75,000 members. The Assemblies of God, begun in Hot Springs, Arkansas, in 1914, had 400,047, and the Church of God in Christ, originated in the same state in 1895, claimed 343,928 members. The area was still basically Protestant. While a survey made by the Bureau of the Census in 1957 showed that Protestants over fourteen years of age were a minority nationally, in the South they composed a majority of 82.8 per cent.[13]

In 1972 the Baptists, with 27,309,000 members, were the largest Protestant denomination in the United States, and within that denomination, the Southern Baptists accounted for nearly half—11,827,000—not including the Negroes' National Baptist Convention, U.S.A., Inc., with 6,487,000 members, and the approximately 2,000,000 that belonged to splinter groups. In the preceding decade, more than 1,000 new members had been baptized every day, and in 1972 the Southern Baptists had 34,441 churches, worth more than $2 billion, and ran seven seminaries, forty-four colleges and universities, and twelve academies and Bible schools. In addition, they were supporting thirty-six hospitals, nineteen old people's homes, and 2,500 foreign missionaries, and were engaged in publishing twenty-three weeklies and scores of monthly and quarterly magazines.

In many respects, however, religion in the South had come to a

[13] "Church News," *Christian Herald*, LXXI (April, 1958), p. 13; "State of the Church," *ibid.*, LXXI (October, 1958), p. 13.

cross-road. The older denominations enjoyed wealth and prestige un-paralleled in their history; yet these very things brought threats to their security. Prosperity caused envy and complacency among the members. Moreover, in the influx of industrial management, much of it Northern, came new and aggressive church members who often grew dissatisfied with evasive Southern church leadership. At the same time, the migration of poor and uneducated countrymen to towns and cities created pressure for less sophisticated churches. Eventually, the status-conscious churches simply abandoned these people and followed the elite to the suburbs, leaving the city proper to the various pente-costal groups.

In all areas of human relations, the Southern church was con-fronted by problems inherent in the changing South. Often the way out was to ignore the issues by concentrating on expanded recreational and educational programs or by focusing missionary zeal on the plight of African natives or Oriental children. At least these objectives seemed safer and more exciting than the distasteful problems of city slums, in-dustrial strife, and explosive racial relationships. The Southern black indeed posed a dilemma with his insistence that desegregation be viewed as a moral as well as a social problem. Although historically the black church had been conservative, in the sixties and seventies it became a powerful institution for social change. The Southern Christian Leadership Conference and Nobel laureate, Martin Luther King, Jr., introduced a program of passive resistance which greatly affected events concerning segregation.

The period after 1950 was indeed a time of philosophical and social upheaval in all Southern churches. For years some white de-nominations and ministers had taken forthright stands on the church's responsibility to meet the new social problems. After the 1954 Supreme Court decision on school integration, the representative bodies of every major religious group in the South made some pronouncement in support of the Court's position. Later events proved that sometimes they were ahead of their membership. There were instances of out-right revolt by individual congregations and removal of ministers for their support of integration. Gallup polls between 1959 and 1970 show regularity of Southern church attendance declining from 51 per cent to 44 per cent, second to the Midwest's 47 per cent in 1970. That same year, however, Southern college students led the nation when 50 per cent declared that organized religion was a relevant part of their lives. Thus, as a projection, it would seem safe to assume that religion would remain one of the most significant elements in retaining the distinctiveness of the South.[14]

14 Simkins, "The Rising Tide of Faith," pp. 92-103.

# 19

## THE BACKWARD SOUTH

"BACKWARD" IS AN EPITHET which has long been applied to the South by reformers and liberals who despair of the conservative and retrospective attitude of the Southern people. How unique and applicable this label is can only be shown by the cold logic of history and actual facts and figures. The various causes for such denunciations have all existed at one time or another outside the region. The same conditions which fostered child labor, lynching, convict-lease systems, race riots, and demagoguery, to mention only some of the more commonly denominated examples of "backwardness," were American rather than Southern in origin, but because they were coexistent in the South in the period after the Civil War, Northern criticism focused upon them as distinctly Southern.

As shown earlier, one of the issues upon which the North was bitterly outspoken in the closing decades of the nineteenth and early years of the twentieth centuries was that of child labor.[1] Ignored was the fact that Northerners themselves were far from blameless in this respect and that it was a national rather than regional problem. Child labor was a part of early stages of manufacturing and usually declined sharply, if it did not disappear, with the coming of industrial maturity.

[1] For a discussion of this condition in the South, see chapter XI.

Only slowly was it recognized that what was needed was a joint national program to protect children from exploitation throughout the country.

Even more a subject for censure was the prevalence of the practice of lynching in the South. Traditionally, lynching was a frontier method of justice which existed only in the absence of courts, with the victim usually being given the semblance of a trial. Modern versions, however, were perpetrated in settled regions where there were courts; yet there were no trials, the accused was assumed to be guilty, and the penalty was usually death, often accompanied by torture. Lynchings after 1865 had racial connotations which made the practice more closely identifiable with the South. Before that time, however, of the more than 300 persons said to have been hanged or burned by mobs in the United States between 1840 and 1860, less than 10 per cent were Negroes. Mob action of this sort was taken against the abolitionists in both North and South, as witness the Boston attack upon William Lloyd Garrison, the assaults upon James G. Birney by the citizens of Cincinnati, and the Illinois murder of Elijah Lovejoy. Joseph Smith, the Mormon leader, also fell before a mob.

In the 100 years after the Civil War, the South was the chief culprit and the Negro the principal victim of lynching. While the excessive lawlessness during reconstruction is hard to classify as lynching, the practice rose steadily in the two decades after 1880, stabilizing around 1910 and beginning a steady decline about 1922. Figures vary considerably according to source and definition of what constitutes a lynching. According to a tally kept by the Chicago *Tribune,* there were 3,337 unofficial executions between 1885 and 1903, representing every state except New Hampshire, Vermont, Rhode Island, and Utah. Of these the South had 2,585, the West 632, and the East and Midwest 120. For the decade 1890-1899, some 87 per cent of such offenses were in the South, and 72 per cent of the total number of victims were Negroes. Statistics collected by Tuskegee Institute show that a national total of 4,730 persons were lynched between 1882 and 1952; 1,987 of these lost their lives in the twentieth century. The annual national total dropped below ten only after 1935 and then virtually disappeared. Even the passion-ridden civil rights disorders of the 1960's produced few cases of the types of violence that have historically been defined as lynchings.

Many efforts have been made to explain this social aberration, which for over a century amounted almost to a national characteristic. One defense was that lynching naturally grew out of the frontier spirit — red-blooded Americans just naturally take the law into their own hands. As indicated above, however, the conditions under which post-

Civil War lynchings took place showed little resemblance to those of the frontier.

SELECTED LYNCHINGS IN THE UNITED STATES, 1882-1952

| Location | White Victims | Negro Victims |
|---|---|---|
| United States | 1,293 | 3,437 |
| Mississippi | 40 | 534 |
| Georgia | 39 | 491 |
| Texas | 141 | 352 |
| Louisiana | 56 | 335 |
| Alabama | 48 | 299 |
| Colorado | 66 | 2 |
| Nebraska | 52 | 5 |
| Indiana | 33 | 14 |
| California | 41 | 2 |
| Illinois | 15 | 19 |
| Arizona | 31 | 0 |
| Ohio | 10 | 16 |
| Minnesota | 5 | 4 |
| Oregon | 20 | 1 |

The most common defense offered in cases of Southern lynchings was the protection of white women from sex crimes. This is refuted, however, by the fact that murder was the victim's alleged crime in almost twice as many cases as was rape, the latter being the excuse in only a fourth of the occasions. In the year 1914, for example, of fifty-two lynchings, only seven (two white and five Negro), or 13 per cent, were charged with crimes against women, and three of the lynched parties were female.[2] Other charges were widely scattered, including such things as arson, rioting, plotting uprisings, maiming, robbery, and such trival things as slapping a white child and bringing suit against a white person. Women, themselves, discredited the sex pretext by forming anti-lynching societies and denouncing this form of protection.

A more logical explanation was the unreasoning fear of the Negro, especially in the South, and the widely-held belief that he was more prone to give vent to his animal passions, especially against the whites. Undoubtedly, much of the hatred of the Negro which broke out in the form of lynching parties and race riots stemmed from the fact that

[2] For a breakdown of reasons given in that year for lynchings, see University Committee on Southern Race Questions, "Open Letters, January 5, 1916," in *Negro Pamphlets,* III. University of Virginia Library.

after 1865 the race became the symbol of defeat in the war and of exploitation during reconstruction. Caught up in emotions of terror and despair, such events were attempts of self-reassurance by performing the ritual of white supremacy. Race hatred magnified the Negro's offenses, whether serious or trivial. Growing out of this was a quick and passionate resentment by the whites against any gesture of the Negro toward equality.

Although some foreign observers wrote off such affairs as proof of the sadism among Americans, the answer, at least in the South, lay in more tangible things. In a region where educational standards were practically nonexistent, there was a corresponding ignorance of law and social justice. During the period of highest incidence of Southern lynchings, incomes were low, archaic political systems were in a state of collapse, and economic competition between the races was becoming acute for the first time. Inept public officials, poor and ineffective social institutions and legislative programs, malnutrition, disease, and crime — all combined to prevent a proper respect for the agencies of the law. Because of such conditions, large segments of the Southern population were incapable of understanding or respecting the majesty of law. Common justifications offered by a community which had instigated a lynching were the weakness of the courts, the delays and legal chicaneries, uncertainty of the jury system, and weak and insecure jails.

The University Commission on Southern Race Questions declared in 1916, "Lynching is a contagious social disease." The South after the Civil War certainly furnished ideal conditions for its spread. Poverty and fear formed background factors, for the actual participants in lynching mobs were usually members of the frustrated lower strata of Southern whites. In general, most lynchings did not take place in the "Black Belt" counties but in those where the Negroes were a minority, especially where they numbered less than one-fourth of the population. It was also mainly a rural and small-town act; it occurred more frequently in poor districts, although after 1914, lynchings in any Southern town of more than 10,000 people, regardless of location, became practically nonexistent. The trivial justifications assigned in many cases indicate that, in principal, lynching was often more than punishment of an individual: it was a disciplinary move against the whole Negro race. Fear of being economically displaced by the Negro was mixed with a social fear: the dark race was "getting out of its place" and threatening white supremacy. These facts, plus the isolation and dullness of everyday life in rural and small towns, provided the tinder for lynchings.[3]

Although factually untrue, the desire to protect white women from

[3] Southern Commission on the Study of Lynching, *Lynchings and what they Mean* (Atlanta, 1931), pp. 12-14, 28, 31.

attack by Negroes was the most common justification given for lynching in the South. Men who denounced the crime for any other cause still often supported it in such cases. Typical of this argument was that offered by Ben Tillman of South Carolina, who delighted in telling Chautauqua audiences that the African was biologically inferior, incapable of assimilating white culture, and must therefore be kept in an inferior caste to prevent racial amalgamation. He boasted that, although as governor of South Carolina he had taken an oath to support the law, "I would lead a mob to lynch any man, white or black, who ravished a woman, black or white." To Tillman, such a culprit put himself outside both human and divine law, and white women were in "a state of siege," surrounded by black beasts. Education, sponsored by Northerners, stimulated impossible ambitions, fostering discontent and leading to crime. As late as 1903, he saw a "war of the races" as inevitable.[4]

Although eventually economic and social conditions improved and Southern public opinion forced a rapid decline in lynching totals, the number of race riots increased, giving some validity to Tillman's assertion. Early post-Civil War race riots had been restricted almost wholly to the South, such as the Memphis and New Orleans incidents and the famous conflicts in Cainhoy and Hamburg, South Carolina. These were the results of animosities growing immediately out of the War and the first chaotic years of freedom. Later, friction was caused by political conflict, inequality before the law, economic frustration, and the general failure of the Southern agrarian system. A notorious riot scare in 1882 was the Jack Turner incident in Alabama, when a group of Negroes planned a surprise attack upon the white population. The secretary of this group lost his minute book, which fell into white hands. The plotters were hanged, but fear of an uprising continued. The famous clash in Wilmington, North Carolina, in 1898 was born of a hot white-supremacy political campaign and editorials by a Negro editor suggesting that many of the Negroes lynched for rape had actually been caught in clandestine love affairs with white women.

The drive for political disfranchisement of the Negro at the turn of the century made race relations critical. In August, 1904, the Statesboro riot in Georgia took place against a background of hatred and suspicion. The immediate occasion was the conviction of two Negroes for murder of a white family, fanned by such claims as that of one newspaper editor that Negro Mafia societies existed in the state. Feelings ran high, and two Negro women were whipped for allegedly crowding white women off the sidewalk. A rumor that the Negroes in the community were planning to free the murderers led to their seizure

[4] Francis B. Simkins, "Ben Tillman's View of the Negro," *Journal of Southern History*, III (May, 1937), pp. 161-174.

by a mob and being burned alive. This was a signal for wholesale terrorism, in which houses were wrecked and Negroes were attacked without discrimination.

The next most sensational event was the Atlanta riot of September, 1906. The city was booming, a magnet for both whites and Negroes from surrounding areas. *The Clansman,* based on a lurid reconstruction novel by Thomas Dixon, was being performed in the city. A heated campaign to disfranchise the Negroes had just ended in Georgia, and a crime wave existed for which the Negroes were chiefly blamed. Yellow journalism was at a peak, as the *Journal* and *Evening News* struggled for subscribers. One editor called for a revival of the Ku Klux Klan, and another offered a reward for a "lynching bee." One night the *Evening News* issued a series of extras about a supposed case of rape. On Saturday, September 22, newspapers told of four successive assaults on white women. Panicky residents, joined by country folk in town for the day, blindly attacked every Negro they could find, and for several days the city was virtually paralyzed as the riot progressed.

Up until 1900, race riots were confined almost entirely to the South, the home of 90 per cent of the Negro population. The years of the First World War, however, saw Negroes moving in large numbers to the industrial centers of the North and West, causing a steady increase in racial friction of all sorts, beginning with a major conflict in East St. Louis, Illinois, in July, 1917; during the preceding year and a half, about 18,000 Negroes had moved into the town. The same month saw a three-day riot in Chester, Pennsylvania; in August, Negro troops and white policemen were the principals in a bloody conflict in Houston, Texas. The year 1918 was relatively quiet, but the return of international peace brought new disorders on the home front. Seventy Negroes were lynched in 1919, some still in uniform, and there were twenty-five race riots in such scattered urban centers as Washington, Chicago, Omaha, Knoxville, Longview, Texas, and Elaine, Arkansas. The Southern episodes were sparked by such things as the report by a Negro schoolteacher to a Chicago newspaper of a local lynching, the death of a white woman who fell while fleeing from a Negro, and the efforts by Negro tenants to organize and force fair crop settlements. After a relatively quiet year in 1920, the next was scarred by a major riot in Tulsa, Oklahoma, which saw ten whites and twenty-one Negroes killed, 10,000 Negroes made homeless, and property loss of over $1,000,000.

World War II brought a renewed outbreak of major race riots, totaling eight in the nation between 1942 and 1946.[5] These were lo-

[5] *Negro Yearbook, 1941-1946* (Atlanta, 1947), pp. 232-255.

cated in Detroit, Michigan (two); Mobile, Alabama; Beaumont, Texas; Los Angeles, California; Harlem, New York; Columbia, Tennessee; and Athens, Alabama. Like those following the First World War, they were largely the result of increased economic competition from large numbers of Negroes moving into an area, in addition to a general feeling that the Negroes were "getting out of their place" in a segregated society, and just pure racial prejudice. Pent-up frustrations, rising expectations, isolated acts of white violence, the emergence of a new type of black leadership, and a changed attitude among the blacks led to a rash of violent confrontations across the country in the 1960's.

Springing from much the same source was the Southern attitude which viewed the rise and spread of the convict-lease system with equanimity. Since it, too, primarily involved Negroes, it could therefore be ignored or passed over lightly. This system also had its roots deep in the past, having been used in Northern states until organized labor and public opinion compelled its abolition. Like child labor, the modern form of convict leasing was almost entirely a Southern monopoly. The absence of strong unions and public unconcern gave it protection, while the economic stringency of the post-Civil War days made it seem a necessity.

Convict leasing, although referred to as the South's "unique system," probably had its American origin in a Massachusetts law of 1798 permitting the wardens of houses of correction to hire prisoners to anyone who would furnish employment. In 1828 Kentucky turned over its whole prison population for five years to a merchant, Joel Scott, for an annual payment of $1,000. Other states also experimented with some variety of hiring out prisoners to private contractors before the Civil War.[6] In general, most authorities were of the opinion that their prison populations should not be allowed to serve time in idleness and that prisoner work could be a valuable part of the rehabilitation program.

The main question was how this best could be accomplished. Four systems gradually evolved: (1) In the contract system, the contractor employed the convicts at a certain agreed-upon price per day for their labor. The prisoners worked in the prison under the immediate direction of the contractor or his agents, and the institution furnished the power and sometimes the machinery. (2) The piece-price system was a variation of the contract system in which the contractor furnished the prison the proper materials and received the finished

[6] William E. Blatner, "Some Aspects of the Convict Lease System in the Southern States" (unpublished Master's thesis, Dept. of History, University of Oklahoma, 1952).

product at so much per item. (3) In the public account system, the inmates worked for the benefit of the state, and any marketable products were sold for its profit. (4) The lease system permitted the institution to lease the convicts to a contractor for a fixed sum and period, the lessee usually assuming responsibility for clothing, food, health, and maintenance of proper discipline among the convicts.[7]

The first three types became the most common in the states outside the South (only Nebraska, Washington, and New Mexico used the lease in 1886), but the lease system dominated below the Potomac for historical reasons. In the Old South, many crimes had been punished on the plantations, although most states had penitentiaries. A few were even advanced in that respect, but war halted this progress. Troops from one side or the other burned the penal institutions of Georgia, South Carolina, Virginia, and Mississippi, and the rest were badly damaged or misused during the war.[8] A wave of destruction and an aftermath of poverty left the South helpless to deal with a crime rate which almost doubled after emancipation. The existing penitentiaries were in deplorable condition, and money to build new jails or subsist prisoners was nonexistent. A report on the Nashville prison in 1878 told of two and three men locked in cells seven by three and a half feet in dimension, lacking toilet facilities and subject to recurring epidemics, and of a hospital "lacking in the decency and comfort of a pig-sty."

Faced with an increased number of Negro prisoners, a regional shortage of labor, and impoverished state treasuries, the governments of the South proved very susceptible to the financial lures of the lease system. During the decade 1867-1877, all of the Southern states adopted such schemes, a period, incidentally, which coincided with the reign of carpetbag government. By such a move, an item of expense was made profitable to the state, as well as to the man who did the hiring. Much, if not most, of the railroad mileage in the twenty years after the Civil War was laid with convict labor. The great expansion in mining operations was also largely based on the blood and sweat of these men, women, and children. Senators Joseph E. Brown and John B. Gordon were members of penitentiary companies which hired Georgia's convicts for a 20-year period; state warden John H. Bankhead of Alabama grew rich through such connections; Edmund Richardson and James S. Hamilton of Mississippi based their fortunes on such labor; and "penitentiary rings" sprang up in many states to monopolize the profits

[7] Commissioner of Labor, Second Annual Report, 1886 (Washington, 1887), p. 4.
[8] Fletcher M. Green, "Some Aspects of the Convict Lease System in the Southern States," James Sprunt Studies in History and Political Science (Chapel Hill: Univ. of North Carolina, 1949); George Washington Cable, "The Convict Lease System in the Southern States," Century, V (February, 1884), pp. 582-599.

available by hiring labor for a few cents a day. The convicts, chiefly Negroes, became enmeshed in a system which functioned without social planning or humanity, soulless chattels in the eyes of the law.

When prisoners were leased, the state generally surrendered all control over them, leading to almost unbelievable brutalities. There was no segregation as to race, age (some being as young as eight years old), sex, or type of crime. The discipline was harsh and rigorous, and the convicts were underfed and overworked. The more the contractor worked them and the less he fed them, the greater were his profits. The system lacked even the deterrent found in slavery in that the contractor had no cash investment of his own in their welfare.

Georgia in 1871 leased all of her convicts to three companies for twenty years. So profitable was this that by 1900 the convicts were bringing to their employers almost twice the profit to be made from free labor.[9] South Carolina first used the system temporarily in 1873, when the superintendent of the penitentiary was forced to lease convicts in order to feed them when the legislature halved his appropriation. Governor Daniel H. Chamberlain then suggested in 1876 that the system be extended, in view of the expense of maintaining prisoners in idleness. The next year the Bourbon governor, Wade Hampton, was able to secure passage of such a bill, and the first contract was made with the Greenwood and Augusta Railroad for 100 convicts at $3.00 each per month and maintenance. By 1878 South Carolina had 221 prisoners working on railroads, in phosphate mines, and on private plantations. In two years' time, 153 prisoners had died — the death rate on the Greenwood and Augusta being 50.52 per cent — 82 had escaped, and many of those returned to state custody were so disabled they could not walk. An investigation showed the prisoners to be suffering from malnutrition, vermin, and beatings, and from living in indescribable filth. About the only result of this report, however, was to make the state diversify its prison employment by putting some convicts on contract and public account projects.

A federal survey in 1886 showed that Alabama leased all of its state and county prisoners, 1,435 males and 100 females, to seventy-six contractors, who used them indiscriminately in coal mining, farming, and lumber production. They worked eleven hours a day for thirty-five cents. The state penitentiary alone showed an income of $42,987.13, against expenses of $13,917.65. The survey also showed that Arkansas leased 518 males out of a total of 564 prisoners to a single contractor, to be worked ten hours daily for a return to the state of fourteen and

[9] American Society for Extension of University Teaching, *Syllabus of a Course of Six Lectures on the American Negro* (Philadelphia, 1900), p. 4, in *Negro Pamphlets*, V. University of Virginia Library.

one-half cents per man per day, while Florida's prison population was leased primarily for the production of turpentine. Georgia's state prisoners, described as especially overworked and treated barbarously, all resulting in a very high death rate, were leased to three contractors; the forty females were engaged in making bricks and farming, and the males in brick-making and mining, for eleven hours a day at a price of five and one-half cents each. Kentucky leased 847 males and 25 females for two and two-thirds cents a day for coal mining, railroad construction, and laundry work. In addition, some 214 were used in public account work, constructing a prison and quarrying stone. Louisiana leased its men and women for farm, railroad, and levee work at about seven cents per day for an income of $20,000, against expenses of $14,871.55. Mississippi's system was described as very bad, with a high death rate and extensive overwork. Its state and county prisoners, male and female, were leased to thirty-four contractors, chiefly for farm labor, for $39,420 to the state. North Carolina leased prisoners for railroad construction while using others to make brick and construct a governor's mansion. South Carolina's prison population in 1886 was engaged variously in phosphate mining under a lease; in making boots, shoes, and hosiery under a contract; and on public account projects. In Tennessee, the Tennessee Coal and Iron Company was the lessee of most of the state's prisoners, using both sexes for mining. The state received $101,000, against expenses of only $9,900. The company found such labor not only profitable but also indispensable in breaking strikes and discouraging unionization among free miners. Texas used the bulk of its inmates on public account projects, as well as contracting the labor of some for making saddle trees and similar objects. Virginia used the contract system altogether, employing her prison population in making shoes and barrels and processing tobacco.

Southern exponents of the leasing system, as contrasted to those favoring the other three types, argued that 90 per cent of the laborers were Negroes of the lower class who benefited from being worked regularly. Also, since they were accustomed to outdoor life, this was more humane and healthful than cooping them up within walls. The convicts were more reliable and productive than free labor. Mine owners, in particular, claimed they could not work their pits at a profit without the lowering effect on wages of convict-labor competition. Undoubtedly, however, the biggest asset in the minds of the penny-pinching Bourbons was that the state enjoyed a clear profit, around 372 per cent of operating expenses. The only cost was for a superintendent and one or two other officials, for under such a system a prison was not even necessary.

These advantages were outweighed in more compassionate eyes

by the obvious disadvantages. Allowing the prisoners to escape or die was cheaper than guarding them; pecuniary interest was set in opposition to humane ones; the system made possible greater punishment than that imposed by the courts; to look after the health of the victims was impossible, leading to awe-inspiring death rates; the prisoners could not be segregated; the chances for reformation of the criminals were reduced to a minimum; and the system was used to debase free labor. Few realized the extremes of the system, and they were easy to ignore, as the prisoners seldom came in contact with the public. Consequently, the only real solution — abolition of the lease system — seemed to involve expenses which the taxpayers did not wish to assume.

Nevertheless, opinion slowly formed against leasing the convicts when experience showed that the abuses were virtually impossible to eliminate. Gradually, around 1890, the system was discarded in state after state, being replaced by the contract or public account systems. The most common employment was in state-owned enterprises within the walls of the prisons or on state farms. By 1904 the lease was used in only four Southern states — Alabama, Florida, Georgia, and Virginia — and involved only 3,528 prisoners, 17.1 per cent of the productive convict laborers, Virginia leasing only 4.4 per cent. (Wyoming, the only state outside the South using the system, had 123 inmates so employed.) Virginia moved to end leasing by legislative action in 1901, Georgia followed in 1908, and Florida in 1924; Alabama closed the door on this "relic of barbarism" in 1928. Only one stain remained: Georgia, in replacing the lease system, inaugurated another of doubtful improvement. Instead of leasing to private individuals, that state began leasing her convicts to individual counties for road work, giving rise to the infamous "Georgia Chain Gang." Continued protests by citizens and welfare agencies and the introduction of modern road-making machinery finally ended this practice in 1943.

Another channel for man's inhumanity was revived in the twentieth century in the form of another relic of the past, the Ku Klux Klan, which flourished following World War I. According to popular legend, this was a renaissance of the Southern Klan of early reconstruction days. Actually, this version had little in common with the original except name and a mistaken belief that it was following the earlier tradition. It cashed in on the glamor of the "Lost Cause," using the historical regalia and ritual, and it fed upon the folklore that Anglo-Saxons nobly took the law into their own hands in times of turmoil. The original Klan had been strictly Southern, aimed at the Yankee through the Negro. The new organization became national and was never anti-Northern even in the South. Throughout the country it flourished on old inherited prejudices against minority groups — Negroes, Mexicans, Jews, Catholics, foreigners, and liberals. To the Americans troubled by the science of Darwin, it reaffirmed the Old-Time Protestant religion; to a nation troubled by the rise of communism, it supported the capitalistic system; and to an Anglo-Saxon majority, it promised control of the non-Nordics, who allegedly threatened their way of life. Its strength lay in the fact that it was all things to all men. In one state it fought chiefly against the Catholics; in another it was a censor of morals; and in yet a third, it was denouncer of evolution. It summed up the whole hierarchy of hates and fears of a troubled time.

The second Klan dated from October, 1915, when Colonel William J. Simmons, preacher and salesman of Atlanta, Georgia, and a group of thirty-four Georgians met atop Stone Mountain near Atlanta and, in the light of flaming torches and a cross, declared, "We are dedicated to the exalted privilege of demonstrating the practical utility of the great, yet almost neglected, doctrine of the Fatherhood of God and the Brotherhood of man, and to maintain forever White Supremacy in all things." Despite the reflected glamor afforded by the popular motion picture, *Birth of a Nation* (1915), the movement attracted little attention outside of its native state for the first years of its existence. With at best a membership of a few thousand, in 1920 Simmons hired Edward Y. Clarke of the Southern Publicity Association and Mrs. Elizabeth Tyler, both professional publicity agents, to lead a national campaign for membership.

The time was ripe for an organization which stressed "Native, White, Protestant" supremacy. The Negro had been "spoiled" by high war-time wages and experiences of racial equality practiced in France during army service, and he needed to be "put in his place." Jews were viewed as radicals and conscienceless profiteers; immigrants were out to destroy American institutions and the purity of "American" blood; and Catholics set religion above patriotism. The Klan's secrecy and ritual was bait for lovers of the bizarre and secret adventure who lived hopelessly drab and aimless lives. In the words of Frederick Lewis Allen, "Here was a chance to dress up the village bigot and let him be a Knight of the Invisible Empire." Here, also, was a chance for the suppressed classes to work off their frustrations at the expense of minorities and feel patriotic while doing so. To the sponsors, needless to say, the organization had great potentiality as a moneymaker, with memberships being sold for ten dollars each.

Enrollment began to grow by leaps and bounds. According to Simmons, in 1922 the average increase was 3,500 a day. At its peak the Klan claimed 5,100,000 members, and its ghostly rituals could be witnessed in all parts of the country. In the South, white supremacy was at first its chief objective, but later, opposition to the Jew and, especially, the Catholic proved more popular. As local Klans enjoyed considerable freedom of choice in deciding upon what "evils" they wished to clean up, there was considerable variation. In some areas they fought labor organizers, punished immoral women, and opposed birth-control advocates, internationalists, and those favoring repeal of prohibition. They worked closely with the more fundamental denominations, although there was no official connection between the Klan and any sect, and a few Protestant ministers were known to be Klan officials.[10] Its membership was chiefly from the common whites, the less educated and less disciplined elements of the white Protestant community, industrial and rural.

In the North the same groups were attracted, and the Klan's professed aims were usually anti-communistic. In the East and Middle West, it absorbed the old anti-Catholic sentiment; in California and Oregon, an expanded program exploited anti-Oriental, anti-Semitic, and anti-foreigner prejudices. Especially in Oregon, the Klan fought against parochial schools, hiring "escaped nuns" to spread stories of priestly immorality.

The years between 1920 and 1922 were ones of great violence laid to the account of the Klan. According to an exposé of the Southern Klan by the New York *World* in 1920-1921, the organization was responsible for four murders, two mutilations, forty-one floggings, twenty-seven tar-and-featherings, five kidnapings, and the driving of forty-three persons from their homes. Oklahoma was allegedly the scene of 2,000 Klan outrages within a 2-year period. These acts of violence were more shocking than numerous but spread fear and consternation throughout the country. The fight of the *World* not only aroused public opinion against the Klan but also led to a Congressional investigation. This, in particular, showed up the Klan's financial dealings. The Imperial Wizard had been given a $25,000 home, and the Klan hierarchy received huge rake-offs.

Unfavorable publicity caused a split within the organization and the end of its first period. Simmons was "bought out" for a reputed $140,000, and control passed to a faction which took the pretensions of the group seriously and was not out primarily for the money, as had been the Simmons clique. The new Imperial Wizard, inaugurated in December, 1922, was Hiram Wesley Evans, a Dallas, Texas, dentist, who referred to himself as "the most average man in America." The new leadership preached the same intolerance. Evans wrote in 1924,

[10] Robert M. Miller, "A Note on the Relationship between the Protestant Churches and the Revised Ku Klux Klan," *Journal of Southern History*, XXII (August, 1956), pp. 355-368.

"The Negro is not a menace to Americanism in the sense that the Jew or Roman Catholic is a menace. He is not actually hostile to it. He is simply racially incapable of understanding, sharing in or contributing to Americanism." As to his definition of "Americanism," he stated two years later that to the Klansman it "is a thing of the spirit, a purpose and a point of view, that can only come through instinctive racial understanding. . . . He believes also that few aliens can understand that spirit." The new administration also shifted the emphasis from violence to political activity, and from 1923 to 1928, political intrigue rather than brute force typified the Klan's actions.

Politicians were drawn to the Klan almost from the beginning, and it became a political power throughout the country. It attracted Republicans and Democrats, being stronger among the Democrats. It dominated for a time the states of Oregon, Oklahoma, Texas, Arkansas, Indiana, Ohio, and California, while in Kansas, Missouri, and Maine it was too strong to be ignored. It elected governors and Senators and dominated counties. So powerful was it in the national Democratic party that in the convention of 1924, the Klansters, by a vote of 546 15/100 to 541 85/100, were able to defeat a resolution denouncing the Klan by name. Instead, a general, evasive protest of "un-American" groups was passed. But public pressure throughout the nation formed more heavily against the organization, and in 1928, Wizard Evans ordered the Klan to unmask. Even this move was not enough to save it, and its waning strength showed in the Democrats' nominating a Catholic for the Presidency that year. During the Depression years, membership fell to practically nothing, and in 1944 the Klan was disbanded as a national organization.

After World War II, on May 9, 1946, another meeting was held on Stone Mountain to rally the faithful to meet new threats to Americanism. The new leader, Dr. Samuel Green, announced that the "cardinal principle of the Klan is white supremacy" and urged those to join who "truly desire to do your part for Christianity, your Country and your Race." The appeal went largely unheeded until the Brown decision of 1954 aroused the prejudices upon which it fed. Under Imperial Wizard Robert Shelton, and headquartered at Tuscaloosa, Alabama, blacks and civil rights "agitators" were its targets, and dynamite its weapon. Its membership was small, and the press and pulpit were almost unanimously hostile. The failure of Southerners to heed its call marked the end of a myth and new hope for the future.

Closely allied with the Klan in the public's mind and profiting from the same economic and social disorders were the political demagogues. Throughout all history demagogues have sprung out of social maladjustments regardless of region, section, or nation, where they fill the social vacuum which "good" politicians neglect. They are deformed results of an effort to meet a human need which actually could have been more adequately met in another way. According to Allan Nevins, the demagogue is generally the "product of some wrong, some neglect, some falsehood, for which society bears a responsibility."

Like most epithets, however, difficulty arises in defining the terms and in agreeing on those to be so labeled. Historically, demagoguery has assumed many forms, of which the ranting of a Southern Vardaman is only one. Class-conscious harangues by irresponsible labor leaders and sectional diatribes by Northern Congressmen are equally appeals to passions rather than to reason and are designed for one purpose: to win votes. One scholar wrote of the phenomenon: "The term is not absolute, since there exists a bit of demagoguery in the most lofty of statesmen and, sometimes, some constructive qualities in a few of those universally conceded to be demagogues."[11] Webster's definition is more delineated: "An insincere politician, orator, or leader who stirs up popular prejudice to gain office or influence." In the same vein, Huey P. Long once said: "I would describe a demagogue as a politician who don't keep his promises." Consequently, the label generally has no geographical or class boundaries,[12] but rather is most often defined in terms of techniques and intentions, with the worst being those guilty of using reprehensible means for selfish ends.

The entering wedge for American demagogues came with the introduction of liberalized suffrage provisions. Would-be officeholders quickly learned the necessity for creating issues which appealed to many. Presenting these issues in colorful language, including personal abuse, was a lesson reinforced by experiences in the Jackson era. In the 1830's, Franklin Plummer of Mississippi and Ely Moore of New York repeatedly won election to Congress by extravagant promises to their respective piney-woods and workingman constituencies, but neither became conspicuous for reform efforts. James H. Lane of Indiana and Nathaniel P. Banks of Massachusetts exploited the anti-slavery issue basically for their own benefit. W. R. W. Cobb of Alabama won a seat in Congress by singing "Uncle Sam is Rich Enough to Give Us All a Farm." Fernando Wood of New York was the self-appointed "protector of the poor," and Ben Butler of Massachusetts was a long-time self-proclaimed friend of the workingman and later a "bloody

[11] Reinhard H. Luthin, *American Demagogues* (Boston: Beacon, 1954).
[12] In his list of Northern demagogues of the twentieth century, Luthin includes James M. Curley of Massachusetts, William H. Thompson of Illinois, Frank Hague of New Jersey, Vito Marcantonio of New York, and Joseph R. McCarthy of Wisconsin.

shirt" demagogue.[13] These men and their successors exploited class, race, and religion in their campaigns for power. They were emotional rather than rational, talented exhibitionists, adopting distinctive costumes and picturesque language, yet all the time identifying themselves with their audience. Basically, they were all anti-intellectual, ignoring the issues or presenting oversimplified, emotional answers to the problems of the day. And all were enemies of the "interests."

Despite this long history and broad geographic spread, the Southern demagogue was the one which became a national institution. Although relatively few in number, his fame is general, and he seemed to exemplify all his section's ills and many of those of the nation. This widespread awareness of his presence, and the general condemnation that usually followed, was based upon his bitter attacks upon the Negro, violent language, and bizarre manners, all of which he deliberately cultivated to provide the conspicuousness upon which his political success in the South depended. Yet few of these so-called demagogues were uneducated men, many having law degrees in addition to college training. Neither were they from the lowest strata of Southern society. All showed hostility to large corporate and financial power, and most used the Negro as a regional scapegoat.[14] Their election resulted from great promises on behalf of the electorate, and while their achievements rank low historically, they often seemed large to the voter in comparison with the do-nothing attitudes of their predecessors.

The New South provided a fertile ground for these rabble-rousers. The region's illiteracy, considerably higher than in other parts of the country, was reinforced by the elements of provincialism, one-crop farming, inadequate credit, sharecropping, and weak social institutions. The seeds of discontent were nurtured by the festering wounds of Civil War and reconstruction, exploitation by Northern capitalists and their Southern allies, and lack of national political patronage. The heavy percentage of Negroes gave the demagogue an issue with which to rouse the Negro's chief economic rival, the "poor white." This type of politician was the natural result of one-party politics, where power was in the hands of the well-to-do, who were in turn supported by the Democratic organizations, the press, the bar, and the more prominent clergy. Revolters had to find their support chiefly among those ignored by the "ins"— the rural tenants, mill workers, and lower classes still politically self-conscious after the failure of the agrarian revolt — and by appeals which would be heard, if for no other reason, by their very violence.

[13] Reinhard H. Luthin, "Some Demagogues in American History," *American Historical Review*, LVII (1951-1952), pp. 22-46.
[14] Daniel M. Robison, "From Tillman to Long: Some Striking Leaders of the Rural South," *Journal of Southern History*, III (August, 1937), pp. 289-310.

Thus, campaigns were based on personality rather than issues, and a premium placed upon stunts to attract attention. The candidate would present himself as the defender of the people, boast of prejudices and humble backgrounds, and pander to the pride and bigotry of the "wool hat," "red neck," and "lint head" voters. Once in office, the rebel would be unfettered by party machinery and would use his position to build his own machine and perpetuate himself in office.

Among those twentieth-century Southern politicians most commonly denoted as demagogues,[15] the following are typical. Idol of the underprivileged in South Carolina was Coleman L. "Cole" Blease. Blease, a small-town boy, attended Newberry College and received a law degree from Georgetown University. He quickly fell under the influence of Ben Tillman and was elected as a Tillmanite to the state house of representatives in 1890, where he served as Tillman's floor leader. After service in both the house and senate of South Carolina, in 1910 and again in 1912, he was elected governor, despite the opposition of a now hostile Tillman. In 1924 he went to the United States Senate.

Although unable to maintain the friendship of Tillman, Blease had learned his lessons well and, in fact, improved on Tillman's techniques. Besides the farmers who formerly supported Tillman, Blease made a specialty of appealing to the downtrodden cotton-mill workers, whom Tillman had described as the "damned factory class." He even excelled his former mentor as a Negro-baiter, promising to "wipe the inferior race from the face of the earth." In regard to lynching, he stated that "whenever the constitution comes between me and the virtues of the white women of the South, I say to hell with the constitution." He was more lavish in his promises, succeeding in enchanting the mill workers, tenant farmers, and poor whites generally. Yet on reaching office, he repeatedly betrayed them by opposing governmental programs that would benefit them. While constantly criticizing the privileged classes, he opposed compulsory education —"I have never heard a common sense argument in favor of it"— killed labor bills, opposed child labor laws, and hated national unions. Bizarre in manners and morals, dressing in frock coat, striped trousers, and a shoe-string tie, his two terms

[15] The difficulty in discussing this problem in relation to the South is that of agreement concerning who should be on the list. Many would include the leaders of the agrarian revolt, such as Ben Tillman and Tom Watson. While it is true their methods were demagogic, there is little doubt concerning their sincerity. Modern politics has produced little more agreement. For example, Allan A. Michie and Frank Ryhlick, *Dixie Demagogues* (New York: Vanguard, 1939), include in their discussion such names as John Nance Garner and Martin Dies of Texas, James F. Byrnes of South Carolina, Byron "Pat" Harrison of Mississippi, Josiah W. Bailey of North Carolina, Millard Tydings of Maryland, and Carter Glass and Harry F. Byrd of Virginia.

as governor were marked by graft, corruption, damaging attacks upon the state university, and the wholesale pardoning of prisoners. Although his rule as governor was the worst in state history, the people loved him for voicing their hatreds and frustrations.

In Arkansas, Jeff Davis, son of a Baptist minister and educated at the University of Arkansas and the law schools of Vanderbilt and Cumberland universities, inherited the mantle of the agrarian reformers. Dressed in a Confederate-grey Prince Albert coat which became his trademark, Davis was elected attorney general in a campaign in which he stated that "the war is on, knife to knife, hilt to hilt, foot to foot, knee to knee, between the corporations of Arkansas and the people." Described by the Helena *World* as "a carrot-headed, red faced, loud-mouthed, strong-limbed ox-driving mountaineer lawyer, and a friend of the fellow who brews forty-rod bug-juice back in the mountains," Davis quickly made a reputation as a friend of the little man by bringing suits against insurance companies, American Tobacco Company, Standard Oil, and the "Cotton Seed Oil Trust." Opposed by what he called the "high-collared roosters," the "silk-stocking crowd" of Little Rock, and the newspapers, he campaigned for governor by pitting class against class and claiming that the only people who would vote for him, according to the newspapers, were the people living in the "forks of the creek" who wore "patched breeches and one gallus." As governor from 1901 to 1907, he achieved needed but temporary success against insurance companies and some labor reform legislation. Not one to take the truth too seriously, he juggled the state finances to make it appear that the state was out of debt, and the legislature voted a tax reduction. He exploited this achievement to a seat in the United States Senate and left his successor to worry about the ensuing deficit.

James E. and Marian Amanda Ferguson of Texas made a unique contribution to American politics. Jim, or "Pa," as he was most commonly known, was the son of a poor Methodist minister and farmer. After a country-school education and a period as an itinerant laborer, he studied law, married the daughter of a well-to-do farmer, and became a banker. Over one-half of Texas farmers were tenants in 1910, and so Ferguson decided to run for governor on a platform calling for rent reductions for tenants, cheap money, and aid to rural farmers. An artist on the political stump, his demagogic methods and manners alienated the better classes but proved highly attractive to the larger class of the poor. Upon election, his rent bill was passed but not enforced. He did succeed in securing additional establishments for the mentally ill and greater appropriations for rural education. Claiming his first election was a triumph of "the great masses of plain people of Texas," he won a second term in 1916. In a fight with the University of Texas because of faculty and student opposition, he vetoed its appropriation. He was impeached in 1917 and barred from holding any future "office of honor, trust or profit under the State of Texas" on charges of having appropriated certain state property to his own use, of having deposited state funds in his own bank, and of having accepted a "loan" of $156,000 from brewery interests without provision for repayment. Although ineligible, he ran for governor in 1918 as a martyr of the "University crowd" and for the presidency of the United States in 1920 on the American party ticket. In 1922 he unsuccessfully sought a seat in the Senate on the slogan, "Kill the Rent Hog and the Interest Hog," after which he added anti-Semitism to his list of appeals.

He then discovered a new technique. He ran his wife "Ma" for governor in 1924. She campaigned on the platform of clearing his name for the sake of his children and grandchildren and the slogan, "The people of Texas will have two governors for the price of one." Victorious and becoming simultaneously one of the first women elected governor of a state, she had "Pa's" impeachment erased from the senate record. She failed of re-election in 1926, partly because of the issuance of over 2,000 pardons for state prisoners in twenty months and charges of irregularity in the maintenance and construction of highways. But she won in 1932. Although little was done for the poorer whites of Texas, the Fergusons remained the darlings of that class until displaced in its affection by the greater showmanship and more lavish promises of W. Lee "Pass the Biscuits, Pappy" O'Daniel. His platform of the Golden Rule, the Ten Commandments, and $30-per-month old-age pensions led him to the governorship and later the United States Senate.

In Alabama, J. Thomas Heflin, nicknamed "Tom Tom" because of his continual breast-beating, reached the House of Representatives and later the Senate by joke-telling and diatribes against Negroes, corporations, Yankees, and Republicans. Son of a country doctor in eastern Alabama, he was chosen to a seat in the state legislature by fighting against the Populists. He soon sensed this to be a dead-end cause and joined the "people," winning advancement to Congress in 1904 on a platform of prohibition and white supremacy. Customarily dressed in a black coat, white vest, fawn-colored pointed shoes, flowing tie, candy-striped socks, and pince-nez, and wearing his hair long, he quickly became a well-known figure in Washington. National publicity followed his shooting of a Negro on a streetcar and his announcement that he carried a pistol to protect himself against anti-prohibitionists. He sought the support of the second Klan and became a violent anti-Catholic, even claiming to have discovered a popish plot to poison him. The fact that his name did not appear on any important legislation was blamed on "Republican stenographers and printers."

The heir to Tom Watson as the idol of the Georgia masses was Eugene Talmadge, the "Wild man from Sugar Creek." Characterized as looking like a "cross between a ventriloquist's dummy, and a sour-faced owl," he catered to the "wool hat" boys, showing that despite a college education he was still one of them by his double negatives, "cracker" drawl, and flaming red suspenders. A candidate in every state-wide Democratic primary except one between 1926 and 1946, he ran three times for commissioner of agriculture, twice for the Senate, and five times for governor. He first achieved the position of commissioner of agriculture after a race waged as "just a plain ol' dirt farmer," attacking the Chicago meat packers. Later threatened with impeachment for misuse of funds, he told the farmers, "Shore, I stole; but I stole it for you." Elected governor on the promise of $3-automobile tags, he became a virtual dictator, putting down opposition with the state militia. His attacks upon Georgia's institutions of higher education on the grounds that some of the administrators favored integration of the races caused the schools to lose accreditation. He pardoned large numbers of convicts — 3,000 during his term beginning in 1940 — claiming that they would help solve the World War II labor shortage. He made good use of the county-unit system, under which underpopulated rural counties were able to outvote the more populous urban centers.

He favored low wages and opposed unions; strikers were treated as revolutionaries and placed in concentration camps. Of the national relief program during the Depression, he said, "Let 'em starve! Any man can find a job, if he really wants to work." Yet he campaigned for the Senate in 1938 on the grounds that he would "provide a homestake and a grubstake for the unemployed. I will protect the farmer and worker with high tariffs. I will expand the CCC camps. Why, fellow Georgians, I will make America another Garden of Eden!"

James K. Vardaman, the "White Chief" of Mississippi, rose to power following a long period of Bourbon control in which business had been favored and scandals had developed in the treasurer's office. After serving in the state legislature, beginning in 1890, he was defeated for the Democratic nomination for governor in 1895 and 1899. The adoption of the direct primary in 1903 made it possible for him to win the nomination in 1904 by capitalizing on his support from the hill counties. He knew how to captivate his audience. Wearing long flowing hair, dressed in immaculate white, and riding on a lumber wagon drawn by white oxen, he campaigned on two main issues: his status as a "son of the soil" and enemy of large corporations, and advocacy of white supremacy. The Negro was a "lazy, lying, lustful animal which no conceivable amount of training can transform into a tolerable citizen," with a nature that "resembles the hog's." Lynching was justifiable, and the Fourteenth and Fifteenth Amendments should be repealed. This was a theme he used for three decades of office-seeking. As governor, he did accomplish the passage of laws restricting corporations and established a state textbook commission. His elevation to the Senate cleared the way for his successor as chief prophet of racial antagonism, Theodore G. "The Man" Bilbo.

Bilbo, a lay preacher, opened his political career by admitting acceptance of a bribe of $645 and being declared by the legislature as "unfit to sit with honest, upright men in a respectable legislative body." Nevertheless, the "red necks" elected him to the governorship and later to Congress. In 1934 he won a Senate seat by denouncing "farmer murderers, poor-folks haters, shooters of widows and orphans, international well-poisoners, charity hospital destroyers, spitters on our heroic veterans, rich enemies of our public schools, private bankers who ought to come out into the open and let people see what they are doing, European debt cancellers, unemployment makers, Pacifists, Communists, munitions manufacturers, and skunks who steal Gideon Bibles." He also proposed to solve the unemployment problem by shipping 12,000,000 Negroes back to Africa.

In a class by himself was Huey P. Long, "Kingfish" of Louisiana, and the most controversial of Southern figures.[16] He was born in 1893 in Winn Parish, a poor area of small farms and cut-over timber lands with a record of having been cool to secession and a center of Populism and later of Socialism. Seventh in a family of nine children, Huey knew from firsthand observation the pinch of poverty and the backward social conditions which blighted the lives of thousands of Southern families. As a boy, he traveled the state peddling books, soap, a lard substitute, and a cure for "women's sicknesses." Sharp and shrewd, with borrowed money he completed a three-year law course at Tulane in less than a year and at the age of twenty-five became a candidate for the Louisiana railroad commission on a platform which stressed that two per cent of the people owned from 65 to 70 per cent of the nation's wealth. Elected, he began his running fight, to last through most of his career, against corporations, especially Standard Oil, which had large holdings in the state.

His position on the railroad commission was used as a springboard for the governorship, a position he attained in 1928 with the biggest majority in the state's history. As governor, Long initiated a definite

[16] See, for example, T. Harry Williams, "The Gentleman from Louisiana: Demagogue or Democrat," *Journal of Southern History*, XXVI (February, 1960), pp. 3-21; compare Allan P. Sindler, *Huey Long's Louisiana* (Baltimore: Johns Hopkins, 1956).

program of action and was ruthless with those who opposed its adoption. Through use of the patronage, he built up a political machine which gave him more power than most Latin American dictators. He openly forced contributions from companies which got state contracts and used strong-arm tactics when he thought they were necessary. But in the final analysis, the source of his power rested in support by the common people. Although he was vulgar, crude, and often obscene, he kept faith with the people and they with him. He gave them what he promised, and the corporations paid for it. His appeal was seen in the fact that he could command support from the Protestant back country of the state as well as from the Catholic Southern part.

He promised good roads and built them. He gave free textbooks to the children, rather than to the schools, to keep down the issue of state aid to parochial schools; appropriations for higher education were increased, and over 100,000 illiterates of both races received free night-school training. Free bridges were constructed; a state board of health with real authority was set up, and hospitals and institutions for the unfortunate were built that rivaled any in the South. The poor man was allowed to vote without payment of poll taxes and was benefited by cheaper utility rates and the shifting of some of the tax burden to the well-to-do. Standard Oil was brought to heel by a law which allowed the governor to impose a variable tax upon refined oil.

Long was a master politician. On one occasion his legislature passed forty-four bills in twenty-two minutes. His best weapon was stinging sarcasm and mastery of the art of satire. Of Postmaster General Farley he said, "Jim can take the corns off your feet without removing your shoes"; Harold Ickes was described as "High Lord Chamberlain, the Chinch Bug of Chicago"; Henry A. Wallace was labeled "Honorable Lord Destroyer of Crops, the Ignoramus of Iowa." General Hugh Johnson of the NRA was described as "Hugh Sitting Bull" and the organization as "Nuts Running America." He himself, however, was invulnerable to caricature or ridicule. When the "March of Time" sent movie cameramen to interview him with the intention of showing Americans how dangerous he was, he defeated them by posing as a buffoon whom no one could think of taking seriously. He conducted state business from his bedroom and dressed in garish fashion; yet when events threatened to get out of hand, he became the master. When, after less than a year in the governor's office, he was impeached and tried on twenty-five charges that included bribery, misappropriation of state funds, removal of school officials for political reasons, kidnaping, and misconduct in public places, among other things, he brought popular pressure against the legislature and was acquitted. "I used to try to get things done by saying 'please,'" he grimly announced. "That didn't work and now I'm a dynamiter. I dynamite 'em out of my path." For a time in 1930, he was both governor and United States Senator and upon relinquishing the former position was able by shrewd, if not illegal, tactics to place his own man in the governor's chair.

On the national scene, he quickly became an opponent of President Franklin D. Roosevelt through his Share-Our-Wealth Plan, a rival to the New Deal in its appeal to the underprivileged everywhere. In an undated handbill, Long wrote, "There is no need of hunger in the land of too much to eat; no need of people crying for things to wear in the land of too much cotton and wool; no need of homelessness in the land of too many houses." By confiscating and redistributing the great fortunes of America, he proposed to insure every "deserving family" in the nation a home, an automobile, a radio, and an education for its promising children; in accordance with the title of his book, he would make *Every Man a King* (1933). By 1934 he had built the slogan "Share Our Wealth" into a national club with no dues, claiming 3,000,-000 members. That he intended to ride this appeal into the Presidency was evident from the title of his next work, *My First Days in the White House* (1935). His program scared both conservatives by its radicalism and reformers by its popular appeal. Before it could be put to the test of the ballot box, however, Long was assassinated on a visit to his new state capitol in September, 1935.

This controversial man was characterized by his contemporaries variously as a man of the people, a Fascist, a demagogue, an ignorant clown, and a would-be dictator. Yet none denied his talents in offering a program which would appeal to the "forgotten man" in the language he could understand. His program was not Marxist but approached it. He concentrated on economic and social problems, being one of the few Southern leaders of the masses who felt it unnecessary to pander to racial or religious bigotry in search of votes. A natural orator, he offered material benefits in return for loyalty and support. He had the capacity to make his promises come true, as he was a good, practical administrator, always doing enough for his constituents to be able to say that he had kept his promise to them.

Huey Long, and others of his type, were the symptoms of a condition, not the cause. These causes were listed at Long's funeral by the Reverend Gerald L. K. Smith, president and national organizer of Long's Share-Our-Wealth Club: "His body shall never rest as long as hungry bodies call for food, as long as lean human forms stand naked, as long as homeless wretches haunt this land of plenty." Yet, despite the prevalence of need in the South, demagogues were not typical of the rank-and-file of Southern politicians but were the picturesque exceptions. True need for reform will always nurture demagogues; when there is a discontented and underprivileged group which sees no hope of relief under the prevailing order, it will always follow any leader who promises help.

Demagogues, as well as other evidences of a Southern cultural lag, were graphic examples of the duality of the Southerner as an American. On the one hand, the South was still bound by certain institutions and practices long since rejected by most civilized communities. The situation was further complicated by two factors. First, most of these social ills came to public attention at a time when the nation, still under the influence of the post-Civil War "devil theory of history," was critically observing the South and ready to believe the worst concerning the people and their motives. The South, on the other hand, used the North as a scapegoat, blaming local conditions on the loss of the War and the ensuing reconstruction. Moreover, the South's reaction to outside criticism was either to deny or defend the existence of such conditions or to declare that they were of no concern to any but Southerners.

Thus, in public the South often presented a face which justified the opprobrious title of "backward." Yet, simultaneously, the region quietly carried on programs of domestic reform against tremendous odds and, on an individual level, showed typical American concern for human welfare. Surrounding all was the determination to share in the benefits of a democratic society.

# 20

# THE PROGRESSIVE SOUTH

THE SOUTHERNER TRADITIONALLY RESENTED and resisted reform pressure when externally applied. But on the other hand, he has, as prompted by his own conscience, made progress toward amelioration of the social maladjustments of his region. Specific reforms often came later than north of the Potomac, the delay often, as in the case of the child labor problem, complicated by factors other than social inertia. In an area slowly climbing back from the economic and social ravages of war, to arouse a lethargic public to action in regard to specific abuses was difficult. Yet at no time in its history, even during the abolitionist crusade, did the South lack men and women willing to devote their lives to improving the lot of their fellow men, black as well as white. Often forgotten by history and abused by their contemporaries, nevertheless, they cumulatively left an important legacy to their homeland.

The first national period of reform with which the South came in contact after 1865 coincided with reconstruction. The pressure for change was applied from outside the region, and most of the changes were intended for or at least identified with improvement of the lot of the Negroes. Unfortunately, Southern resistance was automatic and paralleled the tendency to equate social change with the infringements and events of reconstruction. The reforms resting upon federal law, such as the Civil Rights Act of 1875, suffered at the hands of the courts or from the loss of Northern interest in the welfare of the Negroes, while those improvements provided by reconstruction constitutions were either omitted by later conventions or nullified by the dollar-hoarding tactics of the Bourbon or Redeemer governments. Since many white Southerners had never enjoyed these social benefits, they were slow to realize that they, as well as the Negroes, were harmed by this retreat into conservatism. In the Southerners' zeal to recapture their governments from Negro-Republican domination and to ease the financial burdens of taxation, many reforms were associated in their minds with the period of reconstruction and thus were lost — reforms which had to be regained after long and bitter struggles later.

It would be only a slight exaggeration to say that at the beginning of home rule in the South virtually every area of human life was in need of reformation. Yet the Southern people were weary of strife and concerned only with regaining peace and improving their economic position. Ironically, the solution to the economic problem was the "New South" movement, which preached the Northern gospel of diversification through industry. The arrival of industry brought in its wake a new set of social and economic problems to add to the existing unique ones, but at first they were not apparent to the people in general. So pressing were the economic deprivations that work under any condition was hailed and employers cited as public benefactors. Exploiting employers gained immunity by the existence in the South of a philosophy of paternalism, for the tradition of proprietary responsibility which had characterized the essentially paternalistic plantation economy carried over into the New South. The region had traditionally been the stronghold of rank individualism, and laissez-faire had gained wide acceptance there. Thus, the inherited absence of any feeling of need for legal protection for workers, the lack of a labor movement, and the existence of strong religious and economic fundamentalism — all made the South slow to recognize the reality of such problems and to take action on them.

One of the reactions to defeat was a solidly defensive spirit toward all things Southern which made even native criticism extremely difficult. Nevertheless, the region did produce social critics.[1] Most failed to acquire national reputations, since they tended to confine themselves to Southern problems. They were also more temperate in their approach and often were supporters of white supremacy. Their appeals rested less on government intervention and more on individual humanity. By

[1] Herbert J. Doherty, Jr., "Voices of Protest from the New South, 1875-1910," *Mississippi Valley Historical Review*, XLII (1955-1956), pp. 45-66.

way of example was George W. Cable.[2] Born of a Northern mother and Southern father and raised in New Orleans, after service in the Confederate army he became a newspaper man in his home city. He first attracted attention in 1870-1871 through his protests concerning corruption in the local government, the mud and filth of the streets, and the lack of even rudimentary efforts to protect public health. The following year, while continuing this work, he began a campaign against the Louisiana Lottery, characterizing it as a "heinous offense against society," a "crying shame," and a "subtle poison" that "cankers the morals of the rising generation." So bitter was his condemnation that two of his editorials led to a suit by the company against the newspaper.

Cable was one of the prime movers and principal defenders of the Auxiliary Sanitary Association, founded in 1879 by a group of private citizens to supplement the work of the state board of health. By their efforts more than $100,000 was raised and spent on drainage; funds considerably in excess of those provided by the local government were provided to buy pumps, fill cesspools, clean gutters, disinfect contaminated areas, inspect toilets, and provide free smallpox vaccine. Public pressure was used to force doctors to disclose the existence of cases of yellow fever or cholera. So successful were the activities of this group that its example was cited as precedent for other similar reform groups throughout the South.

Cable also attacked conditions in local prisons and asylums, demanding the formation of a special board to oversee such matters. When such an agency was established in 1881, he continued to rally public support behind it through the medium of his newspaper columns. He personally made a study of the most advanced systems of the East and created the Prisons and Asylum Aid Association, comprised of leading local citizens. In addition to better buildings and care of the inmates, the group sponsored establishment of juvenile homes and houses of industry and sought employment for released prisoners.

Most of these efforts met with general approval. However, when Cable turned his reforming zeal to the problem of the Negro, the response was different. His defense in 1875 of the unsegregated schools of New Orleans gave the first indication of his feeling that the Negro should be given equal rights. A growing reputation as a local-color writer brought him a national audience, which he was quick to exploit in behalf of his reforms. At the meeting of the National Conference

[2] Arlin Turner, "George W. Cable's Beginnings as a Reformer," *Journal of Southern History*, XVII (May, 1951), pp. 135-161, and *George W. Cable, A Biography* (Durham: Duke Univ., 1956).

of Charities at Louisville in 1883, he bitterly indicted the convict-lease system in the South for its inhumanities and the especially heavy force with which it rested upon the Negro, views circulated nationally by *Century* magazine the next year. This was followed by an address before the annual meeting of the American Social Science Association in Saratoga, New York, on "The Freedman's Case in Equity." Despite the fact that he recognized social equality as a "fool's dream," he continued his attacks upon Negro injustices. His most important critical essays were collected in *The Silent South* (1885) and *The Negro Question* (1888), both clarion calls for civil equality — the Negro must have the vote and an education which would qualify him to use it. As could be expected, he was bitterly attacked by the Southern press for his "misguided" views, which were blamed on his maternal background. The hostile reception to his stand on the race question was undoubtedly a factor in his decision to move to Massachusetts in 1886. Most Southerners, far from lamenting the loss of a great literary figure, rejoiced at the loss of a critic who persisted in washing the region's dirty linen in public view.

Yet another Southerner to win national attention was Walter Hines Page. Born before the Civil War of middle-class parentage in North Carolina, he began as editor of the Raleigh *State Chronicle* in 1883. His editorials against the "ghosts" which were strangling North Carolina and the rest of the South (the Confederate dead, religious orthodoxy, and Negro domination) and his demands for greater educational opportunities for its people brought not action but enmity. Discouraged by his homeland's apparent hostility to change, he moved to New York in 1885. While carving out one of the most distinguished journalistic careers in American history, he never ceased being a friendly critic of the South. Active in reform, he was influential in inducing John D. Rockefeller to make large gifts for Southern education and was himself a member of the Southern Education and the General Education boards which did so much to aid the South. He also used his friendship with Rockefeller to initiate the Rockefeller Commission for Eradication of Hookworm Disease when it was found that almost 60 per cent of all Southern school children were so infected. The Cooperative Farm Demonstration program under Dr. Seaman A. Knapp of the United States Department of Agriculture owed much of its success in the South to the support given by Page. A man of the world, his first loyalty was always to the South, where, although his criticism was often resented, much improvement resulted from his efforts.

The nearest approaches to region-wide reform movements in the South coincided with the farm revolts, which, in turn, were sparked not only by economic grievances but also by the demand for greater

services from the governments. As has been seen, the Granger movement which helped downtrodden Western farmers largely bypassed
the South, so not until the rise of the Alliances did Southern farmers
become vocal. In 1874, the first state department of agriculture was
established in Georgia, and seven of the states with such organizations
in 1895 were Southern. In the 1870's and 1880's, Southern governments also created railroad commissions, though they generally proved
unequal to their tasks. The decade of the nineties was marked by increased activities to control business. With the death of Populism as a
political force, the small businessmen and urban middle class joined
the discontented farmers in a war against the threat of monopoly, with
the newcomers taking over the leadership and aligning their attack
with the progressives of other regions.[3] The issues were such as could
command wide support: replacement of outmoded forms of government, railroad and public utility regulation, public education, penal
reform, prohibition, internal improvements, and the extension of public
control over government.

Often their efforts were fought by Southern apologists of the
"foreign" interests, politicians who were strongly entrenched within
the established Democratic party and frequently controlled it through
state machines. This led to factional battles within the party between
the conservatives and the new leaders of the reform group. One of the
first objectives, therefore, became revision of party machinery, with
the direct primary for nominations the most important objective. By
1890 every county in South Carolina was using a limited version of the
primary system for naming local officers and legislators, and by 1896
the use of the primary was state-wide. The movement spread, and a
good majority of the Southern states were using it by the time it was
adopted in Wisconsin (1903).[4] Now able to secure the nomination of
candidates representative of the reformers' points of view, governmental changes came with greater ease, and by World War I, every
Southern state had enacted laws against corrupt practices such as
bribery, intimidation, and excessive campaign expenditures.

Curiously, the practices of initiative, referendum, and recall did
not find the favor in the South that they did in the North. However,
Oklahoma, Arkansas, Mississippi, and Maryland adopted initiative and
referendum before 1918, and Louisiana in 1914 became the first Southern state to accept recall. Although generally failing to win state-wide
approval, these reforms were more successful in local governments,

[3] Dewey W. Grantham, Jr., "The One-Party South," *Current History*, XXXII (May,
1957), pp. 264-265.
[4] Arthur S. Link, "The Progressive Movement in the South, 1870-1914," *North
Carolina Historical Review*, XXIII (1946), pp. 172-195.

where the first noteworthy steps in the United States in improvement of city government were taken. The commissioner form originated in Galveston, Texas, in 1900 and was quickly adopted by most of the larger cities in the South, then spreading to the North. Similarly, the city-manager plan was introduced in Staunton, Virginia, later winning national approval. In 1905, city planning programs were initiated in Columbia, South Carolina, and San Francisco, California, to insure their citizens safer and more pleasant places to live.

Many of these objectives were promoted by a group of reform governors helped into office around the turn of the century by election reforms. Among them were Charles B. Aycock, the "education" governor of North Carolina; Braxton B. Comer, who led the reform force in Alabama; Hoke Smith of Georgia, a political ally of Tom Watson; Napoleon Bonaparte Broward of Florida, who campaigned against the railroads and "land pirates"; and William Goebel of Kentucky, whose fight against the corporations and railroads led to his assassination. Even the demagogues were affected by the fever. All met stiff opposition; yet the number of state railroad commissions were increased and old ones strengthened. The first corporation commission in the United States with control not only over railroads but also over public utilities, banks, and trust companies was set up in North Carolina in 1899. Northern insurance companies, which drained off the capital of the South through high rates and overcharges, came under fire, and in at least one state, it was proposed that the government should enter the business in competition. North Carolina attacked the Tobacco Trust, and Standard Oil became the special target of Texas reformers, with the state seeking over $75,000,000 in fines in 1907 from that combine.

But "foreign" giants were not the only ones slain. State legislatures concerned themselves with local problems, and citizens other than those led by Cable in New Orleans were beginning to make their voices heard. As early as 1874, John Berrien Lindsley of Tennessee had become concerned with health conditions in Southern prisons and published an influential pamphlet, *On Prison Discipline and Penal Legislation*. Wherever one looked, prisons were obviously a fit subject for reform.[5] Foremost among the problems was the convict-lease system, and the first efforts were therefore made to abolish the practice or curb its abuses. With about nine-tenths of the prisoners being Negro, to arouse white opposition to the abuses was difficult. Vested interests which had large financial stakes in the lease system fought every step made by courageous men and women.

[5] Jane Zimmerman, "The Penal Reform Movement in the South during the Progressive Era, 1890-1917," *Journal of Southern History*, XVII (November, 1951), pp. 462-492.

Robert Alston and Rebecca L. Felton of Georgia, Julia S. Tutwiler of Alabama, and governors Hoke Smith of Georgia, George W. Donaghey of Arkansas, and Bibb Graves of Alabama were joined by most of the newspapers of the South in attacks upon this inhuman evil. It is altogether probable that the newspapers gave more attention to the public failure to care properly for its convicts than to any other social maladjustment of the period. For example, the press is usually given credit for preventing the introduction of the system into the coal mines of Kentucky, as well as for breaking down the system elsewhere. Aiding in the fight were the forces of free labor; in the 1880's both the American Federation of Labor and the Knights of Labor took strong stands on convict labor. In both 1891 and 1892, Tennessee coal miners struck against such competition. The reason for their concern is obvious in a statement made by Albert S. Colyar, general counsel for the Tennessee Coal and Iron Company: "For some years after we began the convict labor system we found that we were right in calculating that free laborers would be loath to enter upon strikes when they saw that the company was amply provided with convict labor. I don't mind saying that for years the company found this an effective club to hold over the head of free laborers."[6] Prison reform planks were endorsed by the Union Labor party, the Agricultural Wheel, the Farmer's Alliance, and the Populist party.

At first, success came mainly with efforts to ameliorate the existing system. A 15-year Texas lease was terminated by the governor at the end of six years because the conditions had become objectionable; the convicts were re-leased under a contract which gave them greater protection. Despite their profitableness, the state passed a law forbidding future leases in 1886. Alabama forbade, in 1883, subleasing without the approval of the warden and governor and separated whites from Negroes and hardened criminals from first offenders. Mississippi ended leasing by a provision in the constitution of 1890; South Carolina in 1889 forbade its use in phosphate mines and, in 1897, on private farms. By 1900 the drive was for complete abolition of the system, and thirteen years later it was achieved in six states and making headway in others. Prison Reform Associations were active in most areas of the South, and by the middle 1920's, the last vestiges of leasing had been eliminated from the Southern scene.

States were forced to seek alternatives, however, and most turned to employing the inmates at farm work, in road building, or on public projects. Farming, first used as a stopgap measure, seemed particularly attractive, as most of the prisoners had rural backgrounds, and this

[6] As quoted by Thomas D. Clark, "The Country Newspaper: A Factor in Southern Opinion, 1865-1930," *Journal of Southern History,* XIV (February, 1948), pp. 3-33.

profitable work was also a healthier environment with a great variety of tasks. North Carolina officials advocated this as early as 1879 and leased land for such use in 1882. After the abolition of the lease, more and more states established penal plantations. When Louisiana took such a step, it was hailed by Northern reformers and penologists as placing that commonwealth "a century ahead of the methods in common practice in the ordinary prisons North and South." Certainly a tremendous improvement was made in convict mortality rates by the substitution. Eleven Southern states had large prison farms by 1920.

Road construction work could offer many of the same attractions. The concurrent drive for good roads which took place at the turn of the century led many states to view convict labor as a solution to that problem as well. Local prisoners had been used for road work in early colonial days, and in 1873 North Carolina had allowed counties and municipalities to use prisoners so. With pressure for roads increasing, not only were counties in every Southern state allowed this privilege, but state prisoners were so used, sometimes with bad results. Georgia's "chain gangs" became almost as notorious for maltreatment as the lease system. Introduction of modern road-building machinery and protests of reformers gradually led to a discontinuance of primary reliance upon prisoners for road work.

The various local societies for penal reform which sparked the drive for abolition of the lease continued to work for other changes. The most active, the Prison Reform Association of Louisiana (1897) and the Southern Howard Association of Tennessee, worked for reform of criminal law, improved prison management, juvenile reformatories, aid for discharged prisoners, and the like. These and similar organizations in Georgia, Virginia, North Carolina, Texas, and Alabama could boast among their achievements the introduction of the parole system and the suspended sentence, night schools, libraries, and prisoner grading. In May, 1912, greater unity of effort was afforded by the meeting of the first Southern Sociological Congress and the establishment of state boards of charity. By 1915, out of twenty-six such boards in the United States, six were in the South.

Before the Civil War, the North had adopted the principle of segregation of sexes and had made the care of juvenile delinquents a charity distinct from the penal systems. The South, on the other hand, had largely escaped these problems until Negro women and boys began to appear in large numbers in criminal courts after 1865. Yet, only after long agitation was attention at last given to the recommendations of the charitable-minded that special provisions should be made where these classes could be segregated from evil influences. Texas, North Carolina, and Virginia were the first to provide such facilities, and

Alabama soon followed their example. Texas organized a reformatory for boys under age seventeen in 1890; the Virginia Prison Reform Association established a private one; and the creation of such an institution was unsuccessfully demanded in Arkansas by the Populist party. The agrarian constitution of South Carolina in 1895 permitted such an organization and was implemented with a reformatory for Negro boys in 1900 and for whites in 1906, primarily because of the efforts of the state Federation of Women's Clubs. All Southern states, except Florida and Mississippi, had made provisions by 1912 for juveniles, and all were making an effort to give some religious or educational training, either under sponsorship of the state or private groups. Segregation of female prisoners had been accomplished in all states except Tennessee and Louisiana by 1900.

Prison discipline also came under observation, and many unusual or cruel forms were abolished. It was discovered that rewards, in the form of extra privileges or tobacco and the like, could be substituted for punishment as a means to secure discipline. The honor system and the granting of time off for good behavior were begun in the South as early as 1890 but did not become general until after World War I. The first probation law was passed by Massachusetts in 1878, but by 1900, only four other states had followed. Virginia passed the first such statute in the South in 1904. Although the first parole law was enacted as early as 1837, the practice had been approved in only thirteen states by 1900. The first Southern state to adopt parole was Arkansas in 1907, and by 1944 all of the United States had such provisions, with Mississippi being the last to put it into force.

Closely allied with the drive for prison reform were efforts to help other groups of the socially handicapped. Only four years after the first American establishment of such an agency, North Carolina, on April 10, 1869, set up a Board of Public Charities, but it had little more than advisory responsibilities and no budget.[7] This weak beginning is not too surprising in light of the fact that by 1904 only fifteen states had such agencies to coordinate the various public welfare services. By 1931 only Arkansas and Mississippi, along with three Western states, had not made such provisions.

Organized movements for protection of public health were slow in developing in the United States because of a general ignorance as to the causes of disease. By 1878, however, most of the larger cities and sixteen states had set up boards of health, eight of which were Southern. Even so, as could be expected from low incomes, a shortage of doctors, and a bad previous health record, this element of Southern

[7] A. Laurance Aydlett, "The North Carolina State Board of Public Welfare," *North Carolina Historical Review*, XXIV (1947), p. 1ff.

progress left much to be desired. Epidemics were a common phenomenon, and the region had a virtual monopoly on hookworm and pellagra. The few early organized health movements were primarily concerned with the problems of the periodic onslaughts of malaria and yellow fever, and preventive medicine made slow progress because of public indifference and political interference. The first state board of health in the United States did not make an appearance until 1867 in Louisiana, and during the 1870's similar organizations appeared in Virginia, Maryland, Alabama, Georgia, Tennessee, Kentucky, and North Carolina. However, the last, established in 1877 had an annual appropriation of only $100.[8] Functions usually included the power of quarantine, abatement of health nuisances, supervision of vaccines, and, later, inspection of drinking water. County health departments were notably lacking or, at best, consisted of volunteers from the county medical societies. While North Carolina's state board was the first in the nation to begin publication of monthly reports, in 1886, by 1898 the only Southern state boards spending as much as one cent per capita on public health were those of Florida and Mississippi.

After the major yellow fever epidemic of 1905, aided by new medical discoveries and the reforming zeal of the Progressive period, Southern health began to show steady improvement. The widespread hookworm infestation of the South had been dramatically publicized in 1902, while almost simultaneously the carriers of malaria and "Yellow Jack" were identified and pellagra diagnosed for the first time. Within a decade, boards of health were established in the remaining Southern states and old ones rejuvenated and reorganized. More money was appropriated, and a start was made in establishing county boards. Sanitariums and boards of control were established for tuberculosis; bacterial laboratories sprang up in the Southeastern states; governments undertook to secure wider distribution of serums, vaccines, and antitoxins. Walter Hines Page, as a member of President Theodore Roosevelt's Commission on Country Life in 1908, became convinced of the hookworm's responsibility for much of the South's ills. After being told by the discoverer of the parasite that the typical Southern patient could be cured with "about fifty cents worth of drugs" and that at least 2,000,000 Southerners were so infected, he interested the Rockefellers in helping. Although Northern newspapers satirized such efforts as looking for the "germ of laziness" and some Southerners felt the region was being slurred, the Rockefeller Sanitary Commission for the Eradication of Hookworm took long strides toward curing many of the afflicted and eliminating the disease.

[8] Jane Zimmerman, "The Formative Years of the North Carolina Board of Health 1877-1893," *North Carolina Historical Review,* XXI (1944), pp. 1-34.

Similar massive attacks were waged against other Southern scourges. The fight against malaria, one of the most important in the region's history, saw significant strides being made between 1917 and 1930 in mosquito control. New Deal assistance came with the draining by 1938 of almost 2,000,000 acres of swamp through CWA, FERA, and WPA programs. The introduction of DDT in the 1940's helped complete the job to such a degree that by 1950 a case of malaria became a medical rarity. Typhoid and dysentery control was advanced by federal projects that constructed 2,300,000 sanitary privies by September, 1939. Scarcely a Southern institution was left untouched by the twentieth-century drive against venereal diseases, and, simultaneously, tuberculosis was dislodged from its primary position as a Southern killer.

Health department expenditures increased 81 per cent between 1910 and 1914 and continued to grow. Once converted to the need for public health services, the Southern states lagged primarily from a shortage of doctors per capita and lack of governmental financial resources. The national average of per capita public expenditure for such services in 1940 was $1.90, ranging from $0.76 in Tennessee to $4.26 in Nevada. Seven Southern states spent less than $1.00 per capita, and only Louisiana ($2.43) exceeded the national average. Increased federal assistance helped narrow the gap, with the result that mortality rate differences between the regions slowly narrowed.

Aid for the insane, blind, deaf, and dumb was also limited before the twentieth century by the financial distress of the South. The South had established the first three state institutions for the insane in the United States — Virginia (1773), Kentucky (1824), and South Carolina (1828) — and all states below the Mason-Dixon line except Florida had such care by 1861. After the War, Virginia opened the first Negro insane asylum in 1870, marking an initial indication of responsibility for the race. Although help for the blind, deaf, and dumb was not as great, a start was at least made. By 1909 thirty state institutions in the South cared for the insane, though they still lagged in providing for the feeble-minded and epileptics, and every state provided for the blind, deaf, and dumb. Progress continued into the twentieth century in helping the insane; although the South listed the lowest insanity rate per capita, it had one of the highest totals for first admissions to treatment.

Concern for paupers primarily was shown by establishment of "almshouses," "poorhouses," and "workshops" and through private charity. There was, in general, no lack of agencies but a lack of knowledge of how to use them. In the absence of state regulatory bodies, the need was first met by private organizations, such as the New Orleans

Conference of Charities, organized in 1883 for the purpose of protecting the community, eliminating duplication of gifts, aiding through work relief, and elevating the "home life, health and habits of the poor." This and similar groups suffered from lack of adequate financing. Again, not until the turn of the century was substantial progress in welfare work made, when the social-welfare people undertook region-wide action. A leader in the movement was Kate Barnard, young Commissioner of Charities and Corrections in Oklahoma, upon whose instigation the governor of Tennessee called a Southern conference on social problems. This resulted in the organization of the Southern Sociological Congress in 1912 to promote abolition of child labor and the convict lease, better provisions for children and defectives, public health, and improved race relations. Strongly supported by church groups, the Congress set up a center to promulgate social-welfare information, and annual conventions were planned. To coordinate welfare work, and especially gifts, the larger cities began using the community chest system, and by 1920 four of the fifty-two cities employing this technique were Southern. Since that time most communities above 20,000 population have utilized chests or similar organizations.

Aside from necessary financing, the most serious Southern problem in social work was a shortage of trained personnel, a not surprising situation in view of the fact that the first social-work school in America was not opened until 1898. In 1929 the region had only 234 out of the total 3,487 membership of the National Conference of Social Work; yet even this was a gain, for in 1894 there had been only twenty-five Southern members. Part of this problem was met by establishing professional training courses in such colleges and universities as Tulane, Atlanta, North Carolina, Tennessee, William and Mary, Texas, and Oklahoma. By 1952 the South had four schools of public health, Johns Hopkins, Tulane, and the universities of North Carolina and Oklahoma, and fifty-five offered some instruction in working with handicapped children. The Southern Regional Education Board has also been a powerful agency in encouraging better training facilities for social workers.

Public financing of welfare programs showed a steady gain, and Southern states by 1948 were spending a larger proportion of their incomes on such programs than was spent in the rest of the nation, when 20.6 per cent of all expenditures for state and local government went for public welfare, compared to 19.5 elsewhere. Ranking especially high in this regard were Texas and Oklahoma. As in the case of education, however, these figures are misleading, for average payments still were lower in proportion to other states. The bulk of the expenditure went for aid to children, relief for the blind, general assistance, and old-age assistance. Kentucky was the fourth state in the Union to provide old-age pensions (1926). The efforts of the New Deal were especially beneficial in getting social welfare programs started and encouraging such new programs as workmen's compensation laws, minimum wages, and women and child labor regulations.

Although Southerners at first took a very philosophical view of children working, Northern protests would not have allowed them to remain complacent, even if they had so desired. The rise of the textile industry in the South spotlighted the role played by juvenile workers. Again the fight for improvement was spearheaded by organized labor, the press, church groups, and dedicated individuals. The threat of federal action was a further stimulus. Probably the most active and influential individuals were Edgar Gardner Murphy and Alexander J. McKelway. Murphy, a native of Arkansas and Episcopal minister in Montgomery, Alabama, played an important role in the organization of the Alabama Child Labor Committee to fight for a protective law in that state. He was a prolific writer on the subject, turning out newspaper articles, pamphlets, and books, with his *Problems of the Present South* proving particularly influential. Recognizing the working child as a national rather than a regional problem, he was instrumental in the formation of the National Child Labor Committee in 1904, which united the efforts of all the reformers and included, among many Southerners, Ben Tillman and Hoke Smith.

McKelway, born in Pennsylvania but raised in the South, was a Presbyterian minister.[9] As editor of the *Presbyterian Standard* in the heart of North Carolina's textile district, he became an outstanding spokesman against child labor after falling under the influence of Murphy's writings. At first interested almost exclusively in the problem in textiles, he soon broadened his attack to include canneries, mines, cigar factories, night messengers, and the like. In 1903, at the same time that Murphy was leading the fight for state action in Alabama, McKelway, with the support of such newspapers as the Raleigh *News and Observer* and the Charlotte *Observer*, secured passage of a mild law which provided a minimum age of twelve and a maximum work week of sixty hours. The next year, at Murphy's urging, he accepted the post of assistant secretary for the Southern states of the National Child Labor Committee, becoming a full-time lobbyist, detective, and writer on the subject. He traveled throughout the South, working with local reform groups to secure desired legislation. In 1905, for example, he became secretary of the Child Labor Committee in Georgia and,

[9] Herbert J. Doherty, Jr., "Alexander J. McKelway: Preacher to Progressive," *Journal of Southern History*, XXIV (May, 1958), pp. 177-190.

with the support of the Atlanta *Constitution* and *Journal* and the backing of Governor Hoke Smith, achieved victory.

By 1907 virtually every Southern state had child labor laws,[10] but the problem then became one of low standards and poor enforcement. In that year the National Committee shifted its drive from state to federal regulation and supported a bill of Senator Albert Beveridge of Indiana. Murphy opposed this tactic and resigned from the Committee, but McKelway heartily supported it and went to Washington to lobby in vain for the measure. The failure to secure federal regulation was not, as often claimed, the sole responsibility of the South; the proposed Twentieth Amendment in 1924, establishing federal supervision in this area, proved to have little appeal even in the North. As late as 1938, the Amendment was turned down by New York, Massachusetts, and Mississippi. Southern states which had refused approval generally pointed out that child welfare bureaus, largely created by the efforts of McKelway and the Committee or similar organizations, had already been established by state action and that there was no need for federal interference.

In yet another area, Southern reformers of the late nineteenth century moved to end a Southern problem which had assumed national importance. Lotteries, generally abolished in the North before the Civil War, had a revival in the war-torn South. Although chartered in Alabama, Mississippi, Georgia, and Louisiana, markets were national, as state prohibitory laws were successfully evaded. One by one, local reform groups secured repeal until only the Louisiana Lottery Company was left. So profitable had it become that it could offer the state $1,250,000 annually for its franchise. Yet, spurred by the knowledge of local evils resulting from its operation and the national disrepute it brought the state, the people of Louisiana in the election of 1892 voted 157,422 to 4,225 against rechartering the company.[11]

Not only did women, such as the Ladies Auxiliary to the Louisiana Anti-Lottery League under Mrs. William Preston Johnson, play a major role in many of the reform movements taking place in the South, but they also were the beneficiaries, albeit sometimes disinterested. Although the enfranchisement of the Negro inspired militant suffragettes of the North, Southern women showed little interest in the ballot for themselves, while Southern men had even less. A Texas constitutional convention in 1868 reported that voting was "unwomanly" and that the sex should avoid "mingling in the busy noise of election days." A similar group in 1875 noted only two men interested in votes for

[10] Elizabeth H. Davidson, *Child Labor Legislation in the Southern Textile States* (Chapel Hill: Univ. of North Carolina, 1939).
[11] Ezell, *Fortune's Merry Wheel,* chap. XIII.

women. Not until the 1880's, with the rise of the prohibition movement and the belief that female votes would be cast for reform, did the woman's suffrage movement gain momentum.

In the meantime, Southern ladies were more interested in educational and economic opportunities. Here they met with continued success. By 1882 the vast majority of "higher institutions for women" were in the South, and they granted 684 of the 904 higher degrees awarded women in that year, although presidents of women's colleges were quick to state that they were "not teaching women to demand the 'rights' of men nor to invade the sphere of men." By the 1890's women not only had achieved colleges of their own but were successfully invading the state universities on the same basis as men.

At that same time, the special legal disabilities of wives were being removed, with Mississippi being one of the first three states in the nation to eliminate them entirely. In most states wives could now own and control property, retain earnings, make contracts, and sue and be sued. So widely was civil equality recognized that only time was required to erase the few remaining discriminations from the statute books — discriminations such as Georgia's and Louisiana's recognition of the husband as head of the family; North Carolina's, Kentucky's, and Texas' refusal to allow divorce except for adultery when the wife was the offender; and South Carolina's denial of divorce on any ground whatsoever.

The endorsement of woman suffrage by the Woman's Christian Temperance Union in the 1880's seems to have provided the chief source of initiative to fight for voting rights, and most such Southern clubs date from that period. There is no doubt that at first the majority of Southern women were lukewarm or opposed to the idea, some even joining the National Association Opposed to Woman Suffrage. Suffrage clubs grew slowly in number and were subject to internal factionalism and periods of undulating interest. By 1898 the limited right to vote on tax questions in Louisiana was the only achievement. Expanded activities of Southern women during the First World War and the success of women in winning the right to vote in the West increased desire for the same privilege among Southern women. Arkansas allowed women to vote in Democratic primaries in 1917 and Texas in 1918, while Tennessee in 1919 gave them the vote in presidential and municipal elections.

Supporters for votes for women stressed the discrimination according to sex, the role of women in winning the War, and their need to have the ballot to protect homes and children. Opponents stated that woman suffrage and socialism went hand in hand; women would be forced to serve "on juries in murder cases, commercialized vice cases, and whiskey cases." The woman voting would mean racial equality of the sexes and another period of Radical reconstruction featuring female carpetbaggers. Finally, to end all arguments, the movement was fostered by reformers and busybodies from the North.

In June, 1919, the Nineteenth Amendment was sent to the states for ratification. Despite the argument that this was a violation of states' rights and would cause the above-mentioned horrors, Texas in a special session of the legislature became the first Southern state, and the ninth in the nation, to give approval. By the summer of 1920, eight other Southern states had followed, and the amendment had thirty-five of the necessary thirty-six approvals for adoption. Tennessee called a special session of the legislature and after a bitter fight achieved the honor of casting the deciding vote which put the amendment into effect.[12]

The South had also played a dominant role in the adoption of another amendment which was viewed as a reform by that generation. That was the Eighteenth, or Prohibition, Amendment. Despite the fact that the region was known before the Civil War as the "land of Dixie and Whiskey," the temperance movement had been present, championed by some of the prominent political leaders, and excessive drinking was considered grounds for dismissal in most of the Baptist and Methodist churches. In 1852 there were some 265 temperance societies in the state of Kentucky alone, and in 1855 the "dry's" ran a candidate for governor in Georgia. Mississippi had taken a long step toward state-wide prohibition before the War, but only Delaware had completely yielded to the dry forces which were sweeping the North at this time.

The Civil War provided a setback to the prohibitionist forces everywhere, and in 1865 only Massachusetts and Maine were dry, but the former soon fell from grace. The reformers, however, renewed their efforts nationally. Within three months, the Friends of Temperance were organized at Petersburg, Virginia, and temperance advocates were busy in every Southern state by 1870, as old orders were revitalized and new ones begun. The Sons of Temperance was probably the strongest of the early groups, pressing its program with lectures, picnics, rallies, mass meetings, and full-dress parades. Bands of Hope were established to work with the children; the Order of Good Templars was especially active with the Negroes; and the Woman's Crusade tried to close saloons by holding prayer meetings on the premises.

12 For accounts of the woman suffrage movement in these two key Southern states, see A. Elizabeth Taylor, "A Short History of the Woman Suffrage Movement in Tennessee," *Tennessee Historical Quarterly*, II (September, 1943), pp. 195-215, and "The Woman Suffrage Movement in Texas," *Journal of Southern History*, XVII (May, 1951), pp. 194-215.

The Crusade was the parent of the Women's Christian Temperance Union, formed in 1874, which became a power in the South by the 1880's. Foes of liquor worked for state-wide prohibition and also sought to dry up areas by local option. The Tennessee legislature, for example, was literally swamped with local option petitions in 1881. Numerous are the accounts such as that appearing in the Taylor County (Texas) *News* on February 19, 1886: "The Temperance ball is still rolling, and at every turn it gains in numbers and strength, and Sweetwater will soon be noted for its sobriety." In this particular case, there was undue optimism, but local option was notably successful in drying up many areas in the South. Tennessee turned down a constitutional prohibition amendment by popular vote in 1887 but did enact a measure making it illegal to sell intoxicants within four miles of any school.[13] During the eighties every state enacted laws requiring the teaching of temperance in public schools, and in 1892 the American Temperance University was established at Harriman, Tennessee.

In addition to the traditional arguments against strong drink, the South added others with a racist flavor. Although probably not a decisive factor, it was argued that prohibition was necessary to keep alcohol from the Negroes. Drunken freedmen would be especially dangerous in the rural areas, and, considering their naive state, they should also be protected from the evils of the saloon. Deprivation of strong drink would make it easier to keep them in their place. The chief move which eventually brought success was a combination of religious groups, chiefly Methodist and Baptist, with urban progressives. The reform governors, notably Smith of Georgia and Comer of Alabama, played key roles.

The work of decades finally bore fruit in 1907, when Georgia became the first Southern state to adopt state-wide prohibition, after having first dried up all but a handful of its counties by local option. In short order, success crowded upon success, and William Archer, traveling through the area in 1909, reported: "Everyone agrees that the most remarkable phenomenon in the recent history of the South is the 'wave of prohibition' which has passed, and is passing, over the country. There are 20,000,000 people in the fourteen Southern States, 17,000,000 of whom are under prohibitory law in some form.'"[14] It was literally almost a wave, for within nine months of Georgia's action, four more states had done likewise. Again, the way had been prepared by drying up most of the counties by local option. The single city of

[13] Grace Leab, "Tennessee Temperance Activities, 1870-1899," East Tennessee Historical Society, *Publications*, XXI (1949), pp. 52-68.
[14] William Archer, *Through Afro-America* (London: Chapman & Hall, 1910), pp. 146-155, discusses the effects of prohibition in the South.

Chicago had more saloons than all the states of the South by 1914. By December, 1917, when the Eighteenth Amendment was submitted for ratification, the South was almost totally dry. So strong were their convictions that Alabama had forbidden the possession or sale of anything which "tastes like, foams like, or looks like beer" or of bottles shaped like whiskey flasks. Georgia outlawed even non-alcoholic drinks "made in imitation of or as a substitute for beer, ale, wine or whiskey" or the like.

With the submission of the Prohibition Amendment, Southern states were the first to approve and proved staunchest in supporting it against later attacks. With the repeal of national prohibition, Kansas, North Dakota, and Oklahoma and five other Southern states chose to remain dry. Although others fell by the wayside, until only Oklahoma and Mississippi were left, there was still much dry sentiment in the states of the South, and many counties remained dry by local option even after repeal. It was not solely by chance that after Oklahoma voted for repeal in 1959, the last remaining bulwark of prohibition until 1966 was a Southern commonwealth, Mississippi.

At a time when no evil seemed too small to be unworthy of scrutiny, Southern reformers showed at least one blind spot of remarkable size: their attitude toward the Negro. Alexander J. McKelway, for example, fought not only for child labor laws but also for temperance, prohibition of gambling and the convict lease, employers' liability, workmen's compensation, public education, initiative, referendum, recall, state aid to needy families, and women's suffrage. Yet he could hail Negro disfranchisement and even attempted to justify the Atlanta race riots. Cable also opposed social equality, and Charles H. Otken, a Baptist minister of Mississippi and author of the muckraking *The Ills of the South* (1894), believed the only future for the Negro lay in removal to Africa.

With the Southern leaders of reform accepting the regional decision to disfranchise the Negro politically and isolate him socially and economically, improvement of the lot of the race seemed remote. The apparent abandonment by former Northern friends and the Republican party, combined with dilatory or prejudiced courts, were sources of further discouragement and seemed to point to flight from the South as the only means of escape. The legacy of submission, induced partially by the constant threat of violent physical reprisal for insistence upon rights, was reinforced by Booker T. Washington, the major leader of Southern Negroes, who counseled patience rather than action. In some respects, this was wise advice, for the low economic and educational status of Southern Negroes precluded any real background for effective action. Even after the formation of the National Association for the Advancement of Colored People in the North in 1910, most Southern Negroes were either unaware of its existence, too frightened to join, or hostile or unconvinced of the wisdom of its methods.

As has been shown, lynchings and race riots became all too common phenomena; yet the very same men and states which opened the door to this mob violence were often trying at the same time to curb the forces which they had unleased. Ben Tillman, the main architect of the Negro's disfranchisement in South Carolina, was also chiefly responsible for a provision to eradicate lynching. South Carolina's constitution of 1895 provided for removal of sheriffs guilty of "negligence, permission, or connivance," and a Tillman amendment held the community in which a lynching occurred liable to damages of not less than $2,000, to be paid to the heirs of the murdered person. On one occasion, a South Carolina governor pardoned three Negroes who lynched a white man for raping a Negro girl on the grounds that he would "not discriminate against Negroes. These men had seen the law broken and lynchers go free countless times." This act was generally approved by the public, for as one editor said: "If lynchers are allowed to go free in other incidents then these ignorant Negroes should not be made to suffer. They are following in the footsteps of their enlightened white neighbors."

State after state provided laws against mob action and stripped their courts of many technicalities which slowed the progress of speedy trials in the type of cases which led to lynchings. Gradually the number of aborted lynchings grew, until by 1921 the total was greater than those completed, and numbers of states were able to show long spans of years without a single incident. Although still comparatively safe from conviction, white members of mobs found officials and the courts more sensitive on the subject of prosecution. Between 1922 and 1926, grand juries investigated seventeen lynchings and indicted 146 persons, and from 1913 to 1929, threatened lynchings were prevented in 569 cases, 85 per cent of which were Southern.[15] The number of actual lynchings declined drastically during the late twenties and thirties, virtually disappearing, indicative of the development of an enlightened public opinion.

The forces responsible for this maturing were many. One which deserves much credit was the Southern press. After 1900 most of the newspapers were at least nominally against mob violence, although some still apologized for it in specific cases, citing the weakness of the courts, delays, the depraved nature of the Negro, and like arguments. Despite the fact that, if the editor were too critical, he ran the risk of

[15] Southern Commission on Study of Lynching, *Lynchings and What they Mean* (Atlanta, 1931).

bodily harm or at least public censure for degrading the South, the large majority believed that mob violence threatened the whole structure of law and order. Most would have agreed with the editor of the Greensboro, Georgia, *Herald-Journal*, who wrote: "I feel sorry for the South that this blot is upon her. It affects us all over the world. It robs us of prosperity and the high moral and social position to which we are entitled. It ruins the worth of our investments. If it is not stopped then shut the school houses, burn the books, tear down the churches and admit to the world Anglo-Saxon civilization is a failure."

Groups of all sorts were soon on record in opposition to law by violence. Voices from the pulpit denounced lynching. Methodist Bishop Warren A. Candler of Atlanta, not a noted liberal, declared that it was "due to race hatred and not to any horror over any particular crime, [and] unless it is checked it may involve anarchy; for men will go from lynching persons of color to lynching persons on account of religion or politics, or their business relations." The fact that mob terrorism was one of the reasons assigned for large Negro migrations from the South awakened the region to its need for Negro labor and helped turn the face of business against the practice.

Since violence was most often justified as being necessary to protect white females, one of the most effective organizations was the Association of Southern Women for Prevention of Lynching, composed of women of high social rank in every county, which brought pressure on officials and made studies which were publicized by the newspapers.[16] The Commission on Interracial Cooperation, the Southern Commission on the Study of Lynching, and the University Commission on Southern Race Questions tried to break down the myths which justified mob action. The last-named was composed of Southern college professors, who in 1916 and 1917 addressed open letters to the college men of the South attacking the problem of lynching, discussing Negro education and migration, and praising the Negro's role during the First World War.

The revival of the Klan, with its racial connotations, met opposition from most religious groups, with the Southern Baptist Convention denouncing mob violence in 1922 and in 1923 and 1927 adopting resolutions condemning the "cowardly and diabolical" actions of masked mobs. Similar stands were taken by Methodists and Presbyterians, and virtually none of the prominent church leaders joined the organization. Again, the press was significant, with the Montgomery, Alabama, *Advertiser* and the Memphis, Tennessee, *Commercial Appeal* winning

16 Anne F. Scott, "After Suffrage: Southern Women in the Twenties," *Journal of Southern History* XXX (August, 1964), pp. 298-318.

Pulitzer prizes for their opposition. In every state, editorial writers, ministers, and courageous politicians like Carter Glass of Virginia, Oscar W. Underwood of Alabama, and Thomas W. Hardwick of Georgia were outspoken enemies of the Klan and must be given much credit for its death.

Often, the approach to improved relations between white and Negro was bi-racial and national in scope. Among the more important organizations were the Union League (1910) and the Commission on Interracial Cooperation (1919). The League, feeling that economics lay at the root of much racial friction, made its attack along those lines. With a national office in New York and a Southern field branch in Atlanta, it soon had branches in the principal cities of the South. With local units governed by interracial boards, and often supported by community chests, it did social work, found jobs for Negroes, and served as a pressure group for playgrounds, housing projects, schools, and the like. The Commission also had national headquarters in the North, with Southern branches whose leaders and officers were Southerners. By 1921 it had 800 county interracial committees whose aim was "not work *for* colored people, but work *with* colored people for community betterment." Working through other organizations, it tried to get the best elements of the two races together "to quench, if possible, the fires of racial antagonism which were flaming . . . with such deadly menace in all sections of the country." Its principal approach was conciliation, moral persuasion, and education. One of the Commission's greatest services was to make interracial work socially acceptable in the South.[17]

Yet another variation was that provided by the Southern Regional Council, established in 1944. Recognizing the fact that the impoverished condition of Southern whites was as important a factor as that of the Negroes, this organization of both white and Negro members sought to further equal opportunities for all Southerners. Through twelve state affiliates, usually called Councils on Human Relations, it sought to coordinate Southern thought and leadership in meeting racial and economic problems through the use of conferences, fact-finding, reason, and persuasion.

The one approach to the problem of race relationships which brought the hottest reaction from Southerners was that of federal intervention. Late in 1919 the National Association for the Advancement of Colored People began agitation which culminated in 1921 with the passage by the House of Representatives of the Dyer Bill to

---

[17] Gunnar Myrdal, *An American Dilemma* (New York: Harper, 1944), pp. 837-850.

prevent lynching. This was killed in the Senate, and similar bills after that time met the same fate. Southern Senators, often using the filibuster technique, argued that such measures would be violations of states' rights and, moreover, that they were unnecessary, as the South was taking care of the problem in a satisfactory manner. The same reaction was evident toward efforts to insure Negroes equal employment opportunities through the Fair Employment Commission in 1941, Franklin Roosevelt's "Second Bill of Rights" to equalize opportunities, and the 1945 bills for Fair Employment Practices and to outlaw lynching and poll taxes. Removal by the Supreme Court of the legal support for "separate but equal" facilities and the efforts of President Truman in behalf of Negro rights were all factors in the Dixiecrat revolt of 1948.

The era of the 1960's was marked by civil rights efforts on many fronts. The federal government took jurisdiction in cases involving violence and willful interference in regard to school desegregation. The Civil Rights Act of 1964 also provided penalties for employers or labor unions who followed discriminatory employment, promotion, or firing practices, while also banning discrimination by businesses offering food, lodging, gasoline, or entertainment to the public. Federal machinery for registering voters and seeing that they got to vote was set up while both major parties championed equality of races. Southern blacks themselves became increasingly active in their own behalf. The NAACP philosophy and leadership emerged in stronger positions, while the teachings of Booker T. Washington went into eclipse. By this time, blacks had progressed educationally and economically to the point that they produced leaders in virtually every state, commanding respect not only from their own people but also from the more intelligent and educated whites as well. Approaches ranged from the passive resistance of Dr. King to the "black power" of the Student Nonviolent Coordinating Committee (SNCC) and the Congress of Racial Equality (CORE).

In retrospect, most of the improvement in race relations came from a growing Southern awareness that the region could no longer remain unique in a democratic society. By the 1970's a majority was at least resigned to the irrevocable fact that black constitutional demands had to be granted; only a handful clung to the illusion of segregation or that violence could prevail. A mute struggle against acceptance of this new image of the black still persisted in the minds of many, but only because it also meant acceptance of a new image of themselves. If not a change of heart, then at least there was a change of action. The South began making the best of losing the segregation battle, for after all, the situation was not as bad as some whites had predicted it would be. The new phenomenon in the mid-seventies was Southerners pointing with pride to a new racial harmony which they felt could set a national pattern.

By the mid-seventies many of the faults of the South remained, faults which had forced endurance of outsiders' condescension and reformers' stinging rebukes. The Southerner still did not completely fit the mold of a progressive American. Yet, despite his different folkways, he had, in the last analysis, gone along with the main currents of progressive American life. Although he might still boast its individuality, in the roughly 100 years after the Civil War the South had progressed from being the despair of reformers and liberals to a point where most of the remaining inequalities were such that they could be removed with more money and time. The reasons for most Southern reform efforts lagging by a generation in comparison to the North were the legacy of history, the difficulty of reform in a poverty-stricken region, and the necessity for educating Southerners to the need for such action. Once the need was recognized, the South did not lack for leaders. Their one great omission has been the failure to include the blacks and women as equal partners in Southern life—problems not unique to that region. But again, the glare of publicity concerning the pending federal Equal Rights Amendment, an enlightening Southern conscience, and the insistence of both blacks and females themselves have determined that neither could no longer be ignored.

# 21

## TWENTIETH CENTURY POLITICS

v. o. key, jr., a leading authority on Southern politics, stated in 1949 that writers customarily relied upon a couple of caricatures to describe Southern politicians: as statesmen of the old school, spokesmen for sound economics, defenders of the Constitution, and enemies of "subversive and foolish proposals," or as representatives of a ruling class wedded to reaction, intent upon repressing both the white and Negro masses, and conspiring with the evil forces of Wall Street. He concluded that in "both caricatures there is a grain of truth; yet each is false," because "the politics of the South is incredibly complex."[1]

Certainly, to assume that the demagogue was typical of twentieth-century Southern politics is an error; yet, those who would ignore him are confronted with the dilemma of "Boss" E. H. Crump, Theodore "The Man" Bilbo, W. Lee "Pass the Biscuits, Pappy" O'Daniel, and James E. "Kissing Jim" Folsom, "The Little Man's Big Friend." These men are indeed necessary for a truthful portrayal of the region but not as central figures. They are merely the colorful exception to the rule that at the end of the Agrarian revolt Southern politics returned to a conservative, but not necessarily reactionary, position. Much less color-

[1] V. O. Key, Jr., *Southern Politics in State and Nation* (New York: Knopf, 1949), p. ix.

ful, but more typical, were such reform governors as Charles B. Aycock, Hoke Smith, Napoleon B. Broward, and Braxton B. Comer. On the national scene, having served political apprenticeships in their native states, were men who were able to win political preferment without relying upon the emotional appeals and prejudices of the demagogue: Carter Glass and Harry F. Byrd of Virginia; Joseph T. Robinson and J. William Fulbright of Arkansas; Oscar W. Underwood and William B. Bankhead of Alabama; Cordell Hull and Estes Kefauver of Tennessee; Claude Kitchin and Gordon Gray of North Carolina; Richard Russell and Walter George of Georgia; James F. Byrnes of South Carolina; and Vice-Presidents Lyndon B. Johnson and John Nance Garner of Texas, to name only a few.

Southern politics have been complicated by their encompassing not only all the usual and common problems but also special ones which demanded ever greater degrees of political sagacity, patience, and persistence. These included the effect of history, a unique problem of racial adjustment, a legacy of poverty and unprogressive agriculture, and a lack of political participation by the masses. Overshadowing all, of course, was the concern for maintaining white supremacy. The two great political crises of the South, the Civil War and the Agrarian revolt, in both of which Negroes played a vital role, dug deep furrows sown with bitter memories. Despite the Civil War's residue of Republican enclaves scattered through the region as continuing evidences of a lack of unity, there was simultaneously generated a greater degree of solidarity against the outside world than ever before. Then, the defeat of Populism, while the movement did seed the habit of radicalism in some areas, also strengthened the hold of the conservative Democratic party by the revived specter of Negro domination. The South was not able to repress all political dissent, but it did keep down rivals to the dominant party, with the result that the so-called Democratic party in the South became essentially a holding company for a number of changing, warring factions which carried the same name. This situation in itself usually forces a conservative approach to politics.

One point on which all the factions agreed was the role of the Negro voter. At the end of the Agrarian revolt, the South deliberately set out to eliminate the Negro as a voter by the use of such techniques as the poll tax, residence requirements, and the literacy test. The poll tax, of such antiquity that even Aristotle had complained of it, in general proved a boomerang. The small sum, from one to two dollars a year, although cumulative in some states, was not in itself sufficient to discourage anyone seriously desiring to vote and became less so with economic improvements. The nuisance value of having to go down to the courthouse six or more months before an election to pay probably disfranchised more, white and black, than did the cost. Moreover, its proposed effect was overestimated, seen by the fact that all but a handful of states (Alabama, Arkansas, Mississippi, Texas, and Virginia) abolished it without any startling increase in voting participation.

Literacy tests proved more efficient as a means of eliminating the Negro voter, but they too had a discouraging effect upon white participation, despite the many loopholes provided to prevent such exclusion. The killing of the "grandfather clause" by Supreme Court action in 1915 removed a relatively easy method of discrimination, and other substitutes, while discouraging the would-be Negro voter, did little to stimulate whites to greater political action. In the dramatically exciting national election of 1912, one of the hardest-fought in American history, participation in the lower South ranged from 15 to 24 per cent of the registered voters, while the upper South, North Carolina and above, could show only 26 to 48 per cent. The region as a whole had only 33 per cent participation, as compared to a national average of 60. Lackluster elections fared even more poorly — the election of 1920 evoked Southern participation ranging from eight per cent of the registrants in South Carolina to 44 per cent in North Carolina.

Although tests other than understanding the constitution were added to the literary provisions in the twentieth century, the South came more and more to rely upon yet another technique — the closed, or white, primary. This was based on the thesis that while the Constitution prevented a state's denying a person the right to vote because of his color, the Democratic party, a private organization, might discriminate in any fashion it desired. The closed primary was a gradual development growing out of the history of the region. At first virtually all of the Negroes were Republicans, and the white Democratic party was little troubled over the theoretical question of whether Negroes would be admitted or not. As the Southern states began to adopt during the Progressive period the direct primary method of nominating candidates, they continued the practice of not admitting Negroes under the authority given parties by state laws to establish the qualification for voters in the primaries. By central or county party rule, participation in primaries came to be formally limited to whites. By 1930 Negroes were barred from primaries by state party rulings everywhere except Florida, North Carolina, and Tennessee, where they were kept out in some counties by local option. The significance of this move was obvious: in the one-party South, the primaries were the election, with the general election merely a formality to confirm Democratic party victors in office. If the Negro were barred from the primary, it made little difference if a few of them voted in the general election.[2]

[2] For discussions of the nature and relative value of disfranchisement techniques, see *ibid.*

A still newer departure came in 1923, when Texas closed the primary by law. When this was successfully challenged in 1927, the act was repealed, and another law provided that each party's executive committee would prescribe qualifications for party membership. This, too, was successfully attacked, and the state withdrew all legislation upon the matter, leaving such rulings up to the state conventions of each party. This method was upheld by the Supreme Court in 1935. In 1944, however, the closed primary was contested in Texas upon the grounds that the primary was a part of the necessary machinery for choosing officials and that the state, by condoning such party action, was violating the Fifteenth Amendment. In April, 1944, the Supreme Court, in Smith *v.* Albright, ruled: "It may now be taken as a postulate that the right to vote in such a primary for the nomination of candidates without discrimination by the state, like the right to vote in a general election, is a right secured by the Constitution. By terms of the Fifteenth Amendment that right may not be abridged by any state on account of race."

This decision was a serious blow to those wishing to prevent Negro suffrage and was not accepted without attempts to find other means of control, especially in the deep South. Efforts to dissociate the state completely from the primary, reinforcing its private nature, were blocked by the courts. More stringent literacy requirements were added, as well as oaths which Negroes could not be expected to take willingly. In South Carolina, for example, in 1948, all voters in the Democratic primary had to take oaths opposing the FEPC and favoring racial segregation and states' rights. Eventually, the closed primary was conceded as lost. Most Southern states either accepted the right of the Negro to vote or concentrated on techniques preventing his registering, an evasion made increasingly difficult by the growing hostility of the courts and federal government toward any form of discrimination.

Enveloping all of the politics in the South after 1900 was this bitterly futile attempt to hold down Negro participation in government. Traditionally, the region had come to expect national opposition to such a program to come from the Republican party, and therefore the white Southerners placed their hope in the Democratic party. Few were the times that the Southern voter deserted the national Democratic cause, and even then the politicians did not always follow their constituents' desires. Although the South was generally conceded to be "solidly" Democratic, rifts within the party often caused hope among the national Republican leaders that a two-party system might successfully be reintroduced into the South.

Although the region had been in the Democratic column in every election since the end of reconstruction, the general dissatisfaction of conservative Southerners with the drift of the national Democratic party under the leadership of William Jennings Bryan inspired the Republican party under Theodore Roosevelt and William Howard Taft to its greatest efforts to woo the South. But that party split before any gains were consolidated. Nevertheless, Roosevelt viewed the rupture in 1912 as an opportunity to base the Progressive party in the South upon those businessmen who naturally found their views coinciding with those of the Republican party but who would, for historical reasons, vote for no organization carrying that name. He was embarrassed by the fact that his friendship with Booker T. Washington and the objectives of the new party immediately attracted the support of the Negroes, for he knew that if the party were to succeed in the South, it must not openly seek such support. Thus he tried to leave the matter of Negro participation to each state organization but finally concluded that Southern leadership should be put in the hands of "intelligent and benevolent" white men. In actuality, although his tariff plank appealed to Southern industrialists, more were repelled by the party's stand on social issues, and the Progressives made little impression upon the South.[3]

If the Progressive party was too progressive for most Southerners, it was not liberal enough for some. This was borne out by the relative strength of the Socialist party in portions of the South. Generally strongest in the upland areas where the Populists had been most successful, the Southern version of Socialism rested upon many of the social aspects of Populism. In 1912 the Socialist Presidential candidate, Eugene V. Debs, supported chiefly by unsuccessful farmers and unskilled workers who had been indoctrinated by the radical Industrial Workers of the World (IWW), received support varying from 20 per cent of the voters in Oklahoma to .32 per cent in South Carolina.[4] Even this small outlet for grievance, however, was quickly closed, for during World War I, Southerners tended to equate Socialism with foreign "isms" and thus as "un-American."

Dissatisfaction with the Democratic party was quickly forgotten. The election of Southern-born Woodrow Wilson, the first from the region since Andrew Johnson, gave Southerners a reason for pride and hope. Seven members of his cabinet likewise were of Southern origin, while Southern Senators and Representatives dominated the 1912-1914 Congress. The degree to which they influenced the progressive pro-

[3] George E. Mowry, "The South and the Progressive Lily White Party of 1912," *Journal of Southern History*, VI (May, 1940), pp. 237-247; Dewey W. Grantham, Jr., "The Progressive Movement and the Negro," *South Atlantic Quarterly*, LIV (1955), p. 461ff.

[4] Grady McWhiney, "Louisiana Socialists in the Early Twentieth Century: A Study of Rustic Radicalism," *Journal of Southern History*, XX (August, 1954), pp. 315-336.

gram of Wilson's administration is debatable,[5] but as chairmen of key committees and numbering about 35 per cent of all Congressional Democrats, Southerners played an important role. Whether the influence of the residue of Southern agrarianism committed the administration to the New Freedom or whether Southern Congressmen were merely "instruments" of that policy — willing followers for the rewards which could accrue — the fact remained that Southern names such as Underwood, Simmons, Glass, Clayton, Smith, Lever, Owens, and Adamson appeared on most of the important legislation of that period. Only on such reform matters as child labor, woman suffrage, and liberalized immigration policies did the Southerners break with the administration.

War found the region and its representatives supporting the President. As early as 1914, Wilson chose his closest advisor, Colonel Edward M. House of Texas, for the delicate task of taking a trip to Europe to try to prevent the outbreak of fighting. When the President reached the conclusion that war between the United States and Germany was inevitable, only four Southern Congressmen refused their approval. The South went to war with about the same enthusiasm as the rest of the nation, and still others of her native sons assumed high positions in leading the war effort. William G. McAdoo headed the Railroad Administration Board, Carter Glass became Secretary of the Treasury, Walter Hines Page served as ambassador to Great Britain, and Colonel House renewed his travels as roving ambassador to Europe. State Councils of Defense and county committees throughout the region showed their zeal by publishing the names of all persons who did not buy Liberty Bonds or were slackers in other ways. Vigilante groups made life miserable for Socialists and members of the Industrial Workers of the World and also laid the foundations for the rise of the second Ku Klux Klan.

In 1918 the South, faced with local dissatisfaction over the peace program and loss of Wilson's leadership, all augmented by a national reaction against liberalism, began to lose political solidarity. Socially and economically the region was changing, bringing the inevitable political repercussions. The Republican Harding carried Oklahoma and Tennessee in 1920, while shifts of around 18,000 votes in Arkansas and 36,500 in North Carolina would have added those two states to his column. Four years later the Republicans ran better percentage-wise in the South than did the Democrats in the North, although only

[5] Compare Arthur S. Link, "The South and the New Freedom," *American Scholar*, XX (1951), pp. 314-324; Dewey W. Grantham, Jr., "Southern Congressional Leaders and the New Freedom, 1913-1917," *Journal of Southern History*, XIII (November, 1947), pp. 439-459; and Richard M. Abrams, "Woodrow Wilson and the Southern Congressmen, 1913-1916," *ibid.*, XXII (November, 1956), pp. 417-437.

Kentucky and West Virginia ended in Coolidge's camp. But these were only straws in the wind. Southern politicians were as apathetic in this period of "normalcy" as those of the rest of the nation and showed little interest in upsetting the one-party system. Of more pressing and immediate concern were the activities of the Klan and the Negro problem.

This political complacency was soon shattered, however. For years the South had been said to put its faith in only three things — hell, calomel, and the Democratic party. Hell had suffered a serious blow three years earlier at the Scopes trial, and new medicines were challenging calomel. Left was only the Democratic party. But in 1928 even that rock was shaken loose from its foundations, and the most serious challenge to its power in the South since the Civil War was made. Alfred E. Smith — a Catholic, a "wet," a product of Tammany Hall's infamous politics, and already rejected once by the South in 1924 — was made the Democratic party's nominee for President. The national party, in effect, asked the rural, Protestant, and prohibition-minded South to support a candidate diametrically opposed to all things close to Southern hearts. Smith, in brief, represented nearly everything antithetical to the South except Republicanism.

This time the loyalty of the Southerners was stretched too far. The Republicans, on the other hand, offered a Protestant dry, untainted with the polygot "isms" of the big city. These were the type of emotional issues which affected a region well known for past emotionalism. Although the name Republican had been anathema since reconstruction, many Southerners, encouraged by church and rural leaders, cast their first Republican ballot. It did not mean that the South had turned Republican but that it would no longer "vote for the devil if he were on the Democratic ticket." Only the facts that a good proportion of the large newspapers and professional politicians supported Smith and that a Southerner, Joseph T. Robinson of Arkansas, was the Democratic nominee for the Vice-Presidency prevented a worse rout.

Smith carried only the Southern states of South Carolina, Georgia, Alabama, Mississippi, Louisiana, and Arkansas. Analysis of the vote shows that the whites of the Black Belt generally voted for Smith, while those in areas with less Negro population shifted to Hoover. In the two states with the heaviest concentration of Negroes, South Carolina and Mississippi, Hoover received only 4.6 and 17.4 per cent of the vote, respectively. In Arkansas alone did the "white counties" support Smith, and that was probably because of the influence of Robinson. The power of the Democratic press in the South was most strikingly seen in Alabama, where only 7,100 votes kept that state in the Democratic column.

The South was not suddenly and miraculously a two-party region, however. Once its point had been made and the Catholic menace removed, the South returned to the Democratic fold. Southerners felt no inherent objection to one-party domination as long as it was liberal enough on the local level to permit wide differences of opinion. Then, too, economic factors were strong enough to make them feel the national Democratic party best represented their views.

So well was the breach healed and so strong the economic pressures that in 1932 the region enthusiastically supported a "wet," though Protestant, New Yorker. Franklin D. Roosevelt's aristocratic manners appealed to Southern traditionalists, while his stirring words in behalf of the underprivileged aroused the masses. The traditionally poverty-stricken South was quick to see the advantage in an administration which was so openly generous. And once more, as a result of the seniority rule in Congress, Southerners held key positions.

The New Deal had a greater impact upon the South than even the New Freedom of Wilson. Addressing itself directly to the South, it encouraged the spread of liberal ideas, stimulated Negro leaders to reconsider their traditional Republican alliance, fostered the rise of the infant labor organizations, and aroused the hopes and political interests of those normally left unmoved by traditional Southern politics. The Roosevelt personality and program was injected into state and local politics to a degree heretofore unknown in the South. By giving Southern leaders a prominent part in the administration, it tended to pull Southern politics and politicians into the national orbit. The New Deal, likewise, by union assistance and a great increase in Negro voting in the South, strengthened the liberal wing of the party, especially in urban areas.

At first Southern public opinion embraced the New Deal, and its representatives in Congress generally supported the program faithfully. The impact of World War II augmented this, but changes were in sight. The administration seemed to Southerners to become more liberal, and this trend, plus its centralizing tendencies, alarmed a growing number, especially industrialists and businessmen. While flouting Southern prejudices, Roosevelt more and more shifted his appeal to urban voters, members of organized labor, and city Negroes, groups mainly concentrated outside the South — alarming evidence to conservatives that the Democratic party no longer considered Southern votes indispensable to victory. Eleanor Roosevelt also stepped up her personal campaign for better treatment of the black race; moreover, the discontented and neglected groups in the South began threatening the controlling political cliques as they had not been threatened since the days of the Agrarian revolt.

With Southern conservatives genuinely alarmed, soon a number of the region's Congressmen were openly sniping at the administration's racial, financial, and labor policies and voicing concern over the court reorganization plan. After 1936 the Republican presidential vote began increasing in those parts of Southern cities inhabited by the growing business groups. (Labor became politically activated at a much slower rate. Only 51 per cent of the Southern skilled and semi-skilled voted in 1952, in contrast with 80 per cent outside the region. For the unskilled, the figures were 28 and 78 per cent, respectively.) Even financial aid lost some of its lure with the return of prosperity. One Georgia planter retorted, when reminded of the amount of Northern money being sent in for relief and other activities: "We oughta be gittin' some of it back; they stole enough from us in the war." Despite Roosevelt's effort to purge some of his worst Southern tormentors, other names stayed high on the list of his most faithful supporters — men such as Pat Harrison of Mississippi, Alben W. Barkley of Kentucky, James F. Byrnes of South Carolina, Robert L. Doughton of North Carolina, Joseph T. Robinson of Arkansas, Cordell Hull of Tennessee, and Hugo L. Black of Alabama — and the rank and file of Southern voters still continued to show approval of Rossevelt the man, if not his policies, at the polls.

Northern disregard of the doctrine of states' rights and the party's abolition of the unit and two-thirds majority rules for voting and nomination weakened the South's position in the national party. Nevertheless, Roosevelt carried all the Southern states in each of his campaigns and continued to find some of his strongest supporters as well as detractors in that region. However, the establishment of the Fair Employment Practices Committee (FEPC) in 1941 to eliminate racial and religious discrimination in war industries and the fight in 1942 over repeal of the poll tax, prevented only by a Southern filibuster, weakened the unifying effect which the outbreak of World War II had had in moderating Southern discontent. Thomas Dewey, the Republican nominee in 1944, received almost as much support in the South as Hoover had in 1928, although the region remained solidly in the Democratic column. Southern Congressmen voted more often with the Republicans than formerly. Less than one-twelfth supported the administration in 90 per cent of the votes during 1944, and more than one-third of the Southern members of the House during that session voted against their party on over 35 per cent of the issues.[6]

Once more, as in Populist days, the Negro was made the central, if not always the real, point of contention which separated the Northern and Southern wings of the party. Southerners felt that the national

[6] C. Van Woodward, *Reunion and Reaction*, 2nd ed., revised (Garden City, N. Y.: Doubleday, 1956), p. 271ff.

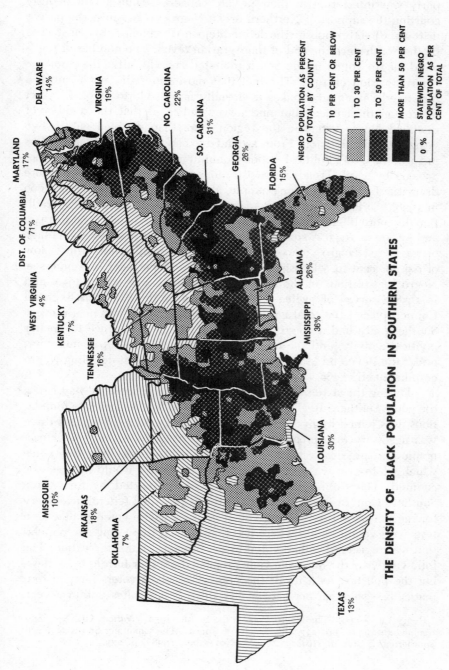

THE DENSITY OF BLACK POPULATION IN SOUTHERN STATES

NEGRO POPULATION AS PERCENT OF TOTAL, BY COUNTY

10 PER CENT OR BELOW

11 TO 30 PER CENT

31 TO 50 PER CENT

MORE THAN 50 PER CENT

0 %  STATEWIDE NEGRO POPULATION AS PER CENT OF TOTAL

*Reprinted, with permission, from the New York Times of March 18, 1956*

DELAWARE 14%

VIRGINIA 19%

NO. CAROLINA 22%

SO. CAROLINA 31%

GEORGIA 26%

FLORIDA 15%

ALABAMA 26%

MISSISSIPPI 36%

LOUISIANA 30%

TEXAS 13%

OKLAHOMA 7%

ARKANSAS 18%

MISSOURI 10%

TENNESSEE 16%

KENTUCKY 7%

WEST VIRGINIA 4%

DIST. OF COLUMBIA 71%

MARYLAND 17%

party was interfering in their private concerns while simultaneously courting the support of Northern urban Negroes. Certainly, the party's drift was directly opposite the deliberate course which had been steered by the South since the end of the Agrarian revolt. The number of registered Negro voters in the South mounted steadily after the Supreme Court decision of 1944. The fact that most states did not identify a registered voter's race makes it virtually impossible to arrive at exact figures on the subject, but one survey indicated that the number of qualified Negro voters in the region more than doubled within two years after the decision. From around 150,000 to 250,000 Negro voters in 1940, the CIO's Political Action Committee estimated that there were 750,000 by 1948. Trends in registrations in specific states were more dramatic. In Louisiana, for example, Negro registrants numbered 2,000 in 1936; 880 in 1940; 1,600 in 1944; and 7,500 in 1946. Virginia, traditionally more liberal, had 25,400 in 1941; 32,500 in 1943; 44,000 in 1945; and 57,800 in 1947. A study made in 1947 showed that the percentage of registered Negro voters to adult Negro population ran from a low of 0.9 per cent in Mississippi to a high of 25.8 per cent in Tennessee. Negro registrations in the South approximated 900,000 by 1950, and in 1958 a survey of twelve Southern states by the Southern Regional Council placed the total at 1,238,038.[7] By that time practically every Southern city had a Negro voters' league to spur the race to greater political activity, and the Southern Christian Leadership Conference, under the Reverend Martin Luther King, set its goal at doubling Negro enrollments by 1960.

During the sixties help came from many directions. In May, 1962, the white Southern Regional Council, financed by three private foundations, was joined by five black groups to spearhead a drive. This drive was necessary to overcome the lethargy based upon the fear of economic and physical reprisals — a belief that it made little difference which white man was elected, and that black votes would not even be counted. The Voting Rights Act of 1965, supported by forty-three Southern Congressmen, assisted greatly. It provided federal machinery for registering and protecting voters in areas where voter-qualification tests were required and where less than half of the voting-age population was registered or had voted in the previous national election. The following year the Supreme Court removed another hurdle by outlawing the poll tax. As a result the number of black voters jumped dramatically — some 50 per cent in five deep South states within a year.

[7] Henry Lee Moon, "The Negro Vote in the South: 1952," *Nation*, CLXXV (September 27, 1952), pp. 247-248; Lewis W. Jones, "The Changing Status of Negro Southerners," *Current History*, XXXV (November, 1958), p. 273.

Slow but steady increases found better than half (3.5 million) of the eligible blacks registered in 1972, although the number was not as much as some black leaders had hoped. More important, there were now black office-holders. Before the act of 1965 there had been only seventy-two blacks in elective offices in the South, but nine years later there were 1,314, an 1,800 per cent increase. The result was that not a single Southern state was without a black legislator. Thus, democracy took on new meaning to most blacks.

The growing political participation of the Negro, the encouragement given him by national Democratic administrations, and the use of federal authority in his behalf to break down the barrier of segregation precipitated the first formal revolt by the South against the Democratic party in the twentieth century. Unlike the uprising in 1928, when the Black-Belt counties stood firm, the Dixiecrat Rebellion of 1948 came from an alliance of the areas of greatest Negro concentration and the industrial centers. Both of these groups found reasons to feel aggrieved by the racial, labor, business, and agricultural policies of the New Deal and of President Harry Truman. Essentially representing the conservative wing of the Southern Democratic party, the Dixiecrat leadership was furnished by corporation lawyers, well-to-do businessmen, representatives of industry, and Black-Belt landlords.

The revolt actually began as early as 1944, when anti-Roosevelt movements started in South Carolina, Mississippi, and Texas. The only success they achieved was in helping to defeat Henry Wallace for the Vice-Presidential nomination, although they did close the popular vote margin in the fall election to the narrowest it had been in twenty-eight years. By 1947, Roosevelt was dead, and the country seemed to be moving to the right, politically, to the encouragement of the conservatives. Yet, currents were running underneath which soon disrupted the peaceful scene. The South had willingly joined the World War II crusade for the "Four Freedoms" without feeling the necessity of extending them to their Negro citizens, although liberals of all shades and varieties were pointing out the inconsistency between what America preached and what the South practiced. Negroes became more restive after the War, and ever larger numbers followed those who had moved north earlier. Communists, labor leaders, newspapermen, minority leaders, and Northern politicians clamored for reform, and many viewed the Northern Negro vote as politically more important than that of the white South.

In response, President Truman appointed a Committee on Civil Rights, composed of thirteen Northerners and two Southerners, whose report, published on October 29, 1947, called for sweeping government action for an end to most forms of segregation, a federal anti-lynching law, abolition of poll taxes and "white" primaries, and a federal Fair Employment Practices Act. Pressure on the South was justified on the ground that it was "sound policy to use the idealism and prestige of our whole people to check the wayward tendencies of a part of them." Calling these demands an "American charter of human freedom," Truman asked for Congressional implementation.

To many Southerners this seemed little less than a declaration of war against the region. Already feeling that Roosevelt and Truman had been deliberately seeking to undermine the rights of the states, they based their defense upon states' rights. Even before Truman requested action, Governor William M. Tuck of Virginia declared that federal policy, if continued, would result "in the virtual abolition of the states," while Mississippi's Senator James Eastland saw proof that "organized mongrel minorities control the government." Governor Fielding Wright of Mississippi, in his inaugural address, called for a break with the Democratic party if its leaders continued to try "to wreck the South and our institutions." Although the racial implications were stressed, the oil interests of the region were also unhappy with federal efforts at regulation and the Supreme Court decision in the tidelands oil cases.[8] Private power companies complained of competition with TVA and similar governmental agencies, while businessmen in general chafed under wage and hour regulations and other aspects of the labor program.

Governor Wright took the fight to the Southern Governors Conference, organized in 1937 to secure cooperation in solution of common regional problems, demanding that it take a stand against any further efforts to enact civil rights legislation and call a "Southern Conference of true Democrats" to plan a course of action. The governors decided, however, to first approach the Democratic National Chairman to see if he would use his influence to have the controversial legislation withdrawn and if he would favor a return to the old two-thirds rule for Democratic nominations for the Presidency, which had been dropped under Roosevelt in 1936. When this was refused and Truman, after the failure of Congress to pass the desired laws, announced that he was going to campaign on the issue, the governors' committee recommended that state Democratic conventions go on record as opposing the nomination in 1948 of Truman and any candidate favoring civil rights.

Within the Southern states, local Democratic organizations were the scenes of internal strife between the factions willing to defy the national party and those willing to yield if necessary. In Alabama the delegates were pledged to vote against any nominee who was unsatisfactory on civil rights, and about half pledged themselves to walk out

[8] Ernest R. Bartley, *The Tidelands Oil Controversy* (Austin: Univ. of Texas, 1953).

of the national convention if a Truman-type civil rights plank were adopted. The state Democratic executive committee of Mississippi called a regional meeting of "all true white Jeffersonian Democrats," those "volunteer citizens" who supported states' rights and opposed the trend of the national party. At this conference, meeting in Jackson, Mississippi, on May 10, 1948, the group, dominated by delegations from Mississippi and South Carolina, called upon each state to choose delegates and presidential electors opposed to objectives of the Truman administration. If the civil rights program were supported by the party's national convention, the group called for another meeting, to be held at Birmingham, Alabama, to plot future strategy.

At Philadelphia, scene of the national convention, the Northern and Western delegates showed little inclination to yield to the demands of the Southern faction. After the Southerners rejected the platform committee's compromise plank and demanded acceptance of the Southern view, the majority of the delegates then adopted an even more radical platform than at first proposed. It "highly" commended Truman for his "courageous" stand, refused to reinstate the two-thirds rule, and urged enactment of the civil rights program, leaving even moderate Southerners stunned at this repudiation of the South by the Northern and Western wings of the party. With this, to the chanted strains of "Dixie," thirty-five delegates, chiefly from Alabama and Mississippi, walked out of the convention. Those remaining vainly tried to block the renomination of Truman by uniting in support of Richard B. Russell of Georgia. Equally unavailing were their efforts to dictate the Vice-Presidency, which went to Senator Alben Barkley of Kentucky, a Southerner willing to support the national party platform.

Two days after the end of the national convention, on July 17, a "conference" was held at Birmingham, Alabama, consisting largely of Mississippi leaders, Alabama conservatives, followers of Governor J. Strom Thurmond of South Carolina, and hundreds of curious citizens from the surrounding areas, including a large bloc of college students out for a lark. The majority could not be said to have had any special political importance, representing no one except themselves. But viewing the national Democratic party as being anti-Southern and the Republican party as being little better on civil rights, besides being handicapped by its traditional stigma in the region, the group decided to organize the States' Rights party, more commonly called the Dixiecrats. After maneuvers which indicated little of democracy in action and much of behind-the-scenes control, Governors Thurmond of South Carolina and Wright of Mississippi were unanimously recommended to carry the standard of the new party in support of a "declaration of principles" which primarily rejected national interference in state affairs.

The political strategy behind the move was the belief that in a close election no candidate could win without Southern votes, thus forcing a choice by the House of Representatives. There, the Dixiecrats believed, all Democrats would unite in support of a Southern Democrat rather than see the victory of a Republican. With Henry Wallace already campaigning on a "Progressive" ticket, the strategy had some chance of success if the former Confederate states would only unite behind Thurmond.

On the other hand, the Dixiecrats faced a hard task. Thurmond was not personally or politically strong; the party was immediately suspected by the Southern liberals of being reactionary; politicians remembered the political fate of leaders who had bolted in 1928 and shuddered at the possible loss of patronage. Moreover, the movement was openly flouting one of the most sacred historical shibboleths of the South: the necessity for Democratic party regularity under all conditions. Despite Dixiecrat denials of being reactionary and their passionate avowals that this was not a bolt but that they instead were the "true Democrats," opposing "totalitarianism at home and abroad," they were not able to unite the Southern wing of the Democratic party behind them. The progressive elements and the ruling politicians mostly stayed in the Truman ranks. In North Carolina, Virginia, and Tennessee, they were held in line from fear that a Democratic split would give local victory to the Republicans, a possibility the Dixiecrats tried to avoid by having the regular Democratic electors instructed to vote for Thurmond and Wright. Essentially, the movement failed because it was unable to win the Southern electoral votes. It carried only the states of South Carolina, Alabama, Mississippi, and Louisiana and garnered only thirty-nine electoral and 1,169,000 popular votes.

The people of the South were not ready for a full-scale revolt. Despite the fact that the old party had proven unreliable on the race issue, they were unwilling to go over into the hated Republican camp, which seemed to offer little that was more suitable to Southern wishes, or make the final break by supporting a third party. Prophetically, in all the states which the Dixiecrats carried, they had been successful in having their candidates declared the representatives of the Democratic party.

The period of the fifties was one marked by political uncertainty in the South. Despite the talk of retaliation, the Truman administration tried to hold the South by giving its leaders key appointments. Moreover, Truman's efforts to make good on his civil rights program continued to meet defeat, largely through the agency of Southerners holding key committee posts in Congress. In 1952 the Democratic party showed itself eager to heal the breach made by the Dixiecrats.

The convention refused to bind all delegates in advance to support the party nominee and wrote into its platform moderate provisions on civil rights and minimum wages. When first place on the ticket went to Adlai E. Stevenson of Illinois, the convention, in another move calculated to appease the South, chose Senator John J. Sparkman of Alabama as its candidate for Vice-President. Nevertheless, in the election that followed, the region showed its continued disapproval of the New and Fair Deals, although the two major parties avoided most head-on issues. Despite the growth of a Southern labor movement which tended to support liberal candidates and increased Negro participation, prosperity had created many businessmen and professional and middle-class citizens who felt their interest more closely tied with the Republicans.[9] The fact that Dwight D. Eisenhower had not been active politically before his Republican nomination, the hold of the "great man tradition," and the urgency of the Korean War — all favored his candidacy. Southern "Democrats for Eisenhower" clubs helped remove the stigma of voting Republican. Although in 1952 the only states Stevenson carried were Southern or border ones, the voters of Virginia, Tennessee, Florida, Texas, and Oklahoma put their states into the Eisenhower column. In South Carolina, Louisiana, and Kentucky, the Democratic margin was very narrow.

When the election of 1956 proved a repetition of 1952 and Eisenhower this time carried Florida, Kentucky, Louisiana, Tennessee, Texas, Virginia, Oklahoma, and West Virginia, there was considerable speculation as to what had happened to the "solid South." But, while the region did not appear as solidly Democratic as once had been thought, in another way it was as firm as ever. Despite what seemed to be a growing tendency to vote Republican in national elections, voter registration remained true to the traditional party, and non-presidential Republican candidates still had little hope of success. The region still remained unique in the habit of viewing all political questions from a racial angle, in its citizens' habit of not voting, in the unity of its Congressional delegations, and in its custom of seeing little relationship between state and national politics.

Democrats found encouragement for the future in these facts and in two new areas during 1956-1960. Uncertain economic conditions and chronic unemployment were joined by a flare-up in race relations. The Supreme Court decision in 1954, in Brown *v.* Board of Education of Topeka, had been a bitter blow to school segregationists but was generally blamed on the Court rather than the Eisenhower administration. Little Rock, Arkansas, became the focal point of the Southern

[9] Dewey W. Grantham, Jr., "Politics Below the Potomac," *Current History*, XXXV (November, 1958), pp. 262-265.

resistance to integration in 1957, as Governor Orval E. Faubus used the National Guard to prevent nine Negro children from entering the city's Central High School. President Eisenhower countered by providing the children with federal military protection. His administration also passed the first civil rights laws after reconstruction, giving protection to Negroes wanting to vote by allowing federal judges to intervene when state officials refused to register qualified persons.

The Democrats took a calculated gamble in 1960 with the nomination of a Catholic, John F. Kennedy, for President. To mitigate the effect that this might have on the South, the party chose Lyndon Johnson of Texas for his running mate. With the injection of the new issue of religion and the growing awareness on the part of Southerners that there was little difference on the race issue between the parties, the contest obviously would be close in the South. As anticipated, Southern Negroes and organized labor were generally for Kennedy, and in the last analysis Johnson's influence probably saved the election for the Democrats by holding at least forty-six Southern electoral votes in the Democratic column.

Despite the fact that former Vice-President Richard M. Nixon, the Republican candidate, carried only the Southern states of Florida, Kentucky, Oklahoma, Tennessee, and Virginia, he increased the Republican vote and outran Eisenhower in six states, four of which were in the deep South. In the eleven states of the old Confederacy, he polled 4,723,981 votes (47.7 per cent), as against Kennedy's 5,179,550. This compared to 50.5 per cent for Eisenhower in 1956 and 26.8 for Dewey in 1948. Nixon's chief support came from the cities of the South, and the Republicans held their five House seats in Florida, North Carolina, Texas, and Virginia (2), though running behind in every other contested Congressional race. Mississippi was carried by a slate of eight independent electors, who with seven others from Oklahoma and Alabama cast their votes for Senator Harry F. Byrd of Virginia in a futile gesture of defiance.

The first of two assassinations which shook the South occurred with the shooting of President John Kennedy in Dallas on November 22, 1963 (the second being that of Martin Luther King, Jr., in 1968). For a brief period the question of regional complicity was raised, for Kennedy's death brought a Texan to the White House, the first Southern resident since Andrew Johnson to hold the office. Lyndon Johnson in his early career was a Southern liberal and great admirer of Franklin Roosevelt. After Roosevelt's death he briefly moved to the right, especially on civil rights, voting against six such bills, although refusing to sign a Southern Manifesto protesting the Supreme Court's desegregation decision. But as Senate Majority Leader he fought for passage of the Civil Rights Act of 1957, although some still suspected him of being a secret segregationist. As President, however, his administrations produced the Civil Rights Act of 1964, the Voting Rights Act of 1965, the Fair Housing Act of 1966, and the Federal Jury Reform Act of 1968.

In 1964 Johnson was the Democratic presidential candidate, while the Republicans chose Barry Goldwater, whose political philosophy was much closer to that of the conservative South than that of its native son. The candidacy of segregationist George Wallace, governor of Alabama, proved popular in Northern states such as Wisconsin. However, he withdrew when he feared he would serve only to defeat Goldwater. In the election, however, Goldwater collected votes more like the Dixiecrat, Strom Thurmond, than like the Republican, Dwight Eisenhower, for the Southern votes he received were mainly influenced by the race issue, coming from the Black Belt rather than the urban centers. Altogether, Goldwater carried only the five deep South states of Alabama, Georgia, Louisiana, Mississippi, and South Carolina. A North Carolina Republican elector even cast his ballot for Wallace. The region gave Johnson 52 per cent of its votes.

The first Southerner to be elected since Woodrow Wilson, Johnson's "War on Poverty" and his "Great Society" were to fall short of his own expectations, but social legislation dealing with civil rights, education, health services, housing, welfare, urban and rural renewal, and preservation of scenic America was most impressive. One of his goals was to free his fellow Southerners from the onus of being segregationists and to end their feeling of alienation from the rest of the nation, but these efforts did not bring him the popularity he craved. He was saddled with the blame for an unpopular war in Vietnam and his social reforms brought little praise, even from those who benefitted most. Johnson was haunted by his past as a Southerner and believed it was this that prevented his getting a fair hearing as President. He also felt that it subjected him to ridicule and, finally, helped force him from office. In his memoirs he commented on that "disdain for the South that seems to be woven into the fabric of Northern experience."[10]

When Johnson announced he would not be a candidate in 1968, his party chose then Vice President Hubert Humphrey. George Wallace became the candidate for the new American Independent Party, calling for patriotic rededication and states' rights, while insisting that he was a segregationist, but not a racist. The Republicans turned once more to Richard Nixon, hoping he could rescue that party from the conservative stance which had brought political disaster four years

[10] T. Harry Williams, "Huey, Lyndon, and Southern Radicalism," *Journal of American History*, LX (September, 1973), 267-293.

earlier. Their "Southern Strategy" in the main, appeared to be based upon a "go slow" policy as regarded civil rights, an active wooing of the South politically, and promises of conservative appointments, especially to the Supreme Court. The choice of Spiro Agnew of Maryland as his running mate was generally ascribed to this policy. Nixon polled only 350,000 more popular votes than Humphrey and was hurt in the South by Wallace, who carried Alabama, Arkansas, Louisiana, Mississippi, and Georgia. But his appeal to the South was seen in the fact that the Democrats carried only West Virginia, Texas, and Maryland. Thus, his 37 per cent of the Southern vote gave him his national margin of victory.

Although in retrospect, Nixon's "Southern Strategy" can be criticized in many details, it did have some unexpected dividends. It acknowledged the necessity of restoring the South's sense of belonging to the Union and did bring that region back into national political councils. The Presidential attention lavished on the area was duplicated in 1972 when the Democratic presidential aspirants courted the South more eagerly than ever before. Nixon was much more acceptable to the Southerners, however, than the liberal Democrat, George McGovern. In the election of 1972 Nixon became the first Republican candidate in the nation's history to carry every Southern state.

Although the South had shown increasing tendencies to vote Republican in national elections, conservative Democratic control on state and local levels was successfully maintained by use of time-worn tactics. The most important of these was the invoking of the race question. For almost 100 years, this technique had successfully forced rebels into conformity and prevented the development of a more realistic and democratic political system. The Democratic party glossed over economic and social cleavages by forcing into the same camp such natural antagonists as the social conservatives from the hills and the economic conservatives from the lower country. Antiquated apportionment practices and the overwhelming weight of rural areas in state politics added to the strength of the conservatives and were a potent force against change. Furthermore, as long as conservative Democrats, loyal to the interests of industrialization, could control the state governments, there was no need for a separate conservative group led by Republicans. For that matter, as long as the potential nucleus of a Southern Republican party raised no serious complaints against the local Democratic administrations, it had little chance of becoming a major threat in the South.

Although state and local governments remained essentially oriented to the one-party system, the twentieth century, nevertheless, saw some significant changes. In general, this resulted from the acceptance of a broader view of the purposes and duties of the state government, especially in the direction of increased public services. Budgets grew steadily, while the administrative machinery groaned under the new and enlarged tasks of providing protection, education, sanitation, and agencies of social betterment in ever-increasing volumes. States strove desperately to escape the stigma of low educational rank, poor roads, and low health standards. Correspondingly, budgets also increased for library extension service and for institutions for the unfortunates. As early as 1930, Virginia budgeted its revenue on the basis of 7.0 per cent for general government, 1.3 for conservation of natural resources, 1.0 for health and sanitation, 40.6 for highways, 9.9 for charities and the like, and 32 for education. These were percentages which approximated those of New York State, except that the latter spent more on conservation and charities and less on highways. Virginia was not an exception; Mississippi, for example, the same year divided her efforts: 6.0 (general government), 1.7 (conservation), 3.0 (health and sanitation), 19.2 (highways), 11.7 (charities), and 45.3 (education). For fiscal 1972 the median amount paid by citizens for support of state and local governments was $461; among Southern states, only Maryland and Delaware exceeded this amount. Because of the greater relative poverty of Southern states, this meant that these governments were especially concerned with devising tax systems which would support these increased burdens. Most criticism of Southern backwardness in governmental functions should be directed at the lack of money with which to accomplish the desired goals, rather than at a callousness concerning their need.

Less commendable, however, was the way in which rural white political control was used to sustain white supremacy. It is doubly ironic, therefore, that a Southern-initiated test case provided the vehicle that broke rural domination and produced one of the major state-level reforms of this century. The mayor of Nashville, Tennessee, seeking better representation for his city and its home county in the legislature was upheld by the Supreme Court in Baker v. Carr. That now famous, "one man, one vote," decision in March, 1962, forced legislative reapportionment in recognition of the fact that most Americans are now urban residents. However, to date, legislative philosophy has been slow to reflect this change. Also, while the South originated the two major systems for municipal reform in this century — the commissioner and city-manager plans — its county governments proved themselves increasingly ineffective. This, too, was not a unique Southern problem but a general American one. While the chief solution will probably lie in the area of county consolidation, few states were willing to act. However, action was taken in the 1950's toward abolishing the antiquated county court system, and some states passed permissive statutes for county managers.

A backward look over the political history of the South during the last quarter century makes three developments stand out. First and most dramatic, because of the accompanying passions and violence, was the effective enfranchisement of the Southern blacks. In 1964 civil rights advocates concentrated their attention upon voter registration. Almost predictably, violence struck as it had the previous year when Medgar Evers, the black Mississippi civil rights leader, had been murdered, and a bomb killed black children at a Birmingham, Alabama church. This time three young men engaged in a summer voting project were killed near Philadelphia, Mississippi, by lawless elements which included law officers. In 1965 tactics used by local white officials against voter registration efforts so outraged and frustrated Dr. King that he led a protest march in Selma, Alabama. When this peaceful demonstration was brutally attacked, thousands of blacks and whites from throughout the nation poured into that town, and additional lives were lost in new confrontations.

President Johnson, in a strong, nationally televised speech, denounced the actions of his home region: "It is wrong, morally wrong, to deny any of your fellow Americans the right to vote in this country." He touched the hearts of many black Americans by challenging the nation to cast off the "crippling legacy of bigotry and injustice" and then he closed his talk with "We Shall Overcome," the slogan of the civil rights movement. Congress responded with the Voting Rights Act of 1965. The result was the steady increase in both registrations and in the election of black officials. The latter were placed in state legislatures, on city councils, as county commissioners, and in Congress. The 1901 valedictory of Congressman George White of North Carolina had at last come true: "This, Mr. Chairman, is perhaps the Negroe's temporary farewell to the American Congress; but let me say that, Phoenix-like, he will rise up and come again."

The second political phenomenon of the last twenty-five years was the active presence of two, and occasionally three, party operations, after virtually a century of one-party domination. Although the Republican party had existed in the South since Reconstruction, it held little attraction for most Southerners, but served mainly as a means of registering a protest vote against national Democratic policy. In the sixties, however, Southerners seemed more willing to admit agreement with the Republican party's principles. The States Right ticket proved to be a halfway house toward Republicanism (its leader, Strom Thurmond, later became a Republican), and after the 1948 election the South did not cast a solid electorial vote in a single election until 1972 — and then for a Republican.

By 1952 Southern Republicans had begun contesting elections, even on the local levels. They were aided by Eisenhower's candidacy which made it more respectable to vote Republican. New recruits also helped to break the hold of the Old Guard in several states. Urbanism and higher incomes both proved to be in the Republicans' favor. The urban South's support of the GOP nominees indicated a regional difference which could be explained by the weakness of organized labor, absence of an immigrant bloc, and the new white-collar, management-oriented industry. Similarly, the party offered more opportunities for leadership to the ambitious young than did the entrenched Democratic party.

The success of John Tower in winning Johnson's old Senate seat in Texas was inspiring elsewhere. In 1962 Oklahoma Republicans elected Henry Bellmon their first governor, and Senatorial candidates made serious challenges in Louisiana, South Carolina, and Alabama. In Congressional races in the South, Republicans picked up four additional seats for a total of eleven. Two years later the party had organized all but 138 of 1,140 counties in the deep South, contested 84 of 119 Congressional districts, and won in eighteen, including five new ones. On the state level, they held 44 senate and 137 house seats. The 1966 elections gave them two more Senators, seven Congressmen, and three governors. More significant for the future was the fact that millions of Southerners had voted Republican, often for the first time, and the party had acquired a respectability never enjoyed previously. But generations of tradition and past voting habits were still bolstered by long-held Democratic posts, and the Republican party would continue to struggle to maintain its viability as a political option for Southern voters.[10]

A third political characteristic of the third quarter of the twentieth century was the rise of a new moderation in Southern politics. This may well be a partial result of the first two. Long the center of radical stands, the South has seen the rise of a new breed of moderate politicians who have been winning elections. One straw in the wind was the creation in 1967 of the Southern Committee on Political Ethics, which included leaders in religion, business, communications, labor, law, and civil rights. It had as its goals: full political participation by racial minorities, voter education, dignifying the profession of politics, and establishment of a climate favorable to free discussion of public issues. That voter tastes changed is seen not only in the more moderate stance of George Wallace, but also in the recent elections in Virginia, South Carolina, Georgia, Florida, and Arkansas of one Republican and four Democratic governors. These new politicians frankly and openly stood for an end to racial discrimination and the necessity for their states to align themselves with the rest of the nation.

[10] George B. Tindall, *The Disruption of the Solid South* (New York: W. W. Norton & Co., Inc., 1972).

# 22

# SOUTHERN ECONOMIC DEVELOPMENT
# SINCE 1930

THE TWO MOST POWERFUL economic influences upon the "New South" were the Great Depression, beginning in 1929, and the succeeding World War II. As has been indicated, regardless of the shock which the Depression caused among non-agricultural classes, its onset was no surprise to the Southern farmer, who had been in economic distress since 1920. Up to 1930 there had been a steady increase in tenancy and a decline in the number of farm owners. None of the efforts of distraught politicians had proven effective in stemming the drop in farm prices. Suddenly, the rest of the country found itself confronting similar circumstances, and its predicament only made the Southern farmer's situation worse.

What happened to cotton was a typical example. As the world demand for cotton goods declined, mills cut production. This, in turn, curtailed orders for raw cotton at a time of maximum acreage, for growers in desperation had increased output to offset low prices. In 1929 the Southern cotton crop totaled almost 15,000,000 bales and was competing on the world market with a foreign production of 11,500,000 bales. The price dropped from twenty to twelve cents a pound. By the next year, it fell to eight cents. In 1931, despite warnings, the region grew 17,000,000 bales, and the New York quotations skidded to five cents. On Southern markets it was even lower.

This was immediate disaster to tenant, landlord, banker, and those dependent upon cotton. The farmer had gotten $1,245,000,000 for his 1929 crop; the larger output in 1931 brought only $484,000,000 — a reduction of 62 per cent — and in 1932 he received only $374,000,000. In the same year, forced farm sales in the United States were 46 per 1,000, but in North Carolina they were 68.2 and in Mississippi 99.9. The South was dazed. Many farmers abandoned their land altogether and fled to town, as in all states a huge cityward movement began. There they found their situation little improved. The basic industries were curtailing employment, and there were few alternative occupations. Only the tobacco industry showed signs of stability. The category formerly known as "Negro jobs" was virtually erased, as whites began to compete for that work. Ignoring their preachers, who said they were paying for past sins, Southerners, white and Negro, blamed the Yankee, Wall Street, and especially that man in the White House. Their scorn took the form of naming makeshift wagons constructed of old automobile chassis "Hoover buggies" and their expanding slums "Hoovervilles." Southerners agreed that there must be a change and probably all greeted Roosevelt's election with greater over-all glee than people elsewhere in the country.

Reformers looking toward the South saw a region with approximately one-third of the nation's area and population, yet only one-fifth of its wealth. There lived 20 per cent of the wage earners who obtained only 15 per cent of the national wages. About 97 per cent of the nation's cotton and 87 per cent of the tobacco was grown there, but only 16 per cent of the manufacturers were Southern in origin; 27 per cent of the nation's property value was there, but only 14 per cent of the bank deposits and 32 per cent of the state government debts. Wasteful methods of agriculture and progressive deforestation had long since squandered many natural assets. With the largest number of farms of any region, per-farm acreage was the smallest. Much of the mineral wealth and hydroelectric potential was untouched. While rural poverty was notable, industrial laborers averaged sixteen cents per hour below the national average. Half of the region's people were ill-housed; 60 to 88 per cent of the city dwellers were ill-fed; sickness and death rates were the highest anywhere in the country.

No President since the Civil War showed as much concern for the South as did Franklin D. Roosevelt. Along with those of the rest of the nation, the attack upon the South's specific problems began in 1933. The Southern states were among the first to suspend their banks: Louisiana in February, 1933, with Alabama, Kentucky, Mississippi, and

Tennessee following by March 1. On March 9, the President sent to Congress an Emergency Banking Bill, permitting sound banks to re-open and providing them with greater stability. The varied program of the New Deal furnished government credit, debt adjustment, crop controls, soil conservation, crop loans, aid to tenants to purchase homes, and a variety of efforts to rehabilitate farmers. Basically, its efforts were directed against tenancy, the one-crop system, and the poor financial arrangements in the South.

Of especial concern were the Agricultural Adjustment Acts of 1933 and 1938, aimed at regulating farm production and maintaining purchasing power at levels which had existed before World War I. Throughout the South, farmers slaughtered animals and plowed under crops which had been declared excess. Millions of dollars from the federal treasury flowed southward in payment. While, for the first time in over a decade, Southern agriculture produced a little more than a mere living, too large a share of the profits went to the landlords. Benefit payments were made directly to the planters, who often kept most of the money in payment of cropper's debts, real or imaginary. Crop restrictions threw thousands of tenants and sharecroppers off the farms and onto relief. Especially hard hit were Negroes; by one estimate, over 70,000 Negro farmers were displaced by whites between 1930 and 1935. Efforts by the government to force landlords into a more equitable sharing were generally unavailing. In many cases planters dropped the sharecrop system and rehired their tenants as wage hands without right to benefits. The Department of Labor estimated that perhaps as many as half of the landlords opposed any change in relief techniques for fear that it would cause loss of control over croppers.

In an attack upon the problem of rural credit, Congress in 1933 created the Federal Farm Mortgage Corporation for low interest loans on agricultural lands and passed the Farm Credit Act to provide loans for production and marketing of farm produce. These were followed by a five-year moratorium on farm foreclosures. The Farm Security Administration Act of 1937 attempted to deal with the financial problems of "bad credit risks," going so far as to try to set up cooperative villages and farms. Over $300,000,000 was loaned to tenants and sharecroppers to buy livestock and equipment. Some efforts, largely ineffectual, were made to close out marginal farms in the South and to resettle their inhabitants.

The National Industrial Recovery Act of 1933 sought essentially the same goal for industry as the farm program envisioned for farmers — relief, recovery, and reform. The hope was that industry could expand employment while at the same time recognizing the rights of labor and improving wages and hours of work. The increased wages and shorter hours of the NRA, however, caused many Southern employers to dispense with as many employees as possible and to use the "stretch-out" to get a maximum effort for those remaining. Machinery surplanted individuals whenever possible. These facts gave the newly-flowering Southern labor movement just grounds for demanding still more federal intervention.

The Public Works Administration and the Works Progress Administration, in their Southern phases, left indelible marks upon the region. The PWA constructed new courthouses, post offices, libraries, bridges, hospitals, college and university dormitories, and the like. The WPA built sidewalks, drainage ditches, sewer systems, and roads, as well as a multitude of ephemeral projects. As a by-product, it surveyed historical records, placed murals in public buildings, gave free entertainment, and conducted classes for illiterates. The Civilian Conservation Corps helped to some extent in reforestation and the battle against erosion, while old-age and unemployment insurance and old-age assistance programs, operated under the social security system, gave thousands of low-income Southerners financial help. The Federal Housing Administration's slum clearance program in the South was particularly helpful, especially to the Negro, with the region getting roughly half of all such projects in the nation. The Rural Electrification Administration made cheap electrical power available to remote rural areas which had been bypassed by private utilities, making possible the development of diversified farming, establishment of small industries, and enhancement of the general attractiveness of these areas.

While some of the New Deal programs which concerned the South were ill-advised and misfired, the general effect was good. About the only substantial bloc of farmers who felt the over-all result had been bad were the sugar producers. Nearly half of the sugar land was idle by 1939 because of quota reductions, and these growers felt they had been sacrificed to the administration's "good neighbor policy," despite the argument of Secretary of Agriculture Henry A. Wallace that it was an "inefficient industry" and should be eliminated gradually by competition.

There was also abuses of the programs by Southerners. The rise of cotton prices brought complaints that they were not higher and denunciations of the crop restrictions. Individual landlords cheated on their acreage allotments and applied fertilizer to their crop to such a degree that, in 1937, the average production per acre was 267 pounds, fifty more than former records. The total crop hit a record-breaking 19,-000,000 bales, which dropped the price from the previous eleven-to-fourteen-cent-range down to eight cents a pound.

On the other hand, Southern taxpayers objected to the WPA, CCC,

and similar agencies on the grounds that they were havens where loaf-
ers were supported at public expense and that, by offering shorter
hours, lighter work, and year-round employment, they interfered with
the labor supply. Although relief payments in the South were about
half that of other regions, they were generally more than a sharecropper or many tenants could make when employed. The Southern industrial worker, even though his chances for employment were fewer and
his pay scale lower than elsewhere in the nation, could rejoice that at
least the factories were operating and hours were shorter than he had
ever known. To the masses, the fact that much of the philosophy of the
New Deal ran counter to established Southern ideals was no problem,
and they were almost solidly uncritical supporters of Roosevelt. They
were willing to try almost any change to be saved.

One federal project in the South was of such monumental scope
that only history can effectively evaluate it: the Tennessee Valley
Authority. In the words of one of its first directors, David E. Lilienthal,

> A new chapter in American public policy was written when Congress in
> May of 1933 passed the law creating the TVA. For the first time since
> the trees fell before the settlers' ax, America set out to command nature
> not by defying her, as in that wasteful past, but by understanding and
> acting upon her first law — the oneness of men and natural resources, the
> unity that binds together land, streams, forests, minerals, farming, indus-
> try, mankind.[1]

Based upon the World War I development at Muscle Shoals and embracing some 40,000 miles in seven states, the Authority was empowered to acquire, construct, and operate dams in the Tennessee Valley,
manufacture and distribute nitrates and fertilizer, generate and sell
electric power particularly with a view to rural electrification, inaugu-
rate flood control through reforestation, withdraw marginal lands from
cultivation, develop the river for navigation, and advance "the economic
and social well-being of the people living in the said river basin."

This was a region of varied agricultural and industrial potential,
with rich natural resources and water power which was going to waste;
here was undertaken a long-range program of economic and social
planning. Despite obvious need for reform in all of these categories,
there were loud complaints that TVA marked a radical departure from
American rugged individualism, mixed with bitter comments from
private utility men, such as Wendell Willkie, who averred that as a
yardstick for measuring electric rates the TVA was "rubber from the
first inch to the last." There can be little question, however, that it
provided a better level of living to thousands of people in the area by

[1] David E. Lilienthal, *TVA — Democracy on the March* (New York: Harper, 1944),
p. 46.

development of cheap and efficient fertilizers, education in soil conservation, reforestation, and provision of less costly electricity. In 1934 only one farm in thirty in Mississippi, Alabama, Tennessee, and Georgia received electricity; five years later, the proportion was one in seven. The government invested $831,329,978 in TVA and in fifteen years more than trebled electric generating capacity in the area. The efforts not only were beneficial to the citizens of the valley but also to the nation as a whole. TVA played a vital role in the military effort of World War II. It made possible a great expansion of aluminum production and provided the power for the atomic project at Oak Ridge. It promoted industry where it was most needed and raised incomes in one of the most depressed parts of the South.

TVA and the social reforms undertaken by the New Deal were the most controversial aspects of its Southern application and suffered the most opposition and criticism. Other measures, though often falling short of the goals proposed, generally were acknowledged to have been beneficial in the main. One unexpected result of the program of rehabilitation was to spotlight the dark areas of Southern life. While this created a national demand for reform, sensitive Southerners were sometimes embarrassed. Reports of the dire conditions of tenant farmers, Negroes, and shoeless people, while basically true, brought angry retorts.

The South was especially vulnerable and reacted with greatest heat to criticisms of the Negroes' status. The Negroes were often the hardest hit by the Depression, since most of them were engaged in agriculture. Throughout the area, they were hurt not only by crop restrictions but then by federal action abolishing sweatshop jobs. Losing out on the farm, they began to migrate in large numbers, South Carolina and Georgia losing approximately 10 per cent of such population, and all states saw a huge cityward movement. Few bettered their condition, for in the urban centers they came into competition with unemployed whites. By 1933 over two million Negroes were on relief, double the total which should have existed in view of their percentage of the population. Often, too, there was discrimination in the relief programs. In Mississippi, where they numbered slightly more than half the population, only nine per cent of them were receiving aid in 1933 as compared to 14 per cent of the whites.

Outside of agriculture, the largest number of Negroes worked in personal and domestic services in 1930, some 70 per cent of those so employed, or 806,000. Continued hard times and white competition lowered this percentage by 5.1 per cent during the next ten years. Negroes had made up 33.1 per cent of the total employed labor force in 1930, but twenty years later, this dropped to only 22.6. Southern

Negroes displaced in agriculture were not assimilated into other fields of work as fully as were the whites, and many left the region entirely.

By 1949 the median income of Southern non-white families was $995, approximately half that of their white neighbors and only a third of that of whites in other sections. Less than 12 per cent of the Negroes had incomes of $2,500 or more. Tenant farmers of both races declined by 622,000 between 1930 and 1945, and white owners increased by 270,000. Negroes represented over 35 per cent of the decrease (223,-000) but only four per cent of the increase in ownership (11,000). By 1940 only 40 per cent of Southern non-whites were still employed in agriculture.[2]

These, as well as conditions in general in the South, had earlier come to the attention of the President. Roosevelt, in a letter of July 5, 1938, to members of the Conference on Economic Conditions in the South, wrote: "No purpose is closer to my heart at this moment than that which caused me to call you to Washington. . . . It is my conviction that the South presents right now the Nation's No. 1 economic problem — the Nation's problem, not merely the South's. For we have an economic unbalance in the Nation as a whole, due to this very condition of the South." He called upon the National Emergency Council to determine a clear picture of the total situation, including, in his opinion, the "wasted or neglected resources of land and water," the abuses of its soil, the need for cheap fertilizer and power, and the requirements of its people. Other problems encompassed the region's capital resources and the absentee ownership of these; effects of the new industrial era and absentee ownership of the new industries; labor and employment and the necessity of protecting women and children; farm ownership, tenancy, and farm income; and taxation, education, housing, and health.

In its report the Council considered the thirteen states from Virginia south and westward through Texas and Oklahoma.[3] Here was an area with a population of over 36,000,000, 97.8 per cent native-born, of which 71 per cent was white and 29 per cent Negro. In this crescent of 552 million acres, nature had been generous with her wealth, but the people as a whole were the poorest in the country. No other region had such diversity of climate and soil, with opportunities to grow such a wide variety of crops. It had 40 per cent of the nation's forests, good transportation facilities, abundant fish and game, more than 300 differ-

[2] Lewis W. Jones, "Reconstruction Number Two," *Nation*, CLXXV (September 27, 1952), pp. 255-256.
[3] U. S. National Emergency Council, *Report on Economic Conditions of the South* (n. p., 1938). For a report on Southern farm conditions between 1934-1937, see T. J. Woofter, Jr., and A. E. Fisher, *The Plantation South Today* (Washington: Government Printing Office, 1940).

ent minerals, water-power potential, petroleum deposits, and the like. But, despite its wealth in grass, output of livestock lagged, and the annual production was only one-sixth of the nation's total. With a fifth of the coal deposits, less than two per cent had been tapped; while mining a tenth of the nation's iron ore, the South originated only seven per cent of the pig iron. From 27 per cent of the total hydroelectric generating capacity came only 21 per cent of that actually produced, and the region contained 13 per cent of the country's undeveloped power. This story of wealth in natural resources which had been made to yield but poor returns was typical in all areas of the Southern economy.

One reason for this was the lack of machinery to convert this largess to use. The area had only 16 per cent of the factories, machines, and tools with which people made a living. More than half the nation's farmers had less than one-fifth of its farm equipment. Only 15 per cent of the factory horsepower was in the South, despite its wealth in coal, oil, gas, and water power. Without means to manufacture its own products, the region had been forced to trade its natural wealth and the labor of its people for goods manufactured elsewhere — a traffic which had been unequally balanced against the South. As a result, the richest Southern state ranked lower in per capita income than did the poorest elsewhere. The average income for the region in 1937 was $314, compared to $604 for the non-South. About 53 per cent of the farmers were without land of their own, with tenant families averaging only $73 per person for a year's work, and sharecroppers from $38 to $87 per person — or from ten to twenty-three cents a day!

Southern industrial wages were also the lowest in the United States, the average annual return being $865, compared to $1,219 elsewhere. Per capita income from dividends and interests showed the same lag — $17.55 as against $68.97. The assessed value of taxable property averaged only $463 per person in the Southern states and $1,370 in the Northeast, meaning three times as much property per capita for support of schools and other institutions. This was reflected in 1936 by state and local government collection of $28.88 per person in the South against a national average of $51.54. In July, 1937, Southern banks held less than 11 per cent of the nation's bank deposits — under six per cent of savings deposits — and its insurance companies had only 2.6 per cent of such assets in the nation. This capital shortage was reflected by the higher interest rates charged and the necessity of looking outside the South for capital.

Much of the potential capital had flown northward as a result of absentee ownership. The public utilities, the major railroad systems, the richest deposits of iron ore, coal, and limestone, and most of the aluminum-producing bauxite, zinc deposits, sulphur, and the like were owned and controlled from outside the area. Cotton manufacturing, the South's major industry, found many of the larger mills with non-Southern owners, and the same was true to an even greater degree of the plants making artificial fibers. In short, the practice of shipping away its products in a raw or semi-finished form meant that the South usually received nothing but the low wages of unskilled and semi-skilled labor. The end profits went to financial institutions in other regions.

These were the facts as presented by the National Emergency Council, a presumably neutral governmental agency, to the public in 1939. Obviously, conditions which had developed over generations and even centuries were not to be corrected overnight; in fact, in modified form, these problems confronted the South and the nation well past the middle of the twentieth century.

The final assessment of the New Deal's contribution to the South was positive, however. It did more for the Negro than had any other administration since the Civil War, in the form of relief funds, housing projects, rural resettlement, parks, picnic grounds, education, and health. Southern whites, to an even greater degree, profited from such measures. But perhaps the greatest contribution was an intangible one — the focusing of sympathetic national attention on the problems of the South. Not only did federal assistance continue, but private aid came from many sources. In 1934 the National Planning Association, with a special Committee of the South (1946), was formed as an independent, nonpolitical, nonprofit organization to blueprint national policy. If the nation were to reach its goal of high-level employment and production with a rising standard of living, the underdeveloped resources, markets, and manpower of the South had to be utilized. National policies and programs had to be provided to create a favorable environment for vigorous, rapid expansion in the South. Southern liberals, too, were encouraged to act by the New Deal. Over 1,200 met in Birmingham in 1938 as the Southern Conference on Human Welfare, with Negro leaders playing a prominent role. This and similar organizations continued to keep the South's problems before its own people as well as the nation.

In the long run, however, it was the outbreak of World War II which brought real prosperity to the nation and to the people of the South. With a rapidly expanding American and world market, the traditionally impoverished South enjoyed its greatest prosperity, as agricultural prices rose steadily and thousands went to work in war plants and war-expanded Southern cities. Between July, 1940, and June, 1945, manufacturing facilities alone grew by over $4,442,000,000 in thirteen Southern states. In value terms alone, this probably represented a doubling of the region's 1939 industrial capacity. Moreover, to the sums spent for agricultural products and manufacturing facilities, more than $4,000,000,000 went into military establishments located in the South — 36 per cent of such expenditures in the nation.[4] War contracts and allocations distributed by federal agencies and British purchasing missions, exclusive of foodstuffs and contracts for less than $50,000, reached $17,848,556,000 by September of 1942, and a year later totaled $28,425,411,000.[5]

A number of areas had their first experience with large-scale industry, as many of the new factories were located in communities which had little or no industry prior to 1940. In addition, one of the most important benefits was the changes in skills and perspectives of workers and administrators. The ability of Southerners to produce the goods needed during the war undoubtedly served as a base for future expansion.

The average per capita income in the South rose sharply from 1940 to 1946. While it mounted 109 per cent in the nation, thirteen Southern states increased from 112 per cent in Virginia to more than 170 in Alabama, Arkansas, and Mississippi. The average Southern income in 1948 was 170 per cent above the 1929 level, while that of the non-South rose only 96 per cent. Southern purchasing power had increased 93 per cent, compared to 40 elsewhere. Total Southern income payments (wages, salaries, farm income, etc.), which stood at only 13.8 per cent of the national total in 1931, reached 19.8 by 1945. During 1940-1944, this represented an increase from 12.5 billion to 29.7 billion dollars; in the same period, federal payrolls disbursed in the South rose from 18.7 to 27 per cent. These significant changes were further accelerated by the outbreak of the Korean War in 1950.

Manufacturing was responsible for most of the South's improvement. Income from agriculture in 1929 had been approximately two-thirds greater than industry's; in 1948, it was just a tenth more.[6] In the short span of one generation, the South added 653,684 persons to its manufacturing force. The importance of this as measured in terms of "value added by manfacture" was a growth from $1,750,000,000 to $7,500,000,000. At the same time, its farm income rose from two to four billion dollars. Changes in agriculture were mirrored by the report

[4] Frederick L. Deming and Weldon A. Stein, "Disposal of Southern War Plants," National Planning Association Committee of the South, *Reports*, No. 2, pp. 17-18, 42-43.
[5] *Blue Book of Southern Progress* (published annually by the *Manufacturers Record*), 1942, p. 13; *ibid., 1943*, p. 19.
[6] Calvin B. Hoover and B. U. Ratchford, *Economic Resources and Policies of the South* (New York: Macmillan, 1951), pp. 44-64.

of the Federal Reserve Bank of Atlanta that, in the six states of its district, 250,000 new tractors were bought between 1940 and 1950. Thus, not only were mules and farm hands displaced, but also there was a steady increase in the size of farms. For example, South Carolina farms averaged 297 acres in 1960 and 389 in 1970. Southern farm totals dropped in this decade from 1,460,000 to just over 500,000.

The decline in relative importance of agriculture in the Southern economic picture was not the only significant change it experienced. Three transitional stages went on simultaneously: (1) diversification of output; (2) a shift to fuller usage of mechanization — a conversion pretty well completed by 1960 in the Mississippi Delta area; and (3) an adjustment of the region's economy to the broadened markets accompanying industrialization. King Cotton, whose despotism had been under attack since the end of the Civil War, lost further ground. For one thing, foreign competition mounted steadily. Total foreign output of cotton in 1920 had been around 7,000,000 bales, a figure which grew to 18,000,000 by 1936. During the six years prior to World War II, as a consequence, foreign purchases of American cotton declined almost half, while use of non-American cotton grew almost 70 per cent. Competition from synthetic fibers rose steadily, also. As a result of this situation, economic law and the efforts of the New Deal led to a steady reduction in Southern cotton acreages. Between 1929 and 1948, acres in cotton shrank by more than half, with almost one-fourth of the farms which had previously produced the staple dropping out. The government attempted in 1933 to reduce output by one-fourth; in 1943 laws were passed penalizing overproduction. From 42,-000,000 acres in cotton in 1929, totals fell to 18,000,000 in 1944 and rose only to 25,900,000 in 1949.

The old Southeastern cotton belt found itself caught in a relentless vise. The region, cropped since colonial times, faced depleted soils, mounting fertilizer costs, reduced markets for its inferior short-stapled cotton, and a rough topography which forbade extensive use of labor-saving machinery and large-scale farming. Not only was there foreign competition to worry about but also new American competitors. By 1949 over half of the entire crop was being grown on the richer soils of Oklahoma, Texas, New Mexico, Arizona, and California, and 60 per cent of the total was raised west of the Mississippi River. Although the total number of cotton farms dropped from 1,600,000 in 1940 to 850,000 in 1957, yield per acre increased from an average of 151 pounds in 1929 to 250 in 1940 and 409 in 1957, most of this increase coming from outside the old cotton belt. The only thing which made it possible for this area to stay in cotton production was the government's cotton support program, a program which in 1957 cost the taxpayers more than $1,000 for each farm growing cotton. Moreover, this expensive program prevented the natural shift of cotton to the low-cost, highly-productive, flat lands and irrigated areas of the Southwest and West, keeping cotton prices so high that they provided an umbrella for foreign growers and a powerful incentive for consumers to shift to synthetic fibers.

The South's number two crop, tobacco, suffered many of the same experiences. Returns dropped rapidly in the early days of the Depression, and the government followed a similar program of reduction of output in an effort to raise prices. Although the value of the tobacco crop declined 61 per cent between 1929 and 1932, its recovery proved more rapid, since consumption did not decrease materially and no satisfactory substitutes were found. By 1937 it was worth 24 per cent more than the 1929 value and by 1948 was 257 per cent higher. Production averaged 1,339 million pounds per year between 1929 and 1931; with the boost afforded by the war, it reached 1,917 million in 1948. Between 1929 and 1948, prices doubled, primarily because of the great increase in domestic consumption, especially in the form of cigarettes, which saw a jump from 526,000,000 pounds to 1,181,000,000 in 1948. During this time foreign sales rose only slightly. Acreages remained fairly constant because of governmental controls, but, as a result of better seed, new techniques, and disease and pest control, the yield per acre improved from an average of about 775 pounds before 1930 to approximately 1,033. Despite cancer scares and other hazards of the business, the tobacco market had a steady growth. In the ten years after the Surgeon General's warning about cigarettes, total consumption increased from 523.9 billion in 1963 to 583 billion in 1973, when American smokers numbered approximately fifty-two million. The production of tobacco added approximately $1,500,000,000 annually to the income of Southern farmers.

The ensuing thirty years after the Depression saw several notable changes: fewer farmers depending upon one crop for their source of income; a large shift in farm population with a positive decline in total numbers, especially among tenants; an enormous drop in cotton production, both absolutely and relatively; an increase in the production of most other farm commodities, including the number and value of livestock; and a continued problem of governmental controls and creeping inflation. From 1930 to 1940, farm population declined 22.2 per cent — 611,000 Negroes and 602,000 whites. During the next decade, the loss was 25 per cent, representing some 597,000 whites and 468,000 Negroes. The pattern was to continue. Alabama in 1950 had 211,512 farmers, but these drifted away, until there were only 176,956 in 1954 and 115,610 in 1960; Mississippi's farm total fell by almost one-half between 1920

and 1960. Of the 134,000 farms that disappeared, over 105,000 were
Negro. Part of this resulted from substitution of machines for human
and animal energy — the pattern of farming changed, while the required labor dropped. The number of tractors alone increased over
300 per cent between 1940 and 1947. Improved farming practices,
hybrid corn, new grasses, and other improvements were made.

Even with this great exodus of personnel from agriculture, the
South, nevertheless, continued to produce a surplus. The tendency
toward larger farm units — Alabama farms averaged 71.9 acres in 1935,
with 52 per cent in the 10-40 acre class, while 32 per cent were over
the 100-acre mark in 1960 and the average was 143 — marked the development of agricultural techniques in which the small farm, whether
owner-operated or tenant-staffed, was at a distinct disadvantage. Further efficiency could conceivably lead to an additional reduction of
about one-third in Southern agricultural population dependent directly
on farming as a major source of income.

Especially affected by these changes was the Southern tenant. Up
to 1930, the trend had been to the increase of tenancy and the decline
in the number of farm owners. The proportion of tenant-operated
farms and acreages reached its record high peaks in 1929-1930, though
the absolute number of tenants did not hit its apex until 1935. During
the period from 1930 to 1945, the percentage of tenant-operated farms
dropped from 57 to 42 per cent of the total. Between 1930 and 1950,
the percentage of tenant farmers dropped approximately 20 per cent,
while in the next decade they decreased in the Southeast from 426,174
to 157,162. The cumulative impact can be seen in a single state, Alabama, where 65 per cent of the cotton growers in 1911 were tenants,
as compared to only 27 per cent in 1960, or in Arkansas where the percentage of tenancy dropped from 24.3 in 1959 to 12.6 in 1969. By the
latter year only 11.7 per cent of the region's farms were tenant
operated.

The South had 776,000 sharecroppers in 1930; by 1954 the total
had fallen to 273,0000 and by 1960 was probably below 200,000. A few
cases illustrate what had happened. One Mississippi plantation reported the loss of 1,800 people in twelve years, laborers that had been
replaced by thirty cotton-picking machines and 180 tractors. The huge
Delta & Pine Land Company of Scott, Mississippi, in 1956 had a total
of 24,000 acres under cultivation in all crops. Whereas it had formerly
had as much as 16,000 acres in cotton, utilizing 5,000 tenants and
1,200 mules, in 1956 there were only 7,800 acres of cotton, and the rest
were in corn, rice, alfalfa, sorghum, oats, and barley. There were 15
mules, 200 tractors, 1,500 steers, and the few remaining tenants were
tractor drivers and repairmen. On the small farms, on the other hand,

the individual crop allotments were so small that farmers could not make a living from cotton. Only 36 per cent of the Southern farmers in 1958 produced any cotton, and the acreage was the smallest since 1876.

TENANTS IN THE SOUTH, 1930, 1950, 1959, AND 1969

*% of Tenants to Total Farm Population*

| STATE | 1930 | 1950 | 1959 | 1969 |
|---|---|---|---|---|
| Alabama | 64.7 | 41.4 | 27.9 | 10.0 |
| Arkansas | 63.0 | 37.6 | 24.3 | 12.6 |
| Florida | 28.4 | 12.3 | 5.9 | 6.6 |
| Georgia | 68.2 | 42.8 | 25.3 | 9.1 |
| Kentucky | 35.9 | 22.5 | 17.2 | 9.2 |
| Louisiana | 66.6 | 39.6 | 24.6 | 16.0 |
| Mississippi | 72.2 | 51.6 | 32.3 | 9.0 |
| North Carolina | 49.2 | 38.3 | 31.4 | 14.9 |
| Oklahoma | 61.5 | 31.4 | 19.9 | 14.1 |
| South Carolina | 65.1 | 45.3 | 31.8 | 12.3 |
| Tennessee | 46.2 | 29.2 | 20.5 | 7.5 |
| Texas | 60.9 | 30.4 | 21.7 | 16.5 |
| Virginia | 28.1 | 17.1 | 14.7 | 8.3 |

Whereas in 1937 less than three per cent of the South's cropland was occupied by truck crops, gardens, and orchards, diversification had now become common in the region. A parallel development was the increased concern with soil conservation. Cotton was still an important income-producing crop, but had been toppled by agribusiness. Just as sharecroppers were replaced by new machinery, new cash crops, forests, and livestock idled cotton gins and made rural entrepreneurs out of once largely unprosperous farmers.

Various crops supplanted cotton and tobacco. Georgia, North Carolina, Alabama, and Virginia became important producers of peanuts, with the lowly "goober" providing over 11 per cent of the value of all farm products in Georgia in 1958. Soybean acreage more than doubled in the South between 1938 and 1954; citrus fruits increased 550 per cent, hay 42, wheat 66, and truck crops 34 per cent in the years from 1929 to 1950, as increasing urbanization and improved transportation took place in the South. By the 1970's peanut production was so large that it had been frozen by law; the Southeast's share of the annual cotton crop had dropped to 10 per cent; soybean acreage had passed a half million in each of ten Southern states; and Florida was producing 80 per cent of the nation's citrus fruits and was second only to California in vegetables. Also, even in the older crops the yield per acre was going up because of fertilizer and improved seed and techniques.

Many of these new products were more adaptable to mechanization than were the traditional staples. Approximately 14 per cent of Southern farmers in 1945 reported owning tractors; by 1954 the figure was nearly 40 per cent. In Alabama, for example, there were 7,638 farm tractors in 1940, as compared to 75,000 twenty years later. In 1948 around 1,000 mechanical cotton pickers operated in the South; eight years later, there were 11,645, and about a quarter of the cotton in Mississippi, Arkansas, and Louisiana was harvested in this fashion. By the mid-seventies, better than half of the cotton was mechanically picked. Mechanical and chemical weeding techniques also made outstanding progress after 1930.

While the number of farms was declining, the size was increasing, and net income per farm was approximately double twenty years after 1938.[7] This was all to the good. Without benefit of crop supports, cotton production could well be wiped out east of the Mississippi River, and the older area of the South would be forced to look to new resources for capital. Even with the progress made since 1930, farm incomes and standards of living were low compared to those in most other regions of the United States. A 1955 Department of Agriculture survey of low-income farms found six of nine problem areas and half of the farms classified as "low production" to be Southern. Obviously, only a part of the farm population in the South will find a future on the land. This is particularly true of the Negroes, and, eventually, non-agricultural pursuits must absorb all but a minority of these dispossessed farmers.

One of the most successful developments was the increase in livestock and allied products, which provided not only additional income but also an improved diet. Between 1930 and 1947, the South made greater gains in livestock than the rest of the nation in all classes except horses and mules, with beef cattle jumping 76.6 per cent. Supplementary to the long-established areas of Texas and Oklahoma, the center of the new cattle industry became the old cotton South, plus Florida.[8] By 1952 over 25,000,000 acres of improved permanent pasture had been planted in the area, giving it winter grazing for the first time in history. Four years later, 41 per cent of the land in Mississippi, Georgia, Alabama, and Tennessee was in grass. The land not only supported more cattle per acre than rival regions but also by the fact of

[7] Gilbert C. Fite, "The Revolution in Southern Agriculture," *Current History*, XXXV (November, 1958), pp. 266-270.
[8] William A. Emerson, Jr., "Cattle Rush Down South," *Colliers*, CXXIX (April 5, 1952), p. 27ff.

winter forage took advantage of high spring markets for cattle. Florida boasted ranches of over 200,000 acres and ranked twelfth nationally in the number of beef cattle. Alabama cash income from beef was $7,605,000 in 1940, $37,000,000 in 1950, and 55.8 per cent of farm income in 1960. Montgomery referred to itself as the cow capital of the old South. By 1971 dollar returns from livestock exceeded that of farm crops in six of eleven states; Georgia alone had over 2,000,000 head of cattle; and there were 250 feed mills and twenty packing-houses in the South.

While beef cattle tended to dominate on the large farms in areas of scarce labor, dairying sprang up on the smaller farms near market centers. Between 1930 and 1947, the number of milk cattle increased one-third, and from 1940 to 1954, the sale of whole milk more than doubled. From 1947 to 1952, alone, the number of grade A dairies in North Carolina doubled, reaching 4.300. The record of such states as Arkansas, Kentucky, Virginia, and Tennessee was outstanding in the 1950's, and the whole South became one of the most promising frontiers for increased milk production, a fact borne out by the increasing numbers of processing plants. The South by 1970 had a better balance between livestock and crop economy than it had at any time since the Civil War.

In addition to enlarged sheep and hog production, spectacular gains were also made in poultry output. Notably in Texas, northwest Arkansas, the Shenandoah Valley of Virginia, and northern Georgia, poultry increased beyond even the hopes of agrarian reformers. With the advantages of year-round outdoor raising and savings in construction costs, Southern farmers profited from the fact that rival producers primarily went in for egg production, leaving the South a chance to fill the gap by concentrating on chicken for meat. Poultry products in 1950 brought Virginia farmers $45,800,000, as compared to tobacco's $55,000,000. Between 1939 and 1954, Georgia farmers increased the income from the sale of chickens from four to 117 million dollars, which in the later year brought two-thirds as much as the cotton crop. By 1970 four Southern states ranked among the top six producers of chickens in the nation, and the region was annually producing fifteen billion eggs — three times more than 1958's production — and 1.6 billion broilers.

Ironically, these agricultural developments which have been heralded as notable achievements left in their wake groups of Southerners who did not prosper, and, more important, were worse off than before. As the impact of mechanization and agricultural diversification resulted in steady declines in tenancy, small farms, and staple-crop agriculture, most Americans probably assumed, if they thought of it at all, that the former tenants had improved their lot by going into industry and migrating into town, or to the North.

Two examples prove that this was not always true. During the 1930's the South became attractive as a producer of pulpwood, and thousands of acres of farm lands were converted to forests, displacing additional farmers. Many (an estimated 200,000 in 1972) became cutters or haulers, nominally independent contractors selling wood to dealers, who in turn sold it to the paper companies. They were neither covered by minimum wage legislation, nor did they receive company payments for retirement, sickness, or unemployment. With no assets but their labor, most were quickly in debt and at the mercy of their dealers, who loaned money for trucks and equipment. It has been estimated that, even in good years, their income is well below the poverty level. The important timber industry has become as dependent upon exploited labor as cotton sharecropping was before it.

Better known and more numerous were the thousands who permanently joined the ranks of the seasonal migrant workers, moving from area to area to harvest perishable crops. Largely a byproduct of the great expansion of truckfarming, they became an important part of the labor force after 1940, gathering tons of food along the Gulf and Atlantic coasts. As they moved from farm to farm, they lacked even the small degree of permanency that they or their parents had as tenants. While most were native whites or blacks, Mexican-Americans and "wetbacks" also labored on the Texas side of the Rio Grande. Their wages tended to remain low while their "temporary" living quarters annually deteriorated. Authorities have found some to be literally in a state of peonage. Some of the worst cases of mistreatment were by the big argricorporations, especially producers of frozen foods. In 1970 a Senate subcommittee member described their living conditions as "undoubtedly the worst in America." The existence of groups such as the woodcutters and migrants helps to explain why 46 per cent of the country's poor live in the South, though the region has only 21 per cent of the total population.

A major part of the hope for full employment lies in the strides taken in industry, however. Until the beginning of the twentieth century, the South moved from agriculture toward business and industry less rapidly than did the nation as a whole. Even after the industrial expansion following World War I, agriculture still accounted for 34 per cent of the total working force in 1940, as compared to 19 per cent for the nation. Manufacturers employed only 15 per cent of the workers, as compared to a national average of 23. The decade from 1930 to 1939 was marked by three years of precipitous employment decline, followed by seven years of low and irregular recovery, although the decline was not as great as in the non-South. The region began recovering more quickly, due to possession of fewer of the heavy industries, a textile boom in 1933, and upward trends in paper, petroleum, and cigarette production. Total Southern manufacturing in 1939 was just about where it had been in 1929, except that wages were around nine per cent lower and "value added by manufacture" down about two per cent, a much better showing than for the nation as a whole. Regionally, manufacturing employed 1,362,027 workers producing products valued at $8,253,143,800 in 26,516 plants. The textile industry, with 476,000 production workers, was in first place, with increased relative importance. Lumber and timber products were second with 203,000 employees but had declined in relative importance. The food-products industry, with 126,000 workers, was the only other hiring as many as 100,000. North Carolina was still in first place as the leading Southern industrial state.

As has been seen, however, the years of World War II saw massive gains in manufacturing output. Between 1939 and 1954, production increases ranged from 353 per cent in Alabama to 533 in South Carolina. During the same period, non-agricultural employment rose by 58.2 per cent in the United States but by 64.7 in Virginia, 70.5 in Georgia, 73.3 in South Carolina, and 105.7 in Florida. The *Census of Manufactures* showed the number of such establishments to have doubled, production workers increased by almost the same percentage, value added by manufacture mounted fivefold, and the South's proportion of the total national value added by manufacture risen from 12.7 to 15.2 per cent. The war brought new shipyards, airplane factories, munition plants, and the like. Wages and salaries increased even faster than employment.

Some of this gain was illusory, however, as the South experienced a faster demobilization of its "war industries" than did the non-South, and these lines had created the biggest expansion in employment. A larger-than-average share of the region's new facilities was of somewhat dubious convertibility to peacetime use, products of federal construction.[9] A fifth of the value of Southern war facilities was in explosives and ammunition. Those, plus some of the chemical plants, were held in stand-by conditions and could not be added to active productive capacity. Nevertheless, effective capacity probably increased about 40 per cent over pre-war levels, and the South's normal industries maintained production somewhat better than such firms elsewhere. The period and years which followed brought significant expansion in chemicals, farm equipment, tires, automobile assembly, electronics, electrical supplies, aluminum, and food products, as native and outside capital moved in to exploit the natural resources of the South.

Back in 1889, Henry Grady, in his pleas for originating Southern

[9] Deming and Stein, *op. cit.*

industry, had told of the funeral of a Georgia farmer in which the punch line had been: "The south didn't furnish a thing on earth for that funeral except the corpse and the hole in the ground." Yet, by 1960 that farmer's family could select a polished marble monument from more than a dozen big manufacturers in seven Southern states. It could buy a fancy casket, with nylon lining made in the Carolinas, from two score Southern producers. It could get nails, shovels, and other hardware from almost 200 Southern steel fabricators or from over 100 big foundries, using metal from any of twenty-odd rolling mills. It could dress him from the skin out in fashionable clothes made in 700 different apparel plants in the South and with shoes from 100 different factories. It could send him to the cemetery in style in a hearse made in Alabama, using oil and gas and rolling on tires and tubes available from several Southern states. In fact, there would not be a thing needed for that funeral that the bereaved could not buy in the new industrial South.

The rapid recovery and continued expansion of industry showed in the per capita income: four times as much in 1955 as in 1930, climbing from 44.7 per cent of the national average of 64.1 per cent. In only ten years, 1939-1949, total financial resources grew by 242 per cent, compared to 135 per cent elsewhere, and banking assets in the region increased phenomenally. During the next decade, the Southern gain in personal income was nearly 85 per cent, with Florida alone showing a jump of about 175 per cent. Although the region's gain between 1966 and 1971 was 48.4 per cent — compared to the East's 39.8 — and Mississippi showed a jump of 51 per cent, by 1972 that state's per capita income of $3,137 was still lowest and only Maryland exceeded the national average of $4,492. Yet, despite this continued lag, the South had reason for optimism.

Among the older industries, progress was continuous, while new ones came in ever increasing numbers. These elements accounted for this accelerated pace: in a free economy, industry seeks a profitable position regarding resources, labor supply, and purchasing power. The South had always had an abundance of the first two but lacked purchasing power, as seen in the low income of its inhabitants. As already pointed out, parity payments brought large sums into the region during the Depression, and for the first time, the South met its living requirements and had some left over. World War II greatly increased this reservoir of purchasing power. A study in 1949 of eighty-eight plants, all established after the war, representing investments from $100,000 to $10,000,000 and covering all major types of industry except tobacco, showed the determining factors in the location of these plants in the South to be: first, and primary, the importance of the region as a market; second, materials and energy resources; and third, labor in terms of availability. Some 45 per cent of these establishments were market-oriented, while the last two factors accounted for 30 and 25 per cent, respectively. In cost and size of working force employed, the labor-oriented plants came last. The first two categories were also the ones which paid the highest wages. No longer could anyone say of the South that it was merely a source of sweatshop labor.[10]

Most of the 1940-1970 industrial development was branch plants directed and financed by national manufacturing concerns. A common saying in the South ran, "Cotton goes west and cattle comes east, the Negro goes north and the Yankee comes south." Along the lines of the Southern Railroad alone, 142 new plants and 107 plant additions were built in 1950. During the next year, the South sprouted one new multimillion-dollar factory each working day for a capital accretion in excess of $3,000,000,000; agricultural employment dropped to only 21 per cent of the total; and industry definitely drew ahead of agriculture as a major regional source of income. Industries were more diversified than formerly, with chemicals, synthetic fibers, food, pulp, paper, farm machinery, building materials, and apparel being conspicuous by their growth. The wage trend rose, as a tightening labor market forced old industries to increase their scales.

The South had four-fifths of the cotton-textile industry by 1952 and was getting almost all of the new chemical-fiber plants, while making inroads into woolens and worsteds as well. Already, the textile machinery manufacturers were considering moves to the area of their best customer. As of that date, the chemical industry had located more than half of its new installations in the South, and the fastest growing chemical empire in the world was developing along the Louisiana-Texas Gulf Coast. The trend in the new plastic industry was also southward. By 1953 the value of Dixie's chemical products exceeded that of its textile output for the first time. Between 1947 and 1953, value added by manufacture increased 51 per cent in the five states of Alabama, Georgia, Louisiana, Mississippi, and South Carolina, while New England saw a rise of only 45 per cent. South Carolina's textiles rose 13 per cent, and Massachusetts' declined 25. Louisiana chemicals soared 139 per cent and New York's 48. Georgia's output climbed 139 per cent and Wisconsin's only 59. All of this took place despite the growing awareness that the South could no longer offer a guarantee of lower costs than the North.

Part of this growth must be credited to rising Southern consciousness of the importance of industrial research. In 1942 there was only a

[10] Glen E. McLaughlin and Stefan Robock, "Why Industry Moves South," National Planning Association Committee of the South, *Reports*, No. 3.

handful of industrial research laboratories in the South; ten years later, 160 company and thirty independent consulting laboratories were engaged in 4 per cent of the industrial research going on in the nation, as well as ten manufacturers of scientific instruments. During the 1960's "research" became a magic word because of the belief that it was essential to economic development. By the end of that decade there were more than 800 separate, nonprofit research agencies, 160 of which were primarily concerned with the social sciences.

Probably the most spectacular industry to grow out of a test tube was a discovery by a Georgian, Charles H. Herty, of a process for producing newsprint from slash pine. Worthless as timber, these trees, which covered much of the South, became a valuable asset, and in 1939 the first such factory went up at Lufkin, Texas. By 1965 Georgia had replaced Wisconsin as the leading state in production of paper and paperboard; 1.8 million Southerners were growing trees commercially; and the region had more than two-thirds of the nation's tree farms. Five years later the South had 40 per cent of its land in forests, as well as 300 pulp and paper mills. The financial impact of this new industry was evident by the fact that in 1971 Mississippi got $491.6 million from its farm crops, $542.7 from livestock, and $600 million from timber products, while the comparable figures for Tennessee were $327.4, $419.1, and $500 million. After a Floridian discovered the trick of concentrating frozen citrus juice, new fields of frozen foods were opened, and several supplementary industries grew up for processing the by-products.

This march of expansion showed no sign of faltering by 1970. South Carolina acquired new Orlon plants, while Georgia produced goods from airplanes down to home appliances. Big aluminum plants operated in New Orleans, Baton Rouge, Mobile, and Listerhill (Alabama). The carpet industry spread to Mississippi; Texas was an electronics center, with such giant firms as Texas Instruments; on the South Carolina-Georgia border and at Oak Ridge, Tennessee, were huge nuclear plants; and of twelve large duPont post-war chemical plants, ten were located in the South. In 1956, 1,059 new factories were established below the Potomac, and the decade of the 50's saw the Gulf South area become the site of one-sixth of all industrial construction in the country, a value of $3.25 billion. The South in 1957 had 33,700 manufacturing establishments with an output of $62.25 billion, representing 36 per cent of the chemical industry, 80 per cent of the cotton textiles, 70 per cent of the rayon and the new synthetic fibers, 80 per cent of the petrochemicals, and 38 per cent of the petroleum manufacturing facilities. Over 90,000 Southerners worked in electronics. General Electric had by that time constructed nineteen major plants

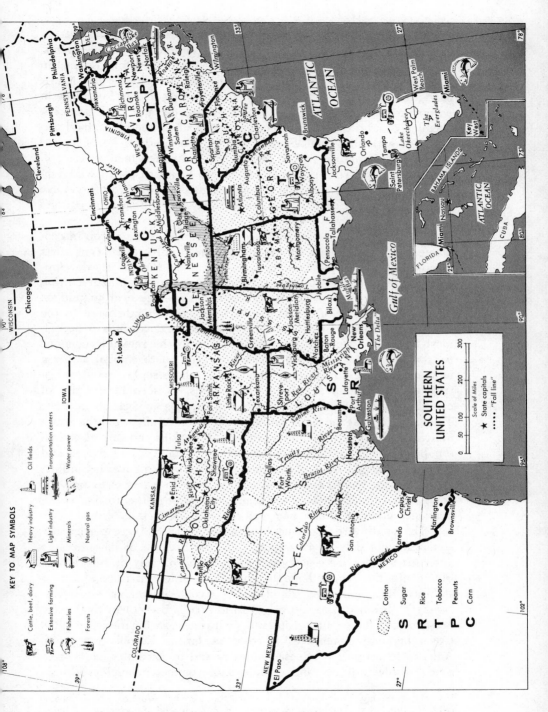

*Israel, Boemer, and Durand,* World Geography Today (*New York: Holt, Rine-hart, Winston, 1960*), 449.

employing 30,000 workers. There were 110 aircraft and missile plants, with a major research and development center at Redstone Arsenal in Alabama, as well as the major launching pad in Florida and NASA headquarters in Houston, Texas. Food processing rose to first place in economic importance in 1957, followed by oil and coal products, chemicals, and textiles. At the end of the decade of the fifties, food was still first, with an output value of $13,239,000,000, but chemicals had moved into second place ($9,785,000,000), although textiles was still the largest employer. At that time, $65,100 Southern plants were employing 3,770,000 persons and producing goods worth $79,583,000,000. Southern ports accounted for approximately one-third of the nation's export-import business.[11]

During the 1960's the South continued to lead the nation in economic growth. Although agriculture produced only 10 per cent of its income, net income per farm more than doubled. But the big development came in manufacturing and financial resources. Manufacturing wages rose by 58 per cent, *versus* a national average near 50, and six of the ten states with the largest national growth rate were in the deep South. In the single year, 1971, industrial developers added almost $4,000,000,000 and 200,000 new jobs to the region's economy. By the seventies it was also obvious that the South was attracting a new and more desirable type of industry: those sophisticated industries which demanded more rigorous skills, as seen in the rise of capital investment per job from $6,269 in 1962 to $32,148 in 1970. The very fact that these special businesses were coming into the South indicated that they were finding the requisite skills and capital. Southern banks, such as Republic National Bank of Texas, Citizens and Southern National Bank of Georgia, and Wachovia of North Carolina among others, passed the $1,000,000,000 mark in assets. Although the South was certainly not self-sufficient in capital in the 1970's, its dependence upon the North had just as surely lessened.

The southward movement of outside capital was particularly significant not only by its amount but also because of its entry into enterprises which were new or comparatively so. Only by such attraction could the region hope to enjoy indefinite expansion, business stability, and improving standards of living. Beginning with Mississippi's "Balance Agriculture with Industry" (BAWI) in the 1930's, no section of the country displayed such eagerness for foreign capital. Governors and committees traveled as far as Europe and South America in search of increased industry and trade. States, cities, railroads, public utilities, and chambers of commerce employed high-

[11] Frank J. Soday, "Southern Industry on the March," *Manufacturers Record*, CXXVI (June, 1957), pp. 7-23; *Industrial Development and Manufacturers Record*, CXXIX (May, 1960), pp. 4-24.

powered salesmanship tactics, featuring tax holidays, free plant sites, special work-force training programs, railroad spurs, and highway access concessions, as well as national advertising in trade journals, newspapers, and popular magazines. They sang siren songs about plentiful water, raw materials, cheap labor, research advantages, rich markets, recreation, and sunny climate. Spending by states on promotion and advertising reached $500,000 a year or more in tax monies by 1960. The South no longer was hostile or indifferent to the wealthy outsider, but placed at his disposal every possible aid to his business. In North Carolina, for example, a privately financed Business Development Corporation was established; discriminatory corporate taxes were repealed and the business interests of that state financed the nonprofit Research Triangle Institute, utilizing the scientists at the University of North Carolina, Duke, and North Carolina State to help industries in research needs. The Southern Research Institute at Birmingham was opened in 1946, and fifteen years later, scarcely a major university or college in the South was not eager to offer its facilities for economic research of every sort.

Joining those seeking to lure the businessman were representatives of a new major Southern industry — the tourist trade. After World War II, a steady stream of travelers moved south to find sun and recreation, to see this controversial region, and to share the glamour of the "Lost Cause." Some 4,000 motels and tourist courts were built by 1954. To ease travel, the South also constructed more new roads in 1956-1959 than in the 141 years before 1930. In excess of $2,000,000,000 was brought in by this hospitality in 1958, and visitors became in many states a better-paying crop than agriculture. The celebration of the Civil War Centennial meant a new bonanza for Southern landlords, curio stores, gasoline stations, and battlefield guides, as the aura of the past blended with the prosperity of the period. Florida could boast an annual tourist income of $3.6 billion; Texas, $1.5 billion; Virginia, 1.0 billion; and not a single Southern state reported less than $200 million. The Bi-Centennial celebrations held hopes of attracting thousands more to relive the past and view a region that was fast losing much of its distinctiveness — at least some of its worst aspects.

The great economic progress of the South after 1930 affected virtually every facet of Southern life. In 1930, of every $100 in demand deposits, the non-South had $77.98 and the South, $10.65; in time deposits, $81.76 and $6.64; in federal income tax payments, $85.30 and $5.60. Twenty years later, the same three categories showed the South's proportion to have risen to $19.83, $12, and $16, marking an increase of virtually 100 per cent.[12] The same period saw a rise in per

[12] Walter Prescott Webb, "The South and the Golden Slippers," *Texas Quarterly,* I (1958), pp. 1-13.

capita income of 119 per cent in the North and 225 in the South. In its sources of income, the Southern pattern became remarkably like that of the nation as a whole. As early as 1940, the similarity was striking. By 1947 the South was getting $6,911,000,000 from agriculture, $10,529,000,000 from manufactures, $13,888,000,000 from trades and services, and $6,013,000,000 from the government.

In real per capita income between 1929 and 1955, in terms of 1947-1949 dollars, of the eight states showing the highest gains ($625 and over), three were in the South. Four more were above the national average ($540); an equal number fell just below in the $470-539 category. Of the nine showing a gain of less than $470, only two, Mississippi and Arkansas, were from the South. Although the region had yet to close the gap in per capita income averages, each year the difference became less. In virtually every category of financial progress, the South advanced at a faster rate than the North.

Though much had been accomplished by the 1970's, there were still no grounds for complacency. The South was still the poorest region in the nation. In per capita income, it was still more than a third lower than the average, and the gap between its rich and poor was greater than in other parts of the country. Despite success in attracting industry, only a handful of the major industries listed in *Fortune*'s "500" had headquarters in the South. The black had still not received his fair share of the increasing economic opportunities, although much progress had been made. Relatively speaking, there were too many uneconomical, sub-marginal, small farms — the home bases of most of the region's poor. All of these factors helped to hold down the region's economy.

Nevertheless, the economic factor was one of the more important ones in the emerging Southern moderation on race. "In prosperity, you don't need scapegoats." When there were enough jobs to go around, Southerners no longer felt the need to blame or apologize for giving them to blacks. Over-all, enough had been accomplished so that in October, 1973, Malcolm S. Forbes, editor-in-chief of the financial magazine bearing his name, would write with confidence: "The South's economy is no longer the country's up-and-coming one. It's arrived."

# 23

# THE SOUTHERN PEOPLE SINCE 1930

WHILE PROBABLY NOT AS DRAMATIC in outward manifestations as the economic revolution which swept the South after 1930, fundamental changes also occurred on the social scene. Some were the result of improving standards of living, others the slow but steady maturation of seeds planted in the distant past. In 1936 an eminent Southern scholar indicted his homeland as a region of homicides, false standards of "honor," factional and interstate jealousies, intersectarian conflict, and illiteracy. Worse than most of these shortcomings were the lack of aesthetic influences, the failure to esteem distinguished effort, and the tendency to discourage original and creative work. To him, if one word characterized the South, it was "waste" — waste of manpower and of women and children in race conflict, in personal antagonisms, in "stubborn opposition to progress," and in undeveloped youth going through life without ever realizing their potentialities.[1]

Any claim that this was merely one individual's disgruntlement was destroyed two years later, when the problems of the South were spelled out in even greater detail in a report to the President of the

[1] Howard W. Odum, *Southern Regions in the United States* (Chapel Hill: Univ. of North Carolina, 1936), p. 374.

United States by a group of distinguished citizens of the South.[2] In the watershed years of the 1930's, the committee considered these Southern problems — the disproportion of adult workers to dependents, the displacement of agricultural workers by machines, the ousting of Negroes by whites from traditionally Negro occupations, and the emigration of its most skilled and productive workers — to be the most pressing faced by the nation. Although the region's birth rate was higher than other sections, this predominantly rural area lost one-fourth of its sons and daughters to Southern cities or to other parts of the United States. Of the 28,700,000 people shown by the Census of 1930 as having been born in the South, only 17,500,000 lived in their natal locality, and 3,800,000 had left the region entirely. About one in every eight born and educated in Alabama and Mississippi lived their productive years in another state. Most serious, this migration from the South took many of its ablest people; nearly half of the Southern-born scientists of eminence resided elsewhere. The loss of the most productive talent left the South a land of the very young and the very old, further complicating the problems of education, relief, and the like.

For those who remained in the South, the average income in 1937 was $314, compared to $604 for the rest of the country, while Southern farmers received less than half that amount. Therefore, the absence in many Southern country areas of many of the decencies of life, as well as the relative rareness of ordinary items such as automobiles, radios, and books, was not amazing. With so many people living so close to poverty, there was great difficulty in providing the schools and other public services necessary in any civilized community. In 1935-1936 in Mississippi, 1,500 school centers were without buildings; instead, lodge halls, country churches, and other public buildings were used.

Where family incomes were exceptionally low, the sickness and death rates were unusually high. The climate was not to blame, for it was healthful for those who had the necessary care, diet, and freedom from occupational diseases. Malaria, which annually infected more than 2,000,000, was estimated to have reduced the industrial output of the South by one-third. The scourge of pellagra, chiefly due to inadequate diet, was almost exclusively Southern, and pneumonia and tuberculosis took higher tolls among Southern workers than others. On the other hand, health protection facilities were most limited. In 1930, for example, per 100,000 population the South had only 29.3 dentists, 95.1 physicians and surgeons, and 129.6 trained nurses, as compared to national averages of 57.8, 125.2, and 239.6, respectively. Furthermore, in 1938 South Carolina had only one-third as many doctors per

[2] U. S. National Emergency Council, *Report on Economic Conditions of the South* (n. p., 1938). Southern members of the committee are given on page 3.

capita as California. The South was deficient in hospitals, clinics, and health workers, with many counties having no facilities at all. Prior to 1936, only one state in the region considered industrial hygiene, despite the knowledge that loss from industrial injuries and illness ran into the hundreds of millions of dollars.

Even though after 1930 the South made about the same progress in reduction of the death rate as other regions, it still remained somewhat higher. The failure to close the comparative gap lay in the fact that the life expectancy for non-whites remained substantially lower than for whites. Although the Southern white death rate was relatively low, the region's inferior record as to health and physical well-being continued to be poor. Much of this was because of the South's being particularly vulnerable to diseases which rank low in fatalities but high in enervation. Historically, these included such as malaria, hookworm, and pellagra. Fortunately, definite methods for elimination of these scourges were found, and considerable progress was made in reducing their toll.

Another corollary was evidenced in bad housing, with its direct relationship to poor health and lessened industrial efficiency. It also encouraged crime, inferior citizenship, low standards of family life, and deprivation of reasonable comfort. The poorly-built rental quarters, often on land which was good for nothing else, were simply convenient barracks for a supply of cheap labor, a slum often built to be just that — a slum. In the least desirable locations, the rows of wooden houses were without proper sanitary facilities and lacked running water, bathtubs, and sinks. About 26 per cent of city or town homes were without indoor flush toilets. This absence of toilets and sewer systems characterized not only a large proportion of homes in small towns and cities but also the great majority of farm and rural domiciles. Hookworm flourished in a region where nearly one-fifth of all farm homes had no toilets at all.

In 1938 there were an estimated 2,500,000 substandard houses in the South. Rural areas had the oldest farm dwellings, of lowest value and in greatest need for repairs, of any in the United States. More than one-third lacked even screens to keep out mosquitoes and flies. One-eighth of all Southern residences housed an average of more than one and one-half persons per room, while in the nation as a whole, only one-fourteenth was so crowded. By conservative estimates, 50 per cent of all families in the South needed to be rehoused.

However, the principal blame for the South's over-all need for improvement could not be assigned to the world-wide economic distress of the period. Compared to the rest of the United States, the South had been in a depression for generations, and the characteristics and effects were of long duration. Some Southerners despairingly questioned whether the South had made the right decision in the 1880's to emulate the industrial North, and they proposed a return to the agrarianism of Jefferson and the pre-Civil War South. By the 1920's a school of young Southern writers centered at Vanderbilt University had already issued a series of essays, *I'll Take My Stand,* in which they sentimentally reviewed what seemed to them a golden age when success and money had not ruled. But their South had never really existed; nor were the malformed features of the twentieth century solely the fault of the introduction of industrialization and commercialism.

This same despair, however, was one reason why the average Southerner greeted the election of Franklin D. Roosevelt with such anticipation; here was a man, he believed, who would remember the "forgotten man," who recognized the Southern situation for what it was — a national problem. Southerners did not contemplate a break with the American tradition but simply wanted a greater share of what the rest of the nation took for granted. They were ready for a shift within the system.

Southerners willingly went to war in 1941. Support by their Congressional delegation made possible the draft extension and revision of the neutrality acts. The old Confederacy was hostile territory to the America First Committee, whose members were ostracized. Hitler's barter system and Japan's Greater East Asia Co-Prosperity Sphere seemed personal attacks upon Southern markets, while religious fundamentalism easily delineated the struggle as one between good and evil. In its zeal, the South was blind to the paradox it created: "When the land of the Ku Klux Klan, chattel slavery, Judge Lynch and the poll tax starts whooping it up for the four freedoms, that alone ought to be enough to make it suspicious to the minds of all thinking men everywhere."[3] Apparent contradictions notwithstanding, the South was staunchily American, and even the most rabid "Yankee hater" protested with violence any slur on his national patriotism; along with these protestations, however, the Southerner kept a conviction that there was a superior, distinctive civilization below the Mason-Dixon line.

This mutual egocentricity blinded him to the social upheavals that swirled through the South. Most Southerners in 1941 were unaware of the sweeping changes occurring even during their own lifetime. Municipal slum-clearance projects, old-age pensions, and social security became a part of everyday life. Child labor almost disappeared, along with lynching and race riots. At the heart of the social transformation were shifts in population patterns. Despite its traditionally high birth

[3] Wayne S. Cole, "America First and the South, 1940-1941," *Journal of Southern History,* XII (February, 1956), pp. 36-47.

rate, the South from 1910 to 1950 lost fertility more rapidly than the rest of the nation — from 19 per cent higher in 1910 to 16 in 1940. Like other parts of the United States, there was a population spurt during the war years of the forties, but the Southern increase was slower, and its comparative fertility continued dropping. This is evidenced by the fact that its proportion of the nation's population held firm at approximately 28 per cent from 1910 to 1970. More and more, the South resembled the rest of the country in its patterns of family size, and rural-urban fertility differentials narrowed as a result of urbanization and a decreasing black agrarian population.

Only in the 1930's did the South have a higher percentage of population gain than the rest of the country, because of the drastic decline in migration. In fact, as has been suggested, the region's principal export was human beings. In normal or boom years, the South gave away thousands of young men and women, principally between the ages of 14 and 35. During the years of the Depression, the demand for their services decreased, and the South kept its young people until the market revived. During World War II, migration was heavier than ever before — 1,600,000 between Pearl Harbor and March, 1945.

An interesting characteristic was the increasing proportion of whites involved, Negroes comprising only one-third of the net emigration during the War. The 1950's brought further increases in white migration from the South — a loss not significantly offset by immigrants into the South. For the years 1953-1957, emigrants exceeded those coming in by approximately 200,000, while foreign-born inhabitants of the region numbered less than two per cent of the population. Although declining, relatively, between 1950 and 1960, the Southern birth rate remained somewhat higher. In this period, the rate for the South increased 16 per cent, as opposed to 32 to 36 per cent in other regions. The higher rate resulted from the rural character of the South (farm women of childbearing age averaged 2.1 children, compared to 1.6 for urban wives) and the younger average age of Southerners. This meant not only more women of childbearing age per 1,000 but also a greater percentage of nonproductive workers and thus a lower per capita income. Whereas the 1960 census had shown three Southern states (Arkansas, Mississippi, and West Virginia) as having a net loss of population, ten years later only West Virginia was smaller and only Alabama and Tennessee were significantly below the national average of 13.3 per cent growth.

Until 1930 the South's economy was primarily agricultural and this was reflected in her population, with some 5.5 million (42.8 per cent) engaged in farming, compared to 5.3 million elsewhere. In the early thirties, farm population increased somewhat as the Depression drove thousands back to the farms, but with the coming of World War II, the trend was sharply reversed. Between December, 1941, and March, 1945, gross intra-state migration in thirteen Southern states amounted to 3,200,000 persons, and interstate movement within the region accounted for 1,600,000 more. Of 1,333 counties, 714, predominantly rural ones, lost population between 1940 and 1950. The exodus was such that agricultural workers fell to 3.2 million and constituted only 21.3 per cent of Southern population. In the twenty years between 1950 and 1970 an additional 2.7 million Southerners left the farm for good, and only five of sixteen Southern and Border states did not show a rural decline in the 1970 census.

Negro migration had a decided effect upon the population ratios in the South. Traditionally, the Negro was the first to migrate; thus his numbers increased more slowly. In the twenty years after 1930, white population growth was ten times greater than the Negro's, while the number of Negro inhabitants doubled in the rest of the country. The result was a steady drop in the Negro percentage of total Southern population. A decline in the number of Southern counties in which Negroes made up 50 per cent or more of the inhabitants began during World War I. As early as 1940, significant changes were obvious. For example, between 1900 and 1940, the number of predominantly Negro counties in Alabama declined from twenty-two to eighteen, in Arkansas from fifteen to nine, in Florida from twelve to three, in Georgia from sixty-seven to forty-six, in Louisiana from thirty-one to fifteen, and in Texas from twelve to three. Many were also leaving the region as well as the farm, seen in the fact that Negro percentages of total population in the same period fell from 44 to 27 per cent in Florida, 47 to 36 in Louisiana, and 58 to 43 in South Carolina. A look at Virginia gives one example of what was happening. That state's percentage of Negro population declined from 35.7 per cent in 1900 to 22.1 in 1950, when only 83 per cent were Virginia-born. The majority of the newcomers arrived from the deeper South. Likewise, most of the emigrants from Virginia went north and northeast.

Between 1940 and 1950, according to Census Bureau figures, seven Southern states lost an over-all total of 249,360 Negroes, while their white population increased by 2,046,511. For the region as a whole, its percentage dropped from 23.8 to 21.6. In 1950 the State of Georgia had more blacks than any other state, but by the end of the decade New York had moved into first place. Washington, D.C. had by this time become the only major city in America which had more blacks than whites. While blacks showed a 25 per cent national gain between 1950-1960, the increase in the South was roughly 9 per cent. Their concentration in central cities had far reaching effects at every level. If black Southerners who migrated to urban areas created fears and brought problems with them, they also carried the potentials of change. It was there, with the aid of many whites, that they were able to launch strong protests against existing injustices. The political effect of the blacks who lived in the cities, whether North or South, was obvious to politicians, and it is not surprising that racial reform became a reality in the years of the sixties.

Migration patterns after 1960 showed some interesting changes which could affect the entire country in the future if they continue. First, black population by 1970 had increased by 43.4 per cent in the Northeast, 56.1 in the West, and only 5.8 in the South, but the rate of migration had dropped from an average annual net Southern loss of 152,000 before 1960 to 88,000 per year by 1970. The cumulative result was that blacks made up only 19 per cent of Southern population with only 53 per cent of the nation's blacks still living there. In the entire nation there were sixteen communities above 25,000 which were more than half black; ten of these were outside the South.

The other characteristics of the 1960's were more surprising. The 1970 Census showed that for the first time since the Civil War the combined white and black in-migration was greater in the South than the total out-migration. This partially was attributable to a decline in the latter figures, but it also reflects the fact that in addition to the usual white business representative who moved South, there was also a reverse migration of blacks. So far, this return has been relatively small, but civil rights leaders and others agree that it is happening at an expanding rate. The Census Bureau reports that it is coming chiefly from middle and upper class blacks. John Lewis, former head of SNCC, said, "Black people are coming back because of the significant changes in the social, economic, and political climate of the region." When James Meredith returned to Mississippi after six years in New York, he said, "On a person-to-person, day-to-day basis, the South is a more livable place for blacks than any other place in the nation." The Gallup Poll took his statement and found in 1971 that nationally 48 per cent of the blacks agreed, 30 per cent disagreed, and 22 per cent had no opinion. In the South, 63 per cent agreed. This increased attractiveness of the South sufficiently alarmed some Northern businessmen to the degree that in 1972 a committee of the Institute of Life Insurance warned its members that if this reverse trend continued it would "serious exacerbate conditions in Northern cities" and that they should "develop counter incentives to potential emigration of talented blacks before the condition [became] irreversible."

Cities had particular attraction for the Negro. Traditionally, race relation taboos were more difficult to enforce in metropolitan areas. Urban growth broke down housing patterns and furnished more capital for improving individual housing status. There was more opportunity for self-expression and more job opportunities at a higher occupational level. The city Negro also commanded greater purchasing power, which in turn brought more self-respect and greater acceptability from the whites. Closer proximity, newspapers, leaders, plus more liberal sympathetic whites to aid him made launching organized protests easier for the reform groups.

From the Delta the Negroes streamed into Memphis or Little Rock; from Alabama farms to Birmingham; in Georgia to Atlanta and Augusta; and from South Carolina to jobs in Charlotte, Durham, Greensboro, or Winston-Salem in North Carolina. By 1950, however, they no longer tarried briefly and then moved north as they did during the war days. More and more became content to remain in the South. As early as 1950, 48 per cent of all Southern Negroes were urban dwellers. This swift influx became the number one problem of the large American cities, for sociologists estimated that the Negro's adjustment to urban life would be a challenge "not for a decade but for generations." Dr. Philip M. Hauser, former acting head of the Census Bureau, stated in 1958 that the "startling fact . . . is that for only a little more than one generation has the Negro been drawn into the main stream of American civilization represented by urbanism and metropolitanism as a form of life," despite the fact that he had been an American longer than the average white person.

After World War II, Negroes stayed in Southern cities in greater numbers, because as a rule they were successful in getting better jobs at better wages and faced less discrimination. Essentially, what happened was that the Negro enjoyed a share, although a minor one, in the industrial boom which swept the South during these years. He probably could have earned more money in Northern centers, but Southern pay scales, plus lower living costs, seemed to satisfy him. The percentage of urban Negro families in the United States earning less than $1,000 annually decreased from 90 to 40 per cent between 1936 and 1954. The fact that one-half had incomes of more than $2,500 indicated their greatly improved economic status. Their average annual income in the latter year was 56 per cent of that for urban whites. Even that looked good, however, when compared to the figure of $749 for rural Negro families, and Southern Negro farm population dropped from 1,500,000 in 1940 to 770,000 in 1960.

Racial barriers in employment were slowly beginning to crack, and by the seventies, they were crumbling. Constant pressure was

applied by blacks themselves, federal and state government, and many
enlightened employers. Increasingly, blacks were employed in a variety
of jobs and industries formerly reserved for whites. For example,
blacks made up a fifth of North Carolina's textile workers by 1971.
Two things had contributed to these gains in the years prior to the
fifties: a growing labor scarcity and voluntary programs which fostered hiring and promotion irrespective of color. Few things, however,
did more to advance equal employment opportunity than the Civil
Rights Act of 1964 with its severe penalties for discrimination.

Progress in race relations has continued mostly through the efforts
of new, and in many cases young, leaders in business and politics.
Politicians and businessmen, both white and black, were determined
to avoid letting racial conflict interfere with the economic development of the South, believing that the stability already achieved has
been a big plus in attracting business and people to the region. In
pursuit of their economic goals they sponsored the tremendous expansion in vocational education and apprentice schools. These leaders
also directed the conscious shift from seeking labor-intensive industries to those which were capital-intensive. The South no longer has
a labor surplus to squander, and both of these developments have
been reflected in more and better jobs for both races.

Except for a lag of almost fifty years, urbanization of the South
progressed in much the same manner as the United States as a whole.
In 1940, for example, the percentage of urban dwellers in the South
was equal to that of the nation in 1890. However, since 1930, the rate
of Southern urbanization was so rapid that the lag dropped propor-
tionately. Between 1930 and 1970, the movement to the city was twice
as fast in the South as in the nation.[4] This is shown by Census returns
based upon percentages of population living in towns of 2,500 or more.

In 1920 the South had only seven of the top fifty cities of the
United States ranked by population, a figure which doubled during
the next twenty years. This proportion had not increased by 1950, but
the cities represented moved higher up the scale, with Houston, Texas,
occupying the fourteenth place. By 1960, the Census showed that
Houston had grown by 56.4 per cent and occupied sixth place in size
in the nation.

Ten years later, eleven Southern cities had made the top fifty in
size. Much more spectacular than the growth of large metropolises
was the increase in urban centers (2,500 inhabitants or more). Only
one Southern state, Florida, was more than 50 per cent urban in

[4] Rupert B. Vance and Nicholas J. Demerath, eds., *The Urban South* (Chapel Hill:
Univ. of North Carolina, 1954).

1940, and there were only forty-two cities of more than 50,000 population in thirteen Southern states. Three, Arkansas, Mississippi, and South Carolina, had no city of over 100,000 people. Yet, in the next ten years, the region's urban residents increased by 35 per cent, the fastest rate of growth in the nation. About half of the Southern counties, including nearly all of the rural ones, lost population, as the South became the only region to show an absolute decline in rural farm dwellers.[5]

By 1950, of 4,284 urban centers in the United States, the South had 1,217, or 28.4 per cent. What was significant, however, aside from the rise in urban population, was the disproportionately large share of the smaller centers: only one-fourth of all settlements of more than 10,000 were in the South, while almost one-third of the smaller ones were Southern. Of thirty-three "metropolitan areas" with over 500,000 inhabitants, the South boasted only seven. Yet, the Southern percentage of urbanization had risen from 15.2 in 1900 to 64.4 in 1970 (U.S. average was 73.5). Florida was one of ten states that exceeded 80, and West Virginia, Mississippi, and the Carolinas were the only Southern states below 50 per cent. As the factors responsible for urbanization were still strong, it was likely that Southern urban centers, large and small, would continue to multiply.

Although the South resembled the North in its multiplication of cities, the city did not dominate the Southern thought pattern. Instead, there is evidence that the country conquered the city.[6] Rural religious habits were strengthened by the migration to town, voting characteristics did not obviously change, and the ultimate dream of the Southern businessman continued to be retirement to a country estate. The coming of industry had little effect to the contrary. Given a choice between a heavily industrialized area or a small non-industrial town with adequate transportation, most concerns will choose the more rural area. Many factory workers also preferred commuting to the small-town plants from rural homes. Thus, because of the motor truck and the automobile, the South will probably continue in a pattern of many small cities and only a few very large ones. By 1970 there was the interesting phenomenon that manufacturing was growing faster in its rural areas, where two-thirds of the poor were located, than in the urban centers.

Yet, adjustments were necessary. Sparked by city dwellers, and in the face of bitter opposition from the clergy, prohibition and many

[5] Wilbur Zelinsky, "The Changing South," *Focus*, II (October 15, 1951), p. 2.
[6] Walter Sullivan, "The City and the Old Vision," in Rubin and Kilpatrick, *op. cit.*, pp. 117-128.

blue laws were repealed. In 1941, for example, the city council of Charlotte, North Carolina, voted eight to three to allow Sunday baseball, movies, tennis, golf, and swimming. A rapid expansion in slum areas, unemployment, and the trials of transition were reflected by greatly increased crime rates. In almost every type, urban crime rates in the South were far beyond those of other regions. In 1937, for example, the South had a murder rate of 23.2 per 100,000 population, as compared to 1.3 in New England, 3.8 in the Middle-Atlantic states, and 4.2 for the Pacific Coast. Over thirty years later, this picture had not changed, and individually owned guns were still more prevalent. However, the suicide rate was the nation's lowest; only Florida, Louisiana, and Virginia exceeded the national average for alcohol consumption; and only 7.0 per cent thought marijuana should be legalized.[7] In short, the South was becoming nationalized, even to the ills that had confronted the North a half century earlier. Better police systems, improved housing, and increased appropriations for health supervision were problems of staggering proportions which faced Southern cities.

In recent years several trends improved these situations. The introduction of black policemen was beneficial, although their numbers did not reflect black percentage of the population. The Federal Jury Selection Act of 1968 and state actions increased black representation and, it is hoped, instilled greater confidence in the court system. Another notable accomplishment came in the field of public housing. The nation's first public slum-conversion project began in Atlanta, Georgia, with eleven blocks replaced by a housing project. Throughout the South, similar undertakings were made, with rentals pegged to the low incomes predominant in the region. As a consequence, the most conspicuous beneficiaries were the urban blacks, yet by the 1970's approximately one-third of that race lived in sub-standard housing, compared to one in twelve whites. Although much remained to be done in solving large-city problems, obvious areas needing attention were the small and middle-sized communities. These were the most backward in providing adequate protection from crime, disease, fire, and the like. One asset which prodded even these was the growing awareness that to attract industry they had to make their communities attractive and safe.

This fact was particularly true with regard to education. To the Negro and white alike, one of the most potent lures of the cities was the chance for educational betterment. But while both did improve

[7] Sheldon Hackney, "Southern Violence," *American Historical Review*, LXXIV (February, 1969), pp. 906-925.

their educational chances by moving to the city, the Negro was destined to be disappointed, for the gap between theirs and comparable white schools was the more evident. In 1930, for every $7 spent for whites, only $2 went to Negroes, and five years later the ratio was almost the same — $37.87 to $13.09. The value of Negro school property per pupil was less than one-fifth as great as that for whites. The Depression hit Negro education especially hard, for little room for improvement could be found in the already overstrained budgets. The Negro teacher's lot was especially hard, despite the fact that teaching was the principal Negro profession. Relegated to segregated schools, he had a heavier teaching and pupil load and less education — the last fact often serving as an excuse for discriminations in salary.

While Negro educational levels were undeniably poor, they were just one facet of the over-all serious educational picture in the South. The region had a large backlog of illiteracy, more children to educate per capita, less money, and fewer adults. In Arkansas, for example, during 1933-34, the average annual salary of public school teachers was $465, compared to $2,361 for New York state. Southern states in 1936 spent an average of $25.11 per child in school, about half that for the country as a whole and a quarter of that for New York. Nowhere was the number of pupils per teacher higher than in the South.

During the Depression the number of elementary students showed a decline from 7,128,000 in 1930 to 6,950,000 in 1950, although since that time the South, like the rest of the nation, was faced by a tremendous increase. The fruits of the past and the Depression were reflected in the figures of the 1940 Census. In the former Confederate states, an average of 5.7 per cent of the rural native white males over twenty-five years of age reported having had no schooling, and an average of 20.3 per cent had attended only from one to four years. This survey found 851,000 adults in the Southeastern states (including Kentucky) who had not completed a single year, while the average for persons over twenty-five was 8.5 years for urban dwellers, from 7.2 to 4.5 for rural citizens, and 4.9 to 2.8 for Negroes.

Despite these facts, however, 85.4 per cent of all children between the ages of five and seventeen were enrolled in Southern schools in 1940, as compared to an average of 85.2 in the other regions of the United States. By 1945 the Southern states were spending 1.78 per cent of their income (wages, salaries, farm income, etc.) for education, as compared to 1.71 per cent for the rest of the country, but because of lower incomes and larger numbers of children, this superior effort was producing only $72.21 per pupil, comparable to $137.87 elsewhere. The average number of days attended by each pupil had risen until it was 96 per cent of the national rate. Yet, of the World War II draft registrants who could not sign their own names, nine of ten were Southerners, and six of the nine were Negroes.

Despite the fact that a Gallup Poll in 1941 showed that approximately half of the white people of the South favored equal public school advantages for the Negro and that North Carolina had become the first state to equalize teachers' salaries, discrimination was evident. The percentage by which cost per white pupil exceeded that per Negro pupil in 1943-1944 ranged from a low of 43 per cent in North Carolina to a high of 499 per cent in Mississippi. Educational expenditures mounted continuously, but there was simply not enough revenue to maintain two first-class systems of public education, and so, while both fell short of national averages, the Negro suffered first and hardest.

By 1947 educational appropriations per population unit ranged from $15.03 in Mississippi to $23.60 in Texas, as compared to an average of $26.05 in non-Southern states. By the next year, 39 per cent of all expenditures of Southern state and local governments went for schools, as compared to 25.5 elsewhere. From 1940 to 1952, school revenues increased over three and one-half times, and the average number of school years completed by whites went up to 9.7 years and for non-whites to 7.0 years. Part of the explanation for the improved Negro situation lay in the fact that by 1952 they were getting nearly three-fourths as much per pupil as was being spent on the whites. Beginning with South Carolina in 1951, all Southern states made determined efforts to equalize white and Negro schools. Within a few years, the differential was largely eliminated in all but expenditures. The length of the school term was approximately the same, as was the number of pupils, teacher training, and pay scales for similar qualifications.

Still remaining, however, was the problem of inequality in expenditure between rural and urban schools, an average of $44 per pupil, with extremes of $265.75 a pupil for metropolitan districts in Kentucky to $56.46 in Mississippi rural districts. It was estimated in 1957 that to close this gap would cost the South about $240,000,000 and that replacement of inadequate buildings and equipment would require another $1.7 billion — about one-third of which would be for Negroes. To meet this problem, Southern states began to engage in larger degrees of state aid to poorer school districts.[8]

One of the primary reasons for improvement of Negro education, aside from an increase in enlightened public opinion, was the changing attitude of the Negro. No longer was he willing to submit passively to

[8] George B. Tindall, "Problems of the Southern Schools," *Current History*, XXXII (May, 1957), pp. 273-277.

injustices but was more apt to demand aggressively equal rights and opportunities. Ever since the Civil War, the race had been characterized by its zeal for education and the belief that increased knowledge was the Negro's best ally for improvement of his position. Therefore, that school segregation became one of the focal points of attack is not surprising. As has been shown, the first efforts were aimed at professional education and were marked by a favorable court attitude and success.

Upon shifting their attention to segregation in the public schools, the Negroes won their first significant victory on May 17, 1954. In Brown v. Board of Education of Topeka, the Supreme Court ruled that "we must look . . . to the effect of segregation itself on public education," rather than to historical precedent.

> Segregation of white and colored children has a detrimental effect upon the colored children. The impact is greater when it has the sanction of the law; for the policy of separating the races is usually interpreted as denoting the inferiority of the Negro group. A sense of inferiority affects the motivation of a child to learn. Segregation with the sanction of law, therefore, has a tendency to retard the educational and mental development of Negro children and to deprive them of some of the benefits they would receive in a racially integrated school system.

Therefore, the Court decided that "separate educational facilities are inherently unequal" and that "segregation is a denial of the equal protection of the laws."[9] On May 31, 1955, the Court implemented this decision by declaring that district courts were to require "a prompt and reasonable start toward full compliance" and to take such action as necessary to bring about the end of racial segregation in public schools with "all deliberate speed."

Oliver Brown's victory, however, was a bitter one, as the South rose to the defense of Jim Crow. The region fell back upon its old stand that race relations were purely a Southern problem and should be solved locally, that if Northerners and reformers would leave the South and the Negro alone, peaceful adjustment of the race issue could be made. Otherwise, they were fomenting race riots which would in the long run hurt both white and Negro, and the nation as a whole. Symptomatic of this feeling was a letter written to an Alabama editor by an "Ex-Yankee from Ohio, who loves the South and all of its principles." This man wrote, "If some folks don't like the way we grit-eaters run things down here in the South, why in the world don't they pack

---

[9] Brown v. Board of Education of Topeka, 347 US 483, Sup. Ct. 686, 98 L.Ed. 873 (May 17, 1954).

their bags and move up north. We have trains, buses and airplanes that leave here every hour of the day for all points north."[10]

Another point of resistance was the organization of White Citizens Councils. They apparently had their origin when fourteen men met in Sunflower County, Mississippi, and formed the first council in July, 1954. As the movement spread throughout the lower South, they quoted with approval a speech by Senator James O. Eastland of Mississippi, who said,

> It is essential that a nation-wide organization be set up. . . . A people's organization to fight the Court, to fight the CIO, to fight the NAACP, and to fight all the conscienceless pressure groups who are attempting our destruction. We will mobilize and organize public opinion. . . . We are about to embark upon a great crusade, a crusade to restore Americanism, and return the control of our government to the people. . . . The choice is between victory and defeat. Defeat means death, the death of Southern culture and our aspirations as an Anglo-Saxon people.

The councils not only stressed the threat to the South but tried to appeal to the more respectable classes and shake off the onus of the Klan by disavowing violence.

In other areas of influence, however, the stand was also taken that the Supreme Court had exceeded its authority in the school decisions. As late as August 23, 1958, the Conference of State Chief Justices adopted a critical report, holding that the United States Supreme Court had "too often . . . tended to adopt the role of a policy maker without proper judicial restraint." A poll by *U.S. News & World Report* (October 24, 1958) showed that of the judges of the District and Circuit Courts of Appeal who answered in eleven Southern states, 55.5 per cent agreed with this point of view and only 28 per cent voiced disagreement.

Meanwhile, the Southern states adopted various measures of defiance. Most of the resistance fell into three broad categories: shutting off funds to integrated schools; granting of broad authority to school officials in pupil placement; and exercise of extraordinary police powers. Most states enacted legislation aimed at curbing NAACP activities. School districts were gerrymandered so that segregated housing could be the apparent reason for separate education. By 1958 some 196 laws had been passed in the eleven states of the lower South to permit legal circumventions, even to the extent of abolishing public education and beginning a system of state-subsidized private schools on the

[10] Birmingham, Alabama, *Post-Herald*, September 28, 1957.

argument that the states were under no federal obligation to provide free public education. "Pupil placement" acts regulating the conditions of assignment, attendance, and enrollment were popular because they were based not on race but on state police powers and because they put placement in the hands of local school boards. Other legislative sanctions penalized teachers sympathetic to integration and repealed or relaxed compulsory attendance laws.

As the Supreme Court and lower federal courts slowly dismantled these defenses, violence broke out. Integration of Negro students into white high schools brought mob violence to Clinton, Tennessee, and to Clay and Sturgis, Kentucky, in September, 1956. A year later federal troops were sent into Little Rock, Arkansas, when National Guardsmen under orders from Governor Orval Faubus prevented Negro children from entering Central High School. The next year the governor ordered all four Little Rock high schools closed. In Virginia, the Warren County High School was closed rather than admit Negroes in 1958.[11] In 1960 the scene of friction shifted to Louisiana and Texas.

Despite such incidents of open resistance, integration of schools made progress. During the school year 1955-1956, Negro children in integrated situations increased by 250,000. The Southern Education Reporting Service announced in 1957 that, three years after the Brown decision, in the seventeen states and the District of Columbia where segregated schools existed by law, 700 school districts had been desegregated out of some 3,000. Only a handful of those integrated were outside the border states, yet some 2,000,000 Southern white children and 325,000 Southern Negroes were involved in integrated situations. No progress had been made in Mississippi, South Carolina, Georgia, Florida, and Alabama. Whereas integration moved rapidly in Delaware, Kentucky, Missouri, Maryland, Oklahoma, and West Virginia, only spasmodic progress was evident in Louisiana, North Carolina, Tennessee, Texas, and Virginia. By the end of 1958, some 377,000 of the South's 2,924,000 Negro students were in school districts which gave outward compliance to integration; 792 districts had begun or completed integration by this time. Only fifteen of these, however, were found below the border states, none within the deep South.

Progress continued haltingly as the task became harder. Six years and scores of lawsuits after the Supreme Court had ruled school segregation unconstitutional, of the seventeen affected states and the District of Columbia, only West Virginia and the District were completely desegregated, and only 6.3 per cent of the Negroes attended integrated classes. In four states, Alabama, Georgia, Mississippi, and

11 Joan Lee Barkon, "Southern Schools in Transition," *Current History*, XXXV (November, 1958), pp. 292-296.

South Carolina, even token integration was nonexistent. In 1961 some additional 1,000 Negro children were assigned to bi-racial schools. Atlanta accepted Negroes in white high schools, the first desegregation in Georgia below the college level, and even Little Rock opened its junior high schools to Negroes for the first time. Delaware permitted Negroes in all grades in all of its schools, and expanded integration took place in many states.

More important than the slow progress indicated by these statistics were the new sentiments developing in each race. By 1961, according to George Gallup's polls, 76 per cent of the Southerners generally conceded that desegregation was inevitable. The Georgia legislature abandoned massive resistance laws which had been heralded as sufficient to keep the schools segregated for "1,000 years." The Negroes, on the other hand, became self-conscious of their legal and moral rights and were determined to look after themselves. White paternalism, which flourished before 1954, vanished. Whites who once sincerely regarded Negroes as content with their lot were finally aware that this was no longer true. Aspects of segregation which once were of no concern became embarrassing under the focus of national and international attention.

The integration fight in the public schools made two points clear: first, no longer could the Negro be ignored, and second, Southern education even at its best could still stand improvement before reaching the national average.[12] Integrated schools would not solve the basically economic problem of Southern education but might well make it worse. For example, North Carolina's drive, which had begun when "Education Governor" Charles B. Aycock inspired that state to build a new school building every day for ten years, by 1959 had reached the point where, although it gave 76 per cent of its budget for education, its average teacher salary ranked it only thirty-eighth in the nation. The highest ranking Southern state was Florida in sixteenth position, while Mississippi occupied the last place.

On the other hand, North Carolina in 1959 had a per capita income of only $1,317, Florida of $1,836, and Mississippi $958, compared to New York's $2,578, California's $2,523, Massachusetts' $2,335, and Indiana's $2,010. The majority of the Southern states spent a greater percentage of their citizens' income to support their schools than did the richer states elsewhere; yet the ten lowest states in expenditures per pupil were all Southern or border states. Compared to a national

[12] Patrick McCauley and Edward Ball, eds., *Southern Schools: Progress and Problems* (Nashville: Vanderbilt Univ., 1959); Ernst W. Swanson and John A. Griffin, *Public Education in the South, Today and Tomorrow* (Chapel Hill: Univ. of North Carolina, 1955).

average of $340 and New York's high of $535, Mississippi and Alabama ranked lowest of all states with expenditures of $181 and $164, respectively. Yet, Mississippi allotted 3.8 and Alabama 3.3 per cent of their total personal income payments for school support, as compared with New York's 3.2.

This seemingly irremediable situation led to demands that the educational problem of the South be viewed as national rather than regional. Children should be educated to become Americans rather than Virginians or New Yorkers and a lag in some states hurts the whole nation. Thus, federal aid was prominently suggested as a means for correction of the inequalities between the regions. The case for federal aid grew out of the fact that it was the only apparent way in which the discrepancies could be immediately eliminated; with more children and less income, the South's facilities were still inadequate, despite praiseworthy efforts. Also, much of the region's wealth was actually siphoned off by absentee ownership to other states, together with the fact that the South subsidized education in wealthier non-Southern states through the migration of Southerners who left after completing their education. It was estimated that the total cost of educating the more than 7,000,000 who left the South in the decade of 1940-1950 was two to three billion dollars. While there was some reverse migration from richer states, it was much smaller.

Southern objections to this solution were based on the arguments that political considerations would require more money than enough for equalization alone. In turn, a huge school fund distributed from Washington would invite pressure groups and eventually put public school organizations into federal politics. Most important was the fear that substantial federal aid would inevitably bring federal control of educational policy. Campaign promises made by the Democrats in 1960 were redeemed by the beginning of federal aid to public education. Although equality of public education had not been achieved fifteen years later and some grumbled over threats to withhold such aid if integration were not pressed more vigorously, most of the dire predictions had not come true and Southern education had certainly benefitted from the infusion of federal funds.

The Southern Negroes were beneficiaries not only of the general improvement in education and economic opportunities which took place in the South after 1930 but also made social gains as well. Before 1930 they had little reason for optimism, but the next forty years was a time of great change. For one thing, the old doctrine of racism as a scientifically respectable concept was exploded, with the result that segregation became logically difficult to defend as a good within itself. The emphasis of the New Deal upon human rights and equality had its effect on reforming politicians, while at the same time the Democratic party discovered that Negro votes had value. Negro and other minority groups learned the importance of standing together and brought pressure to bear, particularly upon industrial unions. The outbreak of World War II, with its demand for manpower, opened a period of general prosperity which eased economic competition and permitted Negroes to rise in occupational status. Nazi racism and the Allies' goal of the Four Freedoms made obvious the glaring shortcomings of American democracy. The end of that conflict in turn brought a large number of countries into prominence whose people were also non-white and whose aid was coveted in the ensuing "cold war" with Russia. The decade of the fifties, with its prosperity, growth of suburbs, and general domestic stability, helped to ease racial tensions, aside from those growing out of integration of tax-supported institutions. Racial violence declined, and federal courts and governmental agencies showed more awareness of the Negro's problems.[13] The Negro himself was not only more willing to use the courts but also grew more determined to gain his rights by use of economic boycotts, "sit-ins," and other forms of passive resistance against discrimination in transportation, eating facilities, libraries, theaters, and the like.

Much of the social progress was a result of economic gains. Between 1940 and 1950, non-agricultural employment in the South expanded by almost 60 per cent for white women, almost 40 for white men, 30 for Negro men, and seven for Negro women. Despite this imbalance, the urban employment of Negroes, even at occupational levels lower than those of whites, was a distinct improvement over their previous agricultural employment. On this basis, the Negro middle class grew, with more working in professional, semi-professional, and service occupations. Consequently, the Negro's economic importance increased, with marked consideration being given the Negro market, both in terms of numbers of consumers and of the money they had to spend.

The Census of 1950 reported that 29 per cent of the Negroes in the United States were farmers, compared to 15 per cent of the whites, with an average income of $691. About 45 per cent of all non-white persons, urban and rural, were classified as unskilled laborers, household workers, or service employees, as compared to only 13 per cent for the whites. Six per cent more Negro women found it necessary to work outside the home than did whites, while three per cent fewer Negro males than whites were employed. Nineteen of 180 skilled trade

[13] Oscar Handlin, "Desegregation in Perspective," *Current History*, XXXII (May, 1957), pp. 257-259; Lewis W. Jones, "The Changing Status of Negro Southerners," *ibid.*, XXXV (November, 1958), pp. 271-276.

unions excluded Negroes altogether, while an additional ten put them in segregated organizations. In creature comforts, seven out of ten white dwellings had hot and cold running water and private toilets against less than four for Negroes. The death rate was ten and seven per thousand for white men and women, as compared to fourteen and eleven for Negro citizens.

Such figures do not tell the whole story, however. Opportunities for Southern blacks were greater than ever during the decade of the fifties. Although largely restricted to black clientele, they made small but spectacular beginnings in banking, building and loan associations, and life and burial insurance. Black social workers became increasingly common, as did black postal workers, policemen, and firemen. Over 140 Southern cities were employing black police by 1954. More and more members of the race became taxpayers, home owners, and dependable citizens. They succeeded in getting their feet planted firmly on the political road leading from second- to first-class citizenship. In the words of black publisher John H. Johnson, "Every Negro is a Horatio Alger. . . . His trek up from slavery is the greatest success story the world has ever known. . . ."

Yet these very successes gave the black a keener sense of the opportunities he had missed, but might have shared had his skin been white. To gain these, he was now willing to take risks. His drive for equal opportunity under law, and the support it engendered, shook the entire nation during the 1960's. The movement, beginning during the previous decade, was founded upon non-violence and profound idealism as it set out to dramatize the need to overhaul racist institutions. Early black efforts were directed primarily at educational and social discrimination. The Montgomery, Alabama boycott over segregated busses brought the first major victory. The early fifties also saw the Supreme Court chipping away at segregation in higher education, paving the way for the historic Brown decision of 1954. Although a few blacks attended white colleges and universities, they were notably absent from state universities in the lower South. In 1956 Autherine Lucy enrolled at the University of Alabama, but left shortly afterwards. The courts then opened the University of Georgia, but this time the black students had the support of the Governor in their efforts to enter the school. But in 1962 came one of the sternest tests of black determination, federal sincerity, and Southern resistance. James Meredith, a black Air Force veteran, secured a court order admitting him to the University of Mississippi. The Governor and other officials chose to defy this order. President Kennedy, hoping to avoid a state-federal confrontation, went on national television to urge compliance and restraint, but even as he was speaking, riots broke out on the campus that left two dead and scores injured. The President's firm action in nationalizing the state Guard and sending in federal marshals, though unpoplar with some, clearly proved that integration was a reality.

While victory had been won in higher education and the public schools were starting the slow march toward conformity with the Brown decision, the sixties saw parallel drives to capitalize on Martin Luther King's victory in the Montgomery boycott. This period, which might be called the "King Era" of civil rights, was basically characterized by the concept of "passive resistance" and King's eloquence in stressing the power of love and belief in the brotherhood of man. The year 1960 saw the onset of "Freedom Riders," sponsored by CORE, to test segregated interstate facilities, while SNCC coordinated hundreds of students in "sit-ins" in opposition to segregated eating facilities. In 1962 King personally led the assault in Birmingham, which he called "the most thoroughly segregated city in the United States," as he and thousands of protestors carried their demonstrations to the streets. Brute force, in the form of dogs, fire hoses, and hundreds of arrests, was used by police authorities, shocking the nation as the scene was replayed over national television.

President Kennedy used the same media to denounce publicaly all segregation as morally wrong and to call upon Congress for redress of black grievances. When the civil rights legislation faltered, in August, 1963, some 200,000 blacks and whites held a march on Washington. This provided the background and occasion for Dr. King's memorable and stirring "I Have a Dream" speech. Despite a seventy-five day filibuster, spurred on by public opinion and the tragic death of President Kennedy, the Civil Rights Act of 1964 was finally passed with the strong support of President Johnson. It banned discrimination in businesses offering food, lodging or entertainment, and by employers or labor unions in hiring, firing, or promoting. Penalties for violations included provisions for suits by the Attorney General and/or withholding of federal funds. Altogether, it proved a major victory in the fight for racial equality.

The years after 1965 were characterized by black efforts for political equality, more rapid desegregation of public schools, and the rise of "black power." Although the phrase, "black power," was used following the wounding of James Meredith in 1966, the movement's genesis lay in the continued opposition of die-hard whites and the rising impatience of younger blacks. Stokely Carmichael, former SNCC worker, became its leading advocate. Carmichael and black college students rejected the approach of King and most of the older organizations. With the assassination of King in Memphis in 1968, most black youths took the position that passive resistance had been killed by

James Earl Ray's bullet. In the wake of this event came riot after riot throughout the country, but chiefly in the North. The violence that ensued fragmented the civil rights movement (now viewed by some as a drive for "liberation"). It created a political "backlash," and made "law and order" and the "Southern Strategy," key elements in Nixon's presidential victories.

Against the violence of the sixties, integration of public schools moved distressingly slowly for the blacks but inexorably fast for some whites. In the decade between Brown v. Topeka and the Civil Rights Act of 1964, integration was chiefly of the "token" variety. The main attack weapon was the power to withhold federal funds from states and school systems which had not desegregated. A year after its use began, black enrollments in white schools of the ex-Confederate states increased sixfold, yet in 1967, 86 per cent were still in segregated schools. Again the courts moved to speed the process by ordering school boards to submit geographic zoning plans and by removing "freedom of choice" options. These moves meant literally mixing the schools, and for the first time whites were as liable to be bussed to black schools as the blacks to white schools. White reaction was largely non-violent, more often compliant, with the adamant taking refuge in private "segregation academies." It has been estimated that in 1972 some 7.0 per cent of school-age children were so enrolled. Yet in April, 1973, the Department of Health, Education, and Welfare could report that nationally almost 2.5 million black students, or 36.8 per cent, were in majority-white schools, compared with 44.4 per cent, or 1,405,000 in the deep South.

Public attitudes had also changed. Polls in the seventies showed that only one white in six Southerners still opposed school desegregation. There were also drastic declines in proportions that would object to voting for a black for President or having blacks move into their neighborhood. Meanwhile, 73 per cent of Southern blacks said "things had gotten better" for them in the last five years, and 65 per cent believed they could win black rights without violence. Sweden's Gunner Myrdal, returning to the South for the first time since his classic study of racial injustice, stated his belief that that region would probably solve its racial problems before the rest of the nation did.

With exceptions, all the more noticeable because of their comparative rarity, the South continued to have a good record insofar as other minority groups were concerned. Protestant-Catholic relations had not achieved that of brotherhood, but they were not violent either. The relative unimportance of that issue in most Southern minds was dramatically illustrated by the presidential election of 1960. During the troubled days of the Depression, one of the most fanatical of anti-Semitic groups was William Dudley Pelley's Silver Shirts, originating in North Carolina. Despite its obvious patterning on the moribund Ku Klux Klan, leading one wag to comment on the "great shift from sheets to shirts," the group had little success in attracting widespread support in the South. Another episode took place in 1958, with bomb attacks on synagogues in such cities as Miami and Jacksonville, Florida, Nashville, and Atlanta. The general tendency was to blame these on Communists or on a few radical extremists who claimed that Jewish money from New York was financing the NAACP in its drive for school integration. No evidence could be found connecting the Klan or White Citizens Councils with the outrages, and none of the rabbis connected with the bombed temples had been identified with the integration movement. Jewish leaders believed that they had been instigated by "old-line anti-Semitic agitators" and pointed to the great increase in anti-Semitic literature which had come in during the months preceding these incidents. With less than 6.0 per cent of its people foreign born in 1970, the region's other minorities — Indians, Mexican-Americans, and the like — all benefitted from the various civil rights and fair employment legislation. Like the blacks, they also became more militant, and successful, in their demands for equal treatment.

In the years after 1930, Southern women continued the steady erosion of artificial barriers to their equality with men. They were so successful that any evidence of legal discrimination was soon viewed as an archaic relic of the past, and by 1960 Southern females could and did enjoy essentially the same rights as their Northern or Western sisters. Among the few exceptions that continued was the refusal of Alabama, Mississippi, and South Carolina to allow women jurors, and in Florida and Texas (along with California, Nevada, and Pennsylvania) married women were required to get court permission to go into business for themselves.

The emancipation of the female was marked not only by her increased participation in politics, clubs of every sort, sports, business, and the professions, but also by the fact that more of them worked outside their homes. Between 1940 and 1950, employment of females increased 37.2 per cent in the South. Of the total increase in Southern civilian employment of more than 2.4 million, 43.5 per cent was supplied by women. Whereas they had constituted 23.5 per cent of the labor force in 1940, as compared to a non-Southern percentage of 25.3, ten years later they made up 26.9 per cent as against 28.3. These years also saw a sharp drop in the numbers in agricultural and domestic service, and the biggest gains were registered in clerical and craft work. By the 1970's, however, as a result of state and federal fair employment laws and "Affirmative Action" plans, female workers found themselves in favored positions in virtually every field and at every level of employment. The probable passage of the federal Equal Rights Amendment would theoretically remove the last vestiges of sexual discrimination.

In fact, by 1975 few areas of Southern life could be said to be distinctively different from the North. Those which could be pointed out were usually mental and emotional, long-established traditions from the past. Agrarian attitudes still dominated, although the farm continued losing out to the city. Personal independence and conservatism held the growth of labor unions below that of industrialization. The "Solid South" appeared a thing of the past, but while the Republican party seemed firmly based for future growth, it had not yet achieved anything close to equality in the deep South. Despite the election, with Southern support, of a Catholic president in 1960 and the continued growth of liberalism, fundamentalist religion continued a potent conservator of the Southern way of life. Over-all, the Southern people still showed the influence of their unique history. The South would continue the most supersensitive region of the United States as long as the situation described by Gunnar Myrdal existed: "When . . . Northern journalism discusses wrongs at the North or at the West, it criticizes the *wrongs,* but when it discusses wrongs at the South, it criticizes the *South.*"

Although the "changing South" was still the South, in 1975 it was a region which was content to be a member of the Union and sought to rival the North only in terms of Northern standards. Military amalgamation, begun during the Spanish-American War when Southerner and Northerner united against a common foreign foe, was completed in the World Wars which followed. The growth of industrialism, with the accompanying Northern investors; Northern philanthropists; patronage of Southern literature; and Northern acceptance of the "Lost Cause" — all helped soften the scars of the past. Urbanism broke down some of the Southern provincialism, as did increased educational opportunities, the rise of the tourist trade, and migration between regions. Only in religion, politics, and certain areas of public opinion, such as attitudes of race, were there large gaps in reconciliation between the South and the rest of the nation. This degree of progress was possible because Americans were fundamentally one people, with common aspirations, whose leaders essentially have been men of good will.

The legacies of the past, therefore, were still the regional characteristics of the South, and every nation has its regions. However, on every hand the evidence was clear that the South was moving back into the "mainstream" of American life.[14] That there had been change is undeniable, and many would agree with the observation of historian C. Vann Woodward that "recent changes are of sufficient depth and impact as to define the end of an era of Southern history." By the 1970's the tenant shacks had largely disappeared. Both country and urban homes were usually substantial, with access to electricity. Plumbing, runnng water, and refrigeration were standard equipment, to say nothing of radio and television, for the South's relative position of wealth had improved in almost every category since 1930. Between 1960 and 1970, for example, median income for whites rose 71 per cent and 178 for blacks, as the Southern economy continued to grow faster than the nation as a whole. Southerners were healthier and better educated; black faces appeared in newspapers, on television, and in business offices. The principal cities had their major-league sports, as well as theater companies, art museums, and symphonies. The young Southerner was interested less in where the South had been but more in where it was going. In Richmond, Virginia, General "Stonewall" Jackson's stuffed horse, Old Sorrel, was moved out of the vacant Confederate Old Soldier's Home to make way for a new Virginia Institute of Scientific Research. In Camden, South Carolina, the marble Confederate monument was shifted from the center of town to clear the street for increased traffic to a new orlon plant. Another historic chapter came to an end when the 1959 Southern Governors' Conference demanded more adequate tariff protection for their region's industrial products.

In the last analysis, the South had consciously, perhaps unconsciously, moved haltingly in the direction of accepting the advice of the man who personified the "Lost Cause," General Robert E. Lee. After the Civil War, he declared the primary need of the region to be "the thorough education of all classes of people" and that the major aim of every Southerner should be to unite in "the allayment of passion, the dissipation of prejudice and the restoration of reason." Above all, he urged the South to "abandon all local animosities and make your sons Americans."

Slightly more than one century after the Civil War, the question, "What is the South?" should instead be phrased, "What was the South?" Even for those who argue that this is not accurate — that the South continues to be a distinct and separate region — there, nevertheless, can be only one valid definition for that uniqueness — a state of

[14] George B. Tindall, "The South: Into the Mainstream," *Current History*, XL (May, 1961), p. 269ff.

mind. Granted this, then the words of Robert E. Lee carry even more vital implications for the South of 1975. Few nations have been given the opportunity for ideological leadership in the world as has the United States of America. The South, a region apart within the nation, must not shirk its obligations to its country and to Western civilization.

The sources and literature for a cultural history of the South since 1865 are of enormous proportions. The following list makes no claim of being definitive but is intended to be a selective guide for further reading for the general student rather than the research specialist. Emphasis, therefore, has been placed upon books and monographs that will serve as an introduction to most of the myriad subjects that comprise a history of Southern society. In most cases, newer works have been cited on the grounds that they are more likely to be available and contain the latest results of historical research. Some of the older, standard works are included because of the feeling that they still have much to offer or because they have not been superseded by later historians. A particular effort has been made to include in the footnotes articles that have been particularly valuable in this study; therefore, these citations should be used in conjunction with those that follow. As there are many elements of Southern development that have been ignored in the usual politically-oriented histories, it has been necessary to include works sometimes excluded from historical bibliographies.

In the list that follows, the bibliography will be divided into large subject categories, with an indication of textural chapters that deal with these themes. Under each major heading, the bibliography for special topics will be grouped.

*Chapter I*

There is only one other single-volume work that deals exclusively with Southern history since 1865: T. D. Clark and A. D. Kirwan, *The South Since Appomattox* (New York, 1967). The nearest approach to a multi-volume history of the South during this period is the later volumes of the projected ten-volume series, *The History of the South*, published by the Louisiana State University Press. At this time, the series has not progressed beyond 1945. This set will supersede the older J. A. C. Chandler and others, *The South in the Building of the Nation* (13 vols., Richmond, 1909-1913), although the older work still is a valuable source of information for some features of the South before 1909. T. D. Clark, ed., *The South Since Reconstruction* (Indianapolis, 1973), is an excellent set of readings for the period since 1880. The only multi-volume history of the United States that gives adequate treatment of the broad phases of Southern culture is A. M. Schlesinger and D. R. Fox, *The History of American Life* (13 vols., New York, 1927-1948), and this does not progress beyond the Depression period. Harvey Wish, *Society and Thought in Modern America* (New York, 1962), contains valuable information on the South.

The best general histories of the South include W. B. Hesseltine and D. L. Smiley, *The South in American History* (Englewood Cliffs, N. J., 1960); F. B. Simkins and C. P. Roland, *A History of the South* (New York, 1972), and M. L. Billington, *The American South* (New York, 1971). The only one-volume collection of documents is I. W. Van Noppen, *The South: A Documentary History* (Princeton, 1958). Much valuable information is included in the various issues of the *Journal of Southern History, Journal of Ameircan History*, and the *American Historical Review.* Virtually every state historical society or archives has its publications, although these lean heavily toward political, military, or genealogical history. The best key to this type of material is J. R. Masterson and others, *Writings on American History* (Washington, 1909-      ). Two short bibliographical works sponsored by the American Historical Association's Service Center for Teachers of History are O. A. Singletary, *The South in American History* (Washington, 1957), and Hal Bridges, *Civil War and Reconstruction* (Washington, 1957). In addition, there are histories of the individual Southern states, although these are uneven in quality.

There are also certain books on the South that are so broad in their scope and interpretation that they cannot readily be categorized. Among these should be mentioned C. V. Woodward, *The Burden of Southern History* (Baton Rouge, 1968); W. H. Nicholls, *Southern Tradition and Regional*

*Progress* (Chapel Hill, 1960); B. B. Kendrick and A. M. Arnett, *The South Looks at Its Past* (Chapel Hill, 1935); H. W. Odum, *An American Epoch* (New York, 1930), *Southern Regions of the United States* (Chapel Hill, 1936), and *The Way of the South Toward the Regional Balance of America* (New York, 1947); Hodding Carter, *Southern Legacy* (Baton Rouge, 1950); and C. G. Sellers, Jr., ed., *The Southerner as American* (Chapel Hill, 1960). Four works are worthy of special mention because of unique qualities: the classic study of Southern culture is W. T. Couch, ed., *Culture in the South* (Chapel Hill, 1935); P. H. Buck, *The Road to Reunion 1865-1900* (Boston, 1937), is a magnificent work showing the breaking down of sectional hostilities; R. B. Vance, *All These People: The Nation's Human Resources in the South* (Chapel Hill, 1945), is an excellent source of statistics of all sorts; and W. J. Cash, *The Mind of the South* (New York, 1956), is one of the most provocative studies written by a Southerner about his native region.

As background studies of characteristics of the "Old South" that might be expected to influence the development of the "New South," most of the general works mentioned above have merit. In addition to these, however, should be mentioned other excellent studies of special value. These include Clement Eaton, *A History of the Old South* (New York, 1975), *Freedom of Thought in the Old South* (Durham, 1940), and *The Growth of Southern Civilization, 1790-1860* (New York, 1961); the familiar U. B. Phillips, *Life and Labor in the Old South* (Boston, 1929); and an interpretation of the Southern image in W. R. Taylor, *Cavalier and Yankee: The Old South and American National Character* (New York, 1961).

*Reconstruction*
*(Chapters II, III, IV, V)*

There is not as yet, and probably never will be, a completely satisfactory account of Reconstruction, one free of racial and sectional prejudices, that blends political, economic, and social forces. Reconstruction history has recently been restudied on a broad scale. Relatively conservative approaches can be found in E. M. Coulter, *The South During Reconstruction* (Baton Rouge, 1947), J. G. Randall and David Donald, *The Civil War and Reconstruction* (Boston, 1961), and Avery Craven, *Reconstruction: The Ending of the Civil War* (New York, 1969), while J. H. Franklin, *Reconstruction: After the Civil War* (Chicago, 1961), and K. M. Stampp, *The Era of Reconstruction* (New York, 1965), represent "revisionist" viewpoints. Congressional hearings can be found in H. L. Trefousse, ed., *Background for Radical Reconstruction* (Boston, 1970), while the black role is emphasized in LaWanda Cox and J. H. Cox, *Reconstruction, the Negro, and the New South* (Columbia, S. C., 1973), and Robert Cruden, *The Negro in Reconstruction* (Englewood Cliffs, 1969), and P. H. Buck, *The Road to Reunion 1865-1900* (Boston, 1937), is still unsurpassed as a study of sectional tensions and the forces at work to overcome them. The best collection of documents on the subject is still W. L. Fleming, ed., *Documentary History of Reconstruction* (2 vols., Cleveland, 1906-1907). Hal Bridges, *Civil War and Reconstruction* (Washington, 1957), is a brief survey of issues and bibliography.

Studies have been made of Reconstruction in each of the various Southern states. However, the bulk of these fall within what is called the "Dunning School" and are marked by a Democratic bias and hostility toward Negroes, Carpetbaggers, and Scalawags. Here, especially, one must make use of the revisionist articles that have appeared in scholarly journals in recent years. Among the best of the state studies are: W. L. Fleming, *Civil War and Reconstruction in Alabama* (New York, 1905); J. W. Garner, *Reconstruction in Mississippi* (New York, 1901); Alan Conway, *The Reconstruction of Georgia* (Minneapolis, 1966); F. B. Simkins and R. H. Woody, *South Carolina During Reconstruction* (Chapel Hill, 1932); Ella Lonn, *Reconstruction in Louisiana after 1868* (New York, 1918); and T. B. Alexander, *Political Reconstruction in Tennessee* (Nashville, 1950).

Travel accounts give valuable general pictures of the South after the war. Among the more significant are Sidney Andrews, *The South Since the War* (Boston, 1866); Whitelaw Reid, *After the War: A Southern Tour* (Cincinnati, 1866); Edward King, *The Great South* (New York, 1875); Robert Somers, *The Southern States since the War* (London, 1871); Charles Nordhoff, *The Cotton States in the Spring and Summer of 1875* (New York, 1876); and J. T. Trowbridge, *The [Desolate] South, 1865-1866* (Hartford, 1866 [1956]). Accounts of Southerners that fled after defeat can be found in A. J. Hanna, *Flight into Oblivion* (Richmond, 1938); L. F. Hill, *The Confederate Exodus to Latin America* (N. p., 1936); A. F. Rolle, *The Lost Cause: The Confederate Exodus to Mexico* (Norman, 1965); and A. J. and K. A. Hanna, *Confederate Exiles in Venezuela* (Tuscaloosa, 1960).

All of the Lincoln and Johnson biographies deal extensively with Reconstruction under these two presidents. Special authorities on this subject include: J. G. Randall, *Constitutional Problems Under Lincoln* (Urbana, 1951), and *Lincoln in the South* (Baton Rouge, 1946); W. B. Hesseltine, *Lincoln's Plan of Reconstruction* (Tuscaloosa, 1960); H. K. Beale, *The Critical Year: A Study of Andrew Johnson and Reconstruction* (New York, 1930); and E. L. McKitrick, *Andrew Johnson and Reconstruction* (Chicago, 1960), which challenges many of Beale's conclusions. W. A. Dunning, *Essays on the Civil War and Reconstruction* (New York, 1904), continues to be valuable for its discussion of constitutional issues. A special study of importance is J. T. Dorris, *Pardon and Amnesty Under Lincoln and Johnson* (Chapel Hill, 1953).

Radical plans can be found in B. B. Kendrick, ed., *Journal of the Joint Committee on Reconstruction* (New York, 1914), as well as in biographies of the various Radical leaders. Special aspects are treated in G. R. Bentley, *A History of the Freedman's Bureau* (Philadelphia, 1955); S. D. Smith, *The Negro in Congress* (Chapel Hill, 1940); H. H. Donald, *The Negro Freedman: Life Conditions of the American Negro in the Early Years After Eman-*

*cipation* (New York, 1952); H. M. Hyman, *Era of the Oath* (Philadelphia, 1954); R. P. Sharkey, *Money, Class, and Party: An Economic Study of the Civil War and Reconstruction* (Baltimore, 1959); Jacobus Ten Broek, *The Antislavery Origins of the Fourteenth Amendment* (Berkeley, 1951); J. B. James, *The Framing of the Fourteenth Amendment* (Urbana, 1956); R. E. Morrow, *Northern Methodism and Reconstruction* (East Lansing, 1956); G. R. Woolfolk, *The Cotton Regency: The Northern Merchant and Reconstruction* (New York, 1959); and H. L. Swint, *The Northern Teacher in the South, 1862-1870* (Nashville, 1941). Two books by or about Carpetbaggers are: H. C. Warmoth, *War, Politics, and Reconstruction in Louisiana* (New York, 1930), and Jonathan Daniels, *Prince of Carpetbaggers* (Philadelphia, 1958).

Many of the works mentioned above treat of the overthrow of Radical Reconstruction. Two additional books should be mentioned: G. W. McGinty, *Louisiana Redeemed: The Overthrow of the Carpet-bag Rule, 1876-1880* (New Orleans, 1941), a state study, and the most influential of recent studies on the general subject, C. V. Woodward, *Reunion and Reaction: The Compromise of 1877 and the End of Reconstruction* (Boston, 1951).

*The South at Work*
*(Chapters VII, VIII, IX, XII, XXII)*

The best specific works dealing with the economic development of the South after the Civil War are E. Q. Hawk, *Economic History of the South* (New York, 1934); C. B. Hoover and B. U. Ratchford, *Economic Resources and Policies of the South* (New York, 1951); and M. L. Greenhut and W. T. Whiteman, eds., *Essays in Southern Economic Development* (Chapel Hill, 1964). C. V. Woodward, *Origins of the New South, 1877-1913* (Baton Rouge, 1951) and G. B. Tindall, *The Emergence of the New South, 1913-1945* (Baton Rouge, 1967), give well-integrated pictures of the South that contains much economic material of value to the student. Economic change is also featured in Virginius Dabney, *Below the Potomac: A Book about the New South* (New York, 1942), and T. D. Clark, *The Emerging South* (New York, 1961), is especially valuable for showing changes since 1930. Most of the general histories mentioned above treat some aspects of economic development.

For agriculture, F. A. Shannon, *The Farmer's Last Frontier: Agriculture, 1860-1897* (New York, 1945), has some valuable chapters on the South. Works dealing with Southern agriculture in general include H. H. Bennett, *The Soils and Agriculture of the Southern States* (New York, 1921); A. M. Tang, *Economic Development in the Southern Piedmont, 1860-1950: Its Impact on Agriculture* (Chapel Hill, 1958); W. A. Range, *A Century of Georgia Agriculture, 1850-1950* (Athens, 1954); H. H. Donald, *The Negro Freedman* (New York, 1952); C. H. Otken, *Ills of the South* (New York, 1894), a competent statement by a contemporary; R. B. Vance, *Human Geography of the South* (Chapel Hill, 1932); C. S. Johnson and others, *The Collapse of Cotton Tenancy* (Chapel Hill, 1935); R. B. Vance, *Human Factors in Cotton Culture* (Chapel Hill, 1929); J. C. Robert, *The Tobacco Kingdom* (Durham, 1938); National Emergency Council, *Report on Economic Conditions of the South* (Washington, 1938), a good brief account of agriculture during the Depression; A. F. Raper, *Preface to Peasantry: A Tale of Two Black Belt Counties* (Chapel Hill, 1936); A. F. Raper, and I. D. Reid, *Sharecroppers All* (Chapel Hill, 1941); J. H. Street, *The New Revolution in the Cotton Economy: Mechanization and its Consequences* (Chapel Hill, 1957); T. J. Woofter, Jr., and A. E. Fisher, *The Plantation South Today* (Washington, 1940); and Victor Perlo, *The Negro in Southern Agriculture* (New York, 1953). H. D. Woodman, *King Cotton & his Retainers* (Lexington, 1968), is an excellent study of the financing and marketing of cotton before 1925. Much agricultural history can be found in accounts of the Agrarian Revolt; see, for example, Theodore Saloutos, *Farmer Movements in the South, 1865-1933* (Berkeley, 1960).

Business and industrial developments are highlighted in C. V. Woodward, *Origins of the New South* (Baton Rouge, 1951); G. B. Tindall, *The Emergence of the New South, 1913-1945* (Baton Rouge, 1967); T. D. Clark, *The Emerging South* (New York, 1961); H. L. Herring, *Southern Industry and Regional Development* (Chapel Hill, 1940); Broadus and G. S. Mitchell, *The Industrial Revolution in the South* (Baltimore, 1930); W. P. Webb, *Divided We Stand* (Austin, 1944); T. D. Clark, *Pills, Petticoats, and Plows: The Southern Country Store* (Indianapolis, 1944); Edwin Mims, *The Advancing South* (Garden City, 1926); J. M. Maclachlan and J. S. Floyd, Jr., *This Changing South* (Gainesville, 1956); R. P. Brooks, *The Industrialization of the South* (Athens, 1929); J. V. Van Sickle, *Planning for the South* (Nashville, 1943); F. L. Deming and W. A. Stein, *Disposal of Southern War Plants* (Washington, 1949); G. E. McLaughlin and Stefan Robock, *Why Industry Moves South* (Washington, 1949); and National Emergency Council, *Report on Economic Conditions of the South* (Washington, 1938).

The views of contemporary supporters of diversification and industrialization can be found in H. W. Grady, *The New South* (New York, 1890), speeches by one of its most vocal advocates. See also R. B. Nixon, *Henry W. Grady, Spokesman of the New South* (New York, 1943), and G. T. Winston, *A Builder of the New South: D. A. Tompkins* (New York, 1920). A modern critic of the agrarian tradition and proponent of Southern industry is W. H. Nicholls, *Southern Tradition and Regional Progress* (Chapel Hill, 1960). For the views of those feeling that the region made a mistake by industrializing, see Twelve Southerners, *I'll Take My Stand* (New York, 1930). A milder and more modern approach can be found in L. D. Rubin, Jr., and J. J. Kilpatrick, eds., *The Lasting South: Fourteen Southerners Look at their Home* (Chicago, 1957). The problem of alien ownership is discussed in E. G. Arnall, *The Shore Dimly Seen* (Philadelphia, 1946).

For accounts of developments in various industries, see Broadus Mitchell, *The Rise of the Cotton Mills in the South* (Baltimore, 1921); M. A. Potwin,

*Cotton Mill People of the Piedmont* (New York, 1927); J. C. Sitterson, *Sugar Country: The Sugar Cane Industry in the South, 1753-1950* (Lexington, 1953); J. F. Stover, *The Railroads of the South, 1865-1900: A Study in Finance and Control* (Chapel Hill, 1955); N. M. Tilley, *The Bright-Tobacco Industry, 1860-1929* (Chapel Hill, 1948); J. K. Winkler, *Tobacco Tycoon: The Story of James Buchanan Duke* (New York, 1942); C. H. Candler, *Asa Griggs Candler* (Emory University, Ga., 1950); C. C. Rister, *Oil! Titan of the Southwest* (Norman, 1949); Ethel Ames, *The Story of Coal and Iron in Alabama* (Birmingham, 1910); and S. F. Horn, *This Fascinating Lumber Business* (Indianapolis, 1943). Closely aligned with industrial development is the history of the TVA. Its story is told in D. E. Lilienthal, *TVA, Democracy on the March* (New York, 1944), and G. R. Clapp, *The TVA: An Approach to the Development of a Region* (Chicago, 1955).

While labor problems are discussed in most of the works on industry, there are some special studies that should be mentioned. Representative approaches include F. R. Marshall, *Labor in the South* (Cambridge, 1967); E. H. Davidson, *Child Labor Legislation in the Southern Textile States* (Chapel Hill, 1939); National Emergency Council, *Report on Economic Conditions of the South* (Washington, 1938); G. S. Mitchell, *Textile Unionism in the South* (Chapel Hill, 1931); H. J. Lahne, *The Cotton Mill Worker* (New York, 1944); and H. L. Herring, *Passing of the Mill Village* (Chapel Hill, 1950). Two government publications are worthy of special mention: US Commissioner of Labor, *Second Annual Report, 1886* (Washington, 1887), and US Department of Labor, Bureau of Labor Statistics, *Labor in the South* (Bulletin no. 898, Washington, 1947). The best account of Negroes and the union movement is S. D. Spero and A. L. Harris, *The Black Worker: The Negro and the Labor Movement* (New York, 1931). An account by an organizer is L. R. Mason, *To Win these Rights: A Personal Story of the CIO in the South* (New York, 1952).

*Southern Society and Culture*
*(Chapters X, XI, XIII-XX, XXIII)*

Among the best general accounts of the South with strong social and cultural emphasis are W. J. Cash, *The Mind of the South* (New York, 1941); C. V. Woodward, *Origins of the New South, 1877-1913* (Baton Rouge, 1951); G. B. Tindall, *The Emergence of the New South, 1913-1945* (Baton Rouge, 1967); T. D. Clark, *The Emerging South* (New York, 1961); W. T. Couch, ed., *Culture in the South* (Chapel Hill, 1935); H. W. Odum, *An American Epoch* (New York, 1930); P. H. Buck, *The Road to Reunion, 1865-1900* (Boston, 1937); R. B. Vance, *Human Geography of the South* (Chapel Hill, 1935); C. G. Sellers, Jr., ed., *The Southerner as an American* (Chapel Hill, 1960); F. B. Simkins, ed., *The South in Perspective* (Farmville, 1959); L. D. Rubin, Jr., and J. J. Kilpatrick, eds., *The Lasting South: Fourteen Southerners Look at their Home* (Chicago, 1957); A. F. Scott, *The Southern Lady: From Pedestal to Politics, 1830-1930* (Chicago, 1970);

Twelve Southerners, *I'll Take My Stand* (New York, 1930); Virginius Dabney, *Below the Potomac* (New York, 1942), and *Liberalism in the South* (Chapel Hill, 1932); Hodding Carter, *Southern Legacy* (Baton Rouge, 1950); H. W. Odum, *The Way of the South* (New York, 1947); R. B. Vance, *All These People: The Nation's Human Resources in the South* (Chapel Hill, 1945); R. B. Vance and N. J. Demerath, eds., *The Urban South* (Chapel Hill, 1954); G. L. Simpson, Jr., *The Cokers of Carolina: A Social Biography of a Family* (Chapel Hill, 1956); W. H. Stephenson, *The South Lives in History: Southern Historians and their Legacy* (Baton Rouge, 1955); W. H. Nicholls, *Southern Tradition and Regional Progress* (Chapel Hill, 1960); and K. D. Lumpkin, *The Making of a Southerner* (New York, 1947). Two unusual attempts to explain the South are found in David Bertleson, *The Lazy South* (New York, 1967), and E. E. Thorpe, *Eros and Freedom in Southern Life and Thought* (Durham, 1967).

For study of the social caste system and class and race struggles, see R. W. Shugg, *Origins of Class Struggle in Louisiana* (Baton Rouge, 1939); John Dollard, *Caste and Class in a Southern Town* (New Haven, 1937); Allison Davis and others, *Deep South: A Social Anthropological Study of Caste and Class* (Chicago, 1941); and A. F. Raper and I. D. Reid, *Sharecroppers All* (Chapel Hill, 1941). For a discussion of particular white groups, the best works are: M. A. Potwin, *Cotton Mill People of the Piedmont: A Study in Social Change* (New York, 1927); Horace Kephart, *Our Southern Highlanders* (New York, 1922); and Shields McIlwaine, *The Southern Poor-White from Lubberland to Tobacco Road* (Norman, 1939).

The literature on the Negro and the South is almost endless. Among the best studies are: J. H. Franklin, *From Slavery to Freedom, A History of American Negroes* (New York, 1967); Gunnar Myrdal, *An American Dilemma: The Negro Problem and Modern Democracy* (New York, 1944); C. V. Woodward, *The Strange Career of Jim Crow* (New York, 1974); E. F. Frazier, *The Negro in the United States* (New York, 1949); R. W. Logan, *The Negro in American Life and Thought: The Nadir, 1877-1901* (New York, 1951); L. R. Harlan, *Booker T. Washington* (New York, 1972); H. H. Donald, *The Negro Freedman* (New York, 1952); W. E. B. DuBois, *The Souls of Black* (Chicago, 1903), and *Black Folks, Then and Now* (New York, 1939); C. H. Nolen, *The Negro's Image in the South* (Lexington, 1967); and the classic, B. T. Washington, *Up From Slavery* (New York, 1901).

The volumes of the *Negro Yearbook*, published by Tuskegee Institute, are a vital source of information on all aspects of Negro life and especially relations with the whites. Important monographs dealing with special aspects of Negro life include G. B. Tindall, *South Carolina Negroes 1877-1900* (Columbia, S. C., 1952); V. L. Wharton, *The Negro in Mississippi, 1865-1890* (Chapel Hill, 1947); L. D. Rice, *The Negro in Texas, 1874-1900* (Baton Rouge, 1971); F. A. Logan, *The Negro in North Carolina* (Chapel Hill, 1964); E. D. Cronon, *Black Moses: The Story of Marcus Garvey and the Universal Negro Improvement Association* (Madison, 1955); Hortense

Powdermaker, *After Freedom: A Cultural Study in the Deep South* (New York, 1939); C. S. Mangum, Jr., *The Legal Status of the Negro* (Chapel Hill, 1940); C. G. Woodson, *A Century of Negro Migration* (Washington, 1918); S. D. Spero and A. L. Harris, *The Black Worker: The Negro and the Labor Movement* (New York, 1931); E. F. Frazier, *The Negro Family in the United States* (Chicago, 1939); Wilson Record, *The Negro and the Communist Party* (Chapel Hill, 1951); and E. L. Tatum, *The Changed Political Thought of the Negro, 1915-1940* (New York, 1951).

There has been a deluge of material in recent years on the problem of integration. For a typical view by a radical segregationist, see T. G. Bilbo, *Take Your Choice, Separation or Mongrelization* (Poplarville, Miss., 1947). More scholarly works dealing with this problem are T. D. Clark, *The Emerging South* (New York, 1961); L. R. Harlan, *Separate and Unequal: Public School Campaigns and Racism in the Southern Seaboard States, 1901-1915* (Chapel Hill, 1958); R. P. Warren, *Segregation, The Inner Conflict of the South* (New York, 1957); A. P. Blaustein and C. C. Ferguson, *Desegregation and the Law: The Meaning and Effect of the School Segregation Cases* (New Brunswick, 1957); Brooks Hays, *A Southern Moderate Speaks* (Chapel Hill, 1959); William Peters, *The Southern Temper* (Garden City, 1959); W. D. Workman, Jr., *The Case for the South* (New York, 1960); Harry Ashmore, *Epitaph for Dixie* (New York, 1957); Henry Savage, Jr., *Seeds of Time: Background of Southern Thinking* (New York, 1959); Don Shoemaker, ed., *With All Deliberate Speed, Segregation-Desegregation in Southern Schools* (New York, 1959); Gary Orfield, *The Reconstruction of Southern Education* (New York, 1969); L. D. Reddick, *Crusader Without Violence: A Biography of Martin Luther King, Jr.* (New York, 1959); C. E. Lincoln, *Martin Luther King, Jr.: A Profile* (New York, 1969).

Other social problems and the efforts made to reform them are discussed in E. G. Murphy, *Problems of the Present South* (New York, 1909); C. H. Otken, *Ills of the South* (New York, 1894); C. W. Pipkin, *Social Legislation in the South* (Chapel Hill, 1936); Elizabeth Wisner, *Social Welfare in the South* (Baton Rouge, 1970); and E. H. Davidson, *Child Labor Legislation in the Southern Textile States* (Chapel Hill, 1939). Two studies dealing with reform during the Progressive Era are H. C. Bailey, *Liberalism in the New South* (Chapel Hill, 1969), and J. T. Kirby, *Darkness at the Dawning* (Philadelphia, 1972). The best biography is H. C. Bailey, *Edgar Gardner Murphy* (Coral Gables, 1968). The Woman Suffrage movement is discussed in the general histories of that subject, and A. E. Taylor, *The Woman Suffrage Movement in Tennessee* (New York, 1957), is a good account of the movement in a key Southern state. Discussions of the problem and prevalence of lynching can be found in the various issues of the *Negro Yearbook;* A. F. Raper, *The Tragedy of Lynching* (Chapel Hill, 1933); C. H. Chadbourn, *Lynching and the Law* (Chapel Hill, 1933); and Southern Commission on Study of Lynching, *Lynchings and What They Mean* (Atlanta, 1931). A brief survey of the convict leasing system can be found in F. M. Green, "Some Aspects of the Convict Lease System in the Southern States," in Green, ed., *Essays in Southern History* (Chapel Hill, 1949), while J. F. Steiner and R. M. Brown discuss another phase of the problem in *The North Carolina Chain Gang* (Chapel Hill, 1927). There is not an adequate study of the Ku Klux Klan, but C. C. Alexander, *The Ku Klux Klan in the Southwest* (Lexington, 1965), is best for the part of the South covered. Little has been written on the social conditions leading to the rise of the demagogues, but R. H. Luthin, *American Demagogues: Twentieth Century* (Boston, 1954), and A. A. Michie and Frank Ryhlick, *Dixie Demagogues* (New York, 1939), can be used with care. The story of the fight for prohibition is covered in Virginius Dabney, *Dry Messiah, The Life of Bishop Cannon* (New York, 1949); J. B. Sellers, *The Prohibition Movement in Alabama, 1702-1943* (Chapel Hill, 1943); J. L. Franklin, *Born Sober: Prohibition in Oklahoma* (Norman, 1971); and D. G. Whitener, *Prohibition in North Carolina, 1715-1945* (Chapel Hill, 1946).

Descriptions of education can be found in C. V. Woodward, *Origins of the New South, 1877-1913* (Baton Rouge, 1951); G. B. Tindall, *The Emergence of the New South, 1913-1945* (Baton Rouge, 1967); C. W. Dabney, *Universal Education in the South* (2 vols., Chapel Hill, 1936); and Edgar Knight, *Public Education in the South* (Boston, 1922). Descriptions of specific situations can be had in S. P. Wiggins, *Higher Education in the South* (Berkeley, 1968); H. W. Mann, *Atticus G. Haygood* (Athens, 1965); Franklin Parker, *George Peabody* (Nashville, 1971); O. H. Orr, *Charles Brantley Aycock* (Chapel Hill, 1961); J. P. Rice, *J. L. M. Curry, Southerner, Statesman and Educator* (New York, 1949); H. L. Swint, *The Northern Teacher in the South, 1862-1870* (Nashville, 1941); L. D. Rubin, Jr., ed., *Teach the Freedman: The Correspondence of Rutherford B. Hayes and the Slater Fund for Negro Education, 1881-1893* (2 vols., Baton Rouge, 1959); Louise Ware, *George Foster Peabody: Banker, Philanthropist, Publicist* (Athens, 1951); M. B. Pierson, *Graduate Work in the South* (Chapel Hill, 1947); Willard Range, *The Rise and Progress of Negro Colleges in Georgia, 1865-1949* (Athens, 1951); and R. S. Suggs, Jr., and G. H. Jones, *The Southern Regional Education Board: Ten Years of Regional Cooperation in Higher Education* (Baton Rouge, 1960). Especially valuable for statistics are E. W. Swanson and J. A. Griffin, *Public Education in the South, Today and Tomorrow* (Chapel Hill, 1955), and Patrick McCauley and E. D. Ball, eds., *Southern Schools: Progress and Problems* (Nashville, 1959). There is no good work covering public libraries in the South. The best single source is T. D. Barker, *Libraries of the South: A Report on Developments, 1930-1935* (Chicago, 1936).

The varied aspects of Southern literature have attracted many writers, most of whom are not historians. The best general accounts can be found in W. T. Couch, ed., *Culture in the South* (Chapel Hill, 1935); J. B. Hubbell, *The South in American Literature, 1607-1900* (Durham, 1954); Donald Davidson, *Southern Writers in the Modern World* (Athens, 1958); L. D. Rubin, Jr., and R. D. Jacobs, eds., *Southern Renascence: The Literature of the Modern South* (Baltimore, 1953); L. D. Rubin, Jr., *The Faraway*

*Country: Writers of the Modern South* (Seattle, 1963), and L. D. Rubin, Jr., *The Writer in the South* (Athens, 1972). Southern writers, through their works, are one of the best sources of Southern cultural history. Satisfactory studies of individual authors include P. M. Cousins, *Joel Chandler Harris: A Biography* (Baton Rouge, 1968); Arlin Turner, *George Washington Cable* (Durham, 1956); L. D. Rubin, Jr., *Thomas Wolfe* (Baton Rouge, 1955), and *No Place on Earth: Ellen Glasgow, James Branch Cabell, and Richmond-in-Virginia* (Austin, 1959); and H. H. Waggoner, *William Faulkner: From Jefferson to the World* (Lexington, 1959).

Southern newspapers are discussed in F. L. Mott, *American Journalism: A History of Newspapers in the United States through 260 Years: 1690 to 1950* (New York, 1950). This should be supplemented by T. D. Clark, *The Southern Country Editor* (Indianapolis, 1948), and studies of individual papers, such as E. L. Bell, *The Augusta Chronicle: Indomitable Voice of Dixie, 1785-1960* (Athens, 1960).

There is no one description of non-literary arts in the South. The best general source is the essays in W. T. Couch, ed., *Culture in the South* (Chapel Hill, 1935). The best works on Southern architecture are Lewis Mumford, *The South in Architecture* (New York, 1941), dealing with the early part of the period, and Edward and Elizabeth Waugh, *The South Builds: New Architecture in the Old South* (Chapel Hill, 1960), which emphasizes recent trends. There is no single study of Southern painters, but Walter Pach, *The Art Museum in America* (New York, 1948), gives information upon that aspect. The only book-length study of a Southern sculptor is J. I. Fortune and Jean Burton, *Elisabet Ney* (New York, 1943). Gilbert Chase, *America's Music* (New York, 1955), is a good study of general developments, while M. C. Hare, *Negro Musicians and their Music* (New York, 1936), discusses contributions of that race.

For accounts of Southern recreational developments, one is almost totally dependent upon periodical literature. A. M. Weyand, *The Saga of American Football* (New York, 1955), has a chapter on the South. R. C. and Victoria Case, *We Called it Culture: The Story of Chautauqua* (Garden City, 1948), discusses adequately Southern developments in that field, and Philip Graham, *Showboats: The History of an American Institution* (Austin, 1951), is best on that subject.

Just about every phase of religion is well covered. The various census reports are valuable sources of information, statistical and narrative, as are the various issues of the *Yearbook of American Churches*. W. T. Couch, ed., *Culture in the South* (Chapel Hill, 1935), is also valuable. Special aspects of the subject can be found in S. S. Hill, Jr., *Southern Churches in Crisis* (New York, 1967); W. G. McLoughlin, Jr., *Modern Revivalism: Charles Grandison Finney to Billy Graham* (New York, 1959); N. F. Furniss, *The Fundamentalist Controversy, 1918-1931* (New Haven, 1954); W. W. Barnes, *The Southern Baptist Convention, 1845-1953* (Nashville, 1954); R. B. Spain, *At Ease in Zion: A Social History of Southern Baptists, 1865-1900* (Nashville, 1967); J. L. Eighmy, *Churches in Cultural Captivity: A*

*History of the Social Attitudes of Southern Baptists* (Knoxville, 1972);
H. D. Farish, *The Circuit Rider Dismounts: A Social History of Southern
Methodism, 1865-1900* (Richmond, 1938); R. F. Johnson, *The Develop-
ment of Negro Religion* (New York, 1954); C. G. Woodson, *History of
the Negro Church* (Washington, 1945); Leonard Dinnerstein and M. D.
Palsson, eds., *Jews in the South* (Baton Rouge, 1973); and E. T. Clark,
*The Small Sects in America* (Nashville, 1947).

### Southern Politics after Reconstruction
### (Chapters VI, IX, XXI)

Almost all of the general works mentioned earlier concern themselves
with Southern politics. C. V. Woodward, *Origins of the New South, 1877-
1913* (Baton Rouge, 1951), and G. B. Tindall, *The Emergence of the New
South, 1913-1945* (Baton Rouge, 1967), are the best of the general Southern histories in political coverage. Already virtually a classic is V. O. Key, Jr.,
*Southern Politics in State and Nation* (New York, 1949).

For politics during the "Bourbon" or "Redeemer" period, see W. B. Hesseltine, *Confederate Leaders in the New South* (Baton Rouge, 1950); V. P.
DeSantis, *Republicans Face the Southern Question: The New Departure
Years, 1877-1897* (Baltimore, 1959); R. B. Nixon, *Henry W. Grady, Spokesman of the New South* (New York, 1943); C. C. Pearson, *The Readjuster
Movement in Virginia* (New Haven, 1917); W. J. Cooper, Jr., *The Con-
servative Regime: South Carolina, 1877-1890* (Baltimore, 1968); A. J. Go-
ing, *Bourbon Democracy in Alabama, 1874-1890* (University, Alabama,
1951); J. F. Doster, *Railroads in Alabama Politics, 1875-1914* (University,
Alabama, 1957); W. A. Mabry, *The Negro in North Carolina Politics Since
Reconstruction* (Durham, 1940); A. D. Kirwan, *Revolt of the Rednecks:
Mississippi Politics, 1876-1925* (Lexington, 1951); and Paul Lewinson,
*Race, Class, and Party: A History of Negro Suffrage and White Politics in
the South* (New York, 1932).

Historians of national agrarian discontent have not neglected the South.
Among the standard works are S. J. Buck, *The Granger Movement* (Cambridge, 1913), and *The Agrarian Crusade: A Chronicle of the Farmer in Poli-
tics* (New Haven, 1921), and J. D. Hicks, *The Populist Revolt* (Minneapolis,
1931). General accounts of value on the subject, but more specifically Southern, include B. B. Kendrick and A. M. Arnett, *The South Looks at its Past*
(Chapel Hill, 1935); C. V. Woodward, *Origins of the New South, 1877-1913*
(Baton Rouge, 1951); and Theodore Saloutos, *Farmer Movements in the
South, 1865-1933* (Berkeley, 1960). The best contemporary accounts are
C. H. Otken, *The Ills of the South* (New York, 1894), and the essays by
farm leaders in E. A. Allen, ed., *Labor and Capital* (Cincinnati, 1891).

Special topics are treated in A. D. Kirwan, *Revolt of the Rednecks: Mis-
sissippi Politics, 1876-1925* (Lexington, 1951); R. C. Martin, *The People's
Party in Texas* (Austin, 1933); A. M. Arnett, *The Populist Movement in
Georgia* (New York, 1922); R. P. Brooks, *The Agrarian Revolution in Geor-*

# General Bibliography 491

*gia, 1865-1912* (Madison, 1914); S. A. Delap, *The Populist Party in North Carolina* (Durham, 1922); F. B. Simkins, *The Tillman Movement in South Carolina* (Durham, 1926); W. D. Sheldon, *Populism in the Old Dominion* (Princeton, 1935); C. V. Woodward, *The Strange Career of Jim Crow* (New York, 1974); H. G. Edmonds, *The Negro and Fusion Politics in North Carolina, 1894-1901* (Chapel Hill, 1951); W. A. Mabry, *The Negro in North Carolina Politics Since Reconstruction* (Durham, 1940); and Paul Lewinson, *Race, Class, and Party: A History of Negro Suffrage and White Politics in the South* (New York, 1932). Among the leading studies of agrarian leaders are D. M. Robison, *Bob Taylor and the Agrarian Revolt in Tennessee* (Chapel Hill, 1935); Stuart Noblin, *Leonidas LaFayette Polk: Agrarian Crusader* (Chapel Hill, 1949); F. B. Simkins, *Pitchfork Ben Tillman: South Carolinian* (Baton Rouge, 1944); C. V. Woodward, *Tom Watson: Agrarian Rebel* (New York, 1938); and R. C. Cotner, *James Stephen Hogg* (Austin, 1959).

The best general coverage of Southern politics since the agrarian revolt is V. O. Key, Jr., *Southern Politics in State and Nation* (New York, 1949), and *American State Politics* (New York, 1956). Other general works of a broad nature include C. A. Ewing, *Primary Elections in the South* (Norman, 1953), and *Congressional Elections, 1896-1944: The Sectional Basis of Political Democracy in the House of Representatives* (Norman, 1947); E. A. Moore, *A Catholic Runs for President* (New York, 1956), an account of the 1928 election; Wilson Record, *The Negro and the Communist Party* (Chapel Hill, 1951); E. L. Tatum, *The Changed Political Thought of the Negro, 1915-1940* (New York, 1951); J. B. Shannon, *Toward a New Politics in the South* (Knoxville, 1949); Taylor Cole and J. D. Hallowell, eds., *Southern Political Scene, 1938-1948* (Gainesville, 1948); G. E. Mowry, *Another Look at the Twentieth Century South* (Baton Rouge, 1972); G. B. Tindall, *The Disruption of the Solid South* (New York, 1972); W. C. Havard, *The Changing Politics of the South* (Baton Rouge, 1972); and H. M. Hollingsworth, ed., *Essays on Recent Southern Politics* (Austin, 1970).

Topical studies of special interest include A. A. Michie and Frank Rhylick, *Dixie Demagogues* (New York, 1947); D. M. Potter, *The South and the Concurrent Majority* (Baton Rouge, 1972); Frank Freidel, *F.D.R. and the South* (Baton Rouge, 1965); Gunnar Myrdal, *An American Dilemma* (New York, 1944); D. E. Lilienthal, *TVA, Democracy on the March* (New York, 1944); G. R. Clapp, *The TVA: An Approach to the Development of a Region* (Chicago, 1955); E. R. Bartley, *The Tidelands Oil Controversy* (Austin, 1953); E. D. Price, *The Negro and Southern Politics: A Chapter of Florida History* (New York, 1957); N. R. McMillen, *The Citizens' Council: Organized Resistance to the Second Reconstruction* (Urbana, 1971); R. P. Warren, *Segregation, The Inner Conflict of the South* (New York, 1957); Brooks Hays, *A Southern Moderate Speaks* (Chapel Hill, 1959); Harry Ashmore, *Epitaph for Dixie* (New York, 1958); W. D. Workman, Jr., *The Case for the South* (New York, 1960); and Reg Murphy and Hal Gulliver, *The Southern Strategy* (New York, 1971).

Although the contemporary South is best revealed through periodicals, there are biographies of Southern politicians of value. Some of the best include D. W. Grantham, Jr., *Hoke Smith and the Politics of the New South* (Baton Rouge, 1958); Samuel Proctor, *Napoleon Bonaparte Broward: Florida's Fighting Democrat* (Gainesville, 1951); Josephus Daniels, *The Editor in Politics* (Chapel Hill, 1941); Charles Jacobson, *Life Story of Jeff Davis* (Little Rock, 1925); A. S. Coody, *Biographical Sketch of James Kimble Vardaman* (Jackson, 1922); G. C. Osborn, *John Sharp Williams* (Baton Rouge, 1943); A. M. Arnett, *Claude Kitchin and the Wilson War Policies* (Boston, 1937); J. F. Rippy, ed., *Furnifold Simmons, Statesman of the New South* (Durham, 1936); J. E. Palmer, Jr., *Carter Glass, Unreconstructed Rebel* (Roanoke, 1938); A. P. Sindler, *Huey Long's Louisiana, State Politics, 1925-1952* (Baltimore, 1956); Stan Opotowsky, *The Longs of Louisiana* (New York, 1960); and T. H. Williams, *Huey Long* (New York, 1969).

Aaron, Henry, 337
Abbott, Lyman, 32
abolitionists, 10, 18–20, 42; free Negroes and, 13
absentee ownership, 122, 435, 470
academic freedom, 274, 276
actors and acting, 326–327
Adams, Henry, 191
Adams, Herbert, 317
Adams, John, 23
Adjuster party, 109
Africa, slavery and, 11–12
Age of Reason, 18
Agee, James, 295
Agrarian Revolt, 250, 406, 413; politics and, 407
Agricultural Adjustment Acts, 430
agricultural education, 264
Agricultural Workers Labor Union, 211
agriculture, 4; crop changes, 1929–48, 442; crop failures, 53; crop–lien laws, 120; diversification in, 130–131; improvement in, 437; industrialization and, 136–138, 153, 450–452; labor organizations and, 210–211; pattern of, 15; post-Civil War problems of, 46, 53, 115–135; single-crop system, 121; unity and, 22
Agriculture Department, U.S., 122, 128, 154, 386
Alabama, convict leasing in, 367; destruction of in Civil War, 26; reconstruction in, 89; University of, 259, 265, 472
Alabama Polytechnic Institute, 260, 267
Alcorn, James Lusk, 90, 101
Alcorn Club, 85
Alderman, Edwin A., 254
Alkahest circuit, 330
Allen, Frederick Lewis, 370
Allen, Henry W., 35–36
Allen, James Lane, 286, 292
Alliance of Texas, 159–162, 167
Alston, Robert, 389

America First Committee, 456
American Art Annual, 317
American Association of University Professors, 276
American Civil Liberties Union, 276
American Colonization Society, 190
American Cotton Oil Trust, 144
American Council of Education, 270
American Federation of Labor, 188, 204, 208–209, 212, 215, 389
American Freedman's Union Commission, 45, 50
American Independent Party, 422
American Library Association, 308
American Missionary Association, 45, 261
American Revolution, 23
American Teachers' Association, 269
American Telegraph Co., 238
American Tobacco Co., 146–147
Ames, Gen. Adelbert, 90
Amnesty Proclamation, 64
amusements and sports, 322–339
Anderson, Marian, 316
Anderson, Maxwell, 290
Andersonville prison, 32
Andrews, Sidney, 39
Anglican Church, 18, 322, 340
Anglo-Saxon Southerners, 11, 224, 370
anti-Catholicism, 352–353, 370–371
anti-evolution laws, 354
Anti-Lottery League, 396
anti-lynching bill, 403–404
Anti-Saloon League, 348
anti-Semitism, 352, 354, 370, 377, 475
apathy, political, 427
Archer, William, 399
architecture, 308–312
aristocracy, 8, 222
Arkansas, convict leasing in, 367–368; destruction of, 26; reconstruction in, 89–90, 110; war debt, 110
Arkansas Gazette, 305
Armstrong, Louis, 315
Armstrong, Gen. Samuel, 193
Arp, Bill, 330

Union League, 85, 95, 403
union organizing, 209–210
unions, strength of, 203–205, 212–213
Unitarian Church, 18, 341–342
United Cigar Stores, 146
United Confederate Veterans, 103
United Daughters of the Confederacy, 317, 333
United Mine Workers, 206, 210, 212
United States Steel Corporation, 148, 153
United Textile Workers, 205
unity, forces working for, 22
Universal Negro Improvement Association, 190
University Commission on Southern Race Problems, 196
university courses, vs. college programs, 263–264
University of the South, 274–275
university presses, 273–274
*Up From Slavery*, 294
upper class, 222
Urban League, 196
urban population, growth of, 234

vagrancy laws, Negro and, 49
Valentine, Edward V., 317
Vance, Z. B., 34
Vanderbilt University, 261, 264–266, 293, 456
Vardaman, James K., 378
Veazey Convent Inspection Act, 353
Virginia, Negro population in, 458; reconstruction in, 87–88, 109–110; University of, 19, 258, 261, 264, 337, 341; war debt in, 108–109
Virginia Military Institute, 275
Virginia Museum of Fine Arts, 319
*Virginia Quarterly Review*, 274, 299
*Voice of the People, The*, 287
Vollmer, Lula, 289, 320
voters, number of, 408; *see also* Negro voting and suffrage
Voting Rights Act of 1965, 416, 427

Wade, Benjamin, 64
Wade-Davis bill, 65, 68
wage earners, number of, 152–153
wage rates, 201, 435
Walker, Margaret, 294
Wallace, George, 422, 427
Wallace, Henry A., 380, 417, 420, 431
Walthall, Edward C., 103–104
War of 1812, 16
Waring, Robert P., 37
Warmoth, Henry Clay, 84, 91–92
Warren, Fuller, 272

Warren, Robert Penn, 293, 295
Washington, Booker T., 55, 97, 184, 226, 243, 275, 294, 332, 400, 404, 410; life and work, 193–195
Washington and Lee University, 317
Watson, Thomas E., 169–172, 177, 181, 337, 353, 378, 388
Watterson, Col. Henry, 103, 175, 304
wealth, industrial boom and, 152; shrinkage of in Civil War, 28
weather and climate, 4
Weaver, James B., 169
*Web and the Rock, The*, 291
Webster, Daniel, 57
Weeks, Edward, 290
welfare programs, 393–395, 425
Welty, Eudora, 293, 295
West Virginia, formation of, 61–62
Wharton, Vernon L., 91
*What Price Glory?*, 290
Whig party, 9, 104–105
White Citizens Councils, 467
White, George, 426
Whiteman, Paul, 314
whites, "poor," *see* poor whites; poverty of after Civil War, 30
white supremacy, education and, 251, 371–372, 474
white trash, 10
Whitney, Robert, 316
Whittier, John Greenleaf, 280–281
Wilcox, Cadmus M., 35
William and Mary College, 258, 318
*William and Mary Quarterly*, 274
Williams, John Sharp, 5
Williams, Tennessee, 293, 320
Williamsburg, Va., restoration of, 310
Willkie, Wendell, 432
Wilmer, Bishop Richard H., 38
Wilson, Henry, 32, 72
Wilson, Woodrow, 216, 410, 413
Winthrop, R. C., 248
Wirz, Capt. Henry, 32, 35
Wisconsin primary, 387
Wolfe, Thomas, 290–291
woman suffrage, 397
women, emancipation of, 228–231; higher education for, 397
Women's Christian Temperance Union, 348, 397, 399
women's clubs, 335, 391
women's colleges, 263–265
Wood, Fernando, 373
Woodrow, James, 349
Woodson, Carter G., 294
Woodward, C. Vann, 102, 477
work, as religion, 220